The "ISMS"

A History and Evaluation

THE "*ISMS*"

A HISTORY AND EVALUATION

By EUGENE O. GOLOB

Essay Index Reprint Series

BOOKS FOR LIBRARIES PRESS, INC.
FREEPORT, NEW YORK

LIBRARY OF CONGRESS CATALOG CARD NUMBER:
68-20302

PRINTED IN THE UNITED STATES OF AMERICA

CONTENTS

v

Part IV. Theories of Corporatism and an Approach to the Middle Way

PREFACE

The twentieth century, it is said, is a time of chaos, of transition, of the collapse of old values, of the breakdown of order. It is not at all strange that this should be so, for those disturbing words and phrases can properly be applied to almost any period of history. The human truth is that change is our only constant. But our era is, of course, quite different from the past in many ways, as a number of stock phrases make us acutely aware. This the age of mass production, of total war, of a world shrunken into one. This is the atomic age. And it is the age of ideological conflict.

Never before have the policies of so many nations been so clearly influenced by ideological considerations. Never before has so large a proportion of the population of the earth thought and argued in such consciously ideological terms. Words ending in "ism" have so proliferated that they almost form a special department of the vocabulary. And words ending in "ist" are bidding fair to monopolize the language of political invective. The "smear" tactic of the present is to label the other fellow "communist," "socialist," "fascist," "economic royalist," or what have you. There is in addition a highly specialized category of opprobrium, of which "Titoist," "Trotskyist," and "warmongering imperialist" will serve as adequate examples.

In a way this is a good thing, and bespeaks a rise in the level of public debate, for it means that a good deal more of political argument now concerns major issues of policy and principle, so that there is less time for picayune disputes. But the old truism that every gain has its costs applies here too. Aside from the fact that in our time ideological conflicts are those least open to compromise, the triumph of the "isms" places a much heavier burden on the active intelligence of the citizen. For, unlike the simple Anglo-Saxon expletives, these words put us under the obligation to know what they really mean, and whether it is accurate to apply them to the man on the other side of the fence. Personal tragedies have resulted from unclear conceptions of what "communism" or "fascism" actually represent, and from the facile and legally indefensible process of determining guilt by association. More sweeping, if less poignant, tragedies have resulted from official errors in judging what a "communist" or "capitalist" nation was likely to do, and to what extent it would be guided by adherence to the doctrines of "communism" or "capitalism."

The growing awareness of these differing social theories results from the fact that more and more people appear to find them useful in clarifying practical thinking and action. This makes it all the more necessary that the theories themselves be clarified, and that is what I have tried to do in this book. Only in the very broadest sense, however, is it a study in semantics, and only to a limited degree is it a systematic analysis of doctrine. The writer, as it happens, is a historian, and therefore professes the belief that no institution or idea can be abstracted from its past and still be properly understood. The historian believes that the past lives on in the present and into the future. Not the entire past, of course, although this be true in a purely logical sense. Ideally, the historian's task would be to select, from all that is known, those facts that are most relevant to the question he has chosen to ask, and then to arrange them in a meaningful order. In the more modest world of reality, the good historian tries to answer his question by discovering what facts are most relevant, and ordering them intelligibly. Obviously then, the standards by which the historian judges relevance become the most important element in the success or failure of his quest.

Now this might seem to place an intolerable burden upon the subjective judgment of the individual historian. It might even threaten to raise the old question, Is history really scientific? Or is it merely the expression of one man's opinion on how and why things came to pass as they did? I do not think this question is particularly meaningful. If the most rigorous and number-minded physicist were to try his hand at historical analysis, he would find himself using precisely the same processes of thought he had employed in the laboratory. He would find that his results were of a lower order of certainty, that insight counted for more, and measurement for less, in his new work, and that some trusted methods were not too useful. But he would be as objective in one role as in the other, for all that objectivity in analysis means is a decent and abiding respect for the facts, and a cheerful willingness to discard a favorite hypothesis when the evidence fails to support it. This, and simple integrity, are the only safeguards against a search for just those particular facts that will prove whatever it is desired to prove.

On this view, there has obviously been a good deal of needless confusion over the matter of objectivity. It cannot mean wallowing in a mudbank of undifferentiated data which then somehow shapes itself into scientific truth, nor does it mean suppressing one's opinions. They are present in the original act of asking one question rather than another, in the principle of selection on which one proceeds, and in the interpretive answer to the how and the why. For a historian, or economist, or political scientist to conceal his own outlook on society and his own preferences is no more than a bit of labored coyness. It derives from the fact that that eternal model of objectivity, the physicist, is quite indifferent to the fate of a tungsten filament, as is the biologist to that of a fruit fly. Even this neutrality no longer exists unimpaired, however, at least in the Soviet part of the world. And neither the physicist nor the biologist is or should be indifferent or neutral with respect to the fate of his society. "Objectivity through self-effacement," then, is not only illusory, but is actually self-defeating. Its practitioners forget that there are always at least two parties to any act of communicating an idea. They forget the reader. And the reader will be in a much better position to reach an objective judgment of a book if he is clearly told where the writer stands and to what values he holds.

All of the foregoing is by way of explaining why I have not tried to hide behind a curtain of neutral words the point of view which led me to undertake this book. I feel very strongly that every American with a mature conception of what citizenship means has two special obligations: first, to gain as accurate as possible an understanding, and as keen as possible a critical judgment of the ideologies that are now competing for world favor; second, to devote himself to the very considerable effort of working out the content of the American ideology and the principles by which policies and actions should be decided. In short, I believe that there is an American ideology, shared in varying degrees by most of the democratic half of the world, to which I subscribe. Its core is belief in the essential dig-

nity of the individual, the realization of which is the purpose of our
political and economic systems. The American conception of political democracy may be stated, very shortly, as representative government under the Bill of Rights. The fundamental social and economic
principle is a rough equality of opportunity for individual achievement, and the objective of social policy is a proper balance between
security and individual freedom of action.

This is, of course, not to claim perfection, which is eternally denied to the sons of man. We fall short of the mark in respect of each
of these values and aims, but that is no reason for rejecting Arthur
Koestler's observation that a partial truth is preferable to a total lie.
Our limited success in achieving our goals is at least deserving of
limited praise. Nor should an emphasis on the individual be taken as
a confession of faith in laissez faire, which I regard as being as absurd in its own way as are the regimented Utopias. The position
from which this book is written may suitably be described as a moderate conservatism, not merely accepting but welcoming change, and
asking only that it harmonize with and perpetuate what was best in
the past. It is not especially concerned with system building and, indeed, rather fears the application of tight logic and abstractions to
the loose patterns of human behavior. Unfortunately, I do not know
of any striking catchword or phrase to characterize this point of view,
but this is not an unmitigated loss, for their very seductiveness is one
of the greatest failings of the fetching "isms." I am offering a middle
of the road position (a good friend has suggested the word *viamedi-
anism*), and it is always extremely difficult to speak for moderation
in the clarion tones of either the fearlessly new or the resolutely ancient.

The purpose of the book has naturally dictated its organization.
A number of the leading contending ideologies will be analyzed
from three standpoints, as historical developments, as bodies of doctrine and in terms of their significance for contemporary America.
The order of treatment runs from laissez faire through varying degrees of statism to totalitarianism. This arrangement has its disad-
vantages, such as, for example, the separation of the discussions of
communism and socialism by an intervening section on anti-Marxian
British Labour. Moreover, the plan makes it necessary to refer to the
same epoch in more than one context. The historian is rather like a

tourist, however, seeking and finding something fresh every time he visits his favorite city. Where such seeming repetition occurs, the viewpoint is different in each case. The organization has advantages too, for it tends to bring out more strongly the fundamentals of doctrine, and to point up theoretical relationships between points of view that are strongly opposed in practice. The pages on Christian social philosophy and on the types of corporatism serve as a convenient bridge between criticism and affirmative suggestion.

One of the embarrassments of critical writing, to which most of this book is devoted, is that it invites the challenge, if from no other source than the critic's conscience, to come up with something positive. And this the honest critic may not be prepared to do. I have nevertheless tried, in the last chapter, to meet this challenge in a tentative sort of way, in the belief that very little harm can come of it, save to the writer's own pride, and that it may yield the good that results from offering other critics a substantive target to shoot at.

The various chapters are not as equal in length as perfect literary organization would seem to require, but I have preferred to economize where possible in order to give greater space to less familiar and more controversial subjects. I have been similarly guided in supplying factual and statistical evidence, and in citing its sources.

At the end of each chapter are remarks about some books the reader may find interesting, or valuable, or happily even both. These comments and booklists do not constitute a bibliography, and are therefore very brief.

The very writing of a book is a confession of the author's self-esteem, but pride of authorship is displayed in sharply divergent ways. There are the writers who secrete their manuscript and place it under the highest security until it bursts into the advertising columns and the reviews. And there is the very different breed of writers who seem to wish their work to be all but a community project, the direct benefit of which they would of course monopolize. Such authors deliberately misconstrue the courteous interest expressed by unwary friends as offers to read and criticize and, losing such restraint and consideration for others as is customary to them, press drafts of their work upon the good folk unfortunate enough to be with them when they are possessed of this frenzy of authorship. I belong to the latter, undignified and greedy school, and have ruthlessly exploited my friends and expropriated the value they have added to my work. The apologies and deep-felt thanks I now offer to them, in an interval free from the manuscript madness, can be but slight amends.

Lyle C. Fitch took time from better things and gave unstintingly of his expert knowledge and wisdom. His keen and perceptive criticism served me both as a guard against error and a guide to useful inquiry. The contribution of Edith B. Golob will be evident to anyone in a position to judge the advance of this work, very imperfect though it be, over my normal usage and expression. The residual strength of conscience limited my burdening of others to parts or chapters of the book: S. Hugh Brockunier, Lester V. Chandler, and Charles W. Cole read Part I; Carl E. Schorske read chapters 8 and 9 and part of chapter 12; Burton C. Hallowell and Willard M. Wallace read chapter 11; Michael Cherniavsky and Harry Schwartz read chapter 12; Sigmund Neumann and William A. Spurrier read chapters 13 and 14. I am grateful to the Wesleyan Research Committee for its assistance; to Gertrude M. McKenna and her colleagues at Olin Library who were always kind and helpful; to Marilyn Kwayauskas, Mrs. Esther B. Carling, and Mrs. Ellen D. Heye, who typed the manuscript.

> Herewith I launch thee, paper ship
> To sail a wordy ocean.
> Skim through the churnings of the critics' slip
> Set greater waves in motion.

E. O. G.

Middletown, Conn.
December, 1953

PART I

The Ideology of Capitalism

1.

CLASSICAL CAPITALISM

Liberty, Opportunity, Prosperity:
Individualism and the Industrial Revolution

Iᴛ ɪs not unnatural that in responding to the onslaught of collectivism, twentieth-century Americans should fall into the common
error of thinking that individualism has always been the order of the
day. We tend to assume that individual initiative and unregulated
enterprise have always been the rule in the economic system, that
government intervention in social and economic affairs was never
more than a temporary departure from the historical norm. Another
all too prevalent error is to think that politics and economics, philosophy and religion, cultural tradition and social custom, can each
be analyzed "scientifically" without regard to the others. Such misconceptions make it difficult for the modern American to get a clear
view of the problems of his society, and leave him rather befuddled
before the glimmering galaxy of "isms." But it is precisely the function of historical perspective to sweep away such obstacles to an un-
distorted view. And the historical record is exceedingly unkind to
some of the assumptions most easily taken to be true.

In point of fact, collectivism of a certain kind was increasingly
dominant from the late days of the Roman Empire to the fifteenth
and sixteenth centuries. Land and agriculture were the basis for the
major institutions of society, and as time went on the manorial sys-

tem became the prevailing pattern for the organization of social and economic activity in Europe. It was a system under which the large agricultural estate attempted to be self-sufficient, to make its own tools and to produce what it consumed. It thrived during a period when the little man needed protection and the mighty based their power on wealth in land. And it declined as towns grew and prospered on the sites of Roman encampments, or beneath the walls of castles and monasteries, as trade by land and sea became more secure and more fully developed. But the towns, although bringing upon the scene a new social power, the middle class or bourgeoisie (*bourg*=town), did not at once produce the individualistic values and society we now take for granted.

Town life, like all other aspects of medieval civilization, was under the strong influence of Catholic philosophy, then as now in fundamental opposition to materialistic individualism. The cities, moreover, were as subject as the countryside to other pressures that pervaded Europe in the Middle Ages, an intense need for economic and military security, fear of famine, necessity for the community to live at peace with itself. They could not afford the luxury of untrammeled individualism. Craftsmen and merchants gained control over the towns, and secured charters which gave them privileges, liberties and increasing freedom from the nobility, but the bourgeois carried on their trades within their own system of strict regulations. They were organized into gilds possessing many of the combined features of contemporary trade associations, labor unions and fraternal orders and, in addition, frequently constituting a religious congregation within the gild chapel. Through their gilds they prohibited such business practices as cornering the market, purchasing goods before they were offered for public sale, having more than a specified number of apprentices, and the like. The live or painted clock standing before our twentieth-century watchmaker's shop, the boot hanging over the door of some of our shoe stores, are a reminder that the medieval gildsmen believed this was as far as one could properly go in calling the public's attention to one's wares. They had the surprising notion that quality was the only legitimate advertising technique, and advertising as we know it today they would have considered immoral.

Of course, there were wide variations in rules and their observance from place to place and over the course of years. As trade and crafts grew and produced accumulations of capital, violations of medieval law and of the medieval spirit became common and accepted practices. The discovery of new worlds and new products, the importation of vast quantities of gold and silver led to an inflation in the sixteenth and seventeenth centuries that shattered the relatively static contractual system of the Middle Ages, and gave the middle class increased power and prestige. But the bourgeoisie could not yet stand on its own. Struggling to free itself from the control of the landed nobility, it entered into alliance with that other enemy of the nobles, the king. For the monarchs of Europe had been striving to crush the independence and autonomous power of their dukes and counts, who were in some instances their sworn enemies and more powerful than they. Thus the rise of the middle class was at first part and parcel of the rise of absolute monarchy. As the kings of France and England rose from a position of relative equality with their higher nobles to one of clear superiority, their middle-class allies rose with them. But, freed from the nobles, they became the servants of the king. Through the sixteenth and part of the seventeenth centuries in England, and even later in France, modern capitalism, the bourgeois economic system, developed under royal, mercantilist control.

At this stage there was far more room for individual initiative than in the thirteenth-century town. Not that the kings had turned over control of economic affairs to their bourgeois supporters. Far from leaving the economy to its own working, the royal governments tried to extend over *the whole country* a system of control in many ways similar to that of the medieval city. This was mercantilism, the economic power policy of the ambitious absolute monarchy. In its highest form under the administration of J. B. Colbert from 1661 to 1683, during the reign of Louis XIV of France, mercantilism included regulation of labor, methods of production, type and quality of product, prices and methods of merchandising. It comprised subsidies, monopolies, tariffs, interest-free loans to businessmen, importation of foreign artisans, and the prohibition of emigration of skilled French subjects. It was an all-pervasive system, but inclusive and seemingly severe that it was, it still effectively encouraged and stimulated private business. And, given an inch, private business began to try for additional yards of freedom. There were three main reasons for this. First, while laws were much stricter in those days, enforcement was far more difficult than with modern facilities of communication. Second, government help did get many businesses under way. The St. Gobain mirror works, established with Colbert's aid, is still in operation today. Third, the mercantilist administrator had to work out his program of national economic development through and by means of the individual businessman or firm. The king's officials would, of course, try to fit the entrepreneur's self-interest into the administrative scheme of national interest, and the merchant or manufacturer was pressed to find a place within the program. But, even while the mercantilist state condemned the bourgeois for his selfishness, it had to use him to further its own ends, and it had to give him considerable liberty within the limits it prescribed.

England was the first large nation to veer from state development of the economy. In the fifteenth and sixteenth centuries the nobles had been so thoroughly subjugated by the Tudors that the throne no longer feared them. The crown was supreme, and so towered above its bourgeois allies that it could safely hand over the administration of social and economic laws to local middle-class officials without danger of losing its ultimate control. Of course the royal government could and did step in from time to time, but its hold slowly slackened. By the mid-seventeenth century the British middle class was ready to revolt and cut off the monarchy as well as the King's head. Oliver Cromwell's Puritan Revolution did not endure, King Charles II was recalled to the throne in 1660, but British mercantilism never again showed the degree of control over internal social and economic affairs that was taken for granted in Elizabeth's day.

Capital, trade, and invention progressed more rapidly in the fluid English society born of revolution than on the Continent of Europe. But government was not yet reduced to the hands-off role of the passive policeman. While internal restrictions fell off, Great Britain attempted to maintain some regulation within her colonies, and a great deal over the trade of the Empire as a whole. The colonies of North America, however, evaded internal regulation and eventually were forced into revolution by their inability to live and prosper within the limits of the British mercantilist system.

By the year 1788 it was an accepted principle in the United Kingdom and the United States, and to lesser degrees in other lands, that economic initiative should normally come from interested individuals, and the right of the public authority to intervene within the national boundaries was being questioned. The next year, 1789, saw the beginning of the French Revolution that spread the doctrines of individual freedom through half the world.

Even in the extremely sketchy form in which this story has been told, it brings out two striking points. First, some of the precepts and institutions we now tend to take for granted were not characteristic of Western civilization during twelve of the fourteen and one-half centuries since Rome first fell into non-Latin hands. Second, individualistic principles and capitalist institutions came into being very, very slowly over a period of approximately five hundred years and reached toward maturity only at the end of the eighteenth century. Their gradual development paced that of industry and technology, and our individualistic principles reached the advanced status of commonplaces only with the extremely rapid growth of industry in the late eighteenth and nineteenth centuries. Individual liberty, individual opportunity and individual prosperity as the way to the greatest good for the greatest number, are not timeless truths. They were, however, the ideological keystone of the industrial revolution.

Expansion and Enterprise: The Historical Setting

The eighteenth century has been called the Age of the Enlightenment. This flattering description is often disputed, for a variety of reasons, but whatever else the term may imply, the period was certainly one in which thinking men tried as never before to bring all nature's phenomena and all man's ways into logical systems of natural law. The curse of specialization, the experts' Tower of Babel, had not yet settled too heavily over Western civilization and a man could still be master of several branches of knowledge.[1] There was, therefore, an inevitable tendency to seek analogies among the different fields of learning, and to apply the same methods of reasoning in social philosophy as were used in physics.

[1] This strengthened the sense of the unity, rather than the departmentalization of learning. For example, James Watt, inventor of the first practical steam engine and many other useful gadgets, referred to his work as "philosophy," and regarded himself as a natural philosopher in the field of mechanics.

Eighteenth-century thinkers built upon the practical and theoretical achievements of an earlier age that produced the physics and mathematics of Newton, the political science of Locke, and the physiology of Hartley. For every aspect of the world and human society that came under their observation, they sought to discover natural laws logically harmonious with and similar to the laws established in the physical sciences. The philosophers of the Enlightenment believed in the power of human reason to deduce universal law from axiomatic truths and from what had been observed. Consciously in some cases, unconsciously in others, they tried to think through to the political and economic equivalents of the law of gravity. Their outlook was mechanical, not evolutionary, for they thought in terms of the workings of a finished machine rather than of a growing and changing organism.

The end products of this point of view can be seen in the political theory of the separation of powers and checks and balances that so influenced the framers of the American Constitution, but nowhere more clearly than in the systematic economic theory that now developed for the first time in history. In the Middle Ages, economics was necessarily approached from a religious standpoint; in the sixteenth and seventeenth centuries, economics might generally have been described as the study of particular problems of business, and of government in the economic sphere. The Industrial Revolution called for explanation of economic phenomena and the thinking of the times demanded that explanations be stated in terms of natural law. Classical economists therefore conceived of their subject as the "science" of the natural laws of the production and distribution of goods. It is a pleasant paradox: the economic theory of the hard-headed, individualistic businessman of the Industrial Revolution, was far more abstract than that of the royal bureaucrat of the seventeenth century.[2] And yet this is understandable, for the hard-headed businessman was only asking for his equivalent of the laws of the equally hard-headed physicist. They were not then aware, as we are in this Atomic Age, how very abstract the physical sciences are.

[2] Classical economics actually *was* the businessman's theory. It is impossible to insist too strongly that everyone is a theorist, consciously or not. The industrialists of Manchester and Birmingham who backed the campaign to repeal British grain tariffs prior to 1846 were fully conscious of the classical theory of rent and wages, and based their campaign on their theory.

Classical economics provided a set of logically consistent answers to the questions raised by this era of rapid social change. Adam Smith's *Wealth of Nations*, published in 1776, brought together the earlier efforts at this new kind of rationalistic analysis, but this masterpiece still reveals the moral philosopher who is aware of the complexities of man and his works. The clergyman T. R. Malthus, the broker David Ricardo, and the other founders and popularizers of classical economics squeezed out of Smith his deductive method and tight reasoning, and tossed away as pulp the richness of his human observation.

The Economic Man and Equilibrium: Some Assumptions

At a time such as ours, when rationalism and even rationality command less respect than they have for centuries, a moderate degree of conscious effort is needed to appreciate the spirit and the methods of the fathers of the classical school. An analogy with Euclid, whose prestige has in fair part survived the invention of new forms of mathematics, may possibly help. Euclid's plane geometry is a logical system based on such axioms as that parallel lines never meet, or that quantities equal to the same or equal quantities are equal to each other. Classical economics was a sort of economic geometry based on a series of logical deductions from presumably self-evident truths.

One basic assumption was "the economic man." Every individual acting in the economic sphere was thought to operate in a purely rational way. His objective was profit, and the means to this end he chose through a rational analysis of his own self-interest. No other considerations entered into his decisions; ethics and psychology were as rigidly excluded from the science of economics as they were from the science of physics.[3] The Ten Commandments and the

[3] There was, of course, an implicit ethic, based on the sanctity of unlimited property rights and on the underlying assumption that the existing distribution of property was equitable. It can be argued that Adam Smith's belief in economic individualism was built upon a conception of the individual as guided by an understanding of the bonds which united him to his fellow men (*Theory of Moral Sentiments*, published in 1759, seventeen years before the *Wealth of Nations*). If this be so, that aspect of Smith was not taken over by later classical economists.

A theory of psychology was also inherent in the concept of the economic

Sermon on the Mount were irrelevant to the life of the economic man, as were neuroses and duodenal ulcers. Furthermore, as Newton's laws operate equally well in France or Russia, England or Tasmania, as carbon is carbon whether in Siberia or the Transvaal, the laws of economics were held to be of universal validity and the economic man was held to be the same wherever found. Nineteenth-century critics were quick to point out that this assumption disregarded the obvious influence of national habits, cultural differences, and traditions. But the Enlightenment spirit was cosmopolitan as well as rationalist, and its social philosophers were not especially concerned with historical accidents which could hardly affect the fundamental identity of the human race.

Another assumption was that, since the whole is equal to the sum of its parts, the group interest is equal to the sum of the individual interests of the members of the community. This proposition ran counter to a view widely held among seventeenth-century mercantilists, that individual interests were likely to be of a short-term character and might be contrary to the general welfare. For example, the great French administrator, Colbert, observed that a landowner might wish to fell an entire stand of timber to take advantage of a sudden rise in prices. But this might mean a dangerous shortage of timber for the French navy—and hence for the nation—a few years later. French law, therefore, provided that forests could be cut over for firewood and the like only once in 40 years, and for timber only once in 120 years. Such a policy would not have been acceptable to classical economists, believing as they did that there was no distinction between individual and general interests, and that an "invisible hand" guided selfish and often conflicting individual desires to the welfare of the group as a whole. As Adam Smith wrote, "What is prudence in the conduct of every private family can scarce be folly in that of a great kingdom."[4]

A third classical assumption was that, as water seeks its own level, the economic system would find its proper and most efficient alloca-

---

man: the idea, borrowed from Jeremy Bentham, that man's actions were dictated by a rational calculation of the pleasures and pains involved in alternative courses. This bears little resemblance to psychology in any modern sense of the word.

[4] *Wealth of Nations*, New York, Modern Library edition, 1937, p. 424.

tion of resources if unhindered by artificial, man-made obstacles. In the absence of tariffs, subsidies, wage and hour laws, and the other outcroppings of government intervention, labor would go where it was needed, capital where it could be most fruitfully employed. Where the mercantilist had established qualitative social standards, believing, for example, that foundries, because of their wartime potential, were more useful to the nation than equally profitable or more profitable import firms, the classical school had no community standards. A good business was one that existed without artificial support. The decision as to whether an undertaking should exist was not to rest with bureaucrats but with a natural force. Mercantilist interference, said Adam Smith, could only compel "the trade of a country into a channel much less advantageous than that in which it would naturally run of its own accord.[5]

Alone and unaided, the first two assumptions could produce nothing but chaos and the third would be meaningless without an activating factor. The economic man following his own self-interest would have to possess a divine degree of enlightenment to be able to discover through reason the point at which selfishness might boomerang. Nature, however, each part of which goes its own way, is order rather than chaos. The third assumption, that the economy would seek its proper level, pointed the way to the notion of economic harmony that duplicated the harmony of the physical world. A force was still necessary for the machine to function; it could not operate without some equivalent of Newton's dynamics. This force was competition, which regulated the economic natural machine while the economic man's desire for profit propelled it. Competition, the fourth major assumption, would produce those adjustments in prices and production, in the supply and remuneration of capital and labor that would yield the best results of which the economy was capable. As this competition was for the consumer's shilling, it was the consumer's choice as to how to spend the fruits of his labor that governed the destinies of competitive enterprise. The consumer was guided by his interest to seek the most for the lowest price. The producer's self-interest led him to meet this requirement in competition with other producers. The result, achieved as if by the working of the "invisible hand" of a higher power, was to maximize

[5] *Wealth of Nations*, p. 473.

production at minimum prices, in an order of natural harmony.

Upon these four propositions—the idea of the economic man, the idea of self-interest, the idea of the automatic flow of labor and capital where needed, the idea of competition—the theory of classical capitalist economics was built. By weaving these concepts together and by following out their logical implications, economic theorists and practical men of affairs built an ideology which was used to explain and defend the capitalist, free enterprise, industrial system of society.

From Division of Labor to Laissez Faire: Main Doctrines

It should be borne in mind that this individualistic ideology arose in western Europe toward the close of the era of mercantilism, in the latter part of the eighteenth century. Like all new social theories, it was elaborated as a criticism of what had been the established principles of government intervention as well as a herald's call to a new era of expansion and progress. Ripe targets for this criticism, to be found in both international and domestic policy, were the specific issues to which the classical assumptions were applied.

One of the chief preoccupations of the mercantilists had been to assure the nation an adequate supply of gold and silver, not, as has often been said, that they believed precious metals to be the only form of wealth. They were not so short-sighted. But in an age when credit facilities such as banks, commercial paper and national debts were inadequately developed,[6] there was good reason to argue that gold and silver excelled all other forms of wealth in several ways. They were the most liquid form of wealth, since they could at any moment be exchanged for any other goods, or services; they did not deteriorate physically, and were always in demand. Consequently gold and silver were regarded as superior to all other forms of wealth in serving the needs of both war and peace. An adequate supply of precious metals meant that soldiers could be hired and

---

[6] National debts, called by Alexander Hamilton a national blessing, have a long history and a tradition of almost uninterrupted growth behind them. French *rentes* were an early sixteenth-century development, Dutch bond issues began in the late sixteenth century, and the British national debt, started in 1693, provided the basis for the foundation of the Bank of England the following year.

supplied in time of war, and that commodities and services would be produced, bought, and sold in time of peace.

With the expansion of trade and industry in the eighteenth century and the development of credit facilities, the advantages of the precious metals over other commodities declined. Armies could be paid and equipped with the proceeds from the sale of government bonds. Commercial paper and bank loans afforded business concerns the necessary funds to maintain activity. Specie was still the base upon which the paper money structure rested, but it was now at most the foundation and no longer the whole edifice.

The facts of history were therefore running with him when the many-sided genius David Hume turned his attention to the flow of gold and to the mercantilist doctrine of the favorable balance of trade. The mercantilists had argued that if the nation's economic objective was to secure precious metals, this could be done either by mining them or by exporting more goods than were imported. This was the favorable balance of trade, the balance being received in gold or silver. Western Europe was not a gold or silver mining area, therefore treasure had to be sought in foreign trade. Since the nations of western Europe were quite similar in their production of raw materials, wheat, wool, iron, and timber, the greatest markets and highest profits would be developed in the export of manufactured articles. This called for protective tariffs on the importation of manufactured goods, or even for prohibiting their entry; conversely, the logic of the favorable balance of trade indicated duty-free imports and sometimes export prohibitions for raw materials, to keep them in adequate supply. Since some commodities were more exportable and more profitable than others, the mercantilists had devised subsidies to create the chosen industries, and regulations to ensure quality. The immediate objective of all these measures was the acquisition of a large supply of precious metals.

The whole theoretical structure of mercantilist government intervention would accordingly be undermined if the doctrine of the favorable balance of trade could be proved false. Hume set out to do just this. He argued from the quantity theory of money, known since its statement by Jean Bodin in 1568, and from the classical principle of the automatic flow of labor and capital. The quantity theory, simply put, was that prices would rise with an increase and fall with a decrease in the amount of money in circulation. If a country increased its supplies of precious metals through a favorable balance of trade, said Hume, prices in that land would rise, and foreigners would buy less from it. After a time, the value of that country's exports would fall below the value of its imports, and it would have to pay out gold to make up the balance. As its gold supply declined, its prices would fall, and its export trade would recover. A favorable balance of trade could therefore not continue indefinitely. Like water in two connected vessels, trade and gold would seek their natural level. Protective tariffs and government intervention in general were at best futile, and even injurious. A country's supply of precious metals would inevitably be proportioned to its actual needs in business and industry, and laws and decrees would avail as little as did the words of Canute against the Channel waves.

But the argument could be carried further. The other aspect of the automatic flow principle was that capital and labor would, if unhindered by man-made obstacles, go where they could most profitably be employed. David Ricardo, possibly the most influential of the classical economists in Parliament and out, developed this reasoning into the law of comparative advantage, the cornerstone of free trade and laissez faire economics. If, for example, England could produce both cutlery and blankets more efficiently than France, but cutlery more efficiently than blankets, it would be profitable to England to concentrate labor and capital on cutlery and import its blankets from France. And, if Great Britain did not impose a protective tariff on blankets, her producers would tend to switch from the less to the more efficient and favorable cutlery industry. If all nations were to adopt complete free trade, each would concentrate its efforts in the field in which it could best specialize, and the total world product would be at its optimum. Even should one or more countries remain blind to the truth of this natural law of economics, it would still be profitable for England to follow a free-trade policy, since every single act of government intervention, anywhere in the world, by diverting labor and capital from its naturally most efficient and profitable channel, would decrease the flow of income.

This was the argument that the commercial and industrial class of England and their spokesmen, such as Ricardo, Cobden, and Bright, triumphantly fought through their own Parliament and attempted, with far less success, to sell to the nations of the world. Ricardo's law of comparative advantage was merely the international aspect of the great principle of the division of labor, based on the axioms of the automatic flow of productive forces directed by the self-interest of the economic man.

Applied to the domestic economy, these propositions were destined to create the theoretical symbols that stand for individualistic free enterprise; freedom of contract, competition, and laissez faire. They were revolutionary enough to bring with them a host of disturbing and momentous issues. It was clear enough that the subsidies and legal monopolies (in such common commodities as matches) of the mercantilist era would have to go. The gilds too, an institution dating to the Middle Ages, which regulated crafts and trades and closed them to all but their members, had no place in the new age of individualism. And, following classical logic, together with the removal of barriers to competitive private enterprise went the imposition of restrictions on labor organization. Banding together to force higher wages or better working conditions was held to be an interference with the laws of economics and with the freedom of the individual to make contracts.

The new industrialism called into existence large cities such as Birmingham and Leeds, and a new social class, the propertyless wage laborers, who were to be named the proletariat in the radical philosophies of the nineteenth century. A revolution in British agriculture, the enclosure movement, completed the change from small-scale farming for subsistence to large-scale farming for profit. Common pastures were eliminated and the strip holdings of the free peasantry consolidated, leaving them with acreage insufficient for self-support. They moved to the squalor of the new cities and huddled beside the factories that would employ them. Herein was the death of Merrie England and the birth of the Workshop of the World.

Effective labor organization had been prohibited by the Combination Acts of 1799 and 1801 (later modifying laws did not materially change the situation). Left to the beneficence of natural law, the condition of the working class deteriorated. The wretched life of factory labor led to protests by landed aristocrats, who saw their traditional leadership threatened by the new industrialists. And they were joined by workers, radical intellectuals, and clergymen in an effort which secured the enactment of some largely ineffective remedial legislation.[7] Ethical and moral principles furnished the basis for most of the protest, but what place did ethics and morals have in a system of natural law?

The answer of the industrialists to their critics, radical and reactionary, was phrased in the logical arguments of T. R. Malthus and Ricardo. Malthus, a Church of England minister turned economist, contemplated the misery of the poor, and found an explanation for it in terms of natural law. Observing the phenomenal rise in population of the young United States of America, and the slow increase in agricultural production of the fields of old England, Malthus, with a peculiar consistency, reached the conclusion that population tended to increase much more rapidly than the means of subsistence. Population, he claimed, inevitably pressed upon food supply, and hunger and starvation were the equally inevitable result. Nature charitably prevented this tendency from working too strictly by such checks as wars and vice, floods, and plagues. If the workers sincerely desired to improve their lot, it was for them to limit their numbers by the exercise of what Malthus called moral restraint, or chastity. The manufacturer was not responsible for his employees' sufferings; the workers were bringing the curse upon themselves by excessive breeding. His doctrine, Malthus said, "attributes the greatest part of the sufferings of the lower classes of society exclusively to themselves."[8]

Ricardo carried Malthus's reasoning further. He drew a distinction between real wages, the goods and services the consumer could afford to buy, and the money wages the worker received. And then he argued that however money wages might vary, real wages in the long run would hover about the subsistence level, beneath which workers would not marry and beget children. Applying the population theory, if real wages were to rise above the level that would merely afford habitual subsistence to the earner and his family, that family would obviously increase. Hence the supply of labor would

<hr/>

[7] A trend toward state intervention in England came into being while classical doctrine was still fighting for dominance. See pp. 261, 547.

[8] *Essay on the Principle of Population,* London, 9th ed., 1888, p. 417.

rise, and since labor is one commodity among the rest, whose money price is set by supply and demand, money and real wages would fall. This would drive real wages below the subsistence level for the increased population. The excess labor supply would eventually die off, and wages would return to the level which, said Ricardo, would "enable the labourers, one with another, to subsist and to perpetuate their race, without either increase or diminution."[9] This was the iron law of wages (the German socialist Lassalle called it the "brazen law of wages") which, like the population theory itself, freed the employer from any moral responsibility for the misery of those who worked in his shop.

Society was warned against such vain sentimentalities as poor relief and child labor restriction, for to enable the poor to reproduce was merely to help them multiply their troubles. Harriet Martineau, English observer of the American scene and author of fictionalized economics for people of good breeding, wrote:

. . . legislation *cannot* interfere effectually between parents and children in the present state of the labour-market. Our operations must be directed towards proportioning the labour and capital, and not upon restricting the exchange of the one for the other,—an exchange which must be voluntary, whatever the law may say about it. . . . The case of those wretched factory-children seems desperate: the only hope seems to be that the race will die out in two or three generations, by which time machinery may be found to do their work better than their miserable selves.[10]

The British Poor Law Reform of 1834, which ended the old Elizabethan system of home relief and established the workhouses that Dickens castigated in *Oliver Twist*, was but a logical response to the revealed natural law of economics.

Although the classical school had in this fashion satisfactorily out-

[9] *Principles of Political Economy and Taxation*, London, Everyman Edition, 1911, p. 52.

[10] Maria Weston Chapman (ed.), *Harriet Martineau's Autobiography*, Boston, 1877, vol. 2, p. 215. This was with reference to the British Factory Act of 1833, which prohibited employment in textile factories of children under nine years of age, and limited working hours to nine a day up to the age of thirteen and twelve a day from thirteen to eighteen. By "proportioning the labour and capital" Miss Martineau meant decreasing the proportion of working-class population to capital through celibacy in accordance with Malthus's doctrine. The "race will die out" presumably refers to Malthus's "natural checks" on increase: disease and vice.

lined the role of government as a passive policeman and had explained away squalor and disease, although it had brought to the social science of economics a prestige similar to that of physics, it still had to demonstrate that the social machine did in fact function smoothly, in a machinelike manner. It was obvious and correct to point out that the Napoleonic wars ending in 1815 had constituted an artificial, man-made dislocation of the instruments of the economy. As the war years receded into the past, however, the economy did not follow an unchanging course of prosperity. There were depressions, with unemployment, social disturbances, plummeting profits.

Did the natural order provide for these mechanical breakdowns? The French classical economist, J. B. Say, proved to the contentment of most fellow theorists that it did not. There could be no general overproduction, for the supply of one commodity constitutes demand for others, and the production of one creates the ability to purchase others. Some goods could, of course, be overproduced relative to effective demand, and others underproduced. But this could only mean a short-run improper allocation of resources. The factors of production would soon shift to adjust to demand, from the industries in which there was excess supply to those in which supply was short. The consumer was lord of the economic universe, producer balanced against producer, and a long-run glut was a logical impossibility. Rational mankind had merely to come upon the natural laws of political economy and eliminate man-made impediments to their smooth functioning. In Ricardo's confident words,

> By an adherence to these [principles of economics], governments cannot fail to promote the welfare of the people who are submitted to their sway. What more clear than the advantages which follow from freedom of trade, or than the evils resulting from holding out any peculiar encouragement to population?[11]

Say's law of markets completed the main outlines of an optimistic social philosophy. It did not have the transcendent optimism of medieval mystics, who envisioned the journey of the mind of man to God, or the unrestrained optimism of anarchists who believed man was infinitely perfectable once he had freed himself from the

[11] James Bonar (ed.), *Letters of David Ricardo to Thomas Robert Malthus,* Oxford, 1887, p. 171.

shackles he had himself created. It was a bourgeois optimism, derived from a naïve faith that it rested on a reasoned view of the "law of nature." Imbued with the spirit of progress, individual man could and did seek his fortune, new products were developed, technology and science sped forward. All countries felt the pressure of England's salesmen, and heard English publicists urge the nations to follow their well loved Workshop and Banker of the World along the road to free trade and nonintervention, to economic liberalism at home and abroad. Imperialism lost favor in the metropolis of the world's greatest empire; the British sought trade rather than colonies, and the flag followed the merchant only when he found local authority inadequate to business security. Britain's liberalism, displayed with the prestige of her diplomacy and supported by her awesome fleet, was more important than the Monroe Doctrine in guaranteeing the independence of the new Latin American republics. British interests called for peace, stability and the advancement of democracy. In the nineteenth century, democracy and political liberalism were linked with the rise to power of the middle class, and this favored the adoption of the economic liberalism that meant good business for Great Britain.

It is all too easy to allege hypocrisy in this Victorian Age. One can point out that England adopted free trade only when her lead over the rest of the world enabled her to overcome any competition. She called on other nations to follow her when they were so far behind industrially that her exports would flood their markets. Criticism of imperialism came ill from the great imperial nation. The industrialist who worshiped gravely with his family on Sunday, contributed generously to charity, condemned slavery, and accepted the extension of the suffrage was the man who spent his week in a single-minded search for profits and paid his workers little enough to make them objects of charity. He remained undisturbed by the fact that they were economic and social, although not political, slaves. The ideology of classical economics, of economic liberalism, by which the time, the country, and the man lived, resolved these apparent contradictions. It was a nonhistorical system of thought, and the fact that England's rise to industrial greatness had commenced under a system of mercantilist regulation and stimulation escaped notice. It was believed that her industrial growth simply coincided with her adoption of the program of economic liberalism. Hence British economic liberals could in all good conscience urge other lands to follow this policy.

As for imperialism, the British swept away the last of the Navigation Acts, measures restricting colonial commerce, in 1849, and the gates were open to anyone's trade. And if the Union Jack trailed British investments into Egypt, South Africa, and a dozen points around the globe, the operations of the Royal Navy could often be justified by the danger that another, less liberal power would step in and close a promising market.

Nor was the hard-driving businessman a conscious hypocrite. The ideology of economic liberalism divorced economics from Christian ethics, and he could conveniently feel as righteous in his weekday greed as in his sober devotions on the Sabbath. Chattel slavery, as practiced in the American South before the Civil War, clashed with both systems of thought, violating both freedom of contract and Christian principles, and the British manufacturer condemned it. The industrial worker, on the other hand, free in civil law, was enslaved only by rigorous natural, economic law whose inevitability carried the implied moral sanction of the universe. While the Victorian businessman favored extension of the suffrage in order to weaken the old landed aristocracy, he still believed actual political power should rest in the hands of those with strong material interests in the country, especially the commercial and industrial propertied class. As Malthus had put it, "the middle parts of society are most favorable to virtuous and industrious habits, and to the growth of all kinds of talents."[12] Unfettered by aristocratic concern for the poor, guided by reason and imbued with a zeal for work and knowledge, the middle class could best take the lead in casting off ancient prejudices, cutting government expenditures, and building squalid factories as monuments to progress.

The Victorian Age was one of great material progress, in which even the factory laborer shared, despite the iron law of wages. It was an age in which humanitarianism (arising from religion, custom, and simple good will) and able public administration (arising from the conviction that wealth and position carried the responsibility for public service) tempered the harshness of a rationalistic

[12] *Essay on the Principle of Population,* p. 473.

ideology and helped produce what we now look back to fondly as the good old days.

NOTES ON BOOKS

There are a number of good histories of economic theory which will be helpful for the doctrines of the classical school and their successors: C. Gide and C. Rist's *History of Economic Doctrines* has almost become a classic in its own right; Erich Roll's *A History of Economic Thought* is more detailed, and gives a better picture of the development of particular classical concepts than it does of the doctrine as a whole; Alexander Gray's *The Development of Economic Doctrine* is brief, witty, and in many ways the most satisfactory.

In none of these books, however, is classical economics described as part of history. The social background is there, of course, but it is not allowed to intrude too much upon the seemingly autonomous growth of theory. In this respect the histories of economics resemble classical economics itself.

One should turn to the classical writers themselves, but it must be said that they lost not only much of Smith's breadth of view but his attractiveness as a writer.

2.

THE CLASSICAL DOCTRINE
IN AMERICA

World Trade and Local Industry:
Capitalism in the Young American Republic

Victorian values now carry little weight in their homeland and economic theory in the tradition of the classical writers has lost most of its influence in its old strongholds, the British universities. The prestige of doctrine dies hard, however, especially when it rests upon unquestionable economic triumphs well within the memory of living men, and when there are still strong groups in society to whom it continues to be serviceable in the defense of their interests. The task of upholding the values of nineteenth-century England and the theories of its classical economists has largely passed into the hands of certain sections of the American public who have popularized the phrase "free enterprise system." This has become an effective slogan, for it has been used as a symbol for the things that are America's pride: democracy, opportunity, and progress. But once again historical perspective casts a strong shadow of disapproval, for the history of the United States reveals no close and direct relationship between our success as a nation and the ideology derived from the theories of Malthus and Ricardo.

The young United States was largely British in civilization. Political traditions and institutions, business practices, religious organizations, and the arts and crafts were either transplants of or derivations from British originals. The influence of settlers from elsewhere than the British Isles was distinctly secondary. The British version of western European civilization was modified by the colonists in accordance with the conditions of their American environment, but these modifications were all the more striking because of the essential similarity between the Old and New World cultures.

The United States had never had a genuine class system based on the land, family, and status distinctions of the medieval order,[1] while the industrial revolution was only in the process of breaking down the rigid class structure of the mother country. American society of the early nineteenth century was, of course, not equalitarian, but differences in the New World were based on wealth, education, occupation, and religious affiliation, rather than on inherited rank.[2] Consequently, class fluidity and the opportunity to rise in the social and economic order were from the first characteristic of American civilization. Farmers' sons could become merchants or lawyers, and the vast lands west of the original settlements offered opportunities unnumbered.[3] The respectability of the middle class was assured

[1] The Southern planter aristocrat is comparable to the British country squire rather than the feudal noble. However gracious their mansions and manners, however great their family pride, they were essentially in the business of farming for profit, unlike the Norfolks of England and the Rohans of France.

[2] The slaves, amounting to 18 percent of the population in 1790, obviously do not come under these generalizations. Slavery established so extreme and rigid an exclusion from the general patterns of society, however, that it is possible to speak, as Aristotle did, of an essentially democratic society existing above and not including these living chattels. Slavery did, of course, contradict the central value of a democracy born in the Christian tradition: the essential dignity of the individual human being, irrespective of status. It was therefore incompatible with a democratic society in the long run.

[3] I am aware that the recent trend in American historical scholarship has been to correct an earlier overemphasis of the role of the frontier and its cultural implications. But it cannot be denied that the frontier did promote both individualism and a type of community spirit. To point out that this historical fact differentiates the United States from, let us say, Belgium or Wales, does not imply unseemly flag waving. It is merely another way of saying that energetic sons of European civilization took advantage of the opportunities inherent in living in a rich area with a low population density. De Tocqueville wrote: "The chief circumstance which has favored the establishment and the maintenance of a democratic republic in the United States is the nature of the territory that the Americans inhabit. Their ancestors gave them the love of

from the very beginning and there was no struggle for social equality with an old landed aristocracy. The struggle that was to mark American history was between sectional and economic interests rather than social castes. Business has clashed with the farmer, capital with labor, but they have fought as social equals in the eyes of the law.

Young America did not have the kind of industrial proletariat that existed in England as a result of the enclosure movement. There was no excess agricultural labor to be forced into the urban working class. As in most newly settled areas, land was plentiful, and wages were higher than in Europe. Farming was a practical alternative for a sufficient number of people, so that labor tended to be in short supply. Workers had to be imported from the old world for such projects as the Erie Canal, and eventually to staff the factories of the New England textile towns. The result was that American labor was not placed in the completely dependent and forlorn position of the English working class, and each successive wave of immigrants was quick to seek and eventually to gain the independence and self-respect of its predecessors.

In colonial times industries had been on a small scale and were geared to the local market; the large enterprises and fortunes were to be found in trade and shipping. When America became an independent nation it continued to import a large proportion of its manufactured goods from Great Britain (in 1790 the British Empire accounted for nearly two-thirds of America's international trade). But the industrial capacities of the Northern states soon began to develop. Samuel Slater built New England's first textile mill at Pawtucket in 1790, and the iron industry had been started in 1643. The plantation economy of the Southern states continued to produce cotton and tobacco and import the manufactures of the new industrial society. This difference in economy was reason enough for disagreement between the two sections, for the North soon came to think that its potential as a manufacturing area could best be developed behind a tariff wall protecting it from England's greatly superior industry, while the South naturally would suffer from the resulting higher costs of goods imported from Europe or from the North. The greater

equality and of freedom; but God himself gave the means of remaining equal and free, by placing them upon a boundless continent" (*Democracy in America*, New York, Bradley edition, 1945, vol. 1, pp. 290–291).

wealth, industrial development and population of the North enabled
it gradually to overcome Southern and Western resistance and set
America on the road to industrialization with the aid of protective
tariffs.

The United States never accepted the wage, population, or tariff
theory of British classical economics, showing the same reluctance to
follow the new "science" as did the nations of Continental Europe.
France and Austria, for example, sharply modified the conclusions of
Adam Smith's successors in accordance with their vigorous and lasting mercantilist tradition, and America transposed classical doctrine
in the light of its own unique characteristics and requirements. As a
result, while the nations of the Old World were working out a compromise between the interventionist system of the absolute monarchy
and the utter individualism of the classical school, the young American republic was at the same time developing a capitalist economy
and ideology that included Continental as well as British features
but differed from both in many of its values and practices. For the
moment, we shall only sketch the most general characteristics of this
development, for we are still concerned primarily with the classical
outlook and its continuation into the present. The greater part of the
American story belongs in another context which, for want of a more
pleasing word, we have called neomercantilism. The classical principles did, however, have an important role to play in American history, and its nature must be suggested.

The American Way: Laissez Faire Behind a Tariff Wall

Two main factors conditioned America's choice of policy in her
development as an industrial nation: the need for protection and the
vastness of the land. Her people had no fixed system of economics
that they accepted as fact. In many respects, they followed the individualistic doctrines of the classical school, but the country's needs
quickly modified pure theory. American individualism, moreover,
was not so rigid as to prevent the individual from seeking and obtaining benefits from the state when he could not secure them
through his own efforts. He would permit the state to help, but
would not allow it to control: American individualism was willing
to accept gifts, if there were no strings.

The Republic had opened its career under the leadership of the

Federalist Party of Washington and Alexander Hamilton who, as first Secretary of the Treasury, was a theoretical and practising mercantilist. We have already observed that the mercantilist emphasis on gold and silver, which made good sense in the seventeenth century, had less and less validity as the economy progressed and credit institutions developed. Mercantilist writers of the latter part of the eighteenth century were aware of this fact, and began to stress instead the development of industrial productivity as the aim of national policy.[4] Hamilton naturally shared this later view. His famous *Reports,* on the Mint, on the Bank, and particularly on Manufactures, offered Congress a program for the rapid industrial development of the United States.[5] Although Hamilton's plan was only partially enacted, the fact remains that he had presented it with no fear of being labeled visionary or subversive,[6] and that Federalist policy was designed to promote the same industrialization by less extreme measures.

The election of Jefferson in 1800 brought about a shift in emphasis from industry to agriculture, but despite his agrarian inclinations, several of the new President's acts served as a spur to industry. His response to British and French interference with American shipping in the course of the Napoleonic wars was to secure the passage of the Embargo and Non-Intercourse Acts of 1807 and 1809. The first limited American shipping to coastal trade and the second excluded the ships of the offending nations from American ports, and forbade American vessels to enter belligerent waters. Naturally, this led the Yankee merchant mariners to wail loudly, but it operated as an insurmountable protective wall benefiting Yankee, New York, and Pennsylvania industrialists. In 1816 the first high-tariff bill became law. In succeeding years tariffs fluctuated with the conflict between Northern manufacturers and Western and Southern agriculturalists, but as the trend toward industrialization continued, so did the policy of protection.

This trend was furthered by "the American system," closely linked with the name of Henry Clay, the "great Compromiser" in the clash of north and south over the admission of new states to the Union. He

---

[4] Trends in mercantilist thinking are discussed in p. 89 ff. below.
[5] See p. 101 ff. below.
[6] He was properly charged, however, with favoring class legislation.

favored the central bank and a land settlement policy that would bring in the revenue to support other aspects of his program. Clay called for federal planning, construction, and financing of internal improvements such as roads and canals. Such projects, he said, were the grant to the inland citizenry that would balance federal benefactions to the coastal population in the form of lighthouses and harbor facilities. Henry Clay's American system was part of America's expression of mercantilist, rather than classical economic thinking.

America's emerging ideology drew from both these sources to create an effective amalgam. Through the ups and downs of political struggle, the American policy—protection, internal improvements, land settlement, the economic linking of the agricultural West with the industrial East—continued to develop.[7] Although Andrew Jackson vetoed appropriations for a road from Maysville to Lexington, in Kentucky (on the ground that while it might form a link in a national road, it lay entirely within one state and was beyond the proper limit of federal activity), he did support interstate highway construction. In the great period of railroad building, before and after the Civil War, private capital was aided greatly by federal, state, and local governments through grants of land and subsidies and chartering of monopolies. There was some state rate regulation from the beginning of railroad development, but federal supervision did not come into being until the passage of the Interstate Commerce Act in 1887, which followed the unsuccessful efforts of agriculture to secure relief through the states from high charges and unfair practices of the railroads.

The same pattern of sectional disputes, shifting alliances and battles between agriculture and industry, government aid and relatively slight government regulation, is shown in the history of our navy in its relation to the steel industry, of federal aid to education in the land grant colleges, of our imperial efforts abroad. In the great heyday of American industrial expansion following the Civil War, when the Republican Party embodied the union between Midwestern farms and Eastern factories, this pattern was stabilized and its

[7] The implementation of this general policy was sometimes more and sometimes less democratic. Clay followed Hamilton in tending to favor the interests of those better situated in society, while Jackson followed Jefferson in tending to favor the interests of the large population groups.

ideology crystallized as the American free enterprise system.

There were sharp conflicts, such as the money controversy of the late nineteenth century, but the basic political, social, and economic institutions of the country were not attacked by any large section of the population on ideological grounds. In practice, free enterprise gave business freedom to compete or merge, freedom from the opposition of highly organized labor, freedom from regulation and, through protective tariffs, from foreign competition. The ideology of free enterprise was illustrated in the use of federal troops to support management in the Pullman Company strike in 1894, to preserve order *and* freedom of contract from interference by unions. It was illustrated in the action of the Supreme Court, in 1886, in reversing previous decisions in order to extend to corporations protection, under the due process clause of the Fourteenth Amendment, from restrictive legislation. It was illustrated even in the Sherman Anti-Trust Act of 1890, which sought to prevent competitive private industry from being stifled by huge private combinations. It was illustrated too in the Supreme Court's rejection of minimum wage laws, as late as 1923, as unjustifiable extensions of the police power of the states.

In internal social and economic policy, America appeared to remain truer to the ideology of classical capitalism than did Great Britain, where the doctrine had originated. With the major exception of the governmental gifts to business mentioned above, the United States seemingly exhibited a deep allegiance to the spirit of laissez faire. At the same time European nations were working toward more effective regulation of hours and working conditions in factories and controlling child and woman labor. On the other hand, in external policy, America early departed from classical doctrine to become and remain protectionist.[8]

Classical Theory and Contemporary Fact

It may seem strange that the ideology of capitalism—individualistic, materialistic, mechanistic—to which classical economic theory

[8] While the final triumph of protectionism as a principle did not come until the 1880's, "tariffs for revenue only" was an unachieved slogan even in the low-tariff era from 1833 to 1861.

in particular contributed so heavily should remain relatively unchanged for over a century. The economic doctrine itself did develop, but by working out new theoretical devices and analytical refinements rather than by changing its basic assumptions. In no sense is this intended as a dismissal of the work of the great neoclassical economists who carried the Ricardian tradition into modern times. The fact is that they studied and wrote about a theoretical, flexible, and competitive capitalist economic system, and thought in terms of such a system. Their major assumptions, generalizations, and conclusions therefore had no need to be changed, except in detail.

As the society grew more complex, however, the simple mechanistic approach to understanding it proved less adequate than ever and had to be modified. Distinguished economists such as the Austrians Menger and Böhm-Bawerk, the British Jevons and Marshall, the Americans John Bates Clark and Fisher, and many others, developed a far more refined and acute theory of capitalist economics than that of the original classical school. Their revisions of the theory of value, wages, and capital in some instances held far broader social implications. Since they were of an abstract nature, however, these implications did not immediately affect the working ideology of capitalism. The neoclassical method of analysis, marginalism,[9] was

[9] In marginal analysis, demand as a psychological fact, the relationship between demand and supply as expressed in terms of price, and the relationship between costs and quantity of production are all explained in terms of the last unit of demand, supply, or production entering into the equation. This last unit is at the limiting *margin* of demand or supply, and there will be no more units beyond it at the particular price. For example, assuming that there is a state of perfect competition in a market (where no one seller or buyer can significantly influence price) then the price of a pair of shoes will be set at that point at which the seller's desire to offer shoes and the buyer's desire to take them meet. This point is the price at which the last pair of shoes is sold, and becomes the price for all transactions in shoes in the given market. The price of the marginal unit, in short, will be the price of all identical units in this strictly theoretical, nonexistent market. The individual buyer arrives at his marginal demand unit in this way: if he is extremely hungry and only one loaf of bread is for sale, he will offer perhaps $100 or more for it. But he would offer far less for a second, still less for a third, and so on. Moreover, there is also a price at which sellers would cease to sell, since they would lose money. Thus there is a scale of demand and one of supply, depending on price. The point at which these two scales intersect will be the actual market price. This reasoning is thoroughly consistent, but is a purely theoretical *interpretation* of how the process works in real life.

more effective than the old in describing the psychology of the economic man, but this too left the essential classical conclusions undisturbed. Neoclassical economists still assumed the existence of the economic man, of perfect competition, of the tendency of the economy toward optimum production at lowest prices in the absence of artificial hindrances. When they did agree to government intervention, it was as a very particular exception. The ideological core of the theory remained almost intact. The integrated economics of Alfred Marshall and John Bates Clark made explicit the governing role of consumer choice that was implicit in classical theory. This intellectual refinement, however, came toward the close of the nineteenth century when a host of factors, including the growth of monopoly, were weakening the consumer's actual influence on the market economy. The greatest theoretical accomplishments of economics in the classical tradition came at a time when corporate concentration, increasing government intervention and the rise of labor organizations were widening further the gap between fact and theory.

There was one important respect, however, in which the newer, neoclassical theorists departed from the old. Ricardo and Say had denied the possibility of depression in an unfettered capitalist economy. It could hardly be argued at the close of the nineteenth or in the twentieth century that depressions were not a recurrent economic phenomenon. It was necessary to explain them as a phase of capitalism. The new generation of economists accepted the challenge, and there came in this century a profusion of theoretical explanations of what came to be called the business cycle.[10] They ranged from underconsumption to overproduction, from sunspots to variations in interest rates, from the description of precise ten- or twenty-year cycles to historical explanations in which each rise and each fall was given its own special causation. Beyond the theorizing lay the in-

[10] While the lead in studying the business cycle was taken by Wesley C. Mitchell and other economists who departed from the orthodox pattern, neoclassical economists such as Jevons, and writers in this tradition such as Hawtrey, contributed their share to the stock of cycle theories. Aside from these men, who accepted private property as the core of the economy, there were basic critics such as Thorstein Veblen, who believed depression inherent in capitalism. Long before, Karl Marx, attacking the whole property concept, had argued that capitalist depressions would inevitably recur and become more severe.

evitable question as to what, if anything, should be done. This was one of the two great problems out of which arose the disillusionment with liberal, capitalist economics that has swept Europe and invaded America in recent times. The other was the question as to how competitive really was the free enterprise society with its huge and stifling monopolies.

Both questions, however answered, seriously endangered one of the major articles of faith of Ricardo and his successors: the belief that the desires of the consumer were the ultimate ruler in capitalism. As long as it could be said with Adam Smith that "consumption is the sole end and purpose of all production; and the interest of the producer ought to be attended to, only so far as it may be necessary for promoting that of the consumer";[11] as long as it could be argued that it was the consumer who determined, through demand, what was to be produced, in what quantity, and at what price, the essential economic democracy of capitalism could be demonstrated. But many theories of the business cycle, and the fact and theory of monopoly, served to dethrone the consumer, and cast doubt on the effectiveness of competition as a regulator. Inevitably it was asked, If the producer rules, who is to rule the producer?

In short, increasing awareness of economic fluctuations and the trouble they brought, and of the rise of monopoly, placed in doubt some of the basic tenets and much of the inherent optimism of the whole liberal outlook. The consumers' democracy of classical doctrine had been linked ideologically with the growing political democracy of the Western world. When an aura of doubt began to replace the aura of faith that had surrounded economic liberalism, belief in political liberalism itself soon began to sag. This began to occur in Europe at the turn of the century, and totalitarianism eventually took hold. America might have had a similar experience had the depression of the 1930's not been overcome. Economic dislocation was a fact, and not the least of its by-products was that it invited those who still believed in political liberalism, although they were compelled to doubt its economic corollary, to intensify their reëxamination of the very heart of classical thought.

Were there to occur a strange disruption of historical continuity, a theory created to explain the facts and to meet the intellectual re-

[11] *Wealth of Nations*, p. 625.

quirements of one place and time might conceivably prove even more suitable to the facts and conceptual demands of another place at a far later time. No such supernatural aid, however, came to natural-law economics as developed by the classical writers and their latter-day heirs. Their assumptions and conclusions do not fit our current ideas regarding psychology and human nature, or our institutions and ways of living.

The "economic man," their prime assumption, has been a target for criticism since his birth a century and a half ago. Some have denied his existence and others have called him unchristian and brutish. To begin with, he was an abstraction. Ernst Mach, nineteenth-century Austrian scientist and philosopher, once illustrated the process of abstraction in this way: You start with an object possessing a number of characteristics; then think of the object as if one characteristic were removed, and you can still conceive in your mind of the whole object; remove another characteristic, and this will still be true; a third, and so on, until there is nothing left of the object; but you still imagine you have a conception of it. This is the kind of abstraction of which the economic man is an example.[12]

Every individual, however, lives and acts as a whole person. The ideas, things, and persons with which he has been brought up are at all times a part of him. Religious beliefs, artistic judgments, ethical concepts, thoughts on science and nature, habitual ideas, are as integral to a man as the reason which enables him to discover his self-interest. No one is at all times a reasoning creature. He is more likely to depend on reason in deciding what price to ask or to offer than in his family, social, or political life, but more than reason is involved even in his economic behavior. The heavy sale of manuals of business charm, the importance of fraternal and recreational organizations, the power of family relationships to overcome mediocrity of talent, all argue the obvious, that the human being always acts as a whole, as a compound of his own personality and the in-

[12] Ernst Mach, *Popular Scientific Lectures* (T. J. McCormack, trans.), Chicago, 1895, p. 200. Of course, the "economic man" stops just short of this absurdity, for *one* trait is taken to represent the *whole* man. But the mental process involved in creating him is the same. Abstractions can be useful analytical tools, provided it is never forgotten that they are only abstractions and tools, and not reality.

fluences of environment and tradition. The economic man is an unrealistic abstraction from the total man. Only the schizophrenic displays a truly split personality.

Nor can the notion of self-interest be restricted to the economic field. The shape it will take, the goals the individual will set for himself, are also the result of all that the individual is and has been. The closest approximation to the economic man was the entrepreneur who rode roughshod over competitors and employees weekdays and salved his conscience with prayer and charity week ends. But even he was acting morally, according to the standards of his day. There may have been reasonable facsimiles of economic men in the Victorian Age when the prestige of the theory made the behavior relatively respectable; this very respectability, which most men are apt to seek, colored their actions perhaps as much as reasoned self-interest. Business, like political morality, has changed, however. No twentieth-century Commodore Vanderbilt would say, "The public be damned!" He would instead spend millions in advertising to secure the public's good will.

Thus, instead of the economic man, we have to think of the modern American and his social and economic ideas and ways. He, like all people, is likely to desire prestige among his associates and family, material comforts and security. He is unlikely to ignore a chance to make an honest profit, will often press his opportunities to the very limit of the letter of the law, and will occasionally exceed it. He is more apt to be aware of a moral code in business than was his grandfather, and has consciously added security to his economic goals. Money as an end in itself is less attractive than it was two generations ago.

The second basic assumption of classical economics was the harmony of community and individual interests. Isolated from the other pillars of the classical scheme, this can rest only on some very unrealistic logic-chopping. We would have to say that individual interest, properly defined, means *long-run* interest, and in the long run individual interest depends on the welfare of the community since wealth means little when the country collapses. Therefore *short-run* individual interest must also harmonize with community interest. Yet this is evident nonsense, as is demonstrated by such occurrences as the Teapot Dome scandal, price gouging in times of shortage, and the waste of natural resources. Short-run individual interest may or may not run counter to the welfare of the community, but when it does, the community is properly annoyed and may seek to defend itself through law. This classical assumption was not meant to stand alone, of course, and was linked with the idea of the "invisible hand" guiding labor and capital to the most profitable and hence most beneficial endeavors through competition.

.In the first place, it is not necessarily true that the most profitable is the most beneficial employment of resources.[13] This was obviously false in wartime, and could be false whenever any social or community goals are set. The question resolves itself, therefore, into whether or not the community has the right to set goals. The American tradition says it does. Protective tariffs, grants to railroads, the Prohibition Amendment, laws against dope peddling and prostitution, all revealed economic or social objectives. With respect to the proposition that "profitable equals beneficial," it must be said that it depends upon the particular case.

In the second place, the proposition that capital and labor would automatically flow to their most efficient employments itself rests upon an assumption, that of perfect mobility, that capital and labor are free to seek the most profitable employment. The latter, in turn, rests upon a capacity for ignoring reality. Again the economic man appears in the argument, but if his family prefers to live in East Town rather than move to West Town some miles away where his employer's competitor is offering higher wages, he will stay in his old job despite all rational economics. Even when a particular area is stricken by act of nature or by technological change, it will be some time before labor deserts it for a more prosperous region. The reluctance of people to leave their home grounds constituted one of the most difficult labor problems during the Second World War,

[13] Profit as used in ordinary speech usually means the return on investment, and to persons untrained in the terminology of economics may even include entrepreneurial wages. The classical writers distinguished between returns on investment and an excess return called "profit." Since the "invisible hand" would guide capital to those endeavors which showed profit in the short run, competition among the increased number of producers would eliminate this excess and returns on investment would fall to the general average. Thus, owing to the weight of the "invisible hand," there could be no "profits," strictly speaking, except in the event of interference with the sleight of the "invisible hand."

and a high price had to be paid to bring workers to new production sites.

When technological unemployment strikes, as it did when machines replaced men in the cigar-making trade, for example, the classical argument that the workers would switch to another trade proved false. They were cigar makers, not machinists or stevedores. Some did, of course, go into other lines of work, but others opened small shops of their own where they continued to make cigars by hand. Aside from the factor of place, labor could move freely from one type of work to another only when skill and experience were not involved.

As for the mobility of capital, if a man's money is tied up in a furniture works which he manages, he cannot easily and suddenly skip into the textile business. Two things are involved here, skill and knowledge of the particular business, and ability to convert his investment into cash. He may be a good furniture man, but little else in the business way, and he may not be able to sell out quickly and profitably. Then too, as modern industry has followed its path to increasing complexity and higher investment in machines and plant, it has found it ever more difficult to change its course. Retooling for a new model is a major and terribly costly operation for the automobile manufacturers, and conversion to war production and reconversion to peacetime uses was so huge a task that the resources of the United States government had to be called into play.

Capital in the sense of productive facilities is not mobile, and liquid assets, such as cash or gilt-edge securities, have little to do with the automatic flow of capital to the most profitable line. The word *flow* means moving from one place to another, and in the modern world it is very hard for capital invested in industry to shake loose in order to move. A stockholder may sell his shares, but the investment remains. It is true, of course, that "in the long run," capital will shift from the less to the more profitable field, but when we are considering mobility of capital and labor as aspects of the mechanism of automatic adjustment that keeps the economy spinning at its optimum speed, the "long run" offers slight consolation. As Lord Keynes remarked, "in the long run we are all dead."

Competition was the most important of the classical assumptions. It was the force that would hold the whole system together and by which individual self-interests would be evened out to the benefit of all. By putting a premium upon efficiency and natural advantage, competition would drive out high-cost producing units and bring about the most advantageous distribution of capital and labor. If there were unusual profits in one type of business, new investors would be attracted and competition would bring prices down, and profits to the general average. The factor of competition would therefore protect the general welfare against excesses of individual self-interest.

The founders of classical economics took for granted perfect competition (where no one buyer or seller would exert a significant influence on price, and where consumers and producers are informed as to all relevant factors):[14] but not even their most orthodox descendant would claim that such a state now exists. They believed, furthermore, that competition normally operated through reductions in price; this never was and is not necessarily the case. Competition certainly exists today, but in widely varying degrees, and beside wide varieties of controlled production and selling.

Economists, of course, did not make a practice of closing their minds and senses to what was going on about them. As a group, they were rather among the most assiduous and best-informed observers of society. And they had always been disturbed by the clash between complex realities and the "spirit of system," the almost hypnotic desire for a thoroughly integrated set of doctrines. In pages that Keynes was later to make famous, Malthus had questioned Say's so-called law of markets, the principle of general equilibrium of supply and demand, but succeeding generations ignored his unorthodox views. John Stuart Mill, the last great classical writer, was so torn between the wish for a neat theoretical scheme and his sense of ethics that he tried to fit certain types of social legislation into the classical framework. He was thereby able to satisfy his moral principles, but he only succeeded in undermining the structure of natural-law economics.

When a theoretical system is claimed to represent the law of nature, it must be consistent and it must be exclusive. It cannot borrow elements from other systems based on opposing principles without

[14] The subsidiary assumption regarding the economic man's knowledge of all the facts of the case is a self-evident absurdity.

destroying the universal validity to which its own principles pretend. Mill fell into this trap. As a result, his interventionist beliefs were taken up by socialists and other thoroughgoing opponents of capitalism. Those who regarded Smith and Ricardo as the founders of a natural science could not, however, follow Mill too far, and remained noninterventionist in principle. They adjusted to the irregularities of social change by consenting to occasional exceptions to their laws, and continuing to incorporate new refinements into the old body of theory. One of the most intelligent escapes from the clash of economic abstraction with reality was that of John Bates Clark, who declared that the effectiveness of the natural laws of the imaginary static society was limited by the operation of natural laws of change in the real world of men. This left the laws of change to be worked out and analyzed, but it did not add reality to static theory.

The doubts have persisted, and the jarring facts could not be wished away. Economics in the classical tradition is fundamentally unrealistic, and rests far too much on a group of primary axioms. Beyond these, there are a number of methodological assumptions necessary to its analysis—"in the long run," "other things being equal."[15] Contemporary defenders of this tradition in economic thought usually follow J. B. Clark's lead, and reply that they are fully aware that their theory often fails to fit the facts, but that for purposes of analysis they set up ideal hypothetical cases, draw conclusions and then make the proper adjustments for the realities of life.[16] But that is easier said than done. It is like the old Ptolemaic astronomy, which employed "ideal" circular orbits, which were then adjusted toward reality by the addition of complex epicycles. A scientific generalization or law is accurate to the extent that it de-

[15] The assumption "other things being equal" is particularly unsafe. The "other things" thus set aside usually include the whims of fashion, of politics, and of mankind in general, as well as more strictly economic phenomena which are disturbingly fickle rather than constant. The assumption is essential, however, to all classical and neoclassical reasoning, which depends on the singling out of one factor or group of factors for consideration while the rest are to oblige by remaining unchanged.

[16] This approach was worked out by the German sociologist Max Weber, as the method of "ideal types," abstractions which are to be used only as a basis for comparative analysis of real situations. Too many who use it, however, fall in love with their ideal types and confuse them with the real objects of study.

scribes or predicts behavior, and its worth is placed in question the moment it has to be adjusted in order to *approach* what is actually observed.

The vitality of theory in the classical tradition does not rest on its obviously limited validity as a science of economics. Its wide appeal is certainly not as an analytical device, and the explanation for its popularity lies elsewhere. Like so many of its own elements, it has itself become an abstraction and a symbol. When Americans speak of "the free enterprise system," and then go on to talk of supply and demand and other elements of classical and neoclassical doctrine, they imply far more than the specific words actually mean. "The free enterprise system" has become the symbolic phrase for a great many things, noneconomic as well as economic: individual initiative, class fluidity, the chance for every lad to become President and for every messenger boy to become Chairman of the Board. Through a process of ideological free association, the theory of the unfettered market economy has come to be credited with tremendous industrial expansion and the conquest of the continent, political democracy, a high standard of living, plumbing, the automobile, education and increasing cultural opportunities, the ideas of toleration and fair play.[17] These things are true of America, but the magic phrase tends to make us forget the protective tariffs, federal grants, state and federal social legislation, the frontier, and the waves of immigrants, among many other factors which contributed to our social freedom and our economic development. Once the phrase "free enterprise" is taken as the symbol for our national achievements, people slip into an uncritical acceptance of some of its strictly economic implications. Thereafter, although the symbol be historically inaccurate and the theory unsound, symbol and theory are

[17] F. A. Hayek offers a good example of this kind of association. The virtues of the Anglo-Saxons, he says, were "independence and self-reliance, individual initiative and local responsibility, the successful reliance on voluntary activity, non-interference with one's neighbor and tolerance of the different and queer, respect for custom and tradition, and a healthy suspicion of power and authority." These virtues "are largely the product of the institutions" the "collectivists" are "out to destroy" (*The Road to Serfdom*, Chicago, 1945, pp. 215–217). Granting for the moment that the British do excel nearly all others in these noble qualities, it remains to be asked whether the Black Prince and the mercantilist Elizabeth possessed them, or whether British social and constitutional development was carried out by a committee of learned Ricardians.

united in a broad ideology which is claimed to represent modern American society. The tensions of the twentieth century have so sharpened debate that in coming to the legitimate defense of our political liberty, our relative social equality and our unequaled economy, we have defiantly proclaimed "free enterprise" as our slogan. And a good many of us have gone on from there to state a firm belief in a classical variety of economics.

If the issues of today were not so rigidly drawn in ideological terms, if our traditional anti-intellectual, antitheoretical attitude were not a handicap in deciding our policy and presenting it to the world, the gap between the classical type of theory and American practice would not seriously matter. We could then let the rest of the earth carry on with gross misconceptions of what the United States is like, and what it is trying to do, as we did in the nineteenth century. We could proceed with our daily work and political squabbles in the comfortable trust that our basic qualities and the wealth of our land would carry us through to success in the end.

But, if we are to have Two Worlds, or more, instead of a peaceful and progressing One, we must be able to chart a clear course, and explain it with equal clarity to the nations we would like to have join our ideological fraction of the planet. The economics of Ricardo and his successors is increasingly unpopular in most of these countries. We fail ourselves, and we fail them, in allowing this confusion to persist. For what we mean by the "American way of life" is not described or represented by the simple slogan "free enterprise" or by an ideology in the classical spirit. America has a limited, modified capitalist system, always in process of change, that bears little resemblance to the imaginary, static, "pure" capitalism that was supposed to have existed in England one hundred years ago.

And yet, flying in the face of the facts, the abstract theory of the self-regulating economy is the basis of many of our school and college texts, of the statements of business leaders, and, not surprisingly, of more than one political pronouncement. As recently as 1944, one of the twentieth century's most noted exponents of nineteenth-century economics wrote:

There is no other possibility than either the order governed by the impersonal discipline of the market or that directed by the will of a few individuals; and those who are out to destroy the first are wittingly or unwittingly helping to create the second.[18]

In a word, whatever its shortcomings, economics in the classical tradition continues to be a live issue. Its very vigor is in a way disheartening, for it is an extremist position. If it were indeed true that there were no middle ground between the "impersonal discipline of the market" and the "will of a few individuals," there would be no escape from despair. For we know the first to be impossible, and the second to be hateful. But history, which has been called the record of human calamities, can also be a source of hope: along with failures, it records the improvisations and accommodations of succeeding generations, and the triumphs of the wisdom of peoples over the strict logic of the prophets of doom. The history of the classical doctrine itself reveals one of these improvisations: the history of what an arch enemy of our way of life, Lenin, called "monopoly capitalism," is the record of one of these accommodations, as yet uncompleted.

NOTES ON BOOKS

Since American classical thinking was part of the main stream of British economic doctrine a separate treatment of the history of American classical theory as such would hardly be justified. Joseph Dorfman's *The Economic Mind in American Civilization* contains a wealth of theoretical and factual material, but its organization is not such as to reveal the broad sweep of ideological development. V. L. Parrington's classic *Main Currents in American Thought,* Merle Curti's *Growth of American Thought,* and R. H. Gabriel's *The Course of American Democratic Thought* are not, of course, primarily directed to economics, but they all contain valuable discussions of economic thinking in its social context. T. C. Cochran and W. Miller's *The Age of Enterprise* and L. M. Hacker's *The Triumph of American Capitalism* are extremely useful for background, and J. F. Normano's *The Spirit of American Economics* is a brief discussion of the history of American economic theory. The books suggested for chapter 1 are also pertinent here.

[18] Hayek, *Road to Serfdom,* p. 199.

3.

MONOPOLISTIC CAPITALISM

Mass Production and the Financiers: The Historical Setting

THE decline of competition should be sufficient to explode the myth of a "pure" capitalism, but the rise of monopoly has happily not yet encompassed the society as a whole. Since our economy is of too complex and variegated a nature to admit of a simple characterization, the myth of pure competition tenaciously refuses to be shattered by either reason or reality.[1] The idea of monopoly, moreover, is generally unpopular. One result of perpetuating the old and failing to replace it with a new myth is the common error of picturing the restraint of competition as the work of economic pirates who forced honest businessmen to the wall and proceeded to bleed the public at large.

There are good historical reasons for the growth of what is loosely

[1] Lord Keynes observes, with respect to the power of the classical myth: "I remember Bonar Law's mingled rage and perplexity in face of the economists, because they were denying what was obvious. He was deeply troubled for an explanation. One recurs to the analogy between the sway of the classical school of economic theory and that of certain religions. For it is a far greater exercise of the potency of an idea to exorcise the obvious than to introduce into men's common notions the recondite and the remote" (*The General Theory of Employment, Interest and Money*, New York, 1936, p. 351). Bonar Law was leader of the Conservative party, Chancellor of the Exchequer during the First World War and Prime Minister in 1922–1923.

called monopoly. Actual monopoly, where one seller controls the entire supply of a salable product, is quite rare, except in legalized cases such as public utilities. Limited competition, where there are a few producers or sellers of a commodity, where there may be agreements or understandings about price and the degree and kind of competition that should exist, is quite common. Both monopoly and limited competition are as old as Western civilization, if not older. Certain types of the former were far easier to establish in days of poor communications, and commodity monopolies (as distinct from public utilities) were frequently granted by the mercantilist states of the seventeenth century. Limited competition was characteristic of the medieval gild system, though in forms different from today's. The common law, on the other hand, was generally opposed to restrictive practices, which had to be based on charters or statutes. The ancient predisposition against monopoly was therefore something to be slowly undermined by the specific interventions of government. But that is not the crux of the story, for even a most perfect state of competition would have intrinsic characteristics that tend toward its own destruction.

For one thing, it is a normal tendency for any entrepreneur to seek monopoly. The small shopkeeper hopes, through competition, to acquire all the trade in his neighborhood, the manufacturer hopes to win away his competitor's customers. And so it goes. Time was when the competing producers were small, when machinery accounted for but a very low percentage and labor and materials for a very high percentage of their costs. Under these conditions, when a relatively small capital investment enabled a man to enter a particular field, the force of competition soon arose to thwart monopolistic ambitions. But the progress of industrialization has meant an increasingly high investment in machines, with overhead costs accounting for an ever larger proportion of the total cost of production, and direct costs (labor and materials) an ever smaller share. This means that far more capital is required to begin a business. The skilled craft worker finds it almost impossible today to build up through savings a capital sufficient to launch him as a producer in his own right. When Henry Kaiser, who could hardly be compared with an artisan, decided to break into the automobile business, he went to the bankers for capital. In the case of such a large venture, a syndicate of financiers is created to distribute securities to the public; the project is too big for one investment banker.

Classical economists did not think in terms of the modern corporation, and with good historical reason. The fantastic speculative frenzies of 1720, the Mississippi Bubble in France and the South Sea Bubble in England, set a standard for both credulity and panic that modern times have found hard to equal.[2] A deep distrust of the corporate form of enterprise resulted. From 1721 to 1825 a special act of Parliament was necessary to form a joint-stock company in England. General incorporation provisions were not enacted till 1844, and limited liability was not legalized till 1855. The companies authorized by Parliament in the century following the Bubble were largely in such fields as road and canal building and insurance. The various forms of partnership dominated the industrial and commercial world, so that Adam Smith felt justified in writing:

> The only trades in which it seems possible for a joint stock company to carry on successfully, without an exclusive privilege, are those, of which all the operations are capable of being reduced to what is called a routine, or to such a uniformity of method as admits of little or no variation.[3]

The corporate form prospered despite Smith's doubts, and its triumph was a jarring note to his successors. John Bates Clark, the greatest American neoclassical economist, wrote in 1907 that "individual enterprise and generally free competition" were endangered by corporations:

> . . . this free action is in process of being repressed by chartered bodies of capitalists, the great corporations, whom the law still treats somewhat as though in its collective entirety each one were an individual. They are building up a semi-public power—a quasi-state within the general state—and besides vitiating the action of economic laws, are perverting governments. They trench on the freedom on which economic laws are postulated and on civic freedom also.[4]

Smith had written that one necessary justification for incorporating an undertaking is "that it requires a greater capital than can

<hr />

[2] Perhaps the prize swindle conceived by an agile promoter during the boom phase of the South Sea Bubble was a "Company for Design Which Will Hereafter Be Promulgated."

[3] *Wealth of Nations,* p. 713.

[4] *Essentials of Economic Theory,* New York, 1907, p. 377.

easily be collected into a private copartnery."[5] What he could not foresee was that the new industrial age would, in its most important aspects, not only require the formation of vast units but would progressively exclude the small. Revolutionary technological changes substituted steel for wood and iron; steam and then electricity for water, wind, and muscle; railroads and steamships for carts and sailing vessels. Technological change made possible large-scale machinery and the economies of mass production, vastly wider markets and the increased demand and supply of an expanded and more active economy. Producing and distributing enterprises met Adam Smith's criterion in ever growing number: the "private copartnery" could not gather the capital or provide the organization necessary to the new industrial order.

Machine production, calling for large corporations and large investment, was the essence of industrial capitalism. The fact of size not only meant that the entry of new firms had been restricted, but that the large firm had tremendous advantages over the existing small competitor. Some of these are rather obvious: a more impressive credit position in most cases, better bargaining power in buying as well as selling, greater capacity to expand production when needed, the ability to withstand higher merchandising costs. Higher mechanization and proportion of overhead costs also meant greater endurance in bad times and acted as a spur to mass production and expansion, for *average* costs are lowered when overhead is distributed over a large output.

There has been another tremendously important corollary to the growth in size of the business unit. When firms were small, and the owner was the active manager, his policies were governed by the simple maxim, Keep costs low and prices the highest at which the product could be sold. His simple object was profit: he would pour income back into the firm if he desired to expand, he would not build reserves for their own sake. As firms grew to giant size, however, ownership and management were divorced. The owners might indeed be the "widows and orphans" who held shares of stock, the managers were administrators who might or might not have money invested in the firm. The mass of scattered owners were content to receive dividends (or merely to hold the shares until their market

[5] *Wealth of Nations*, p. 714.

value rose), and were inarticulate and powerless when it came to determining corporate policy. In the first place, they were apt to be ignorant of the particular business and uninterested in anything but their investment profits. In the second place, the average owner held too few shares to have any influence. Thus control over business policy moved from the legal owners to the managers—and the financiers. As few stockholders ever bothered to vote their shares, possession of a relatively small block—perhaps 5 percent of voting stock—would bring control over the policies of a vast enterprise. Out of this situation came the interlocking directorates and the domination of producing industry by investment bankers (well illustrated by the replacement of Andrew Carnegie's leadership by U.S. Steel).

The shift of control over industry to financial powers brought about a change in business objectives. The financiers, of course, were still interested in producing goods for sale, but they were likely to be equally, if not more, interested in the profits to be made from issuing securities, and the power to be gained in arranging mergers and combinations. They were apt to be more interested in stabilty than competiton, in steady rather than competitive pricing. Furthermore, when the owners and managers of money became the controlling forces in corporate boards of directors, they were less than anxious to make capital available to entrepreneurs who wanted to set up in competition with the firms they ruled. Closing the field to newcomers, or at least making it far more difficult for them to enter, led toward monopolistic or limited competition among a few large firms.[6]

In short, industrial capitalism could not help but bring about the decline of competition. This was an intrinsic process, and, as the economy matured, the development was only intensified. Size and a high proportion of overhead cost may indeed make it possible for

[6] It is worth noting the comment of Herbert Hoover on the meat packing industry, when he was Food Administrator during the First World War: "Entirely aside from any conspiracy to eliminate competition amongst themselves and against outsiders, it appears to me that these five firms closely paralleling each other's business as they do, with their wider knowledge of business conditions in every section, must at least follow coincident lines of action and must mutually refrain from persistent sharp competitive action towards each other. They certainly avoid such competition to a considerable extent." Quoted by A. R. Burns, *The Decline of Competition*, New York, 1936, p. 164.

a firm to survive a depression, but they tend to produce stable, "sticky" prices in normal times.[7] Great volume of business and high fixed costs require long-range planning of expenditures on equipment, materials, and advertising and, therefore, of selling prices. It is difficult to shift prices with any frequency (the act itself is a major bookkeeping operation for some of our industrial giants). The result is that the prices of the few big competitors in a field such as automobile manufacturing are very similar. Price competition disappears, to be replaced with quality competition and increased advertising, often with advertising alone. While competition may continue in this sense, it is not the same thing as price competition which, under classical theory, was to result in the uniform market price that would equate supply and demand and thus govern production and the whole economy. In quality and advertising competition, each firm tries to differentiate its product from the rest in order to gain some of the advantage it would have if its product actually were unique, and sold by a monopoly. There results a hectic struggle to monopolize the consumers' eyes and ears, which is all very beneficial to the radio and television performer, to advertising agencies, to contest winners, and perhaps, who knows, even to the public at large. But this kind of competition cannot provide the automatic adjustment necessary to the classical version of free enterprise. If anything, it hinders it.

Major policies of the great corporations were set by small groups among whom nonowning managers and absentee bankers came to predominate. And these were the men who demanded a free hand in conducting their operations, calling upon the spirit of free enterprise. As is so often the case where personal interests intrude,

[7] "The statements of the steel producers indicate fairly clearly the origin of their desire for stable prices. The demand for their products is subject to wide cyclical fluctuations; they are anxious above all to avoid price cutting in times of diminished demand because of their heavy overhead costs and their (doubtless well-founded) belief that in any given condition of business the demand for steel products cannot be greatly stimulated by price reductions. They also appear to pin some faith to the belief that if they maintain their prices buyers can be discouraged from holding off the market in the hope of further reductions. The policy of stable prices springs, therefore, from a dual source, the hope of eliminating price cutting from a situation in which it may be very costly, and the hope of mitigating the cyclical fluctuations in demand which lead to undue price competition" (Burns, *Decline of Competition*, p. 216).

half a story had been remembered: the classical critics of mercantilism had condemned *both* private monopoly *and* government intervention. In the latter part of the nineteenth century, however, leading capitalists generally limited their fire to government interference and worked hard to create private monopolies. These rugged individualists were hard fighters, who believed that nearly all was fair in their campaigns to acquire the wealth, power, and prestige that came from the establishment of great industrial or financial domains.[8]

The Carnegies and Fricks, Morgans and Rockefellers gave the new, mushrooming capitalism of American big business a lusty, dramatic, and effective leadership that aroused bitter condemnation and opposition. Great Britain, the home of laissez faire, watched almost undisturbed the less advertised growth of such huge combinations as Lever Brothers. France, with a mixed tradition of interventionism and laissez faire, brought forth the powerful steel association, the Comité des Forges.[9] Germany, where full-scale industrial development began only after the formation of the Empire in 1871, not only tolerated but encouraged combinations in restraint of competition, such as the Rhenish-Westphalian Coal Syndicate (1893). Only in the United States were antitrust laws passed, beginning with the Sherman Act of 1890. For, not only, as we have said, did the classical tradition survive to a greater extent in America's domestic policy than in that of any other major country, but there was a wider popular base for antimonopoly sentiment.

English agriculture had all but passed out of the picture. French agricultural and industrial leadership lay in the same hands. German agriculture and industry had entered into a mutually profitable intimacy. But the alliance between American agriculture and in-

[8] If they were inclined to be ruthless and to disregard considerations of public interest, they frequently tried to square their debt to their fellow men by giving huge fortunes to institutions that served the community. Some may have been moved by guilty consciences or the desire to perpetuate their names in stone; others by the simple business fact that they had no banking correspondents on the far side of the Styx; still others, like Andrew Carnegie, expounded the doctrine that great riches came to men of superior talent whose duty it was to employ their wealth for the benefit of the public. (See Carnegie's *The Gospel of Wealth*, published in 1900.)

[9] Price fixing agreements were illegal in France until 1884, as were effective labor organizations. It is interesting that both prohibitions, born of the classical tradition, were removed in the same year.

dustry embodied in the Republican Party was an arrangement between two relatively independent interests. The agricultural society that had so recently developed in the new lands of the American West was vigorous, youthful, and independent in spirit. The farmers had to be shown that the terms of agreement with industry brought them a net profit, and were ready to fight whenever they were convinced that "Wall Street" was taking advantage of them. Without their ready belligerency the Sherman Anti-Trust Act (which called for government intervention to preserve competition) and the Interstate Commerce Commission Act (which provided for government regulation of the railroads and other interstate carriers) would never have been passed, and William Jennings Bryan's appeal for free silver would never have been made, or would have had little meaning in American history.

The decline of competition continued, nonetheless, despite federal law and the opposition of various social groups. Restriction of the free play of market forces took numerous forms. In addition to factors that gained influence imperceptibly over the course of years, such as the tendency to replace price competition with differentiation of product through advertising, there have been the overt and obvious trusts and pools, mergers and holding companies, basing point agreements and price leadership. At the heart of each and all is the simple proposition stated by Adam Smith, the father of the classical tradition: "People of the same trade seldom meet together, even for merriment and diversion, but the conversation ends in a conspiracy against the public, or in some contrivance to raise prices."[10] This should not be taken to mean that businessmen are subversive conspirators, but simply that competition is often curtailed in the convivial atmosphere of the nineteenth hole, as men legitimately seek to further their interests. It means the force of competition, which the classical school relied upon to save competition itself and the public interest, has proved inadequate to the task. Adam Smith understood, as most of his followers in the classical tradition did not, that when men meet, agreements are made.

The inherent nature of modern technology calls for large-scale organization. The corporation and corporate devices such as the holding company facilitate concentration of control and separation

[10] *Wealth of Nations,* p. 128.

of ownership and management. It is the ordinary desire of men to increase their wealth and power. These are the factors which, together with its own self-limiting nature, led to a "decline of competition." This is an irritating phrase to most Americans, one that induces a feeling of resentment and a tendency to cling to old beliefs and slogans to restore an injured sense of security. Yet pure competition meant a state in which no one seller or buyer or likely group could exert a significant influence on the market. Even if this be strictly theoretical, competition as past generations conceived it meant that no one business unit could markedly influence price, and that every field was open to the entry of new competitors. The decline of competition may therefore be seen in the concentration of industry into a small number of large firms, and in the fact that prices of goods made by the concentrated industries were relatively stable in the Great Depression, while their production decreased. In a more competitive system, a handful of firms would not be as important as they are in ours. In a more competitive system, a depression would lead to less curtailment of output and more price cutting to attract the weakened demand.[11]

The degree of concentration in the American economy is illustrated by the fact that in 1937 the 100 largest companies produced 34 percent of the total value of products, and employed 21 percent of all wage earners.[12] In the same year, 1937, the 394 largest corporations filing income-tax returns (0.09 percent of the returns) owned about 45 percent of all corporate assets. And 55 percent of all these firms owned only 1.4 percent of the total assets. Of the 192,028 corporations that reported net incomes in 1937 (285,810 reported no net income), 248 or 0.1 percent received 40 percent of the total reported net income, and 65 percent received only 1.7 percent of the total.[13]

The fields in which this concentration was marked were just those

---

[11] Whether competitive price cutting is more or less desirable than monopolistic rigidity during a downswing is not the question here (see p. 57 ff.). The point is only that rigidity has tended to replace price cutting.

[12] The next largest 100 companies added only 7 percent in value of products and 5 percent in workers, making the figures for 200 companies 41 percent and 26 percent respectively.

[13] *Investigation of Concentration of Economic Power, Final Report of the Executive Secretary to the Temporary National Economic Committee,* Washington, 1941, pp. 46, 169.

which showed great reductions in production together with stable prices during the depression, contrary to the theory of classical capitalism.[14]

	Percent Drop in Prices	Percent Drop in Production
Agricultural implements	6	80
Motor vehicles	16	80
Cement	18	65
Iron and steel	20	83
Auto tires	33	70
Textile products	45	30
Food products	49	14
Leather	50	20
Petroleum	56	20
Agricultural commodities	63	6

Whether or not the relationship between concentration and stable prices indicates monopolistic pricing and unfair imposition on the unfortunate consumer in time of depression, does not concern us here.[15] We are not trying to prove that the public has been gouged by big business, but that concentration and price stability are traits of the major mass-production lines that give modern industrial society its distinctive character. Neither concentration nor price rigidity goes with automatic adjustment and the classical natural laws of competition and supply and demand.

Prior to the New Deal, the responsibility for the decline of competition was generally ascribed to big business alone. The interventionist policies of Franklin D. Roosevelt focused attention on big government, and the strikes after the Second World War on big labor, as forces seeking to destroy the competitive economy. All three are unquestionably involved. In an extension of the old

[14] Gardner C. Means, *Industrial Prices and Their Relative Inflexibility*, 74th Congress, 1st Session, Senate No. 13, Washington, 1935, p. 9.

[15] This is a highly controversial point, for the stable prices occurred most frequently in durable, and the flexible prices in nondurable, goods. Naturally, demand for goods used over a period of years, such as automobiles, will be the first to fall off in a depression. Against this it is argued that prices are flexible for durable goods whose production is not concentrated, and are inflexible for nondurable goods whose production is concentrated (National Resources Committee, *The Structure of the American Economy*, Part I, *Basic Characteristics*, Washington, 1939, pp. 142–143).

American practice of seeking government aid when favorable to the interested party, business, labor, and agriculture have all sought government regulation when it would benefit them. Until recent years, labor and agriculture were far more likely than business to demand regulation as a cure for competitive ills, but NRA and bituminous coal legislation show that business too will ask Washington to help it curtail competition within its own ranks when the free play of the market is unsatisfactory. As for public policy itself, it has operated against competition in four main respects; first, by deciding that competition is wasteful in certain lines and by legalizing monopoly; second, by deciding that competition must be protected in other lines and by outlawing competitive practices that might make it difficult for small competitors to survive; third, by deciding, upon some basis difficult to discover, that competition in certain fields might lead to "price cutting" (an integral part of classical capitalist ideology) and by deciding accordingly that retailers must charge prices fixed by manufacturers; fourth, by determining that the free play of the market is apt to produce injustice, and by legislating in the interests of competitively weak social groups.

Examples of the first type of public policy are legion, covering the entire range of public utilities. In return for the efficiency and economy of monopoly the people are to be protected by government regulation of rates. But if the public is to benefit, regulated monopoly must ask lower prices than would unregulated competition among smaller and presumably less efficient units. This is not necessarily so, especially if the utility has sufficient influence over the regulating agency. Furthermore, the public utility concept may be employed to prevent the rise of new competing forms, such as truck and bus transportation. It involves the paradox of sacrificing even the *possibility* of public protection through classical competition for regulation that *always* preserves the monopolies.

An example of the second type of governmental attack on competition is the Robinson-Patman Act of 1936, a federal law that prohibited pricing which discriminated between individuals or areas, and price cutting whose object was to destroy competitors. Its purpose was to protect small firms, particularly retailers, against large competitors such as chain stores. But this raises another paradox, for by preventing large organizations from crushing small competitors, it eliminates the only kind of competition—in prices—that is really vital in the automatic adjustments of competitive capitalism.

The third type of public retreat from competition is illustrated by the "fair trade" laws that have been passed in many states—a good instance is the New York alcoholic beverages law of 1947. These acts provide for price maintenance agreements under which the public can buy only at prices fixed by the manufacturers in blithe disregard of the "natural law" of supply and demand that is regularly invoked whenever the public begins to complain of excessively high prices.[16] Again government intervention has been employed to stifle competition, all in the name of the competitive system.

The fourth class of government attack on competition includes wage and hour and agricultural parity legislation. Such laws are desired by large sections of the nation, but they nevertheless interfere with the functioning of the theoretical natural-law economy.

In addition, the law sanctions another restrictive procedure: patents are a form of monopoly and, furthermore, make it possible to *retard* technological progress. Behind patent protection a firm can prevent a new process or machine from being used, in order to protect current prices or other advantages, and current capital investment. Yet patents are necessary to protect the rights of inventors.[17]

As for big labor, few today will question labor's right to organize. But the delicate mechanism of competitive capitalism could function only when prices were actually set in the market by the interaction of supply and demand, when costs and wages were similarly adjusted in a natural, automatic fashion. The struggle of labor for better wages and conditions (a perfectly legitimate object from the competitive standpoint) has resulted in widespread and well-knit

[16] This kind of law was given federal support in the Miller-Tydings Act of 1937, which legalized price maintenance agreements for goods in interstate commerce in any state which itself legalized such agreements. The Act was emasculated by a Supreme Court decision in 1951, and a new law passed to circumvent this decision became the subject of further litigation.

[17] "Until about 1898 patents were required to be utilized if the right was to be preserved. In 1896, however, it was held for the first time that the suppression of a patent was within the rights of the patentee, and the principle was acknowledged by the Supreme Court in 1908 and again in 1916" (Burns, *Decline of Competition*, p. 15).

unionization. But this means that it is extremely difficult to lower wages (if it is at all possible, at present, without mass layoffs on a depression scale followed by rehiring at a lower level). Labor has thereby placed another barrier in the path of the machine, one that will gain in effectiveness when the annual wage movement really gets under way.

The point is simply that flexibility is an essential attribute of competitive capitalism, and the rigidity introduced by big labor combines with those created by big business and big government to make that kind of capitalism nonexistent in fact, although not in ideology. Neither labor, nor business or government, is engaged in a sinister plot for control based on a lust for power, although the power motive does carry great weight in all three fields. Labor and business are led to establish rigidities by two main desires, to improve their economic position and to make it as secure as possible against the dangers of depression. Government is similarly motivated, sometimes in the interest of less fortunate groups, sometimes in what is sincerely believed to be the interest of all. The very nature of modern industrial society requires labor, government, and business to be "big," and their bigness renders impossible the functioning of the older, smaller-scale, simpler, and more flexible capitalist system.

The Rugged Individual and the Octopus: Monopolistic Capitalism Attacked and Defended

The strange thing about our new economic order is that no great ideological defense has appeared thus far. Along with essentially the same political institutions and doctrine, we continue to talk the language of our old economic ideology, although the economic structure has drastically changed. The new order has been attacked from all sides, and yet its main defense consists in praising the virtues of the old system it replaced.

Aside from Marxist and other fundamental assaults on capitalism itself, the new limited capitalism was attacked by two groups that accepted the basic idea of private ownership and initiative. The first, holding to the orthodoxy of small-scale capitalism, condemned big business for taking advantage of the consumer, the farmer, and the small competitor. This group regarded huge corporations as the work of evil connivers, power-mad tycoons, and could see no economic justification or rationale for the great combinations. Its remedy was in antitrust legislation, which may have changed the appearance of the tide, but certainly did not stem it.

The other group was composed of the new liberals,[18] reformers who looked to government to cure specific social ills as they arose. They agreed with the complaints of the first group, and approved the antitrust laws. In addition, however, they felt that government should combat social injustice and inequality by regulation and by social legislation. In general, both groups recruited among the intellectuals and laborers of the Eastern cities, and the farmers and political leaders of the Midwest.

The defense of concentrated big business was along two main lines. At first emphasis was placed on the public benefits to be gained from business combination. Large-scale operations, it was argued, brought economies, research, and new methods which produced further economies to be passed on to the consumer. As time went on, and the consumer continued to complain about costs and denied receiving any benefits, another angle received equal stress.

---

[18] This is one of the most confusing words in current use. Few are the American political leaders who do not claim to be liberal. Hoover and both Roosevelts, Wilson and Hughes, Robert A. Taft and Truman, all have worn the badge of liberalism. While they do in fact have a great deal in common, there are also many differences among them. The confusion arises from the fact that the word has two very pleasant and honorific connotations, and at least three historical meanings. Men like to think they are liberal because the word suggests a warm and friendly attitude toward people, and a "progressive," forward-looking outlook. Historically, the word should really not be used without a modifying adjective. *Political* liberals believe in representative government under law and within a Bill of Rights, self-determination, and a moderate form of nationalism. Although it was foreshadowed in earlier ages, political liberalism developed as a major mass movement in the first third of the nineteenth century and recruited among the middle class. *Economic* liberalism is another term for classical economics. Before 1848 most political liberals tended toward economic liberalism, but in later years this became less common, as many convinced political liberals began to call for government intervention and social reform. *Reforming* liberals, therefore, are men who believe in political but not economic liberalism. Robert A. Taft and Harry S. Truman, for example, are both obviously political liberals, but when the issues change from political to social and economic, Taft is by and large an economic liberal, while Truman is a reforming liberal. The word *liberal* should be less confusing if these distinctions are kept in mind.

This was the astonishing doctrine—astonishing in a rabidly capitalist country—that competition was wasteful.

This was put more dramatically by Arthur Jerome Eddy, whose book *The New Competition* ran through seven editions between 1912 and 1920. He proclaimed: "Competition is War, and 'War is Hell.'" Competition, he said, destroyed honest merchants and artisans and undermined business ethics. Combination, or association, on the other hand, meant coöperation and harmony. Mr. Eddy distinguished between combinations that were designed to raise prices (farmers' coöperatives and labor unions) and those that were designed for efficient production and lower prices (large corporations). He urged the establishment of open price associations in the various lines of business. Prices, bids, and orders, he said, should be filed with a central office, and competition for orders would then be conducted in an open and gentlemanly fashion. He denied that this would raise prices, but conceded it would tend to stabilize them. The least that can be said is that this device produces a narrower price range, probably with a higher floor, if not with a higher ceiling.

Mr. Eddy's basic idea, that price competition implied warfare and waste was neither new nor original with him. The famous "Gary dinners" are an instance of this spirit in action. Judge Elbert H. Gary, head of the U.S. Steel Corporation and founder of the Iron and Steel Institute, brought the leaders of the various firms in the industry together at dinner meetings in order "to prevent if I could, not by agreement, but by exhortation, the wide and sudden fluctuation of prices which would be injurious to everyone interested in the business of the iron and steel manufacturers." Competitors of U.S. Steel were given to understand that if they declined to be coöperative, Big Steel would be able to come out on top in "unreasonable and destructive competition."[19]

Although a fairly good technical case could be made for U.S. Steel's policy, it was one that was very difficult to popularize. Indeed, the customary American glorification of the common citizen is an intrinsic obstacle to acceptable praise for one who has risen too far above the average level; unless, of course, it can be shown that he succeeded through an unusually zealous application of the

[19] Burns, *Decline of Competition,* p. 79.

ordinary virtues. Although this would fit the case of Horatio Alger, it is exceedingly hard to apply to something as impersonal and unglamorous as a corporation.

The defenders of business combination therefore appealed to America's pride in its industrial achievements by hailing the economies of mass production and warning of the waste and immorality of unrestricted competition. Their opponents had an easier time in condemning what they saw as the growth of despotic private powers, and demanding both legislation to protect competition, and regulation in the public interest.

There was accordingly good enough reason why the case for big business continued to be stated in terms of small-business theory. Men like Arthur Jerome Eddy were not too numerous, and his point of view could not be readily assimilated to the greater part of the traditional American outlook. The professional economists, on the whole, were not easily ruffled. Until the 1920's they generally persisted in theorizing about the old hypothetical system of perfect competition, but a new type of analysis finally began to develop. This was the economics of imperfect or monopolistic competition, worked out by such writers as Piero Sraffa, Joan Robinson, and Edward Chamberlin. Essentially, the new approach was a continuation of the classical and neoclassical tradition, in that it dealt with the theoretical workings of a capitalist economy abstracted from society as a whole, an economy whose main institutions were exempt from the process of historical change. It was different, however, in two main respects. First, it employed a different series of assumptions. Second, its ideological implications have not yet been developed, and, indeed it is extremely unlikely to produce a general social ideology comparable to classical capitalism or Marxism.

Instead of assuming perfect competition, and all the other perfections of classical theory, the economics of imperfect (or monopolistic) competition worked with hypothetical cases covering the range from one firm (pure monopoly), to two firms, several firms, an unlimited number of firms (pure competition with free entry of new competitors into the particular field). It paid close attention to differentiation of products and abandoned the doctrine of consumer sovereignty. In both these respects it was far more realistic than classical or neoclassical theory. It succeeded in establishing a series of theorems indicating what business policy and pricing would be under the various circumstances. It can deal theoretically with specific cases, and can undoubtedly contribute to the comprehension of particular actual situations. But while it can add to an understanding of how modern limited capitalism operates, it is not designed to produce an ideology by which to live.

An ideology involves values, no matter how "scientific" it aims to be. It involves notions of good and bad, and this recent development of theory does not approach this most important problem of all. Operating with the facts of limited competition, it can help explain them. But it tells very little about their relation to the total society we live in. One important contributor to the economics of imperfect competition defended its limited horizons on the ground that the more comprehensive classical approach had failed:

> The conclusion to be drawn is not that our economic institutions . . . deserve moral approval or indignation "en bloc," but rather that they are perfectly indifferent to the moral and social contents of their workings. . . . We are rightly dissatisfied with the distorted picture of economic life which classical theory has bequeathed us. Subconsciously, however, we keep hoping for some other grand formula that would unravel as simply and elegantly the infinite complexity of our modern world. For economics to progress, it must give up its youthful quest for a philosophers' stone.[20]

In short, we are offered a little assistance in ascertaining what society we live in, but none whatever in answering the great question that rises in this divided world, Which society do we want?

Thus the strictly theoretical debate over the decline of competition has been rather unfruitful. Orthodox economic thought, the scholasticism of the twentieth century, has withdrawn into itself. A few minds trained in the Ricardian mystery, however, have dared to take a more positive approach to the problem of monopoly and competition. K. E. Boulding has argued that the restrictions of competition on the part of both business and labor merely result from the understandable desire of private persons and groups to achieve some security against the threat of deflation and depression.

[20] Robert Triffin, *Monopolistic Competition and General Equilibrium Theory*, Cambridge, 1940, pp. 187, 189.

Since government has failed to provide adequately for economic stability, he feels, the individuals directly concerned can hardly be blamed for trying to provide for themselves. Boulding defends monopoly against the charge that price rigidities prevent the free adjustment of the market, and therefore accentuate depressions: deflation can spiral like inflation, he argues, and the rigidities created by monopolistic capital and labor act as brakes on the deflationary process of depression. He defends quality and advertising competition as against price cutting for the same reason. But Boulding's defense of monopoly is admittedly half-hearted. He offers no ideology of monopoly capitalism, and merely contends that monopolistic policies make a good deal of sense in the modern world once the classical abstractions have been discounted.[21]

Another defense of monopoly, in some ways similar to Boulding's, is offered by one of the most distinguished economists of our time, the late Joseph A. Schumpeter of Harvard. He reminds us that the English-speaking world has had an emotional bent against monopoly since before the days of Adam Smith but argues that the greatest achievements of capitalism can nevertheless be credited to its monopoly phase. The capitalist economy, says Schumpeter, is always in a process of change, which he calls "creative destruction," the replacement of old methods and products with new. This, he believes, is the vital form of competition which brings the benefits of technological progress to the consumers, price competition being a short-run, unsettling factor. But the risks of "creative destruction" requires short-run stability to make them worthwhile, and monopolistic rigidities are therefore an aid to long-run advance. So runs Schumpeter's thesis, bolstered by the argument that monopolistic practices check rather than intensify slumps.[22]

Aside from the fact that his thesis is by no means universally accepted,[23] let it not be thought that Schumpeter has worked out a

---

[21] K. E. Boulding, "In Defense of Monopoly," *Quarterly Journal of Economics*, August, 1945, pp. 524–542.

[22] Joseph A. Schumpeter, *Capitalism, Socialism, and Democracy*, New York, 2d. ed., 1947, especially chaps. 7 and 8.

[23] G. H. Hildebrand, Jr. (*American Economic Review*, September, 1943, pp. 591–601), raises the question whether the great economic progress of the last three generations was due to large firms and monopolistic practises or to the achievements made where competition was stronger.

systematic ideology of monopoly capitalism. On the contrary, he sets a sharp limit to his case for monopoly by predicting the downfall of capitalism as a whole! The gap between fact and social philosophy, therefore, still remains to be filled.

Until very recently, the majority of our business leaders and large numbers of the population at large continued to lean on the classical or neoclassical system of theory, lagging behind a dynamic and changing economy. Because the tradition of economic analysis was rationalistic rather than historical, the historical factors operating against competition were lost sight of for many years. During all those years we told the world, as we told ourselves, that we were the great example of the benefits of a system of competition (perfect competition, implied).

For some years past, and particularly since the end of the Second World War, when we have been on the defensive psychologically, we have changed our tune somewhat. For example, Russell Porter, of the *New York Times*, defended the American system against Thomas Mann's implication that we practiced "'absolute' and unplanned free enterprise in nineteenth-century European fashion." Mr. Porter added, correctly I think, that "Europeans seem to believe that American free enterprise is something they have tried and failed with and, therefore, it is doomed to failure here also." This erroneous belief comes, according to Mr. Porter, from the fact that Europeans were so accustomed to absolutism in one form or another that in the nineteenth century they also accepted "absolute, if disguised, power by super-governments of businessmen. This led (as Marx predicted) to monopoly and cartels, class war, imperialism and world war." America, on the other hand, has always rejected absolutism and, says Mr. Porter, "the whole internal history of this country has centered around the struggles of the people as a whole to keep any group—government, business or labor—from wielding too much power." He then recalls the various measures, from the National Banking Act of 1863 to the TVA, that bespeak government intervention, and he concludes, "Nor is the American economy entirely unplanned, as many Europeans believe. It is planned by the people themselves in a way to offer incentives for the maximum production of goods and services."[24]

[24] *New York Times*, September 14, 1947.

This is a capable argument in many respects, but there is some confusion in it, and it raises at least two questions that it does not attempt to answer. Mr. Porter is right in stressing European misconceptions about America, although he fails to see that the ideological label *we* have been using fits the facts they think they observe here far better than what actually exists. We have never done much talking about the interventionist side of our social and economic history, and we have fairly boasted about the competitive side. Mr. Porter is also correct when he says that we have planning by the people themselves. But, if he means that the economy is planned by the whole population as consumers, then he must believe that that pure competition exists which he denies. For it is only through pure competition, as we have seen, that consumer control—or planning —can operate. Actually, we have a large measure of consumer control in many branches of our economy (the independent professions, some parts of light industry and of merchandising), but at the same time we have a large measure of producer control in those very fields in which the American economy is celebrated the world over (heavy and mass-production industry). The decline of price competition means that we have a degree of nongovernment planning which is nevertheless not ruled by the whole of the people as consumers but by small groups of leading producers.

And what alternative have we? If we are to have the benefits of modern mass industry we cannot escape the type of management that goes with them and that brought them about. Nor can we indulge in dreams of restoring competition. In the first place, the overwhelming majority of our business and labor leaders proclaim by their daily actions that unlimited competition is not desirable. In the second place, let us repeat that the benefits of mass production require stability and a large degree of planning by somebody. The simple truth is that we cannot afford too much competition. We can go along with the classical economists if we wish and agree that if and where perfect competition could exist it would not only not be wasteful but would lead to the most efficient use of resources. But competition is the antithesis of stability, and our great economic machine is so complex that instability and change throw it out of kilter. If it be true that the growth of modern industry cast sand into the bearings of the small-scale competitive machine, the converse also holds, that excessive competition throws an even worse abrasive into the far more productive machinery of monopolistic capitalism.

There is no simple answer to the problem of monopoly and the decline of competition. We cannot establish perfect competition, and do not want to anyway, but it is not a sufficient alternative to adopt the slogan of more government intervention. State regulation does not eliminate problems: it is only one way, and by no means always the best, of trying to solve them. It increases certain social and economic costs which should not be accepted lightly without careful thought about their relation to long term social objectives. We should not and cannot honestly proclaim classical capitalism as our ideology, but it is not enough merely to say that we have a generally effective system of limited capitalism, with producer leadership in its most important branches. No matter how well the economy may function, we cannot afford to confess reliance on statesmanlike guidance by these leaders, for this conflicts with our democratic principles. To do so would satisfy neither the American tradition nor our needs as a nation engaged in ideological conflict.

The question reduces to one of values. Economics and social philosophy in general can only tell us whether or not we are working toward the values we hold, it cannot equip us with the values themselves, the standards which determine the objectives we set for our lives. Classical economics conflicts with both today's facts and traditional values, for it has a set of its own. The spokesmen for limited capitalism still tend to ignore these conflicts and repeat classical dogma, while disregarding most of it in practice. The new imperfect competition economics claims to be neutral in regard to values, for otherwise it would make little sense. Thus we have acquired no new ideology to fit our changed society, and accordingly no standards by which to guide or with which to publicize our policy toward basic social and economic problems. Values, ideology, and institutions have moved apart in the last 150 years, and they must be brought together again.

NOTES ON BOOKS

Among the brilliant and suggestive theories regarding the growth of monopoly are those of Marx and Thorstein Veblen, but the reader is advised to give primary attention to Part II of J. A. Schumpeter's *Capitalism, Socialism, and Democracy*. For the facts of the case, and analysis, in addition to various TNEC monographs, major works are A. R. Burns' *The Decline of Competition*, A. A. Berle and G. C. Means' *The Modern Corporation and Private Property*, and the Twentieth Century Fund studies by G. W. Stocking and M. W. Watkins, *Cartels in Action; Cartels or Competition?* and *Monopoly and Free Enterprise*.

PART II

The Mercantilist Tradition

4.

NEOMERCANTILISM:
THE NATION STATE
AND NATIONALIST ECONOMICS

Group Interest and Government Intervention: Statism Defined

As RED herrings go, the charge of statism is one of the milder varieties, used chiefly when it would be manifestly absurd to accuse an opponent of either socialism or communism. Its lower "bogey potential," however, makes the word easier and safer to employ, and it has accordingly experienced a sharp rise in popularity. Yet statism—the doctrine that government should concern itself with stimulating, guiding, and regulating various aspects of the people's lives —is probably as old as human society.[1] The degree of intervention and control was highest in the earliest form, family society, and in primitive communities where property is owned in common, government could almost serve as a synonym for everyday life. From the monarchies and empires of the ancient world to the nation states of seventeenth-century Europe, the idea of statism, the right of the government to intervene in social and economic, religious and cul-

[1] Until a few years ago it was considered the depth of poor taste to use the word *statism* instead of the French *étatisme*, which has precisely the same meaning.

65

tural affairs went essentially unchallenged. There had been many struggles over the issue of centralized versus decentralized power, but the almost unlimited extent of that power itself was hardly questioned. Only when an industrial society was rising on the foundation of the age-old agricultural order did its middle-class creators propose the strange, new and revolutionary doctrine that government was to take the role of a "passive policeman."

The theoretical basis for statism of course varied over the centuries. In a family society, sovereignty and property were vested in the head of the family, by virtue of his position. The absolute monarchs of the seventeenth century, basing their claim to undivided power on the grace of God and on medieval law,[2] likened themselves to the paterfamilias, and claimed ownership of all the realm. King James I, writing the *Trew Law of Free Monarchies* in 1598, declared that the king was "Lord of all goods," and "inflexible Lord of the whole realm," and that the "king towards his people is rightly compared to a father of children, and to a head of a body." Louis XIV of France may or may not have said, *"L'état c'est moi,"* but he did write that "Kings are absolute Lords and naturally have free and full rights over all properties, lay as well as ecclesiastic, to employ them as wise stewards, that is according to the needs of their state."[3] Thus the theoretical basis for the intervention of the seventeenth-century mercantilist monarchy was the king's claim to own his whole kingdom, parts of which were held by his subjects by his royal grace. There was no limit to the king's theoretical right, and in theory no redress from bad government save through divine intervention. In the eighteenth century, the age of so-called enlightened despots such as Frederick the Great of Prussia, the monarch's duties were given more emphasis, and his rights somewhat less. But his powers were as great and extensive as ever, even if based upon his obligations to his people rather than on an unquestionable right. Frederick of Prussia wrote, "The prince is to the

---

[2] The theoretical case for absolute monarchy was grounded on sacred writings, on the hierarchical nature of feudalism (land being held under grant from the king or intermediate lords), and on the historical doctrine that states had been formed when a king led his people into a region and then divided it among them.

[3] E. Lavisse, *Louis XIV, de 1643 à 1685* (Ie Partie), vol. VII–I of *Histoire de France Illustrée*, Paris, 1911, p. 391.

nation he governs what the head is to the man; it is his duty to see, think and act for the whole community, that he may procure every advantage of which it is capable."[4]

Almost a century before Frederick wrote these words, the Glorious Revolution in England had established the fundamental principles of the limited monarchy, under which the British king "reigned but did not rule." George III was able to exercise some personal power because he was wealthy, had the prestige of the throne, and was an assiduous politician, not by virtue of royal right. It was the power of the monarch, not that of government, that had diminished, however. Even though Adam Smith and earlier critics in England and on the Continent attacked many of the practices of government intervention, their opposition was generally on grounds of expediency or of natural law (that a particular policy was harmful to the nation or was contrary to the "law of nature" in economics and, therefore, could not conceivably be beneficial).[5] The right of the state to make and administer social and economic policy had not yet been seriously disputed. The debate that raged between the precursors of classical economics and the defenders of the mercantilist tradition of statism was over the wisdom of government intervention, not over the political principle itself.

These defenders had other justifications for statism than divine right or the father-child or head-body analogies. As we have seen, the classical school believed the general interest was equal to the sum of individual interests: statists on the other hand have always drawn a sharp distinction between community and private interests. They have held that it was the function of government—absolute or republican—to guide social and economic activity for the general welfare. F. V.-D. de Forbonnais, one of the outstanding mercantilists of eighteenth-century France, wrote that while an individual merchant might profit from importing goods that compete with home products, the nation would lose at each step of the manufacturing and distributing process. The country as a whole profits from the

---

[4] Frederick II, *An Essay on Forms of Government*, 1777, trans. by Thomas Holcroft in 1789 and reprinted in *Introduction to Contemporary Civilization in the West*, New York, 1946, vol. 1, pp. 916 ff.

[5] This despite the obvious fact that almost the whole of man's life is taken up with efforts to shape nature to his ends, rather than to accommodate himself to nature.

work performed at every link in the chain from raw material to consumer, but "the merchant's gain is solely the excess of the sale price over the purchase price." The great minister Colbert condemned merchants for thinking "only of the small immediate profit they can make," and declared that it was "necessary to override the motives of small private interests which do not deserve consideration among the general motives of the good of the state."[6]

Discarding the purely theoretical claim of absolute monarchs to own every living thing, object, or land their armies surveyed, the ideology of statism therefore rested on an assertion of the supremacy of community over individual interest. This did not challenge the right of private property, but it did mean limitations on the way in which property could be used. Some of the revolutionary philosophies of the nineteenth century, however, denied the institution of property itself and, accordingly, took it for granted that the community, acting through its government, should manage the possessions that were common to all.[7] Hence from the right wing of the old absolute monarchy to the left wing of socialism, the basic principles of statism were accepted. They were part of sharply differing ideologies, as they had been current within widely varying societies over the long centuries. The economic liberals of the classical tradition alone offered a serious challenge to statism, and this was severely limited both in time and space: to the period roughly between 1815 and 1914, and largely to western Europe and the English-speaking lands across the seas.

Statism is a fundamental characteristic of ideologies—both capitalist and socialist—that have been active competitors for public favor in our own time. Its tradition has been continuous and strong. It has appealed to lofty motives of morality and patriotism, and to simple motives of interest and gain. Unfortunately, the supremacy of the classical tradition in our schools and writings for a century or

[6] F. V.-D. de Forbonnais, *Elémens du Commerce*, Leyden, 1754, Part I, p. 49; Charles W. Cole, *Colbert and a Century of French Mercantilism*, New York, 1939, vol. 1, p. 334. Forbonnais contributed the leading articles on economic subjects to the *Grande Encyclopédie*.

[7] Anarchism also denied the right of private property, but argued that since the evils of human behavior resulted from the perversions introduced by a social system based on this right, elimination of property would end these evils and remove the need for government. This is a logical step beyond the "passive policeman" state of classical capitalism.

more has so distorted our view that ideologies rooted in ages past are made to appear radical and revolutionary, while the classical newcomer is cloaked with the black gown and mortarboard of ancient academic respectability. It is true, of course, that socialism, communism, and fascism are relatively recent arrivals, their birth having followed hard upon that of economic liberalism itself. The moderate statist ideology of neomercantilism, however, has forebears as old as the medieval parliaments that grew into our institutions of representative government. If age lends interest and dignity, therefore, neomercantilism must be approached in a spirit of respectful inquiry.

National State and Nationalist Economics: The Historical Setting

However enhanced by historical seniority, neomercantilism is an unattractive word, and, furthermore, is not descriptive of the outlook it represents. Neomercantilism is the nineteenth- or twentieth-century edition of mercantilism,[8] the statist ideology that ruled the Western world from the sixteenth through most of the eighteenth century. The word *mercantilism* itself was coined by critics who contrasted what they thought was a mistaken stress upon the merchant and trade with their newer emphasis on labor and production. Mercantilism was therefore largely misunderstood.[9]

In many respects, mercantilism was an adaptation of some of the principles and practices of medieval town and gild regulation to the purposes and needs of the national monarchy.[10] Viewed as a consistent program, and before allowance has been made for deviations owing to the sinfulness of mankind, these medieval institutions add up to a plan and pattern for a functional society, a society with an understood and accepted purpose. This aim was to help each man to achieve salvation and the life everlasting by living as a Christian in his station in society. This great guiding purpose meant a moral

[8] *Neo* = "a new and different period or form."

[9] Even so distinguished an economist as the late Lord Keynes discovered mercantilism only years after he had won international renown. Chapter 23 of his *General Theory*, published in 1936, contains a frank confession of his sins of ignorance and misunderstanding in this regard.

[10] See p. 71.

approach to economics, and a lack of emphasis on material progress. From this religious goal stemmed medieval provisions designed to prevent the quick-witted trader from gaining unduly at the expense of his fellow men—"let the buyer beware" was a precept abhorrent to the law of the medieval Church, for seller and buyer had moral obligations toward each other. St. Thomas Aquinas declared, *"In all contracts the defects of the salable commodity must be stated; and unless the seller make them known, although the buyer has already acquired a right to them, the contract is voided on account of the fraudulent action."*[11] From this otherworldly outlook stemmed too the restrictions on the number of workers a master could employ, on sales techniques designed to increase business, and the laws forbidding those of one class to ape the manner and attire of those above them—for honest work is noble in all stations of life, and "it is easier for a camel to go through the eye of a needle than for a rich man to enter into the kingdom of God."[12]

But the desire for money, which is the root of all evil, distorted this pattern of Christian social justice while some of its details were still being traced. The desire and the opportunity to fulfill it had developed together. For we must not forget that there was another stimulus for the medieval social system, material rather than religious. Stability and justice may have been stressed because of otherworldliness, but security was sought against the armed attack and the danger of want that were both ever threatening. As trade became safer and extended over wider areas the need for local security measures decreased, fluidity began to replace stability, and worldly ambition came into its own. An important characteristic of this development was the growth of stronger governments controlling larger areas than before. Counts and dukes made real their theoretical control over the nobles beneath them, and then the kings began to achieve success in their long struggle to subject the counts and dukes.[13]

[11] Original italics, reference to St. Ambrose: *Summa Theologica*, Dominican Fathers' translation, London, 2d rev. ed., 1920–1929, reprinted in *Introduction to Contemporary Civilization in the West, A Source Book*, New York, 1946, vol. 1, p. 89.

[12] Matthew 19:24; Mark 10:25.

[13] An example of this process is the celebrated conflict between the dukes of Burgundy and the kings of France. In 1363 a son of King John the Good of

Royal influence on medieval social policy, and therefore on the patrimony of mercantilism, has not received adequate attention.[14] The unity between religion and social and economic practice in towns and manor—the medieval synthesis—is intellectually so attractive that we tend to pass over the efforts of the medieval kings to establish and execute economic policy. They had always wished to be kings in fact. They issued kingdom-wide regulations and used economic devices to strengthen their own power, as well as employing their power to strengthen trade and the economy according to the conceptions of the day.

An interesting example of royal economic policy in the Middle Ages is offered by the history of the Mediterranean port of Aigues-Mortes, now silted up and inland, built by St. Louis as an embarkation base for the Crusades. His successors attempted to concentrate all French Mediterranean commerce at this port, at the expense of the long established leader, Marseille, which was under the Count of Provence rather than the king. They also tried to direct inland trade in southeastern France to the royal city of Nîmes, at the expense of other towns independent of the French crown. Italian merchants were invited to come to Nîmes, but were forbidden to trade elsewhere. All this was to strengthen the king by channeling trade through his towns, and to give commerce itself the benefit of royal support.

Even a random glance over French and British economic legislation in the Middle Ages reveals the wide extent to which the central authority tried to assert its control. In England, the Great Winchester Assize of 1203 established national customs duties, and made

---

France became Duke of Burgundy, and this branch of the royal house built the duchy into a major power (including the Low Countries) that was a thorn to the French crown. In 1477, following the death of Duke Charles the Bold, King Louis XI seized the important duchy, reaping there the benefit of the centralizing work of the dukes, and further centralizing France as a whole.

[14] Even Eli Heckscher's great *Mercantilism* (2 vols., London, 1935) tends to underemphasize the part played by medieval kings in shaping social and economic policy. While he refers to a good many royal measures (mostly English), his work is organized around a series of categories such as bullionism and "the fear of goods," with the result that the influence of institutional factors through the changing course of history is slighted. The medieval royal effort to legislate for the whole kingdom is far more important in establishing precedent for later ages than its relative lack of success at the time would indicate.

food exports subject to license, in accordance with the medieval policy of safeguarding against shortages. In 1299 the Parliament of Edward I severely restricted the export of coin and precious metals. In the fourteenth century, England followed a Venetian precedent in limiting a merchant's imports to an amount equivalent to his exports; in 1381 Richard II issued the first Navigation Act, designed to strengthen the royal navy by stimulating English merchant shipping. In the same century, French kings used the gild system more and more to gain control over the economy, and English laws established nation-wide regulation of wages and of the terms of labor, setting the basis for Queen Elizabeth's famous Statute of Artificers. In the fifteenth century, the Duke of Burgundy prohibited the importation of English wool cloth and yarns, the English Parliament blamed foreign competition for unemployment in the silk industry, and a French decree of 1466, designed to favor silk production, took note of the loss of precious metals resulting from the importation of silk.[15]

These are a few of the many instances of royal mercantilism in the Middle Ages. Later mercantilist policies, such as insuring adequate supplies of raw materials and precious metals, protection of manufactures and regulation of industry and labor, had been shaped by royal hands from the thirteenth century on.

Between the fifteenth and seventeenth centuries, the monarchs succeeded in their struggle for undivided power; the oligarchy of feudalism was replaced with the absolute rule of a king. The unrelenting efforts of the kings involved immensely complicated intrigues, wars, and political marriages. They engaged in alliances of convenience as well as of interest with each other, and with middle-class opponents of the nobility. Royal maneuvers to obtain supremacy were an old story, however. What finally crowned them with success was the diminished capacity to resist of the landed nobles. The growth of trade and industry and the increased wealth and power of the towns, the price revolution that followed the conquest of American treasure and the opening of new European mines, all combined to undermine the position and prestige of a nobility whose strength had lain in relatively fixed land rents and in

---

[15] The instance of Aigues-Mortes was suggested by Professor Robert Lopez of Yale; the others are taken from Eli Heckscher's *Mercantilism*.

private armies.[16] The establishment of absolutism came at different times in different countries. Henry VII in England (1485–1509) and Henry IV in France (1589–1610) reigned supreme. A last stand of the French nobility in the 1640's only showed that England was about a century ahead of her great rival in social and constitutional development. But nearly everywhere in Europe, from the mid-fifteenth century on, the tide was running with the crown. The new order of capitalism therefore came into being within the framework and under the control of absolute monarchy; capitalism under royal guidance was mercantilism.

State Guidance for Private Initiative: Main Doctrines

Mercantilism is not a synonym for bullionism or protectionism, but a well-rounded ideology covering political and social as well as economic policy. Unlike classical economics, however, mercantilism is not based on a series of presumed natural laws which have only to be discovered and then followed. It is grounded on this proposition, that social policy is a matter for human, not natural law, and that when social objectives have been established, those means should be employed to reach them which are found to work best, and for just so long as they work. In short, a twentieth-century writer in the mercantilist tradition might suggest aims and means different from those of a seventeenth-century writer, which is hardly astonishing in view of the fact that a good many things have

[16] The feudal obligations of the peasantry to the lords gradually changed from work to payments in money. But payments were generally fixed, and inflation meant that the lords received less and less real purchasing power. After an age of stability, prices skyrocketed in the sixteenth and seventeenth centuries. The French nobility was especially hard hit: the lord Bertrand de Preignan "is found begging for a commoner's name so as to get his share of wood from the communal forest with other villagers. The wife of a debt-encumbered lord keeps herself alive after his death by running an ale-house. . . . In 1530, in the Gévaudan, 121 *seigneurs* had an aggregate income of 21,400 livres: one had 5,000, another 2,000, the rest an average of 138 livres each. And there were merchants in the town with incomes up to 65,000 livres" (*Cambridge Economic History of Europe*, vol. 1, Cambridge, 1942, p. 557). As for private armies, as early as 1296 King Philip the Fair of France had ordered royal officials not to permit the presence of armed men in their districts, and St. Louis had previously prohibited private warfare. These prohibitions gradually became effective.

changed over the last three hundred years. But they would both be interested in establishing objectives suited to the times: they would agree that government is the proper agency to express these ends and to choose the means; and they would be primarily concerned with promoting the welfare of a particular nation rather than the world at large.

Thus the medieval kings, in order to promote prosperity and increase the royal revenue and power, tried to attract trade and foreign merchants; to prevent shortages, they restricted exports. The mercantilist kings of the sixteenth and seventeenth centuries, to achieve similar ends, likewise limited certain exports, both to prevent shortages and to keep industry supplied with raw materials, but they favored the export of manufactured goods. Nineteenth-century neomercantilists were more interested in the home market and less in foreign trade. But they all regarded national welfare and security as conscious goals, and agreed that it was the state's duty to see to their attainment. Indeed, considering the vast changes that have occurred over the last three centuries, the continuity of the force of economic nationalism is tremendously impressive; for the main doctrines of mercantilism reveal a much narrower gap between the seventeenth and twentieth centuries than the classical economists had taught.[17]

Granted its medieval origins, mercantilism was essentially the ideology of the central, royal states that overcame feudalism in the late fifteenth and sixteenth centuries. The main object of the monarchs, as we have said, was to elevate their power within the realm and abroad. They had to increase their revenues, which enabled them to hire and equip soldiers and to support a display of royal magnificence which would enhance their prestige. Warfare was far less a matter of productive capacity, and the arts and crafts far less a matter of producer's goods than today. Hard money was therefore of supreme importance. Unless mines were conveniently located within the realm (as in modern Russia or South Africa), precious metal could be obtained only through foreign trade. The acquisition of bullion through foreign commerce was not the *objective* of mer-

---

[17] Every interpretive treatment runs the risk of oversimplified generalization. This is particularly the case in dealing with nationalist systems which, by definition, vary from country to country.

cantilist policy, it was one of the most efficacious means to the *end* of increasing royal and national wealth and power. But, by its very nature, money does occupy a central place in the logic of economic reasoning, and is a convenient pivot around which to describe mercantilist doctrine. There were two main aspects to mercantilist monetary aims: first, to secure hard money through foreign trade and to keep it in the country through the restriction of precious metal export and of the importation of foreign manufacturers; second, to keep it in circulation and readily and cheaply available for the needs of commerce and industry.

Money was to be kept within the country by the sternest of measures, including death for its unauthorized export. In its early forms this policy was applied to individual transactions: no merchant could export bullion without special license. In the seventeenth century a new view won acceptance: it was the overall balance of imports and exports, and the net import of money that counted, not the individual transaction, for one pound of silver exported might bring back two or more through profitable trade. The volume of international trade had increased, and its nature had changed. Gold and silver had to be shipped to the Far East to buy spices and cloths (which might then be reëxported at a profit), and skilled foreign artisans who could domesticate new industries were sought after by each national state. Aside from the Oriental trade, the emphasis shifted increasingly to manufactures, and the doctrine of bullionism shifted with it. And while mercantilists frequently used the words *money, wealth,* and *capital* interchangeably, they were not so stupid as to believe what Adam Smith thought they believed, that "wealth consists in money, or in gold or silver."[18] The mercantilists did think, and rightly in their day, that the precious metals were an exceptionally important and convenient form of wealth.

Once bullion had been acquired, the mercantilists believed a rapid rate of circulation actually multiplied the effect of a unit of money. Referring to grain trade and shipping, the French eighteenth-century mercantilist Forbonnais wrote, "At least one hundred fifty thousand men will have been employed and thenceforth nourished by this production and this shipping: and if we assume that this revenue circulates only six times a year, it will have fed and

[18] *Wealth of Nations,* p. 398.

employed nine hundred thousand men."[19] If the supply of money were inadequate, they believed, the economy would slowly stifle. Here was an additional theoretical justification for the efforts to gain precious metals through foreign trade, and when New World shipments of bullion began to decline after the mid-seventeenth century, attention was given to other means of increasing the supply of the circulating medium. Banknotes and commercial paper were praised as means of expanding national money, and in the eighteenth century numerous schemes were advanced for paper money, to be based on the public debt or on land.

Of great importance to the mercantilist, both in maintaining the supply of money and its circulation, was the interest rate. In this connection, a mixed argument was given for a low rate of interest, in part drawn from medieval moral and religious doctrine, in part from secular economic thought. While the Church had always opposed the taking of interest on scriptural, ethical, and economic grounds (the doctrine that money was sterile), canon law had actually met the needs of the economy. The taking of interest was allowed on commercial loans, generally speaking, and the word usury (from Old French *usure*, meaning use) came to be applied only to excessive rates of interest and to interest on consumption loans, particularly in cases of need.[20] A general antipathy to moneylending survived, however, supported by the feeling that a man who lived on loan interest was lazy and unproductive. In addition, the mercantilist theory of interest held that high rates crushed economic activity and drove a country into decay.[21]

[19] Forbonnais, *Elémens*, Part I, p. 114. For further examples see Heckscher, *Mercantilism*, vol. 2, pp. 208–209.

[20] Religious economic doctrines will be discussed more fully in chap. 13.

[21] By "interest," the mercantilists obviously meant the price paid for a loan of money. This may seem to be self-evident, but the classical emphasis on real wealth rather than its symbol, money, sometimes creates difficulties. Thus Heckscher ridicules John Locke's mercantilist view on interest with the statement that it "would be irrefutable if capital were synonymous with money, and interest with the price for the loan of money; as this is not so, it is entirely irrelevant" (*Mercantilism*, vol. 2, p. 204). While the mercantilists were well aware of the representational character of money, they also recognized that borrowers might desire it for this very reason, since money is the most liquid medium of exchange. In short, the mercantilists were conscious of what Lord Keynes was to call the "liquidity-preference" factor. (See chap. 23 of Keynes' *General Theory*, and chap. 7 below.) Keynes' "speculative motive" for hoarding was, like the liquidity preference itself, more influential in mercantilist days than now.

Forbonnais, for example, argued that interest arose when some people saved, instead of spending money. The consequent shortage of money would lead those in need of it to offer a price for its temporary use. A high rate of interest, therefore, betokens an excessively unequal distribution of incomes leading to excessive saving. "The less the working population is in a position to consume," wrote Forbonnais, "the less equally distributed is the capacity to consume, the easier it will be to stock money, the scarcer money will be in commerce." The withdrawal of money from circulation produces a lack of confidence, leading to a further withdrawal. When a country has a high interest rate, he concluded, the working class will be in more difficult circumstances and there will be many poor: a picture of what we would now call a deflated economy.

The interest rate must therefore be kept low, and mercantilists of the sixteenth and even seventeenth centuries generally approved legal maximum rates. Later writers and administrators, as we have suggested, stressed instead means to increase the quantity of money in circulation, through a favorable balance of trade and the development of credit devices.[22]

The mercantilists, of course, employed many other approaches to secure an adequate volume of money. Even their attitude toward luxury contributed to this major economic end. Here too we find the combination of motives—religious and moral, secular and economic —that influenced interest policy. Here too, the policy became increasingly secular in spirit as time went on. The medieval moral condemnation of luxury, like that of usury, yielded first place to an economic argument. In the Middle Ages, the wearing of ornaments and finery had been restricted according to social status: a bourgeois, for example, was forbidden to wear the velvet cloak and gold chains befitting a noble. The medieval consciousness of hierarchy combined with the religious condemnation of luxury as a worldly vice. Mercantilism adopted these two considerations, and added a

---

[22] Forbonnais, *Elémens*, Part II, pp. 91 ff. Although he attributes a high rate of interest to inequality of incomes and a consequent shortage of money resulting from saving by the rich, it is interesting that Forbonnais does not suggest, as a social objective, increasing the incomes of the poor, as do some modern underconsumption theorists, but limits himself to the standard mercantilist proposals.

A similar point of view is presented more systematically and with much greater precision in Keynesian economics. See chap. 7.

third, which soon became dominant. This was the monetary argument that all luxuries, when imported, diminished the national supply of precious metals by affecting adversely the balance of trade, and that gold and silver ornaments and utensils made at home produced the same result by withdrawing specie from monetary circulation. Thus mercantilist legislation came more and more to resemble the modern practice of levying high tariffs on imported luxuries and excise taxes on those produced at home.[23]

The process of secularization was completed when mercantilists condemned thrift, in a manner consistent with their theory of interest and money, and went on to oppose only those expenditures on luxuries which led to a decrease in the amount of hard money in circulation. Their attitude toward luxury brings out a curious conflict between thrift and spending that has existed in capitalist thinking from the very beginning. On the one hand, the individual was cautioned to be penny-wise, and on the other hand, nations have been warned that if their citizens are penny-wise they will, as a community, prove to be pound-foolish. The English mercantilist Bernard de Mandeville, who wrote his amusing and irritating *Fable of the Bees, or Private Vices Publick Benefits* in the early eighteenth century, pointed out that if individuals stopped spending freely and even wastefully, trade and industry would decline. Sobriety would gain, at the expense of prosperity.

It is characteristic of mercantilism that the way in which its different aspects interlock can best be traced in actual policies rather than by following a logical chain, as in classical economics. The power objectives of the national monarchies, monetary policy, and the attitude toward luxury were mutually consistent and interdependent, and this holds true for colonial expansion and imperial policy, for internal economic development and regulation, and for the social views of the mercantilist state.

Foreign trade was desired because it secured bullion, but also because it created employment at home. The merchant marine was important, because otherwise goods would have to be carried in

---

[23] Modern luxury taxes are based on the principle of equity in taxation, that is, of placing a heavier tax burden on articles that are not necessities; like their seventeenth-century equivalents, they bring protests from the producers of the taxed goods, who point out that they are providing employment and contributing to national income.

foreign ships at a cost in money, but the merchant marine also provided trained crews and even ships for the royal navy, as in the case of the British fleet that defeated the Spanish Armada in 1588: hence the Navigation Acts, tax differentials, and subsidies designed to stimulate the national merchant fleet.

The needs of colonial expansion and trade further justified the mercantilist shipping policy, and the colonies themselves formed an integral part of the mercantilist scheme. Even Brandenburg, which had not yet developed into the Prussia that was to be the seed of the future Germany, engaged in a colonial venture. In 1683, Frederick William the Great Elector founded a colony on the Guinea coast of West Africa. As Brandenburg was a relatively backward Baltic state, the attempt failed. In 1698 Scotland, at the time a poor country whose sons were only beginning their peaceful infiltration into positions of leadership in England, tried unsuccessfully to found a colony at Darien, in Panama. As is always the case, these nations copied the practice of the leaders, ignoring the fact that the big powers' colonization rested on a well-developed base at home. The "colonial compact," which governed colonial relations with the mother country, was designed to help the European nation's manufactures in a number of ways. First and most important, the colony was to supply the mother country with raw materials for industry and with such products as sugar that were not grown at home. Second, the colonies were to serve as a market for home manufactures, and, third, as distribution points from which to capture more foreign trade. Conversely, the mother country was to buy the colony's products and supply it with manufactures, and provide it with the services of government as well as financial and military support. Each was to respect the other's special position in this arrangement, as is well illustrated by the regulations governing the relationship between Great Britain and the thirteen American colonies. For example, the Hat Act of 1732 protected British hat makers by prohibiting intercolonial trade in hats and limiting American producers to hiring two apprentices, to keep their output at a low level. On the other hand, King James I protected American tobacco planters by destroying a promising English tobacco culture by force of arms (the King was tempted, it is true, by increased import duties on what he had once called a "Drug" owing to which "the Health of a great number of our People is impaired, and their Bodies weakened and made unfit for Labour").[24]

Mercantilist imperial policy was obviously directed to the needs of a growing industrial society, but the colonial compact could also be defended on grounds of bullionism and the favorable balance of trade. For aside from possible colonial mines or treasure, cheap colonial raw materials would aid home industries in winning markets abroad, and there was money to be made in triangular trade. And there was still a further justification for colonial expansion: national and royal power and prestige would be increased by the possession of "plantations beyond the seas."

The close interrelationships of the various programs are equally evident in mercantilist domestic policy. Here the emphasis was on the industries which were to secure a favorable balance of trade and increase the nation's stock of precious metals. But manufacturing enterprises would also provide employment for a large, industrious population, the nation's greatest wealth as the mercantilists believed. The export of luxury products would bring the country prestige as well as money, and the less refined work of iron foundries would add directly to military power. Therefore the mercantilist state did everything in its power to create new industries and expand the old.

The work of Colbert, France's administrative genius, provides the best example of mercantilist industrialization. Every branch of seventeenth-century industry felt the touch of his helping, guiding, and regulating hand. For example, mirrors, which changed the faces of the world when they came into general use, had been a Venetian monopoly. Colbert spent much money and effort to smuggle Venetian craftsmen into France, and in 1665 established with royal funds the private company that developed into the celebrated St. Gobain corporation of our own day. A Dutch Calvinist clothmaker, Van Robais, was established at Abbeville, with royal funds, special privileges, and the sole right to set up such a mill within ten leagues of Abbeville. This firm lasted until the French Revolution. The making of iron and iron products, guns and naval stores, watches and stockings, books and soap, tapestries and swords, statuary, paintings, of anything that would increase the wealth of the country and the

[24] Heckscher, *Mercantilism*, vol. 2, p. 292.

power and prestige of the monarch, was fostered and watched over by this unbelievably industrious statesman and his assistants.

In choosing a method to help a particular industry, Colbert was not hampered by worries about possible vengeance at the hands of natural laws of economics. Without fear of such retribution, he could and did use every trick of the trade, trying only to select what seemed to be the best device for the situation before him. Whenever possible, stimulation of private enterprise was preferred to state operation and ownership. In some instances, he granted twenty- or thirty-year monopolies to entrepreneurs to get a business under way. He usually tried to avoid this extreme, however, and preferred to throw a field open to competition rather than renew a monopoly when its term had been reached.[25] Exemptions from taxes and military obligations, a grant of naturalization to foreign workers, the right to establish a brewery to provide employees with beer, the right to use the phrase "Royal manufacture" and to wear royal livery, gifts, interest-free loans, pensions, heavy purchases by the royal household and government; protective tariffs on competing goods and exemptions from raw materials duties; these were some of the devices used by Colbert to start and expand industries. Mercantilism believed neither in competition nor monopoly as a perfect state of economic organization; both were simply means to the overall end of wealth and power, to be called upon as the situation demanded. In the Middle Ages, there had been a greater degree of competition and vocational fluidity than a stylized picture of the gild system would indicate; the same is true of the mercantilist era, despite the enforced extension of the gild system in a country such as France.

Colbert did not, however, rely on competition to maintain the quality of goods or to protect the consumer. He believed, in accordance with long-established tradition, that quality was the best advertisement, and that quality therefore had to be uniform and high for goods to sell abroad. Since he recognized the almost universal human tendency to short-measure and short-weigh, however, he

---

[25] The chartered company, usually a joint stock organization with a grant of monopoly, was an important mercantilist device. Examples include the British East India Company, the Bank of England, and John Law's celebrated Mississippi Company in France.

tried to overcome this mortal frailty by regulation and inspection. He used royal and local officials, intendants and mayors, and in addition a group of roving functionaries in his own service, who worried over the projects of special interest to Colbert and tried to correct any lack of zeal on the part of resident officialdom. Colbert's own men had no local ties that might divert them from executing his policy, although some of them were not above taking "honest graft" (a much more inclusive category in those days than now). But no government could hire enough bureaucrats to enforce the tremendous number of varied regulations that were issued in the name of Louis XIV. For the broad base of the regulatory pyramid which he topped, Colbert used the organization and techniques of medieval town and gild regulation, expanded and adapted to the needs of his time.[26] Very often a gild was instructed to draw up the rules for the conduct of its own trade, which were then given royal sanction, if satisfactory. In many instances Colbert issued the regulations for a local gild directly, and general ordinances were established covering the entire kingdom. In trades where no organization existed, they were sometimes created by the government, as when the lemonade sellers of Paris were forced to organize into a gild.

Thus the two major aspects of medieval interventionism, town and gild regulation and royal ordinance, were joined together by the mercantilist state. Businessmen were to govern themselves, but under the supervision and according to the policies of the monarchy.[27] Naturally enough, labor too felt the stimulating and regulating hand of the state, although in its case the hand was far heavier. The aim of public policy was national wealth and power, and while middle-class merchants and manufacturers inevitably became rich in the

[26] The French Woollens Regulation of 1669 is an excellent illustration of how detailed and severe Colbert's regulations could be. Its fifty-nine articles occupy ten and one-half pages of Cole's *Colbert* (vol. 2, pp. 383 ff.) on which this discussion of Colbert is based. Lengths and widths are prescribed for various types of cloth, with detailed provisions for inspection and measuring; dishonest manufacturing techniques are forbidden, the name and place of the maker is ordered woven, not sewn, into the cloth, and the rules of gild operation are established.

[27] Both to regulate and facilitate business practice, uniformity of weights, measures, monetary units, and law was sought by the mercantilist state, with varying success. Colbert had drawn up and issued codes of criminal, civil, and commercial law, but was less successful in standardizing units of measurement.

process of achieving this aim, it must not be forgotten that *their* gains did not themselves constitute the objective of mercantilism under the absolute monarchy. King and country were in a sense synonymous words; royal wealth and power were the goal, and middle-class wealth was an inescapable by-product of royal success. If it seems paradoxical to think of national wealth and prosperity as something apart from the wealth of the individuals who comprise the nation and carry on its economic activity, it can at least be said that the middle class, the working agents of mercantilist capitalism, did not suffer materially from this purely theoretical distinction. Under mercantilism, and indeed through mercantilism, they prospered to the point where they were eventually able to overcome the monarchy and make national policy in their own name. But the curious paradox and the strange distinction did hold with respect to labor. Not, as has often been said, that a low wage policy was intrinsic to mercantilism: this error arises from generalizing from the English examples. It was rather that the lower orders of society were not expected to surpass the standard of living suitable to their status. The level was, in the eyes of French and other Continental mercantilists, neither to be depressed nor significantly raised. In short, the strict class lines of medieval society were yielding before the thrust of the bourgeoisie, but were holding firm before workers who were still several centuries away from a bid for power.

The gild system under mercantilism therefore offered labor low wages, strict regulation and little opportunity for advancement. There were three main levels in the gild structure. At the lowest was the apprentice, both learner and worker. He entered upon his term, often of seven years, when a boy in his teens, and learned his trade working in his master's shop. In return for this labor, and for help around the house, the master furnished the apprentice with instruction, room and board, and supposedly with fatherly guidance and protection.

After serving his term, the apprentice became a journeyman (from *journée* = day, hence worker paid by the day), and the journeyman might eventually become a master, working in his own right. Entry into the master's rank was restricted, however, sometimes severely, and family connections were always important and frequently essential in making this step to the status of an independ-

ent producer or merchant. As journeyman's associations were prohibited, the gild served as a mechanism for the control of labor, as
well as of the entrepreneurial class. Regulation of labor went beyond wages and hours to include penalties for loafing on the job
and for stealing the employer's tools, provision for religious devotions, and prescriptions concerning mealtimes and food, hiring,
firing and leaving a job. Rules varied widely, as did their enforcement, and the gild was only one of the agencies through which the
mercantilist state sought to regulate labor in the interest of increased productivity. Municipal and royal officials played their
part, and all coöperated with religious and civic leaders in an effort
to relieve the labor shortage that had characterized European economies since the Black Death in the mid-fourteenth century. Paradoxically, this shortage was accompanied with widespread vaga-
bondage—the "sturdy beggars" of Elizabethan literature—for the
culture of urban capitalism had not yet replaced the overwhelmingly agricultural civilization of the late Middle Ages, and the
values and outlook of the modern wage laborer had not been
adopted by peasants torn from their land.

A partial solution to the problem of increasing the labor supply
was therefore at hand. Mercantilist administrators and churchmen
joined in following medieval precedent: idleness was sinful, and at
the same time, it was society's duty to help the needy.[28] Seventeenth-century French mercantilism sought to overcome this particular sin, aid the poor and secure workers through the device
of the *hôpitaux généraux,* or general hostels. Here the poor were
compelled to live and work, receiving maintenance and vocational
training, save for the sickly and the aged, who were given relief at
home. At first sight the *hôpitaux généraux* would seem to have been
merely a seventeenth-century variant of the Victorian workhouse,
but there were a number of differences. The workhouse was quite
similar to a jail for vagrants; the French hostels, however restrictive,
were also centers of religious charity. The workhouses of Victorian
England were to add to the labor force by making any outside job

---

[28] It is a curious historiographical error to regard industriousness, thrift, and
sobriety as social virtues born of the Calvinist Reformation. This point will be
treated more fully in chap. 13.

seem desirable in comparison with the misery of Her Majesty's establishments for the poor; the *hôpitaux généraux* made it possible for a man to attain to the master's certificate after the required years of training, and therefore to social respectability and achievement. The British workhouses were instituted in accordance with one of the theories of classical economics, the Malthusian law of population; the French hostels stemmed from the medieval idea of social obligation as well as from the mercantilist desire to add to the number of artisans.

As with any system based on the nation as a unit, there were wide differences from country to country in mercantilist labor policy. England, where the complete victory of absolute monarchy occurred a century and a half earlier than in France, followed her characteristic pattern of nationwide legislation and localized administration. The gilds were far less important as an agency for indirect control than on the Continent, and, indeed, the principal Elizabethan statute regulating labor was designed in part to stem the flight of industry from town to country to escape the control of urban gilds. This was the Statute of Artificers of 1562. It provided that certain trades could be taught only in the towns, others in the country as well; it established apprenticeship regulations, and decreed that all who did not have a trade, except the gentry and professionals, should work as farm laborers; to prevent labor from moving about in search of better jobs and higher wages, the law required a worker to present a letter of recommendation from his old employer when seeking employment in a different parish; and the justices of the peace were empowered to fix wages. This Statute was complemented with Poor Law legislation, especially the famous Act of 1601, which provided for relief for the infirm, jobs for the able bodied, and punishment for the physically fit who refused to work, all to be administered locally. With modifications, the Statute of Artificers and the Poor Law continued as the basis of England's labor policy into the nineteenth century.

The mercantilist state was often extremely beneficent to the skilled craftsman, but certainly somewhat less than generous toward the common laborer and the lower grades of artisans. Yet there was nothing inherent in mercantilist doctrine that made the effort to keep wages low inevitable. This was an English pattern.[29] Under the Tudors, the workers were thought of as obviously necessary productive factors, whose wages had to be low if the country's goods were to compete successfully in foreign trade. When the Whig coalition of businessmen and landed aristocrats—both capitalist now—gained power in England through the overthrow of the Stuarts in the seventeenth-century revolutions, the position of the laboring classes remained the same. It even deteriorated somewhat, for the absolute monarchy was paternalistic, and was still moved by the medieval concept of the obligation toward the poor, while the rising manufacturers were free from any fatherly sense toward their workers. As we have suggested, they eventually even found in classical economics a theory by which they could liberate their consciences.

A high-wage argument could also be built upon mercantilist premises, however. Even in England, Elizabeth and James I enacted minimum wage provisions. In France, the tendency was actually to favor higher wages. Colbert wrote to a provincial official urging the establishment of new manufacturing facilities: "These manufactures will perhaps force the masters to give something more to the workers, and will produce at least this advantage, that the masters of a single manufacture do not dominate the workers and give them only what they see fit." Forbonnais declared that when employment is inadequate, the wise state "provides for its laborers, or supplies them with work."[30] The labor policies of the mercantilist state varied, in short, with the ruling idea as to what the state actually was, and according to the interests of the social and economic groups that were identified with those of the particular nation at the particular time.

When the English monarchy found it necessary to use the middle class to establish its own power, the tendency toward oppression of labor was strong. After absolutism had triumphed, but was beginning to meet with opposition from an increasingly self-confident bourgeoisie, as was the case with James I and Charles I of England, the king's tendency was to return to paternalistic ideas of social

[29] On England see E. S. Furniss, *The Position of the Laborer in a System of Nationalism,* Boston, 1920; P. W. Buck, *The Politics of Mercantilism,* New York, 1942.

[30] Heckscher, *Mercantilism,* vol. 2, pp. 168 ff.; vol. 1, p. 257; Cole, *Colbert,* vol. 2, p. 455; Forbonnais, *Elémens,* Part I, p. 62.

justice, and to make the bourgeoisie bear the costs. In France, on the other hand, absolutism was strong enough to insist at least on the maintenance of the traditional status of the working class. When later neomercantilist economics was allied with political and social democracy, as in the United States, high-wage doctrine triumphed outright, and the mercantilist device of protective tariffs was hailed as a defense against the competition of cheap foreign labor.

The principles held by the ruling group provided the criteria for making plans and laws, as well as the basic attitudes toward justice and morals, individual welfare, war and peace. As social and economic conditions changed with the overseas expansion of Europe and the growth of capitalist productivity, new problems arose to be judged according to these criteria. In this process, the standards themselves were modified, and the interpretations of underlying values too were shifted as new social groups secured a share in government and in the procedures of policy making. In this process lies the explanation of the changes that occurred in mercantilism in the latter part of the seventeenth and the eighteenth centuries, and of its transformation into the neomercantilism of the nineteenth century and of our own times.

Under the absolute national monarchy, lasting till 1689 in England and 1789 in France, the dominating values were those of a paternalistic king, who recognized no distinction between his own and the nation's interests. With his corps of administrative servants he sought to guide his country according to his standards of success and welfare, within the framework of traditional views of social justice. Given the economic conditions and beliefs of the time, the monarchs felt it to their interest and therefore to the nation's to have a plentiful supply of hard money in circulation, to have a low interest rate and a favorable balance of trade; they felt it proper to stimulate and regulate industry and commerce, as well as labor and the professions. Louis XIV regarded supervision of the arts as a normal part of the activities of his state.[31] In several instances the

[31] The French state went beyond the rest in its interest in the arts, although royal courts in general were patrons of artists and writers. Colbert and Louis XIV treated the creative arts as just another industry that would enhance the glory of the crown. Artists were hired by the state, and Versailles was their best market. As with other trades, regulation was instituted to ensure quality of artistic production and performance. For example, in 1672, Jean Baptiste Lully

combination of kingly standards and current economic beliefs produced policies utterly abhorrent to modern Western standards of decency. The British, for example, believed that the needs of their navy justified shanghaiing merchant seamen or other able bodied subjects of the Crown. The French used courts of justice to provide galley slaves for their Mediterranean war vessels.[32]

Although less shocking because it was more impersonal, the mercantilist attitude toward war gives equally strong evidence of the change in the ethical standards of public policy in Western civilization. Mercantilists generally believed that the amount of wealth and trade was more or less static, and therefore that one country could increase its share only at the expense of the others.[33] Warfare was

---

"was given the right to form the Royal Academy of Music at Paris, and his permission was therefore necessary for any musical presentation employing more than two instruments. Aided by the state and supported by Colbert, Lully enforced his monopoly and fixed the Italian opera upon France as the dominant form of musical entertainment." The theater was similarly handled, Colbert establishing the Comédie française with a monopoly in Paris (Cole, *Colbert*, vol. 1, p. 316).

Despite the superficial resemblance between Colbert's approach to the arts and that of modern totalitarians, it should be noted that the seventeenth-century control was far more civilized than that of our day. Its object was the maintenance of good taste, arbitrarily defined, rather than perversion of art forms to crude propaganda aims or in accordance with pseudo-scientific aesthetics. It resulted in an excess of formal refinement, but that is not to be classed with the systematic vulgarity of modern propaganda art. While a breach of the official canons of taste might result in a loss of favor and revenue under Louis XIV, it did not lead to the artist's suppression, as a "non-Aryan" or to his being forced to issue preposterous apologies, as is the Soviet practice. Colbert's methods are hardly to be recommended today, but they are one of many instances of the superiority of royal absolutism over party dictatorship.

[32] Practices of this type are familiar in modern times through their employment by totalitarian governments. The recently abolished Georgia chain gangs were somewhat different, in that the work project seems to have been more or less incidental to the punishment.

[33] Seventeenth-century mercantilists were well aware of the tremendous economic changes that had occurred prior to their time. They believed the economy to be static only in the sense that they felt further major changes to be improbable. "Colbert recognized that the opening up of 'some new commerce' might upset the static world trade which he posited. But he regarded such an event as 'very uncertain' and too unlikely to base commercial policy on" (Cole, *Colbert*, vol. 1, p. 342). Some justification for this view might be found in the fact that the second half of the seventeenth century was a period of stable or declining prices and of relatively slower expansion and colonization, compared to the highly inflationary and brilliantly expansionist century and a half preceding.

consequently a proper means to national welfare, and economic justification was provided for the territorial ambitions of dynastic monarchs. War was not glorified in the manner of twentieth-century fascists: it was merely accepted as a normal instrument of national policy.

Both the concept of a static economy and the mercantilist view of warfare were slowly overcome, the former by two centuries of remarkable economic expansion, and the latter by the growth of mass public opinion and the development of total war. Militarism, of course, has proved to be one of the most persistent of human institutions, for pacificism did not become an attitude seriously to be reckoned with until the twentieth century, in which armed conflict has thus far had the upper hand. Other characteristic practices and theories of mercantilism, however, were sharply modified or disappeared entirely.

Bullionism, we have said, fell victim to both new economic fact and to the rising position in society of the middle class. The new fact was the development of public and private credit devices: bond issues, commercial paper and banking. As a result of the heightened influence of the bourgeoisie, the always intimate relationship between wealth and power was slowly reversed: to the absolute monarchy wealth was sought as a means to power, as well as for its own sake; to the middle class power was originally sought as a means to wealth, as well as for its own sake. The former implied a high preference for liquidity in riches, the latter a preference for the riches of productive enterprise. This shift in emphasis is well expressed by Marshal Vauban, the great military engineer of Louis XIV:

It is not a large quantity of gold and silver that constitutes the great and true wealth of a state, since there are very large countries in the world which have an abundance of gold and of silver, and which are not thereby more prosperous nor more happy. Such are Peru and several states of America and of the east and west Indies which have an abundance of gold and precious stones, but which are lacking in bread. The true wealth of a kingdom consists in the abundance of the commodities whose use is so necessary to the life of men that they would not be able to do without them.[34]

[34] Quoted by Paul Harsin, *Les Doctrines monétaires et financières en France du XVIe au XVIIIe Siècle,* Paris, 1928, p. 96. Vauban wrote at the close of the

The mercantilist attitude toward bullionism therefore changed. In the eighteenth century, a large supply of precious metals was given less and less weight as a national objective, and emphasis was placed upon the stimulating effect on the economy of an *increase* in the amount of money in circulation. At the same time, a two-century-old contradiction in mercantilist thinking was swept away. The quantity theory of money, stating essentially that an increase in the supply of money would lead to an inflationary price rise (other things being equal), was in obvious conflict with the aim of simple bullionism, to increase the national stock of gold and silver. Eighteenth-century mercantilists avoided the contradiction by admitting that the initial effect of an influx of bullion would be inflationary; they went on to argue, however, that the purchasing power of money would soon not only recover but rise, owing to increased competition, lower interest rates, and expanded productive capacity. In short, they stressed the stimulative effect of the introduction of new money into the national economy, rather than the supply of bullion itself.[35]

This modified attitude toward bullionism implied a further relaxation of government control over the export of precious metals. But the reduction in the role of the state was not limited to this matter of hard money. Regulation, under the absolute monarchy, was basically only one means of state stimulation of the economy, and as economic initiative passed slowly from the hands of the government into those of the middle class, the regulatory function of the bureaucracy also diminished. By the mid-eighteenth century neither regulation nor stimulation was as necessary as a hundred years earlier. The role of government was gradually being transformed from central guiding agency to general arbitrating agency, through which public judgment could be passed on the conflicting interests of private groups, and through which national policy could be made

---

seventeenth century. An even earlier writer, Scipion de Gramont, argued that the monetary function of gold and silver, as a way of stating the value of goods, was the result of human choice, and "not founded on nature." The superiority of gold as money, according to Gramont, derived from its physical attributes (Harsin, *Doctrines*, pp. 60 ff.).

[35] See J. W. Angell, *The Theory of International Prices*, Cambridge, 1926, chaps. 2, 8, and especially his analysis of Forbonnais, pp. 208–209, 216–218. Modern expressions of this view are discussed in chap. 7 of this book.

that would be binding on all. The right of the state to intervene was not questioned. The initiative which sought to turn this intervention into one or another path now came more from the commercial and industrial middle classes, and less from the administrative officials.

Where the absolute monarchy had the influence and power of the going concern, as in France, the gilds became an agency for the preservation of members' privileges rather than for carrying out governmental policies for economic development. Where the absolute monarchy had been overthrown, and where a Parliament served as the bargaining table at which group conflicts could be compromised, as in England, the gild system disintegrated and the crafts and arts became open to all who could afford to enter them. In general, internal guidance and control either lost its dynamic quality or simply fell away, bit by bit. Not that the noninterventionist dream world of the classical economists came into existence; but the central conception and impetus, which gave the thoroughgoing mercantilism of Colbert many of the characteristics of a planned economy, were no longer present. The basic mercantilist proposition that it was the duty of the state to promote national prosperity and welfare was not seriously challenged until the day of the classical economists. Mercantilists of the eighteenth century redefined the standard of welfare to emphasize productivity rather than military power and bullion, and stressed the economic and political devices that would work best toward their modified objectives. In France, inheritances from the old order, such as the monopolies that Colbert had viewed as a necessary if unpleasant expedient and the internal tariffs that he would have eliminated had he been able to do so, came under renewed and redoubled attack. In England, vestiges of the old order could still be seen in poor relief and in a chartered monopoly such as the East India Company, but state intervention in the domestic economy was governed by the will of the commercial and landlord oligarchy that had triumphed over the absolutist aspirations of the Stuarts.

The decline of the Colbertian variety of centralized, sweeping, and dynamic mercantilism was accompanied with the numerous protests that bespeak a changing and confident society. Later generations of writers, pursuing the scholar's favorite game of tracing influences and finding "precursors," viewed these criticisms from within the mercantilist family as faint flickerings of the great light that was to burst forth with Adam Smith and the classical school. To a limited extent this holds true, for Smith leaned as heavily on his predecessors as did Malthus and Ricardo on Smith. But the mercantilists who criticized one or another practice did not think of themselves as pioneers clearing the brush for the glorious march of a new science as yet unborn. It is faulty perspective to regard eighteenth-century mercantilism as a "precursor" of classical economics, instead of the practical adaptation of policy to changed facts and needs that it actually was.[36]

The continuity of mercantilist economics, from the sixteenth-century monarchy to present times, is clearly seen in the history of protective tariffs. Internal regulation developed and expanded, declined, and rose again: tariffs, on the other hand, might well be coupled with the death and taxes that are always part of the mortal scene. According to Colbert, a proper tariff policy involved "reducing the import duties on goods used in the internal manufactures of the kingdom" and "increasing the duties on the importation of manufactured goods."[37] These two points, by no means original with Colbert, have remained part of the protectionist program. Tariffs are not an end in themselves. They are a device used to carry out objectives of national policy that have varied over the years, and the

[36] Because of his attacks on the traditional antiluxury attitude of mercantilism, Mandeville is generally viewed as a precursor of classical economics, rather than as a mercantilist. A similar case is that of David Hume, who prepared the classical attack on bullionism (see p. 13 above). Hume was essentially a mercantilist, and his theory of the international flow of specie was like that of some contemporary mercantilists, such as Forbonnais. Hume wrote, "It is of no manner of consequence, with regard to the domestic happiness of a state, whether money be in a greater or less quantity. The good policy of the magistrate consists only in keeping it, if possible, still increasing; because by that means he keeps alive a spirit of industry in the nation, and increases the state of labour in which consists all real power and riches. A nation, whose money decreases, is actually, at that time, weaker and more miserable than another nation, which possesses no more money but is on the increasing trend" ("Of Money," *Essays Moral, Political and Literary,* London, 1882, vol. 1, p. 315). Forbonnais took the same view, but stressed the fact that, as a nation always had competing neighbors, it was essential to keep the stock of bullion high and rising.

[37] Cole, *Colbert,* vol. 1, p. 346.

arguments for protectionism have varied accordingly. But protectionism has always appeared in mercantilist platforms.[38]

Even more striking evidence of the continuity and modernity of the mercantilist outlook is to be found in the field of public finance and fiscal policy. The general attitude, to be sure, was similar to what became classical orthodoxy: the national budget was to be balanced, the function of taxes was exclusively to raise money for governmental needs, and the public debt was essentially an evil that had sometimes to be tolerated, but that was to be reduced as soon as opportunity afforded. This was the view of even so sophisticated a mercantilist as Forbonnais. But in the latter half of the eighteenth century a different conception of fiscal policy developed, assigning to it a positive role in the direction of the economy.

A number of mercantilist writers, among whom Sir James Steuart (1712–1780) was perhaps the most outstanding, wove together old and new concepts to form a pattern astonishingly similar to contemporary Keynesian economics. They argued that a domestically held public debt was different from all other forms of property, and in particular from private debts, in that it was at one and the same time both a sound equity for its owners and the basis for the monetary and credit system. In a period of business stagnation, therefore, an expansion of the public debt would increase the amount of money in circulation, and the expenditures financed by the new issues would create work and therefore demand for goods. The wheels of trade would turn more rapidly. In a period of full economic activity, however, it would be the better part of wisdom for governments to refrain from such monetary expansion. The amount of an internally owned national debt was little cause for concern, unless it was outrageously high, for the real burden on the state was not the debt itself but the interest to be paid on it. Following a war, therefore, fiscal policy should be aimed at establishing prosperity,

[38] There have been protectionists, typified by American high-tariff leaders such as William McKinley, who believed that this was the only legitimate exception to the natural law economics of the classical school. They desired the state to intervene in the market economy by erecting high customs barriers, but believed that any internal interference for purposes of welfare or social equity was unnatural and improper. This highly inconsistent attitude on the part of those whom we might call "simple protectionists" is not neomercantilism, which does not argue from natural law for one part of the program and from practical expediency for another.

rather than paying off the war-swollen debt, for only a prosperous country will be able to deal with financial burdens.

Steuart and others approached policy from the demand side of the economic equation: if employment were high enough at wages sufficient for the people to spend enough to maintain full economic activity, other economic problems would all but take care of themselves. Both debt management and taxation were to be directed toward establishing that level of economic activity which would support employment and demand.

A good deal of the modern ring to this argument is, of course, lost in the eighteenth-century phrasing, but the basic ideas were there. Not the least of the triumphs of the classical economists was to interrupt this line of thought for over 150 years, until it was revived in twentieth-century dress and technical refinement by Lord Keynes.[39]

Mercantilism is a continually developing doctrine of the role of the national state in economic and social affairs, and the term *neomercantilism* is merely a means of distinguishing between the absolutist or oligarchical form and that of a more democratic society. The dividing line between mercantilism and neomercantilism can be drawn in that momentous epoch between 1776 and 1830, when the middle class gained a degree of power and influence it had never before achieved; when the factory system came into its own and the railroad gave new meanings to geography; when nationalism, the glorification of a mystic entity considered greater than the sum of its parts, replaced the simpler patriotism which had meant love of

---

[39] See Sir James Steuart, *An Inquiry into the Principles of Political Oeconomy*, 1767 (the 1805 edition by General Sir James Steuart, the author's son, runs to six volumes, of which vol. 4 is especially relevant); W. F. Stettner, "Sir James Steuart on the Public Debt," *Quarterly Journal of Economics*, May, 1945, pp. 451–476; *An Essay on Circulation and Credit . . . From the French of Monsieur de Pinto*, London, 1774 (the translator as of the title page is the Rev. S. Baggs, but the McCulloch catalogue indicates it was actually Sir Philip Francis); Melon, *Essai politique sur le Commerce*, in E. Daire, *Economistes financières du XVIIIe Siècle*, Paris, 1843, pp. 802 ff.; aspects of this general position may be found in mercantilists of the first part of the eighteenth century as well, including Cantillon, Forbonnais, and John Law. See also H. Grossman, "The Evolutionist Revolt Against Classical Economics," in two parts, *Journal of Political Economy*, October and December, 1943; E. B. Wilson, "John Law and John Keynes," *Quarterly Journal of Economics*, May, 1948, pp. 381 ff.

king and countryside; when history came to be regarded as the key to understanding, and as the foundation of national right and vitality; when Romantic writers led men to think in terms of growth and feeling, rather than the mechanistic balances of the followers of Newton or the matter-of-fact precepts of royal bureaucrats.

The conception of national interest changed as one social group after another achieved the power to influence public policy. Two ideas remained constant: that the nation was a basic entity in economic affairs, rather than a political intrusion into economic reality; that national welfare was the objective consciously to be worked for, under the overall guidance of the state. For about a half century following 1830, these fundamental propositions of neomercantilism almost lost their standing as intellectually respectable guides for economic policy, under the propaganda blows of classical theory. The last three generations have seen a sharp revival of neomercantilist thinking and practice throughout the world, a development in which America has played an extremely important role.

NOTES ON BOOKS

There is no adequate, brief history of mercantilism in English, so far as I know. J. W. Horrocks' *A Short History of Mercantilism* is more helpful, despite its classical bias, than G. F. von Schmoller's *The Mercantile System and Its Historical Significance*. E. S. Furniss' *The Position of the Laborer in a System of Nationalism* and P. W. Buck's *The Politics of Mercantilism* are useful for British mercantilism, despite a tendency to criticize men of an earlier age for shortcomings in terms of twentieth-century public morality. E. A. J. Johnson's *Predecessors of Adam Smith* and J. W. Angell's *Theory of International Prices* are important for mercantilist theory. Small's *Cameralism* is the available treatment of the significant and, in the Western countries, neglected development of mercantilism in Central Europe.

The monumental works in English in the field are Heckscher's *Mercantilism*, a vast source book whose value is not lowered by the author's classical predispositions and excessive use of abstractions, and C. W. Cole's *Colbert and a Century of French Mercantilism*, which gives a splendid picture of the system under Louis XIV.

Some of the reasons why mercantilism deserves renewed interest in the twentieth century are given by J. M. Keynes, in chap. 23, "Notes on Mercantilism . . ." of the *General Theory of Employment, Interest and Money,* but this only serves to emphasize the need for a good, brief history of mercantilist thinking in its social setting. The standard histories of economic theory regard mercantilism as prehistorical, and, when they mention modern mercantilists at all, write them off lightly as "unorthodox."

5.

AMERICAN NEOMERCANTILISM: HAMILTON AND HIS SUCCESSORS

The Europeans who came to America in the seventeenth century were not revolutionaries. A good many were dissenters in religious matters, but even these brought with them the economic and social ideas that were taken for granted in their countries of origin. It is true that the colonists were less concerned than the inhabitants of the Old World with promoting the glory of the state, although each colony desired to become well ordered and prosperous. But American social thought began in the spirit and traditions of mercantilism and developed under continuing European influence. Differences in environment explain adequately American deviations from the general stream of European economic and social thinking. Commonplace though this be, the classical myth has become so deeply ingrained in American thinking that the colonists are sometimes depicted as devout believers in unrestricted individualism, hard money, and laissez faire.

From Massachusetts to Virginia, the ministers of the Gospel and the political leaders who gave voice to the social ideology of seventeenth-century America proposed essentially the same policies as the Catholic bureaucrats of Louis XIV and the royal Stuarts of England. In New England, where religious influences were especially strong, moral and spiritual arguments for public policy were given particular prominence. But here, as everywhere, the secularization of ideology and institutions proceeded rapidly, and the end product

97

was an American neomercantilism that kept pace with and, from the time of Alexander Hamilton, exerted a strong influence on European economic thinking.

The new world of the Puritans was a wilderness to be conquered for the Lord, and the leaders of New England gave considerable thought to the economic arrangements best suited to both their physical and spiritual salvation. Although the human task was to strive for the greater glorification of God, the search for moderate wealth and comfort was regarded as entirely legitimate for both individual and community. Following the failure of the initial collectivist experiment of the Pilgrims of the Plymouth colony, individual property rights and private initiative were accepted as necessary to the general welfare, but this of course did not mean that the regulative role of public authority had been rejected. Along with other colonists, such as Thomas Budd in Pennsylvania, Robert Beverley, the historian of Virginia, and her governor, Sir William Berkeley, Puritan leaders asserted the duty of the state to assist and guide the development of the economy.

Having accepted interventionism from the very beginning, the colonists went on to adopt a whole series of mercantilist principles and policies. They drew a distinction between individual profit and general welfare. Increase Mather, famous Puritan divine and father of Cotton Mather, wrote: "Sometimes one man by seeking to advance himself has brought great misery on whole nations."[1] They believed in state stimulation of industries, in the restriction of imports of foreign manufactures, as entailing a loss of specie; they thought the precious metals should not be exported, and they believed in the favorable balance of trade. They approved of regulation to ensure the quality of goods, and of the grant of monopolies and other privileges to stimulate production. They brought to the New World medieval conceptions of the just price, and were as stern as any European bureaucrat in their denunciations of idleness and of demands on the part of labor for what they considered to be excessively high wages. As a matter of fact, the typically colonial combination of scarcity of both goods and labor initially led the New

---

[1] Increase Mather, *The Excellency of a Public Spirit*, quoted by E. A. J. Johnson, *American Economic Thought in the Seventeenth Century*, London, 1932, p. 89.

Englanders to adopt views and actions far more extreme than those of the mother country.

For example, in 1639 a Captain Robert Keayne (or Keaine) was defendant in a well-known case tried before both magistrates and clergy of Boston, the accusation being that he charged excessive prices on such goods as gold buttons, bridles, and nails (which were in great demand for building and in short supply). Keayne did not defend himself with the claim that a merchant had the right to charge the highest price he could get, but confessed that he had been "misled," as Governor John Winthrop reported, "by some false principles, as, 1. That if a man lost in one commodity, he might help himself in the price of another. 2. That if, through want of skill or other occasion, his commodity cost him more than the price of the market in England, he might then sell it for more than the price of the market in New England." "These things," continued Winthrop, "gave occasion to Mr. Cotton, in his public exercise the next lecture day, to lay open the error of such false principles, and to give some rules of direction in the case." And the Reverend John Cotton proceeded to offer a clear statement of the doctrine of just price, denying that "a man might sell as dear as he can and buy as cheap as he can," or that "as a man may take the advantage of his own skill or ability, so may he of another's ignorance or necessity."[2] In 1641, Cotton proposed that both prices and wages be fixed by government. But the Puritan leaders soon realized that they had neither the apparatus nor the accounting principle with which to set prices, and that the availability of land for the opening of new farms made wage controls ineffective.

The colonial mercantilist ideology was soon secularized. The initial Puritanical condemnation of luxury yielded to the view that expenditures on unnecessary and decorative objects provided employment and enhanced prosperity, except when they involved imports that drained money from the land. Early Massachusetts debates on usury ended with the setting of a legal maximum interest rate of 8 percent. Arguments over prices and wages shifted from the moral to the monetary field, and here the colonists showed all the inventiveness and ingenuity for which Americans have become famous. They had always agreed that the circulating medium should

[2] N. S. B. Gras, ed., *Business History*, Cambridge, 1936, vol. 1, chap. 3.

be in ample supply and of stable purchasing power, but their initial dependence upon Europe for manufactered goods led to a shortage of gold and silver. As a result, as early as the 1680's, leading citizens of Massachusetts and other colonists were issuing proposals for banking and monetary systems based on personal credit, on stocks of grain and other commodities and on land.[3] A number of paper money schemes were enacted, receiving a degree of public support they were unable to gain in old Europe in the early years of the next century.[4]

The colonies grew within the confines of the British mercantilist system to that degree of maturity that led them to revolution. Until the imperial victory of England over France in 1763, however, the colonial compact, limiting the colonies to supplying the mother country with raw materials and buying her manufactures, was loosely enforced. Furthermore, smuggling was an effective and large-scale corrective to unwelcome legislation. When her triumph in 1763 enabled England to turn to the task of tightening the mercantilist system of empire, tension between colonies and mother country grew rapidly. The colonies, particularly in the North, had long outgrown the plantation status: their own mercantilist desires clashed with those of Great Britain. The colonists' protests against perfectly ordinary mercantilist enactments rose to a crescendo over the relatively minor matter of a tea monopoly bestowed upon the British East India Company. A movement for autonomy came into being and developed into a war for independence.[5]

In short, the United States of America grew out of a background that shared the thinking of late eighteenth-century mercantilism. The mercantilist spirit was evident in the Philadelphia Convention

---

[3] Unlike later cheap money movements, initiated by debt-ridden farmers, the early proposals were made by outstanding figures in colonial trade and commerce, whose descendants were to be sturdy defenders of conservative monetary policies.

[4] For American social and economic thought and policy prior to the Revolution see especially E. A. J. Johnson, *American Economic Thought in the Seventeenth Century,* and "Some Evidence of Mercantilism in the Massachusetts Bay," *New England Quarterly,* July, 1928; Joseph Dorfman, *The Economic Mind in American Civilization,* New York, 1946, vol. 1.

[5] It is not suggested that the incompatibility of colonial and British mercantilism "caused the Revolution." The Revolution was an intricate and developing phenomenon, involving the whole social complex, and certainly including the economic issues of the time.

that drafted the Constitution, and it was to the mercantilist tradition that the first Secretary of the Treasury, Alexander Hamilton, fell heir. Hamilton, who was fully aware of the classical theory of his time, rejected Smith's proposition that government intervention could only "transfer the natural current of industry from a more to a less beneficial channel." He argued against the Jeffersonian lovers of agriculture, that industry was at least as productive as farming, and offered far greater opportunity for the exercise of ingenuity and skill. He stated one of the fundamental points of nineteenth-century neomercantilism when he wrote that the purely agricultural country would always be relatively poor and in a state of economic subjection to foreign suppliers of manufactured goods. He stressed the importance of economic stability, a point that was eventually to become the chief preoccupation of the capitalist world. Another of Hamilton's principles was to remain part of the neomercantilist creed: a nation whose economy specialized in a few staple commodities was subject to all the strains and fluctuations of the world market and had no control over its own course, while the nation with a diversified economy, whose producers were sufficiently protected to dominate the home market, was guaranteed a stable floor upon which to build prosperity and growth.

The all-important problem, as far as Hamilton was concerned, was how to go about creating this diversified economy in the undeveloped but potentially wealthy United States. While he admitted that history gave many examples of excessive and unwise state intervention, he felt that this was no reason to throw out the good with the bad. National independence and security, he said, "appear to be materially connected with the prosperity of manufactures. Every nation, with a view to those great objects, ought to endeavor to possess within itself, all the essentials of national supply. These comprise the means of subsistence, habitation, clothing and defense."[6] Hamilton accordingly proposed that the federal government undertake to stimulate the growth of industry in America. Competition from abroad, and the force of custom and fear of novelty at home, made it inadvisable to trust exclusively to individual initiative and interest. He urged Congress to enact protective tariffs, to offer

[6] *Report on Manufactures*, in *Papers on Public Credit, Commerce and Finance*, by Alexander Hamilton, ed. by Samuel McKee, Jr., New York, 1934, p. 227.

subsidies and prizes, to prohibit the export of industrial raw materials, to improve facilities for transfer of money, to provide for better credit mechanisms and internal communications. He called for "Judicious regulations for the inspection of manufactured commodities," as being

. . . not among the least of the means by which the prosperity of manufactures may be promoted. It is, indeed, in many cases, one of the most essential. Contributing to prevent frauds upon consumers at home and exporters to foreign countries, to improve the quality and preserve the character of the national manufactures, it cannot fail to aid the expeditious and advantageous sale of them, and to serve as a guard against successful competition from other quarters. The reputation of the flour and lumber of some States, and of the potash of others, has been established by an attention to this point. And the like good name might be procured for those articles, wheresoever produced, by a judicious and uniform system of inspection throughout the ports of the United States. A like system might also be extended with advantage to other commodities.[7]

Hamilton felt that federal guidance and regulation was far preferable to that of the states, and expressed the wish that Congress, being "the body in this country, in whose councils a local or partial spirit is least likely to predominate, were at liberty to pursue and promote the general interest, in those instances in which there might be danger of the interference of such a spirit."[8]

Hamilton recognized that his program meant giving special advantages to particular groups, and justified this short-run burden with the argument that in the long run the nation as a whole would benefit. He conceded that subsidies would initially represent a cost to all the people to help a few establish an industry; that tariffs would at first raise prices and thus amount to an indirect subsidy, although less efficient; that to restrict raw material exports would create hardships for domestic raw material producers. But, he insisted, once American industry had become established with the aid of the state, prices would fall owing to domestic competition, and industry's contributions to national welfare in the form of employment, security, and markets for raw materials would more than balance the initial costs.

[7] *Report on Manufactures,* pp. 244–245.
[8] *Report on Manufactures,* p. 247.

This broad sector of the Hamiltonian program was topped with a board to consist of "commissioners, not less than three . . . officers of the government and their successors," who were to administer a fund "for promoting arts, agriculture, manufactures and commerce." They were to employ the fund

. . . to defray the expenses of the emigration of artists and manufacturers in particular branches of extraordinary importance; to induce the prosecution and introduction of useful discoveries, inventions, and improvements, by proportionate rewards, judiciously held out and applied; to encourage by premiums, both honorable and lucrative, the exertions of individuals and of classes, in relation to the several objects they are charged with promoting; and to afford such other aids to those objects as may be generally designated by law.[9]

Hamilton was also the eighteenth-century mercantilist when it came to monetary and fiscal policy. He favored a national bank and the assumption of state debts by the federal government because these measures would tend to unify the country economically and would put its credit on a conservatively sound basis. He believed that a funded national debt would help agriculture, industry, and commerce by increasing the circulating medium and lowering the interest rate, twin objectives of mercantilist policy.

In outlook as in time, Hamilton stands at the turning point of the eighteenth into the nineteenth century, of mercantilism into neomercantilism. He leans somewhat more heavily upon direct government intervention than his immediate successors, both political and theoretical. His emphasis upon security and the home market rather than on a belligerent campaign for foreign trade reflects the transfer of power from the absolute monarch to a well-to-do citizenry. His argument that American entrepreneurs could afford to pay higher wages than their European competitors revealed the conditions of a youthful economy and eliminated from American mercantilism the low-wage doctrine that might have made it incompatible with a growing democratic society.

Hamilton thought of himself as an aristocrat, and his policies were frankly designed to favor the growth of a class whose interests would make them conservative and devoted to stability as a social

[9] *Report on Manufactures*, p. 274. "Emigration" from Europe to America.

good. But his justification of national interest and of government intervention in its behalf carried forward the tradition of mercantilist thinking in America. He placed an obstacle in the path of the importation and assimilation of classical economics, and thereby helped make it possible for a later, more democratic age to feel at ease in making its own adaptations of mercantilist doctrine.

We have already shown that only part of the Hamilton program was adopted, and that the general spirit of American neomercantilist policy during most of the nineteenth century was one of generous help to business, with but very little guidance and even less regulation. In a country expanding rapidly both geographically and in productivity where a proletariat in the European sense did not come into being, there was less urgent demand for the restrictive aspects of state intervention. It is generally correct to say that the scope of neomercantilism, in Europe as well as America, narrowed during the 1850's, '60's, and '70's, laying greatest stress on the creation of a varied, stable, and relatively self-sufficient economy, and relying largely upon internal competition to protect the interests of the people as consumers. Only toward the latter part of the century, when the working class developed effective and vocal organizations and the farmers similarly felt the need for banding together, did state intervention in the domestic economy return to its old place in schemes of mercantilist doctrine. But many threads bind the two periods and the two viewpoints together.

To begin with, the practice of government intervention did not fade quite so rapidly as the laissez-faire mythologists would have it. While economically liberal Britain was busily scrapping the vestiges of her Navigation Acts and grain protection, she was at the same time enacting factory legislation designed to mitigate somewhat the hardships of industrial labor. In the United States, recent studies show that interventionism was vigorous and lively into the decade preceding the Civil War. This picture is somewhat obscured by the fact that intervention was more striking at the state than the federal level. But an active "state mercantilism" had survived the colonial period, and state jealousies did as much as ideological conflict to restrict the national government to protective tariffs, inland improvements and various forms of subsidies.

"The laissez-faire argument," write the Handlins with reference to the period before the Civil War,

. . . found no place in Massachusetts thinking. . . . Failure to develop a case against all government economic measures acquired particular significance when liberal humanitarianism placed ever heavier emphasis upon the police and reform functions of the state. There was no counterpart in America of the transatlantic tendency to transpose objections against privilege into objections against government regulation. In the United States the people who favored reform were not held back by a fear of the state; the people were the state.

Two hundred years after the landing at Plymouth, the editor of the *Boston Commercial Gazette* regarded as " 'manifestly erroneous' the notion that industry should be left alone, that the people individually, and not the government, 'are the judges of their interests and consequently should be allowed to regulate them unobstructed.' That principle was 'subversive to the end and aim of all governments; and . . . utterly impracticable.' "[10]

In Pennsylvania, the mercantilist tradition was even stronger than in Massachusetts. The state held investments in 150 enterprises, stimulated railroad and canal construction, and lent money to private business. In the famous case of *Sharpless vs. Mayor of Philadelphia* (1853), involving the right of the city to engage in subscription toward the building of the Hempfield railroad, Pennsylvania's Chief Justice Black held that state investment had "from the earliest times" been carried on "in pursuance of laws which no one ever doubted to be constitutional." The judge wrote:

It is a grave error to suppose that the duty of a state stops with the establishment of those institutions which are necessary to the existence of government: such as those for the administration of justice, the preservation of the peace, and the protection of the country from foreign enemies. . . . To aid, encourage and stimulate commerce domestic and foreign, is a duty of the sovereign as plain and as universally recognized as any other.[11]

[10] See O. and M. F. Handlin, *Commonwealth, A Study of the Role of Government in the American Economy: Massachusetts, 1774–1861*, New York, 1947, pp. 54–55, 262.

[11] Quoted in Louis Hartz, *Economic Policy and Democratic Thought. Pennsylvania, 1776–1860*, Cambridge, 1948, p. 122. Hartz comments that "the grave error which the Chief Justice described is perhaps as adequate a definition as any of that amorphous concept known as 'laissez-faire' which is often alleged to have governed the thinking of the period before the Civil War. . . ."

Legislators of the Keystone state made the typical mercantilist distinction between individual and public wealth, defining the latter by the productive capacity of the community. To increase productivity they favored public investment, even if it involved deficit financing. So widespread was this point of view, that even many of its opponents were willing to concede the necessity of public investment until fully adequate private capital were available. In Pennsylvania prior to the Civil War, the mercantilist tradition of colonial days was fused with a democratic outlook that gave it increased scope and vitality.[12]

Government intervention was therefore anything but an "un-American" importation of either European royalism or European radicalism, depending upon one's tastes in epithets. It was, indeed, declining just prior to the Civil War, and this decline was not arrested till the close of the century. But the period of laissez faire (behind a tariff wall, at that) was hardly long enough to break the thread of interventionist tradition. The tradition was carried on in thought as well as practice, although the form of neomercantilist analysis and writing did undergo a distinct change during the nineteenth century. Hamilton thought and expressed himself in the manner of eighteenth-century mercantilism, working up a group of harmonizing proposals to cover the aspects of the national economy in which he was interested. His successors in what became the academically unorthodox branch of economic thinking in America were forced to concern themselves first with the latest pronouncements of the classical school. Although their practical conclusions were for the most part in sharp opposition to those of Ricardo, Malthus, and Say, such men as Daniel Raymond, Henry C. Carey, Friedrich List, Stephen Colwell, and Simon N. Patten felt compelled to deal with generalizations about rent, value, profits, wages fund, etc. They tended to present their own viewpoints in broad strokes, basing them upon their own abstract propositions or sweeping historical generalizations, such as Carey's law of harmony and List's law of the stages of national development. They fought their main battle for the principle of the national economy, and the protective tariff became their chief governmental device to stimulate national economic and social growth. Nineteenth-century neomercantilist writings show little of the precise analysis of particular measures to

[12] Hartz, *Economic Policy*, pp. 169, 177, 301 ff., 306–307.

promote national welfare that characterizes the work of those who had not yet felt the weight of the classical pretensions to a natural and universally valid science.

List, an unhappy German who drew his inspiration from French mercantilism and his personal observations in the United States, was willing to accept the classical dogma of laissez faire—for the distant future in which all nations would have achieved equal stages of economic growth, and could therefore engage in competition without risk of suicide. For all practical purposes, however, he claimed that England's industrial superiority would prevent the other nations from ever starting the development to economic maturity that was their national right. Hence he called for an historical method of economic analysis that would enlighten national governments as to the proper policies for the time, and condemned the abstractions of the followers of Ricardo.[13] Henry C. Carey, the son of one of List's American friends, the Philadelphia publisher Matthew Carey, first fell under the spell of the classical school, and then turned sharply against it. Unlike most neomercantilists, Carey tried to work out a system of universal, natural laws of economics, based on the principle of association or harmony rather than competition. He urged protection and dependence upon a secure home market, and placed great weight upon the type of association and coöperation to be found in the joint stock company. Carey's friend, another learned and influential Philadelphian, Stephen Colwell, doubted that economics could be developed as a natural science, and contented himself with a vigorous criticism of the classical tradition along the lines prepared by List, together with a bitter protest against a type of social thinking that divorced itself from Christian ethics.[14] All these men were spokesmen for industrialization in an age when the su-

[13] List offers a good example of one of the dangers inherent in nationalist economics, particularly in German hands, for his nationalism ran away with him. Since his prescription for a country capable of thorough economic development includes the requirement of adequate size and seacoast, he decided that the Netherlands would simply have to become part of the future united greater Germany (*Introduction to Contemporary Civilization in the West*, vol. 2, p. 288).

[14] When we recall that the descendants of Colwell's Whigs were the gold Republicans of 1896, it is amusing to note that Colwell was an outstanding opponent of Andrew Jackson's Democratic hard money policy. Colwell, who favored the Bank, took what is now a modern, "sophisticated" view, that credit in adequate supply was the real basis for monetary circulation, and that specie had little to do with it.

premacy of industry over agriculture was far from conceded. Their personal interests and ideological viewpoint were those of the industrial upper middle class. They preached the harmony of national groups and interests, but the harmony was centered in their own group. We have pointed out that while mercantilists of different times might agree on a major principle, such as the right of the state to determine social ends and means, and on particular measures such as protective tariffs, their views on other matters, particularly the status of the various social groups, would depend upon how democratic was their conception of society. Colbert spoke for an absolute royal master; Hamilton, and his nineteenth-century successors we have mentioned, spoke for an aspiring aristocracy of industrial and commercial leadership. The democratization of neomercantilism was far from complete.

Ignoring variations in theoretical approach and in detail, neomercantilist doctrine as of about 1850 reached the following principal conclusions: (1) the nation is the most important economic reality, and classical economic theory, ignoring national differences and offering policies based on a nonexistent cosmopolitanism, is utterly unrealistic; (2) national agriculture, industry, and commerce are mutually interdependent, and it is to the long-run interest of each for the nation to develop a diversified economy in secure control of its home market and thus insulated against the ruinous fluctuations of world markets; (3) relative self-sufficiency is desirable, but total self-sufficiency (autarky) is not; (4) it is the duty of the central government to stimulate the diversified economy by appropriate measures of protection, finance, and improvements; (5) protection should not be so extreme as to subsidize inefficiency, or to diminish foreign trade; trade will be greatest among highly developed industrial states; (6) with respect to domestic policy, principal reliance should be placed upon the force of internal competition to regulate prices and the distribution of rewards.

This set of precepts is but a pale continuation of the comprehensive mercantilism of Colbert, but it was sufficient to keep alive the seeds of a renewed expansion of the role of the state when a proper climate was provided by the growth of monopoly capitalism and organized labor, and of the problem of agricultural surpluses. The basic conception of the right and duty of the state to establish and execute national objectives was maintained. The idea of nationality carried with it a condemnation of unbridled individualism and furthered a belief in the interdependence of the welfare of all citizens that could easily justify government intervention in internal social and economic affairs.

In the last two decades of the nineteenth century the scope of neomercantilist doctrine widened once more. It is not surprising that this expansion should have occurred first and most clearly on the continent of Europe, where nationalism was acute and industrial problems pressing, and where the Colbertian tradition was still strongly revered. Using List and Carey as starting points, a man such as Paul-Louis Cauwès, Dean of the Paris Law Faculty, urged a broad policy of state intervention in both domestic and foreign business, in the interests of national welfare and social justice. In contrast to List's reliance on competition to maintain equity and prosperity at home, Cauwès echoed a theme stressed by Social Catholics, the organization of voluntary, coöperative groups for mutual betterment—an adaptation of the medieval and mercantilist gild system to modern industrial society.[15] In Germany, nationalist and interventionist doctrines were proclaimed by such influential men as Adolf Wagner and other historical economists, and the Junker Otto von Bismarck enacted a program of social insurance, high protection and imperialism. In "classical" England, Joseph Chamberlain's campaign for social reform and tariff protection stirred debate over economic laws that had been regarded as undebatable, and in 1900 Parliament outlawed usury in a gesture of defiance against the omnipotent automatic market.

Each nation naturally produced its own version of modern neomercantilism. Common to all was an emphasis upon nationalism, and what was essentially a moral protest against suffering and injustice surrounded by wealth and privilege. The formal arguments of the classical economists were no obstacle to the spirit of nationalism, or to indignation based upon ideas of right and wrong that were drawn, in at least some instances with due credit, from the ethics of the Western religious tradition. In the United States, the people we have called "reforming liberals"[16] combined with nation-

---

[15] See chap. 13 for a discussion of Social Catholicism.
[16] See note on p. 54.

alists to restore the breadth of neomercantilist doctrine and policy. To neither group was man a disembodied economic mind, to neither was he just one of the factors of production. Henry Charles Carey had declaimed against the classical "analytical process that selects only the 'material parts' of man—those which are common to himself and the beast—and excludes those which are common to the angels and himself."[17] This was the spirit that moved such a man as Simon N. Patten, perhaps the outstanding American neomercantilist thinker of the turn of the century.[18] He rejected not only the classical laws of wages and population, but their conception of the economy itself, which he condemned as static. His own view was of a progressing economy, which could achieve a sufficient surplus above the subsistence level for economics to be concerned with problems of consumption rather than production. He favored a high-wage, diversified system for America, not only guarded but stimulated by protective tariffs. He approved of government intervention to gain desired social ends, preferring state and local initiative to federal, where possible. Patten did not elaborate a system, but he was an extremely influential teacher of a nationalist and interventionist point of view that was to dominate American public policy in the twentieth century.

American politics at the turn of the century was, as we have indicated, quite preoccupied with the problem of trusts, and reformers were at least as active in blasting big business as in calling for state intervention for social welfare. At first sight they would appear to be guilty of asking for both more and less competition at the same time, but since they were not trying to work up theoretical systems, but to fit practical means to social objectives, the inconsistency is not a real one. Monopoly was felt to be threatening democracy, both social and political, and trust busting was hailed as a way of limiting the concentration of excessive power in the hands of a few business leaders. The reformers also believed that economic

[17] Carey, *Principles of Social Science,* Philadelphia, 1858–1859, vol. 1, p. 31.
[18] Patten was Professor at the Wharton School of the University of Pennsylvania from 1888 to 1917. Among his many students who later became prominent was the New Deal economist Rexford G. Tugwell. The sharp distinction must not be lost sight of between neomercantilists like Patten and "protectionists" pure and simple, the advocates of "laissez faire behind a tariff wall" who clamored for high tariffs but fought unions and social reform.

abuses that amounted to sins against morality existed in the sweat-shops of the cities and in some of the labor practices of large corporations, and they regarded the government as the logical agency to correct these evils. Even those who stressed the restoration of competition, rather than regulation for social ends, helped build the structure of modern American neomercantilism. They wanted government to play an active but a negative role, but they helped accustom people to the idea of an active state, and thus made easier public acceptance of government that was active *and* positive.

Since the days of Theodore Roosevelt, an increasing share of public debate has been given to the question of government's role in society. Interventionism has been the winner thus far, although there is general agreement it is to be limited at some point as yet undefined. The two Roosevelts and Wilson have been the heaviest contributors to the resurgence of interventionism. But while Theodore and Franklin Roosevelt were outspoken neomercantilists, Wilson was among those who almost unwillingly strengthened the hand of the state and enlarged the domain of its activity. The New Freedom of Woodrow Wilson was a highly individual creation that leaves one with the uncomfortable feeling that this great humanitarian had not the fullest understanding of the relationship between political and economic life, or of economic life itself. While Theodore Roosevelt was in the White House, Princeton's famous political scientist expounded his belief in the competitive system of the classical economists, and his trust in the patriotism and morality of businessmen to protect the nation from the evils of monopoly. At the same time he was an ardent exponent of dollar diplomacy, taking the sharply interventionist position that "since trade ignores national boundaries and the manufacturer insists on having the world as a market, the flag of his nation must follow him, and the doors of the nations which are closed against him must be battered down."[19] By the time he had entered the Executive Mansion, however, Wilson had come to believe that the only way competition could be saved was by breaking the tie between big business and government, and by enacting legislation to outlaw economic practices that stifled competition. In short, he had reached the conclusion that state in-

[19] Quoted by William Diamond, *The Economic Thought of Woodrow Wilson*, Baltimore, 1943, p. 141.

tervention was needed to save the noninterventionist competitive economy. He had also changed his view on foreign economic policy, now insisting on unrestricted world competition and an almost hands-off policy on the part of government.

In practice, however, Wilson's adherence to the tradition of British economic liberalism meant very little.[20] He denounced the protective tariff, but the Underwood Tariff of 1913, which he saw through Congress, merely rationalized American protection, and brought it down to a more sensible level. The Clayton Act stopped several loopholes in the antitrust laws, but there were fewer prosecutions under Wilson than there had been under Taft. Although Wilson, as president, had completely reversed his earlier support for dollar diplomacy, he continued the policy of his predecessors in such acts as the Bryan-Chamorra Treaty of 1913, which gave the United States imperialistic privileges in Nicaragua. Despite the fact that his New Freedom was to arise almost entirely from the revival of competition, and despite the fact that he had once spoken out against labor unions and in defense of the open shop,[21] Wilson found himself regulating business and supporting the interference of labor unions with the free play of the market. He favored government inspection and regulation of working conditions, and workmen's compensation laws; he signed the LaFollette seamen's bill and the Adamson eight-hour-day law for railroad workers.

The failure of the original Wilsonian ideal of simply restoring competition was the downfall of the last systematic and intelligent effort to base public policy on nineteenth-century economic liberalism. When Wilson turned from his earlier reasoning and backed unions as the common man's weapon against the trusts, he implicitly acknowledged the fact that twentieth-century competition was to be among various types of groups, rather than between individuals. His chief departure from Theodore Roosevelt lay in his belief that there was a vast difference between big business and the ogre of monopoly: "I am for big business, and I am against the trusts," said

[20] Except in connection with the peace negotiations, where he joined Herbert Hoover and Bernard M. Baruch in firm opposition to the continuation of wartime international economic controls. He stood staunchly on the rock of international laissez faire, from which the British were trying to induce him to leap. See Diamond, *Economic Thought*, pp. 181 ff.

[21] Diamond, *Economic Thought*, p. 70.

Wilson.[22] Roosevelt had come to recognize, by 1912, that bigness was an inevitable aspect of industrialization, and that with bigness came inevitable rigidities. The New Nationalism of Theodore Roosevelt thus bore a much closer ideological relationship to the New Deal of Franklin Roosevelt than did the New Freedom under which F. D. R. made his first appearance in national affairs.

The two Roosevelts, neomercantilists in a democratic age, tried to democratize the Hamiltonian outlook; Wilson had fallen into the impossible difficulty of trying to rebuild a small-business society in an age in which it had decreasing significance. Although this ran counter to his deepest political convictions, Wilson was forced by the process of meeting practical problems to extend further the sphere of government intervention. And his own dynamic conception of the role of the presidency furthered the neomercantilist tradition, though this was not his intent. Wilson had written that the president should be

. . . a man who will be and who will seem to the country in some sort an embodiment of the character and purpose it wishes its government to have—a man who understands his own day and the needs of the country, and who has the personality and the initiative to enforce his views both upon the people and upon Congress.[23]

He did not realize that in twentieth-century industrialized society, forceful executive leadership could hardly be displayed in the negative policy of removing bars to competition, that it would inevitably assign to government a far more positive role.[24]

[22] *The New Freedom*, New York, 1913, p. 180.

[23] Quoted by C. B. Swisher, *American Constitutional Development*, Boston, 1943, p. 568. Wilson's failure to think through the relationship between economics and political science is brought out by the fact that while he had once regarded himself as a Federalist, he was bitter in his condemnation of Hamilton; while he attacked Jefferson on philosophical grounds, his own vision of a society of small, competing economic units was a reasonable twentieth-century facsimile of Jefferson's agrarian ideal. See R. Hofstadter, *The American Political Tradition and the Men Who Made It*, New York, 1948, pp. 239 ff.

[24] Toward the close of his second term, Wilson may have experienced a second ideological shift. He said: "The world is going to change radically, and I am satisfied that governments will have to do many things which are now left to individuals and corporations. I am satisfied, for instance that the government will have to take over all the great natural resources . . . all the water power, all the coal mines, all the oil fields, etc. They will have to be government-owned.

"If I should say that outside, people would call me a socialist, but I am not

With a degree of consistency above the average for political leaders, and surprisingly high for one of his flamboyant temperament, Theodore Roosevelt had taken a neomercantilist position through most of his public life. Fair allowance must be made for the facts of Roosevelt's political career: he was somewhat slow in adding mature judgment to the enthusiasm he always displayed, it was only when he was elected president in his own right in 1904 that he felt free to urge a positive reform program, and it was not until he began to pave the way for his 1912 campaign as an independent that he expressed his views as a consistent theory of government and society.

The historical approach characteristic of neomercantilism came naturally to Roosevelt, who was himself an historian. In the 1912 campaign, Wilson had attacked the Progressives as being much too interventionist, and had preached the New Freedom of restored competition. Roosevelt replied,

The key to Mr. Wilson's position is found in the statement . . . that "The history of liberty is a history of the limitation of governmental power, not the increase of it."

This is a bit of outworn academic doctrine which was kept in the schoolroom and the professional study for a generation after it had been abandoned by all who had experience of actual life. It is simply the laissez-faire doctrine of the English political economists three-quarters of a century ago. It can be applied with profit, if anywhere at all, only . . . in a community before the days of Fulton, Morse and Edison. To apply it now in the United States, at the beginning of the twentieth century, with its highly organized industries, with its railways, telegraphs and telephones, means literally and absolutely to refuse to make a single effort to better any one of our social or industrial conditions.

Moreover, Mr. Wilson is absolutely in error in his statement, from the historical standpoint.

So long as governmental power existed exclusively for the king and not at all for the people, then the history of liberty was a history of the limitation of government. But now the governmental power rests in the people, and the kings who enjoy privilege are the kings of the financial and industrial world; and what they clamor for is the limitation of governmental

a socialist. And it is because I am not a socialist that I believe these things. I think the only way we can prevent communism is by some such action as that. . . ." (Hofstadter, *American Political Tradition*, p. 273).

power, and what the people sorely need is the extension of governmental power.[25]

A striking example of Roosevelt's historical outlook is his approach to the great problem of monopoly. There were people, he said, who

. . . tried (by the Sherman-law method) to bolster up an individualism already proved to be both futile and mischievous; to remedy by more individualism the concentration that was the inevitable result of the already existing individualism. They saw the evil done by the big combinations, and sought to remedy it by destroying them and restoring the country to the economic conditions of the middle of the nineteenth century. This was a hopeless effort, and those who went into it, although they regarded themselves as radical progressives, really represented a form of sincere rural toryism. . . . On the other hand, a few men recognized that corporations and combinations had become indispensable in the business world, that it was folly to try to prohibit them, but that it was also folly to try to leave them without thoroughgoing control. These men realized that the doctrines of the old *laissez-faire* economists, of the believers in unlimited competition, unlimited individualism, were in the actual state of affairs false and mischievous.[26]

It is true that the famous Roosevelt motto might well have been changed to "Talk loudly, carry a big stick, and use it softly," for this theatrical statesman certainly exaggerated both his intentions and his achievements. But here too fair allowance must be made for the generation during which Roosevelt fought and campaigned, and historians must avoid the error of estimating his achievements according to the magnitude and nature of the problems through which they themselves are living. In linking elements of the reform program of Bryan's Democracy with a Hamiltonian approach to public policy, Theodore Roosevelt went about as far in word and deed as it was realistic for a popular American statesman to go in his day and age. He preached in the name of public interest, both in attacking business evils and calling for conservation and public control of natural resources. In typically mercantilist fashion he cared as little for perfectionist dreams as for the ostrich-minded prophets of doom

[25] *Works*, New York, 1925, vol. 19, pp. 419 ff. Note the similarity to Franklin Roosevelt's attack on "economic royalists."
[26] *Autobiography*, New York, 1924, pp. 424–425.

who regarded any change as for the worse. He looked upon himself as a conservative, but said:

> True conservatism . . . is also the embodiment of the wise spirit of progress. It . . . acts conservatively before that has happened which will enflame men to madness.
>
> The worst enemy of wise conservatism that I know is the type of conservative who tries to prevent wrongs from being remedied because the wrongs have existed for a long time; and, on the other hand, the worst enemy of true progress is the demagogue, or the visionary, who, in the name of progress, leads the people to make blunders such that in the resulting reaction they tend to distrust all progress.[27]

The basis of Roosevelt's attitude was his belief that "it is necessary to invoke the aid of the government" in order "to preserve the general welfare."[28] For twentieth-century America he was convinced that this meant breaking the hold of big business over government, and he originally placed his hope in vigorous enforcement of the Sherman Act, gaining the rather undeserved name of "trust buster." By the time of the 1912 campaign, however, he had reached the conclusion that "monopoly" was an inevitable characteristic of mass production industry, and that the answer to this private usurpation of sovereignty lay in government regulation rather than in a futile effort to prevent combination. At the same time he wanted to change the rules of the game in order to give labor a better opportunity, and this meant unionization, hours and compensation legislation, income and inheritance taxes, the outlawing of child labor, and a revision of the tariff so that it would protect high wages rather than the privileges of a small group of producers.

Theodore Roosevelt unquestionably grew more "radical" as the years went on. But his essential belief was in a capitalist society, even if it was to be one in which "every man holds his property subject to the general right of the community to regulate its use to whatever degree the public welfare may require it." Taken as a

---

[27] *New Nationalism,* New York, 1911, pp. 42, 59.

[28] *New Nationalism,* pp. 54–55. He followed Hamilton and foreshadowed Franklin Roosevelt both in his broad interpretation of the idea of general welfare and in his preference for federal rather than state action in a good many instances. He anticipated his cousin's fear of a "twilight zone," in which neither state nor national government could act, and his belief that nation-wide activities called for national regulation.

whole, his career shows a steady development of an interventionist outlook. What had led this New York aristocrat and intimate friend of Henry Adams and Elihu Root to preach the gospel of the New Nationalism and the Square Deal was, he believed, a strong sense of moral righteousness. It was this moral emphasis, a recurring note in modern neomercantilism, that led him to temper his vigorous defense of the institution of private property and of property rights with the injunction that they must place second to welfare and to human rights, and to criticize the Supreme Court because it was not "interested primarily in human welfare rather than in property."[29] But the moral fervor that appeared in Wilson as a wish to punish violators of the laws protecting competition, appeared in Roosevelt as a desire to use government as a positive force for moral good. Roosevelt was also a typical neomercantilist in his strong emphasis on national interest, on the role of the central government and of the presidency, in the sharp contrast between the ready expediency of his practical politics and his continued and obviously sincere reiteration of moral principles. His hold on the popular mind for two decades is a good indication of the strength of the mercantilist tradition in American society, even when due allowance is made for the fact that he was the magnetic type of leader who could undoubtedly have attracted wide support for a program to invade the moon. For it must not be forgotten that Theodore Roosevelt was not a socialist, nor even a wild-eyed Bryan Democrat: he was a Republican, and despite his many squabbles and feuds, was one of the top Republican leaders till the day of his death.

The Roosevelt spirit left the White House in 1909, but a good part of his policy stayed on. When William Howard Taft, his chosen successor, entered the presidency, it is true that he became somewhat less interventionist than he had been. But Taft actually continued the Roosevelt program as it stood in 1908. This fact was obscured for most people by the new President's flair for unfavorable publicity and his conservative manner and bearing. Taft's mild progressivism foundered on the rock of Old Guard Republican opposition. Men like Senator Aldrich and Speaker Cannon were as sadly out of touch with the realities of public opinion as were their successors in the Republican leadership a generation later. In 1904 and in 1908

[29] *New Nationalism*, pp. 23, 28.

the people had voted Republican because the GOP was the party of Roosevelt's intelligent and forward-looking conservatism. With his departure from the Executive Mansion the party leadership fell back into "standpatism," and into the service of special interests. Taft's efforts to carry out the program on which he had been elected were generally blocked in Congress. A group of Republican insurgents became the core of the Progressive movement of 1912, the men whom Senator Moses of New Hampshire was later to call the "sons of the wild jackass." The Democrats won the House in 1910, and Roosevelt's speech at Osawatomie, Kansas, paved the way for the three-cornered fight that resulted in the election of Woodrow Wilson.

While the Taft administration was marked by a renewed splurge on the part of the "malefactors of great wealth," it was not a break, only a partial pause, in the development of modern American neo-mercantilism. And, as we have said, Wilson, in both peace and war, helped carry forward the Hamiltonian tradition despite his principled opposition to it. As much as Roosevelt, and perhaps even more, Wilson contributed to the democratization of the active, interventionist state. It was only after his retirement, with the election of Warren G. Harding, that the American government, under the leadership of men who claimed descent from Hamilton, turned away from a positive interventionist tradition.

The so-called "Golden Twenties" are a curious period, which may at best have taught us the lesson that "all that glitters is not gold." It is hard to detect any genuine or consistent outlook in public policy. If in anything, the Harding and Coolidge administrations were consistent in working from short-run judgments. What happened had been forseen by the wise conservative, Colonel Henry L. Stimson, when he warned Theodore Roosevelt against bolting the Republican Party:

> To me it seems vitally important that the Republican Party . . . should take the lead in reform and not drift into a reactionary position. If, instead, the leadership should fall into the hands of either an independent party or . . . the Democrats . . . and if the solid business Republicans should drift into new obstruction, I fear the necessary changes could hardly be accomplished without much excitement and possibly violence.

To Stimson the Republican Party was "the descendant of the Federalist party and the historic party of positive government. 'Throughout its existence,' he wrote, '. . . it has contained within its membership the men who believed that the Government was not a mere organized police force, a sort of necessary evil, but rather an affirmative agency of national progress and social betterment.' "[30] The GOP had drifted into "new obstruction": the slogan of "normalcy" was even emptier than generally believed, for there was no genuine conception of what was "normal." Once again, the government was made the agent of small groups: it was once again to be the negative "police force" of laissez faire behind a tariff wall. But now, in keeping with the spirit of real-estate and stock-market booms, the tariff wall was to be as high as the latest skyscraper. Aside from the tariff, interventionism survived in many lesser ways even in the era of normalcy and bathtub gin. And it should not be forgotten that the isolationism that swept the country in the 1920's was a nationalist movement, and nationalism is likely to breed demands upon the state. Part of the ideological confusion of the '20's stems from the fact that leading social reformers and interventionists in matters of domestic policy such as LaFollette and Norris were isolationists with respect to foreign affairs. The Democratic Party stumbled along in fairly negative fashion, preaching low tariffs and "clean" government. And the only reasonably cohesive group that believed in an active government at home and abroad, the Roosevelt Republicans, had gone into eclipse. The confusion over the role of the state is heightened by the fact that this was also the time in which most leaders of both major parties accepted a remarkable piece of government interference with individualism, Prohibition.

The end of normalcy did not wait for the stock-market crash: it came with the inauguration of Herbert Hoover, a strange and com-

[30] Henry L. Stimson and McGeorge Bundy, *On Active Service in War and Peace*, New York, 1947, pp. 22, 62. It is interesting to speculate on what might have happened had Roosevelt followed Stimson's advice. Wilson might well have triumphed in 1912 in any event, but there would have been nothing to stop TR from having another try in 1916. Given the closeness of the 1916 election, Roosevelt would probably have won, which would have placed the League under Republican auspices, making American adherence quite likely. Control of the GOP would have remained in the hands of its progressive wing, and the Harding-Coolidge era might never have occurred.

plex personality. Hoover was a humanitarian, yet at times gave the appearance of being hard-hearted. He preached the gospel of rugged individualism, yet consciously expanded the role of the state in social and economic affairs. In some ways he is reminiscent of the early Wilson. Wilson in 1912 had attacked Rooseveltian excesses, "the prevailing principles of regulation, the principles which the Republican party has introduced and carried to such radical lengths." He argued for the rule of laws and their enforcement through the courts, rather than regulatory commissions. As we have said, Wilson had once believed the ills of big business could be cured by a moral regeneration among businessmen, in which government would assist by jailing the lawbreakers.[31] Herbert Hoover, of course, found the reforms of Roosevelt and the later Wilson an accepted part of the American scene when he entered the Cabinet in 1921, and he too seems to have accepted them fully. Hoover argued for regulation of business, as the middle way between a laissez faire he thought impossible and a government ownership that was tyrannical. But regulation was to be by law, rather than by agencies of the executive. Like the Democratic president under whom he first became a national figure, Herbert Hoover believed that higher moral standards were the prime requisite for curing the evils of business.[32] Like Wilson, Hoover accommodated himself reluctantly to the needs of a swiftly developing crisis. But there, the resemblance, never more than superficial, stops. Where Wilson finally seized upon the crisis of war as an opportunity to further his principles, and turned an essentially defensive conflict into a crusade for world-wide political liberalism, Hoover remained uncertain and hesitant as the depression wore away the security of the nation.

While Hoover may have been closer in outlook to Wilson than to Theodore Roosevelt, his basic views on the problems of big business were closer still to those of Arthur Jerome Eddy.[33] Hoover did not go so far as to say, with Eddy, that "competition is war, and war is hell," but he did espouse the principle of business coöperation. Bigness was inevitable, he felt, and could become dangerous. Where

[31] Hofstadter, *American Political Tradition*, pp. 245 ff.
[32] R. L. Wilbur and A. M. Hyde, *The Hoover Policies*, New York, 1937, pp. 294 ff., 301 ff.
[33] See p. 55.

necessary, as in the case of legal monopolies, the government should regulate. But regulation was to be held to a minimum, and voluntary codes of business ethics, entered into and enforced by trade associations, were to be the main weapon for eliminating business abuses. As Secretary of Commerce, Hoover spurred the creation of these codes and their promulgation by the Federal Trade Commission, and felt that they were "the strong beginning of a new force in the business world."[34]

When Hoover became president he expected the continuation of what was regarded as exceptional prosperity, and he planned an administration based upon the elaboration of policies following cautious and systematic fact gathering. Then the cloudburst descended.

The question, What caused the Great Depression? is not particularly relevant here. What is relevant is the fact that President Hoover, however reluctantly and hesitantly, gave the federal government a more active role in social and economic affairs than ever before in time of peace. Even before the stock-market crash, the administration through the Agricultural Marketing Act (June, 1929) took steps to relieve the pressure on farm prices caused by huge agricultural surpluses. This law was an attempt to carry into agriculture the policy of self-help with government aid that Hoover had urged upon business as Secretary of Commerce. Farmers' cooperatives were to be given financial and administrative help to keep surpluses off the market when supply was heavy, and thus to maintain free market prices high enough to enable the farmers to live decently. The only trouble was that the farmers were even more rugged individualists than the President wanted them to be, and produced even more than before in anticipation of artificially supported high prices. The result, of course, was a squandering of federal money and the accumulation of greater surpluses which further depressed farm prices.

After the depression struck and the unemployment rolls began to mount, the administration increased federal public works and con-

[34] Wilbur and Hyde, *Hoover Policies*, pp. 304–305. These authors comment, "Hoover enlisted the cooperation of the Federal Trade Commission to assure that these codes had no element of violation of the Anti-Trust laws. . . . There was no force attempted or implied. They were solely voluntary." And they note, "The attempt of the NRA to make these codes of ethics compulsory at once lost the moral lift."

sented to loans to states for support of relief. Under the pressure of public demand, farmers were given seed and implement loans and farm and home owners were given assistance in maintaining mortgages. The most important device for government intervention was, however, the Reconstruction Finance Corporation, which rescued banks and aided business and manufacturing enterprises.[35]

Throughout the Hoover policies ran the theme that the depression was to some degree a scaling down of speculatively inflated values, almost a natural phenomenon, and that the solution lay in reviving confidence and in stimulating production. Confidence was to be restored by exhortation and example, and by adhering firmly to hard money and the gold standard. Production was to be stimulated largely by easing credit, but this was in no wise to take the form of overt monetary inflation.

Hoover's interventionism was, of course, anything but wholehearted. The federal government was to help business help itself. The government was to intervene only when and in the degree absolutely necessary. The President was assuredly neither blind nor indifferent to the suffering of individual Americans during the depression, but as long as he was convinced that actual starvation could be prevented by local government and private charities, he remained opposed on moral grounds to direct federal relief. Only when local agencies could no longer prevent acute physical privation would he regard it proper for the federal arm to go into action.

The boundaries of the Hoover program were set both by the self-help doctrine and by an overemphasis of the production side of the economic equation. Despite the President's consent to the intervention of the national government in economic affairs, the prejudice

[35] The contrast between RFC generosity to large corporations (including an $80,000,000 loan to ex-Vice President Dawes' Chicago bank) and the administration's extreme reluctance to provide assistance to the lowly, was one of the most important factors in its loss of public support. It also gave rise to the feeling, widespread at the time, that Hoover was a hard-hearted engineer who could become wrought up only over the fate of the most important economic machines, the great corporations. It would be closer to the truth to suggest that Hoover was sincerely convinced that relief to needy individuals was debilitating, and that the solution to everybody's problems was to get production going again by direct financial support to the producers. This would enable income to trickle down to the mass of the people. This approach has been derided as the "dripolator theory of economics."

contained in the old classical law of markets—production creates its own demand[36]—was an unfortunate brake upon effective action. Easing credit for big business was a sound procedure, for it prevented catastrophic major bankruptcies, but our industrial giants were not aided in finding customers. Furthermore, there was a lingering refrain from Adam Smith's old song, "What is prudence in the conduct of every private family can scarce be folly in that of a great Kingdom."[37] While the administration recognized that public works provided employment, it did not realize that if the government, like a private family whose income had fallen, cut expenditures and strove to increase revenues, it would exert a deflationary influence upon the economy. The right hand fought against the left: the Treasury worked for a balanced budget by paring expenditures and raising taxes in a desperate effort to avoid adding to the national debt, and thus undermined the inflationary efforts of the Reconstruction Finance Corporation and other agencies.

In effect, the Hoover administration attempted to carry out a program of government intervention based upon the noninterventionist assumptions of the classical school. It was none too successful. In many fields, however, it prepared the way for the more thoroughgoing intervention of the New Deal, and it certainly killed, at least as a matter of practical politics, public support for the old myth of the passive policeman state. The succeeding administration had far fewer inhibitions, and a pragmatic attitude of fitting economic policies and underlying theories to changing fact that was somewhat bewildering but, to most Americans of the time, rather refreshing.

NOTES ON BOOKS

In view of the dominance, until recent years, of the classical tradition in American universities, it is not surprising that two of the most useful books on American interventionist thinking were written by the English-born E. A. J. Johnson, *American Economic Thought in the Seventeenth Century*, and by a Frenchman, Ernest Teilhac, *Pioneers of American Economic Thought in the Nineteenth Century*. L. M. Hacker's *The Triumph*

[36] See p. 18.
[37] *Wealth of Nations*, p. 424.

of American Capitalism will be valuable for background. Joseph Dorfman's *The Economic Mind in American Civilization* is, as with respect to American classical thinking, a treatment of sources from a very particular point of view. A. D. H. Kaplan's *Henry Charles Carey, A Study in American Economic Thought* is a competent analysis. H. R. Seager's introduction to Patten's *Essays in Economic Theory,* edited by R. G. Tugwell, is a helpful prelude to Patten's unsystematic writings.

Several chapters in Richard Hofstadter's *The American Political Tradition and the Men Who Made It* are especially relevant to both early and later phases of this subject, and H. D. Croly's *The Promise of American Life,* together with Theodore Roosevelt's *The New Nationalism* and *Autobiography,* will provide an insight into the spirit of Progressive interventionism.

6.

RADICALISM WITH
A CONSERVATIVE HERITAGE:
THE NEW DEAL

FRANKLIN D. ROOSEVELT did not enter the White House with a clear-cut ideology or program. Nor, however, did he fit Walter Lippmann's description of him as an amiable gentleman who would very much like to be president.[1] He had long had an interest in democratic social reform not unlike that of enlightened members of the British gentry. Frances Perkins' rather unfavorable reaction to the somewhat arrogant young aristocrat she first met in 1910 was modified by his "spirited defense of Theodore Roosevelt," whom civic-minded young people of the day regarded as the great torchbearer in the eternal crusade for honest and active government, dedicated to social justice.[2] Such an attitude was only what was to have been expected of one whose young adulthood coincided with the most productive years of Theodore Roosevelt, one who, moreover, had the good fortune to know the President and even to be distantly related to him. The enthusiasm of many New Dealers for breaking links with the past, and the bitterness of many of Franklin Roose-

[1] Basil Rauch, *The History of the New Deal 1933–1938*, New York, 1944, p. 23.
[2] Frances Perkins, *The Roosevelt I Knew*, New York, 1946, p. 9. Secretary Perkins remarks of Theodore Roosevelt that his "attachment to the principles of social justice has never been sufficiently developed by his biographers. . . ." (p. 10).

velt's opponents tended to obscure the importance of this particular bond, but there has been a growing awareness of its significance. Robert E. Sherwood writes that Franklin Roosevelt "had been profoundly influenced by the belligerent progressivism of his cousin," and quotes at length from T.R.'s famous Osawatomie, Kansas, speech of 1910, "because that Osawatomie speech was of such great importance in shaping the structure of the New Deal." Speaking before an assemblage of Civil War veterans, Theodore Roosevelt had said,

The New Nationalism regards the executive power as the steward of the public welfare. It demands of the judiciary that it shall be interested primarily in human welfare rather than in property. . . . I believe in shaping the ends of government to protect property as well as human welfare. Normally, and in the long run, the ends are the same; but whenever the alternative must be faced, I am for men and not for property, as you were in the Civil War.

Reading these words, one is led strongly to agree with Mr. Sherwood:

Theodore Roosevelt died before his fifth cousin achieved any degree of prominence on the national scene and, during the years of the New Deal, the "Oyster Bay Roosevelts" were implacably opposed to the Hyde Park "maverick." However, the words of the great and gallant T.R. and the actions of F.D.R. were curiously in harmony with one another.[3]

Ideologically, at least, the New Deal descended from the New Nationalism. Indeed, much of the bitterness surrounding the Roosevelt policies between 1933 and 1941 may have arisen from the fact that it was the Democratic New Deal rather than the Republican New Nationalism that sponsored them and from the fact that, as Colonel Stimson had feared, the Republicans had lost their zest for reform.

[3] Robert E. Sherwood, *Roosevelt and Hopkins: An Intimate History,* New York, 1948, pp. 41–42. It is amusing to speculate that accidents of residence may have partly accounted for the fact that the two Roosevelts should have belonged to opposing parties. It would be fitting for an able, intelligent, and public-spirited young man of good family to enter politics, if at all, in the party that might war against the entrenched machine: in southern New York, this had long been the Republican party, and upstate the Democratic.

Aside from the strong feelings it still arouses, the New Deal is a difficult subject to discuss, for many of its policies are seemingly contradictory. One act may be seen to harmonize with the ideology of pure capitalism, another with the program of the socialists. In addition, the political tactics of indirection so skillfully employed by Franklin D. Roosevelt give a texture of blurriness to the canvas, and obscure the outlines of the large design. When looked at as a continuation of the pragmatic and historically shaped tradition of mercantilism, however, the long administration of the second Roosevelt is seen to have as much consistency of direction as can reasonably be expected in the field of statecraft, where the infinity of variables precludes high precision of political calculation, and in a time when change was so very rapid and of such tremendous scope.

The New Deal was neomercantilism democratized. Public power was regarded as an instrument for the welfare of all of the nation, rather than primarily for the benefit of a monarch, of a small elite, or even of one or two major groups. In earlier times, all the nation was eventually to benefit, as the interests of all were deemed to be associated with the prosperity of the chosen group: in the New Deal, as in the New Nationalism, this devious route to general welfare was abandoned, and the good of all was made the direct object of national policy. This is not to say, of course, that success was uniformly obtained either in choice or in execution of policy, but the end did sharply color the means. That the Roosevelt regime was essentially conservative can hardly be disputed: American economic life, like American political life, remained in most important respects essentially what it had been before. Perhaps the most convincing proof of this assertion lies in the criticisms of Roosevelt as a revolutionary. These frantic attacks contain unfulfilled prophecies of doom, such as "Grass will grow in the streets"—and vague generalizations, such as "undermining the American spirit." Some of Roosevelt's enemies even predicted, from time to time, that he would prohibit new elections, and set himself up as a dictator. But the grass, the American spirit, and elections have all maintained their proper place in the American scene. At a more mature level of criticism, there are three main ideological viewpoints from which the Roosevelt regime can properly be considered: theoretical classical capitalism, Marxism, and neomercantilism. According to the first two, it was utterly bad; according to the third, largely, although not completely, successful.

Under Roosevelt, the country recovered from the depression, albeit not fully, preserved and extended its democracy, and triumphed in the greatest war effort in history. It can always be argued, of course, that America was on her way out of the depression anyway, in 1933, that democracy survived despite Roosevelt, and that his social and economic policies had little or nothing to do with winning the war. The trouble with this argument is that it is too much like that of the patient who refuses to pay the doctor on the ground that he would have recovered without the medical services. It is an argument that can rarely be proved. The main point at issue, however, is not the success or failure of this or that aspect of the New Deal, but the way in which the Roosevelt regime continued the neomercantilist tradition.

It was neomercantilist in its insistence on the right and duty of the state to intervene in social and economic affairs in order to promote the general welfare, in its maintenance of the rule of private property and ownership in the overwhelmingly greater part of the economy, in its conception of the nation as an economic and social entity, in its use of fiscal and monetary devices, and in its readiness to employ very different tactics toward the same broad end, the advancement of national well-being.

A great deal of the confusion surrounding the nature of the Roosevelt administration arises from two apparently outright reversals of direction. First, although the United States was headed toward economic nationalism in its destruction of the London Economic Conference of 1933, it sped off in precisely the other direction with the Hull Reciprocal Trade Agreements Program which commenced in 1934. Second, although the government, in the National Industrial Recovery Act of 1933, appeared to adopt a policy like that of Theodore Roosevelt, acceptance of monopolistic practices under public regulation, it switched to an intensified antitrust program in 1938, only to drop it once more at the onset of war. These were the great policy changes. They seemed to make the many other shifts that characterized Roosevelt's political tactics fit into a general pattern of aimlessness. Beyond political maneuvers, moreover, there was the broad contradiction between an agricultural policy devoted to eliminating surpluses, and a public works and conservation policy dedicated to increasing national productivity. Add to this the fact that the President attracted the temporary support of various types of doctrinaires, and the enduring, surcharged, emotional enmity of ordinarily cool and hard-headed men of affairs, and it is small wonder that billows of confusion cloud the real nature of the policies of that extraordinarily energetic and able statesman who has been proclaimed both devil and demigod.

If, however, we accept the reasonable proposition that the "Roosevelt Revolution" stood in the line of a mercantilist tradition centuries old, it becomes possible to develop a picture of what it was and what it meant. The picture, of course, will lack the clarity of rigid, abstract doctrine; it can be no clearer than the actual exercise of public affairs in a free society.

Roosevelt was unquestionably a nationalist, as was Cordell Hull. But there are different kinds of nationalism. The word *nationalism* covers the lunacy of a Hitler as well as the reasonable patriotism of a Wilson, and the phrase *economic nationalism* includes both the ridiculous attempts at self-sufficiency made by small and ill-equipped countries and the moderate protectionism of the Roosevelt administration. When the London Economic Conference met in June of 1933, the United States had followed Great Britain in abandoning the gold standard, while a number of nations led by France clung tenaciously to this shining symbol of the good old days. The British pound had already reached an exchange level favorable for British foreign trade, and all the major negotiating powers were prepared to stabilize the relationships among the national currencies. All, that is, except the United States. The emergency suspension of gold trading in March, 1933, had enabled the dollar to fall in gold value, raising domestic prices and at the same time making American goods more attractive to foreign buyers, as they could acquire more dollars for the same quantity of gold. But the devaluation of the dollar had not gone far enough to suit the President. He therefore dispatched his famous "bombshell" message to the Conference, stating that the United States did not consider the simple device of currency stabilization the proper way to open a campaign for world economic recovery, and that America would not be party to a measure that would hinder its domestic antidepression program.

Scarcely six months had passed, however, when the Roosevelt administration decided that devaluation was now adequate, and used its powers under the Gold Reserve Act of 1934 with great moderation. Under the Act, a $2 billion paper profit accruing to the Treasury from devaluation was to be used for stabilization purposes, and now it was Great Britain and France rather than the United States that delayed international currency stabilization until the conclusion of the French-British-American agreement of 1936. And in June, 1934, the first Reciprocal Trade Agreements Act, the Hull program, was passed at administration insistence. This shift in the course of a single year from "nationalism" to "internationalism" was widely taken to mean that Roosevelt did not know where he was heading, or, at the very least, that he had been converted to "internationalism," as indicated by the ascendancy of Cordell Hull and the decline of Raymond Moley in the President's councils. It is quite true that Moley lost influence and eventually broke with Roosevelt, and that Hull gained steadily in power and prestige. But the following statement, in the first inaugural address of March, 1933, provides a common foundation for both the President's London Conference policy and his later efforts for close international collaboration:

Our international trade relations, though vastly important, are in point of time and necessity secondary to the establishment of a sound national economy. I favor as a practical policy the putting of first things first. I shall spare no effort to restore world trade by international economic readjustment, but the emergency at home cannot wait on that accomplishment.[4]

This is an excellent example of the neomercantilist emphasis on the home market and upon sound domestic conditions as the prerequisite for advantageous foreign trade. While the cheapening of the dollar carried out in the fall and early winter of 1933 had not succeeded in raising prices as much as desired (farm prices actually declined), it had brought definite improvement in America's foreign trade position. Given this achievement, the administration was now ready to refrain from pressing unduly the advantage gained through devaluation, and to turn to other means to increase farm income.

[4] *The Public Papers and Addresses of Franklin D. Roosevelt, With a Special Introduction and Explanation, Notes by President Roosevelt*, New York, 1938, vol. 2, p. 14.

The moderate protectionism of the Hull program was to secure the major share of the home market for domestic producers and, beyond this, to expand America's trade abroad. It fled from both dogmatic extremes, the theoretical perfection of autarky, complete self-sufficiency, and the theoretical perfection of classical free trade, which ignored the fact that the nation was in truth an economic entity.

Another seeming contradiction in the Roosevelt policies, between measures designed to promote scarcity and those designed to promote greater productivity is even less puzzling. The first Agricultural Adjustment Act (AAA), of 1933, which paid farmers for curtailing production and brought on the spectacle of the destruction of farm products (including little pigs mourned enthusiastically by the opposition), was intended to lower supply to the level of effective demand.[5] American agriculture had overexpanded during the First World War, and postwar reconstruction and resumption of normal trade left it with inadequate markets. The practical alternatives were the "nationalist" policy of dumping abroad, which would disturb relations with other powers who, moreover, could render it ineffective by tariff and quota restrictions, and the "scarcity" policy of scaling production down to the level of domestic demand and probable exports. The second alternative was clearly the better and more workable, however offensive to the sense of propriety of the many who felt that there was something immoral about destroying food when people were going hungry. When the AAA was declared unconstitutional in 1936, its objectives were carried on, first by the Soil Conservation and Domestic Allotment Act of 1936, which used the device of transferring marginal lands from production to conservation purposes instead of the curtailment contracts the Supreme Court had outlawed. In 1938, when a new and friendlier majority ruled the Court, the second AAA was passed, withdrawing surpluses from the market under a complex storage and parity price scheme, the "ever normal granary" of Henry A. Wallace. The latter aspect of the program, the maintenance of grains in stable supply, hearkened back, if not to Joseph in Egypt as its author suggested, at least to the Middle Ages and the abso-

---

[5] The critics had forgotten that this destructive method of crop control had been suggested by the Farm Board under Hoover, in 1931, in order to reduce the cotton surplus.

lute monarchies. Soil conservation, technical improvement, and the removal of marginal lands from cultivation were intended to improve the farmer's yield, while crop control and parity payments were to increase his income by reducing salable supply. The key to this seeming paradox in New Deal agricultural policy is the neo-mercantilist doctrine of the balanced economy, in which farmers must have sufficient purchasing power to buy the products of the factories, and workers the products of the farms. In short, the higher food prices would be more than balanced by the increased incomes of those who produced for more prosperous farmers. Here, in somewhat disguised form, was the old mercantilist theory that a large amount of money, turning over rapidly, was conducive to general prosperity. In 1933, the emergency objective was to raise farm prices; thereafter the aim was balance between town and country.

In the instance of monopoly policy, the change in attitude was real. The National Industrial Recovery Act of 1933, which brought fame to General Hugh S. Johnson and the NIRA Blue Eagle symbol, dealt with the monopoly problem by allowing all firms great and small at least a theoretically equal opportunity to indulge in practices frowned upon by the Sherman Act. After the NIRA was invalidated by the Supreme Court in 1935, the administration turned to other matters, notably the "pump-priming" program, which seemed for a time to be successful in bringing about renewed prosperity. In fact, by 1937 there was felt to be sufficient danger of a speculative boom for the administration to reduce sharply the flow of money and credit it had been pouring into the economy. In the autumn of 1937 a sharp recession got under way, for which there were offered three major explanations. Roosevelt's opponents argued that the drop was owing to the New Deal as a whole, to its lunatic financial and social policies and to the business community's loss of confidence. The most avid New Dealers contended that the administration had been too hesitant and therefore inadequate in its program of deficit financing. The administration eventually accepted the latter explanation, but it first explained the recession as arising from the restrictive practises of monopolists. The President accordingly asked for an investigation of monopoly, and Congress responded with the creation of the Temporary National Economic Committee (TNEC), which carried out an exhaustive program of research. Professor Thurman Arnold was called from Yale to head the antitrust activities of the Justice Department. A number of carefully prepared antitrust suits were commenced, notably one against the Aluminum Company of America, although there was no campaign of the pre-World War I variety. What might have developed had the policy been maintained without interruption cannot be told, for the onset of World War II brought a general cessation of prosecutions and even a lifting of restrictions against monopoly procedures.

The NIRA was perhaps a logical conclusion to Theodore Roosevelt's position of 1912. The TNEC phase was perhaps a return to Woodrow Wilson's belief in regulation to preserve competition. The war emergency led to policies that strengthened the underlying forces for concentration and bigness. Even if the war period is dismissed as utterly exceptional, the contradiction remains. But this is another way of saying that Roosevelt did not find a clearcut solution to the most difficult problem facing contemporary America: Given a trend toward concentration in private enterprise, what means should be taken to protect both economic and political freedom? The President had no precise theoretical viewpoint from which to proceed. In recommending the NIRA to Congress, he said that the antitrust laws

. . . were properly designed as the means to cure the great evils of monopolistic price fixing. They should certainly be retained as a permanent assurance that the old evils of unfair competition shall never return. But the public interest will be served if, with the authority and under the guidance of Government, private industries are permitted to make agreements and codes insuring fair competition. However, it is necessary, if we thus limit the operation of anti-trust laws to their original purpose, to provide a rigorous licensing power in order to meet rare cases of noncooperation and abuse.

In requesting Congress to create what became the TNEC, however, Roosevelt said that "a realistic system of business regulation has to reach more than consciously immoral acts. The community is interested in economic results. . . . We must find practical controls over blind economic forces as well as over blindly selfish men."[6]

[6] *Public Papers*, vol. 2, p. 202; vol. 7, 1941, p. 314.

Roosevelt's outlook was pragmatic, but controlled by both moral and social ends: he was seeking the best means to secure honesty and fair opportunity in business, and the highest possible national production. Although he did not reach an answer to the problem of monopoly, it was not difficult for him to attempt two different solutions, both of which were consistent with the relative freedom of the neomercantilist in choosing among means to a given end: the collectivism of NIRA, which was a far cry from either socialism or fascism, and the antimonopoly policy of the TNEC period, an equally far cry from any effort to turn the clock back to the mythical day of perfect competition.

It is easy to see why the vast program sponsored under the NIRA was attractive to the leadership of the New Deal. It promised to meet with one stroke the major needs of the industrial population. A good many of America's business leaders wanted some form of organization under which they could stabilize production and marketing. In 1931, Mr. Gerard Swope, President of the General Electric Company, had proposed a plan for price stabilization based upon relaxation of the antitrust laws and upon an expansion of the role of trade associations. President Hoover rejected the scheme, calling it "the most gigantic proposal of monopoly ever made in history."[7] In December, 1931, the United States Chamber of Commerce returned to the lists with a modified version of the Swope plan, but received the same rejection.

Late in the spring of 1933, however, a comprehensive bill to facilitate recovery by regularizing coöperation among employers and stimulating coöperation between employers and laborers was prepared and offered for President Roosevelt's approval by as diverse a group as could be imagined.[8] The National Industrial Recovery Act was passed by Congress by large majorities, and for the first time in American history, the basic idea of corporatism had been accepted as part of the American scene.

Corporatism, the organization of the economic functions of so-

[7] W. S. Myers and W. H. Newton, *The Hoover Administration, A Documented Narrative*, New York, 1936, p. 119.

[8] Among those involved in various phases of consultation or drafting were General Johnson (one of Bernard M. Baruch's aides), Secretary Perkins, William Green, Senator Wagner, Henry I. Harriman, President of the United States Chamber of Commerce, Rexford G. Tugwell, and others.

ciety into groupings of labor and management for each industry, was one of the features of European fascism. But neither in Europe nor the United States was corporatism *necessarily* linked with fascism. If the corporate system were not an integral aspect of the political state, there was no theoretical reason why corporatism should be incompatible with democracy.[9] Under the NIRA, the private trade associations were more powerful than a newly recruited and overburdened administrative staff. The public interest was, if anything, underrepresented. The NIRA was to fail, but it was not to exhibit even a superficial tendency toward fascism.

Under the NIRA, each industry was to agree on a code to govern its own standards of fair competition and labor relations—in effect, to limit production and competition, to raise prices and to standardize labor policies and wage rates throughout the industry where possible. The codes would then have to be approved by the National Recovery Administration (NRA), which might impose its own code if the industry's proposals were unsatisfactory, or if the industry failed to reach agreement. Once a code had been promulgated, it was binding on the entire industry and was enforceable in the courts. Labor's rights to bargain freely through representatives of their own choosing were guaranteed by the famous Section 7-A. Since there was no specific prohibition of employer influence upon labor elections, however, and a majority labor vote for a particular union was not binding on the minority, this section was in no way a bar to the formation of company unions. Business, in any event, was strongly hostile to unionization or even collective bargaining.

The NIRA was invalidated by the Supreme Court in 1935 after two noisy years, and no real effort was made to revive it in different form, as was the case with the first AAA.[10] Its roots had not struck deep. The country was not only not moved to fight for this venture, it was perhaps the kind of venture the country would not choose to embark upon for any length of time. In part owing to administrative failings,[11] in part to the beginnings of recovery, business had tired

[9] Corporatism is discussed more fully in chap. 13.

[10] Partial salvage was accomplished by later measures dealing with bituminous coal and other fields.

[11] Secretary Perkins writes that Bernard M. Baruch had warned her that General Johnson had been his "number-three man for years. I think he's a good

of the Blue Eagle. Small business and its partisans in Congress attacked the NIRA as fostering monopoly. As early as January, 1934, the President issued an Executive Order designed to enforce the rather contradictory antimonopoly strictures of NIRA. In September, 1934, a fireside chat contained a statement that foreshadowed the later antimonopoly policy of the administration: "There may be serious question as to the wisdom of many of those devices to control production, or to prevent destructive price cutting which many business organizations have insisted were necessary, or whether their effect may have been to prevent that volume of production which would make possible lower prices and increased employment."[12] The administration felt that business leadership had not been willing to share the benefits of the legislation with labor. Even as it attempted to diminish the monopoly-strengthening features of NIRA, it was turning to other measures to aid labor organization, and to fiscal measures to spur recovery. After the Supreme Court had handed down its decision invalidating the NIRA the President remarked to Secretary Perkins:

You know the whole thing is a mess. It has been an awful headache. Some of the things they have done in NRA are pretty wrong, though I think it is going better now. We have got the best out of it anyhow. Industry got a shot in the arm. Everything has started up. I don't believe they will stick, except in a few instances. I think perhaps NRA has done all it can do. I don't want to impose a system on this country that will set aside the anti-trust laws on any permanent basis.

I have been talking to other lawyers besides [Attorney General] Homer Cummings, and they are pretty certain that the whole process is unconstitutional. . . . So let's give the NRA a certain amount of time to liquidate. Have a history of it written, and then it will be over.[13]

The NRA died easily, and with it the greatest effort in history to adapt the principles of medieval gild regulation to the industrial

---

number-three man, maybe a number-two man, but he's not a number-one man." The warning came too late, however (*The Roosevelt I Knew,* pp. 200–201). While a steadier administration would have increased respect for the NRA, it would hardly have influenced the Supreme Court, which ruled unanimously in terms of constitutional law. It has been commented that Johnson was temperamentally suited for and was acquainted with fascist corporatism (Perkins, p. 206).

[12] Rauch, *New Deal,* pp. 122 ff.
[13] Perkins, *Roosevelt,* pp. 252–253.

economy of a democratic nation. With it, too, died the effort to approach the logical conclusion of one of the antithetical solutions to the monopoly problem: the permission of monopoly under government regulation. The antithesis, the institution of perfect competition, was impossible even to attempt.

The administration entered its pump-priming phase in 1935, and faced the problems of renewed depression in 1937. Although the theorists of deficit financing could and did argue that the recession had come because the pump had been primed half-heartedly, another explanation was as easily derived from the same "new economics" ushered in by the writings of J. M. Keynes: NRA had helped business management, but monopolists had not been generous enough in their dealings with labor to provide mass purchasing power equal to the needs of full employment. Therefore, along with deficit financing and public investment, it was necessary to strike against monopolistic practices that diminished the consumers' buying power.

In other words, monopolists were now being accused of a somewhat different kind of subversion of the general welfare than a generation earlier. The great trust-busting campaigns of the Roosevelt-Taft era had not been too clear as to their objectives, aside from a general agreement that mere bigness did not call for prosecution, which the Supreme Court had made law in its "rule of reason" in *U.S. vs. Standard Oil* in 1911. This was the principle that only such restraints of trade as were unreasonable under common law were outlawed by the Sherman Act. The most notorious "trusts" prior to the First World War had been amalgamations of producing firms linked with such celebrated names as Morgan and Rockefeller. Trust builders' use of crude power tactics, both economic and political, had justified Theodore Roosevelt in railing against the "malefactors of great wealth." The antimonopoly campaign under the second Roosevelt struck a much more sober note. Utilities, the field in which some of the most striking concentrations had occurred in the twenties and thirties, were dealt with separately under the Public Utility Holding Company Act of 1935. For the rest, there were few targets, with the exception of the Aluminum Company of America, comparable to the old Standard Oil Company and U.S. Steel. The Department of Justice under Theodore Roosevelt, Taft, and Wilson had fought against unfair business methods, in an effort to "restore competition." This theme receded into a secondary position with Thurman Arnold and his associates, who built their cases against what they regarded as unhealthy economic practices. They attacked the patent monopolies of giant firms, and the make-work and cut-work practices of labor unions. They did not attempt simply to "restore competition." Under this new interpretation of the "rule of reason" the targets for prosecution were those whose acts diminished production, investment and employment. Thurman Arnold wrote that "there is only one sensible test which we can apply to the privilege of organization, and that is this: Does it increase the efficiency of production or distribution and pass the savings on to consumers?"

This test means that we should say to every business enterprise: "You may grow as big as you can provided that you can justify the extent of your organized power by showing that it contributes to the efficiency of mass production and distribution. We will protect you against organized groups of small business which attempt to prevent you from giving cheaper goods to the public. We will, on the other hand, attack you if you seek to maintain your system of distribution by using your organized power to prevent experimental developments by others either in production or in distribution or in price policies. Size in itself is not an evil, but it does give power to those who control it. That power must be constantly watched by an adequate enforcement organization to see that it does not destroy a free market." This is the economic substance of the rule of reason.[14]

The new antitrust program fitted with the new policy of functional finance. The specific, concrete approach of NRA—particular codes for particular industries, particular prices and wages—had given way to the general approach of fiscal method which emphasized aggregates of income, investment, and employment. The impact of monopolistic practice upon these aggregates was made the criterion for antitrust prosecution. It is quite clear that the Roosevelt administration heeled over and changed its course with respect to monopoly, but while such shifts would shock the doctrinaire socialist (not Stalinist) or classicist, they could appear quite sensible to the mercantilist mentality. And the least that can be said is that the new

[14] Thurman Arnold, *The Bottlenecks of Business*, New York, 1940, p. 125.

viewpoint toward monopoly was in complete harmony with the outlook that came to dominate the administration following the publication of Keynes' *General Theory* in 1936.

The Keynesian point of view was most apparent, of course, in the all-important matter of money and finance. In 1932, Roosevelt had attacked Hoover for extravagance, and had pledged a balanced budget. After several efforts at deflationary reductions in federal expenditures, Roosevelt in 1935 adopted the fiction of "normal" and "emergency" expenditures, a fiction that had saved the tenure of more than one French Minister of Finance. Expenditures for the regular departments of government, such as Congressional salaries, or the Department of Justice, were to be met out of tax receipts, expenditures for relief were to be met with bond issues increasing the national debt. Operationally, of course, "regular" and "extraordinary" dollars were indistinguishable. Psychologically, however, this accounting device should have made the people more aware of the precise nature of the fiscal policy under which their government was operating. As the "extraordinary" budget swelled, and as the rush of reform legislation ceased, for all practical purposes, with the passage of the Fair Labor Standards Act of 1938, the neomercantilist character of the Roosevelt regime became increasingly clear.

Unlike their opponents of the classical school, eighteenth-century mercantilists, it will be recalled, had regarded money, taxes, and government expenditures as effective and appropriate instruments of national economic policy. The essence of their theory was stated by Sir James Steuart in 1767, and others.[15] It was not reformulated by an economist able to secure a wide hearing until Keynes wrote his *General Theory*.

The bare principle was that a high level of economic activity depended upon a healthy demand for goods and services, that this demand resulted from adequate mass purchasing power, and that business was greatly stimulated by rapid circulation of a plentiful supply of money. Money, in short, was not exclusively the effect of economic activity, as in classical theory, it was also its cause. In Keynes' systematic explanation, the principle was stated as a formula applicable to different levels of prosperity and depression. The less sophisticated idea of "pump priming" was that business

[15] See p. 93 f.

had slipped from a high level that was normal. The infusion of new money into the economy would spark enough private investment and production for the system to be able to continue in high gear, without renewed assistance, on the artificially created momentum. "Pump priming" was the first fiscal recovery policy of the Roosevelt administration which employed the following devices to develop the desired economic momentum: moderate currency inflation through reduction of the gold content of the dollar; easy credit policies, including low Reserve Bank rediscount rates, the Reconstruction Finance Corporation (RFC), farm credit, mortgage relief; increased purchasing power and demand for goods through higher farm prices, the public works program (PWA) and made-work (WPA), and outright relief. Some of these measures were inherited from the Hoover administration (RFC), others from the initial emergency recovery drive of the New Deal (AAA). "Pump priming" obviously was carried out from the very beginning of the New Deal, but it became the dominant antidepression policy with the creation of the Works Progress Administration (WPA) in 1935.

The Federal Emergency Relief Administration (FERA) had been established in 1933, with Harry Hopkins as its chief and with the first Civil Works Administration (CWA) as part of its program. At the same time, NIRA created the Public Works Administration (PWA), to the command of which the President appointed Secretary of the Interior Ickes. CWA had been too limited in scope, however, and PWA, under Ickes' cautious administration, did extremely well in constructing useful and enduring public facilities but failed to employ a sufficient number of those out of work. Accordingly, in 1935, FERA gave way to WPA, and made-work took precedence over simple relief in the drive to eliminate hardship. Billions were spent in projects ranging from the extremely worth while to the relatively useless, there were remarkable accomplishments and numerous instances of waste and inefficiency. The latter did not overly disturb the President, however, for the object of WPA, to employ millions who were jobless, restoring to them both income and a measure of self-respect, was unquestionably attained. The recession of 1937 followed a cutback in works expenditures, and the program was renewed and expanded in 1938.

There was a difference, however. The influence of Keynesian economics and the striking fact that priming the pump had not resulted in an autonomous high level of business activity, led the administration to adopt a point of view that produced the full employment policy of 1945. In his message to a special session of Congress in November, 1937, the President stated his belief "that the country as a whole realizes the necessary connection between encouraging businessmen to make capital expenditures for new plants and raising the total wage income of our working population. . . . What does the country ultimately gain if we encourage businessmen to enlarge the capacity of American industry to produce unless we see to it that the income of our working population actually expands sufficiently to create markets to absorb that increased production? I further believe that the country as a whole recognizes the need of seeking a more uniformly adequate standard of living and purchasing power everywhere, if every part is to live happily with every other part. . . . Political and social harmony requires that every state and every county not only produce goods for the nation's markets but furnish markets for the nation's goods."

This, writes Secretary Perkins, was a "preview of the ideas involved in the struggle for a full employment policy in 1945."[16]

This new outlook, we have seen, harmonized with the changed attitude toward monopoly, and the neomercantilist pattern was becoming better established as time went on. Nor was it confined to the subjects we have discussed. Social security, labor, housing, power, taxation, all brought forth legislation in keeping with the broad lines of neomercantilism in a democratic state. There has been much discussion of the difference between the First New Deal (1933–1935) and the Second New Deal (1935–1939), and there is indeed some reason for this distinction. The First was preoccupied with recovery, and coöperation with the business and agricultural communities; the Second with reform and economic development, and coöperation with labor and agriculture. Big business, at least, broke with the administration. But there was very much in common between the two phases of the New Deal, and there was very much in common between the two New Deals and the postwar domestic program to which the administration was turning its attention as the hostilities in Europe drew to a close.

[16] Perkins, *Roosevelt,* p. 259.

Three principal objectives were present in all phases of the Roosevelt regime, and in all its major enactments: economic security, a higher standard of living, and aid to underprivileged groups. A fourth objective was reform, in the old sense of the Theodore Roosevelt–Wilson era. The latter was exemplified by the Securities Exchange Acts (1933, 1934), the Glass-Steagall Banking Act (1933), and the Public Utility Holding Company Act (1935). These were designed to prevent dishonest financial practices, and soon became almost noncontroversial. The theme of economic security was of course carried out by the Social Security Act (1935), although it is clear that the entire Roosevelt program was directed to this end. The Wagner Act (1935), the Farm Tenancy Act (1937), the Housing Act (1937), and the Fair Labor Standards Act (1938) were among the measures aimed at improving the economic position of those the administration regarded as receiving unfair treatment at the hands of the economically powerful. It is true that the Wagner Act was lacking in provisions to make union leadership more responsible or giving management adequate protection against union malpractices. And it is rather difficult today to think of American labor as weak and defenseless. But it should not be forgotten that this law was a sharp pendulum swing which merely overcorrected the previous situation, in which many businessmen treated unions as something out of the Kremlin. It was as late as 1933 that some of the country's outstanding industrial leaders declined to shake hands with that arch example of American respectability, President William Green of the AFL![17]

All these laws, as well as AAA and NIRA, shared the common aim of building up purchasing power and living standards in addition to the particular objective for which each was written. While New Deal legislation did not fit into a tight theoretical pattern, it did harmonize. America was to be made more productive, largely through private enterprise, but with such government aid as the great Tennessee Valley Authority (TVA), and the country as a whole was to share in the increased productivity. No new conception

[17] Perkins, *Roosevelt*, pp. 221 ff. Note that the Wagner Act was not originally an administration measure. "It ought to be on the record that the President did not take part in developing the . . . Act. . . . It was not a part of the President's program. It did not particularly appeal to him when it was described to him. All the credit for it belongs to Wagner" (p. 239).

of society was offered. American ideals and institutions were to be left essentially unchanged, and improvements and accommodations to changing conditions were to be in accordance with what was felt to be the best aspects of the American tradition. "Radicals," writes Secretary Perkins,

. . . were always getting angry at Roosevelt for not being interested in overall economic and political changes. For him, the economic and political measures were not the end but the means. He was not even a vigorous anti-monopolist. Big enterprises, if morally and socially responsible, seemed entirely all right. Efficiency interested him only as it produced more comforts for more people and a better standard of living. . . . What he cared about was improvement in people's lives. If economic changes were necessary, he would make them, but only to do a specific task.

Some of the President's "high-strung" assistants did perhaps have visions of sweeping reorganization of American society, but "he always laughed them off and used their brilliant analyses for some projects that would do some immediate good to people in distress."[18]

The New Deal had continued the process of democratizing the objectives and benefits of the mercantilist state. It had directed to popular ends some of the devices employed by the seventeenth-century monarchies, some of the conceptions of the aristocrat Alexander Hamilton, some of the methods of American states before the Civil War. It had revived the mercantilist's willingness to experiment and his lack of fear of innovation. It had returned to the ancient principle that government was to interest itself directly in the welfare of the citizenry, but it was now for the citizens rather than their leaders to pass final judgment as to what constituted their welfare. Under the New Deal, neomercantilist policy was vastly broadened in scope, and the eighteenth-century emphasis on money and fiscal management was revived and strengthened. But private property was not challenged, and private enterprise, although subjected to more regulation, remained the fundamental characteristic of the economy.[19] If there was a "Roosevelt revolution," with the one pos-

[18] Perkins, *Roosevelt*, pp. 332, 333.
[19] When numerous coal operators begged the government to nationalize the mines in 1933, Secretary Ickes said: "What in the world would we do with the mines if we took them over? How could the Government operate them? No-

sible exception of its hastening of the inevitable recognition of labor's place in society, it was only in the minds of those who had lost touch with the past. If the New Deal was "radical," it was so only in the sense that it constituted a radical return to the conservative tradition of the mercantilists. It would be far more accurate to describe the New Deal as a rapidly conceived and pragmatically executed conservative program, in the spirit of the conservatism of a Burke, a Disraeli, or a Theodore Roosevelt.[20]

And its author, the "Squire of Hyde Park," ran remarkably true to the type of the enlightened and forward-looking conservative. Condemned by men of wealth as a traitor to their common class, attacked by radical planners of perfection for letting them down after encouraging them to voice their dreams, Roosevelt was able to command a greater majority of the American people than any other modern president. There were basic reasons for his strength, underlying traits of character and viewpoint, which his personal effectiveness and political skill fused into solid popular confidence. He had a distinct antipathy to systems of theory, and, correspondingly, a pragmatic outlook. Yet it was not pragmatism unalloyed, for, however unphilosophically, he held strongly to several beliefs which provided a fundamental consistency to his actions. The people seemed to have sensed this, for they were willing to trust his leadership not because they regarded him as a magician or even because of prior successes, but because of their feeling that the results of his maneuvers would probably be quite practical, and would almost

---

body in this Government knows how to run a coal mine. This isn't a nationalization program we have undertaken with Roosevelt." While Roosevelt agreed that there were some fields in which government operation and ownership was needed (TVA), the President "always resisted the frequent suggestion of the Government's taking over railroads, mines, etc., on that ground that it was unnecessary and would be a clumsy way to get the service needed" (Perkins, *Roosevelt*, pp. 230, 330).

[20] This view is borne out by one of the judgments expressed by a great American conservative, Colonel Stimson. In 1935 he had opposed TVA, despite his long standing belief in conservation and government water power activities. He had feared the inefficiency and dishonesty of a bureaucracy subject to the spoils system. "By 1947 he was prepared to admit—perhaps even to claim—what he had denied in 1935, that the principle of TVA, as an adventure in the effective use of natural resources, was a direct outgrowth of the position he and other conservationists had taken back in 1912" (Stimson and Bundy, *On Active Service*, pp. 43–44).

certainly harmonize with those customary ways of thinking that they, and he, shared. These ideas have been common to most Americans for long enough for Alexis de Tocqueville to have listed them, together with a pragmatic and experimental attitude and a distrust of theory, in his characterization of the American mind:[21] a deep, if often theologically naïve, religious belief; a respect for the individual as such; a sense of community, both as a pressure to conform with habitual patterns and as an impulse to work together; a strong patriotism, coupled with a desire to maintain a moral position among the nations.

A popular consciousness that all of this entered into Roosevelt's make-up goes much further in explaining his hold upon the public than either his celebrated smile and voice or the rather cynical view that the New Deal had bought the votes with WPA. The Roosevelt administration made many mistakes, and fell short of many of its goals. Inevitably, time exercised attrition upon its public support. But the majority of the people, including a fair proportion of those who voted against the Roosevelt regime, were agreed that in spirit and in much of its policy, it expressed the continuing vitality of the American tradition.

NOTES ON BOOKS

From the plethora of books on this topic of controversy one may recommend Basil Rauch's *The History of the New Deal*, Dixon Wecter's *The Age of the Great Depression 1929–1941*, and Broadus Mitchell's *Depression Decade: From New Era Through New Deal 1929–1941*. *The New Deal, An Analysis and Appraisal*, by the editors of *The Economist*, is a stimulating treatment by a distinguished group of British writers.

A good many memoirs have been published by Franklin D. Roosevelt's collaborators, but Frances Perkins' *The Roosevelt I Knew* is still among the most pertinent for domestic policy.

[21] *Democracy in America*, Bradley edition, vol. 2, p. 3 and elsewhere.

7.

J. M. KEYNES AND THE MODERN THEORY OF NEOMERCANTILISM

Even if both the frenetic champions of an undefined "liberalism" and those to whom the name Roosevelt is an apoplectic agent were to agree on the conservative nature of the New Deal, there would remain the question whether the neomercantilism to which America turned after 1933 offers a guide for future action. Were it to be conceded, just for the purposes of the argument, of course, that the New Deal was an almost perfect solution to the problems of its time, there would still remain the question whether this neomercantilism provides an ideology with which to meet the problems of the foreseeable future: the challenge of Stalinism, the need for a consistent and convincing outlook on the great social issues of our age, the need to dramatize and make effective the case for democracy as we understand it.

For it must not be forgotten that it is in the slogans and explanations of theory that people seek the guide lines to their own decisions. Although most people may be willing to judge things good if they seem to work well in the short run, there are always some who feel compelled to think about the complex relationships that make up a social situation. It is this thinking that produces the social theory that drifts back and forth between learned books and the press, until it moves out across the airwaves in the form of slogans that are far more attractive, although much less precise, than their theoretical formulations.

There has been no dearth of either slogans or theory regarding the New Deal. The catchwords and phrases—"forgotten man," "one third of a nation," "pump priming"—come readily to mind. The theory itself has become a catchword under the name of "Keynesian economics," or "the new economics." It may be objected that the New Deal was not simply an economic policy, and that to Roosevelt economics was a means rather than an end. But Lord Keynes was not merely an economist: he was a philosopher and statesman for whom economics was but one aspect of his interest in society. Circumstances led him, as they did the New Deal, to devote special attention to this aspect, but he was a thinker of great breadth, who carried forward the enduring and vital strains of the nineteenth-century liberal tradition. When properly understood, Keynes offers little comfort to those who think the extension of bureaucracy and of administrative control over the economy in a spirit of doctrinaire equalitarianism are ready and adequate answers to contemporary needs.[1]

Like most human creations, Keynesian economics was not really new. There are important and numerous similarities between Keynes and the mercantilists, particularly of the eighteenth century. Parts of his doctrine had also been foreshadowed by Malthus; by theorists little known in the English-speaking world, such as Silvio Gesell; by the distinguished British economist John Atkinson Hobson.[2]

Keynes, in fact, was both more and less novel than he would first

[1] John Maynard Keynes, Lord Keynes of Tilton, was born in 1883 and died in 1946. His father, John Neville Keynes, was a distinguished writer and Cambridge Professor, his mother an active and intellectual lady who served as Mayor of Cambridge. In addition to his tremendously successful academic career, J. M. Keynes was editor of the *Economic Journal* and chairman of *The Nation and the Athenaeum*, was chairman of an insurance company, and directed an investment firm, both with success. He was advisor to the British Treasury and patron of the arts, having founded a ballet and the Arts Theatre at Cambridge. Keynes' influence in Great Britain was not limited to his writings, for, being a member of a respected family, and a man of adequate means and great charm, he knew and could converse effectively with leaders in all aspects and walks of British life. See the *London Times* obituary, reprinted in S. E. Harris, ed., *The New Economics, Keynes' Influence on Theory and Public Policy*, New York, 1947, pp. xvii ff.

[2] Keynes' relationship to mercantilists, Malthus, and Hobson will be indicated below. He credited Gesell, generally classified as a "monetary crank," with having developed an attack on laissez faire that was equally an attack on Marx (*General Theory*, chap. 23).

appear to be. His relationship to the mercantilists was closer than he thought, for he knew them largely through Heckscher's great work, which did not stress the eighteenth-century developments in mercantilist thinking which were strikingly similar to several of Keynes' own ideas. Apart from particular concepts, moreover, he shared with them an important methodological characteristic: unlike the classical school, Keynes did not assume any particular economic situation as a normal one around which fluctuations could occur. Like the mercantilists, Keynes distinguished between good and bad economic conditions, and did not commit the classical error of regarding the good as "natural." Lord Keynes' originality lay in his ability to provide mercantilist policies with a theoretical foundation based upon the closely reasoned analysis of one superlatively well trained in classical economics. He had both the intellectual capacity and the prestige to work out and gain a hearing for what was the first great systematic exposition of neomercantilism in the twentieth century. In this respect, the publication of his *General Theory of Employment, Interest and Money*, in 1936, constituted a genuine revolution in economic thought.

It is hardly an exaggeration to say that immediately before and especially after World War II the countries of the English-speaking world and western Europe, and others besides, were following Keynesian economic policies. The main reason for this was not that the Keynesian formulas had been proved beyond a shadow of doubt, for this is impossible in the social sciences, but rather that this economics harmonized with the traditions of the West, with its political and moral inclinations and, seemingly, with its needs of the moment. Allowing for variations, the postwar policies of the United Kingdom and the British Dominions, the Scandinavian and Benelux countries, France, Italy, and the United States as well as the principal international economic agreements all reveal Keynesian principles and mechanisms.

It is still difficult to estimate with any precision Keynes' influence on the New Deal itself. Secretary Perkins writes that in 1934, "Roosevelt himself was unfamiliar with the economics of Keynes. Others in the administration had read his works, but he had not yet attained popular acceptance." This, of course, was before the publication of the *General Theory*. When Keynes visited America in June,

1934, he "was liberally consulted . . . by a number of . . . people in the government who were anxious to have his comment," and he had a rather unfortunate visit with the President. Keynes spoke in a most professional manner, with the result that Roosevelt later said, "He must be a mathematician rather than a political economist.' Keynes was equally disappointed, remarking that he had "supposed the President was more literate, economically speaking."[3] On December 31, 1933, the *New York Times* had published an open letter from Keynes to Roosevelt, in which the economist criticized the early New Deal along lines that were borne out by subsequent changes in policy. He pointed out that even necessary reform might impede recovery by weakening the confidence of the business community and "its existing motives to action before you have had time to fit other motives in their place." He warned against the unhealthiness of a price rise that preceded rather than followed an increase in output and employment, and urged an expansion of public debt and the institution of a large-scale public works program. He condemned a simple increase in the quantity of money as "'trying to get fat by buying a larger belt.' His recommendations for stabilizing the dollar and lowering the domestic interest rate were followed precisely by the administration. For the first, he urged the President to

. . . control the dollar exchange by buying and selling gold and foreign currencies at a definite figure so as to avoid wide or meaningless fluctuations, with a right to shift the parities at any time but with a declared intention only so to do either to correct a serious want of balance in America's international receipts and payments or to meet a shift in your domestic price level relative to price levels abroad.

For the second, he advised reducing the "rate of interest on your long term government bonds to 2½ percent or less."[4]

The Roosevelt administration, as we have suggested, became more consciously Keynesian after the recession of 1937, and by 1940 the President was prepared to state in a budget message to Congress:

The experience of 1938–1939 should remove any doubt as to the effectiveness of a fiscal policy related to economic need. . . . Government

[3] Perkins, *Roosevelt*, pp. 225–226.
[4] *New York Times*, Dec. 31, 1933, section 8, p. 2.

must have the wisdom to use its credit to sustain economic activity in periods of economic recession and the courage to withhold it and retire debt in periods of economic prosperity.

The President had accepted the Keynesian view that the recession had arisen from, among other factors, "over-optimism which led the Government to curtail its net expenditures too abruptly."[5]

While it is not possible to trace the specific influence of Keynes on a large number of particular Roosevelt measures, two things can hardly be questioned: first, that the general nature of the Roosevelt program was Keynesian, and, second, that as time went on, more and more members of the administration came under the influence of Keynes' *General Theory*.

Keynes had not always been a "Keynesian." He had started his career as an orthodox if brilliant follower of Alfred Marshall and the neoclassical school. Despite his orthodoxy, however, there were early indications of differences, and in 1925 he bitterly attacked Chancellor of the Exchequer Winston Churchill's return to the gold standard. In 1929 he supported Lloyd George's electoral platform of public works and government loans. Three years earlier, in 1926, his stimulating and thoughtful pamphlet, *The End of Laissez Faire*, had carried his attack on the fallacious assumptions and methods of the classical economists and his belief that society, acting through government, would have to take concerted action to guide both fiscal policy and investment and savings. Articles and open letters published during the Great Depression clearly foreshadowed the full-blown doctrine that appeared in the *General Theory* in 1936.

The *General Theory* starts with the proposition that classical economics had actually concerned itself with what was no more than an unrealistic special case, in which the capitalist economy is in equilibrium at full employment. Keynes called his theory "general" because it dealt with the possibilities of a capitalist economy in equilibrium at less than full employment. If depressions are defined in terms of employment, this would mean that chronic depression is within the range of possibilities under capitalism. This conclusion had, of course, been reached and exceeded by socialist writers, who had then proceeded to argue for the abolition of capi-

[5] *Public Papers of Franklin D. Roosevelt*, vol. 9, New York, 1941, p. 12.

talism. But socialists had claimed depressions to be inevitable: Keynes merely argued that they were theoretically as well as practically consistent with capitalism, and argued for the adoption of policies which would prevent them.

The classical economists had implicitly or explicitly assumed Say's law, that supply creates its own demand.[6] Keynes, following the lead of Malthus and Hobson, argued that supply could exceed effective demand, the desire for goods and services that is backed up by purchasing power.[7] The classical economists, following the implication of Say's law, tended to regard money as merely a means of account, a common denominator for different goods. Keynes, going back to the mercantilists, viewed money as an active and influential factor in the operation of the monetary, capitalist economy. Classical economists had tended to believe that involuntary unemployment could not exist in a competitive society. When it did occur, this was owing to the fact that artificial impediments to natural wage adjustments—the actions of labor unions and of governments—prevented wages from falling to their natural, competitive levels. At these levels, the classical economists believed, all the labor offered would be demanded, and no involuntary unemployment could exist. This proposition, of course, assumed that the aggregate demand for goods would remain the same at the lower as at the higher wages, so that there would be no decline in production and, therefore, no decline in employment. Such a theory of unemployment, like Malthus' pernicious law of population, placed the blame for the troubles of labor squarely on their own shoulders. Aside from the annoying fact that labor, in a democratic society, is most unlikely to consent voluntarily to an all-around lowering of wages,[8] Keynes rejected this reasoning on theoretical grounds. He regarded employment as determined not by the rate of wages but by the effective demand for goods and by the amount of investment.

The classical economists carried on the age-old belief in the virtue of thrift, not only to the individual saver but to the economy as a whole, for they held that all savings, directly or indirectly,

[6] See p. 18.

[7] *General Theory,* pp. 363 ff.

[8] One corollary of the classical theory is that a general lowering of wages would reduce prices, thus constituting a shift of purchasing power to those with fixed incomes, particularly the debt-holding or rentier class.

found their way into real, productive capital, and that savings therefore automatically increased production and employment. Keynes, on the other hand, quoted approvingly Malthus' contemptuous reply to the glorification of thrift: "What, I would ask, would become of the demand for commodities, if all consumption except bread and water were suspended for the next half-year? What an accumulation of commodities! *Quels débouchés!* What a prodigious market would this event occasion!"[9] Although Keynes stated that aggregate savings of a society will be equal in amount to its aggregate investments, he contended that this equality, or equilibrium is likely to occur at a level which will not afford full employment.

The classical economists defined saving as an individual's postponement of expenditure in order to obtain future benefits. Such sacrifice was to be rewarded, and interest was defined as this reward. The rate of interest determined the attractiveness and hence the amount of savings. Since investment meant the use of these savings for the creation of producers' goods, or capital, the classical writers believed that the rate of interest was the price which established equilibrium between savings and investment. If savings exceeded the demand for them for investment purposes, their price— the rate of interest—would fall, and if the demand exceeded the supply of savings, the rate of interest would rise, reaching equilibrium at a level which the classical theorists believed to be one of full employment in a perfectly competitive society. Keynes, on the other hand, argued that A's decision to invest was independent of B's decision to save. He defined interest not as a reward for postponing the immediate pleasure of consumption, but as the price at which lenders were willing to do without the advantage of having thoroughly liquid assets, cash. The rate of interest he held to be "the 'price' which equilibrates the desire to hold wealth in the form of cash with the available quantity of cash."[10] This rate would be determined by the degree to which people preferred to hold cash, rather than lend it, and by the supply of cash available. On this basis, the interest rate does not primarily determine the amount of savings or provide equilibrium between savings and investment. It

[9] *General Theory*, p. 364.
[10] *General Theory*, p. 167.

merely sets one of the standards by which businessmen decide whether or not to undertake investment.[11]

Lastly, whereas the classical economists regarded investment, savings, interest, and employment as perfectly interrelated (save for friction and man-made interference) by human nature and Say's law, Keynes regarded investment as largely autonomous. The rate of investment, he held, depended on such factors as population growth, the export market, businessmen's anticipations of the future, and technological innovations.

These many theoretical differences between Keynes and his orthodox contemporaries and predecessors correspond to as many practical differences when theory is transformed into public policy. In fact, if not for the fortunate habit of most economists of ignoring much of their doctrine when called upon to make practical recommendations, the classical economists could theoretically do nothing better than cry "Laissez faire," Let things alone. Their only exception consistent with theory could be vigorous antitrust and antiunion prosecution. Despite the fact that nearly all economists of the classical tradition recognize real situations and discount their theories when they do, huge areas of disagreement remain between them and Keynes. The followers of classical economics tend to favor a balanced national budget; Keynes argued that it depended upon the state of employment. They could hardly believe it possible to stimulate consumption; Keynes thought it necessary and feasible when consumption fell off. After the First World War they tended to favor a return to the gold standard; Keynes thought it was artificial and disastrous. They were willing to make only grudging exceptions to the rule of international free trade; Keynes came to believe that wise protection could be very useful and, in fact, more conducive to international harmony than untrammeled competition among nations.

In short, as a result of their inability to accommodate the facts of economic depression to their theories of equilibrium, classical thinkers were led to accept depressions as natural results of imperfections and frictions in the economy. This was not a promising basis on which to work out programs to combat their ill effects.

[11] See p. 155.

Keynes, on the contrary, easily accommodated his theory to the facts of depression, which he regarded as the result of inherent imbalances in advanced capitalist nations, and he was able to suggest policies which had, at the very least, a good measure of success. It is partly for this reason that Keynes has often been called a "depression economist." It would be more accurate to say that he was a theorist of the national economy, for his interest was in combating not only depression but inflation, and in ensuring a progressively more prosperous nation.

As convenient a pivot as any for Keynesian theory is the simple proposition, long since noted by mercantilists among others, that people with high incomes are apt to save a greater proportion of earnings than those who are lower in the income scale. Conversely, farther down the income ladder, what he termed the propensity to consume is higher: a person at the bare level of subsistence will spend his entire income and save no part of it. Keynes carried this observation a step further: as incomes rose, consumption rose, but by a smaller amount than income, as part of the increased earnings were saved. As incomes fell, consumption also fell, but by a smaller amount than the decline in earnings, for spending habits were somewhat slower to adjust.

These characteristics of the propensity to consume have important and disturbing implications for the advanced capitalist economy.[12] The most striking, which had been noted by other economists, is that as national income rises, consumption expenditures, advancing more slowly than earnings, will account for a decreasing proportion of total income. Savings will therefore take up an increasing share. The question therefore arises, Will these savings be offset by investment in new real capital?[13] Industrial production is of two general types, consumers' and producers' goods. Since consumer demand rises proportionately less than income in the short run, an increase

[12] In a poor and slowly progressing economy the propensity to consume will obviously be very high; the closer an economy approaches to the subsistence level the less danger there will be of inadequacy of demand; a central African tribe may run the risk of famine, but never of a business depression, which is one of the prices that we pay for having an advanced civilization.

[13] Investment, in Keynes, refers exclusively to industrial investment, the creation of new productive facilities. The purchase of securities, or financial investment, merely involves an exchange of assets of differing degrees of liquidity, with no new addition to productive capacity.

of consumers' goods production will flood the market and be brought to a quick halt. An increase of capital-goods production, however, will fill the gap between income and consumer expenditure. Investment, therefore, is the decisive factor in determining whether there is to be full employment in the advanced capitalist economy. If investment is inadequate, there will be successive reductions of employment and income until a low level of stabilization is reached. The fact that the propensity to consume declines at a lower rate than income is a theoretical check to a fall below the subsistence level of economic activity. A far more convincing check, of course, is the threat of social revolution.

Keynes should be called an underinvestment rather than an underconsumption economist, although it is apparent that inadequate consumer expenditure plays an important part in his analysis. A great difference in social outlook is concealed within this distinction and variation in analysis. The underconsumptionist, like J. A. Hobson, is led to accept socialism. Keynes, on the contrary, stressed the community's need for much more ample productive equipment, and tried to find ways of maintaining investment to provide full employment and rising standards of living under capitalism.

According to Keynes, the decision to invest or not to invest depends upon the businessman's expectations regarding the future. Of all things, expectations (or predictions) of this type are the least certain. There is no scientific way of arriving at them. They are better than offhand guesses, of course, but these expectations are necessarily based upon analyses of the present, and predictions of how the present will change into the future. They will be conditioned by the attitude of the business community toward government policy, the likelihood of peace or war, technological innovation, or the development of new markets. More specifically, the decision to invest will be governed by the investor's estimation of future returns from the new capital asset (what Keynes calls the marginal efficiency of capital) as compared with the long-term rate of interest. For if interest is high, expectations of the future have to be optimistic if businessmen are to invest. Conversely, if interest is low, more modest expectations will afford sufficient inducement.

Interest and money are thus more closely integrated into the main body of economic theory than they had been under the classical school. Like the mercantilists, Keynes was ready to concede that there is nothing which can be effectively substituted for money in a monetary economy, where the desire for money cannot be surfeited as can the demand for radios or cabbages (unless people lose confidence in the currency, as in a runaway inflation, in which case the real problem is not so much one of money as the very preservation of social order).

Interest on money offers an alternative to investment. Holders of wealth can choose among buying new capital assets—investing— buying existing assets, or lending money at interest. If the rate of interest is high, the inducement to invest will be decreased. And if investment declines, employment will fall, demand will follow suit, and a downward spiral of spending, production, and employment will ensue. This explains the old mercantilist contention that high-level business activity corresponds with a low rate of interest, and depressed activity with a high rate.[14] As Keynes saw it, if people were extremely anxious to retain cash—what he called a high liquidity preference—the interest rate would have to be high to induce them to lend it out, unless the supply of money were increased by the banking system. It was therefore a prime policy implication of Keynesian economics that a high rate of interest, indicating a high liquidity preference, should be countered by an easy-money program on the part of government.

The rate of interest is thus one of the determinants of investment, but forcing it down it is not a sufficient answer to the problem of inadequate investment. In part, Keynes' emphasis on interest and money derives from his earlier specialization and writing in this field. Since the publication of the *General Theory*, economists who follow Keynes have felt increasingly that interest plays a much smaller part in the whole investment-unemployment picture than he described.[15] Despite continued low rates, private investment has threatened to be inadequate to maintain full employment. The focusing of attention on other aspects of what he believed induced

[14] See p. 76.
[15] Klein, *Keynesian Revolution*, pp. 65–66. It should be noted that the *General Theory* shows less stress on interest as a counterdepression device than Keynes' earlier writings.

people to invest, has led to the so-called "mature economy" or "long-term stagnation" thesis.[16]

This thesis does not mean that capitalism is incapable of introducing further technological or other innovations. Nor does it mean that with the end of the American frontier, in the sense that most of the land between the Atlantic and Pacific has been settled, there are no more investment opportunities. Stated in general terms, largely as given by Keynes but with additions from other writers, the argument would run something like this: As a capitalist economy advances toward ever higher levels of productivity and standards of living, the average rate of return from new investment (marginal efficiency of capital) tends to fall. The proportion of income saved tends to increase, while available investment outlets tend to dry up. The leveling off of population growth and the more restricted opportunities for land settlement tend to limit the expansion of new markets or the increase of old. The growth of monopoly and the transformation of the entrepreneur into the private business bureaucrat further diminish both outlets for new investment and the incentive to take risks. The conclusion, therefore, is not that there are no investment opportunities remaining, or that there is no inducement to invest, or no spirit of initiative leading to investment, but merely that opportunities, inducements, and initiative are tending to become inadequate to maintain full employment.

If this thesis is accurate—and it is very far from being proved—why not reconcile oneself to the doom of capitalism and set about creating a socialist society free from all the troubles of depression, declining investment opportunities, and all the rest? Keynes indeed spoke of the forthcoming "socialization of investment," and of the "euthanasia of the Rentier," but he stressed the virtues and possibilities of a modified capitalist system.[17] Keynes wished to diminish

---

[16] The "stagnation" thesis is present in the *General Theory*, and was stated by Keynes in "Some Economic Consequences of a Declining Population," *Eugenics Review*, April, 1937, pp. 13–17. The outstanding exponent of this thesis is Alvin H. Hansen, *Full Recovery or Stagnation*, New York, 1938; *Fiscal Policy and Business Cycles*, New York, 1941. See Benjamin Higgins, "Concepts and Criteria of Secular Stagnation," *Income, Employment and Public Policy: Essays in Honor of Alvin H. Hansen*, New York, 1948, and Alan Sweezy, "Declining Investment Opportunity," in Harris, ed., *New Economics*, pp. 425–435.

[17] By socialization of investment, Keynes appears to have meant (since he

the opportunities to create huge fortunes and favored a lower ceiling on high incomes, but he had no use whatever for socialism, and an untempered contempt for Karl Marx. His essentially conservative outlook rather called for a change in some of the rules of the capitalist game and for the addition of some new equipment:

I believe that there is social and psychological justification for significant inequalities of incomes and wealth, but not for such large disparities as exist today. There are valuable human activities which require the motive of money-making and the environment of private wealth-ownership for their full fruition. Moreover, dangerous human proclivities can be canalised into comparatively harmless channels by the existence of opportunities for money-making and private wealth, which, if they cannot be satisfied in this way, may find their outlet in cruelty, the reckless pursuit of personal power and authority, and other forms of self-aggrandisement. It is better that a man should tyrannise over his bank balance than over his fellow-citizens; and whilst the former is sometimes denounced as being but a means to the latter, sometimes at least it is an alternative. But it is not necessary for the stimulation of these activities and the satisfaction of these proclivities that the game should be played for such high stakes as at present. Much lower stakes will serve the purpose equally well, as soon as the players are accustomed to them. The task of transmuting human nature must not be confused with the task of managing it. Though in the ideal commonwealth men may have been taught or inspired or bred to take no interest in the stakes, it may still be wise and prudent statesmanship to allow the game to be played, subject to rules and limita-

---

was not interested in blueprinting some future Utopia this point is not spelled out) overall planning of both public and private investment, in which investment by government in roads, schools, hospitals, and the like would fill the gap between private investment and the level needed to maintain full employment. By the euthanasia of the rentier, he meant that permanently low interest rates, high income and inheritance taxes and other checks to saving would lead to the disappearance of the class that lives on income from securities. In a purely theoretical vein he suggested that when productive facilities were eventually built up to the point where they ceased to be scarce, there would be no economic justification for interest, or for the rentier, who "can obtain interest because capital is scarce, just as the owner of land can obtain rent because land is scarce." This does not mean that capital goods would cost nothing, "but only that the return from them would have to cover little more than their exhaustion by wastage and obsolescence together with some margin to cover risk and the exercise of skill and judgment. In short, the aggregate return from durable goods in the course of their life would, as in the case of short-lived goods, just cover their labour-costs of production *plus* an allowance for risk and the costs of skill and supervision" (*General Theory*, pp. 375 ff.).

tions, so long as the average man, or even a significant section of the community, is in fact strongly addicted to the money-making passion.[18]

It would be difficult to find a more effective defense of what Keynes called "the traditional advantages of individualism" than the following:

They are partly advantages of efficiency—the advantages of decentralisation and of the play of self-interest. The advantage to efficiency of the decentralisation of decisions and of individual responsibility is even greater, perhaps, than the nineteenth century supposed; and the reaction against the appeal to self-interest may have gone too far. But, above all, individualism, if it can be purged of its defects and its abuses, is the best safeguard of personal liberty in the sense that, compared with any other system, it greatly widens the field for the exercise of personal choice. It is also the best safeguard of the variety of life, which emerges precisely from this extended field of personal choice, and the loss of which is the greatest of all the losses of the homogeneous or totalitarian state. For this variety preserves the traditions which embody the most secure and successful choices of former generations; it colours the present with the diversification of its fancy; and, being the handmaid of experiment as well as of tradition and fancy, it is the most powerful instrument to better the future.[19]

To the author of this remarkably precise rendition of the conservative philosophy of Edmund Burke,[20] the problem was not how to scrap a useless past and create a rosy-red future, but how to make the past and present work into a better future which retained the genius of old days. It was incorrect, Keynes thought, to regard capitalism as a total failure, or to believe that private allocation of resources was wholly incompetent. When a system employs nine-tenths of those willing and able to work, he wrote, the complaint is not that these men are doing the wrong work, but that there should be work for the remaining tenth who are unemployed. "It is in determining the volume, not the direction, of actual employment that the existing system has broken down."[21] To one who was an avowed member and defender of the middle class and believed in

[18] *General Theory*, p. 374.
[19] *General Theory*, p. 380.
[20] As a student at Cambridge, Keynes won a prize for an essay on the political philosophy of Burke.
[21] *General Theory*, p. 379.

the values of bourgeois culture, Marx, socialism, and Soviet Russia held no attraction. "Marxian Socialism," he wrote in a derisive manner that few classical economists would share, "must always remain a portent to the historians of Opinion—how a doctrine so illogical and so dull can have exercised so powerful and enduring an influence over the minds of men, and, through them, the events of history." Of Soviet Marxism, he asked "How can I accept a doctrine which sets up as its bible, above and beyond criticism, an obsolete economic textbook which I know to be not only scientifically erroneous but without interest or application for the modern world?"[22] He thought the Russian economic system inefficient, and unlikely to develop any new economic methods of interest or value to the outside world.

Since Keynes believed in maintaining the system of private property, his problem was one of devising methods to stimulate consumption and investment, upon which employment hinged. Inducing people to spend more was to be accomplished by social legislation which would give adequate provision for old age or emergencies, creating a sense of security which would forestall excessive savings by the large masses of the population. In addition, high income and inheritance taxes, by shifting a larger proportion of national income to those with a higher propensity to consume, would help in sparking consumer expenditure. Stimulation of private investment, and here we borrow from Keynesians as well as Keynes, would be accomplished by tax policies that favored risk taking,[23] prosecution of harmful restrictions arising from the monopolistic practices of both business and labor, a low interest rate, a currency with a relatively stable purchasing power, stimulation of foreign trade, and investment abroad, supplying more and better economic information to business.

[22] Quoted by Dudley Dillard, *The Economics of John Maynard Keynes: The Theory of a Monetary Economy*, New York, 1947, pp. 322, 324, in an excellent discussion of Keynes's social philosophy.

[23] Aside from the general proposal to keep corporate income taxes, especially for small firms, at a relatively low rate, it has been suggested, in order to stimulate risk-taking, that more generous provision be made for writing off losses against past or future profits through carry-back and carry-forward provisions. In addition, quite a number of ingenious tax policies have been suggested that would offer rewards for risking new investment. See the sections on taxation in P. T. Homan and F. Machlup, eds., *Financing American Prosperity*, New York, 1945.

All these measures, however, might at times still fail to induce enough private investment to provide full employment. Indeed, taking a longer view, in terms of the stagnation thesis, the Keynesian doctrine would seem to predict that the inadequacy will become increasingly more severe. In either case, the gap is to be filled by public investment, and the stagnation thesis merely assigns a permanent and growing role to the governmental part of the work of investment.

We may discard or at least shelve the theory of long-term stagnation, however, for it is the very kind of theory that Keynes himself would not care to follow as a guide to immediate, practical policy. It is not sufficient just to deduce the doctrine from other Keynesian principles. Aside from the fact that an appeal to statistical evidence does not yield a clear-cut answer, even the proved existence of a trend toward long-term stagnation in recent years could not possibly commit the future to behave in similar fashion.[24] The question therefore is, what should be done if, after all available steps have been taken to stimulate consumption and private investment, the latter should still fall below the amount needed to sustain full employment. The answer, according to Keynes, lay in public investment, a works program directly or indirectly increasing the nation's productive capacity. This would range from roads and schools, subsidizing housing and TVA's, to naval and military construction, if deemed advisable. The last, of course, would, in the long run, be *economically* less rewarding than projects with civilian uses. Government ownership was quite unnecessary and beside the point in the great majority of cases, according to Keynes. What was important was demand-stimulating investment, and the actual labor of construction could be handled by private contractors.

These government expenditures, Keynes believed, should be financed by borrowing money and adding to the national debt. Taking a favorite concept of eighteenth-century mercantilism that had been revived and polished a few years before the *General Theory* was published, Keynes argued that each newly created

[24] George Terborgh, *The Bogey of Economic Maturity*, Chicago, 1945, delivers an effective broadside against the whole stagnation thesis. He points out, however, that Keynesian fiscal policy does not have to be based on this thesis, and can be developed entirely without it. Unprecedented levels of investment and prosperity in the United States following the Second World War led American Keynesians to soft-pedal talk of the "mature economy."

dollar[25] injected into the economy in this way would add more than one dollar to national income. For, if the dollar exchanged hands four times, first "given to the grocer, by the grocer to the wholesaler, and by the wholesaler to the farmer . . . you have created four dollars' worth of national income."[26] Allowing for "leakages" owing to savings or friction, and for the lapse of time while the dollar is circulated, this was the principle of the investment multiplier: if, for example, the estimated gap for a given period between intended investment and the amount required for full employment were $12 billion, and the multiplier were three rather than four (one new dollar creating three of national income), the situation would call for a deficit expenditure, through borrowing, of $4 billion.

Aside from minor criticisms, two major attacks have been leveled against the idea of deficit spending. The economic objection is that an endless building up of the national debt is certain to entail unbearable interest burdens in the future and (as a minor theme) that the debt has to be repaid some day somehow. According to Keynes, the latter point is based upon a false analogy between private and public finance (a distinction mercantilists frequently made). The private debtor assuredly does have to repay the second party who lent him the money. But in the case of an internally held public debt there is no second party, for as bonds fall due, new ones can be issued, if the government does not choose to reduce the debt. As an eighteenth-century French mercantilist put it,

. . . the debts of a state are debts of the right hand to the left hand by which the body will not be weakened if it has the necessary supply of provisions and is able to distribute them.[27]

[25] Newly created because the loan arises through the banks' entering demand deposits to the Treasury account. The Treasury then, indirectly, issues checks against these accounts, as is the case with any borrower from a bank. The sale of bonds to private individuals for cash is, on the contrary, deflationary or inflationary, depending upon whether the government uses the money to reduce its debt or spends it.
[26] This was Keynes' explanation of the principle to Secretary Perkins, who adds rather wistfully: "I wish he had been as concrete when he talked to Roosevelt, instead of treating him as though he belonged to the higher echelons of economic knowledge" (*Roosevelt*, p. 226). For an example of the mercantilist version of this theory, which ignored the factor of "leakage," see p. 75.
[27] Melon, in Daire, *Economistes financières*, p. 802.

It can hardly be argued that there will be no market for government bonds, particularly in depressed times when private investment is slack. As to the major theme, that an unbearable interest burden will be created over years of deficit financing, this objection need not hold unless one believes in the stagnation theory. For otherwise, there will be no addition to debt when private investment is adequate. When an inflationary boom threatens in a time of full employment, the Keynesian policy would be the deflationary one of raising taxes and retiring part of the debt. Furthermore, there is the rule of thumb proposition that if interest payments do not increase more rapidly than national income, the burden of interest will be no greater than before. Interest amounting to 5 percent of a national income of $200 billion will be no heavier a load to carry than 5 percent of $100 billion.

There is the additional objection, of a political and social variety, that a public investment program will involve wasteful and demoralizing boondoggling and, even worse, political corruption and excessive centralization of government. Keynes was as bitter an opponent of boondoggling as any columnist of the depression era, but he felt that any made-work was better than unemployment.

If the Treasury were to fill old bottles with banknotes, bury them at suitable depths in disused coal mines which are then filled up to the surface with town rubbish, and leave it to private enterprise on well-tried principles of *laissez-faire* to dig the notes up again . . . there need be no more unemployment and, with the help of the repercussions, the real income of the community, and its capital wealth also, would probably become a good deal greater than it actually is. It would, indeed, be more sensible to build houses and the like; but if there are political and practical difficulties in the way of this, the above would be better than nothing.

He pointed out the direct analogy between digging for buried paper money and digging for gold that is to be monetized, and then went on to write that

Ancient Egypt was doubly fortunate, and doubtless owed to this its fabled wealth, in that it possessed *two* activities, namely, pyramid-building as well as the search for precious metals, the fruits of which, since they could not serve the needs of man by being consumed, did not stale with abundance. The Middle Ages built cathedrals and sang dirges. Two pyramids, two masses for the dead, are twice as good as one; but not so two railways from London to York. Thus we are so sensible, have schooled ourselves to so close a semblance of prudent financiers, taking careful thought before we add to the "financial" burdens of posterity by building them houses to live in, that we have no such easy escape from the sufferings of unemployment.[28]

There can be no question, on the other hand, that heavy governmental expenditures open the door to corruption and excessive centralization but, just as a nation can choose useful rather than useless public expenditure, the Keynesian answer would run, it can guard against graft and vote buying, and can actually turn public investment to the service of decentralization, as in the case of TVA. Keynes himself believed strongly in the largely independent semi-public corporation as an agency of social policy, and, as we have said, saw little virtue in outright government ownership.

The common labeling of Keynes as a "depression economist" is based in large part upon the fact that the *General Theory* does indeed deal at great length with the problem of depression and how to meet it. But Keynes was equally concerned with the danger of booms, and particularly with their concomitant, inflation. The *General Theory* had defined true inflation as the increase in prices following an upsurge of wages in a condition of full employment, and had warned of possible danger points earlier in the process of rising to that level. The Keynesian answer to inflation, published in response to the problem of financing the Second World War, was in effect the reverse of the solution to deflation: instead of favoring consumer expenditures, encourage savings; instead of cutting taxes, raise them; instead of adding to public debt, reduce it; instead of proceeding with public works, postpone them.[29] The objective was to maintain equilibrium at full employment, and fiscal policy would simply vary with conditions. Keynesian economists have been accused of inconsistency in first urging deficit financing and then

[28] *General Theory*, pp. 129–131. While the leaf-raking of the depression era was very much like pyramid building in that the only demand for it came artificially from the government, it should be noted that the war production program, which succeeded in creating full employment, was also a response to an artificial, if terribly urgent demand on the part of the government.

[29] *How to Pay for the War, A Radical Plan for the Chancellor of the Exchequer*, New York, 1940; also, Keynes, "The United States and the Keynes Plan," *The New Republic*, July 29, 1940, pp. 156–159.

measures to check the rise of prices and wages, but they have actually been no more inconsistent than the physician who prescribes different palliatives for the manic and depressive phases of a manic-depressive condition.

There remains the great question of international economic relations in modern neomercantilism as expounded by Keynes, and here he struck a balance between the rapacity of old mercantilism and the fatuousness of classical doctrine. Keynes felt that there had been a good deal of sense to the mercantilist principle of the favorable balance of trade, the commodity (and service) export surplus, for it was equivalent to domestic investment in its effects on employment. Under the Keynesian formula investment equals national income minus consumption;[30] an export surplus adds to income but not to consumption, and therefore has the same effect, enlarged by the multiplier, as new investment at home. In addition, Keynes felt that in the seventeenth and eighteenth centuries when it was most in vogue, the policy of a favorable balance of trade had a further beneficial result. In the absence of modern facilities of controlling the supply of money, the export surplus brought in precious metals, which supported the mercantilist objective of lowering the interest rate.

But Keynes did not follow the mercantilists down the path to deliberate war for economic gain. He believed in using economic policy to secure peace, but denied the classical theory that unimpeded free trade, and an international gold standard, provided the best means of bringing the nations together in the ties of friendly commerce that would shackle the gods of war. This theory, and Ricardo's law of comparative advantage,[31] said Keynes, would hold true only if all the parties to trade were at a level of full employment. Otherwise, the lack of tariff protection, and the need for gold to back the currency, would set the nations into bitter competition

[30] Since savings also equal national income minus consumption, savings equal investment. This well known Keynesian formula does not mean that the amount of savings *determines* the amount that will be invested (the classical theory). It does mean (1) both savings and investment are governed by aggregate income and its pattern of distribution, (2) investment and propensity to consume together determine aggregate income, (3) investment, which is decided upon independently of saving, will bring income and therefore saving up or down to equality with itself.

[31] See p. 14.

for foreign markets, whence, at least in part, the wars of our time. Keynes' solution was, as one would expect, in harmony with his domestic policies. He wrote:

It is the policy of the autonomous rate of interest [managed currency], unimpeded by international preoccupations, and of a national investment programme directed to an optimum level of domestic employment which is twice blessed in the sense that it helps ourselves and our neighbors at the same time. And it is the simultaneous pursuit of these policies by all countries together which is capable of restoring economic health and strength internationally, whether we measure it by the level of domestic employment or by the volume of international trade.[32]

Keynes had freed neomercantilist doctrine from the unashamed belligerency of the absolute monarchies of the seventeenth century, whose attitude had been based upon the very crude "stagnation" thesis that there was to be no further noteworthy change in the amount of wealth in the world.[33] He had also freed neomercantilism from the crude belief in complete self-sufficiency, that was rampant between the two world wars, even among nations for whom autarky could mean only a permanently lower standard of living. He had revived and refined the idea of the nineteenth-century neomercantilist Friedrich List, that each nation that had adequate potential should strive for a balanced, diversified, stable, and progressive economy, and that only among such advanced nations would it be possible to have extended, mutually beneficial and relatively free trade. Keynes urged, in short, that each country organize its economy at a stable level of full employment and, upon this foundation, coöperate with the other nations in seeking a world-wide increase of trade and standards of living through a multilateral reduction of trade barriers and stabilization of currencies. The moment foreign trade ceased to be "a desperate expedient to maintain employment at home by forcing sales on foreign markets and restricting purchases," Keynes saw every advantage and no loss in freer international exchange of goods and services.[34] In this scheme of things, currency devaluation and protective tariffs are legitimate when their purpose is to end a deficit in international payments that drains the

[32] *General Theory*, p. 349.
[33] See p. 88.
[34] *General Theory*, p. 382.

nation's liquid reserves, or to maintain equilibrium in international payments and prevent such a drain from occurring. These protective devices are frowned upon when their intent is aggressive rather than defensive, when they are designed to create or enlarge a surplus in the balance of payments.[35] Keynes' program was one of moderate and coöperative nationalism that would, in practice, involve far more international collaboration than would free trade.

In their broader aspects, the Bretton Woods international monetary agreement and the Anglo-American Loan Agreement of 1945 implemented Keynes' proposals. Under Bretton Woods, the gold price of a national currency was to vary with the needs of national policy, rather than have national policy bend to the will of a fixed gold standard. The International Monetary Fund was to provide short-term relief for a nation whose currency was imperiled by an adverse balance of payments, and Keynes' principle of monetary autonomy *and* coöperation was enacted into law.

The non-Marxist world swung sharply toward Keynesian neomercantilism during and after the Second World War. The Truman administration, with its emphasis on fiscal policy as a regulator of the economy, with its housing, education and conservation programs, even with the Marshall Plan, was certainly no exception. Yet the relative practical success of this neomercantilism serves to highlight its shortcomings as an ideology which could create a sense of purpose rather than groping.

Keynes' total outlook, his general attitude toward the nature and needs of mankind, offer greater hope than his specific economic theories, and with this view I think Keynes would have been quick to agree. The great emphasis neomercantilism places upon the making of concrete policies and the decisions which they require, underlines the fact that human judgment is prone to error. In a way, this brings in nothing new, for the negative decision of pure classical theory, laissez faire, is as much a decision as any positive one, and entails as many consequences. But Keynesian doctrine nevertheless calls upon political leadership to make many more conscious decisions and to do a great many more things. This at least opens the door to many more mistakes.

Nor are the doctrines themselves foolproof. Public investment

[35] Harris, ed., *New Economics*, p. 274.

may have the undesired side-effect of raising certain prices, creating shortages, disturbing the flow of particular economic streams. And it may thereby partly negate itself by cutting private investment. As the economic tide rises toward or reaches full employment, union labor may continue to demand increases in money wages—for labor leaders are always under pressure to show that they are getting "results"—and a genuine inflation might result. If some institutional device, compulsory arbitration or administrative wage fixing, is resorted to to prevent inflation, we shall immediately be faced with the question of how that freedom is to be preserved for the sake of which all our policies should be conceived.[36] Lastly, and this was one of the unquestioned weaknesses of the New Deal, since investment depends in such great part upon the expectations of the business community, if this group is discouraged by pressures from labor and government and from monopoly within its own ranks, if it refuses to drink when led to the spring, the wisest of measures may fail to yield results.

Turning from the domestic scene to world economic affairs, the picture becomes more complex and more discouraging. To begin with, nations may honestly disagree as to what is proper Keynesian policy, assuming they have already agreed to be Keynesians. After all, the one thing a theory of this type cannot pretend to is clearcut, simple scientific certainty equally valid for all times, places, and conditions. Different governments will win varying degrees of popular acceptance for the same programs, and there will be unequal degrees of success and progress, which the slender and delicate instrument of international monetary coöperation will have to translate into a common denominator.

There is an even greater difficulty. Neomercantilism is avowedly a nationalist doctrine. Keynes and, we believe, any likely American leadership would be *moderately* nationalist. But there can be no guarantee that nationalism will not break the bounds of restraint. Of itself, neomercantilism unfortunately offers many temptations to the evil that accompanies the good there is in nationalism. America should not forget the belligerent statements of Theodore Roosevelt, the invasion of Vera Cruz ordered by the internationalist Wilson, Franklin Roosevelt's love for naval construction (fortunate, as it

[36] See p. 645.

happened), and Secretary Ickes' allocation of public works funds to the building of warships until stopped by Congress (unfortunately, as it turned out). These warlike symptoms and many others occurred in the United States, which has always boasted, and I think rightly, of a degree of moderation greater than that of the other big powers. There is at least a conceivable danger in making armaments the "Egyptian pyramids" of a Keynesian policy. They are perfect "pyramids" until used, and it is something quite external to neomercantilism, a love of peace that is traditional and has little to do with economics, that prevents them from being used. And the love of peace is not universal.

Keynesian economics implies for certain nations a type of imperialism that can easily be justified, the investment of capital in backward areas that can be developed into beneficial producers and buyers. It is difficult to see how non-Marxists could object to this imperialism. But, in the past, political and military measures have sometimes, though definitely not always, accompanied this process of investment, and have given rise to legitimate complaints and bitter struggles. Even if only the good in imperialism be perpetuated, the memory of the bad survives. When investment abroad induces a clash of cultures, there is wide opportunity for misunderstanding both the investor's motives and the seeming ingratitude of the less advanced people.

Even at a less acute level, the Keynesian doctrine, applied narrowly and selfishly, can be an active trouble maker for the world. For a nation, using neomercantilist methods, can without too much trouble escape domestic depression by exporting it. Domestic employment can be raised by ceasing to buy foreign goods and by dumping goods abroad at prices ruinous to foreign producers. The defense against this weapon is retaliatory restriction, with unemployment spread to many areas as the multiplier effect is directly reversed.

Keynes himself pointed to the weakness of his doctrines when they are regarded as a self-sufficient ideology, as there had been a tendency for many followers of the New Deal to do. As early as 1925, in comparing Soviet communism with Western capitalism, he felt that the strength of Russian Marxism *as a religion* offset its serious economic weakness, and would enable it to survive. The divorce between religion and economics under Western capitalism, however, required the economy "to be immensely, not merely moderately, successful to survive."[37] This deficiency of capitalism is yet more dangerous than Keynes imagined, for even "immense" success, in terms of a high standard of living and full employment, is no guarantee against the excesses of nationalism in world affairs. More important still, it is no certain defense against the growth of a germ that is actually indigenous to Western, capitalist democracy: equalitarianism. The belief in equality, social and economic as well as political, is almost universally accepted in the West in the limited sense of equality of opportunity. But there is a strong tendency for it to be transformed into a seductive and bellicose belief in equality as an absolute good, and this could lead to the destruction of capitalism as easily as could atomic war, depression, or the onslaughts of totalitarian expansion.[38]

The tendency to abstract economics from the rest of the social categories is as dangerous in neomercantilism as it is in classical theory. The facile slogan of some persons—politicians, intellectuals, bureaucrats—"more planning and more democracy" begs precisely the issues that are important, and leaves as great an ideological void as existed before.

Once again we come up against the disturbing fact that it is far easier for us to know what we like today than to state our purposes for tomorrow, easier to make our defense in terms of goods and mechanisms than of the ideas that people think. This is a weakness inherent in any middle-of-the-road position, in any viewpoint that is moderate and pragmatic at the expense of being comprehensively logical. It is a weakness that escaped both classicism at its purest, and the Marxist and fascist extremes of statism.

NOTES ON BOOKS

The book to read is, of course, Keynes' *General Theory of Employment, Interest and Money* itself. It is far from an example of Keynes' best style, although there are many brilliant passages. But the *General Theory*

---

[37] Keynes, *Laissez-Faire and Communism*, New York, 1926, p. 131.
[38] See p. 655.

will be hard going for those untrained in economics, and for them Dudley Dillard's *The Economics of John Maynard Keynes: The Theory of a Monetary Economy* will be a good introduction. Seymour Harris, ed., *The New Economics: Keynes' Influence on Theory and Public Policy* contains essays of varying difficulty, including an article by Keynes that is one of the best summaries of his position. Laurence R. Klein's *The Keynesian Revolution* is an able but technical book.

Keynes will be understood and appreciated as a "universal man" and one of the great figures of modern Western civilization by the reader of R. F. Harrod's admirable *Life of John Maynard Keynes.*

PART III

Socialism

8.

DREAMS AND LABORATORIES:
THE UTOPIAN SOCIALISTS

The Conditions of Man and the Social Moralists

"A SPECTER is haunting Europe—the specter of Communism." So begins *The Communist Manifesto,* published by Karl Marx and Friedrich Engels in 1848. And it closes with a ringing challenge: "Let the ruling classes tremble at a Communist revolution. The proletarians have nothing to lose but their chains. They have a world to win.

"Working men of all countries, unite!"

A century has passed since this strange pamphlet began the career that was to see it translated into dozens of tongues and become part of the sacred writings of millions. The socialist parties which were once the major carriers of its message have become, after many vicissitudes, one of the great hopes of those who wish to see political democracy survive in western Europe. Communist parties have risen on the left of socialism to become the dominant force between the river Elbe and the Pacific Ocean. The term "middle class" is one of great respectability in half the world, and one of opprobrium in the other half.

In no small part the great sweep of revolution against capitalism is owing to the ideological strength of Marxian, so-called "scientific," socialism. Much of the fundamental, as distinct from the tactical, strength of Marxism arises, however, from ideas wholly intrinsic to Western capitalist civilization. And both the Marxian revolutionary concepts and the revolutionary ideas that are as Western as the principle of representative government have been bountifully nourished by social and economic conditions unsatisfactory to large segments of the population. Old as well as new elements of Western thinking had a socialist potential, but the actual conditions that enabled socialism to become a political force arose from the growth of industrial society in the nineteenth century.

The industrial and technological revolution was ultimately to bring about a general rise in the standard of living which paled the advances of previous history, but not all the people immediately shared its beneficence. In England and to a lesser degree on the Continent industrialism created the vast new class of urban factory workers, who lived under conditions that would have been deemed inappropriate for slaves or domestic animals. For descriptions of whole families living in a single room, without bedding or furniture, of streets without gutters and alleys without light, of densely populated warrens lacking even the appointments called privies, of people dying of starvation in the streets and sleeping, destitute, in the park near the royal palace, of prostitution, disease and vermin —for descriptions of this corruption of humanity in the cities, one has only to turn to a classic of Marxian literature, Friedrich Engels' *Condition of the Working Class in England in 1844.* If this be suspect because of its violence and its authorship, one can read the Parliamentary addresses of the seventh Earl of Shaftesbury, the noble lord who felt that people were an important part of the nation's resources, or go to the vast library catalogued in the bibliographies of J. H. Clapham's *Economic History of Modern Britain.*

The poor in England barely subsisted, and no Marx or Engels was needed to point out what was obvious to five senses, and the moral sixth as well. The conditions of this working class, dependent for its livelihood exclusively upon wages, brought forth demands for immediate reform from members of all levels of British society, including even factory owners themselves. The need for improvement, however, also stimulated a searching beyond reform for an entirely new and better type of society. It was this that brought out the socialist potential of the Western intellectual heritage. The traditional conception of justice embodied in Christianity and Western law became a weapon of attack against the evils of industrialism. Concepts out of the eighteenth century and the American and French Revolutions—the equality and essential goodness of mankind, and its perfectability in a proper social environment—suggested the nature of the cure. Newtonian mechanics and its conception of equilibrium was not carried over only into classical economics; it also appeared in socialist thinking as a quest for a principle of human activity to which an ideal society could be geared. Lastly, there was what would seem to be a deep-rooted aspect of human nature, the desire to blueprint the actual physical realization of an ideal: ideal houses, ideal machines, ideal societies.

Every age has produced Utopias that reflect its own temper and problems, for the propensity to Utopianism is at least as old as Plato. Sir Thomas More's *Utopia* (1516) only added one more title—and a name that came to stand for them all—to the list of descriptions of perfect communities that did not exist, descriptions that were also a sharp criticism of the failings of the actual society of the time. The eighteenth century, however, introduced an unconstrained faith in the power of human reason not only to discover the natural and the good, but to establish it here on earth. Succeeding generations, while refurbishing the philosophy of faith, did not of course eliminate faith in reason, and technological achievements strengthened belief in the capacity of mankind to accomplish a rapid transformation of dreams into actuality. There developed an exaggerated view of the applicability of the methods of the natural sciences, a pseudo-scientific outlook and method which may be called "scientism." While classical economics and Marxism were the most celebrated consequences of this attitude, it had striking and highly original by-products among the Utopians. For nineteenth-century Utopians were not content merely to plan glorious new worlds, they tried to establish them, and originated a rash of uniformly interesting and unsuccessful Utopian colonies—the Brook Farms, New Harmonys, Oneidas that were founded in the United States, where land was cheap, and the tyranny of the past seemed to be less severe.

Dreams and Laboratories: The Utopian Socialists

On entering the mosques of Utopia, the tourist must discard the shoes he wears in the streets of this ordinary world. For in Utopia matter-of-factness is abnormal, and the brilliant sallies of a febrile imagination often verge upon what ordinary money- and earthbound mortals should call the insane. The Utopian's generous love for humanity is the force that has cut the anchor lines of his fancy, but beyond it sometimes lurks the pathos of an unfulfilled desire to escape the confines of the decrepit, but relentlessly living society in which he exists. This desire is revealed in dreams of wish fulfillment whose minute detailing lays bare frustration as fully as does the labor of a psychoanalyst. Despite their unreality and their aura of madness, however, the Utopians are more than curios in the history of ideas, for they had many followers, and even more readers. The Utopians' contribution to the rise of socialism was that they made some of the basic ideas of collectivist society familiar to the Western world two generations before socialism could become a political movement supported by large numbers of the working class.

There is no one doctrine of Utopian socialism: there are only Utopian socialists, many of whom were inclined to think that no one before their particular day had had a proper idea of what people are like or of the way things should be. They had in common a belief that western European capitalist society of the first half of the nineteenth century was wrongly organized and was unjust. Beyond this, each had his own pet principles and scheme. Etienne Cabet (1788–1856) was one of the few complete equalitarians among them: Henri de Saint-Simon (1760–1825) had a hierarchical system which was transformed into a religion; Charles Fourier (1772–1837) concocted a mad scene of perfect harmony, in which physical nature and the animal world coöperated most generously with human communities that resembled nothing so much as a puppet show; Robert Owen (1771–1858), the sanest of them all, planned model communities whose principles were in many ways but improved versions of those of his own Great Britain, and in which education and decent surroundings would produce decent men.

Cabet, who modestly compared himself with Moses, Socrates, and Jesus, borrowed in many ways from Sir Thomas More, Rousseau, and Babeuf, leader of the unsuccessful Conspiracy of the Equals in the great French Revolution. Endowed with the usual Utopian assumptions regarding the goodness and perfectability of man, Cabet believed in reason as the all-conquering power, and that reason argued the equality of men. One institution above all stood in the way of this equality: private property. In Icaria, the mythical land discovered by one of those traveling British peers of whom French writers were so enamored, all property was held by the community, and all people worked as its employees. The society was completely democratic, for all decisions were made and all officials elected by majority vote. As for minorities, there were none, for since all were equal, none could be discontented! According to Cabet, a journalist who had protested bitterly against efforts of the French state to control the press, newspapers as known in Europe were forbidden in Icaria, for the perfect political equality and freedom of all the people rendered anything more than a mere recitation of facts quite unnecessary. There was to be but one paper for each town, its editors directly or indirectly elected. Books and plays were of course subject to license, their purpose being to strengthen the regime of equality.

If, to this point, Cabet's vision seems to call to mind the Utopia of George Orwell, let it at once be said that Icaria was infinitely better ordered. *Everyone* arose at 5 A.M., worked from 6 to 1 (one hour less in winter), dined communally from 2 to 3, and then enjoyed leisure and culture. Even work was pleasurable, however, for after two hours of silence, there were two in which conversation was permissible, followed by two in which people sang, either individually or in chorus. Different people, of course, had different kinds of jobs, but since they could be equally happy in all occupations, this did not matter. Agriculture afforded as much joy as industry, owing to the excellence of roads and proximity of towns, and produced in accordance with lists indicating immediate farm consumption and the demands of the state for the year in course. Returns from work were identical, for, as Babeuf had said, the fact that an individual's work called for greater application and intelligence "had nothing to do with the capacity of his stomach."[1] Equality was also observed in

[1] Quoted by Jules Prudhommeaux, *Icarie et son Fondateur, Etienne Cabet*, Paris, 1907, p. 175.

dress and housing, for both were designed by community boards and produced in complete uniformity.

Cabet, in the spirit of the French Revolution, made a place for religion, which became a cult of reason, together with generous allowance for praise of the founder, the "good Icar, benefactor of the workers, benefactor of families, benefactor of the citizens."[2] In addition, he provided for a rather rigid patriarchal family structure, with presumed equality of women, and something akin to the maturity rites of preliterate communities, as young people completed their compulsory state schooling and training and prepared to become full-fledged citizens. Despite the importance of the family, education was to be in the hands of the state and, foreshadowing one of the "scientific" measures of the Hitlerian Utopia, a committee of scholars and doctors would authorize or forbid marriages on eugenic grounds.

In Icaria all were happy and prosperous, and the common sins of mankind had disappeared, including marital infidelity. If this Utopia should nevertheless seem unpromising, or, at best, horribly boring, it should not be forgotten that it was for the good of mankind, which was grateful—and free. Cabet defined liberty as "no more than the right to do all that is not forbidden by Nature, Reason and Society, and to abstain from all that is not commanded by them."[3]

Here, then, is a brilliant union of equality and what we should call tyranny. But tyranny is an adaptable quality, and Saint-Simonism offers a good example of the union of tyranny with hierarchy in Utopian thought. Henri-Claude de Rouvroy de Saint-Simon, scion of one of the great families of the ancient nobility of France, cousin of Louis de Saint-Simon, acidulous eighteenth-century chronicler of the Court of Versailles, borrowed from the spirit of Francis Bacon's New Atlantis (1622) rather than from More. Saint-Simon was a passionate reformer whose target was merely the whole of Western civilization. In the process of appealing for a new rule of wisdom and science, and for conversion to his new religion, he spread so broad and turbulent a wake as to confuse the course

[2] Cabet, Voyage en Icarie, Paris, 1846, p. 54.
[3] Cabet, Icarie, p. 404.

he was sailing. Saint-Simonism, the religion and the socialist doctrine, was perfected by disciples, notably Rodrigues, Enfantin, and Bazard, and while their handiwork was assuredly attended with chaos and a fitting touch of madness, there was no lack of clarity.

Saint-Simon himself was an excellent example of that naïve "scientism" which the nineteenth century nurtured and the twentieth has yet to cast off. The law of gravity was not only universal, but explained everything in the universe: in fact, it was almost equivalent to God in Saint-Simon's philosophy. From identifying natural law with divinity it was but a short step to the proposition that human society should be ruled scientifically. Social affairs were therefore to be directed by the ablest technicians of industry, finance and commerce. This group, the Executive Chamber of his system, was to take counsel with the Chambers of Invention and Examination, composed of scientists, engineers, scholars, and artists. Wisdom, thus organized for practical action, would govern mankind in peace and increasing plenty. Since such problems as war were considered solved, the chief function of government would be planning public improvements, particularly canals, for which Saint-Simon had a special penchant.

The high store Saint-Simon set upon the engineering outlook, strongly suggestive of the Technocracy of the 1930's, is displayed in his famous *Parable*, which contrasts the effect upon France of the sudden loss of three thousand technicians, artists, and scholars with that of the loss of thirty thousand nobles, ministers, clergy, and landlords. In the latter event, there would be much sorrow, but the state would carry on. In the former, however, the blow would be paralyzing, and it would take the nation years to recover.

But mere technical efficiency was not the entire aim of this prophet. A moral regeneration was necessary, and this called for a reform of religion. Saint-Simon believed that Christianity had done well in its day, but was no longer effective, and in *Le Nouveau Christianisme* he made appropriate suggestions for its improvement. He conceded the perfection of the Word of God, but denied the divine nature of the many extensions therefrom added by the clergy of organized religion. Christianity, in effect, reduced itself to the commandment, "Men should behave as brothers to each other." This implied that the aim of religion was to "direct society towards the great objective of improving as rapidly as possible the lot of the poorest class." The leaders of the Christian church, accordingly,

. . . should be chosen among the men most capable of directing the projects whose aim is the increase of the well being of the most numerous class; thus the clergy should concern itself principally with teaching the faithful the paths they should follow to increase the well being of the majority of the population.[4]

Thus far we have at most a faint suggestion of socialism; Saint-Simon's proposal is rather to entrust the running of society to a group of learned and efficient men, undoubtedly headed by himself. The leaders were imbued with a love for the masses of mankind, whom they would organize on a hierarchical basis for optimum output—perhaps enlightened managerial dictatorship. The socialism, with characteristic Utopian trimmings, was supplied by his disciples after the Master's death.

Saint-Simon had been extremely vague on the question of private property, the root of all evil to most socialists, but had been clearly antiequalitarian. Bazard, Enfantin and the others found in the abolition of all inheritance the solution to the dilemma of reducing the harm of property without instituting an equalitarian system. In this way the luck of birth would be evened out, and all would have equal opportunity to demonstrate the capacities which would lead to their selection by the chief engineers for high positions in society.

As it happened, the Saint-Simonians organized themselves as a Family, with an inner directing College, all headed by two Fathers, Bazard and Enfantin, as combined high priests, scholars, scientists, and managers. They attracted a brilliant youthful group, who literally worshiped them. Enfantin, who had devised a unique vest which could not be put on without assistance, demonstrating the Saint-Simonian principle of interdependence and association, wore the words *"Le Père"* across his chest, and affected a beard in the manner of a Renaissance painting of Christ. As an example of the

---

[4] Saint-Simon, *Son Premier Écrit; Lettres d'un Habitant de Genève à ses Contemporains, 1802; Sa Parabole Politique, 1819; Le Nouveau Christianisme, 1825; Précédés de Fragmens de l'Histoire de sa Vie écrite par Lui-même; Publiés par Olinde Rodrigues, Son Disciple, Chef de la Religion Saint-Simonienne,* Paris, 1832, pp. 104, 108.

extreme devoutness of the sect, Rodrigues, on one occasion, uttered the following credo (he later led a schism):

> In the name of the living God, who was revealed to me by Saint-Simon, the ancestor of all of you, and mine in particular, my first act of faith here must be to proclaim you, Enfantin, the most moral man of my time, the true successor of Saint-Simon, the supreme chief of the Saint-Simonian religion.

The Saint-Simonian newspaper, *le Globe*, had earlier carried this appeal to listen to the words of the Master "as the apostles of a new Evangile, of the eternal Evangile of which that of Jesus was but the sublime preface."[5]

Unfortunately, the Saint-Simonian religion, which was the energizer of Saint-Simonian engineering, collapsed. The Master had mentioned that women should be absolutely equal with men. When the disciples tried to give this injunction a precise definition, they ran into trouble. While upholding the idea of marriage, Enfantin also seemed to recommend promiscuity, and first Bazard with a number of followers and then Rodrigues left the group. Enfantin insisted that the precise place of women could be decided, on the principal of equality, only when "la Mère" arrived to take the chair Bazard had vacated. But the "Lady-Messiah" did not appear, despite a pilgrimage to Egypt in search of her.

If this seems to exceed even the appropriate limits of Utopianism, it must be said that the venture to Egypt led to a project for a canal at Suez, in which de Lesseps for a time coöperated with the Saint-Simonians. Indeed, the only fitting subscript to any discussion of Saint-Simonianism, is that when the group returned to individual careers in the non-Utopian life of France, they were outstandingly successful as bankers, engineers, and writers.[6]

Saint-Simon did not have a seller's monopoly of Utopian socialism in the France of the first half of the nineteenth century. Aside from Cabet, there was Charles Fourier, the wildest and perhaps most in-

[5] See the reproduction of a print of Enfantin, Sebastien Charléty, *Histoire du Saint-Simonisme 1825–1864*, Paris, 1931, facing p. 136; pp. 87, 135.

[6] Among those connected with Saint-Simon or the Saint-Simonians at one time or another were the philosopher Auguste Comte, the engineer and economist Michel Chevalier, Buchez, who was president of the Constituent Assembly of 1830, and Hippolyte Carnot, member of the Provisional Government of 1848 and father of a President of the Third Republic.

fluential of them all. Fourier was keenly aware of the competition his discoveries regarding the true will of God faced at the hands of such patent frauds as the Saint-Simonians and such patent failures as Robert Owen. He denounced them, and accused them of borrowing from him without due acknowledgment. This was true, to a point, for Enfantin's ideas on women and marriage owed much to Fourier. Furthermore, neither Saint-Simon nor Fourier believed in equality. Fourier was actually much more conservative than his illustrious competitor, for while the Master's disciples asphyxiated private property by terminating the right of inheritance, Fourier believed in property and in capital. On the other hand, it has been claimed that it was Fourier who copied Owen.

It will help, in considering Fourier, if it is at once agreed that he was quite mad, harmlessly, of course, and delightfully, but nonetheless mad. The question then arises, how did the ravings of a madman become important? Fourier had the genius that often accompanies mild insanity: he pounced upon the weak points of contemporary society, and his dream world contained flashes of insight that seduced good folk into trying to materialize it, shorn of its lunatic tassels.

Unlike Saint-Simon, Fourier had no respect for the savants of the age. Moralists, metaphysicians, economists were no more than stones on the road to truth that he, Fourier, had kicked aside. "I do not claim," he wrote,

. . . that my vision is great, because it extends where yours has not reached: I have done what a thousand others could have done before me, but I marched to the goal alone, without equipment and without beaten tracks. I alone shall have confounded twenty centuries of political imbecility; and it is to me alone that present and future generations will owe the beginning of their great happiness. Before me, humanity lost several thousand years fighting insanely against nature; I am the first who bowed before her, in studying attraction, instrumentality (*organe*) of her secrets: she has deigned to smile upon the sole mortal who has offered incense to her, she has revealed to me all her treasures. Professor of the book of destiny, I come to scatter the political and economic shadows, and upon the ruins of the uncertain sciences, I erect the theory of universal harmony.

"Exegi monumentum aere perennius."[7] This modest statement appears in the middle of Fourier's first book: preceding and following it are a bizarre cosmology and a plan for an ideal community which, once established, would be imitated until 2,985,984 of these "Phalansteries" constituted the only form of social organization on earth. Fourier believed that the planet had a life of some eighty thousand years, half of "ascending vibrations" and half of "descending vibrations." His age, and ours, was in the fifth stage—civilization —of the ascending scale. Civilization would shortly yield to "guarantism," in which human rights would actually be enjoyed, and then the world would move into the era of "harmony."

The age of harmony was something out of an opium smoker's fondest dream. It was to result from the will of God, the vision of which had been grasped by mankind with Fourier's assistance. The universal law ordained by God is that of attraction (Newton's gravity), and it will come fully into its own in the age of harmony. Each age is in effect a new creation by God, and in the age of harmony there will be a number of marked differences in His arrangements for the natural world. For example, the aurora borealis will in some fashion distribute great warmth to northern climes; lions will be beasts of burden, and whales will pull ships across the seas; the latter, not to be outdone, will consist of delicious lemonade (*de gustibus non est disputandum*); and, to top it off, there will be six live moons to replace the present dead one.

Assuredly, Fourier was not read for such enlightenment as this. The same law of attraction and conception of the will of God that produced these fancies led to a social philosophy that was very influential. As applied to human beings, the law of attraction meant that institutions must correspond with the various facets of human nature so that, when the impulses of mankind had been liberated in

[7] "I have reared a monument more enduring than bronze," Horace's estimation of his poetry. *Théorie des quatre Mouvemens et des Destinées générales: Prospectus et Annonce de la Découverte*, Leipzig, 1808, p. 268. According to Alexander Gray, *The Socialist Tradition, Moses to Lenin*, p. 174, Fourier's book was not printed at Leipzig, apparently a private mystification that must have pleased Fourier. It may have been an echo of the eighteenth-century practice of falsifying the place of publication in order to avoid prosecution by the French censorship. On Fourier, see also the excellent introduction by Charles Gide, *Selections from the Works of Fourier*, Julia Franklin, trans., London, 1901.

this fashion, a most productive harmony would result. Fourier ordained the existence of twelve "passions," which we might call drives or tendencies, of which three were most important from the social standpoint: the "butterfly" passion (*papillone*) which led men to desire a change of activities; the competitive and intrigue passion (*cabaliste*); a third, the composite passion, defies accurate description, since it really cannot be experienced by one who is still in the state of civilization and has not passed into that of harmony. It would seem to be the capacity to experience manifold pleasures in one circumstance, which would obviously derive from the fact that all the circumstances were in harmony.

Fourier's social scheme was based upon the way in which the law of attraction operated principally through the first two passions, although the other ten were also utilized. Since man likes to flit from one task to another, like a butterfly from blossom to blossom, he will work best and most happily if he engages in dozens of different activities, each for no more than two hours. For example, one Lugas worked in the stables from 4 to 5 A.M., in the garden from 5 to 7, in the reapers' group from 7:30 to 9:30 (following breakfast at 7), in a vegetable greenhouse from 9:30 to 11, and so on including amusements from 9 P.M. to bedtime at 10. Like the school child who switches from arithmetic to spelling to history to geography, etc., every forty minutes or so, Lugas would presumably never be bored, and as we know from the behavior of school children, would therefore be industrious in each enterprise.

The competitive or cabalistic instinct would, by the process of association, be transformed from the war of each against all, which hampers efficiency, into an instrument for getting the best out of everyone. Since all work would be group work, the groups would vie with one another for the plaudits of the Phalanstery. This principle would naturally extend to the arts, and Fourier gives a vibrant picture of the contest between an art group from a Japanese Phalanstery and one from Persia, for the edificiation of the members of a Parisian community. He also describes brilliant and dramatic contests between groups of cooks, for Fourier, who was poor, was deeply interested in the predominantly French art of gastronomy.[8]

The law of attraction also took care of other matters that com-

[8] Obviously a prototype for Soviet "socialist competition." See p. 445.

monly disturb those who live in the state of civilization. Particularly ingenious is the solution to the problem of unruly children with a liking for dirt. These would be organized into little Hordes, and would be assigned—obviously—to the dirty work of the community. Angelic children, on the other hand, for Fourier was willing to concede in principle that there might be such, would handle gentler tasks, including their favorite occupation of admonishing their elders when guilty of a lapse in manners.

Thus the Phalanstery, comprising 1,620 persons of various categories, would run in perfect harmony. Its products would be distributed $\frac{1}{3}$ to capital, $\frac{1}{4}$ to talent, $\frac{5}{12}$ to labor. All would be guaranteed a minimum, and the rate of return on investment would be higher for the poor than the rich. In the long run, all would own approximately equal shares of the increasing wealth of the Phalanstery. As the communities spread, there would be greater exchange and coöperation among them, and peace and happiness would reign on earth in accordance with the will of God.

Without going into any further details of Fourier's lush daydream, the Phalanstery building itself, community eating, the various arrangements governing relations between the sexes which legalized what people in the state of civilization would call promiscuity or, perhaps, free love, without further exploration of the mad embroidery, let us extract what seemed at least likely and significant in the fabric itself. Unlike Cabet and the later Saint-Simon, who stressed failings of distribution, Fourier aimed at a reform of the system of production, in which association rather than individualism would bring about higher levels. He was an early critic of the waste which could be ascribed to middlemen in the distributive process, and this theme has continued to be chanted to the present day. The Phalansteries were, in a sense, linked producers' and consumers' coöperatives. He favored decentralization, both in social organization and in living, and preached a flight from overgrown cities at a time when the flight from the countryside was still in full swing. In a way he foreshadowed the syndicalism that was to gain great strength in Latin Europe, and the Guild socialism that was to arise in modern Britain.[9] The very least that can be said is that he helped greatly toward making socialism a common topic of conversation.

[9] See p. 575.

To turn from Fourier to Robert Owen is to move from the bench of a park orator to the carpeted reception room of a philanthropist. Owen's schemes were failures, but they were the failures of an eminently successful and competent man of affairs who pressed his schemes too hard on the heels of his visions. Owen had been apprenticed to a milliner as a child of ten, and then employed by a haberdasher. At eighteen he had his own business, at twenty he was manager of a large textile mill, and at twenty-eight he was part owner and executive of the great New Lanark Mills in Scotland and married to the former proprietor's daughter.

It was at New Lanark that Owen's career as a social reformer began, from business as well as humanitarian motives. He had earlier noted the contrast between the care lavished on machines and the disregard for the welfare of labor, the "living machinery." This was particularly the case with the employment of young children of working-class families, or of pauper children secured from the workhouses. Owen believed, and clearly proved, that his plant would operate more efficiently and yield a higher return, if working hours were reduced from the thirteen that were general, if living conditions of the laborers' families were improved, and if children were given greater education of a more intelligent type than the rote memorization that prevailed.

Owen carried out these objectives at New Lanark. Workers' housing was improved and standards of cleanliness were enforced. The company store was transformed from the excess profit sideline such enterprises frequently are into a nonprofit distributing agency. Schooling was expanded, and the children were taught dancing and singing as well as reading and writing. The old system of rewards and punishments was abandoned, and skilled teaching instilled in the pupils a respect and real interest in participating in their common task. They were encouraged to ask questions, and to understand rather than memorize.

As may be surmised, education was the heart of Owen's plan for reform and his eventual socialism. He believed that while each person was individual and different from the other, environment and education could either improve or worsen all. His great principle was, therefore, "that the old collectively may train the young collectively, to be ignorant and miserable, or to be intelligent and happy" and "the government of any independent community may form the individuals of that community into the best, or into the worst characters."[10]

From this determinist view of human nature that nevertheless allowed full sway for the rule of reason, Owen naturally proceeded to the question of how to change the environment. As an immediate measure he suggested higher wages, for he believed that the mechanization of industry had created unemployment and shrunken demand, which made the workers victims of the wealth they themselves had created. But Owen went far beyond this suggestion and his repeated advice to manufacturers to be more generous with their labor.

In the 1820's, several hundred coöperative societies were formed in accordance with Owen's belief that wealth resulted from labor, and that labor had the means with which to meet its own needs. Members would supply goods to a general store, at which they could buy at cost but where outsiders would pay the market price. Profits would be saved for the acquisition of property on which to establish a full-blown Owenite socialist community. As goods were evaluated for exchange among members in terms of labor, these coöperatives were the prelude to Owen's next great venture, the labor exchange.

Taking his place in the long line of monetary reformers, Owen proposed that currency be based upon labor, and that goods be exchanged on the basis of labor time consumed in their production. In 1832, as a result of his propaganda and promotional activities, the National Equitable Labour Exchange was opened in London. Goods would be deposited and evaluated with respect to materials and labor in ordinary British pounds, which would then be translated into a labor-time denominator, and a labor note would be issued to the depositor. This note would then be used as currency to purchase other goods, and thereby the whole "money mystery," as Owen called it, would be dispensed with.

The Exchange did not succeed, of course, for it was a distinct and arbitrary monetary system existing within the general system of

[10] Robert Owen, *A New View of Society; or, Essays on the Formation of the Human Character Preparatory to the Development of a Plan for Gradually Ameliorating the Condition of Mankind,* London, 4th ed., 1818, p. 122.

money based on gold. Evaluations were arbitrary and uneven, and tended increasingly to be mere translations of ordinary market prices. The notes, for a time, even had limited circulation among unaffiliated tradesmen in working-class districts, but deposits of goods began to fall off, and the Exchange passed away after a life of two years. It was immediately followed, however, by another of Owen's great schemes, the Grand National Consolidated Trades Union, which resembled the modern Guild socialism of G. D. H. Cole.

The Grand National Union was founded in 1834. Owen had written: "We have long since discovered that as long as master [employer] contends against master, no improvement either for man [employee] or master will be possible. There is no other alternative, therefore, but national companies for every trade."[11] Each trade would form a company, and related trades would join in families of associations. These unions were to include owners as well as workers, and eventually become a state within a state, replacing the system of political representation. The Grand National leapt toward a membership of over half a million in several weeks but then, faced with bitter opposition from employers and government, declined and died.

To this list of Owen's failures must be added New Harmony, the colony in Indiana which was to demonstrate to the world the perfection of his scheme for socialist communities, the ultimate toward which all his work and all his other ventures were directed. Known derisively as "Owen's parallelograms," the communities were to be housed in buildings forming a large rectangle, with common dining, service and recreation rooms. Outside the rectangle would lie the workshops and the fields. All property was vested in the community, and all work done coöperatively under community direction. Naturally, there would be ample provision for schooling according to Owen's ideas of progressive education.

Owen had purchased New Harmony from a Rappite religious colony that chose to migrate in 1824. In 1825 a varied group of several hundred persons settled on the land, and for a year or two all seemed to go well. But then dissension broke out. The people were not sufficiently homogeneous in background, character, or capacity. Robert Dale Owen, the founder's son, was successful in directing

---

[11] C. E. M. Joad, *Robert Owen, Idealist*, London, 1917 (Fabian Tract No. 182, Fabian Biographical Series No. 7), p. 26.

the educational system, but the erring ways of individualism could not be eradicated from among the elders. The colony was dissolved into five smaller units in 1827, and the following year the senior Owen bade it farewell, having lost most of his fortune, but none of his zeal. A subsequent venture at Queenwood, in England, lasted longer than New Harmony, but also failed, as did the Orbiston Owenite community established by a Scotch businessman named Abram Combe.

Owen died at the age of eighty-seven, in 1858. After leaving New Lanark and a career of certain success in the business world, he spent his life preaching, with diminishing results. His atheism and advocacy of liberalized divorce lost him much of the prestige and audience his earlier success had brought. Yet his influence has been widespread and lasting. Consumer's coöperation, the labor union movement, syndicalism, and all types and degrees of socialism since have to a greater or lesser degree borne his stamp.

In all, Utopian socialism created much more flurry than accomplishment. Aside from New Harmony, Cabet's colony at Nauvoo, Illinois, and the Fourierist communities of Brook Farm, near Boston, and the Phalanx of Red Bank, New Jersey, all failed after the initial brilliant promise of a perfect life. Comparison between Utopian colonization, based upon dreams that were at least in many ways noble, which foundered so consistently, with the colonization of ordinary merchants and settlers, based frequently upon the most sordid motives, yet so successful, might argue for the inherent evil of man, or of the world. On the other hand, it might only suggest that a debased mankind was not ready to hear the message. Their communities a pathetic failure, the great achievement of the Utopians was to create an intellectual ferment. But it was not their general variety of socialism, featured by concepts of peace and harmony, that profited from the interest and zeal they aroused. They were the unwitting benefactors of Marxism, the socialism of class struggle and revolution.

NOTES ON BOOKS

Alexander Gray's *The Socialist Tradition, Moses to Lenin* is scholarly and extremely well written. It is recommended both as an informative **and** enjoyable book. Other useful treatments are J. O. Hertzler's *The History of Utopian Thought* and H. W. Laidler's *Social-Economic Movements, An Historical and Comparative Survey*. On individual Utopians, there are A. J. Booth's *Saint-Simon and Saint-Simonism*, Charles Gide's able introduction to his *Selections from the Works of Fourier*, G. D. H. Cole's *Robert Owen*, and B. L. Hutchins' *Robert Owen, Social Reformer* and C. E. M. Joad's *Robert Owen, Idealist*, Fabian Tracts 166 and 182. And the Utopians themselves are nearly always interesting.

9.

FROM HEGEL AND RICARDO TO MARX AND ENGELS

The Utopians were the reason Marx and Engels entitled their *Manifesto* of 1848 "communist" rather than "socialist." They felt they were the first to present to a waiting world the true laws of the historical development of society, past, present, and future, and they did not wish to be linked with these vain dreamers or their colonies, vainer still. They regarded themselves as the first wholly objective social scientists, and, instead of envisioning harmonious life under a reformed sky, they did research, and published their conclusions as the results of correct analysis of accurate data.

They claimed to be the first true scientists of society: they still are, to people numbering in the many millions, whose leaders affirm that Marx and Engels established the uniquely correct explanation of the course of mankind.

However dispassionately one approaches the study of Marxism, this is one assertion that must be rejected. Scientifically successful hypotheses tend to become universally accepted as generalizations of fact. Newton surely had few doubters after a century, but Marxism continues to be a subject for acrimonious dispute. We shall therefore have to proceed on the assumption, however shocking to Marxist propriety, that the two prophets *may not* have been all-knowing, indeed, that they *may* conceivably have been partly wrong. This assumption facilitates matters, for it is very difficult to analyze perfection critically.

Marxism was compounded of the metaphysics and philosophy of history of Hegel, the economics of Ricardo and the classical school, the reforming spirit of the Utopians together with at least a glimmer of their love for painting and predicting a new era, and, strange perhaps in this company, the ancient ethics of the Judao-Christian tradition.

Georg Wilhelm Friedrich Hegel (1770–1831) was a German philosopher and Professor at the University of Berlin. It is no exaggeration to say that he has exerted a direct and tremendous influence on spokesmen for almost every type of social outlook. Aside from Marx and Engels and their progeny, the intellectual descendants of Hegel include the French syndicalist Sorel, the Italian liberal philosopher and historian Benedetto Croce, the fascist Benito Mussolini, the eccentric German philosopher Oswald Spengler, and even Arnold Toynbee. The extremes of left and right, and Toynbee in the middle![1]

Hegel's seductive quality was twofold. To an age torn by the French Revolution and Napoleonic wars he offered not just another reiteration of natural order and harmony but a philosophy that built system and certainty out of the very kind of conflict and struggle through which his readers had lived. To an epoch that had seen intellectual certainty challenged by the scepticism of David Hume and only partially restored by Immanuel Kant, Hegel reasserted the invincibility and universality of reason.[2] And he offered not merely

[1] In an editorial of February 23, 1948, *Life* contrasts the false deification of history of Hegel and Stalin with the inspired truth of Toynbee. While any adherent of Western civilization would unquestionably prefer to live under the aegis of Toynbee than Stalin, Toynbee, unbeknownst to the editors, betrays many of the major symptoms of Hegelian philosophy. The fact is that Hegel can be what you wish him to be, just as Aristotelian or Thomistic reasoning can be used to defend either monarchy or representative government, depending upon how you go about it, and despite the personal preferences of Aristotle and St. Thomas.

[2] Hume had argued that general ideas, such as causality, are not objective truths, but rather concepts whose validity rests upon custom and habit. If this were the case, human reason could have no hope of discovering absolutely true ideas, or of developing a philosophical system that would comprehend all of reason and reality. There were many, and still are, who find this admission of weakness intolerable, impossible to live with because it can be made to imply that man is not master of his environment, and because it warns of the humiliating uncertainty of human knowledge. There were some who reacted to Hume's cannonade by a renewed emphasis on faith, which is immune to assault by criti-

a social philosophy, but, going back to the very basis of thought, a new, noncommonsense logic. In place of the tedious method of classification and syllogism, which had become traditional in the Western world and still is, Hegel presented the dialectic. This word has been used to refer to a good many different things, including simple disputation. It has a special meaning in Hegel, and a different one in Marx. The Marxian version is relatively understandable, since, as always with Marx, it refers directly to concrete social situations. The Hegelian dialectic, however, is a wonderful creation, born of an ecstasy of pure and completely disembodied reason. Hegel's world and language are as far from daily life as poor Fourier's state of harmony. In addition, it must be confessed that while Fourier, and even great philosophers can make attractive reading, Hegel simply repels. For example,

> But in that the Spirit is the true Something, and Nature therefore in itself is only what it is in regard of (Gegen) the Spirit, its quality, so far as it (Nature) is taken *per se*, is just this,—to be the Other in itself, The out-of-itself-Beënt. . . .
>
> The Other by itself is the Other in itself, so the Other of itself, so again the Other of the Other; so, therefore, that which within itself is Unequal simpliciter, that which negates itself, that which *alters* and others itself. . . .
>
> Something *maintains* itself in its non-There-being; it is essentially *one* with it, and essentially *not one* with it. It stands, therefore, in *reference* to its Otherwise-being; it is not absolutely its Otherwise-being.[3]

This can be understood in context, when the unique language of Hegelese has been mastered. As it happened, it became a second

---

cal reason. Kant, reserving the autonomy of reason, divested it of the power to impose order on conditions of existence. Hegel, however, met the attack head on, by proclaiming reason an absolute universal. The dogmatism of Hegelian, and indeed, German philosophy in the early part of the nineteenth century is understandable in view of the need for system and certitude that a generation of chaos had induced. Hegel still cherished the ideal of freedom that had originally given the French armies an extraordinary appeal in German society. But he linked it with a strong argument for order and a tedious assertion of the supremacy of reason. He was a rather striking example of a philosopher's effort to meet a real challenge and trial with a new system of words-in-themselves.

[3] From the Complete Logic, in J. H. Stirling, *The Secret of Hegel: Being the Hegelian System in Origin, Principle, Form and Matter*, London, 1865, vol. 1, p. 372. Original italics.

language for all too many Germans, including Marx, and helps account for the modern German tendency to cumbersome word spinning and capacity for self-befuddlement through overgeneralized abstractions. One of the by-products of the study of Hegel would seem to be a disrespect for the ordinary usage of words.

It would be out of the question to offer a systematic summary of Hegel's philosophy. He gave his followers a way of thinking and some specific judgments on economic and political matters, and these are our major concern. Some contemporary Marxists have gone too far in discounting his influence upon their master, however, and to see Marx in proper proportions it is essential to consider the main lines of the Hegelian structure. Hegel was an objective idealist, which means that he believed ideas had real existence, like the physical world of ordinary common sense, even if there were no one to think them. Furthermore, he held that the world of ideas and nature was one of struggle. This struggle, which Marx translated into the war of social classes, was in Hegel's scheme a series of conflicts in logic, between ideas. It was almost a system of grammar. According to Hegel, each finite object, quality or abstraction is defined by its limits and opposites. For example, Being (not this or that being, but Being in general), Hegel's first category, is defined by its opposite, Non-Being. Being cannot be conceived of except in terms of Non-Being; in thinking of Being one is *logically* driven to think of Non-Being. These two categories imply a third, Becoming, which is a synthesis of Being and Non-Being. It is a synthesis of Being (thesis) and Non-Being (antithesis) for both are contained within it. This is an example of the Hegelian dialectic, in the strictly logical type of application which gives form to all of Hegel's work.

One of the aspects of dialectical conflict is negation, since the qualifying character of each phase is in conflict with the succeeding. Following Engels, a plant is the negation of its seed, and the seeds the plant produces are the negation of the negation. Or, for that matter, bourgeois capitalism was the negation of feudalism, but produced the proletariat whose revolution will be the negation of the negation. If this should appear to be a singularly complex way of expressing the well-known fact of continuity in change, it is at least much more impressive.

Another aspect of the dialectic important to both Hegel and Marx is the concept of the struggle of each element for total realization of itself, which was defined as freedom. For example, take the concept whisky-and-soda: the whisky is constrained, prevented from attaining a state of pure whiskyness, and so is the soda. The synthesis, whisky-and-soda, is higher than either element, but perpetuates both.[4]

Finally, after wading through a dialectical marsh of logical categories, Hegel reached the Absolute, which comprised them all. This was the Idea, struggling to be completely free. In this state of complete freedom, it would be fully conscious of itself, hence it would itself be Freedom. Since the process of the Idea fighting its way to self-realization takes place in the realm of consciousness, the history of this struggle is displayed in the history of conscious beings, mankind. "The history of the world," said Hegel, "is none other than the progress of the consciousness of freedom." Translated, this means that history is the progress of freedom in men's minds, to the point where all men have attained the knowledge "that Mind—man as *such*—is free." Since the highest materialization of the Idea through consciousness is the state, history records the progress of state forms till they have reached the stage in which all are free. In states that have attained this blessed stage, the Idea having realized itself, the dialectic comes to a halt.

This train of thought could easily lead to a nice, logical Utopia, but with Hegel it ended in a justification of the status quo. The explanation lies in his view of property. Everything and every person —every entity—strives dialectically to triumph over the fact that its qualities and characteristics create what he calls its "otherness." It struggles to impose itself upon that which limits its freedom, to become "itself in its otherness" (*Bei-sich-selbst-sein-im Anderssein*). Man, facing the material world of things, strives to overcome them, to instill his will into them by directing them to his own ends. The act of appropriating private property was thus the first concrete manifestation of individual will, or reason, and therefore of freedom. Man has asserted his freedom by appropriating, that is excluding

[4] Lenin's more abstenious example concerned a glass of water, which was characterized by its use. It was a glass in the ordinary sense of the word if used to drink water, but was a cylinder if employed to confine a captive butterfly. As a materialist, of course, Lenin was not concerned with pure "glassness" (*Selected Works*, New York, 1934, vol. 9, pp. 62 ff.).

others from, his property and by imposing his will upon it. But, being aware of freedom, he accepts its manifestation as law, and, to Hegel, nearly all civil and criminal law is essentially law of property, and the state is the guarantor of property.

Hegel believed men to be ruled by self-interest, which he called passion, as well as reason. In the ancient Oriental despotism, only one man was apparently free, and not even he. Since there was no limitation on the despot's passion, his freedom was mere caprice. The Greeks and Romans had consciousness of freedom, but also kept slaves, and therefore knew only that some were free. "The German nations," pronounces Hegel, "under the influence of Christianity, were the first to attain the consciousness, that man, as man, is free: that it is the *freedom* of Spirit [mind] which constitutes its essence."[5]

What does this mean? What did Hegel mean by freedom? Words can be exploited more ruthlessly than any proletariat, and they cannot strike or rebel. Freedom and democracy especially have been martyred. Once Hegel had defined appropriation of property as the first act of freedom, the role of the state (aside from materializing the Idea) as protecting property, and had distinguished between passion and reason, it was very easy and quite logical for him to redefine freedom as submission to an authoritarian state.[6]

While Hegel would probably have disliked Hitler, and the Nazis were explicit in their dislike for Hegel (largely because of his relationship to Marx), he did present a case for a system far in excess

---

[5] *Philosophy of History*, J. Sibree, trans., New York, 1899, p. 18.

[6] I realize that there is a good deal of dispute as to whether or not Hegelian freedom ultimately meant freedom as commonly known in the Western world. Herbert Marcuse argues that Hegel's philosophy should have led to freedom in this sense, but that Hegel was "guilty not so much of being servile as of betraying his highest philosophical ideas" (*Reason and Revolution, Hegel and the Rise of Social Theory*, New York, 1941, p. 218). While the point is at least debatable, it is a wise rule to interpret specific portions of a philosophy in the light of its general tenor. Hegel's tone is statist, not individualistic: the general dominates the specific, collective authority is glorified at the expense of individualism. On this basis I do not see how a serious case can be made for Hegel as an apostle of liberty as the word is generally understood in at least the English-speaking world. Ernst Cassirer (*The Myth of the State*, New Haven, 1946, chap. 17), takes the view that while Hegel, more than any other philosopher, provided a theory for totalitarianism, this was not his intent. Hegel's readers are free to choose their own interpretation.

of constitutional totalitarianism. Hegel was acutely aware of the social deficiencies of his time, the very ones upon which the Utopians and Marx were to seize, and he therefore felt that the law, while defending property, tolerated excesses of selfish passion which caused injustice. His solution was simple: the police would become a positive force for justice! This reflected the German tradition of an honest and conscientious bureaucracy, of which even modern German democrats have been inordinately proud. The state, then, suppressing passion through police action, would liberate reason, producing a freedom not unlike that of an army camp.

In its long progress toward self-realization, the Idea acted through men and nations. Thus, at any given time, there would be one nation whose spirit would serve the Idea, the world-historical nation of the age. Its great deeds would be directed by world-historical men, heroes. Neither the nation nor the individual was conscious of working for the Idea, or the World Spirit, which, Hegel acknowledged as he recorded the evil of history, was not above cunning in guiding selfish actions of individuals and groups to its own ends. Nations which did not serve the Absolute were simply not world-historical, they did not count. The Romans and Greeks had been world-historical, but that was in an earlier stage of the Spirit's self-seeking. It was the Protestant Germans, especially the Prussians, through whom the Idea was achieving its goal. Their religion was indigenous and in harmony with their state system. Prussia had both a monarchical constitution of the type Hegel believed best and a system of law and bureaucracy that made the state supreme.[7]

[7] The Lutheran Reformation had been the crucial event in which the German spirit and the World Spirit began their decisive collaboration, according to Hegel. Luther had contended, very conveniently for the Calvinist absolute monarchs of the Hohenzollern family, that the only real freedom was the inward freedom of the individual's conscience in facing his God, and that external slavery had no impact upon this truth. This conception, of course, promoted splendid obedience to authority in all things that were Caesar's and Caesar was ready to leave untouched those inward freedoms that were of God. Hegel held that the individual will, following passion and being restrained by law (and police), turns inward for full freedom. While Hegel changed his mind several times with respect to the supremacy of state over religion, and with respect to the relationship between inward and external (what the ordinary person might call "real") freedom, he did regard the inward variety as essential to realization of the outward. He believed the Germans were well prepared in this connection.

The Germans were the world-historical people, to whom the Idea had given great and mighty privilege:

> Since history is the embodiment of spirit in the form of events, . . . the stages of development are present as direct national principles. . . . To the nation, whose natural principle is one of these stages, is assigned the accomplishment of it through the process characteristic of the self-developing self-consciousness of the world-spirit. This nation is for a given epoch dominant, although it can make an epoch but once. In contrast with the absolute right of this nation to be the bearer of the current phase in the development of the world-spirit, the spirits of other existing nations are void of right, and they, like those whose epochs are gone, count no longer in the history of the world.[8]

This, of course, was not a simple command to conquer the world; but such an interpretation was easily given in later years when it seemed advisable to make the try. At any rate, Hegel believed that with the German ascendancy the Idea would realize itself universally and the dialectic process would automatically cease, there being no more contradiction. This might be called a desiccated Utopia.

Marx and a good many others, we have said, borrowed much from Hegel. Perhaps the most valuable acquisition was his method, for, despite its unique propensity to complicate matters into a negation of the obvious, it produced a strong intellectual curiosity. The dialectic forced men to focus on changing relationships, rather than separate, fixed things or events, on conflict as the source of change, rather than on an imagined mechanical harmony. In this way it led to larger views, the great risk being, of course, that the views would so expand as to rise above reality. Unless one agrees with Hegel to begin with, it is difficult to meet the objection that while the dialectic pattern may assuredly be observed in nature or in the events of society, o may many another pattern. The dialectic is only one way of organizing data and perceptions, it is not inherent in them. It exists, in short, in the mind of the one who employs it, and nowhere in the natural world.

The dialectic can be made to produce whatever one desires of it, and it was not difficult for Marx, the revolutionary materialist, to take over this intellectual device from Hegel, the conservative idealist. It is a bit of a shock at first, however, to find Hegel voicing a

[8] *Hegel's Philosophy of Right*, S. W. Dyde, trans., London, 1896, p. 343.

number of strictly economic judgments that later found their way into the Marxian system.

Starting, as usual, with an involved subject-object relationship, Hegel concluded that the value of labor lies not in the particular production, but in universal, abstract labor. The latter is made material through the exchange of goods, which translates into price their value in abstract labor. But, said Hegel, man becomes a slave to abstract labor and, in a society which is not organized rationally but through the anarchy of the market, mechanization depresses the worker. Furthermore, the labor of some is appropriated by others. From the relations between master and worker, wealth and poverty arise simultaneously:

By generalizing the relations of men by way of their wants, and by generalizing the manner in which the means of meeting these wants are prepared and procured, large fortunes are amassed. On the other side, there occur a repartition and limitation of the work of the individual labourer, and, consequently, dependence and distress in the artisan class. . . . A pauper class arises, and wealth accumulates disproportionately in the hands of a few.[9]

Marx and Hegel reached similar conclusions by very different paths, and where Marx called for revolution as a remedy, Hegel cried for the justice of the police state. But there is no doubt that Marx was struck by Hegel's economic insights as well as by his total philosophy. It would be wrong, however, to think that Marx created a very simple concoction of equal parts of Hegel and Ricardo. Aside from the unusually vituperative style demanded by the Marxist approach, other noteworthy factors had intervened in the generation between the two masters and the *Manifesto* of 1848. Utopian socialism had reached and passed its zenith; the idea of state socialism had been strongly presented by the Prussian Karl Rodbertus; the economic analysis of poverty was being pursued by men of many different persuasions. Of equal importance, for its philosophical influence, was the fact that Hegel's followers had split into two camps, the right, which remained idealist, philosophically speaking, and the left, which became materialist. The materialist left

[9] Quoted by Marcuse, *Reason and Revolution*, p. 205; see also pp. 78 ff., 115 ff.

led by Feuerbach condemned Hegel's logical abstractions, and created a philosophy that centered upon man, rather than the Idea. Marx applauded Feuerbach's advance upon Hegel, but criticized him for not going far enough and continuing to work, if not with the abstract Idea, at least with abstract man.[10]

By 1848, the way had been well prepared for Karl Marx himself, and his great friend and collaborator, Friedrich Engels, his staunch support while he lived, and successor as prophet at his death.[11] Marx wrote about a concrete social situation, not about abstract principles of philosophy. The situation, bourgeois capitalism, had developed historically, and he predicted its demise. Thus the best starting point for a discussion of Marx is the economic interpretation of history, also called the materialist interpretation of history and historical materialism.

Like Hegel, Marx had history moving in a dialectic process to a point of fulfillment, at which conflict would cease. In the materialist Marx, however, there was no talk of the Absolute Idea. The crucial point of his materialism was his belief that "it is not the conscious-

[10] Marx passed over in merciful silence Feuerbach's later degeneration into an absurdly crude materialism which made food the key to all things—"Man is what he eats." Feuerbach hailed the advent of beans as a cure to the fatal weakness brought about by eating potatoes. (See Sidney Hook, *From Hegel to Marx, Studies in the Intellectual Development of Karl Marx*, New York, 1936, chap. 7.)

[11] Karl Heinrich Marx was born in 1818, to a middle-class Jewish family recently converted. He married Jenny von Westphalen, the daughter of a bureaucrat who, like his fathers, had a rebellious streak that enabled him to approve of her marriage beneath her station. After being expelled from Germany for radical activities, Marx finally settled in London, mostly in the British Museum, and with few interruptions remained in England till his death in 1883. He and his family—his devoted wife should certainly be one of the higher martyrs in the Marxist hagiology—lived in poverty. They were supported by Marx's journalistic work (for ten years he wrote articles for the *New York Tribune* of Dana and Greeley), but largely by subventions from the faithful Engels.

Friedrich Engels (1820–1895) was of a prosperous and conservative business family. He met Marx in 1842. During his stay in England as a clerk in the textile firm in which his father was a partner, Engels started his career as a socialist writer. Despite his inclination to spend his life writing and working for the revolution Engels made the sacrifice, and Marx appreciated it as such, of remaining in the textile business, which enabled him to support the Marx family. Engels was always modest, and willing to play second fiddle. He was prepared to admit only "talent" in himself and others, while crediting Marx with "genius."

ness of men that determines their existence, but, on the contrary, their social existence determines their consciousness."[12] In a remark that has become famous, Marx described the dialectic in Hegel as "standing on its head": Marx turned it right side up and placed its feet squarely upon material ground.

Like Hegel, Marx was concerned almost exclusively with the world in its human aspects, hence his materialism was expressed in a dialectic interpretation of history. As Engels said in his funeral tribute to his friend, Marx had "discovered the simple fact, hitherto concealed by an overgrowth of ideology, that mankind must first of all eat and drink, have shelter and clothing, before it can pursue politics, science, religion, art, etc. . . ."[13] Aside from its philosophical implications, this was the old Robinson Crusoe gambit of the classical economists, who loved to start a *Principles of Political Economy* with surmises about the first concerns of a man stranded on an island. Obviously, food, clothing, and shelter came first; or did they? Some strandees might pray to God, others might stamp and curse, and some might commit suicide. In any event, this "discovery," or assumption, was the starting point.

There is no single, thoroughgoing exposition of the Marxian theory of history, and there has been a great deal of dispute among both believers and critics, as to its precise meaning. One of the best statements, however, is that by Engels:

The materialist conception of history starts from the principle that production, and with production the exchange of its products, is the basis of every social order; that in every society which has appeared in history the distribution of the products, and with it the division of society into classes or estates, is determined by what is produced and how it is produced, and how the product is exchanged. According to this conception, the ultimate causes of all social changes and political revolutions are to be sought, not in the minds of men, in their increasing insight into eternal truth and justice, but in changes in the mode of production and exchange; they are to be sought not in the *philosophy* but in the *economics* of the period concerned.[14]

[12] *The Critique of Political Economy*, N. I. Stone, trans., Chicago, 1907, p. 11.
[13] Franz Mehring, *Karl Marx, The Story of his Life*, E. Fitzgerald, trans., New York, 1935, p. 555.
[14] *Herr Eugen Dühring's Revolution in Science (Anti-Dühring)*, E. Burns, trans., New York, 1939, p. 292.

It is in the system of production and distribution, therefore, that we are to seek the explanation for the course of history. In Marxian language, the "instruments of production" (which include equipment and materials, science and technology) shape the "relations of production" (the organization and method of direction and control of human labor), and "instruments" and "relations," which together constitute the "mode of production," shape the "superstructure" of law and government, art and religion, ethics and even science.

This doctrine of economic determinism of history has been subjected to bitter attack from outside the Marxist palisade. It has been claimed, with adequate support in the shape of quotations from Marx or Engels, that the theory really means that technology is the sole causative factor in human history. A second attack is that Marx makes all the noneconomic sides of culture vary directly with the economic. This would seem to make changes in religion and music depend on the latest techniques in making wheels or steam engines. While the supporting quotations are accurate and plentiful, these strictures are not well taken, and Marx is open to enough criticism without adding that which pays little heed to the general tenor of his argument. By "mode of production" Marx certainly meant far more than technics: he included machines and raw materials, the relations among various types of workers and managers, and even the type of distribution or exchange. As for the second argument, Marx was too much of a Hegelian, believing in change and interdependency, to offer any such theory of restricted causation. A fair analogy for his view of the relationship between economic and noneconomic institutions, and one that has the possible advantage of using Marxian terms, would be the determinism of the foundation (*Unterbau*) of a building with respect to its superstructure (*Oberbau*). The foundation determines the size, shape and weight of the building, but does not completely determine the layout of rooms or ornamentation.

Marx tried to see things in their vast and complex interrelationships, and at most he held that the economic factors shape the general character of the noneconomic. Even this would be open to serious objection, however, and at the risk of depending upon a smaller number of quotations, we may amend it to say that the noneconomic such as religion, philosophy, and government, influence the economic, but that the latter are overwhelmingly more important.

But how do the economic institutions exercise this sway? Do not men and their ideas as to what they should do play some part in what is, after all, their lives? Of course. As the Hegelian dialectic of ideas expresses itself through men, so does the Marxian dialectic, through the struggles of men. But where Hegel had his Absolute guiding people through world-historical individuals, great men like Napoleon, Marx talked of classes, not heroes. "The history of all hitherto existing society is the history of class struggles," declares the *Manifesto*. The institution of property, and the division of labor separates men into exploiters and exploited (very much like Hegel). The precise nature of the exploitation, of the relations of production, is governed by the instruments of production. Hand mills call for different relations than do steam mills. Chattel slavery has given way to wage slavery, but there have always been exploiters and exploited. The dialectic, therefore, is the process of the negation of negation, not of ideas, but of classes. The owners of property, the ruling class, shape law and government to their own interests, and, indeed, government may be defined as the means of repression held by the ruling class. Religion expresses their belief, ethics their customs, art their taste, and science serves their practical desires and their type of curiosity.

The exploited, pressed to the point of misery and despair, and conscious of their interests, revolt and overthrow the ruling class. The exploited now become the exploiters, until another class struggle and revolution negates them. Marx pointed to the conflict of "freeman and slave, patrician and plebeian, lord and serf, guild-master and journeyman," and, lastly, bourgeois and proletarian. In the Middle Ages class relationships had been very complex, and so they were in early stages of capitalism, with capitalists, landlords, professionals, *petit bourgeois* and proletarians. But capitalism had the unique quality of simplifying the class structure, and reducing the struggle to one between capitalists and workers. Of this struggle, there would be one survivor, the proletariat.

But what is a class? And how will there be a revolution, unless there are thoughts of revolution? A class is given concrete existence by its ownership or nonownership of the means of production, and by its freedom or lack of freedom as legally and socially recognized. But the relations of production are, in Hegelian terms, only the "ground"; they are not sufficient for the formation of a genuine, Marxian class. For thus far the class exists only by virtue of its differentiation from its antagonist: Hegel would say it "exists in its other." Furthermore, Marx recognizes the force of custom and habit. People will act according to the precepts they have learned, and the exploited will have been taught principles that derive from the superstructure created by the ruling class. This is a force against revolution. But, says Marx, technology and methods of production change more rapidly than and outstrip social institutions. The result is a contradiction within society that causes economic and social distress. The workers will have been taught to obey the laws (of the capitalist state), to respect their leaders (of the capitalist class), to pay more heed to religion (of the capitalist class) and less to earthly troubles. As misery develops, however, material conditions drive the exploited to cast off the fetters of ruling-class indoctrination, to think rationally, and thus to become conscious of themselves as a class. Now they no longer exist in their "other," they exist in and for themselves. Here enters revolutionary theory, for its role is to make the exploited aware of their interests and to enlighten them as to strategy and tactics, following a scientific explanation of how things have come to be and where they are going.

We now have a self-conscious class, ready for revolution for the purpose of its basic physical survival, and we have a theory that teaches them why things are wrong and how they can be made better. The revolution is inevitable, not in the sense that it will happen owing to an external power even if not desired by the workers, but rather because it is inevitable that the proletariat will become conscious of its interests and organize itself into an intelligent, disciplined, and deliberately revolutionary force. But why should the exploited, once awakened to unfettered thought by material suffering, become conscious of themselves as a group? Why should not each try to make the best possible bargain for himself and damn his fellows? At this point Marx introduces an eighteenth-century concept that became the cornerstone of utilitarianism and classical economics: self-interest. They are driven by self-interest to combine as a class. But self-interest, if it means anything, always means self-interest rightly understood, and it must therefore be assumed that Marx's definition of their interest, and his explanation of their conditions upon which his definition rests, was to be taken as "scientific," or uniquely correct.

The growth of the exploited to class consciousness is thus explained, but why should there arise a theory which enlightens them as to their revolutionary destiny? Why should there arise a theorist, Marx for example? The Marxian answer would be that the theory, being strictly scientific, simply arises from the facts, and that if there were no Marx there would be someone else. Perhaps this question of the origin of theory is not too important to Marxian economics, but it is nonetheless disturbing. For example, given a cultural tradition which recognizes (as did Marx and Engels) inequality among men, it might be just as "scientific" to devise a system of hierarchy, as did Plato and Saint-Simon, and private property might then be maintained. "Scientific" Marxism explains that a proletariat is bound to arise and to rebel in its own interest, but this will hold only if we assume to begin with that Marxism is "scientific," uniquely correct, which is obviously circular reasoning. There is only one thing that can decree misery to be wrong, that can spur people to fight, that can lead them to coöperate instead of taking the dog-eat-dog attitude that derives equally well from the principle of self-interest. It is this that explains the appearance of theory, and of Marx: an ethical tradition. People may accept starvation as ineluctable, or eat each other, rather than band against a common enemy, if their ethical and religious tradition leads them to do so. There is no objective truth to a particular conception of self-interest, for self-interest is defined and limited by ethics expressed in religion, custom, and habit. In a word, what Marx did, without recognizing it, was simply to introduce the traditional ethical standards of Christianity, according to which he judged right and wrong, and according to which the proletariat was to understand its class interest. No one can read Marx without being aware that despite his sneers and diatribes against religion and "bourgeois ethics," his caustic and telling denunciations of the sins of capitalism are inspired by a hatred for an injustice that is defined by its "other"—justice as stated in the Decalogue and the Sermon on the Mount.

Returning to the main line of the Marxian thesis, we have passed from the conflict of feudal lord and bourgeois to the capitalist so-

ciety which it ushered in. This capitalism is now doomed, and will
be succeeded by socialism. History has moved into the present, and
economic analysis of the nineteenth century provides the basis for
predicting the next step. Marx's theory of capitalism, outlined in
the *Manifesto* and *Critique of Political Economy*, was more or less
fully developed in the three volumes of *Capital*, the last two of which
were edited and published by Engels after Marx's death. This
analysis, confronting the same problems as met by orthodox economists of the classical tradition, has won not a little respect among the
latter, and has produced limitless controversy. The respect is at least
partly owing to the fact that, while using different words, Marx talks
their language, for he followed Ricardo to one possible logical conclusion. The reason for the controversy is self-evident: Marx calls
into question the continued existence of Western society as we
know it.

According to Engels, the fog of error in the social sciences had
been cleared away by Marx's having made "two great discoveries,
the materialist conception of history and the revelation of the secret
of capitalist production by means of surplus value. . . . With these
discoveries socialism became a science. . . ."[15] However great the
doubts left among nonbelievers by the theory of history, they are as
nothing compared to the troubles of Marx's theory of value, which
has drawn fire from his critics and has caused a horrid grinding
of mental gears among his followers. Some of the latter have tried
to talk it away, saying it was quite unimportant to the whole of his
doctrine, and others have argued that it meant something quite
different from what he said. The first escape must be denied very
firmly: in a system that claims to hold together perfectly, in strictly
scientific fashion, it is not quite proper to discard what its author
regarded as a major part. Furthermore, Lenin, who is a respectable
proletarian authority, says that "the teaching of Marx is all-powerful
because it is true. It is complete and symmetrical." And, he proclaims, "The doctrine of surplus value is the keystone of the economic theory of Marx."[16] The theory must therefore certainly not be
ignored.

---

[15] *Anti-Dühring*, p. 33.
[16] "The Three Sources and Three Constituent Parts of Marxism," in Max
Eastman, ed., *Capital, The Communist Manifesto and Other Writings by Karl
Marx*, New York, 1932, pp. xxi, xxiv.

Essentially, Marx's theory of value is the same as Ricardo's although more detailed and abstract: the value of goods consists in the labor that went into their making. This, of course, resulted from the eighteenth-century proclivity for finding "natural" definitions for everything. All usable goods, unless free in nature, such as air, result from the expenditure of labor upon materials. The materials themselves, such as iron ore, are the product of labor, and machines are also the product of labor. Labor is therefore the common denominator of all production, and all value is an expression of expended labor. Does this explain the value of an emerald stumbled over by some savage in his wanderings? Does it explain the difference between the value of an hour's work by a plumber and of a Cellini? What is meant by value in the case of the emerald is actually not value but price: the second instance Marx handles without too much difficulty.

If we consider the exchange values of a number of commodities, says Marx, we find that the exchange value of grain is different when expressed in terms of iron than when expressed in terms of shoes. But if x grain equals y iron or w shoes, then y iron equals w shoes. In any of these relations "there exists in equal quantities something common to both. . . . Each of them, so far as it is exchange value, must be reducible to this third." This "third" cannot be any of the properties of the article that characterize its utility, for "the exchange of commodities is evidently an act characterized by a total abstraction from use-value." The only thing left is labor, which is common to all commodities. Not their "being products of labor," for rejecting use-value as a denominator means rejecting actual, particular expenditures of labor.

Along with the useful qualities of the products themselves, we put out of sight both the useful character of the various kinds of labour embodied in them, and the concrete forms of that labour; there is nothing left but what is common to them all; all are reduced to one and the same sort of labour, human labour in the abstract.[17]

Like Hegel, the materialist Marx eliminated by a process of abstraction everything from production but a sheer abstraction. An

[17] *Capital, A Critique of Political Economy,* vol. 1, *The Process of Capitalist Production,* S. Moore and E. Aveling, trans., edited by Engels, revised by E. Untermann, Chicago, 1918, p. 45. For a comment on the process of abstraction, see p. 32.

article has value because abstract, undifferentiated human labor has been expended in its creation. Value is therefore to be *measured* in terms of the duration of labor. "As values, all commodities are only definite masses of congealed labour-time." The problem of skilled versus unskilled labor is very easily eliminated, for the former can be regarded as a multiple of the latter: the labor of the skilled craftsman represents the congealed labor time required in his training, and for purposes of analysis all labor can be regarded as average unskilled.

But suppose one unskilled worker takes ten times longer to produce an article than another? Marx introduces into his definition of value the safeguarding qualification of *socially necessary* labor time, "that required to produce an article under the normal conditions of production, and with the average degree of skill and intensity prevalent at the time."[18] This might seem to be rather irrelevant to the class struggle, but its decisive corollary, surplus value, does provide an ethical basis for revolution.

What the worker sells is his labor power, but the capitalist buys much more than he pays for, and this difference yields surplus value. Labor power is purchased at the going rate for laborers, that is, the amount required to maintain customary subsistence, but the worker is at his bench for a longer time than necessary to create just this amount. In addition, he has created value equal to that embodied in the raw materials and the depreciation of machinery. Let us assume that in six hours a worker produces values worth $30 ($5 necessary for his subsistence, $20 necessary to cover raw materials and their embodied labor, $5 to cover wear and tear on equipment); at this stage, says Marx, the capitalist has acquired no more value than he has given up. But the worker is paid for a day, and produces his subsistence in a half day. During the other half he produces surplus value, for if at the end of twelve hours, he has produced values worth $60 ($5 for his subsistence, $40 to cover materials, $10 wear and tear), there will remain a *surplus value* of $5, which the worker has created, but which has been expropriated by the capitalist.

If one objects that the worker might require a full day to meet his subsistence, Marx could readily reply that if this were the case there could be absolutely no accumulation and, since there certainly is

[18] *Capital*, vol. 1, p. 46.

accumulation, this obviously cannot be the case. The theory of surplus value was therefore an excellent theoretical basis for the abolition of capitalism as a system which robs the laborer of part of his creation. What Marx calls the rate of surplus value, the ratio between labor-time necessary to cover subsistence and equipment and the labor-time that yields surplus value, can be held down by labor unions and welfare legislation. Such measures can indeed brake the deterioration of the working class, but they cannot prevent it.

Why this is so is explained by what the capitalist does with the expropriated surplus value he has accumulated. He cannot consume it all, and, in fact, accumulation has become an end in itself for him, so that all his efforts are strained to increasing the quantity of surplus value. To understand this process it is necessary to introduce another of Marx's classifications, this time similar to one used in traditional economics. Marx distinguishes between constant and variable capital. Constant capital comprises "that part of capital . . . which is represented by the means of production, by the raw material, auxiliary material and the instruments of labour, [which] does not, in the process of production, undergo any quantitative alteration of value." Variable capital, on the other hand, is "that part of capital, represented by labour-power, [which] does, in the process of production, undergo an alteration of value."[19] This distinction, of course, rests on the labor theory of value itself. Assuming for the moment that this theory is valid, it will pay the capitalist to have a higher ratio of variable to constant capital, for only the variable can produce surplus value, the object of the capitalist's desires. This would seem to lead the capitalist to employ more labor and fewer machines, but, strangely enough, such is not the case.

There are other ways of increasing surplus value. The capitalist can hire women and children, as competition keeps the price of their labor lower than that of men and machinery makes it equally effective. Or, when this is prevented by law, there is another course, which he actually follows according to Marx. He increases the ratio of machinery to labor for, by enabling the worker to produce his own subsistence in less labor time the capitalist automatically increases the amount of surplus value he can appropriate. The force of competition drives each capitalist to expand his constant capital,

[19] *Capital,* vol. 1, p. 232.

raise its ratio to variable, in the race for higher profits through more surplus value. But what does this mean for the worker? In the long run, the capital that labor and labor alone has created, which the capitalist has expropriated, brings about a decline in the demand for labor relative to capital. Dead labor kills living labor. Thus arises unemployment, and the decline in consuming power that ensues further aggravates it, creating what Marx calls the industrial reserve army, a mass of workers whom the capitalists can hire during periods of prosperity and cast off in depression.

Here we have what Marx regards as one of the great "internal contradictions" of capitalism, as both wealth and poverty increase side by side, as productivity arises along with a decline in consumption. Despite temporary improvements in the conditions of labor resulting from favorable population trends or fortuitous circumstances such as the opening of new possibilities for investment, the working class is condemned to deterioration. This theory of increasing misery—Schumpeter calls it immiserization, with the apology that this is no worse than Marx's *Verelendung*—has given rise to a vast controversy among Marxists, as to whether it means absolute or relative increase in misery. Here again, everyone is free to choose his own supporting quotations, but the general tenor would seem to be in favor of the absolute interpretation.

It is this immiserization which makes the free working class—and freedom in respect of social status is one of the distinguishing features of the capitalist form of exploitation, according to Marx—conscious of its interests as a class, and prepares it for its revolutionary mission. But what of the capitalists? They too are doomed. The Marxian depression theory holds that accumulation of capital increases employment and therefore wages; higher wages mean lower profits, lower profits depreciate capital values and stop accumulation. A crisis develops which brings unemployment and increases the industrial reserve army. The rise in the latter (making low-wage labor available) enhances the possibilities of acquiring surplus value and the economic upswing is on. Thus the business cycle is inherent in capitalism.

In this process small and weak capitalists are destroyed by large and strong, and capital enters into a trend toward centralization. The defunct capitalists sink into the swelling ranks of the proletariat, and the survivors of the competitive game become fewer and more powerful. There is another underlying factor, moreover, which intensifies competition and hastens centralization, and which Marx regarded as tremendously important in his system: "The gradual and relative growth of the constant over the variable capital must necessarily lead to *a gradual fall of the average rate of profit.*"[20] *Total* profits in a capitalist society will rise with the expropriated increased productivity of labor, but this very increase in productivity means that the *rate* of surplus value and of profits will decline. This induces each capitalist to sell more goods at lower prices in order to increase his own expropriation of surplus value, which means greater rationalization and mechanization and, as above, more crises. Thus competition forces the rate of profit down, and leads to greater concentration and centralization and to imperialism, or capital export, in search of a higher rate.

In any event, as time goes on, the process of depression, concentration of capital, and immiserization of labor becomes intensified, and we at last reach the end of the long trail, the collapse of capitalism.

When this "process of transformation has sufficiently decomposed the old society from top to bottom. . . .

That which is now to be expropriated is no longer the labourer working for himself, but the capitalist exploiting many labourers. This expropriation is accomplished by . . . the centralization of capital. One capitalist always kills many. Hand in hand with this . . . expropriation of many capitalists by few, develop . . . the co-operative form of the labour-process, the conscious technical application of science, the methodical cultivation of the soil, . . . the entanglement of all peoples in the net of the world-market. . . . Along with the constantly diminishing number of the magnates of capital, who usurp and monopolise all advantages of this process of transformation, grows the mass of misery, oppression, slavery, degradation, exploitation; but with this too grows the revolt of the working-class, a class always increasing in numbers, and disciplined, united, organized by the very mechanism of the process of capitalist production itself. The monopoly of capital becomes a fetter upon the mode of production, which has sprung up and flourished along with it, and

[20] *Capital*, vol. 3, p. 248. Original italics, qualified by "so long as the rate of surplus value or the intensity of exploitation of labor by capital, remain the same."

under it. Centralisation of the means of production and socialisation of labour at last reach a point where they become incompatible with their capitalist integument. This integument is burst asunder. The knell of capitalist private property sounds. The expropriators are expropriated.[21]

By the time one has reached the close of the first volume of *Capital*, pummeled by eight hundred pages of invective, data, philosophy, and economic analysis, one is almost ready to bow to certainty, and ask the two questions that remain. What will the revolution be like? And what will the New Society be like?

The answers, unhappily, are not as clear-cut as one would wish them to be. The closer Marx approaches to the culmination of his systematic theory, the more cautious he becomes, because he, and Engels, dreaded most of all the pitfalls of Utopianism. Neither wrote a full description of revolution or the new order. There is much talk of bloodshed in Marx's references to the revolution, but there is also mention of the possibility of a peaceful changeover. Once again, the reader can choose. Marx and Engels started out with visions of bloody battle on the barricades, the red flag flying triumphantly over the dead bodies of capitalist lackeys. As the years went on, a smoother transition became possible in some countries, although in 1886 Engels wrote that Marx believed that "at least in Europe, England is the only country where the inevitable social revolution might be effected entirely by peaceful and legal means."[22]

The question is not of very great importance: if the revolution comes we shall certainly know whether or not it is violent. But what will be its outcome? The answers are necessarily given only in general terms. Since the revolution will be in essence political, to make the form of government correspond to the new realities of the economy, we are told that the first phase of the new order will be the dictatorship of the proletariat. This will be a democratic republic, and it will eliminate the vestiges of capitalist oppression. Then will follow the first stage of communism, not perfect, for it will have arisen not on its own bases but from capitalist foundations. In this state, as under the dictatorship of the proletariat, the means of pro-

---

[21] *Capital*, vol. 1, pp. 836–837.
[22] Preface to first English translation of *Capital*, vol. 1, p. 32.

duction will be socially owned,[23] but from the total social product there will be subtracted shares for the replacement of means of production, for their expansion, for insurance against accidents, for the general costs of administration, for public services such as schools and hospitals, for those who cannot work. The vast remainder will be divided, in effect, upon what the bourgeois presume to be the going principle of capitalism, "to each according to his abilities," to paraphrase Marx. Under capitalism this is just a lie to screen exploitation, under stage one of communism it will really work. Then we at last arrive at stage two, and there the visions become understandably even dimmer, for here Marx and Engels ran the greatest risk of Utopianism.

In this "higher phase of Communist society," says Marx,

. . . after the enslaving subordination of the individual to the division of labor shall have disappeared, . . . when, with the development of the individual in every sense, the productive forces also increase and all the springs of wealth flow with abundance—only then can the limited horizon of bourgeois right be left behind entirely and society inscribe upon its banner: "From each according to his abilities, to each according to his needs!"[24]

If this be spelled out, however, we find that our "scientific" socialists have indeed slipped into a Utopianism by comparison with which Fourier seems quite moderate. In fact, their prophecy appears to be an enlargement of Fourier's favorite butterfly passion. Marx and Engels hated capitalist division of labor, which made the machine dominate man, turned skilled labor into unskilled, and was totally degrading, if efficient. In the new society, says Engels, "the former division of labor will disappear," each individual will receive "the opportunity to develop and exercise all his faculties, physical and mental, in all directions; in which, therefore, productive labor will become a pleasure instead of a burden."[25] This may seem too general, or it may be objected that the junior partner can hardly

---

[23] *Personal* private property was under no objection. An equal division of trousers and electric mixers was never implied in any Marxist writings. This is just a common bourgeois misrepresentation.

[24] "The Criticism of the Gotha Program," in Eastman, ed., *Capital,* p. 7.

[25] *Anti-Dühring,* p. 320.

commit Marx, but the following from their joint work, *The German Ideology* (1845–1846), is reasonably clear. Under the division of labor, they wrote, where work is not freely chosen,

. . . man's own deed becomes an alien power opposed to him, which enslaves him instead of being controlled by him. For as soon as labour is distributed, each man has a particular, exclusive sphere of activity, which is forced upon him and from which he cannot escape. He is a hunter, a fisherman, a shepherd, or a critical critic, and must remain so if he does not want to lose his means of livelihood; while in communist society, where nobody has one exclusive sphere of activity but each can become accomplished in any branch he wishes, society regulates the general production and thus makes it possible for me to do one thing to-day and another to-morrow, to hunt in the morning, fish in the afternoon, rear cattle in the evening, criticize after dinner, just as I have a mind, without ever becoming hunter, fisherman, shepherd or critic.[26]

Marx felt that capitalist division of labor led to the production of commodities as an end in itself, and concealed the human relationships that actually were productive. Thus commodities, as exchanged for money, ruled man, and the "mystery" which capitalism attaches to goods, "commodity fetishism," must be dispelled and labor restored to its rightful place. There might seem to be greater mystery in Marx's phrase than in commodities, but it was his laudable stress upon man rather than things that led him to envisage a state in which people would be free to direct their own labor, despite the fact it would be rather difficult to build a Dnieperstroy dam or Moscow subway when the workers were butterflying from carpentry to cattle raising or criticism.

How would leadership and direction be provided in communism, phase two? The curtain over the window to Utopia is drawn tight again. All we are told is that there will be the necessary minimum of administrative organization, that production will result from voluntary coöperation, and as for the state, in Engels' immortal phrase, "it withers away." After the dictatorship of the proletariat has eliminated the remnants of bourgeois form, "as soon as there is no longer any class of society to be held in subjection. . . .

---

[26] R. Pascal, ed., *The German Ideology*, New York, 1939, Parts I and III, p. 22. "Critical critic" is a jibe at a contemporary German intellectual movement.

. . . there is nothing more to be repressed which would make a special repressive force, a state, necessary. The first act in which the state comes forward as the representative of society as a whole [the proletariat]—the taking possession of the means of production in the name of society—is at the same time its last independent act as a state. The interference of the state power in social relations becomes superfluous in one sphere after another, and then ceases of itself. The government of persons is replaced by the administration of things and the direction of the processes of production. The state is not "abolished," *it withers away.*[27]

With a final Hegelian flourish the story ends in a prosperous and harmonious anarchy, there are no internal contradictions in society and the dialectic of class struggle has come to rest.[28] Marxism has given its view of the whole of history as the arduous climb of mankind toward a high plateau where there will be peace and justice amid abundance. It has laid down the economic and historical laws by which man will accomplish his last upward step.

And yet, while Marxism must be respected and even feared for its influence, it need in no wise be accepted on its claims. Aside from the dialectic, which is to persons of non-Hegelian persuasion merely one of many possible patterns imposed by mind upon facts, the economic interpretation of history is not all that it claims to be.[29] In Marx's hands, this formula is inextricably linked with the doctrine of the class struggle, which complicates and even weakens it, but the fundamental assertion that the mode of production in general governs the evolution of society will not bear up. Economic institutions are shaped by legal and political institutions, and by social customs, as well as vice versa. It is useless to ask which came first, for they probably arose together. For example, it would be folly to deny the influence of a Colbert and his system on the French economy, or the part played by the Court of Versailles in directing production toward luxuries. Marx makes the same mistake as the classical economists, forgetting that each individual acts as a whole, and that "institutions" are abstract ideas referring to special aspects

[27] *Anti-Dühring*, pp. 306–307. Original italics.
[28] The dialectic is relegated to the relationship between man and the world of nature over which he is now presumably master.
[29] This is with particular reference to the Marxist variety. There are other, milder types which merely call economics a better key than any other particular aspect of society.

of a number of whole individuals' actions. It is absurd to attribute the power of compulsion to an abstraction of this type.

Apart from such logical objections, how can one apply the economic interpretation to such historical problems as that of the last Tsar of Russia? Had Nicholas II been conspicuously wise rather than stupid, and strong rather than weak, had he been well educated, let us say at Cambridge, and been greatly influenced by John Neville Keynes, he might well have supported rather than fought progressive elements among Russia's middle class and aristocracy. Given the undeniable power of the Tsar, like that of Joseph Stalin, to make binding day-to-day decisions, it is at least conceivable that Russia would have been in far healthier condition in 1914. Of course, the Tsar could not, of his own will, have trebled the Russian standard of living overnight, changed the rate of surplus value, or made the millions of muzhiks adequately baseball- or cricket-minded, but there was much that he could have done and did not do. Without going overboard into the deep blue of a hero theory of history, in the manner of Carlyle, it is surely foolish to ignore the decisiveness of personal qualities so long as there are individuals who have the power to make decisions that control the actions of the many. The Marxist interpretation does just this, however. Engels wrote, "The man has always been found as soon as he became necessary." This expresses in part the sensible proposition that most great men are such by virtue of the popular support they are able to secure, but it tends to ignore the individual's qualities in attracting and holding that support. As Gray observes, "It is indeed by no means overwhelmingly obvious that if Hegel and Marx had died in their infancy, the Hegelian philosophy would have been produced by someone called Schmidt to give a flavour to the three volumes of *Capital*, written by someone named Meyer: on the whole, the chances are against it."[30]

Then too there are historical phenomena which are not readily amenable to a simple economic explanation. Was the German Reformation the effect of the rise of capitalism? If such is the case how are we to account for the fact that it resulted in the subjection of German town capitalism, which dated to the Middle Ages, and to the rule of semifeudal princes? Or consider World War I,

[30] *Socialist Tradition*, p. 307.

which it has been popular to ascribe to economic rivalries among the powers. There were other rivalries, however, and there is the proved fact that at least several of the powers did not want war *at that particular time*. Unimportant, we are told, the war was inevitable, and would have come soon anyway. Perhaps, but unless we resort to a gigantic application of the "other things being equal" clause, it would have been a different war. Had a new liberal revolution succeeded in Russia in 1915, a war beginning in 1920 might have had a radically different outcome, or, indeed, might never have occurred. It is in the nature of a philosophy such as Marx's to be weakest in dealing with short-run phenomena, but such phenomena strongly affect the manifold conjunctures of history, and can influence the deep-lying trends.

The Marxian interpretation of history offers no valid law of historical development but merely a canon for organizing and assessing historical evidence. As such, it is sometimes useful, as is the Hegelian canon, as are others. When wrongly applied, or ill chosen for the task, it is a bad canon, and when applied universally it is bound to be wrong a good part of the time. The nature of society is such that these rigorous canons cannot be applied consistently. Many of the concepts Marx employs, such as "bourgeois," "interest," "private property," have little meaning aside from their foundation in law and convention. His distinction between feudal and capitalist exploitation rests on the *legal* freedom of the wage worker, as against the permanent ties of the serf.[31] The claim that the legal relationships derived from economic factors exclusively would be exceedingly difficult to establish and in reality would result in another futile chicken-or-egg dispute.

But the Marxian interpretation of history is inseparable not only from the dialectic, but from the theory of the class struggle, which helps it not at all. It is undoubtedly a failing of Western thought habitually to regard order and harmony as normal, and crisis and conflict as an erratic intrusion into human affairs. Marx overcorrected this tendency, viewing a state of latent crisis as the norm. At nearly all times, however, the degree of coöperation between classes has been far higher than the intensity of struggle. This has been

[31] See M. M. Bober, *Karl Marx's Interpretation of History*, Cambridge, 2d rev. ed., 1948, pp. 324 ff.

particularly true of capitalist society which, as Marx says, has had a greater record of accomplishment than any other. If this be regarded as a transitory and unimportant phenomenon, there still remains the question of Marx's definition of the class that is to become conscious of its interest and rise in revolution. It was defined in terms of the owning or nonowning of means of production. If we take this literally, a man receiving a yearly salary of $100,000 or more who owns no income-bearing property must be called a proletarian, which is nonsense. Furthermore, if we take the doctrine literally, an employer who himself has to work is not a capitalist, while someone living on a small inheritance is. Were we to sweep away these objections by calling our high-salaried individual a lackey of the capitalists, and the others intermediate and unimportant types, we should face another set of problems.

In the first place, how does capital arise? Marx's explanation is that the original capitalists were in effect robbers and strong men, and that their descendants continued to live on and increase their ill-gotten gains. This is difficult to disprove, for the records of the "beginning" are scanty, but it does not account for the rise of all capitalists in recent centuries. There were many who actually saved from wages and built up their own shops. Perhaps they did have more ability than others, and did show more energy. In that case they would not fit the Marxian theory. Even the initial robbers must have excelled as robbers, unless they possessed a natural monopoly of the capacity to steal, in itself a form of excelling.[32]

In the second place, class consciousness in reality derives from a great many things other than ownership of property. Income is more important, family much more, and in many instances religion or education are defining factors. The most important, perhaps, is consciousness of class itself. Marx's definition of classes exclusively in economic terms, and narrowly at that, led him into the error of minimizing things that have been historically decisive, such as the force of nationalism shattering class lines, and proclaiming a generalization whose greatest virtue is its close fit with the rest of his theory.

The class struggle doctrine does not stand alone in Marx. The proletariat is driven to revolution by its progressive immiserization,

---

[32] Schumpeter's argument in *Capitalism, Socialism and Democracy*, pp. 14 ff. Marx's notion can be found in earlier writers, including Rousseau.

and we are therefore directed into Marxian economics proper. The starting point should be, as it is in Marx, the theory of value. Marx chose abstract labor power as the source and measure of value because he found it to be the only common element to all products. There is another and much less esoteric common factor, however, that became the foundation of the value theory of the neoclassical economists: the human desire to acquire utilities, whether in goods or in services (Marxian theory accounts for the latter only indirectly). Desire creates value, and the willingness to surrender one utility to obtain another explains exchange value. On the scientific (but not Marxian) principle that when the simpler explanation suffices it is to be preferred to the complex, the labor theory would have to be discarded in favor of the psychological. The universality of the desire for utilities can hardly be denied, whereas Marx's labor power is a purely abstract fiction.[33]

Remove the labor theory of value and the whole superstructure of surplus value, accumulation, concentration of capital, immiserization of labor, class consciousness, and revolution comes tumbling down, unless given non-Marxian supports.

The prediction of immiserization need not detain us. The condition of the working class in Western capitalist society has not deteriorated in an absolute sense, and the share to wages out of increasing national income has remained relatively constant. Although proved hopelessly wrong, the prophecy grew logically from Marx's theory, and some Marxists still try to uphold it, in order to save the perfect coherence of the grand system.[34] As for the concentration and centralization of capital, there has been the paradoxical

---

[33] Schumpeter points out that the labor theory would hold only in a state of perfect competition, in which case, however, there could be no explanation for the value of labor itself, "for this would imply that workmen, like machines, are being produced according to rational cost calculations. Since they are not, there is no warrant for assuming that the value of labor power will be proportional to the man-hours that enter into its 'production'" (*Capitalism, Socialism and Democracy*, pp. 24, 27–28).

[34] J. Kuczynski, *A Short History of Labour Conditions Under Industrial Capitalism*, vol. 1, Part I, *Great Britain 1750 to the Present Day*, 2d ed., London, 1944, pp. 11 ff. and elsewhere, tries to prove absolute deterioration. One evidence is declining vitamin content of workers' diets. As if custom had no influence upon quantity and nature of food! Anyone who compares a capitalist banquet menu of 1900 with one of today would, along this kind of reasoning, have to conclude that the meager tables of our time are clear evidence of poverty among the rich.

development of centralization of control, through the giant firm, and diffusion of ownership through widespread securities holding. In any event, expropriated capitalists are frequently dumped, not into the swelling ranks of the proletariat, but into well-paying administrative positions in the expropriator's employ, and, in addition, hold shares in the new and larger firm. The ranks of the middle class, by any realistic test, have not thinned but grown.

The futility of the labor theory led Marx and his followers into other morasses. The classical economists had been hard put to it to prove that capital really earned its share, but Marx, of course, had to argue that it did not. He therefore claimed that capital contributed no gains, despite the fact that an increase in equipment does enhance the productivity of labor, a major point in Marx's immiserization thesis. In reality, this whole theoretical study, among the classical economists as well as Marx, is utterly fruitless. If the task of the economist is to discover *how* the capitalist makes money, that is very simple: an excess of income over payments. Justification, however, is quite another problem. The classical writers confused the two issues, and Marx, the exploiter, profited from their confusion to turn a neat point of propaganda. Orthodox economists plagued themselves with unconvincing theories of abstinence (return being a reward for doing without present pleasures) and Marx decided that capital was not productive. Keynes at least faced the problem realistically when he considered the question to be one of justifying rewards to mere *ownership* of capital as such.[35]

The Ricardian elements in Marx brought him, in one important aspect of economic theory, to agreement with those who are now called reactionaries, when he argued that a rise in money wages meant an increase in real wages, and that a rise in real wages led to unemployment. But perhaps his greatest difficulty, one that caused dispute not merely among Marxists but between volumes I and III of *Capital,* arose from the relation between values as he defined them and prices. Volume I clearly indicates that values are reflected in money language in prices (which obviously assumes a state of perfect competition). Volume III says, on the contrary, that prices may vary considerably from values. The synthesis of this con-

---

[35] See p. 157, the "euthanasia of the rentier"; Joan Robinson, *An Essay on Marxian Economics,* London, 1942, p. 21.

flict involves new complexities that twist like a barbed-wire entanglement: it is much better practice to clear it with artillery than by unraveling it.[36] Clarification is provided by simply undermining the labor theory upon which all this rests. A very able American Marxist, after improving, at obvious effort, Marx's technique of translating values into prices, suggests the real answer when he writes that by holding on to the labor theory of value, "the translation of pecuniary categories into social categories is greatly facilitated. . . .

Price calculation, on the other hand, mystifies the underlying social relations of capitalist production. Since profit is calculated as a return on total capital, the idea inevitably arises that capital as such is in some way "productive." Things appear to be endowed with an independent power of their own. From the point of view of value calculation it is easy to recognize this as a flagrant form of commodity fetishism. From the point of view of price calculation it appears to be natural and inevitable.[37]

Translated into plain speech, orthodox value theory is good bourgeois propaganda. The labor theory of value, and all that goes with it, makes for excellent revolutionary propaganda.

What is left of Marxism? Like an abstraction, or a Cheshire cat, nearly every part of the original can be removed as wrong, and yet Marxism, and in this instance, a bitter yet triumphant smile, remains. Indeed, one must confess that on the pragmatic test, the assault on Marxism is a terrible failure, for it continues to be believed in fully by millions of people, among whom a percentage are intelligent and well trained.

For one thing, Marxism has become a religion, and as such, is completely accepted as a whole, while any particular part may be objectively invalid. Few Marxists have to examine Marx, in fact,

[36] The synthesis is that, underneath it all, values still govern prices. A new abstraction is introduced in which each individual capitalist receives a proportional share of total social surplus value, and the particular variable capital of a firm does not determine its profit (contrary to volume 1) until its own surplus value has been subjected to the mediation of total surplus value and the average rate of profit.

[37] Paul M. Sweezy, *The Theory of Capitalist Development: Principles of Marxist Economics*, New York, 1942, p. 129. See Bober, *Marx's Interpretation of History*, pp. 210 ff., and Robinson, *Marxian Economics*, chap. 3 and elsewhere.

they do well merely to memorize a summary of the broad synthesis and the most catchy phrases, and pay strictest attention to the latest edition of the party line. Furthermore, there is at least a grain of truth in the contention that Marx created, or at least stimulated, the class struggle, which then became his justification.

Another fact that helps explain the paradox of error and acceptance is the all embracing character of the Marxian synthesis. In a time that seems particularly unsettled, when for a great many people religion no longer provides a sense of aim and meaning, when previous objectives and myths such as political democracy appear to have been fulfilled, Marxism is a ready answer to all questions and desires for purpose in life. To use a word that has become very popular, it is a package, and furthermore, at least at first sight, it seems well put together. This is an immediate attraction, especially to youthful intellectuals of the middle class who are primarily anxious to cast off the necessarily false gods of their parents and who find personal lack of security assuaged by adoption of a doctrine that spells certainty and future triumph.

The attractiveness of the doctrine to the insecure and the underprivileged was enhanced by the literary technique of billingsgate and lead-handed irony that was from the first part of the Marxist tradition. How much greater a feeling of certainty does it afford to read that the celebrated German socialist, Karl Kautsky, was not merely "in unfortunate error," as one might say, but was the "renegade Kautsky." It is so much better, for the souls of those who crave the power to dominate and demolish but who cannot do so, to shout "boob," "filthy bourgeois collaborator," "social fascist," "bourgeois formalist and/or cosmopolitan," "traitor to the working class," "left deviationist," "right deviationist," or simply "crook," "pimp," or "idiot," than to criticize in effete bourgeois fashion. It will be objected that this smacks much more of *Pravda* or its English translations than of the scholar Marx. But the coolly scientific Marx could find no better term for one of Feuerbach's ideas than "dirty-Jewish," and no better critical appellation for his contemporary, the German socialist Lassalle, than "the Jewish Nigger Lassalle."[38] Blunderbuss

[38] Sidney Hook, *From Hegel to Marx*, p. 278 and note. Professor Hook calls it "a vicious form of idolatry" to defend such a practice, but regrets the publication "without critical comment" of unimportant correspondence between Marx

invective, which in bourgeois society is theoretically restricted to the proletariat or peasantry, was characteristic of Marx, and Lenin made it almost a requirement of good Marxist style.

Then again, a number of Marx's conclusions appear broadly correct, and his own theoretical approaches to these results can be discarded and replaced with others of greater validity. The conclusions, while different, resemble those of Marx, and lend prestige to his theories. Joan Robinson writes:

> Voltaire remarked that it is possible to kill a flock of sheep by witchcraft if you give them plenty of arsenic at the same time. The sheep, in this figure, may well stand for the complacent apologists of capitalism; Marx's penetrating insight and bitter hatred of oppression supply the arsenic, while the labour theory of value provides the incantations.[39]

For example, Marx predicted concentration of capitalist ownership and control. Concentration has occurred, for different reasons than Marx offered, and it is a different kind of concentration, but concentration it is nonetheless. Marx predicted imperialism and war: the prediction has come true, again for different reasons and with different characteristics, but the general terms are correct. Marx predicted increasingly severe depressions, and the Great Depression of our time would certainly seem to bear him out. But here too, it would be exceedingly difficult to analyze the Great Depression in accordance with the Marxist canon, and antidepression factors, whose existence Marx recognized, may well prove to be far more effective than he judged. Depressions may not be inevitable.

There is, furthermore, a good deal of truth to the Marxian view that pressure for higher wages leads management to increase mechanization in order to obtain greater productivity per worker. But the Marxian corollary that this swells the ranks of the industrial reserve army will not hold if labor secures its share of the benefits of rising

---

and Engels which was "studded with references to 'der jüdische Nigger Lassalle.'" On the contrary, this is in a way more important than the fact that Marx was *not* an antisemite, for it is very revealing that, despite all his scholarship, Marx found mud-slinging necessary. While these instances of Marx's bad manners may be extreme, they are extreme examples of something characteristic.

[39] *Marxian Economics*, p. 27; the thesis of non-Marxian support for Marxist appearances is ably argued by Schumpeter, *Capitalism, Socialism and Democracy*, pp. 32 ff. and elsewhere.

productivity, and consumer expenditure and investment are kept at an adequate level.

Marx predicted the sharpening of the class struggle and its outcome in a socialist society. Class differences there are, but they become Marxian class warfare only when Marxist propaganda has taken hold. His theory of the *Kapitaldämmerung* would seem to be given credence by those representatives of the middle class who bewail every new step of government activity as a fresh leap toward the hell of socialism. But if these Jeremiahs are correct, it is far more likely that we are heading towards a form of bureaucratic state socialism, in which bourgeois legal, religious, ethical, and artistic forms may survive, than into the dictatorship of the proletariat and the age of the state that is supposed to wither away.

Here then is Marxism, a doctrine that is faulty philosophically, historically, and in terms of the very Ricardian economics it employs, nevertheless alive and more powerful after a century than ever before. Despite the blows it has received, the grand abstraction of Marxism persists, partly because it is an abstraction. Developed as an explanation of nineteenth-century conditions that have since undergone sweeping change, Marxism continues to offer a formula to encompass all problems, political and economic. The downfall of classical liberalism, and the failure of Western democratic culture to develop a new unifying ideology, maintain Marxism as a positive challenge which is not adequately met by a negative demonstration of its errors. Marxism still appeals to the almost universal belief in some conception of the equality of man, and its abstractions promise a fuller integration of this Western idea into social institutions than democratic capitalism has been able to offer.

Perhaps a more fundamental reason for the persistent strength of Marxism than any yet suggested is that it does present one very concrete challenge, albeit once more incorrectly phrased. It focuses attention upon the problems of poverty and unemployment in an environment of wealth, upon capitalist depressions and the ever-threatening gap between production and consumption. Stripped of its Hegelian glitter, its compound abstractions and its revolutionary rhetoric, Marxism proclaims that capitalism cannot escape these troubles, and that they will be unknown in socialist society. One may deny that socialism is workable, but capitalism nevertheless remains on the defensive, for upon it still lies the burden of proving that it can overcome its greatest weakness. This is the sharpest question that Marxism poses.

At the midpoint of the twentieth century some Marxists, at least, can present this challenge with all the greater effect that comes from being able to point to an example of socialist success in escaping the travails of depression and unemployment, the Soviet Union. The nature of this achievement calls for close consideration—for unemployment will always be lowered by maintaining a huge standing army and bureaucracy, by withdrawing workers to forced labor camps, and by operating industry at a relatively low technical level; and there can hardly be a gap between production and consumption when production is at best barely sufficient. But when such questions are not investigated there remains only the boast that Russia alone of the major countries escaped the Great Depression.

A good part of the present support for Marxism in general unquestionably derives from its particular application in Russia, and from the organized ability of Communist leaders to do whatever they wish and call it the perfection of Marxian orthodoxy, whether it is or not. But the doctrine had a long history before the revolution of November, 1917, placed Lenin in power and opened a campaign to impose an unheard-of degree of conformity upon all who wished to call themselves followers of Marx and Engels. In those early days, when socialists could debate freely under the protection of bourgeois law, conflicts between original theory and new and evident fact were discussed, and the Marxist movement had an inner vitality that carried it from the British Museum, where its doctrine was elaborated, into the working class in the advanced capitalist nations of Europe, into backward Russia, and into the United States.

NOTES ON BOOKS

There is a vast and still growing library on each and every aspect of this subject, and a complete bibliography of Marxism would run to several large volumes. The following will, however, provide a good start.

On Hegel, and in his relation to Marx, Herbert Marcuse's *Reason and*

Revolution, Hegel and the Rise of Social Theory, and Sidney Hook's *From Hegel to Marx, Studies in the Intellectual Development of Karl Marx.* On Marx himself, Franz Mehring's *Karl Marx, The Story of His Life,* is still as good a biography as one would wish. For Marx's theories, the most useful introduction is M. M. Bober's *Karl Marx's Interpretation of History.* Others are G. D. H. Cole's *What Marx Really Meant* (Alexander Gray suggests someone should write, *What Marx Really Meant, Actually*) as seen by a very moral Englishman. Gray's chapters in *The Socialist Tradition* give both summary and a rather severe criticism. The most acute analysis is in Part I of Schumpeter's *Capitalism, Socialism and Democracy,* whose critique is all the more devastating for being voiced in a kindly and indulgent manner.

Of Marxian writings themselves, the *Communist Manifesto,* the *Critique of Political Economy* and Engel's *Anti-Dühring* will satisfy most appetites which might be surfeited by *Capital.*

10.

THE SOCIALIST MOVEMENT AND
ITS FAILURE IN AMERICA

Marx and Engels did more than write books arguing the decay of capitalism. Wishful thinking led them to expect the imminent collapse of bourgeois society, and they labored hard and long to make ready the other term of the Marxian equation for revolution, the disciplined class-conscious proletariat. The organization of European labor for social, as distinct from simple, trade-union (wages and hours) objectives was in no small part owing to their political efforts, as well as their books. Indeed, the fear that their revolutionists-to-be might be seduced by other, non-Marxian opponents of capitalism not only gave their writings a consistently bitter and maladroit polemic character, but established the tradition whereby one Marxist wing hates the others far more than the common bourgeois enemy.

From the very beginning of his life as a socialist, Marx was associated with small revolutionary groups—one might call them "splinters," if it were proper to speak of a splinter before any wood had come into being. In 1847 Marx and Engels were connected with a German Workers' Association, which developed into the Communist League. But the significant history of Marxian organization for the overthrow of capitalism begins with the International Workingmen's Association—the First International (born in London, 1864, died in New York, 1876). The Association grew out of correspondence and meetings between French and British workers. An executive committee was formed to which Marx was coöpted in the dubious capacity of representative of German workers. His intellectual leadership was almost immediately evident, however, and his inaugural address to the organization was an effective sermon in the Marxian cult.

Throughout its short career the First International was rent by dissension among partisans of three distinct points of view, including that of Marx, regarding both ultimate objectives and proper means. At first, principal competition was offered by the followers of the French social credit radical, Proudhon. Later, the lead was taken by the supporters of Bakunin, the Russian anarchist, and Marx withdrew more and more from fruitless talk into his research. In 1872, on Marx's motion, headquarters of the International were moved to New York, and four years later this first major bid to organize the world proletariat was ended.

As it happened, international socialism really grew only after the movement had established firm foundations within national boundaries. England, as the most advanced capitalist country, should perhaps have furnished the lead. But the British working class, with greater political and organizational liberties than elsewhere in Europe, was becoming less interested in far-off Elysian fields and more in immediate gains. Furthermore, with a keen disregard for the fact that it was, by definition, proletarian, British labor had become stratified, as skilled workers formed strong and advantageous craft unions and the unskilled lagged a generation behind. Nor was a relatively capitalist France to be the home of the first great Marxian socialist party. Aside from the counteracting influences of such competitors as Proudhon and Blanqui, French labor had suffered a terrible setback as a result of the severe suppression of the uprising of the Paris Commune in the spring of 1871. Marx had given his Paris friends the wise advice to remain loyal to the newly formed Third Republic and work for socialism within it, but he fully supported the Commune after it had begun. The excesses of the Commune, and to a far greater extent the horrible repression that ensued, were a blow from which French labor was slow to recover.[1]

---

[1] In the last phase of France's defeat in her war with Prussia, 1870–1871, Paris had undergone a catastrophic siege. The new National Assembly elected to replace the Second Empire and terminate the war had a royalist majority

Marxism made its greatest strides in Germany. This was not mere chance, however, for the Marxian success took place within a culture where such philosophy was regarded as the highest type of intellection.

Even in Germany, however, it was neither Marx nor Engels who brought the movement into being, but a most gallant and least proletarian of socialists, Ferdinand Lassalle (1825–1864). The son of a well-to-do merchant, Lassalle's major political activities came toward the close of his short life.[2] It was only in 1862 that he began his truly meteoric vocation as agitator and political leader of the working class. The flame burned with unheard-of brightness for two years, and then died with him in a duel with a Rumanian prince who had become betrothed to the damsel of his desires.[3] In these two years Lassalle made the Universal German Workingmen's Association a reality, albeit a small one, helped Marx financially, and fell into theoretical and practical disputes with Marx that earned him the scorn reserved for those who dared disagree with the Master. Bismarck, on the other hand, had a high regard for Lassalle, who tried to persuade the Chancellor to support his schemes for producers' coöperatives.

As a theorist, Lassalle was not of Marx's caliber: as a propagandist, he was unequaled. Like Marx, he started with an economic interpretation of history, though far less systematic, and then ex-

which chose to follow a deflationary policy. During the privations of the siege the Commune of Paris had been formed with a very heterogeneous leadership, to hold off the Germans on the basis of equality of sacrifice among all Parisians. This body now rejected the orders of the National Assembly that debt and rent payments should be resumed, and that wages should no longer be paid the national guard. It declared its independence of the Assembly, and there resulted a civil conflict fought with the greatest bitterness and cruelty. Marx and subsequent Marxists tend to exaggerate greatly the part played by his theories and followers in the uprising.

[2] He spent nearly a decade fighting one of the most famous legal battles of the nineteenth century, one that was at the farthest possible remove from righting the wrongs of the working class. A Countess Hatzfeldt had been subjected by her wealthy and aristocratic husband to what a Reno court today might call mental, personal, economic, and social cruelty. Lassalle was all of twenty when he met the Countess and undertook to be her knight errant. When Count von Hatzfeldt spurned a duel with one so far beneath him in every social sense, the modern Galahad took to the courts, and eventually was rewarded with victory for the lady, and an adequate life stipend for himself.

[3] Not Countess Hatzfeldt, of course, but one Helene von Dönniges.

plained capitalist exploitation of labor in terms of a labor theory of value and Ricardo's law of wages, which he called the "brazen and barbarous" law. He believed that salvation for the workers lay in producers' coöperatives and worker-owned factories.[4] Capital was to be furnished by the state, which played a great role in Lassalle's thinking. The proletariat was to use its numbers to win control of the government through the ballot. Then it would be able to institute direct taxation and social security legislation, and get the producers' movement under way. This program had a direct appeal to ordinary workers that the Marxian mysteries as yet lacked. Parts of it made good sense even from a nonsocialist standpoint, which was, of course, one of its failings in Marx's eyes.

Lassalle's party was founded in 1863. In 1867, Wilhelm Liebknecht, of a comfortably situated and notable German family, and August Bebel, a rarity among socialist leaders, having been a genuine worker, founded the League of Workingmen's Associations. Two years later this became the Marxist Social Democratic Workingmen's Party, affiliated with the First International. In 1875, at Gotha, this group and the older Lassalle organization were united, and the great German Social Democratic Party was on the march. For the next sixteen years, the party program contained vestiges of Lassalle's belief in state aid to the working class that Marx had criticized when the merger first took place. During this time, the Party was underground or, more precisely, at ground level, for Bismarck's antisocialist legislation denied it a legal press and meetings. But repression was rather half-hearted and legalistic in the closing decades of the nineteenth century, compared with the achievements in this art in our own time, and Social Democrats were elected to and spoke plentifully in the Imperial German Reichstag. From about a half million votes in 1877, the Party reached one and one-half million in 1890, the year the autocratic Kaiser Wilhelm II gave it full freedom of expression. And the next year, when to ordinary, bour-

---

[4] This was in distinction to a movement for consumers' coöperatives and savings banks that had been founded by Schulze-Delitzsch, some years before. Lassalle's scheme was reminiscent both of Proudhon's plan to solve the problem of poverty through mutual credit banks, and Louis Blanc's National Workshops, government-supported producing units established to absorb unemployment after the French Revolution of 1848. Lassalle, of course, had a more rounded program, and a more specific plan for political action to carry it out.

geois minds it might have seemed that the socialists, gaining in respect and influence, should have cast off the doctrinal rigidity so necessary to the survival of a persecuted group, the Party became completely Marxian in doctrine. It enshrined the theory of immiserization, and of the ultimate withering away of the state.

Since the threshold of resistance to German philosophy was much higher outside Germany, the advance of Marxism was slower and less clear-cut in the other major European countries. In Russia, socialism was truly underground. In England it faced the obstacle of labor's lack of interest, and the discouraging barrier erected by the traditional British empirical outlook with its reluctance to accept theories that are suspiciously too full blown. In France, it continued to meet the opposition of pre-Marxian socialisms, and its progress was hindered by the French proclivity for splitting into factions.[5]

Nevertheless, Marxism became a powerful force in France, assisted by growing antagonism to the Catholic Church, and by the widespread belief that the Great Revolution of 1789 had achieved political, but not economic liberty. The factionalism which characterized French politics was fully present among socialists, and prevented unity in the movement for a generation following the founding of the Federation of Socialist Workers by Jules Guesde in 1879. Aided by Marx's son-in-law, Paul Lafargue, the party grew slowly in competition with a more moderate group headed by Paul Brousse which stressed immediate reforms. Still greater competition was afforded by syndicalism, which triumphed over Marxism in the labor unions. But this doctrine was essentially nonpolitical, and the tendency was for labor to vote socialist in elections, while following the syndicalist line and leadership in the daily business of relations with the bourgeoisie.[6] Unification of the hostile socialist groups seemed on the way in 1893, however, when for the first time a significant number were elected to the Chamber of Deputies. In accordance

[5] This proclivity has been ascribed to the enduring influence of Cartesian logic, and its requirement of the fullest clarity of thought. While French political programs are likely to be drafted with greater concern for theoretical consistency than American, it would be more realistic to explain French factionalism as resulting from the revolutionary tradition; from a development in the constitution of the Third Republic which terminated the executive's power to dissolve the Chamber of Deputies, and thereby undermined its control over the legislature; and from the party system that consequently developed.

[6] See p. 563.

with French practice, which did not imply identity between political parties and groups of deputies, the socialists established a parliamentary group. At this juncture, however, Alexandre Millerand
initiated what became a popular procedure in French politics, moving from the politically unrewarding socialist organization to the
parties of the right. He accepted a cabinet post in a bourgeois ministry, contrary to the Marxian socialist doctrine of noncoöperation
with governments led by class enemies.[7] On the Millerand issue the
socialist family feud swelled to new heights.

Unity was finally accomplished, owing, at least in part, to outside
pressure. In 1889, the Second International, Marxian Socialist, had
been founded, composed of the various national parties of which the
German was by far the strongest. Its Congress of 1904 appealed to
the French to get together, and the following year they obliged by
forming the Unified Socialist Party.

The good old days prior to 1914, of advancing prosperity and
peace among the major powers, were as happy for the socialists as
for the bourgeoisie. But as the parties, and their members individually, prospered, they had to face an exceedingly troublesome
problem that grew out of their devotion to Marxian doctrine—excellent propaganda, but very rigid. On the one hand, as good
Marxians, they preached the revolution: on the other hand, as good
working-class parties, they agitated for and secured very great
advantages for their constituents. The revolutionary objective implied inflexible opposition to the bourgeoisie and its agencies, including the state; the practical and immediate goal of reform called
for a good deal of coöperation with the middle class and widespread
utilization of the legislative and administrative agencies of government. The former found expression in reiteration of Marxian revolutionary dogma and in the political tactic of abstaining from coalition
governments with bourgeois reformers, a tactic that included elements of obstructionism; the latter led to pressure for the eight-hour
day and social legislation, in short, to increasing intervention in the
economy by the bourgeois state in the interests of its underprivileged citizens.

Socialism might have been able to live indefinitely with these

---

[7] Eventually, he became a rightist President of the Republic. Among the
many others who followed Millerand's path to advancement were Aristide
Briand and Pierre Laval.

conflicting aims, the destruction of the bourgeois state and its strengthening along modern neomercantilist lines, if not for two factors. First, there developed within the movement a sharp ideological conflict over the accommodation of Marxist theory to changing fact. Second, the War of 1914–1918 brought this conflict to a head in exacerbated fashion, and created an undying split in the socialist ranks.

The doctrinal dispute was principally concerned with revisionism, whose chief exponent was the German Eduard Bernstein, and among whose protagonists was the scholarly and beloved Jean Jaurès of France. Revisionism started with the proposition that there was nothing sacrosanct about the details of Marxist theory, and that Hegelian philosophy was, in fact, something less than sacred. Bernstein rejected a rigid economic interpretation of history, and correctly described the labor theory of value as merely an eloquent abstraction. Far more significantly, however, he condemned the prevalent tendency among socialists to fasten a distant gaze upon the revolution and the ensuing dictatorship of the proletariat. He chose rather to minimize the importance of ultimate socialism to socialists, and placed highest stress upon the movement as such and its practical achievements. Bernstein went on to attack some of the major Marxian predictions: the rapidly approaching revolution (even Engels tended to agree that he and Marx, too, had erred in this respect), the immiserization of the proletariat, decline in numbers of the bourgeoisie, concentration of wealth and control, crises of higher frequency and intensity. On the contrary, Bernstein argued, while forms did change, the number and prosperity of the middle class was rising; concentration was occurring in industry, but very unevenly and with an infinity of gradations; the condition of the working class was improving as capitalist society as a whole became more prosperous; and there were new factors, the growth of world-wide markets, the techniques of monopolists, and state intervention, that tended to insulate the economy against the spread of depression. On this basis, he urged coöperation with liberal bourgeois elements for the betterment of the condition of the proletariat, the development of consumers' as well as producers' coöperatives and, above all, a conscious and unswerving devotion to the principles and practices of political democracy.

About all that remained of *Capital* and *Anti-Dühring* was love for the proletariat and the catchall adjective, "Marxian." Revisionism was accordingly rejected by the Hanover Congress of the German socialists in 1899, although it did continue to gain adherents, largely because it made good short-run sense. The orthodox, led by Karl Kautsky, chief theoretician[8] of the German party, replied by modifying the obvious absurdities of the received doctrine, but insisting nevertheless on its general accuracy. Kautsky, whom Lenin subsequently dubbed the "renegade," also altered the idea of revolution, to make it essentially the result of a democratic conquest by the working class.

Revisionism was a "deviation" from Marxism to the right, that is, in the direction of moderacy; there was another, and more pregnant deviation, to the left. This was first presented as an issue in international socialism by Lenin in 1903, but failed to gain much support outside of the Russian party.[9] Although Leninism eventually became the most influential of Marxist doctrines, it was not this that disrupted the Second International, but the assassination of one whom the Marxists would have described as a feudal remnant, the Archduke Franz Ferdinand.

The outbreak of the First World War saw nationalism triumph over Marxism in the various socialist parties. Not that Marxism postulated a cut-and-dried opposition to the nation, or preached that under all circumstances peace was preferable to participation in bourgeois warfare. Marx's criterion for selecting a tactic was not one that could be reduced to an unchanging formula, for Marx stated that all policies and events should be judged in relation to the historical interests of the working class. A war that would result in the smashing of feudalism and the promotion of bourgeois democracy could be regarded as favoring the eventual triumph of the proletariat. But underlying beliefs of Western liberalism, such as pacifism, had survived among socialists despite the severity of Marxian logic, with the result that socialism was almost universally regarded as dedicated to the preservation of peace. In fact, it was widely believed in Europe in 1914 that the power of the socialist

[8] The word *theoretician* would be lost to the language if not for the Marxists, for *theorist* serves just as well. A theoretician may be defined as a Marxian intellectual who specializes in interpreting events and history for the politically active comrades. It conveys great distinction in Marxist circles.

[9] Leninism is taken up in chap. 12.

parties and their cohesion in the Second International constituted an insurmountable obstacle to a major war.

And yet, when war came, the great majority of the socialists in each nation rallied to the flag. It was not merely that they chose one of the readily available Marxist "lines" to justify their action; their decision to support their governments, and the approval this course received from the workers, arose from the terribly bourgeois, or perhaps even primitive, feelings of nationalism and patriotism. The Second International was therefore split. International socialist conferences at Zimmerwald and Kienthal in neutral Switzerland in 1915 and 1916, were quite incapable of restoring the solidarity of the working-class parties of the belligerent nations. Aside from neutrals, most of the support for reviving the international aspect of socialism came from the left-wing minorities in Germany and elsewhere who opposed coöperation with the national war efforts and believed that their principal function should always be the preparation of the proletarian revolution. These left-wingers came increasingly to listen to the appeal of Lenin, leader of the Bolshevik wing of the Russian party, to recognize that the Second International was dead and gone, and to create a new Third International upon the principle of single-minded devotion to revolution. It was only after Lenin's triumph in Russia, however, that this project was materialized.

In 1919, the social discipline that had survived defeat in the Great War broke down in the chaos of peace-without-settlement in central and eastern Europe, and the socialists found themselves in revolutionary situations they had not created, and for which they were unprepared. The greatest impetus to seize the moment and establish the dictatorship of the proletariat came from the followers of Lenin, especially since the Bolshevik leader regarded lasting success in Russia as dependent upon revolution in industrial Germany, which had the oldest and strongest of the Marxist movements.

In 1916, the left wing of the German Social Democratic Party, led by Karl Liebknecht, son of one of the founders, and Rosa Luxemburg, had broken away in opposition to the policy of carrying on the war. Shortly after, the left wing of this left wing formed the *Spartakusbund*, the Spartacists, taking the name of the leader of a slave rebellion against the Roman Republic. A great deal of underground revolutionary organization took place in 1917, and the next year saw the formation of Workers' and Soldiers' Councils, the counterpart of the Russian soviets. When the Imperial regime crashed in November, 1918, a revolutionary situation had developed in many cities, including Berlin, which was at least as propitious as that in which the Bolsheviks had been so successful. Two factors were principally responsible for the defeat of the German revolution: a speedy and effective alliance between the right-wing leadership of the old Social Democratic Party, Ebert and Scheidemann, and the Imperial General Staff; and the fact that the left-wing high command wasted time in indecisive theorizing, and declined to swing into action, as Lenin had in Russia, without the proved support of the majority of the working class. Their failure to cast off democratic scruples and frankly adopt Lenin's conspiratorial technique paralyzed the revolutionary forces. Severe repression followed at the hands of the Social Democrat Noske and the Reichswehr. The German revolution, on which Lenin counted so heavily, was put down.

Compared to the German disaster, to be renewed in a wholly abortive revolt in 1923, the destruction of Bela Kun's communist regime in Hungary in 1919 meant little to the Bolsheviks. Of far greater importance was organizational work in the major countries being carried out under the orders of the Third International, the Comintern, founded by the Russians in 1919. The initial reaction of socialists to the new International was very favorable. The old International had clearly failed, especially if the revolutionary establishment of socialism were the criterion. The new organization offered a fighting line and had the tremendous prestige of being the creation of the one truly successful proletarian party, the Bolsheviks. The Social Democratic parties were invited to join the Moscow International, and a number, including the Italian, Norwegian, and at least the leadership of the Swiss party decided to do so. But the Second Comintern Congress of 1920 set forth a list of Twenty-One Conditions for affiliation, and this effectively limited adherents to the left wings of the socialist organizations, which split off and became the new Communist parties.[10] The twenty-one demands called for "democratic centralism," which in ordinary language

[10] The text of these conditions may be found in, among many other places, J. Oneal and G. A. Werner, *American Communism, A Critical Analysis of Its Origins, Development and Programs*, New York, 1947, pp. 378 ff.

meant strict obedience to the decisions of the directing body of the International.[11] The latter, of course, was completely controlled by the Russians. Democratic centralism held little appeal for men brought up in the traditions of Western liberalism, and success in Russia was not sufficient to cow old socialist leaders in more civilized lands who felt that they too knew Marx, and had no desire to submit to Russian dictation. To Rosa Luxemburg, Lenin's whole doctrine was too much of a Russian theory, too heavily colored by the peculiarities of the backward empire and by the impatience of its revolutionaries, and bound inevitably to draw the very breath of life from Marxism. To the aging Karl Kautsky, Lenin and the Bolsheviki were perverters of Marx; for Kautsky and the hundreds of thousands to whom he remained the great teacher were political democrats in the old-fashioned Western sense, as well as socialists.[12] In France, a socialist named Marcel Cachin made the pilgrimage to Moscow, and then led a split from which the French Communist Party was born. But the vast majority of French socialists, among them the extremely intelligent and sensitive Léon Blum on whom the mantle of Jaurès was to fall, remained true to the democracy of free speech and press of the French republican tradition.

Thus the Second International was reborn. It had resumed functioning as early as 1919, and in 1923 the socialists who rejected Moscow were fully reorganized on an international basis in the Labor and Socialist International. Between the two world wars European socialism occupied a middle ground, fighting against communism on the left, reactionary capitalism and landlord groups on the right, and fascism on both left and right, depending on how one chooses to look at it. The era of German domination, and of the German theoretical outlook, was over. In the 1920's and '30's, the reformist attitude of British Labour, the French and Scandinavians became the characteristic socialist point of view. It entailed a thoroughgoing acceptance of constitutional democracy, with or without a king, and coöperation with middle-class and religious reformers.

Pre-1914 socialism had settled into an established role in Euro-

---

[11] See p. 369.
[12] See Karl Kautsky, *Social Democracy Versus Communism*, D. Shub and J. Shaplen, ed. and trans., New York, 1946.

pean society, in which conservative party and trade union officers followed a revisionist policy with little regard for the official revolutionary Marxian dogma. What remained after the war of this watered-down socialism was the word itself, a continuing belief in the ultimate achievement through democratic means of a socialist society that would constitute a higher and better order than capitalism, and a predeliction for the nationalization of public utilities and basic industries. Much of the cant and jargon of Marxism fell by the wayside, although such terms as "surplus value" continued to be employed as much as a token of continuity with the old tradition as for their analytical or propaganda value. Socialism of this variety continued to make headway among the working class, intellectuals, the lower middle class, and some of the agricultural population. But it lacked the dynamic power of fascist nationalism, and only where it could ally with an intrinsically democratic middle class, as in France, England, the Low Countries, and Scandinavia, was it able to withstand the assault of the new and melodramatic lunatic fringe. In Germany, the Socialists, together with the Catholic Center Party, were sabotaged by the fabulous stupidity of the Stalinist Communists. In Italy, the premature radicalism of labor, largely syndicalist rather than socialist, and the nation's political instability, paved the way for the victory of Mussolini. After the end of the Second World War in 1945, European socialism, democratic and statist, with what might prove to be a crucial conflict between these words unresolved, was coöperating with Christian reformers and those of the liberal middle class who still had faith, in a continuing struggle to make the world safe for democracy.

Its speedy recovery after years of suppression by Hitler and Mussolini came as a surprise to many observers, who had expected that the European working class would identify their sufferings with the failure of democratic and pacifist socialism. But the recovery was real, and the socialists were challenged in their new position in the center only by the rather more conservative Catholic parties.

It is against this picture of a movement that struggled, suffered, changed, but remained alive and strongly rooted, that the record of socialism in the United States must be assessed. To put it simply, American socialism has been a terrible failure. Nor can this failure be explained away with the facile thesis that America lags one or two generations behind Europe in social development, and that the day of socialism is therefore yet to come. This view makes no sense at all except on the assumption that the Marxian theory of history (even in modified form) is scientifically valid, and that the United States is therefore certain to catch up with this previously established truth. Even if it were true that America does tend to follow Europe at a respectful distance, and there are no more than superficial similarities to argue for it, there would be no added hope for American sectaries of reformed Marxism. For neither Marx nor socialism as a general idea has been able to take root in American society. There are, of course, Americans who follow Marx, and they are undoubtedly more numerous and influential than the Americans who follow Bahai or Buddha. But they too are proponents of something that is not easily assimilated in the United States. Their eloquence and persuasive scholarship have fallen upon ears that are sometimes tolerantly, sometimes truculently, but consistently deaf. They have not enrolled any large number of workers, although American laborers are certainly not averse to either novelty or excitement. Nor have they converted that principal source of socialist leadership, the idealistic sons of the middle class, among whom socialism has tended to be a passing phase of youth, a harmless outlet for ethical energies.

There are three major reasons for the inability of American socialism to become a significant political movement. First, while obviously far from perfect, the American economy has on the whole been sufficiently prosperous and flexible to prevent the formation of a large and continuously depressed proletariat, despite unfortunate beginnings in New England mill towns and elsewhere. Second, the rising demands of American labor have been increasingly met. Third, and most revealing, American culture has always been extremely hostile to overwound theories. Every intellectual import has found a few adherents, often with extremely able persons among them, but like the dogma of Ricardo or of Sigmund Freud, they have not won acceptance as matter-of-fact propositions familiar and comfortable to most men in the street. This has been the saving grace of American anti-intellectualism. In a famous passage of *Democracy in America,* de Tocqueville described this important facet of the American mind:

I think that in no country in the civilized world is less attention paid to philosophy than in the United States. The Americans have no philosophical school of their own, and they care but little for all the schools into which Europe is divided. . . . Yet it is easy to perceive that almost all the inhabitants of the United States use their minds in the same manner, . . . without ever having taken the trouble to define the rules, they have a philosophical method common to the whole people.[13]

He went on to describe, oversimplifying somewhat, an interest in factual knowledge as a means to improvisation, a tendency to agree with those general ideas that are commonly accepted, yet, most characteristic of all, "in most of the operations of the mind each American appeals only to the individual effort of his own understanding."

Such an outlook which, four generations later, we might call a kind of pragmatism that, pragmatically enough, stops short of logical conclusions, provided poor soil for intricate theoretical systems. Engels himself at least partly understood this obstacle, for he advised Friedrich Sorge, one of the apostles to the Americans, to establish a simple political movement with a short-run program, after which Marxist theory could take effect. Sorge protested that he himself had found the *Manifesto* most persuasive, to which Engels replied: "You were German forty years ago with the German capacity for theory."[14]

During most of the nineteenth century, the American history of socialism in general and of Marxism in particular was largely one of a handful of native intellectuals and immigrant workers organized in foreign language groups. As the latter stream began to dry up, and particularly when communism was able to attract the foreign language elements, socialism became increasingly a small-scale intellectual's movement, and gained wide toleration as one of the voices of a protesting conscience which are so necessary to a democracy. The peak of the American movement came in the years 1900–1920, when socialism was positively stylish for the intelligentsia and well-to-do idealists, and when it even appeared to be developing

---

[13] *Democracy in America*, New York, Bradley edition, 1945, vol. 2, p. 3. We have already had occasion to allude to Tocqueville's brilliant characterization of the American point of view, p. 145 above.

[14] Mehring, *Karl Marx*, p. 338.

some real attraction for American labor, including the AFL. Even at this time, however, foreign born were disproportionately numerous in the socialist movement.

Despite its unbroken record of weakness, American socialism had an early beginning, with imports of various European Utopian varieties starting with Owen's New Harmony in 1824.[15] Brook Farm, first a country refuge of Boston Transcendentalists and then a Fourierist community, was perhaps the most celebrated, as such men as Charles Dana, Ralph Waldo Emerson, Nathaniel Hawthorne, and Albert Brisbane were associated with it. The Oneida Community of John Humphrey Noyes had a belief in both polygamy and polyandry that was more than a bit shocking to ordinary folk, but its economic success was quite exceptional for a Utopian venture. The zest for founding Edens declined toward the middle of the nineteenth century, however, and American socialism began to be linked with the labor movement, and with Marxism and anarchism.

Direct action has long vied with social reform and simple trade union activity within the American labor movement. Violence on the part of both workers and employers has been a frequent misfortune, since before the Molly Maguires of the 1870's and even after the strikes of the Great Depression. But whether arising from the pioneer turbulence that contributed to the spirit of the IWW, from rightful anger at injustice, or from the tortured and neurotic theories of a Johann Most,[16] violence has shaped the main patterns of neither American labor nor American socialism. In the United States as nearly everywhere else, socialism has been a Marxist movement.

Although William H. Sylvis, who founded the National Labor Union in 1864, entered into correspondence with the First International, Marxian organization really began a few years later, when the General German Workingmen's Association developed into Section 1 of New York, of the International in America. In 1876, these Marxists united with Lassallean socialists to found the Workingmen's Party, whose influence was not too great among other im-

[15] There had been earlier religious communist colonies, such as that of the Rappites from whom Owen purchased his site.

[16] Most, a German ex-socialist turned anarchist, came to America in 1882 and attempted to sell his own solution for the problems of the working class—a liberal use of dynamite and assorted poisons.

migrants or native workers who were resistant to the blandishments of the dialectic. Nevertheless, when the nation was shaken by strikes and civil disturbances in 1877, the new party was quick to get into the scramble, and actually held the city of St. Louis for a week.[17] Shortly after, the organization changed its name to Socialist Labor Party, and dominated American socialism until the twentieth century.

The movement continued small, and largely one of foreign-language groups.[18] Americanization of socialism was under way, however, at least among intellectuals. The ideas and New York mayoralty campaign of the single-taxer, Henry George, and the publication in 1888 of Edward Bellamy's Utopia, *Looking Backward,* induced a great many middle-class Americans to think more theoretically about social problems and objectives. From this awakening, American socialism received its outstanding theorist and first notable leader, Daniel De Leon, who, though foreign born, escaped a good part of the immigrant stigma. He was a fluent speaker and writer, having studied and taught law at Columbia, and he won for New World Marxism the highest accolade it has ever received: Lenin himself declared that De Leon was "the only one who has added anything to socialist thought since Marx." He resembled Lenin in that his doctrine was equally severe and harsh, and his toleration for theoretical dissent equally minute.

While De Leon, who soon controlled the Socialist Labor Party, may have hoed a pure and perfectly straight theoretical row, he was a failure when it came to building the Party into something politically significant. His efforts to take over the Knights of Labor, and later the American Federation of Labor, came to nothing. Continually disturbed by disputes with anarchists, the small organization was further shaken by its leader's intransigence, and new and politically abler men began to appear on the scene.

Eugene Victor Debs, leader of the Pullman strike that had been broken by federal troops, was a man of great personal charm and

[17] L. Symes and T. Clement, *Rebel America, The Story of Social Revolt in the United States,* New York, 1934, p. 149.

[18] The spirit of optimism that accompanies the Utopian element in socialism was illustrated by Wilhelm Liebknecht and Marx's son-in-law and daughter (Dr. and Mrs. Edward Aveling), who, on a visit to the United States in 1886, saw great hope for American socialism.

integrity, an effective public speaker and political worker who had neither the taste nor training for dialectics. But he could appeal effectively to actual American workers. Victor Berger was another practical soul, who was building in Milwaukee a socialist organization that would send him to Congress and elect Socialist Party mayors repeatedly. In New York, men like the able lawyer, Morris Hillquit, were rebelling against De Leon's mixture of autocracy, rationality and unreality. From these Midwestern and Eastern groups the Socialist Party was born in 1901. Even before their union had been cemented, Debs had received nearly 100,000 votes in the presidential election of 1900.

The next twenty years were to see what appeared to be a solid growth of Socialist strength. Anxious not to repeat De Leon's error, and organized much more like the great American political parties than the Marxist parties of Europe, the Socialists permitted wide differences of opinion in their ranks, and had a limited attraction for all levels of American society. Members of prominent capitalist families, such as Joseph Medill Patterson, writers such as Upton Sinclair, and numerous ministers of the Gospel joined the movement. For a short time *Metropolitan Magazine*, financially controlled by Harry Payne Whitney, took a somewhat confused but blatant socialist line. Samuel Gompers' control of the AFL was threatened.[19] The Party had 40,000 members in 1908, and almost 120,000 in 1912. Its presidential vote reached 400,000 in 1904, and shot to 900,000 in 1912, the year of the great three-cornered race of Roosevelt, Wilson and Taft. Thereafter the party membership declined, however, and a slight increase in the presidential vote in 1920 proved to be without significance.[20]

The First World War seemed not only to interrupt but to terminate the growth of the Socialist Party. Like its European confreres, it was pacifist, and, since the United States was not initially involved in the conflict it was able to take a firm stand for neutrality without being crushed, although it suffered both in membership and voting strength. But, unlike the great socialist parties of western Europe,

[19] Symes and Clement, *Rebel America*, pp. 223, 266 ff.
[20] The Socialist vote was undoubtedly held down by the party's inability to get on the ballot in some states, but it was extremely small in any event. Only in 1912 did it exceed 5 percent of the total cast. The peak Socialist vote of 919,000 in 1920 amounted to about 3½ percent of the total.

the American organization showed the courage of its pacifist convictions even after the United States entered the war. Prison was the lot of many of its leaders, including Debs, whose 1920 campaign pictures showed him in a convict's suit.

The hysteria against pacifists and radicals that carried into the 1920's was, however, a minor blow to the Socialists compared to that struck by the Bolshevik Revolution in Russia in 1917 and its aftermath in the United States. The Party could have recovered from a wave of persecution of which the American people eventually grew ashamed. It could not recover from the split of the Communists in 1919, which meant the loss of some of its most devoted workers. And the prewar enthusiasm of middle-class supporters waned during the prosperous 1920's and was transferred to the New Deal when depression came.[21]

The advent of the eloquent former minister, Norman Thomas, to Socialist leadership in 1928, symbolized the Party's retreat from Marxism. To the extent that socialism became identified with him in the eyes of the American public, it was regarded as a critical, ethical and rigidly pacifist viewpoint. The concept of revolution had fallen far to the background, and the idea of a socialist society itself aroused little popular discussion or interest. The decline of the Party led its younger elements to seek a more forceful line, encouraged by Communists who infiltrated into their ranks. They succeeded in gaining control of the Party, in 1933, Thomas remaining its leading public figure, but the old guard seceded. The Socialist Party fell away to less than its original strength at the beginning of the century. Like De Leon's Socialist Labor Party, it had become little more than a name.

This sad sequel to the glorious days of the Debs era when the followers of socialism hailed it as a rising tide that would sweep into the White House within a generation, should occasion little surprise. It may be conceded that election results are not necessarily an accurate picture of the potential support for a socialist movement, and that in a time of exceptionally severe crisis (it would apparently

---

[21] The weakness of its appeal to the American electorate is shown by the fact that it was unable to attract the protest vote, contributing little effective strength to the LaFollette campaign in 1924. In 1928, the Socialist national ticket secured 267,000 votes. This rose to 885,000 in 1932, but had fallen to 117,000 by 1944.

have to be worse than 1932) a revived socialist movement might conceivably become a major factor on the national scene. But for this to occur, it would have to develop an appeal and a mass basis of which its history shows it to be utterly incapable. Only a serious misinterpretation of the growth of the movement before the First World War would offer socialists any hope on this score.

In any Marxian movement, conversion of intellectuals is important only insofar as it leads to better organization and the subsequent conversion of labor. The swing of the intelligentsia to socialism between 1900 and 1917 was a fad. It was quite the thing for young college graduates to join the Socialist Party, to prove that they were liberated and forward-looking. In part the intellectuals were attracted to socialism by a simple extension of the democratic spirit, in part by love for novelty, in small part only by Marxian conviction. Few of them were socialists of the European variety. As for labor, it has been most consistent in its antipathy toward involved doctrine. Marxian theory bores and mystifies the American worker. When it is reduced to slogans he is likely to become suspicious of what lurks behind them. Nor does the history of violence in American labor relations imply that there is fertile ground for a revolutionary movement. As a matter of fact, it may be suggested that American labor had wider and earlier experience with direct action than any European movement, so that its abandonment of the gospel of violent struggle may properly be viewed as a positive rejection. The IWW, prior to the First World War, was a generation or more ahead of European Marxism in both its belligerent tactics and the intensity of its hatred for capitalism. That it has not revived is not owing to the forceful manner in which it was repressed. By the time the nation had passed through the era of the Great Depression and the New Deal, a new amendment had entered into America's social constitution, guaranteeing to labor not only its rights as a corporate body, but its share in the increasing productivity of the national economy. It is, to say the least, unlikely that socialist theory could ever outweigh the real advantages of an assured, profitable, and respected position.[22]

The decline of socialism does not, of course, mean that Marxism

[22] See the suggestive leading article, "Workers of the World," London *Times Literary Supplement*, May 5, 1950.

is dead in America, for the Stalinist variety still moves along in its own peculiar fashion. But the acute problems raised by Russian Communism are rather different from the purely potential problems that a democratic socialism may pose. The century of dispute over Marx has produced a great deal of speculation over his interpretation of history and his economics, but relatively little as to what socialism might mean in actual practice. This was not surprising, so long as the achievement of socialism was a distant dream, and so long as Marx's antipathy toward Utopias influenced his followers. But when the government of a major power like England has affirmed its intention to establish a socialist society, and when other advanced nations may follow suit, it is of the highest importance to give thought to what the word *socialism* might imply for ordinary living.

Since there are no adequate working examples of a socialist society, it will be necessary to take a hypothetical situation.[23] To be fair to the socialists, let us imagine the United States as it might be sometime after the year 2000, assuming (1) that the growth of monopoly has continued unimpeded, (2) that socialism has just been voted in by an overwhelming majority of the electorate, in an entirely peaceful and constitutional manner, and (3) that there have been no major institutional changes, so that economic affairs, including labor relations, have always been conducted as they were in the 1950's. Of course, these assumptions are entirely unrealistic, but they do provide a basis for a theoretical analysis of socialism.

We shall further assume that the electorate have chosen socialism because it is determined to put an end to the occurrence of even mitigated capitalist economic crises, and because it believes in equality. In addition, we shall assume that the bourgeois managers and technicians of industry, for years playing the role of civil servants in huge private enterprises, and consequently having lost the

[23] The Soviet Union, of course, calls itself socialist, but it is a very special case. To examine the United Kingdom (see chap. 11) as an illustration of the working out of socialist theory would be fair neither to Great Britain nor to the doctrine. Sweden or New Zealand might be considered, but neither is fully socialist and both are small countries. Furthermore, like all nations, they too are "special cases."

adventurous spirit of the nineteenth-century middle class, will be as willing to work for the government as for the old boards of directors. The government, we assume, will be sensible enough to make use of their skills. The socialist administration will have established a National Planning Board, subject to a Secretary of Economic Affairs, or to a Cabinet committee. The grand Plan will be published as a National Economic Budget, much lengthier and infinitely more involved than the present variety. It will, of course, have to pass congressional scrutiny and, as at present, require a majority vote of both Houses for approval. Because of its complexity, however, the Congress will be even less capable of expert and effective consideration of the budget than it is today. Only major issues will be decided by the legislature, therefore, and the officials of the Department of Economic Affairs will really be in control.

Their objectives will be very much like those of theoretical capitalism: optimum production and distribution, equilibrium between supply and demand, rising standard of living, full employment and security. They will also believe in freedom of consumers to choose when and how they will spend their money, freedom of all people to do the kind of work they wish to do and for which they are qualified, and payment in accordance with ability. As heirs to a democratic tradition, they will firmly believe in freedom of speech, press, assembly, and conscience, and in popular sovereignty expressed through free elections of representatives of the people.

To all of these aims and beliefs the staunch defender of capitalism could say a hearty "Amen." The socialist planners, however, will be working not with private industries, but with plants "owned by the people" and controlled by the state. Furthermore, in place of the myriad decisions and adjustments of millions of individual or corporate "plans" required by capitalism, there will be far fewer decisions to make, and these will be made by an integrated and expert bureaucracy. Whereas the decisions of capitalists are in many instances *reactions* to external market conditions, the planners will have the great advantage of being able to make *substantive* decisions, and control the many factors which are relatively independent under capitalism. Their work will accordingly be far more rational, their predictions far more certain, than in capitalist society. Under socialism the great general plans will be determined centrally, and the numberless local and individual decisions will have to conform. In capitalist society, it is these many small decisions, made without certainty as to their consequences, that establish the general picture of the functioning of the economy.

The great advantage of the planners is that they will be able to do the work of their capitalist predecessors more efficiently—other things being equal. They presumably will have banished that great plague of the capitalist world, uncertainty, and along with it many of its wastes, such as excessively competitive advertising, the legal profession, and income-tax collectors.[24] In most other respects, however, their problems will be precisely the same as those of capitalist management, given our assumption that the public will be free to spend as it chooses. They will have to hit upon the correct prices to move consumers' goods from the shelves, and the correct allocations and prices for producers' goods. Since, for example, they will know that over the past decade an average of x million shoes have been sold at a total cost of y million dollars, they will have no difficulty in deciding to produce x or $x + 1$ million shoes in the first year of the socialist era. If they follow a rational policy[25] and have no more than the luck of the average capitalist in trial and error adjustment of supply and demand, they should have little difficulty in maintaining equilibrium. Of course, their success in trial and error should be much greater, because of their fuller knowledge of and

[24] As all socialist incomes will be earned, and income differentials will be much smaller than now and will theoretically correspond to social usefulness, there would be no need for an income tax. Public revenue could be obtained very easily either by means of the accounting profits of the socialized economy or by a turnover tax. Both methods, as well as the income tax, are in use in the USSR.

[25] They would equate price with marginal cost, which means charging for a pair of shoes the cost to the producer of the last pair made (cost including a charge for overhead, depreciation, materials, labor, and planned profit). On this basis there would be no danger of unwittingly distorting the most efficient allocation of resources that would be inevitable in a purely arbitrary pricing method. Of course, the socialist state could always move prices from this ideal level for its own purposes. For example, raising the price of a necessity would constitute an additional tax. Raising the price of leather would amount to a form of rationing. Or the state might sell vitamins far below cost, as a form of health subsidy.

control over the different elements of the economy. Pricing rationally, and allocating labor and capital according to a consistent plan, they will be able to achieve that optimum utilization of resources which is the dream of capitalist economists.[26]

As for progress, here too the problems of socialism would not be very great. Investment would be planned, subject to congressional approval, and new products and techniques would be introduced very much as under monopoly capitalism, at a rate that would not cause too much disturbance.

In short, there is a good theoretical case for the proposition that socialism could work quite well, as an economic system at least, provided two conditions are met. First, if socialism is to mean the opportunity for both elimination of economic insecurity and a higher standard of living, it must be adopted by an advanced and wealthy capitalist state. Second, the new socialist state must take full advantage of the skills of the bourgeoisie. If socialism enters a backward nation, like Russia, its economic progress is apt to be very slow and costly, and the elimination of unemployment in an underdeveloped region is no great achievement. If a socialist state should attempt to turn over supervision of the complexities of production to either proletarian theorists or good socialist toilers the whole structure would come tumbling down.

That a socialist system could in theory function well from the economic standpoint does not prove very much, however. After all, there has been no greater praise for the productive achievements of capitalism than that which came from the pen of Karl Marx, and there is good ground to believe that depressions can be controlled. Nor is there any reason why the suffering attendant upon unemployment cannot be completely eliminated by public intervention. The relatively greater equality promised by socialism does not provide a useful argument, for as Schumpeter points out, the wages of labor "might well be higher in a commercial society admitting unrestricted inequalities than the equal incomes would be in equali-

---

[26] It should be noted, however, that their mistakes, *even theoretically*, could turn out to be much more disastrous than capitalist errors. Under capitalism, where decisions are decentralized, errors may cancel each other out. When decisions are centralized, errors may be cumulative, operating like self-realizing expectations of a consensus of businessmen, to create a sharp swing of the economy toward boom or bust.

tarian socialism." The elimination of the so-called "idle rich" would add very little to the average wage.[27]

In short, the economic case for socialism must rest on the presumption of its greater productivity. Since it would be childish to deny the competence of capitalist management as a whole, socialist superiority would have to come from its greater rationality, its elmination of waste and friction, and the maintenance of skilled direction. One widely used argument against socialism is that the problems of planning a national economy are too complex for the human mind. Even if the socialist state were intelligent enough to permit a great deal of decentralization of authority, the task of pulling together into one grand decree all the decisions that are made each day by private business would, to say the least, be very difficult. As for the wastes of capitalism, many of these are apparent rather than real. To take one very simple and minor instance, there is every reason to believe that the Red Bubble Chewing Gum Trust would have to advertise, however unsocialistically, if it wished to move its product into the consumers' mouths. Otherwise, they would be very likely to forget to chew, and would spend their coins in other ways.

The great problem of maintaining skill in socialist management is less one of providing incentive, as is so often said, than of providing incentives that will not undermine the classless society on the one hand, or pervert competence itself on the other. For a good many, socialism will itself be the incentive for hard and devoted work. As Schumpeter says, "Socialist bread may well taste sweeter to them than capitalist bread simply because it is socialist bread, and it would do so even if they found mice in it."[28] Without underestimating the importance of socialist zeal, however, we may pass on to other, more tangible incentives. To begin with, managers will draw higher pay than sweepers, even if the gap will be less than it is today. Managers will also have far greater prestige, power, and influence, which is harmful neither to one's ego nor to one's children's chances in life. Even if we assume that Americans of the year 2015 will be too sophisticated to work overtime and overstrenuously to obtain a ribbon or a medal of the Order of De Leon, First Class,

[27] *Capitalism, Socialism and Democracy,* pp. 191 ff.
[28] *Capitalism, Socialism and Democracy,* p. 191.

there are many ways of escaping the severity of relatively equal incomes. For example, the manager of the Debs Auto Plant at River Rouge might be given, as a perquisite of office, the home of the famous old capitalist, Henry Ford. If he were not inspired by this incentive, his wife would certainly consider it a pleasant place in which to live and would instill him with the proper enthusiasm.

The trouble is, of course, that adequate material incentives would tend to create new class lines which, while not as rigid as those of capitalism are said to be, would tend to be self-perpetuating. It is one thing to follow Lord Keynes and expect capitalists to play their skillful game for reduced stakes: it is quite another thing to expect people with the same talents and energy to play the game and remain socialists. Nor is this the most serious threat to a socialist society. The very nature of bureaucracy, which would have to expand enormously, would tend both to establish more rigid class differences and diminish inspiration if not efficiency. Power would itself become an incentive.[29]

In any large bureaucracy there arises a struggle for power and advancement from which factions are born. Thereafter, factional loyalty becomes prerequisite to a successful career. The complexity of government makes the legislature increasingly remote from actual administration and limits its role to policy decisions at the most general level, and to investigation. The actual authority in the hands of the bureaucracy swells, and with it continue to grow the intrinsic urge to gain power and the inherent spirit of faction. Limited only by the watchfulness of a harried legislature, bureaucracy could become the governing state within the nation. The interests of the bureaucracy make it a class that will defend its privileges, and this, together with inescapable nepotism, or simple favoritism to family and friends, would harden class lines. At the same time, the discipline that is essential to bureaucratic efficiency can instill a spirit of conformity that smothers inspiration, while factionalism and the

[29] That even moderate and democratic socialists are aware of the attractions of power is indicated by the following remark of the British socialist, A. L. Rowse, with respect to incentives: "I should say for the sake of running the passenger traffic of London, or of running one of the great Joint Stock Banks, any real man would be perfectly willing to give up his house in Park Lane or his second motor-car, what a *man* wants is power, and not merely the trappings of it" (*Where Stands Socialism Today?* London, 1933, p. 118). (His emphasis.)

struggle to climb the bureaucratic ladder blight efficiency in the higher, productive sense.

This picture of an all-powerful officialdom will seem too ominous in contrast to the traditional businessman's view, that no one worth his salt would be content to work in the civil service, that bureaucrats are second-raters who cannot succeed in private industry. Let it be remembered, however, that while the bureaucracy of today does indeed attract highly skilled persons, it does so in competition with the vastly larger private sector of the economy. This competition would cease under socialism; the stakes for which socialist bureaucrats would fight would be much higher, in terms of power, and the alternative of a struggle for money would not exist. Advancement in life, the achievement of both prestige and comfort, would tend to mean bureaucratic advancement only.

Nor would decentralized administration necessarily survive. Fulfillment of the plan could easily become an end in itself. Disturbing the plan by production more efficient than scheduled would violate the bureaucratic law of conformity. Nonfulfillment of the plan would be equivalent to robbing society, and would be punished as such. All administrative decisions would be influenced by the need for factional loyalty.

Nevertheless, the old bourgeoisie, now the socialist bureaucracy, would not lose too much. Their standard of living might, on the average, rise, their fundamental political liberty would thus far be untrammeled, and their prestige and power would be greater than ever. It is one of the greatest ironies of all that labor might be the chief sufferer at the advent of socialism. Under capitalism, the threat of unemployment and the prospect of better pay are the incentives to efficient work and the foundation of labor discipline. Under socialism, advancement would remain as an incentive, possibly reinforced by love for "socialist bread," and unemployment would be an even more fearful threat. For it would not be the tragic, yet hopeful unemployment of the worker whose plant has closed down, but dismissal for one or another cause that would be equivalent to violation of socialist discipline, a crime against society.

But what of the socialist labor unions? Surely they should be in an even more powerful position than the great labor organizations of today. At first sight labor should be king in a socialist world, and officially it is very likely to be crowned. But the crown could easily become a crown of thorns. Under capitalism, unions are both a defensive and aggressive force, blocking unfair dismissals and securing higher wages and better working conditions. Under socialism, the defensive function would persist for a time, until increasingly minute regulations from above, spurred on by the bureaucracy, by the spirit of system and the desire for uniformity, above all by the need to fulfill the sacred plan, would so routinize all labor relations as to make the enforcement of labor discipline a matter of law and its execution rather than negotiation. The aggressive function would at once disappear, for wages and hours would be determined by the planners in establishing the costs of the National Economic Budget. Under these circumstances a strike would be tantamount to insurrection. The unions would thus become an arm of management, whose chief purpose, the enforcement of discipline, would be sugarcoated by their great efficiency in such matters as securing clean and adequate lavoratories and arranging picnics and softball games.

Labor would still have the ballot, and could conceivably outvote the new bourgeoisie and farm population,[30] getting a more friendly Congress and president. The electoral issue would then be one of greater consumption versus greater investment—indeed the left might be the Consumption Party, and the right the Investment Party. The issue would be exacerbated by the fact that while the workers rather expect to be exploited under capitalism, they are proclaimed the owners of the means of production in socialist society. Seeing the former bourgeoisie in their same old suburban homes (even if their yacht clubs have been socialized), the workers would be likely to demand the fruits of labor's property. The greater skills, the key posts and the armed forces would be in the hands of the bureaucracy (Investment Party). Compromise might be possible, but it would result from the long tradition of bourgeois democracy rather than from the politics of socialism. Or the Investment Party might decide upon a dictatorship over the proletariat and, taking a leaf from the political book written by the two Napoleons,

[30] Agriculture would not have to revolutionized to fit it into the socialist framework. Collective farms would be quite unnecessary, as planting requirements and price juggling would suit the needs of the planners adequately. Our assumption is that the year 2015 would see a democratic socialism, that would not create havoc for the sake of meeting a preconceived blueprint.

Hitler, Stalin, and Mussolini, they might permit the rite of balloting to continue.

By the very nature of the case, the foregoing cannot really be a prediction of what socialism would be like. In plain fact, no one has a truly significant conception of the nature of a socialist society. About the only characteristic socialists are generally agreed upon is public ownership of productive property. This is a legal fiction which in no way defines *control* or *use* of property, and therefore means very little.[31] Otherwise, socialists usually talk about objectives of which any capitalist could approve, and which capitalism can fulfill. A discussion of a hypothetical socialist society is consequently not too revealing. But little more can be done to perceive the socialist future, than a mere excursion into the possibilities of an untried and hopefully democratic socialism as we can now conceive it.

Should socialism be ushered in by a violent revolution and ruthless suppression of the old bourgeoisie, prediction is much easier. The standard of living would tumble, while competent managers were being trained from the ranks of the proletariat. A police state would be needed to create a form of order out of the inevitable chaos. While the "dictatorship of the proletariat" could theoretically also function well as an economic organism, the problem of incentives would be greater than ever, the power of the bureaucracy even more exaggerated, its morality more deformed. Freedom would be a legal fiction, realizable only as a grant from a dictator.

There are several major factors today that some interpret as directing our society toward some form of state socialism: the growth of monopoly, of the interventionist state, of labor organization.[32] But it would be difficult to deny that there remain many years of life and success in the indeterminate state of American capitalism as we know it. During this time ahead it would be futile to gaze at the theoretically workable economic blueprint of social-

---

[31] This fiction plays an extremely important role in Stalinism (see p. 403); its illusory nature has become the subject of much concern to British Labour (see p. 310).

[32] Schumpeter argues that labor is becoming undisciplined, owing to the strength of the unions, the support of government and public opinion, and the apathy of management, and that a situation might arise in which "*socialism might be the only means of restoring social discipline*" (*Capitalism, Socialism and Democracy*, p. 215). (His italics.)

ism, envisaged as an extrapolation from present society. It is indeed a safe prediction that if there are any socialists in 2015 they will think in very different terms from those of today.

In the meantime, it is well to remember that the doctrine of the most democratic of socialists contains hidden snares, and that when an economic goal has been given the character of an absolute all other aspects of life must be subordinated to it. It would also be well to bear in mind Lord Keynes' precept that it "is better that a man should tyrannize over his bank balance than over his fellow-citizens."[33] A socialist regime can obviously commence with democratic aims, but it is at least uncertain that it can maintain them. Proclamations of democracy were not wanting when the Soviet Union was born in Russia, where even middle-class democracy had but recently begun to grow. Protestations of democratic intent would have seemed superfluous when George VI summoned Clement Attlee to form a socialist cabinet in Great Britain, the mother of industry as well as of Parliaments. Perhaps the chief value of an effort to consider what socialism *might* be like is that it may throw some light on what has actually occurred in Labour England and Bolshevik Russia, two strikingly contrasting realities to which the one word *socialism* has been applied.

NOTES ON BOOKS

There are, of course, histories of the various socialist parties, few of which have been translated into English. A good general account is given in H. W. Laidler, *Social-Economic Movements, An Historical and Comparative Survey*, and there is Max Beer's standard work *Fifty Years of International Socialism*. L. Symes and T. Clement's *Rebel America, The Story of Social Revolt in the United States* is a good work covering the important aspects of American socialism, and recent major contributions to this field are Ira Kipnis' *The American Socialist Movement, 1897–1912* and D. D. Egbert and S. Persons, eds., *Socialism in American Life* (vol. 1). Part V of Schumpeter's invaluable *Capitalism, Socialism and Democracy* is a brilliant interpretation of the socialist movement and the reasons for its uneven progress.

For the critique of socialism, there are the outright anti's, such as

[33] *General Theory*, p. 374.

L. von Mises' *Socialism*, but once more the reader will benefit from an analysis that is not colored by an assumption of the validity of classical economics, and may find it in Part IV of Schumpeter's masterpiece. Other works to be consulted are C. D. Baldwin's *Economic Planning, Its Aims and Implications*, F. Zweig's *The Planning of Free Societies*, and B. Lippincott, ed., *On the Economic Theory of Socialism*. P. M. Sweezy's *Socialism* is about as able a statement of the case "pro" as one can expect to find.

11.

SOCIALISM BY APPOINTMENT: BRITISH LABOUR

IN JULY, 1945, Mr. Clement R. Attlee, the son of a successful lawyer, educated at Haileybury and Oxford, became the second Labour Party Prime Minister.[1] The elation of the Labourites was far greater in 1945 than on the earlier occasions when J. Ramsay MacDonald had received the honor. Then they had held only a plurality of the House of Commons, and were dependent on the support of the Liberals and others. Now Labour had 394 of the 640 seats in Commons. The general election of 1945 had astounded most expert observers and, perhaps, a good many Labour voters, by rejecting sharply the Conservative Party that led the victorious war-time Coalition government. As Winston Churchill put it somewhat ruefully, at the end of five years of his direction of the nation, "all our enemies having surrendered unconditionally or being about to do so, I was immediately dismissed by the British electorate from all further conduct of their affairs."[2]

The popular vote was closer, Labour receiving about 12 million, or a little less than 49 percent of the total, and the Conservatives and Liberals together about 250,000 more. It was, nevertheless, a great victory for the Labour Party, and a choice triumph for social-

---

[1] To prevent confusion, the British spelling "Labour" will refer to the Labour Party, the American spelling "labor," to the working class or labor movement.

[2] *The Gathering Storm*, New York, 1948, p. 667.

ism. The United Kingdom, birthplace and citadel of industrial capitalism, the heart of the British Empire, was the first major nation that voted freely to go socialist. This, at least, was Labour's interpretation of the mandate it received. The Party was ready with a program which it believed would place Britain firmly on the road to a socialist society before the next scheduled general election of 1950, and its legislative schedule was in fact completed by the summer of 1949.

Nevertheless, British economy and society were still far from socialism. Many of Labour's favorite measures were also supported by the Tories. Nor could it be said that the country was overwhelmingly certain that Labour should hold England permanently on the course toward an equalitarian, socialist society.

In a word, the socialist mold had not yet hardened and a Conservative resumption of leadership at the will of the electorate would not constitute a counterrevolution. It had been said repeatedly by members of the Labour Party that their dispute with the Tories differed from all previous two-party battles in that for the first time there was substantial disagreement on fundamental matters. They were socialists, the Tories capitalists. This may have been effective propaganda, but the truth was that the two parties traveled a good distance along the same road and the fork that indeed exists had hardly been reached. Socialism remained a matter of promise, and especially of intent, rather than established fact, for many of the intermediate acts of socialist policy were quite acceptable to Conservatives, if it were not intended to use these measures as levers for completing the socialist blueprint. The crux of the difference between the parties therefore lay in Labour's doctrine, which indicated its intentions.

Compared with Marxian organizations on the Continent, Labour had always seemed very moderate, so much so that until the Attlee government began a genuine assault on some of the strongholds of capitalism it was common in the United States to pass lightly over the Party's renewed pledges of socialist faith, and regard it amiably as the genteel English counterpart of the more sober elements of the New Deal, no more. This is incorrect, for Labour is socialist. But British socialism is not easy to characterize, except in that it is assuredly and avowedly not Marxian. Indeed, Mr. Attlee is inclined to lay stress upon the ethical beliefs of a Christian people as the energizing force of the movement that elevated him to the Prime Ministership.[3] British socialism did not spring from the brain of any one philosopher, or from a small coterie of dedicated agitators.

The many and diverse threads of its origins include the works of Tory reformers, themselves an echo of the mercantilist absolute monarchy; the influence of radical agitators, Utopians, clerics, and intellectuals; the solid, practical advances of the trade unions and coöperatives. Without calling him its founder, it is fair to say that during the first half of the nineteenth century Robert Owen dominated socialism in England. His practical successes were slight and fleeting, but his failures were a stimulant to unionization and cooperation, as well as socialist discourse. In this period, the greatest efflorescence of the working class was the Chartist movement, which stood primarily for the extension of political democracy, through universal manhood suffrage, secret ballot and corollary practices. The ultimate goal of Chartism, social and economic betterment for labor, was to be sought following political victory, and the Chartist movement accordingly gave shelter to a wide variety of economic platforms some of which were strikingly incompatible.[4]

Without belittling Francis Place, the gifted tailor who agitated Parliament into repealing the antiunion Combination Acts, or Robert Owen himself, or Jeremy Bentham, James Mill, and the others who called themselves philosophic radicals, high credit for the actual achievement of reform legislation must be given to such Tories as the seventh Earl of Shaftesbury, father of the Factory Acts, and Richard Oastler, the vigorous propagandist who supported him. And among the ablest preachers of and workers for the improvement of the life of the poor were a number of Anglican ministers who became known as Christian Socialists.[5] From none of these sources, however, could a mass socialist movement have arisen. Nor could it have sprung from the elite craft unions that were gaining strength in the middle third of the nineteenth century.

[3] *The Labour Party in Perspective*, London, 1937, pp. 26 ff.
[4] Hodgskin, Bray, and other writers between 1800 and 1850 have recently been resurrected as the "British pre-Marxians" but their influence was negligible. See Gray, *The Socialist Tradition*, pp. 262 ff.; M. Hovell, *The Chartist Movement*, London, 1918.
[5] See pp. 547 ff.

It was only in the 1880's that the first hesitant steps were taken toward what eventually became the British Labour Party, steps that became really significant when the social climate of England had changed. The middle-class democracy of a propertied electorate had bowed to the inevitable, and with respect to universal manhood suffrage only the dotting of the *i* remained. As in all countries, mass socialism could follow only upon the conversion of bourgeois intellectuals, and to these the "esthetic socialist" John Ruskin strongly appealed. The novels, and later the reform measures of the Tory Disraeli carried on the fight for a higher social morality under the ancient banner of *noblesse oblige,* and his outlook was continued by the Tory Democrats, Lord Randolph Churchill and his friends. Socialist thinking was given greater currency by Joseph Chamberlain's proposals for municipal ownership of utilities and for city action toward social reform, which were characterized as "municipal socialism." The stir that Henry George had created in the United States with his proposal for a single tax on land, eliminating the unearned increment of rent, was even exceeded by his reception in England.

By the end of the 1880's socialism was in the air, and it was beginning to take shape on what Marx would call the only true ground. Organized labor, just commencing to tap the immense reservoir of the unskilled, was nearing that state of growth and maturity which would incline it to employ political action as a direct means to economic objectives. The components of socialism were therefore present and, as usual, the theory had preceded their development by a number of years. The theorists and organizers without whom a sentiment cannot become a movement had entered the lists as early as 1881, twenty-five years before the formation of the Labour Party.

Despite the fact that Marx had lived in England since 1849, and was already rather well known on the Continent, *Das Kapital* did not appear in English until the translation by Samuel Moore and Marx's son-in-law, Edward Aveling, in 1887. This indifference to Marx in his home of exile, owing to British distaste for intricate theoretical systems and to Marx's complex and heavy-handed presentation, helps explain the curious manner in which his doctrine was presented to the British. In 1881, one of the English intellectuals of Marx's acquaintance, Henry M. Hyndman, published *England for All,* with an acknowledgment of his debt to an unnamed "great thinker and original writer." Marx, never slow to respond to a slight, dismissed Hyndman's excuse, that the British were wary of foreigners and would accept the truth more readily from one of their own, and terminated their relationship. The fact that his dishonesty, or tactfulness, served to divorce him from Karl Marx in no way discouraged Hyndman from establishing the Marxist Democratic Federation, in 1881, which later became the Social Democratic Federation. Although the Federation was solidly native, unlike the early American Marxist groups, it did not gain many adherents, and was able only to serve as a leaven in other organizations.

Nor did the celebrated Fabian society, founded in 1883, become a mass movement. But since it was not Marxian, lack of numbers was not of great concern. Indeed, it could not have weathered a great surge of affiliations, for there were not many who could exchange ideas with George Bernard Shaw, Sidney and Beatrice Webb, Annie Besant and Graham Wallas. With such quality, quantity could be scorned.

With Shaw as their leading economic theorist, the Fabians described the capitalist system as based upon private, and unearned, appropriation of common wealth. Ricardo's law of rent, as expanded by Henry George, was further extended, and became the key point of the Fabian explanation of the paradox of poverty amid plenty. Ricardo had argued that as population increases relative to food supply, land of decreasing quality, entailing a higher cost of production, is brought into cultivation. Since grain from all qualities of land will sell at the same price, the owner of the better land will benefit from his lower cost of production and receive an unearned increment. George went further, holding that speculation in land increased these undeserved rewards, and constituted the principal reason for capitalist depressions and the unhappy state of labor. Shaw generalized Ricardo's principle to explain all accumulations of riches, in industry as well as agriculture, as the result of private ownership of advantageous economic facilities, and concluded that public ownership of the means of production was the only way to proper and just utilization of resources. This would come about, not through revolution, but through a slow process of extending the sphere of government activity, and through the education of the electorate to the benefits of socialism.[6]

The Fabians accordingly set for themselves a propagandist's role, issuing their message for specific reforms and an eventual democratic and moral socialism in a large number of excellently written tracts and pamphlets, and fighting for particular measures through their favorite tactic of "permeation." Permeation meant persuading the high-placed and the powerful to support reform laws and policies that would contribute to the gradual socialization of the country. Gradualness was the keynote of the Fabians, even in their name, taken from Quintus Fabius Maximus, the Delayer, who had harried Hannibal but avoided a major battle. The Trojan horse might have been a more apt classical allusion, a sleekly carved Trojan horse that would not be out of place in the drawing rooms of the Oxonians and Cantabs among whom socialism was to permeate.

Judged by the ferocious and heroic proportions of left-wing revolutionary Marxism, the Fabian tactic might seem both puny and naïve. But it was rather successful. The incomparable Shaw did not, of course, persuade his wide public to dedicate themselves to socialism, but he did convince many intelligent men and women that it was smart to be "advanced," and that to be advanced meant being highly critical of traditional institutions and manners. At the very least, his wit helped free British socialism, for a time, from the drab and humorless solemnity of Continental Marxism. The most successful permeators, however, were the Webbs, indefatigable researchers, gatherers, and interpreters of social data. Beatrice Webb's family connections were sufficient to open useful doors, and the Webbs' ultrascientific and factual sales talk produced results. For example, to them is due much of the credit for the Education Act of 1902, enacted by the Conservative Balfour government, which remained basic legislation for the English school system for over forty years.

But neither the Fabians nor their later, more radical, and somewhat Utopian offshoot, the Guild socialists, of whom the prolific G. D. H. Cole is best known, could seriously have threatened the Liberal and Conservative parties. The old and efficacious "permeation" from the North was, however, still working. Just as British

[6] See G. B. Shaw, ed., *Fabian Essays in Socialism*, London, 1931.

classical economics had been fathered by a Scot, Adam Smith, so the real political movement of British labor was brought to life by the Scots mineworkers' leader, Keir Hardie, who led the founding of the Independent Labour Party in 1893. The ILP was an enthusiastic propaganda organization, combining a generally socialist message with a trumpet call for political action by workers and their sympathizers and a demand for legislative intervention on behalf of the underprivileged.

The growing political consciousness of the powerful Trades Union Congress and of the British masses in general slowly strengthened the demand for more effective organization, and in 1900 the ILP, the Fabians, the Social Democrats and the Trades Union Congress joined to form the Labour Representation Committee. Even in its prelife—for the Committee was transformed into the Labour Party in 1906—British Labour displayed a pattern that characterized it until the founding generation declined in years and influence. The bulk of support, financial and electoral, came from the unions, who jealously guarded the supremacy in the Party which their voting strength assured them. But, and this may be what is called a typically British arrangement, the unions were generally content to hold their power as a veto in reserve, their viewpoint setting limits beyond which Labour could not go. For example, the Labour Party did not profess socialism until 1918, owing to the opposition of conservative union leaders. This, of course, made little difference with respect to immediate objectives. Organizational matters were left disproportionately in the hands of the politicians of the ILP, and policy formation to the fertile and ready brains of the Fabian intellectuals. It was, at the least, a practical division of labor.

Sooner or later the Labour Representation Committee would have given place to a nation-wide party, and indeed, it is surprising that it lasted as long as it did. In their first electoral campaign, in 1900, the Labour Representation Committee was able to win seats for only two of its fifteen candidates, and one of the victors was the already famous Keir Hardie. This inauspicious beginning failed to shock the movement into reorganization, but a decision handed down in 1901 by the House of Lords, sitting as high court, upset the workers and their intellectual friends sufficiently for them to organize the Labour Party for the next general election in 1906. This legal ruling, in the famous Taff Vale case, held unions liable for damages to a company by individual workers during a strike. Had it been long sustained, the decision would have put the unions out of business.

For the unions to remain powerful and grow, Taff Vale had to be reversed, but this could take place only through legislative action, which called for an increase in the strength of the prolabor element in the House of Commons. This group was not limited to Labour Party members of Parliament. For years, union candidates had been elected as Liberals, and there were other Liberals who were sympathetic to labor and even owed their seats to labor support. If the Labour Party, as such, could make a good enough showing to give it prestige and commit and obligate the Liberals, the Taff Vale ruling could be abrogated.

This is precisely what happened in the election of 1906. Although Labour won only 30 seats,[7] the victorious Liberals were bound both by campaign pledges and union support where the Labour Party did not offer candidates, and they passed the Trades Disputes Act of 1906, which overrode the Taff Vale decision of the Lords. All things considered, the official entry of the Labour Party into British politics was most successful, and the organization continued to prosper. In the two hard-fought elections of 1910, in which Lloyd George's radical budget was the main issue, Labour secured 40 and 42 seats. With the 80-odd Irish Nationalists, Labour held the balance between the two major parties, and voted to keep the Liberals in office.

The next election was not fought until 1918. During the First World War, the youthful Party was naturally torn by conflicts over pacifism, conscription, wages, and the degree of support to be given the Coalition government, in which it was represented. To strengthen the unity of the movement, Labour conferences in 1918 provided the Party not only with a new statement of principles, but with a new and better organization. For the first time, the Party presented a fully rounded social—and socialist—program, based upon the principles stated in *Labour and the New Social Order,* written by Sidney Webb. The unions' opposition to socialism had declined during the stresses of war, and the revolutionary triumphs

[7] The Liberals had 397, the Tories 132, and the Irish Nationalists 83.

in Russia were a powerful psychological attraction leftward. Nevertheless, neither the word *socialism* nor the usual trappings of Marxist cant appeared. Instead, there was the following statement, clear enough in intent, but with fewer hair-raising connotations than the typical Continental socialist proclamation. It was declared to be an objective of the Labour Party.

To secure for the producers by hand and by brain the full fruits of their industry, and the most equitable distribution thereof that may be possible, upon the basis of the common ownership of the means of production, distribution, and exchange and the best obtainable system of popular administration and control of each industry and service.[8]

This objective was never cast aside, and remained the core of Labour policy when Mr. Attlee took office in 1945. With the publication of *Labour and the New Social Order*, the Party was explicitly, although not blatantly, socialist. When we consider the popular reluctance to take statements of principle seriously, however, it is not surprising that Labour was widely viewed as only a moderate reformist, rather than socialist, movement.

Structurally, the Labour Party had been shapeless and hybrid, revealing the diverseness of its founding groups and their desire to remain autonomous of their larger creation. As is usually the case when proudly sovereign entities are pressed together by the force of events, the confederal form of organization had been adopted. The Labour Executive, the Party's high command, had in effect been a council of ambassadors representing autonomous trade unions, the autonomous Independent Labour Party and the extremely autonomous Fabians. Concentration in the head of the Party of a higher degree of control over its sprawling limbs was greatly assisted by a change in membership rules. Membership in the Labour Party had originally been open only through one of its component organizations. The affiliating trade unions had naturally provided the overwhelming majority of members, as the ILP was small, and the Fabian Society almost negligible, in numbers.[9] The new Labour

[8] Attlee, *Labour Party in Perspective*, p. 46.
[9] In 1914 there were about 1,600,000 members affiliated to the Labour Party through trades unions, 30,000 through the ILP, and 3,304 through the Fabian Society. See G. D. H. Cole, *A History of the Labour Party from 1914*, London, 1948, pp. 9 ff.

constitution of 1918 for the first time cleared the way for the creation of a well-organized, centrally directed mass party. The basic structural unit, henceforth, was to be the local Labour Party, open to individual membership, and directly affiliated with national headquarters. The National Executive, which had previously been chosen by the component organizations, was now to be elected by the entire Party Conference rather than by the individual sections. This change made it possible for the trade unions to decide the total membership of the Executive but, as before, they exercised great restraint in employing their power, and the ILP and Fabians were treated with the utmost generosity.

There has always been some dispute among the theorists of representative government as to precisely whom and what the elected legislator is to represent. He can be regarded as a sort of lawyer, speaking for the interests of his particular constituents, and this attitude has been the typical result of the American system of political decentralization, contrary to the wishes of the Founding Fathers. Another theory sees the representative as one chosen for his preëminent qualities to represent the interests of the entire body politic. This loftier viewpoint actually does make some contact with reality, particularly where, as in Great Britain, the political system is relatively more centralized, and the member of Parliament is not required to be a resident of his constituency. Under the British method of representation and corresponding party organization, the M.P. is relatively freer from local pressures than the American Congressman. If this be a gain, as in all social arrangements, the advantage involves some cost, for the member of Commons is much more closely controlled by the central leadership of his party. Labour M.P.'s were accordingly to be subject to the policy decisions of the Labour Party Conferences, and to the discipline of the Parliamentary Labour Party which they constituted. But the dignity and power of membership in Commons would not suffer M.P.'s to be representatives of their party in the lesser, ambassadorial sense. The Parliamentary Labour Party therefore was given an autonomous voice in formulating national Party policy together with the Party Executive and members of the Trade Union Congress.

Such was the Labour Party that entered the lists at the close of the First World War. In 1918 it won 60 seats; in 1922 its strength rose to

142;[10] and in the election of 1923 Labour secured 191 seats, the Liberals 158, and the Tories only 258. As no party held a majority, it rested with the Liberals to decide whether to allow a Tory or a Labour Cabinet to take office, and they chose the latter course. In January, 1924, J. Ramsay MacDonald became Prime Minister and Foreign Secretary, with the financially orthodox Labourite Philip Snowden as Chancellor of the Exchequer. The utter dependence of the government on Liberal votes dictated a policy of moderation and abstention from socialist measures which was, in fact, quite congenial to MacDonald. The first Labour government was able to accomplish little on the home front, although it did acquit itself creditably in foreign affairs. Its tenure was, in any event, extremely brief. In October, 1924, the Liberals joined the Tories in opposition to the government's proposals for bettering relations with and granting a loan to Soviet Russia, and a general election had to be called.

The campaign of 1924 was colored by the appearance of the celebrated Zinoviev letter, which had all the appearances of authenticity, but might have been a forgery. It carried instructions from the head of the Communist International to the British Communists, urging them to support MacDonald's Russian treaties and, in the lurid phraseology favored by the Comintern's literary artists, to hasten revolution on all fronts. Since Labour's policy toward Russia was the principal campaign issue, the letter, unless proved to be forged, would have been a bad political blow under any circumstances. MacDonald's tactical blunders in handling the matter made things worse than ever for Labour, and the new Parliament contained only 152 Labourites, against 42 Liberals and 415 Tories.

Mr. Baldwin was Prime Minister and Great Britain, after experiencing general elections annually for three years, settled down for the legal five-year term of its version of normalcy. The Baldwin government was illuminated by the successes of Sir Austen Chamberlain, the able brother of Neville, in the Foreign Office, but its course was darkened by continued economic difficulties, and, among other events, by the General Strike of 1926. This was not the general strike of the syndicalists' revolutionary dreams.[11] It was a strike by

[10] In 1918 the two wings of the split Liberal Party gained 171 seats and the Tories 374; in 1922, the Liberals fell to 118 and the Conservatives to 347.

[11] See p. 563.

organized labor to help the miners in resisting employer demands for lower wages and longer hours. The difficulties of the mining industry had been long standing, but they were aggravated by Britain's return to the prewar gold standard in 1925. England's underlying economic handicaps became even more severe in the deflation that followed this reconstitution of the golden calf, and the classical economists' remedy of wage reduction and further deflation was but the next requisite step in the perverse logic of that doctrine.

Labor struck, and was badly defeated, owing in no small part to the intrepidity of Mr. Churchill who, though he opposed neither decent wages nor state intervention in economic affairs, rose with his customary vigor against the threat to the state's sovereignty that he perceived in the growing strength of socialism. As a sequel to the crushing of the strike came the Trades Disputes and Trade Unions Act of 1927, which both placed legal limitations on the extent and spread of strikes and delivered a body blow to the finances of His Majesty's Opposition, the Labour Party. Under an Act of 1913, unions were enabled to assess members for political contributions unless they specifically asked to be exempted from this levy ("contracting out," as the British put it). The new law authorized assessments only when specifically assented to ("contracting in"). As a result, the Labour Party, by 1928, had suffered the loss of about 1,750,000 dues payers, and felt outraged, although it could not claim that union members who wished to support it were prevented from doing so.

The general economic trend, however, proved to be something against which the Tory strategists were unable to contend, and Labour prepared for the general election of 1929 with high confidence. A new and wordy program, *Labour and the Nation,* was prepared as a statement of long-term aims. The electoral program itself concentrated on the problem of unemployment, while socialization was all but forgotten. Even with respect to the issue of the day, Labour could claim no radical inspiration, for the Liberals offered a very similar unemployment program. And, as the Liberal proposals were effectively authored by J. M. Keynes,[12] it would later appear that Labour was following a Keynesian policy. As is always the case in

[12] *Can Lloyd George Do It? An Examination of the Liberal Pledge,* London, 1929 (with H. D. Henderson).

a three-cornered race in single-member districts, however, the weakest contestant, the Liberals, secured a disproportionately low ratio of seats in Commons to their popular vote. Labour, with 8,365,-000 votes, won 288 seats; the Tories, with 8,664,000 votes, won 260 seats; and the Liberals, with 5,301,000 votes, only 59 seats.[13] For the second time, therefore, Labour took office at the pleasure of the Liberals.

Although the Liberals, especially their non-Keynesian element, acted as a brake upon Labour's plans for meeting the problem of unemployment, even more serious obstacles to success were Prime Minister MacDonald's ignorance and Chancellor of the Exchequer Snowden's outlook with respect to economics. MacDonald had been losing respect for his party colleagues, particularly those of the left wing, and socialism had gradually come to mean for him little more than a vague aspiration for the distant future. As for Snowden, he was as doctrinaire as any man in England in his devotion to free trade and the gold standard. As long as Snowden was able to enforce his viewpoint, there could be no recourse to either protective tariffs, which might have secured the home market to British producers, or devaluation, which would have improved Britain's position in foreign trade. In addition, Snowden insisted on balancing the budget, although favoring a moderate public works program to increase employment, and tax relief for the lower income brackets. In general, his approach was to cure a deflationary situation with more deflation and, while the poor and the jobless were aided in several ways, the number of registered unemployed rose from 1,160,000 in the summer of 1929, to 2,750,000 in the summer of 1931.

The political position of the Labour government and the economic position of Great Britain were becoming equally untenable. MacDonald and Snowden sought advice and coöperation from conservative business elements more and more, and turned to French and American bankers for loans that afforded only slight relief. As the crisis worsened, MacDonald, in August, 1931, determined to resign, and Labour accepted this decision, with the ex-

---

[13] Cole, *History of the Labour Party*, pp. 218 ff., 479. The Liberal Party's supporters were deserting to the Tories and Labour, a trend accentuated by the General Strike. The Liberals were further weakened by a split between the Lloyd George and Samuel factions.

pectation that the Conservatives would take over and hold a general election. On his return from the palace, the leader of the Labour Party astounded his colleagues by announcing that he would continue as Prime Minister, heading a National coalition cabinet of Tories, Liberals, and a handful of Labourites. To the stalwarts of the Labour Party, the intellectuals of the Fabian Society and the practical men of the unions, this was a great betrayal; to Conservatives and, as it proved, to a great many Englishmen, MacDonald's action was a patriotic leap over party lines in selfless concern for national welfare. In any event, it was not quite cricket and was, for the Tories, a most unorthodox way of regaining power, although it was, of course, entirely legal.

MacDonald's coup took place on August 24, 1931, Snowden and three other Labour ministers moving with him. By September 21, Snowden was ready to abandon that insistence on the gold standard which he had maintained in stubborn, principled fashion while he was a Labour Chancellor of the Exchequer. "Natural law" could apparently be made to yield only by the exigencies of a National ministry. The tariff, it was felt, called for special electoral sanction, and the government went to the country on October 27 with an appeal for what MacDonald called a "doctor's mandate," the right to prescribe what the ailing lion seemed to need. The election showed the full effect of MacDonald's desertion upon the Labour Party: the Tories won 475 seats, against 72 for the Liberals and 52 for the Labour and Independent Labour groups. National Labour, consisting of MacDonald and his coterie, gained 13 seats.[14]

This landslide defeat naturally had great influence upon the character of the Labour Party. Its right wing, led by MacDonald, which had preferred to soft-pedal all talk of socialism in its efforts to obtain office, was now without influence. Its left wing, led by the Independent Labour Party, drew from the "great betrayal" the conclusion that the leadership had to be firmly committed to socialism, and the moral that compromise with capitalism did not pay. En-

---

[14] As a postscript to what Labour remembers as the disaster of 1931, it may be noted that Snowden, who had retired after the election to the House of Lords and the cabinet post of Lord Privy Seal, further relaxed his economic principles to consent to protection as a temporary measure, but left the government in 1932 when tariffs and imperial preference were adopted as standing policy.

couraged by the world-wide shift to the left brought on by the
Great Depression, the ILP attempted to win Labour to a militant
policy characterized by the slogan "Socialism Now." When the
center not only refused to follow the left, but insisted on tightening
party discipline, the ILP split away into complete independence and
political oblivion. The center set about mending organizational and
doctrinal fences. A degree of discipline greater than previously
known to British politics, appeared with the resolution that required
Labour Party members and office holders to adhere to the majority
decisions of the Party congresses, save in matters of conscience.[15]
While the center majority agreed that one of the reasons for the
disaster of 1931 had been a lack of devotion to socialist principle on
the part of the leadership, it would not go so far as to violate the
British constitutional tradition by committing the King's ministers in-
flexibly to the specific decisions of the Labour Party Conference.
Labour decided to remedy this defect in policy formation by working on its programs years in advance of election to office, and here
the contribution of the New Fabian Research Bureau, founded in
1931 under the leadership of G. D. H. Cole, was especially important.
Lastly, but of great significance, after the *affaire* MacDonald, many
of the old leaders began to fade into retirement, and men of the
lower echelons, Clement Attlee among them, began to move up to
the front bench.

It was nine years before Labour was to enter Winston Churchill's
wartime coalition, and fourteen years before it was to regain command of the government. During these long years of Tory ascendancy—under the bourgeois rather than the aristocratic wing of the
Conservative Party—Labour slowly rebuilt its strength within the

[15] It was under this principle that the Party's outstanding legal mind, Sir
Stafford Cripps, was expelled in 1939, for continuing to insist on a popular
front with the Liberals and others opposed to the Chamberlain Tory government after the Party had rejected his proposals. Exactly two years before, Sir
Stafford and some followers had been threatened with expulsion over their
insistence on a united front with the Communists. On still an earlier occasion
Sir Stafford vehemently condemned appeasement of fascism but even more
vehemently opposed voting for arms appropriations since, by definition, any
use to which the Conservatives—Labor's "class enemies"—would put these
weapons would necessarily be imperialistic (Cole, *History of the Labour Party*,
p. 307). Perhaps the distinguished attorney and nephew of Beatrice Webb
sought release from the confining language of his profession in extreme political
pronouncements.

country, and its prestige throughout the democratic world. Like many another leftish or left-of-center movement in the days of the depression, Labour adopted whole-heartedly the gospel of pacifism and disarmament, but a few years later was quick to cry out against appeasement of fascists. There remained confusion even in conversion, however, for some elements of the Labour Party opposed both appeasement and rearmament—under a Tory government. But its very record of pacifism, and opposition to appeasement, together with its representation of the organized workers, provided the basis for a solid comeback, and in 1935 Labour won 154 seats in Commons.[16]

The next few years were dominated by Adolf Hitler's successful aggressions, and Labour's record of vacillation was no worse than that of most democratic groups at the time. Its legacy of doctrinaire pacifism was slow to dwindle, as was its traditional internationalism, expressed in persevering faith in the League. But by the time of the Munich crisis, in the fall of 1938, Labour had faced the facts clearly and firmly, and the Party took a stand against appeasement and for war if that were necessary. When the conflict broke out a year later, Labour gave full support to the Chamberlain government, in which it justifiably had little confidence. It voted for the government's war measures, but declined to enter into a coalition. Labour contributed to the swelling protest against the lack of vigor with which the fight was being prosecuted, and supported Churchill's rebellion within the Conservative Party. When Chamberlain finally realized he had to step down, Labour agreed to serve under its old enemy, the "former naval person," in the coalition that led Great Britain to victory.

Attlee served as Deputy Prime Minister, Bevin as Minister of Labour, Morrison as Minister of Supply, Cripps as Ambassador to Russia and later as Minister of Aircraft Production. Other members of the Labour Party held important government posts. Working relations were on the whole excellent, and the electoral truce, under which the incumbent party was not challenged in by-elections to Commons, was faithfully observed. Although the Labour leadership assured their more radical followers that this electoral arrangement

[16] The ILP won 4, the two wings of the Liberals 54, and the Conservatives 390.

did not imply a "political truce," it must at least be said that party disputes were severely restrained. Labour even accepted, regretfully but gallantly, Churchill's refusal to amend the hated Trade Disputes Act of 1927 on the ground that it was too contentious a matter within the Conservative Party.

The basic reason for this successful coöperation was more concrete than the celebrated British capacity for compromising and getting along. The two great parties, and the Liberals, were agreed on a number of aims other than the overriding one of winning the war. It should not be forgotten that from the time of Disraeli, and even earlier, British conservatism had been actively interested in reform and social legislation. Government intervention in social and economic affairs held no terrors for the Tory mind, and even the Liberals had come to espouse it. The Liberal landslide of 1906 that ended a long period of Conservative rule was in large part owing to the country's addiction to free trade. It was a setback for the protectionism and imperial tariff preference to which the ex-Liberal and "municipal socialist" Joseph Chamberlain had led the Tories, but not for domestic intervention. During the 1880's and 1890's, the rise of the labor movement and of socialism, Fabian "permeation," and also, as Attlee argues, the revolt of the Christian conscience against the inequities of industrial capitalism, had adequately accustomed the public mind to a tremendous increase of state activity in social and economic affairs. The return of the Liberals was no return to the theories of the classical economists. It was, on the contrary, a rather curious combination of intensified domestic intervention with what had become habitual adherence to free trade in foreign commerce. In short, during the Tory ascendancy, the Liberals had reversed themselves. They dropped Ricardo and laissez faire and came to power in 1906 prepared to lead Great Britain into the swiftest leap toward the welfare state it had ever taken.

It was only after the First World War that the Conservatives, under Baldwin and the lesser Chamberlain, Neville, seemed to move in the direction of the American Republican policy of laissez faire behind a tariff wall. But this was more apparent than real, and was so only in the sense that they added to the welfare structure at a slower rate than before the First War and after the Second. During the 1920's and '30's unemployment benefits were paid beyond the period covered by insurance, old-age pensions were instituted, free milk was provided for school children and free medical service for low income groups. A Keynesian low-interest policy was introduced by Neville Chamberlain as Baldwin's Chancellor of the Exchequer, and was maintained by his successors. There was a large-scale program of subsidized low-rent housing. To continue an interventionist policy was natural for Winston Churchill, for, although now a Conservative, he was not of the Baldwin persuasion. In his younger days he had been a radically interventionist member of the Asquith and Lloyd George Liberal governments. When he at last received the Prime Ministership in the days of crisis, he was predisposed not only to wage a vigorous war, but to prepare a positive, interventionist, and welfare program for the time of peace. The politically weakened Liberals, under the influence of J. M. Keynes and Sir William (later Lord) Beveridge, were, of course, equally interventionist, and were no longer even bound to the dogma of free trade.

Churchill's Coalition government was therefore able to agree on a number of postwar measures which, while naturally falling short of Labour's platform, were exceedingly radical, or at least interventionist by American standards. The most sweeping commitments were those taken in connection with the celebrated Beveridge proposals.[17] In a series of White Papers published in 1944, the Coalition government pledged a program of insurance and social services "from the cradle to the grave,"[18] including a national health service, and a policy of maintenance of full employment on the Keynesian principles of compensatory public investment, monetary and foreign exchange management and taxation adjusted to the state of business. Although these were statements of policy, rather than specific legislative enactments, they certainly revealed no basic dispute over what has been called the welfare state. In several fields, the Coalition government passed laws with which Labour was later content

---

[17] Beveridge's first great report, on *Insurance and Allied Services*, was a command publication in 1942. His second, *Full Employment in a Free Society*, was not officially sponsored and its publication was in fact preceded by several months by the White Paper on employment.

[18] Franklin D. Roosevelt had long been fond of the phrase "cradle to the grave," and was somewhat offended that Beveridge should have received credit for it. (Perkins, *Roosevelt*, p. 283.)

or upon which it was able conveniently to build. The Town and Country Planning Act of 1944 gave local authorities the power of condemnation of "blitzed and blighted" areas at 1939 prices, with the function of infusing reason and order into the development of the land, housing and the growth of cities. The Butler Education Act of 1944 provided for a higher school-leaving age, for greater support for what Americans call private schools, more and better buildings, more and better scholarships, higher teacher salaries, a long-range program of compulsory part-time training to the age of eighteen—in a word, for a vast expansion of public education. The Disabled Persons Act of 1944 transferred to the state the obligation and much of the burden of enabling the physically handicapped to live usefully. The Family Allowance Act of 1945 provided five shillings a week for second and further children of all families, even the wealthiest.

Apart from this legislation, the Coalition government had administered the home front as closely as it could upon the principle of equal sacrifices. Excess profits were taxed at the rate of 100 percent. Rationing was equally imposed and rigorously executed. Government control naturally reached into many new fields and increased where it already existed. Indeed, just before war was declared, Imperial Airways and British Airways were amalgamated into the public British Overseas Airways Corporation, and the Coalition planned an extension of this system of public control and mixed public and private ownership to the whole field of civil aviation. Rail and road transport came under ministerial control during the war, and in 1942 the new Ministry of Fuel and Power extended central government supervision over coal and the other sources of power.

Surely this record and, above all, the general social outlook it revealed, should have encouraged all save convinced socialists—and unreconstructed capitalists—to grant further support to the Conservative Party which had led the Coalition. That the British people did not do so, that they dismissed the Tories and called their wartime junior partners to undivided power, could be taken to mean that they had chosen socialism as a way of life, and that they had authorized the Labour Party to enter into a program of the orderly transformation of the United Kingdom into a socialist commonwealth. In general, this was the way the Labour leadership understood its mandate, for their electoral platform, *Let Us Face the Future* (April, 1945), had not concealed their socialist intentions.

This manifesto promised all that could be expected from an elaboration of the employment and insurance policies of the White Papers. It emphasized planning of investment through a National Investment Board, wide insurance coverage, a health service, and special consideration for children and mothers. In addition it pledged tax revision to bear lightly on the lower income groups, a housing program to benefit the masses, relief for economically depressed areas, if need be through government construction of factories, and the development of agriculture, with special attention to the small farmer. There were two further categories of undertakings. One group carried the message of socialism: nationalization of the Bank of England, of the coal, electricity, and gas industries, of rail and road transportation, and of iron and steel. The second set of promises merely involved a tactical decision which, however, might be taken to imply a commitment on principle: this was the promise to maintain wartime rationing and controls where necessary, and especially to fix rents, prices, and priorities so that inflation would be prevented, necessities would not be scarce while production of luxuries flourished, and all would receive "fair shares" instead of being at the mercy of the inequality of incomes.

When a nation votes to accept so full and varied an assortment of policies it is impossible to say which specifically attracted and which were merely taken along with the rest. Labour assumed the people had made a rational, and, of course, extremely wise choice of their program as a whole, and the Party proceeded with an honest effort to carry it through to completion.

There resulted a veritable legislative festival. Old classics were brought forth and given somewhat different renditions. New measures were presented for which great daring and originality was claimed, although critics were tempted to reply that it was merely that old tunes had been given a new and somewhat brassier orchestration. Finally, there were introduced some fresh compositions which, though well advertised beforehand, nevertheless came as a shock to those who had not been previously prepared to accept them. The tempo was at times reminiscent of the famous Hundred

Days of the first New Deal Congress, but with a significant difference. Most of the New Deal's initial legislative effort was devoted
to emergency measures, in which reform often appeared as a means
of meeting the emergency. Labour too had to cope with economic
crisis, quite different in nature and in origin, but nearly all the
necessary powers had been authorized by existing legislation, especially the wartime controls, and the legislative festival was devoted
to the program with which Great Britain was to face the future.

To press the musical analogy to its furthest, we may say that Labour's performance, taken as a whole, resembled a passacaglia in
which England's economic troubles maintained a powerful and
rhythmic theme in the bass while the government's reform melodies
soared, somewhat independently, above. Basically, the problem of
the United Kingdom was that its habitual economic pattern was no
longer viable. For many scores of years it had been a net importer
of commodities, and had balanced these expenditures with gains
from shipping, insurance, and financial services and from investments abroad. Large-scale liquidation of these investments had been
necessary to finance the total war, and the return of peace found the
United Kingdom heavily in debt, not only to the United States, but
to many countries both within the Commonwealth and without. The
war had built up a tremendous backlog of demand for goods, while
leaving the United States, with its hard-to-get dollar currency, as the
principal source of supply. Great Britain, and the sterling area as a
whole, found itself with a seriously adverse dollar account, and
British exporters were unable to accomplish a major increase in sales
to America. Ignoring for the moment the United States tariff barrier,
British plant had deteriorated and in many fields was obsolescent,
as were British marketing methods. And there was no immediate
economic pressure upon either employers or workers to plunge into
the uncharted waters of rising productivity and competitive selling.

Labor was comfortable in a state of full employment, and management with a guaranteed market for all it produced. The latter
was assured by postwar investment and pent-up demand in a protected home market, and by sales to the sterling area. During the
war, the London accounts of such countries as India had been
blocked, and now Indian buyers were allowed to charge purchases
of British goods against these blocked resources. This provided sales

and profits to British industry, and jobs for labor, but from the standpoint of the United Kingdom as a whole it meant only payments on a wartime debt, and brought about no improvement in the country's foreign exchange position. The American loan of 1945 and the Marshall Plan were of great help, but a lasting solution could come only from increased exports resulting from higher productivity. These were essentially long-term goals, and while there might be short-run progress in their direction it would have to be rein forced by a drastic restriction of nonessential imports and by constriction of the standard of living at home.

Here was a basic problem that Tories as well as Labour would have had to face and, given the wide area of agreement between the two parties on such matters as full employment and measures of social welfare, could not have met very differently. The Conservative program of rapid relaxation of wartime controls might have provided incentives for more vigorous business leadership, and this would have been a distinct advantage. But it would have been balanced, and very likely outweighed, by the inevitably greater difficulties the Tories would have met in dealing with organized labor's pressures for higher wages and more extended influence over economic policy. The judgment of Labour Party socialism must therefore rest in greater part not upon the government's management of the economic crisis but upon its program for welfare and socialization, and particularly upon points of difference between Labour and Conservatism. This is not to dismiss the crisis, for there must always remain the question of whether, given so fundamental an economic difficulty, Labour was right in following the course it chose. But this course was assuredly not a response to a shortage of dollars: it was dictated by the Party's fundamental beliefs in welfare policies and in socialism.

To a surprising extent, however, Labour legislation merely followed patterns introduced by the Coalition government, although in a rather more expansive spirit. To this category belongs the whole range of insurance and welfare measures foreshadowed by the Beveridge Report, including the famous National Health Service Act of 1946, which in effect swept the country's medical profession, hospitals, and auxiliary medical groups and functions into one vast organization. This measure was condemned only by the British Medical Association: the Conservative Party as such criticized only in detail. Under this heading of continuity rather than change we must also place the National Insurance Act of 1946, which provided aid in unemployment, sickness, and widowhood, in the expenses of maternity and death, and for retirement. Here too belong the Industrial Injuries Act, which improved workmen's compensation benefits and procedures, the old-age Assistance Act, and the Children's Act of 1948. Save for the unwelcome blemish of government operation, it was an insurance agent's dream come true: the life span was covered.

Two measures formed a very special category which might be entitled wiping out past stains, or paying a debt of honor to the long struggle of the labor movement. Now that all were equally insured, there was no need for singling out the indigent for particular attention, and the Poor Law, dating back to Elizabeth, and reformed uncharitably in 1834, was repealed.[19] This symbolized the advent of all to social equality, but it was at bottom a gesture of sentiment. Labour's cup of grim triumph overflowed when the Trade Unions and Trade Disputes Act of 1927, the penalty imposed for the General Strike of 1926, was erased from the books. There was satisfaction in removing the Act's limitations upon strike activities, although these had not proved crippling. But there was a major political gain in reversing another provision of the Act which, it will be remembered, required the active assent of a union member to contributions to a political organization. The revised law demanded the member's active dissent to political contributions. In view of normal human inertia, and the conspicuousness of "contracting out," this was a significant boon to Labour's finances.

Such induced enthusiasm for Labour's campaign chest, of course, was a measure the Tories did not initiate or approve, and there were two other broad headings of legislation which afforded genuine issues for dispute between the parties: nationalization and economic controls. Labour's case for nationalization had been that

Each industry must have applied to it the test of national service. If it serves the nation, well and good; if it is inefficient and falls down on its job, the nation must see that things are put right. . . . There are basic industries ripe and over-ripe for public ownership and management in the direct service of the nation.[20]

These included electricity, coal, gas, inland transport, and iron and steel. The Conservatives had not been unanimously and dogmatically opposed to nationalization in all its manifestations. The Baldwin government had created the BBC, and it was the Chamberlain government that established the British Overseas Air Corporation. More than once had a prominent Conservative urged resort to public ownership in a particular field, among them Churchill, with respect to railroads, and Harold Macmillan, with respect to coal.[21]

There was accordingly little outcry when the Bank of England was taken over by the state in 1946. For many years it had obediently followed the wishes of the Crown's financial officers. And the measure of this act of nationalization as a symbol of socialist sentiment may be given by the fact that Lord Catto, Governor of the Bank as a private corporation, was willing to carry on for a time, together with the Deputy Governor, when the people became its owners. The new directors who were appointed caused no shock to London's bankers. The *Economist* called nationalization of the Bank "the prime example of the class of projects whose necessity appears to be as small as the damage they will do."[22] Nationalization of the electric power industry, which struck at municipal and local boards as well as private ownership, could be justified on the grounds of the benefits to be expected from integration, and neither this nor the taking over of Cable and Wireless, both in 1947, produced a full scale battle. The Transport Act of the same year, however, began to draw the charge of "nationalization for its own sake," which was thereafter to be hurled at the Labour government. A commission responsible to the Minister of Transport was to take over railroads, docks and inland waterways, highway transportation, and the publicly owned London transit system. The most controversial feature was that dealing with trucking: distance trucking (over forty miles) was to be nationalized, and short-haul truckers carrying their own as well as public shipments were to be limited to forty miles save under special permit (this was later softened). It was protested that

[20] *Let Us Face the Future,* 1945.
[21] Virginia Cowles, *No Cause for Alarm,* New York, 1949, p. 275.
[22] November 10, 1945, p. 669.

the government had been carried away by a desire for complete-ness and perfection of organization, that while there was need for some rationalization of transport, particularly with respect to the vexing problem that highway competition offered the railroads, there was no economic justification for establishing so complete a monopoly and for so severely restricting private competition as an efficiency yardstick.

The great nationalization debate was properly opened, however, when the government introduced its bill to socialize the iron and steel industry, in October, 1948. The British steel industry had long been cartelized, and prior to World War II had not been outstand-ing for its efforts to keep pace with the march of technology. But during the war it had served well and effectively, and had thereafter coöperated fully with the government in an able program of im-provement and expansion.[23] Now Labour proposed to transfer the ownership of the vast and complex industry to the public, and operate it through a board of experts. The component firms were to remain distinct as producing and marketing units, although some of their subsidiaries would either be exempted from socialization or sold to private holders after the state had taken title.

Mr. Strauss, the Minister of Supply, argued that the industry could expand more daringly under public than private control, and that the needs of planning required government operation of this basic sector of the economy. As a concrete justification for so sweep-ing an act of intervention, this thesis was hardly convincing, since the industry was admittedly adding to capacity as much as the gov-ernment investment plans permitted, and had had harmonious rela-tions with the Ministry in working out its role in Labour's economic program. But both Mr. Strauss and Sir Stafford Cripps advanced another motive, with far more force and conviction. This was the old theme of improper concentration of power—even if it were not improperly used—and the time-honored appeal to equalitarianism. Sir Stafford asked "whether such a large measure of industrial con-

---

[23] Robert A. Brady, *Crisis in Britain: Plans and Achievements of the Labour Government*, Berkeley, 1950, p. 188, writes: ". . . while the condition of the steel industry still leaves very much to be desired, throughout the post-war period it has shown some remarkable progress in the enhancement of the volume of production, gaining higher output per employee, and lowering costs of output."

trol by private interests is consistent with present day democratic government," and declared

. . . this challenge having been put forward by private interests, it is essential that democracy should assert its rights, as otherwise it must acknowledge for all time that it cannot touch these citadels of power, and that it is not the electorate but the owners of industrial power who shall determine the economic policies of the country.

It was not disputed that the government had adequate power, under existing legislation, to guide the course of the steel industry and allocate its products. The actual issue was therefore whether policy-making should be more fully centralized, whether the private managers might at some future time fail to coöperate, whether their mere existence as private executives constituted a threat to democracy, whether Labour was demanding socialization for reasons of principle and consistency rather than upon those grounds of efficiency and public need which it had repeatedly advanced.

These questions of principle regarding the fundamental intent of the Labour government also arose with respect to its administration of controls over the distribution and prices of commodities, and the allocation of raw materials, capital, and labor. The same questions were evoked by Labour's tax policies, by its frequent choice of the imposition of further controls when faced with the alternatives of relaxing existing regulations or adding to them. The opposition raised the cry of "control because it is the socialist thing to do"; Labour proclaimed the slogan of "fair shares for all."

The government monopolized imports of such commodities as tea and tobacco, permitting the tightly organized trade associations to arrange for distribution among domestic companies. Food prices were kept low and quite stable by a system of agricultural subsidies, bulk buying, price fixing and rationing. In textiles, a "utilities" classification, established during the war, was maintained: lower-price and -quality goods regarded as necessities were price fixed and tax-free, other grades and types were correspondingly viewed as luxury goods and were subjected to an extremely heavy sales tax. New housing was very largely restricted to public authorities building for rental. Investment in industry needed the approval of government agencies. Owing in part to the dollar shortage, gasoline was severely rationed and price-fixed for both private and commercial users. For similar reasons numerous import and some export quotas were set, in the administration of which government bulk buying and exchange control were reinforced by specific regulations. Income taxes were raised to new and daring heights, and the earnings that remained were notably reduced by other taxes which fell most heavily on the poor: for 1949–1950, tobacco taxes alone brought in about £600 million, and the duty on beer another £275 million.[24]

Labour could not, of course, be accused of total partiality in the application of controls. Wages, too, were stabilized to prevent inflation, and in October, 1947, the Control of Engagements Order authorized government agencies to assign workers where needed. The wage freeze, however, was accomplished through the coöperation of the Party's adherents in the Trades Union Congress. The Control order was applied to only several hundred individuals before it was

[24] In the following table pounds are translated into dollars at $2.80. The first £139 of a single earner's income was tax-free, and exemptions fell to £100 per person for a family of four or five (no other exemptions are taken into account). The rates given are all on earned income, those on investment income were higher and the difference weighed most heavily on small and middle investors. In effect this was a special tax on middle-class savings income. In both British and American figures, only personal exemptions are taken into account.

| | Great Britain (1949–1950 rates) | | | | U.S. (1949 rates) | | | |
| | Single Payer | | Couple and Two Children | | Single Payer | | Couple and Two Children | |
Gross Income ($)	rate per-cent	net $	rate per-cent	net $	rate per-cent	net $	rate per-cent	net $
560	4	539	—	—	—	—	—	—
1,320	14	964	.75	1,012	11	1,176	—	—
1,400	17	1,160	4.5	1,347	11	1,240	—	—
2,800	26.5	2,057	18	2,296	16	2,356	3	2,720
14,000	50	7,034	48	7,273	29	9,998	23	10,752
28,000	64	10,044	63	10,183	41	16,192	38	17,496
140,000	90	14,174	90	14,413	73	37,614	73	38,326
280,000	94	17,674	94	17,913	82	50,596	81	52,564

These figures obviously fail to take into consideration real differences in costs and standards of living, but it is proper to point out that the British were more severe not only with the rich, but with higher-paid workers and the low middle class, as to both rates and personal exemptions.

finally withdrawn in March, 1950. Under the Labour revision of the Town and Country Planning Act (1947) additions to homes, stores, factories, and farm buildings required licensing. These rules were mildly relaxed in May, 1950, in what Minister Dalton described, in an unfortunate phrase, as "an experiment in freedom."[25]

In short, under Labour, Britain had taken very great strides toward the Party's conception of the welfare state, and significant and somewhat uneven steps toward its notion of a managed economy. Parliamentary opposition stiffened as the government moved farther and farther from the circumscribed agreed position of the Coalition. Labour's outspoken adherence to the principle of nationalization threatened to encompass the sugar and cement industries. And the government had another weapon, which fell short of transferring title, but which could prove fully as effective as state ownership in controlling the course and direction of the British economy. This was the Industrial Organization and Development Act of 1947, designed to relieve economically distressed areas by establishing new factories and to rationalize the growth and location of industry generally. Subsidies and buildings were offered to industries as incentives to move, reinforced by the power to prevent expansion in old locations. This law also made it possible to create, by an order laid before Parliament, Development Councils in the various branches of production. These bodies, representing management, labor, and the state, would have extensive powers over their trades. Their functions lead to the interesting speculation that the distinction between corporatism and socialism would seem to lie in the single fact that socialized shares of stock would carry the names of a public board, rather than private owners.

Development Councils did not mushroom, however, and opposition remained focused on steel. The Steel Bill was introduced in Commons in the fall of 1948, and was duly passed by the Labour majority. Then it moved on to the House of Lords, where the Tories, of course, held sway. This body had shown a remarkable capacity for tactful submission to the popular will. Though it was deeply

---

[25] This Act was interesting evidence of the continued vitality of Henry George's economics in England. It sought to prevent future speculation and unearned increments on land by controlling land use and charging fees for the right to develop it. See Brady, *Crisis in Britain*, p. 407.

dyed the Conservative blue—Lords of ancient family, Lords of battlefield and ocean, the life-tenure Lords of the law and the Church,
the Lords of the press, distilleries, and factories—the upper House
of Parliament refrained from frontal attack upon the many Labour
measures which must have been exceedingly bitter morsels to most
of its membership. Instead, the Lords undertook the gentle and important task of improving through debate the bills that would inevitably become law. But the Conservatives elected to fight openly
on the issue of steel. The Parliament Act of 1911 had limited the
power of the Lords to a two-year suspensive veto. The Tories were
therefore in a position to try the patience of Labour for longer than
it could endure, and Labour responded by attacking the constitutional position of the Lords.

It is of course commonplace to say that the House of Lords is an
anachronism in the twentieth century. To the theoretical socialist it
is far worse than that, for there is no basis whatever in the doctrines
of equality or even of representative democracy for a legislative
chamber whose members inherit their seats or who, if first elevated
to the peerage, have a life tenure that they pass on to their heirs
along with the family silver and the newly designed arms of nobility
(the Law Lords and the Lords ecclesiastical of course excepted). It
must therefore be said that Labour met the moderation of the Tory
nobility with a fair share of its own. Drastic reform—even to the
creation of a democratically elected upper house—was indeed discussed, but Labour's Parliament Act of 1949 was content with reducing the Lords' suspensive veto to a single year. As for the Steel
Bill itself, by an ingenious compromise whereby it would not enter
into effect until after the general election of 1950, it became law in
November, 1949. By common consent it was listed as one of the
issues over which the campaign would be fought.

As in most electoral campaigns, however, no single issue would
be decisive. What would weigh most heavily in the final counting
would be the electorate's opinion of its own welfare, and its attribu-
tion of credit or blame to the party in power. And Labour therefore
had good cause for confidence in repeated victory. In the many by-
elections that had occurred since 1945 to fill vacancies owing to
death or retirement from Commons, Labour had established the
unique record of losing not a single seat, although its majorities had

fallen. There were numerous problems unsolved, especially in international exchange and trade, but there was little save frictional unemployment, and real wages had risen for the many.

As the party in power, Labour naturally claimed credit for the state of prosperity and employment. Although it was objected that the pent-up demand of the war years and the needs of reconstruction would have led to high-level economic activity under any government, Labour was able to contrast this satisfactory condition with depression under Conservative rule following the First World War. Labour was on strong ground in boasting of its progress toward the goal of "fair"—or at least more equal—"shares for all." The proportion of total personal earnings after income taxes accounted for by wages rose by about 8 percent and the proportion that went to what might be called "bourgeois" sources of income fell by about 9 percent between 1938 and 1948. The working-class cost of living rose 74 percent between 1938 and 1948, but that of salaried persons rose 82 percent and costs to the upper middle class between 98 percent and 99 percent. The "social revolution" can be illustrated even more effectively, perhaps, through the process of leveling, both upward and downward, that is seen in the changes in distribution of incomes over a period in which national income rose 114 percent: in 1938–1939, 75,000 persons had net incomes of £2000 or over, in 1947–1948 there were 62,000; in the first period there were 605,000 with incomes between £500 and £2000, in the second there were 1,698,000; before the war, 5,320,000 earned £150 to £500, a decade later there were no less than 17,210,000 in this category![26] And in 1947–1948 only 70 persons in the United Kingdom had incomes after taxes in excess of £6000. Labour was approaching its goal, "between £250 and £300 a year net earned income at the bottom of

---

[26] "Bourgeois" sources here include salaries, professional earnings, profits from trading and partnerships, dividends, interest, and rents. Equalization of incomes is further shown by the fact that the number of large incomes fell despite a 114 percent rise in national income, a 98 percent rise in personal incomes, and a 79 percent rise in personal incomes after taxes. See *National Income and Expenditure of the United Kingdom 1946 to 1949,* Cmd. 7933, April, 1950, p. 15; "Redistribution of Incomes," "Changes in Wages," *The Economist,* Jan. 21, 28, 1950, pp. 120 ff., 183 ff.; "The National Income," April 22, 1950, pp. 902 ff.; M. K. Adler, "The Silent Revolution," *Political Quarterly,* April–June, 1949, pp. 146 ff.; R. Lewis and A. Maude, *The English Middle Classes,* London, 1949, pp. 204 ff.

the scale and between £2500 and £3000 a year net . . . at the top, with much the largest group falling within the £250 to £500 a year range."[27]

Labour's particular constituency, the working class, had indeed benefited. Their diet had improved, they had more money to spend on amusements. Their children were better cared for and had greater educational opportunities. New housing was rising too slowly, but what there was of it was heaven compared to the slums, and rents were low. Medical and dental care had always been less than inadequate for the many, and the National Health Service, with free examinations, treatments, drugs, and awards of false teeth, eye-glasses, and wigs proved immensely popular. Tories might protest its cost, though not its principle; the British Medical Association might have continued reservations; and the American Medical Association might condemn it outright; Labour's voters liked it. They appeared to be pleased that the advantages of the rich were limited by rationing and the policy of "fair shares." They were pleased above all by the welcome sense of security in their jobs and in their personal lives that full employment and insurance brought them. Their sense of security was such that tension in world affairs, the cold war between Russia and the West, affected them far less than it did their more prosperous but less satisfied cousins in America.

These facts and moods were Labour's assets. But there were liabilities. Labour needed the support of voters who were not of the working class, and dissatisfaction with the regulations, restrictions, and shortages that accompanied "fair shares" and Sir Stafford Cripp's "austerity" program to restrain consumption affected more than the well-to-do. Controls had been accepted cheerfully during war, and their continuation was tolerated in a spirit of sober patriotism for some time after hostilities ceased. But the British people were tiring of standing in line, of filling out forms, of scarce goods and poor quality. The burden of taxation was exceedingly heavy, and many a middle-class family found itself unable to give its children the excellent and expensive education which had been the hallmark of progress, and the cause for great sacrifices, among those of moderate means. Housing was still scarce, beer was still watery, and tobacco far too costly.

[27] Francis Williams, *Socialist Britain*, New York, 1949, p. 113.

Furthermore, the Tories had come to life. They had recovered from the shock of the 1945 defeat, and were organizing for the 1950 election with a will to win and with adequate resources. The Liberals too had marked 1950 as the start of their comeback, and even the Communists expected to profit from the dissatisfaction of Labour's left wing with the slowness of the government's progress toward full-fledged socialism.

The Labour election manifesto, *Let Us Win Through Together,* rang the changes on what we have called Labour's assets, and upon the failings of the Tories before the war. Its pleas for greater efficiency and productivity reflected the Party's growing concern with some of the underlying factors that troubled Britain's foreign trade and balances. It pledged further steps along the road that had been followed, including nationalization of the sugar and cement industries, meat wholesaling, and water supply, and carried a threat of similar action in the chemical field. Above all, it appealed to the family spirit, to the housewives, and showed deep interest in children—a good electoral tactic in Pittsburgh or Frog Hollow, as well as London or along the Clyde.

The Tory manifesto, *This Is The Road,* reminded the people of the unpleasant fact, to which Labour ministers had attested, that there would indeed have been unemployment if not for United States and Commonwealth aid. It called for lower government spending, and for the liberation of the energies of enterprise. It proposed the abolition of food subsidies, which helped all equally, and suggested instead that larger family allowances be given those in need, while those who could afford would pay the higher food prices. It pledged a halt to the march of nationalization, and vigorous decentralization of government management where it already existed. The Tories too insisted upon the necessity for greater efficiency and productivity, but, unlike Labour, they relied upon relief from controls and taxation to provide stronger incentives to work and earn. Like Labour, the Tories bowed toward the younger generation, but the theme of their platform was a plea for greater vigor and pride in the imperial tradition, rather than for fair shares for all.

The election of February 26, 1950, disappointed the hopes of each of the parties. Instead of the majority of 75 or more it confidently expected, Labour won 315 seats, and a slender majority of 6 over all other groups; instead of returning to power, the Tories won 297 seats; instead of starting a comeback, the Liberals fell from 12 to 9; and the Communists lost the 2 seats they had held. The popular vote showed Labour in a slightly smaller minority than 1945. Its 13,200,000 votes were 46.2 percent of the total, and the Conservatives and Liberals together secured 15,000,000 votes and 52.5 percent.

Labour remained in office, but the frailty of their majority in Commons indicated that it would not be long before a new election was necessary. The time had clearly come for both major parties, and all interested observers, to take stock of the past five years, and of what it was that the British people wanted.

It would be far too simple to say that Great Britain had become split into two hard-set groups of avowed socialists and capitalists. Adventitious and insignificant circumstances are always present and may take on unexpected importance at election time. And the memories of voters are longer than politicians are apt to believe. The meaning of the election of 1950 is much more accessible if Labour's interpretation of its victory in 1945 as a sweeping mandate is replaced with a far more modest view. As the war ended, people were inclined to turn away from those in office, and Churchill had committed the political blunder of assuming the official leadership of the Conservative Party so that he had to campaign as a Tory chieftain, rather than the elder statesman who belonged to all. Although he had always been a man of great vision, and even of genius, Churchill was surprisingly maladroit as a campaigner. He tried to frighten the people into voting Tory, and chose as his arch-bogey Professor Harold J. Laski, who was then chairman of the Labour Party Executive. Now Mr. Laski was an unorthodox Marxist who believed in political democracy. He was given to extravagant conclusions and violent speech, but he remained, essentially, a professor of political science. To picture him, as Churchill did, as a combined Trotsky and Himmler, only stimulated the wry humor of the rather sophisticated British electorate. The chief result of this particular venture in towing a red herring was to revive old doubts as to the Tories' sincerity in pledging a welfare policy. The people feared a return to Chamberlain and the Great Depression, particularly since it was then widely believed that a slump would follow the war.

These disturbing thoughts were reinforced by the Conservative emphasis upon speedily removing controls, which conjured up images of inflation and no shares for the poor. And Labour pledged "fair shares for all."

In 1950, the country felt comfortably prosperous. If it were true that some day the piper would have to be paid, the masses were not aware that he had begun to play. There were indeed many who were displeased with the present and disturbed for the future, and these voted Tory. But the bulk of Labour's support were living better than they ever had, and this tangible fact outweighed the Tory claim that the benefits of full employment had come despite and not because of the government. In addition, Mr. Churchill repeated, albeit on a far lesser scale, his blunder of the first campaign, and so partly offset the efforts of a group of younger Conservatives to work out and sell the Tory doctrine of intervention in positive terms. It would be a reasonable assessment of the 1950 election to say that the country was rather pleased with its state of health and did not desire any grand and sweeping steps toward the theoretical goal of socialism; it felt that intervention was possibly showing signs of going too far; but it nevertheless did not fully trust the Tories, particularly under that greatest of war leaders, Winston Churchill, to carry on the policies of the welfare state in the proper spirit.

Even if this should be a fair description of the attitude of the British electorate taken as a whole, it is obviously an inadequate consideration of Labour policies and the basic issue of the nature and proper limits of intervention. The worth of Labour socialism can be only partly judged in economic terms, since some of its values—equality, security, democratic control—might be held desirable even at economic cost. Nevertheless, Labour defined socialism as the liberation of the cultural and spiritual forces of the individual, as the achievement of individual happiness, through the establishment by socialist techniques of the material basis for a full and rich life. Inevitably, then, the practical success of these techniques must be submitted to judgment, and such a consideration might yield useful hints as to how workable a proposition is the idea of democratic socialism itself.

The United Kingdom and, even more markedly, other countries whose currencies were tied to the British pound, were in need of commodities which could be obtained only for dollars. It was essential, as we have said, both to curtail dollar imports and to expand sterling area exports to the United States. Curtailment meant controls, and the variations in method that would have been available to another government were minor relative to the problem and the need as a whole. Nor did increasing exports offer quite so wide a choice of policies as might at first be thought. One way, almost traditional in the old days of freer market capitalism, was to cut costs by lowering the domestic standard of living. This Labour refused to consider, which is hardly surprising in a democratic socialist party, and the Tories too protested strongly that they had no intention of tackling the problem by reducing real wages. The area of choice would therefore seem to be reduced to alternative methods of increasing productivity, and it is largely at this point that a noteworthy difference in outlook appears. Labour stressed central planning and guidance. Management was called upon to show greater enterprise and efficiency, under pain of further intervention if it did not. The Tories, on the other hand, demanded greater efficiency on the part of government, and relied upon the release of individual imagination and energy to create a new golden age for British industry.

It had become increasingly apparent, by 1950, that nationalization of itself meant very little. It brought no major change for the better, save perhaps in coal, where improvements in productivity resulted from the Coal Board's heavy investment in modernization, an obligation the old owners had failed to meet. Prices still had to cover costs, and costs could not be lowered drastically. When a nationalized industry runs at a loss, the burden is transferred elsewhere in the economy. Consumers had not benefited from lower prices, and there was nothing inherent in nationalized monopoly that would drive prices down. Now that it was working for its "own" government, and theoretically for itself, labor found itself in a rather peculiar position. The old attitude of struggle against the capitalist exploiters was assuredly quite out of place, and a good many workers discovered that it had been easier to deal with a local owner, who might be cursed to his face if need arose, than with the impersonal agent of a board in far-off London. When the unions, with a high sense of responsibility, supported the government's policy of freezing wages, the transformation of their role from agencies of defense and struggle to a means of discipline over labor had gone about as far as it could go in a democratic society.[28]

There were a good number of workers, to be sure, who were dissatisfied with the mere façade of socialization, and demanded worker representation in management beyond the consultation committees that had been established (in both nationalized and private industry). But this raised a most troublesome question: if labor were to participate in making policy beyond the field of labor relations, did that imply that industry's principal function was to provide jobs? If that were the case, Lord Keynes' project for digging up buried banknotes would do just as well as mining coal, and would be much less onerous.[29] If, on the other hand, the function of industry was to provide for the consuming public, it was far from established that workers were technically competent to do more than offer advice and suggestions about methods of production, and to negotiate concerning their conditions of employment. The government, to be sure, had recognized the primacy of the public interest, and had established consumers' councils for each of the nationalized industries. These, however, tended to be ineffectual. As has so often been said, everyone is a consumer. But there are very few professional consumers, and save when he is paying bills that are always too high, the citizen is much more likely to cast himself in his more active and ambitious role of producer. Consumers' councils had only a general interest to protect and advance, and this was not conducive to dynamic activity in groups largely composed of men who were busy and successful in their own fields of endeavor. Suggestions to improve their effectiveness threatened to involve the proliferation of even more councils and tribunals, only adding to the danger that the time might come when the demand for the right type of public servant would far outrun the supply.

There was yet another side to nationalization that gave ground for concern. One of the best-advertised features of the whole program had been the replacement of private monopolists, intent on sating their greed, with servants of the people responsible, through

[28] See p. 255. British experience tended to bear out Schumpeter's prediction as to the place of unions under socialism.
[29] See p. 163.

a minister, to the people's representatives in Commons. To begin with, no wholesale change of personnel occurred, below the level of directors and general managers: there was no reason to undertake such a campaign of disruption. And then it became increasingly evident that whereas the private tycoon could at least be annoyed, ruffled, chastened, and even reformed by public inquiry and pressure, managers of nationalized organizations could hide safe and secure behind boards, who could hide behind ministers, who had no difficulty in evading annoying questions in a House of Commons that had far too much business to transact. Short of scandalous misbehaviour, the normal sociology of bureaucracy would operate, with its tendency to regard the even path as the best. And even in the celebrated "groundnuts scheme," the vast project for growing peanuts in Africa which at a cost of nearly £30 million had produced little but embarrassment for the government by the time of the general election of 1950, questions were evaded and responsibility remained unfixed.

In a word, nationalization not only proved no panacea, it hardly appeared to meet the needs of Labour socialism, save for its avowed desire to transfer power to the hands of the state. Nor could it be argued that growing pains were the chief difficulty, and would soon be over. The nationalized industries were benefiting from the skills of the old staffs, which had not yet fallen full prey to the stultifying effect of tenure bureaucracy, and it remained to be seen whether their successors would be as able.[30] For the rest, the nationalized industries carried on their business, of course, but it was very much business as usual.[31]

The Labour policy of maintaining controls to ensure "fair shares"

[30] See the comments of Sir Arthur Salter, "The Crux of Nationalisation," *Political Quarterly*, April–June, 1950, pp. 209 ff.

[31] Brady's comment on transport nationalization is typical of his conclusions with respect to coal, steel and communications: "The mere fact that all such media have now been nationalized provides absolutely no guarantee that relations of interdependence, complementarity, or even of duplication and overlapping, will be planned and worked out on a scientific basis" (*Crisis in Britain*, p. 282; see also pp. 166, 234, 272, 306, and elsewhere). A more general criticism, in harmony with these observations, is that while Labour had a program for legislation, there was no genuine plan or planning for action, and that even the government had given up the pretense of so doing. See George Schwartz (of the *London Times*), "Farewell to Government Planning," *Barron's Weekly*, May 1, 1950, p. 7.

had some noteworthy achievements to its credit. Prices moved upward, as they were indeed bound to, but rationing and price fixing, supported by the unions' coöperation in stabilizing wages, prevented the kind of inflation that swept the Continent. Perhaps these restrictions did tend to·inhibit the free and expansive breathing of private enterprise and initiative, but they also safeguarded the poor and the working class from the stranglehold of an inflationary spiral, and British society from the ills of social unrest. It can hardly be doubted that this manifestation of "fair shares" was popular, both for its practical effect and because it appealed to the very real and lively sense of fair play that characterized all strata of British society. From time to time members of the government bestowed a politician's recognition upon this popularity by declaring that the policy in general, and many of its particular applications, would be permanent features of British life. As conditions noticeably improved, however, particularly in the campaign atmosphere of 1949 and 1950, what had been precious safeguards began to appear somewhat irksome. The more politically aware Labourites acknowledged this new mood by a hesitant removal of some controls, which they justified by pointing to the party's initial promise to lift *unnecessary* restrictions as soon as possible. But the depth of "fair shares" appeal should not be underestimated: even after the election of February, 1950, surveys showed a decidedly negative reaction to proposals for a "two-tiered" rationing system, with a basic level of rationed quantities at a fixed price, and free purchases at free prices above that amount. Even if everyone were guaranteed their fair share at a price all could afford to pay, it was widely held to be unfair to allow richer citizens to buy more of the given commodity at a cost only they could support.[32]

There was even less question in the minds of most of the British people concerning the value and success of the health service and insurance schemes. Although these had grown from the Coalition program, residual doubt concerning the Tories' sincerity gave the credit to the Labour government in power. It mattered little to the large majority that the health program had produced some initial absurdities, such as a sudden rush for free wigs, spectacles, and prescriptions in unheard-of quantities. In a way, this flocking to what

[32] *The Economist*, May 6, 1950, p. 987.

many prosperous persons have always regarded as symbols of embarrassment, discomfort, and pain, the examining table, the dentist's chair of torture, the druggist's counter, bespoke a long pent-up demand for health itself, which for too many British people had been beyond practical hope of achievement. But the frictions and unexpected inconsistencies of the health program—a bonanza for dentists and inadequate earnings for general practitioners, the line-up for consultations and prescriptions in part for their own sakes, a disturbing rise in industrial absenteeism covered by that best of all excuses, a doctor's certificate—these and other annoying side effects were symptoms of the difficulties which Labour's program generally met as it inevitably clashed with deeply ingrained human proclivities and stumbled over the infinite complexity of social behavior.

Rigidities, friction, inconsistencies, unexpected and unwanted conjunctures proved to be rather more than the growing pains of a bold new program of socialist intervention. They cast some doubt on the validity and workableness of that degree of planning to which Labour was pledged. They did not, of course, reflect upon either the total planning of an authoritarian regime or the *general* planning of a Keynesian type of neomercantilism. But they did raise the serious question whether Labour had gone too far for the latter, while declining to travel the whole distance that the former required.

It is somewhat embarrassing to give specific examples of the difficulties to which we have referred, for one immediately becomes open to the charge of stacking the cards against the Labour government and of employing trivial matters to detract from the impression of Labour's solid accomplishment. It is, moreover, quite out of the question even to attempt to estimate quantitatively the adverse effect these failings might have had upon the British economy. And yet there is good reason to offer illustrations of some of the types of difficulty that have arisen to annoy a democratic socialist party in office. A single case may reveal, although not with scientific certitude, a more general principle.

Take, for one instance, the African peanut growing fiasco, the groundnut scheme. Despite its long-range character and larger social purposes to increase the supply of edible fats and oils, this was the sort of venture upon which a group of capitalists might conceivably have embarked.[33] It is most unlikely, however, that they would have persisted in their losses and discouragement quite so long as a government that had staked a measure of its political prestige upon the project, and had allotted to it not only money but a place in its portrait of the future. This is not to say that it is always improper for states to undertake costly risks that might contribute to an important social objective; it is only to point to the danger that there might be inherent in governmental ventures a reluctance to change means even while retaining the goal. This one experience at least suggests that Labour had not found an adequate substitute for the pressure that red ink exerts upon the humdrum businessman. If this failing were to prove a general characteristic of socialist government the ensuing costs would gravely endanger the higher productivity upon which so large a part of the case for socialism must rest.

Another case illustrates the problem that may arise when restrictions stop short of total control. We have mentioned the wartime classification of "utility goods," perpetuated by Labour, under which, for example, cottons of ordinary grade were rationed and price-fixed, while higher qualities treated as luxuries were heavily taxed and allowed to find their own price level (rationing by price or, income). As raw cotton prices rose, through no fault of Labour, of course, manufacturers were faced with the alternatives of either cutting utility goods quality or reclassifying them into the luxury, free-price group. In either event working-class consumers would suffer, but the government would not raise utilities prices to meet costs both because the increase would be more readily noticed than a slight shrinkage in width or thread count and because the fixed price entered into the cost-of-living index upon which political claims had to be based. Conservative Lord Woolton commented that "one set of controls is defeating the purposes of the other, and all are embarrassing to both traders and public."[34] In a word, the partial

[33] The project was actually conceived by a subsidiary of the huge Unilever firm. It has been suggested that Unilever persuaded the government to handle the undertaking because, although the direct investment was of manageable proportions, the indirect investment—health and conservation measures—were of too great a scope. Unilever was entrusted with distributing the products of the undertaking, and thus offers an instance in which a private "trust" would benefit greatly from government intervention. See Brady, *Crisis in Britain,* pp. 603 ff.

[34] In a report to stockholders, *The Economist,* April 22, 1950, p. 916.

controls had failed, economically, and the real choice lay between extending them to secure effective subsidization of low consumers' prices, and risking political unpopularity by adjusting prices to costs. The logic of Labour policy ruled out the second alternative, and growing dissatisfaction with scarcities and minor regulations made the first a political impossibility for all but the most doctrinaire members of the party.

In another circumstance, already alluded to, the government did seek to correct undesired consequences of regulation by adding further measures of control. Underlying the health service program had been the correct assumption that the mass of the people had been unable to afford adequate medical and dental care, and that the supply of practitioners had been restricted both by educational facilities and by the limited effective demand for their services. Proper service for all would therefore take some years to prepare. But the government would not countenance a merely gradual change-over from the old way of rationing care by ability to pay. Instead of instituting a scale of reduced fees to be paid by the patient, with evolution toward free service for all, it decreed its final goal in one grand swoop. The dentists especially were overwhelmed: and by working longer hours than was advisable for the sake of efficiency or quality, they were able to reap rewards exceptional even for this ordinarily lucrative calling. They found it unprofitable to continue working for the longer-established children's and prenatal clinics, and one unwanted result of free dental care was a severe decline in service for the young and for expectant mothers. The Ministry of Health did not go the whole way to placing dentists on a salaried eight-hour day, but tried, by limiting dental incomes, to remove the incentive to overwork. The excessive popularity of the health service raised outlays to the point where the government was forced to ask Parliament for supplementary appropriations. To limit both expenses and absurdities, the payment of fees for prescriptions was ordered, although the order was slow in being implemented.

Sometimes planners find that actual results do not accord with their estimates. In such an eventuality a totalitarian regime can choose among three responses to the challenge: it can change the plan to suit the facts, it can force the facts to fit the plan and thereby preserve the sanctity of its official documents even at the risk of economic loss, or, and this is an easy and attractive solution, it can insist that results did in truth coincide with desires, since no one not in on the secret will be any the wiser. This simple escape is not available to a democratic government, and embarrassment to the planners can consequently be much greater. Labour had expected that in 1949 about 50,000 commercial vehicles would be purchased within the United Kingdom. Sales actually amounted to about 100,-000. The government estimate had clearly been wrong in point of fact, but it remained possible to insist that it had nevertheless been entirely right in principle and policy, and this was the attitude adopted by Chancellor of the Exchequer Sir Stafford Cripps. The alternative of revising estimates to meet the revealed pattern was discarded, and a heavy tax was placed upon most commercial vehicles, as the Chancellor said, both because the planned figure was adequate for domestic needs, and in order to divert production into exports. The manufacturers protested that their customers felt a stronger need than the government would concede them, that foreign demand was limited and that it made little sense to apply an artificial hobble to domestic productivity. It is not unreasonable to suggest from this instance that one danger in partial but specific planning might be the tendency to pass over the real obstacle to fulfillment—higher domestic demand than anticipated, in this case —in order to devise an additional pressure to follow the plan.

It was also unavoidable that at some point controls for the sake of "fair shares for all" should clash with simple economic efficiency, or, in other words, economic advantage for all. A case in point was that of coal prices and storage. It had been suggested that coal prices be reduced in the summer, following an old practice of the trade, in order to encourage widespread storage and a consequently more even flow of supplies in the winter. Since many persons, among whom the poorer presumably predominated, did not have storage facilities, the proposal was rejected because, in the words of Mr. Philip Noel-Baker, one of Labour's outstanding younger leaders, it "would imperil the principle of fair shares for all." Here was "if-I-can't-have-it-you-won't-either" with a vengeance, the principle of leveling down. The government eventually yielded to common sense in this particular matter.

The welfare aspect of "fair shares" posed an even greater question. The health, subsidy, education, and insurance programs obviously cost a good deal of money—about 43 percent of total governmental expenditures in 1949—and since this was raised by taxation it constituted a redistribution of wealth. From whom to whom? Labour's politically effective answer was from the rich to the poor, but while this was obviously correct in part, was it the entire answer? The ECA Mission to the United Kingdom estimated governmental social expenditures per family in 1949 at 57 shillings a week, and taxes paid by lower-income families in 1948 at 67 shillings 8 pence a week, with beer, tobacco, and other indirect taxes alone amounting to 37 shillings 14 pence. On this basis they suggested that "the social expenditures are chiefly financed by transfers of income within the lower-income group, in accordance with variations in the pattern of consumption, family size, etc., rather than by transfers between different income levels."[35] This is not to imply that if not for the welfare program the poor would have paid no taxes, or that they were not getting their money's worth, for there were many indirect benefits in addition to those directly provided by the welfare legislation. But taxes had risen 185 percent from 1938 to 1948, by far the larger part of the increase being accounted for by rising welfare expenditures, while national income rose 114 percent. The welfare program was therefore not so much a redistribution of income from rich to poor, as a *redirection* of consumer expenditure from, perhaps, more amusements to better food, education, health, housing, and insurance. The people were required to be abstemious and provident and to show effective concern for their own and their children's betterment.

Expansion of welfare services could not be financed by the contributions of the upper classes, but only by greater productivity on the part of labor, and in the economy as a whole. This Labour came increasingly to recognize, as it became apparent that the rich were becoming a worked out gold mine, and as the pressure of the na-

[35] Report of ECA Mission to the United Kingdom, quoted by *The Economist*, "The Cost of Welfare," April 1, 1950, pp. 694 ff.; *Taxes and National Income and Expenditure* . . . Cmd. 7933, pp. 9, 17. Neither taxes nor income corrected for changes in price level.

tion's foreign trade problems increased. And yet the providing of incentives for greater productiveness proved one of the government's most troublesome tasks.

There has long been a feeling, among moralists and socialists, that profits for employers and higher wages for workers, however effective as incentives to produce, appealed to the selfishness and greed in human nature. To summon effort in this way could only reinforce those traits in man which made him sordid and which induced warfare, poverty, and crime. To achieve the ultimate goal—a better, nobler human being—two great efforts had to be undertaken. Economic insecurity and poor conditions of life, the material stimuli to baseness in the mass of the people, had to be abolished, and new incentives had to be supplied that would call upon the more elevated and noble characteristics of the species, generosity and the social spirit. Owing to the postwar boom and to the welfare measures, Great Britain had made a good start toward material betterment, but to establish effective motives for greater productiveness was a more elusive matter. It was all very well to force upon eye and ear with all the techniques of advertising the established fact that the nation needed every bit of inventiveness, efficiency, and energy that her people could muster. But in peacetime the appeal to patriotism was not enough even in this most patriotic of nations that had given one of history's greatest displays of unity and courage in the Second World War.

Managers and owners had little reason to outdo themselves. They could sell just about all they made at home, in the sterling area or in other regions where postwar shortages prevailed. Why, then, should they strive for new techniques or be eager for the trials, costs, and risks of the American market, with its rather nerve-wracking and strident competition? Corporate gain was inadequate inducement, for taxes were high, dividends were restricted, and dollars made in the United States would remain at the disposal of the British Treasury. The old sordid motive of personal gain had even less force, since higher incomes meant higher taxes and "working for the government." The depressing effect of high taxation on initiative has often been exaggerated, but it did exist at tax levels[36] that soaked up about 36 percent (about equally divided between direct

[36] See footnote 24, p. 285.

and indirect levies) of gross personal incomes in 1949. What this amounted to was partial nationalization of consumption.

The energy of middle-class business leadership was at least partly curtailed by a sense of frustration, but the energy of the working class was limited by a sense of satisfaction. The stick that had traditionally driven the human beast of burden to greater effort—the threat of unemployment—was no longer there for the employer to brandish. Although this was generally accepted as a good thing and a mark of progress, it placed all responsibility upon the reward for good performance. And the British working class, it appeared, was almost surfeited with material rewards. That this should have been so was a bitter commentary on their previous condition, but the fact remained that they felt themselves prosperous and secure to an unheard-of degree. They spent their increased wages on a better diet and leisure, rather quickly self-limiting items. Human nature being what it is, at least before the final perfection of the socialist Utopia, there was no startling response to the government's appeal to work harder. Faced with high rates of absenteeism, which indicated satisfaction with less than maximum possible earnings, Labour was led to consider extension of such typically capitalist devices as piece work and productivity bonuses. In the case of coal mining there was even the suggestion that the wartime system of fines for unwarranted absences from work be restored, and that in this case the incentive system of piecework be replaced with hourly wages, to prevent workers from leaving the pits after they had made all the money they wanted in a short working period. Aside from the fact that this limited ambition to earn obviously cast doubt upon the effectiveness of piecework, British unions had traditionally opposed this method of payment as a capitalist speed-up technique. Under the circumstances it was rather an uncertain means of enforcing discipline, one that might actually boomerang, than of providing incentives. Raising wages was ruled out by the need for stabilization against inflation, and even for the working man, income-tax rates reduced the attractiveness of higher pay. For this reason overtime work and pay offered no solution and if, as it was widely suggested, overtime be exempted from surtax rates, the result would be an inflationary pressure, unless the level of productivity were raised.

This, of course, was the crux of the problem. England had to produce more efficiently, more cheaply, but inadequate incentives, and backwardness in technology, organization, and business methods were tied into a Gordian knot which neither management nor labor was predisposed to cut. To a far greater degree than their American confreres, British capitalists had abandoned the gospel of competition. Even more serious, there was no certainty that more competition—or even the larger monetary incentives the Tories promised—would provide adequate stimulation for greater managerial skill. Too many English businessmen were evidence for Schumpeter's thesis that advanced corporate capitalism transforms the imaginative, innovating, risk-taking entrepreneur into an administrator of a going concern, that the modern corporation "socializes the bourgeois mind."[37] Trade associations were given regulatory functions and restrictive agreements covered the British economy, and although Labour inveighed against monopoly, its agencies were employed by the state as part of the structure of government control. The Monopolies and Restrictive Practices Act (1948) did no more than establish an inadequately staffed commission of investigation, and there was no evidence that a clear-cut monopoly policy was being formulated. Not that this was in the least surprising, for the socialist is no believer in capitalistic competition, and the Marxian socialist is even likely to hail monopolistic concentration as foreshadowing the overturn of capitalism itself. Monopolistic firms, being few in number, facilitate government control and planning. In effect, therefore, Labour veered insensibly toward a loosely organized and governed state of corporatism, in which associations of employers and associations of workers would manage their affairs under the general and sometimes specific supervision of the government.[38]

The unions, for their part, displayed an atavistic reluctance to accept new methods of organizing work and new machines and techniques. They would often insist on the featherbedding principle of keeping the same number of men on the task after labor-saving equipment had been introduced, or accomplish the same end by establishing output limits per worker. This behavior derived from the old fear of technological unemployment, which, under the actual

[37] *Capitalism, Socialism and Democracy*, p. 156.
[38] See p. 541 ff.

economic circumstances, was quite irrelevant. Even more basic and influential, however, seemed to be an intangible, the attitude of workers toward their job. On this score the reports of the investigating groups of the Anglo-American Productivity Council that visited the United States are extremely instructive. Machinery per worker was found generally to be much greater in America than England, organization of the industrial process much more expeditious, and standardization of products a great aid to high output. In cotton spinning, for example, British mills required from 1½ to 2½ times as many workers as the American average for the same output, and processes handled by different firms in different places in England were grouped in one factory in the United States.[39] But one theme recurrent in these reports was the superior attitude of the American worker. He was used to putting in a good day's work; with the encouragement of his union, he welcomed new equipment and procedures, and often made valuable suggestions for greater efficiency. American output per man-hour was 50 percent higher even in the archaically organized building trades, where the construction worker "has never acquired the habit of doing less than he is capable of doing," an observation that will startle many an American who has embarked upon the adventure of having a house built.[40] The explanation for the American advantage lay not in the threat of firing, but in labor's share in increased productivity. American labor had been accustomed to benefit from greater efficiency, British labor had long feared it might have to pay the price in technological unemployment. The Marxist stricture against capitalists, that they took advantage of labor-saving devices to cut their wage bill, had had greater validity in England than in the United States. In a word, England was suffering from the generations in which capital had displayed less than the generosity which American conditions enforced. The British worker's zeal was also checked by ingrained low and restricted habits of consumption. He lacked the American tradition of converting higher earnings into a never-ending stream

[39] See Brady, *Crisis in Britain*, pp. 495 ff. Productivity changes were naturally uneven, outstripping the American rate of increase in some lines and falling behind some European countries in others.

[40] Quoted by *The Economist*, May 6, 1950, p. 1023. For prewar comparison see *The Economist*, "Industrial Productivity," August 14, 1948, pp. 273 ff., sources there listed, and Brady, *Crisis in Britain*, pp. 495 ff.

of household gadgets and automobiles, a strong stimulant to labor efficiency. A vicious circle was closed by the scarcity of attractive goods and their high prices (to which a heavy sales tax was added), offering little inducement to such expenditures. The effectiveness of the money incentive was further restrained by the steep climb of income-tax rates.

Attitudes cannot be changed in a day, and there was little evidence that a socialist solution had been found for this overriding problem. In the long run, of course, British workers might adjust to something resembling the American pattern. Expecting and receiving their share of growing productivity, they might strive to excel in order to rise more rapidly in the wage scale. But the spirit of neither British unionism nor socialism was likely to encourage such a development. Owing to their long and historically well-founded fear of insecurity, the unions stressed level rates of performance and uniformity rather than individual effort. And Labour gave preference to long-term investment rather than consumption, a policy both dictated by export needs of the moment and induced by the general socialist tendency to harness all energies to plans for the future while postponing the presumed lavishness of a socialist system of distribution.

Nor was Labour *doctrine* particularly congenial to wage incentives. It was the veteran party organizer and leader of the moderate wing, Herbert Morrison, who had been chief spokesman for turning to capitalistic plans of incentive payment, which smacked of competition among workers. He argued that it was wrong to "condemn those workers who set 'too fast a pace for their less efficient workmates' as traitors to their class and the labor movement," and preached the rather obvious point that "workers who work harder and earn more than the minimum are not only not injuring their fellows but are helping and supporting them."[41] The party theorists and younger firebrands were distinctly unenthusiastic. Theory, indeed, had no ready answer. Writing after the election of February, 1950, G. D. H. Cole, guiding spirit of the New Fabian Research Bureau, said that nationalization "carries with it grave dangers of excessive centralization and of destroying the *spirit of emulation*— which should not be identified with that of competition as it has

[41] *New York Times,* November 7, 1949.

been practised under the profit system."[42] Something that could be called the "spirit of emulation" assuredly exists. It is revealed in the game of keeping up with the Joneses, and on playing fields from Harrow to Notre Dame, but it is at least dubious that this spirit can furnish as much driving power in the serious business of work as it does in play.

The general mood of Labour's Britain was one of controlled stability rather than dynamic change. Productivity was slowly rising under the pressure of technological change and a steady campaign for improvement. Under the stimulation of the devaluation of the pound from $4.03 to $2.80 in the fall of 1949, and owing to the efforts of the export businesses (whether resulting from fear of government compulsion, patriotism, the "spirit of emulation," or a "spirit of doing the job well"), the dollar shortage had markedly eased. But it was at best uncertain that British prosperity resulted from Labour policies. *The Economist,* indeed, argued that

. . . it is simply not true that planning and nationalisation have maintained full employment in Britain in the last five years. Full employment here—as in France and Switzerland, or Scandinavia or the Commonwealth—has been maintained partly by Marshall Aid, partly by the level of postwar prosperity of the United States. What has done the trick has not been the successful application of socialist principles in Britain but the successful working of capitalism in America. In 1949, a mere five percent fall in the level of American business activity was enough to bring Britain to the brink of financial disaster.[43]

The question still remained whether productivity was increasing rapidly enough to enable England to make her way if the North American props should weaken.

There was no doubt that the economy was delicately, but rigidly, balanced. Although Labour might retain a great deal of its popularity while this balance endured, the rigidity did produce one result that was almost universally deplored outside the party orthodoxy. This was that Labour, forswearing its heritage of internationalism, was forced to pursue and became increasingly committed to a policy of nationalism, economic and political. In three of four major

[42] "Labour and Staff Problems Under Nationalisation," *Political Quarterly,* April–June, 1950, p. 169. My italics.
[43] June 17, 1950, p. 1314.

efforts to establish the federal principle in western Europe at the cost of some diminution in national sovereignty, Labour England "dragged its feet," displaying a great deal of caution and reluctance to yield independence of action. Even where the government's attitude was at least partly justified, its manner was such that, wrote *The Economist*, "world opinion believes that Labour Ministers approach all these matters . . . like inverted Micawbers, waiting for something to turn down."[44] The exception was the Atlantic military alliance, where defense necessities were seen in essentially the same light by Labour socialists, American capitalists, and anti-Communist Frenchmen. But with respect to the Council of Europe, which was heavily indebted for its creation to Winston Churchill, Foreign Secretary Bevin prevented its transformation from a debating society into a body with genuine power. His argument derived from the traditional British constitutional theory that it is better for an institution to be the culmination of organic growth than to precede it. Many who fully shared this belief, however, felt that Bevin was unnecessarily hesitant, and did too little to stimulate organic growth.

Even greater coolness was at first shown by Labour toward the European Payments Union, a Continental outgrowth of the Marshall Plan, designed to bring about mutual convertibility of west European currencies in order to facilitate greater and freer trade among the member nations. England objected that she could not risk either the special position of the pound as an international currency nor planned elements of her economy that might be endangered by the removal of restrictions. A compromise was finally worked out, however, so that Great Britain could participate.

But British economic nationalism was felt to be most extreme in the initial reaction of the government and the Labour Party to the proposal of French Foreign Minister Schuman to pool the iron and coal resources and plant of western Europe and place them under the control of a supra-national authority whose decisions would be binding on the participating states. The French aim was at least partly political, to integrate Western Germany fully and peacefully into the democratic orbit, an objective in which the British

---

[44] June 10, 1950, p. 1258. The remark is credited originally to Philip Guedalla, with reference to the Baldwin government's attitude toward the League of Nations.

thoroughly believed. But the government's response to the Schuman plan was chilly, and a subcommittee of the Labour Party Executive, under the chairmanship of left-winger Hugh Dalton, exploded a bombshell in a statement of policy entitled, apparently with unconscious irony, *European Unity*. It took the position that the United Kingdom belonged primarily to the British Commonwealth rather than to any European regional association, and appeared to assume that the only alternatives were Labour's own brand of socialism and almost pure economic liberalism. Meaningful planning, it argued, required the industries concerned to "fit their investment programs into a European plan," and "the Labour Party is convinced that nothing less than public ownership can insure this fully." The timing of its release made *European Unity* appear an outright rejection of the Schuman proposal, and its tone was smug, its manner dogmatic. For example, aside from the insistence on nationalization, one of Mr. Dalton's reasons for condemning a supra-national authority was that it "would have a permanent anti-Socialist majority and would arouse the hostility of European workers."

This bucketful of ice water aroused a storm of bitter criticism from both Continental socialists and American capitalists.[45] It soon developed that the offending document had not been seen by Mr. Attlee, or his chief colleagues, and the embarrassed Prime Minister was led to declare that it was "not a statement of Government policy."[46] The government's objections to the Schuman plan were almost as profound, although more suavely expressed. They feared that the plan would endanger the protected position of the higher-cost, higher-wage British steel industry, and they feared the loss of sovereignty it entailed. In short, the moderate politicians were not

[45] The poor impression created by *European Unity* was helped along by inaccurate reporting, of which even the *New York Times* was guilty in this instance. The latter, under the signature of one of its ablest correspondents, Raymond Daniell, reported (June 13, 1950) the document as recognizing "that 'international planning' was the key to economic unity but that planning for private profit would be worse than useless." The actual quotation is: ". . . international planning of iron and steel is the key to economic unity. But such planning will be worse than useless if it is inspired, like the cartels of the past, exclusively by the desire for private profit" (*European Unity, A Statement by the National Executive Committee of the British Labour Party*, London, 1950, p. 11).

[46] *New York Times*, June 14, 1950.

too far from the theorists, practically speaking, although they de-
sisted from dogmatic and antagonizing statements of principle.

The flurry was not the first evidence of disagreement within the
Labour Party. There had as yet appeared no division of opinion
regarding ultimate objectives, but there were two fairly well-defined
points of view with respect to immediate policy. One, held by Attlee,
Bevin, and Morrison, was inclined to interpret the election of February, 1950, as an order to go slow. They were prepared to suspend
the campaign for nationalization and, indeed, there were indications
that the Steel Bill itself had been forced upon the older, more
moderate political leadership of the Party by the younger left-wing
element. Attlee and his chief lieutenants read the election returns
much as did the Conservatives. Nationalization would only further
frighten the independent voters, and it seemed even to have lost
much of its charm for the working class. The labor force in the
mines continued to fall, despite the Coal Board's recruitment efforts.
Three maritime unions opposed suggestions for nationalization of
shipping with the statement that

. . . there are certain tendencies evident which can conceivably be detri-
mental to British shipping and could possibly be aggravated by the
processes of nationalization. Flexibility in management to meet speedy
and unpredictable changes in trade and commerce is essential if British
shipping is to maintain its preeminence as a world carrier.[47]

In the spring of 1950 a significant number of controls and restrictions
were removed, and no new major socialist bills were brought up.

The other point of view was offered mostly by politicians below
the highest cabinet rank, by younger M.P.'s, and by many of the
Party's intellectuals. Their leading figure was the buoyant Welsh-
man, Aneurin Bevan.[48] Although this was the Party's left wing, it was

[47] *The Economist*, May 6, 1950, p. 1025.

[48] He was not characterized by sedateness. Bevan often managed to speak
like a King's Minister, but he was more adept at billingsgate. One of his gems
was to say that all and sundry Tories were "lower than vermin." It would be
extremely unfair, however, to suppose that this outburst resulted only from
absorption of Marxist literary standards. Fancied by some as another Lloyd
George, to others Bevan seemed to bear a closer resemblance to a more ancient
Welsh hero, Owen Glendower.

Among Bevan's steadiest supporters were M.P.'s such as Tom Driberg and
Ian Mikardo. There was also a more moderate left wing which included much
more prominent Labour figures like Hugh Dalton, Emanuel Shinwell, and John

assuredly not Communist, for opposition to Communism was one matter in which all but a handful of Labour's membership had a consistent record. The left wing was merely in a great hurry to get socialism established, fully and permanently.[49] It feared that a policy of temporizing might become habitual, and interpreted the February, 1950, election as a reprimand to Labour for not having gone fast enough. How they reached this conclusion is extremely difficult to ascertain. In any event, the left wing wanted more, not less, regulation, and more, not less, nationalization, and turned a deaf ear to the grumblings of the middle class. Nor was the left wing without support among the unions. The important Amalgamated Engineering Union insisted that the pressure for socialization be maintained, and that the Labour program should not be watered down "in the hope of placating ill-informed middle-class voters," as the Union's president put it.[50] As the moderates who led the government slowed their pace even further, Labour's left was brought closer to the Tories' right, at least in that they were united in a sense of frustration.

An explosion was inevitable, and it came in April, 1951, when Aneurin Bevan resigned as Minister of Labour and,[51] while professing loyalty to the Labour Party, proceeded to attack its leadership in what was evidently a bid to appropriate their power for himself. Bevan's pretext for deviating so sharply from the rules of British politics was that Chancellor of the Exchequer Gaitskell had swung so far to the right as to prescribe certain minor fees in connection with the public health service. This pretext logically introduced Bevan's major line of attack, that the "curtailment" of social services resulted from the government's excessive rearmament plans, which

---

Strachey. The latter group often joined with Bevan in debates over policy, but were less eager to challenge the Party's leadership, and less willing to make extreme statements.

[49] See the pamphlet *Keep Left*, signed by R. H. S. Crossman, Michael Foot, Ian Mikardo, and others, London, 1947; and *Keeping Left*, 1950. The latter indicated a devaluation of nationalization and a desire to build Development Councils on a grand scale. This would reinforce the corporatist tendencies in Britain. The left wing was strongly influenced by T. Balogh, *The Dollar Crisis: A Report to the Fabian Society*, Oxford, 1949.

[50] *The Economist*, June 17, 1950, p. 1322.

[51] Harold Wilson resigned as President of the Board of Trade and John Freeman from a subordinate position in the Ministry of Supply.

in turn resulted from a slavish support of America's "aggressive" policy toward Russia. A general fear of repeating the 1931 party split and catastrophe helped Clement Attlee to weather the storm, with Bevan retiring from the ministerial bench to leadership of an intraparty opposition. But election day was assuredly brought closer.[52]

The balloting was set for October 25, 1951, and both Bevan and the leaders made every effort to play down the struggles within Labour. The Party ran on what was generally conceded to be an uninspired statement of policy, blaming Britain's economic difficulties almost exclusively on external factors, saying nothing clear-cut about further nationalization, suggesting further taxation of the rich, although the Labour Chancellor of the Exchequer had freely conceded that this would contribute significantly neither to the well-being of the poor nor to the government revenues. Perhaps Labour's most effective political tactic was to play on the residual fear that Churchill might lead the country into war, and Labour did this by mudslinging in a way that the British had always regarded as a mark of American political immaturity.

The third postwar election was as indecisive as the second, but now the Tories received the slight nod and the responsibilities of governing. Labour's share of the popular vote actually rose, from 46.2 percent in 1950 to 48.7 in 1951. But the Tories' gain was greater, from 43.4 to 48 percent, reflecting a decline in the Liberal and "others" vote, from 10.4 to 3.2 percent. The Conservatives won 317 seats, the Liberals 6, "others" 3; Labour returned 294.[53]

Such results as these could not serve as a clear guide, either as to the will of the British people or as to the wisest course for the Labour Party to follow. In opposition to a Conservative government that was cautious, circumspect, and pacific, Labour did not find it easy to develop a new approach upon which to found a new program. To a good many Labourites, the old doctrine and policies—which amounted to reducing the power and privileges of wealth and combating depression—appeared singularly inappropriate to a time marked by inflation, full employment, and a rapid progress toward

[52] See *The Economist*, April 28, 1951, pp. 961 ff., 969.
[53] The election results are given and analyzed in *The Economist*, Nov. 3, 1951, pp. 1024 ff.

equality. Doubts concerning nationalization, class conflict, the welfare functions of the state, even about the meaning of socialism, were
expressed by Socialist Union, a group of Labour intellectuals. Similar
doubts were dismissed or slurred over by the left wing of the party's
theorists: the *New Fabian Essays*, published in the spring of 1952,
showed awareness of the dangers of political as well as economic
power, but were able neither to solve the problems this posed for
socialists nor to prepare a philosophical basis or program for the
future. Almost by default, therefore, they tended to reaffirm their
confidence in what Labour had done in office and, if by no more
than implication, to recommend more of the same.[54]

The debate of the intellectuals was recapitulated on the stage of
practical politics. Attlee's moderate leadership did little more than
carp at and nag the Tory government, for genuinely constructive
opposition was hardly possible without a firm point of view from
which to offer alternatives, while it was necessary nevertheless to
maintain the appearances of vigorous opposition in order to fend off
the energetic Labourites of the left. The latter, led by Bevan, had no
fresh ideas, and so continued to preach the old: Britain must declare
her independence of American foreign policy, which might lead to
war, and was certain to cripple economically the progress of socialist welfare; the advance of socialism must mean more welfare publicly administered, ever fairer shares, and more nationalization.

Since Labour was out of office, it could afford to carry the issue to
its membership, but it was difficult to interpret the members' decision, owing to a change in the character of the Party itself, a
change whose full extent and meaning were as yet unknown. The
three rocks upon which Labour had been founded were the intellectual socialism of the Fabians, the political organization of the
Independent Labour Party, and the voters and executives of the
unions. When way was opened for individual affiliations in 1918,
local Party organizations were established which the voter could
join and in which he could be active. Originally these tended to
coincide with or be dominated by the local Trades Council, the
union association, but as time went on and the Party gained in numbers, its district and constituency units broadened in character and

---

[54] Socialist Union, *Socialism: A New Statement of Principles*, London, 1952;
R. H. S. Crossman *et al.*, *New Fabian Essays*, London, 1952.

grew more influential. In the election of 1923, 18 percent of the winning Labour candidates were sponsored by Divisional parties and 51 percent by labor unions; in 1929 the Divisional party contribution to the victory list was ahead by 44 percent to 40 percent, and in 1945 by 63 percent to 31 percent. In 1928 individual membership in the Labour Party accounted for 9 percent of the total, and affiliation through unions for 88 percent. In 1945 the figures were 19 percent and 79 percent.[55] In short, Labour was slowly becoming less of a unionists' organization influenced by radical intellectuals, and more of a political party.

This development might bring all the dilution of doctrine, the moderation and willingness to compromise that come from greater contact with a broad, nonideological constituency, and thereby strengthen the moderate Party leadership. But the growing importance of the constituency organizations might have the contrary effect: the left-wing Labour theorists, who had accepted a good deal of Marxian prejudice if little formal Marxian doctrine, might gain control of the constituency groups, and through them convert the workers to a doctrinaire socialism.

Superficially, at least, it appeared that such a triumph of the left might be in the making. At the Party's 1952 conference at Morecambe, bluntly expressed anti-Americanism[56] and dogmatic socialism served as a platform for the Bevanites, who won a resounding victory. The constituency parties elected all six Bevanite candidates to Labour's National Executive Committee, displacing, among others, Herbert Morrison, who was second only to Attlee in the Party hierarchy. The trade unions and other groups represented on the Executive gave the leadership twenty-one seats to the Bevanites'

[55] From data in G. D. H. Cole, *History of the Labour Party from 1914*. At the Party's 1950 conference most of the left-wing resolutions came from constituency organizations in middle-class districts (*The Economist*, July 29, 1950, p. 209). This suggests that the most zealous members of the local parties, and of the left, were still disaffected, bourgeois, intellectual radicals. In 1952, right-wing Labourites charged that these elements were behind Bevan's triumph at Morecambe, and this indeed appeared to be the case. If the usual course of political party development were followed, their influence would decline in the long run—unless of course, they succeeded in converting the electorate to socialism as such.

[56] One of the moderates characterized this attitude as "jingoism with an inferiority complex" (*New York Times*, Oct. 2, 1952). Some of the left wing went so far in domestic affairs as to suggest that the strike be used for political purposes, a proposal indignantly rejected by both union and party leaders.

six, and the Parliamentary Labour Party remained firmly in Attlee's hands, but the trend of the constituencies seemed strongly to the left. The moderate politicians and the union leaders made it clear they had no intention of yielding to Bevan. But the influence of the constituency results was suggested in the renewed acceptance of the principle of nationalization by such men as Hugh Gaitskell, who not long before had indicated he was disillusioned with it.[57]

It was certain only that the outcome of the struggle for the control of Labour would be far-reaching in its consequences. Were the moderates to succeed, it might be possible for Labour and the Tories to resume the old gentlemanly game of British politics, much as it had been played by Gladstone and Disraeli. Both could pursue somewhat different degrees of Keynesian neomercantilism, and alternate in office at the will of the electorate without disturbing the serenity of Her Majesty's throne, or the continuity of the basic policies of Her Majesty's Government. But then there could hardly be a place in the Labour Party for the ambitious Bevan and his supporters, who would have to yield or enter the limbo of splinter-party existence. Were the moderates to be displaced from Party leadership, however, and the cautious union chiefs to lose their power to restrain the ideologically convinced socializers, then the older leaders, the men who had made Labour powerful, would be forced to undertake a most trying searching of souls. They would have to choose between breaking the party loyalty that had been a deep-felt element of their credo and entering upon a path in which they did not believe.

Few have seen the real nature of the problem of Labour socialism more clearly than the outstanding socialist intellectual, G. D. H. Cole. Even before February, 1950, had left Labour with a pitifully small Parliamentary majority, he had written:

The plain truth is that the electors voted in 1945, not for socialism as an economic system based on public ownership of industry, but for more speed in developing the social service state, for less social inequality, and for full employment policies as a means to social security.

The greatest task still remained for Labour, to sell the idea of socialism itself, and he confessed his worry that "party leadership is ceasing to believe in socialism as a way of life, and is coming to believe in a 'mixed economy,' not merely as a temporary resting place, but

[57] *The Economist*, October 4, 1952, pp. 1 ff.; January 17, 1953, pp. 119 ff.

as an abiding solution of the social problem." A similar fate had be-
fallen reform movements of the past, and Professor Cole hoped it
was one that Labour would escape. And yet even Labour economists
were ready to concede that the welfare program cost more than the
economy could bear, that it involved taxation, "ruinous in the sense
that it has become a positive disincentive to capitalists to undertake
industrial reorganization and expansion." The theoretical Labour
conclusion was that the welfare state could not be run "on an economic system not made for it. . . . It can only be done if more of
our industry is removed from the realm of financial incentives altogether."[58] If this was in fact correct, the fork in the road had been
reached: practical Labour policy and politics seemed to call for a
stop to socialization, while ideological Labour socialism was said to
demand still further forced marches, until there could be no return.

Nor could Labour evade an even more basic choice, which was
once suggested bluntly and somewhat cruelly by the Conservative
Party Chairman, Lord Woolton:

> The fundamental error of Socialism is that it misjudges human nature.
> . . . Socialism, I am convinced, will not work. . . . It plans but it has
> not the will to take the power to make those plans work. It . . . despises
> the will to excel; it replaces the individual by a committee; it's neither
> one thing nor another. It hasn't the virtues of free enterprise; it hasn't the
> ruthlessness of the totalitarian state.

> But I believe that, once a nation embarks wholeheartedly on the
> Socialist philosophy, it is leading directly to totalitarianism.[59]

But for Labour to take the road to dictatorship would require a
veritable revolution in the personal philosophies of nearly all of its
leaders, and supporters as well. Remembering the profound influence Christian belief has always exerted upon the movement, it
is only proper to hear Sir Stafford Cripps, in a sermon in St. Paul's
Cathedral:

> Today, in any civilized nation most multifarious functions are per-
> formed by the state or by local authorities or other public bodies on be-
> half of the individual.

[58] "The Dream and the Business," *Political Quarterly*, July–September, 1949,
pp. 201 ff. See T. E. M. McKitterick, "Socialist Planning" (review article),
pp. 218 ff.
[59] From an address before the Institute of Fiscal and Political Education,
New York, June 2, 1950.

This is an obvious convenience which enables a higher standard of living to be reached on a material scale through a proper division of labor. But with the extension of group control comes a danger that the administration may become mechanical and impersonal and that the individual may lose all sense of spiritual responsibility for the corporate acts of his society.

To express this in another way, the danger is that the corporate body which administers may have no soul.

And Sir Stafford declared that if the affairs of the state were conducted "in accordance with the teachings of Christ," there could arise a "corporate Christian conscience which will give it the spiritual power to control the material forces that are at its service."[60] Sir Stafford was unquestionably right in this, but if he implied that the progress of socialism should be limited according to the advance of the Christian conscience, he not only turned his back upon the left wing of his party, but conceded a good part of the Conservative case.

Thus the Labour Party was facing the first truly fundamental crisis and decision of its fifty-year history, whether to determine to proceed with the creation of a socialism it had but dimly envisioned or to be content to administer, in accordance with the fluctuating desires of the people, a mixed economy, a system of modified capitalism, a neomercantilist policy. One thing was quite certain, however. Given the unique history of the United Kingdom, and of its social and constitutional development, the variety of socialism that was peculiar to it would not appear on the list of British exports— not even to its offspring, the United States. America's Republicans were clamoring that the Democrats were following Labour in a choice of doctrinaire socialism, but the Democrats were insisting on their devotion to capitalism of the neomercantilist stamp, and quietly hoping that Labour would follow them rather than the socialist dream.

NOTES ON BOOKS

On the assumption that the reader will make his own selection from among the many good histories of England, it need only be said that G. M. Trevelyan's *British History in the Nineteenth Century and After* would
[60] *New York Times*, Jan. 9, 1950.

be an excellent single choice for general background. For the Labour Party itself, one can find all the information that is necessary, and much that is not, in G. D. H. Cole's *British Working-Class Politics, 1832–1914* and his *History of the Labour Party from 1914*. A brief and breezier account is Francis Williams' *Fifty Years' March: The Rise of the Labour Party*, and the same author's *Socialist Britain* gives both the flavor and a sympathetic analysis of the Party's postwar doctrines. On the Fabian Society, the reader may consult E. R. Pease's *History*, and the *Fabian Essays in Socialism*, edited by G. B. Shaw. C. R. Attlee's *Labour Party in Perspective* is, like its author, significant because of his position in the Party, but it does give a clear statement of the moderate Labour view. *The Decline and Fall of British Capitalism*, by Keith Hutchison, is a well-written historical analysis by a Labour sympathizer, who reinforces his likes with an argument from historical inevitability. Most books about Labour are written by its supporters, and stress its benefits to the working class: Roy Lewis and Angus Maude offer an excellent counterweight in *The English Middle Classes*, an historical and sociological consideration of the weakening position of the bourgeoisie, and of their place under a socialist program.

It is still too early for an exhaustive work on the Labour regime to have appeared, and what is called current history is always the most difficult to study. R. A. Brady's *Crisis in Britain* is a long, scholarly and often rather caustic analysis of Labour's legislative program, but it does not deal directly with the effects of that program on British society. The later work by Ben W. Lewis, *British Planning and Nationalization*, is more descriptive than analytical. Any regular reader of that splendid weekly will recognize the writer's debt to *The Economist*. Although it has become probably the most effective voice in criticism of Labour, it is not a "party" publication. It has not departed from its tradition of meticulous reporting and considered analysis, and is as unsparing of the Tories as of their opponents.

Lastly, as a small tribute to one of the very great minds, and works, of our time, the reader is once more advised to turn to J. A. Schumpeter's *Capitalism, Socialism and Democracy*, this time for the sections pertinent to British socialism. His earlier predictions (1942) had been remarkably successful, and his later estimates (1946) would only add to the soul-searching in which Labour and its friends are likely to be engaged.

12.

SOCIALISM BY REVOLUTION: SOVIET RUSSIA

I. *Lenin and the Revolutionary Movement*

STALINISM is the chief claimant to the direct succession from the founders of "scientific socialism," but this pretension matters little to a world preoccupied with Russian Communism. It is the political and social reality of the USSR that makes Stalinism important, and in this light Marxism is significant only to the degree to which it assists in making the Soviet reality comprehensible.

The Soviet Union, in short, cannot be understood, as was the fashion for a good many years, as essentially an effort to put Marxism into practice. But the subsequent vogue swung to another extreme. After Stalin had exalted heroes of old and executed a number of moves which even his own practitioners found difficult to explain in Marxian terms, Russian nationalism and the Russian national character were called upon for a key to the apparently inexplicable. The "bear that walks like a man" was revived, with the old warning that if he were scratched an Oriental would be found beneath his fur. Obviously, the previous history of Russia had a great deal to do with shaping the Soviet Union, but it was no answer to the Russian riddle—"wrapped in a mystery inside an enigma," Winston Churchill said—merely to say that the Russians were, after all, Russians.

Over a century ago, in a passage of uncanny prescience, Alexis de Tocqueville wrote:

There are at the present time two great nations in the world, which started from different points, but seem to tend towards the same end. I allude to the Russians and the Americans. . . .

All other nations seem to have nearly reached their natural limits . . . these alone are proceeding with ease and celerity along a path to which no limit can be perceived. The American struggles against the obstacles that nature opposes to him; the adversaries of the Russian are men. . . . The conquests of the American are therefore gained by the plowshare; those of the Russian by the sword. The Anglo-American relies upon personal interest to accomplish his ends and gives free scope to the unguided strength and common sense of the people; the Russian centers all the authority of society in a single arm. The principal instrument of the former is freedom; of the latter, servitude. Their starting-point is different and their courses are not the same; yet each of them seems marked out by the will of Heaven to sway the destinies of half the globe.[1]

This disquieting prediction would seem to mark the present state of Russia as the culmination of an inflexible and inevitable course of history. It is not that bald, however. De Tocqueville believed the Divine Will had ordained the march of all peoples toward equality of status, but had left to the free will of man the choice between equality under tyranny or equality in liberty. The growth of the Anglo-American spirit tended toward the latter, the growth of the Russian toward the former. And yet the English-speaking world has seen its threats of despotism, and the Russian its upsurges of the spirit of freedom. When de Tocqueville wrote these lines, the reactionary Tsar Nicholas I had seemingly cast an eternal pall over the fleeting progress the idea of liberty had made in Russia. There were moments in later years when the pall lifted, and the Tsarist empire made real strides toward the Western conception of economic advance and democracy, but of all such historical instances these moments were perhaps the most tragically to merit the comment of "too little and too late."

Modern Russia came out of a past radically different from that of the West. Once a flourishing extension of Byzantine Christian civilization, the continuity of Russian relations with Europe was dis-

---

[1] *Democracy in America*, Bradley edition, vol. 1, p. 434.

rupted by the invasion of the Mongols in the thirteenth century. The domination of the Golden Horde lasted almost 250 years, until the rise of a new power in the heart of Russia, the principality of Muscovy. Under such great centralizing monarchs as Ivan III (1462–1505) and Ivan IV, the Terrible (1530–1584),[2] the outlines of the modern Russian Empire began to take shape. In 1613, Michael Romanov was elected Tsar, and under the dynasty he began Russia reentered Europe.

Of the many and far-reaching consequences this renewal of European relations had for Russia, two deserve special emphasis. In their efforts to expand their realm, and to defend its open borders against Swedes, Poles, and Turks, Russia's rulers needed large standing armies. The readiest way to raise these forces was to enserf the peasants, and hold a loyal landlord, indebted to the throne by its grants of land and power, responsible for providing a quota of men and taxes. This imposition of serfdom from above reinforced strong grass-roots pressures toward transforming free peasants into bondsmen: indebtedness and taxes bound legally free men to the land they rented, and drove many a free peasant to seek slavery as a refuge from these burdens. Many others sought escape in simple flight, and Tsarist enserfment laws were a response to the landlords' demands for help in holding their laborers, as well as to the needs of the crown itself.

A second consequence of the European relationship was the effort to establish a Western apparatus of government. Like the first, it was particularly associated with the abler and more dynamic rulers, Ivan IV, Peter the Great (1689–1725), and Catherine the Great (1762–1796), and it too was imposed from above. The Russians took over much of the pattern of government in vogue among the German states, itself to a considerable extent a schematized copy of the mercantilist state of France, created by princes, rather than grown through the years in response to the shifting and often contradictory needs and tensions of a changing society. It therefore had this advantage over the French—or British—state structure, that it was neater, more rationally constituted, much more easily illustrated by one of those organizational diagrams so beloved of the political sci-

[2] A better rendering of Ivan Grozny might be Ivan the Dread, carrying the connotations of mighty and awe-inspiring as well as fearsome.

ence textbook. But it had this great disadvantage, that bureaucracy was established as a thing almost apart from society, that will and initiative were concentrated rather than dispersed, so that the state would lead its people along a path it chose, rather than follow policies which resulted from requirements the people themselves had generated.

In Russia, all power was vested in the Tsar, who had not only to create the forms of an autocratic government, but had even to invent and establish a new social class—the service gentry—to man his offices and agencies. This process, begun by Ivan the Terrible, was fully developed by Peter the Great. The service caste contained a good many Westerners—German, British, French—imported as expert servants of the throne, and its native members were lifted out of Russian society to devote their lives and their descendants' to service in state, army, or church in return for the social standing and wealth that the Tsar bestowed upon them. There resulted a separation, almost a divorce between government and people. Russia was an underworld, moving along, with slow and slight change. Above it was the state, quick to issue orders, slow to hear complaints. Public opinion was the limited expression of those to whom the Tsar chose to listen. Unhampered by the unwieldy mass of a national point of view, the state could make swift and startling changes of policy, while the nation Russia remained unaware or indifferent.[3]

A depressed and unfree peasantry, a ruling class so separated from the people that it could actually be said to belong to a different culture (there were times when French or German, not Russian, was spoken at the Tsar's court), the monopoly of power by a ruler and handful of aides who were responsible to no one, these were some of the legacies passed down to nineteenth-century Russia. The Church, which in other countries had often been the one organization to

[3] Adolf Hitler is reputed to have given his fondest dreams to one of these reversals during his last days in the Chancellery cellar. In the Seven Years War of 1756–1763, Frederick the Great of Prussia, with only British support, was being slowly ground down, despite his victories, by the combined power of France, Austria, and Russia. All seemed hopeless for the brilliant Hohenzollern king when his bitter enemy, Russian Empress Elizabeth, died. Her successor, Peter III, ardently admired Frederick, and switched his armies to the Prussian side. Peter reigned only a few months before his wife Catherine deposed and imprisoned him, but the vitality of the anti-Prussian alliance was gone, and Frederick was able to conclude an advantageous peace.

maintain a degree of autonomy even under the most powerful of despots, had been completely absorbed into the pattern of state. In 1586, during the rule of Boris Godunov, the Russian Church was freed from ecclesiastical subordination to the Patriarch of Constantinople, and in 1721 Peter the Great suspended the independently influential Russian Patriarchate and placed the Church under a Synod headed by one of his lay officials. Its great importance in the lives of a devout people made the Church extremely useful as an agency for what the twentieth century would call thought control. There was dissatisfaction in the land, but it was revealed through sporadic peasant and Cossack uprisings, the most important of which[4] left the regime in secure control, and under no necessity to institute reforms.

There was one gap in the Tsarist armor, however, which, when social conditions were at last ripe, would widen into a serious breach. This was the protest of the free and active intellect. The process of enforced Westernization begun by Peter the Great had had its comical aspects, such as the required shaving of good old Russian beards. It also had its share of irony, as when Catherine II experimented with a periodical press, such as was then in vogue in Paris. It soon developed that there was no want of satirical spirit among the Russian nobility who had imbibed Western ideas, and what more obvious target than Her Majesty's court and government? The experiment was terminated, but there was no way, at that time, of blocking the incursion and absorption of Western thinking, with its restless, critical note. Nor was there any way, in those days, of preventing the comparisons unfavorable to Russia that were drawn by members of the service caste nobility who went to Germany and France as to a finishing school.

This unsettling knowledge of the West was vastly increased by the Napoleonic Wars, when Russian armies fought through Europe and triumphantly occupied Paris. And, as a result, the progress of super-

---

[4] The rebellions of Stenka Razin in the seventeenth century and Pugachev in the eighteenth. The latter uprising, indeed, had an unfortunate influence: Catherine the Great, in whose reign it occurred, had no legal title to the throne, and had to rely on the gentry to maintain herself in power. As a consequence of Pugachev's threat, her authority over the gentry was weakened, her efforts to press reforms against their will fell by the wayside, and the gentry's obligations to the state—which had been the counterpart of their privileges—were greatly reduced.

ficial borrowing that had brought the façade of Western government to the heirs of Muscovy was now repeated at the other end of the scale. Army officers and intellectuals formed secret societies dedicated to the cause of reason, liberalism and nationalism, after the European mode of the day. Unlike the Polish, German, or Italian groups, the Russian organizations had no natural following in a restive bourgeoisie, but that they had been formed at all was a momentous thing.

The Tsar, Alexander I (1801–1825), was, as he conceded, not without blame for the rise of revolutionary liberalism. In his early years he had been much given to liberal ideas, largely manifested, to be sure, in reform projects that were never carried out. He had later experienced a conversion to a reactionary point of view, reflected in the rather preposterous Holy Alliance, and in acts that belied his expressed wishes for a liberal Polish monarchy under his kingship, and that put an end to all thought of reform at home.

Alexander died on December 1, 1825. The succession had been arranged for his younger brother, Nicholas, the elder and reputedly liberal Constantine being quite content not to rule. But there was a delay of some weeks while Nicholas waited for Constantine to proclaim the revised succession publicly. The secret societies decided that this was the time to strike, and on December 26 the liberal rebel officers paraded their troops to the cry of "Constantine and Constitution!"[5] Nicholas replied by declaring himself Tsar without further delay, and the uprising, without plans or organization, was easily put down.

The reactionary Nicholas reigned thirty years, but the spirit and influence of the revolutionists he had crushed, the Decembrists, survived him. Pathetic failure though it was, the uprising of 1825 was nevertheless Russia's first modern rebellion. The Decembrists stood for more than mere dissatisfaction with depressed conditions: they

---

[5] The soldiers, it is told, thought "Constitution" (Constitutsia, in Russian) was Constantine's wife. Stories such as this lend a piquant air of unreality to Russian history. Another, of the same epoch, has Alexander living on, after his official burial, as a monk.

Similar tales are told of the Soviet era: peasants requested pictures of the new Tsar, "Lenin-and-Trotsky," and, after Lenin's death he was convincingly reported, at the muzhik level of reliability, to be going from village to village, incognito of course, redressing wrongs.

had the ideology of political liberalism and constitutional government. Their subsequent influence was out of all proportion to their
achievements. These "conscience-stricken gentry," unable to live at
peace with the oppression of the masses which their own status entailed, became heroes for later revolutionaries to admire. Despite
his efficiency and unwavering devotion to the Tsarist principle,
Nicholas was unable to hand on even a thriving autocracy to his son.
In 1854 Russia became engaged in the Crimean War, where mon-
strous inefficiency revealed the deep-seated weaknesses of a narrow
despotism, and a clear need for reform. Alexander II ascended the
throne in 1855, brought the war to an end a year later, and undertook to improve the condition of the peasant masses and the operation of the Russian state. "Better," he said, "to abolish serfdom from
above than to wait till it begins to abolish itself from below."[6]

Alexander's reform decrees began to appear in 1861, after five
years of preparation, and brought major changes in the four great
spheres of peasant status, provincial government, education, and the
law. The most important and far-reaching of these measures was the
decree on the peasantry of 1861. Serfs dwelling on crown and state
lands were freed and given land. Household serfs of private landlords were liberated, and the farming peasants on private estates
were given legal freedom and the right to buy land from the owner.
The landlords were compensated with government bonds, while
peasant purchases were financed by a state bank, the peasants to
repay over forty-nine years. The land was deeded not to individual
peasants but to the village community, the *mir*, which held tremendous power over the peasant family and individual and served the
state as an agency for maintaining order and collecting taxes.

The reform was a boon to the peasantry, but it also favored the
growth of Russian industry by producing a great movement to the
cities and into the ranks of the industrial proletariat, particularly
among serfs engaged in household or craft work who received freedom without land.

The other reforms were diluted but typical elements of the nineteenth-century liberal creed. District and provincial assemblies, the
zemstva, were created in 1864 with the right to levy taxes and to
legislate in the fields of public welfare and education. They prom-

[6] Bernard Pares, *A History of Russia*, New York, 5th ed., 1947, p. 346.

ised to provide a splendid training ground for political activity on the part of liberal gentry and offered at least the glimmer of a hope of eventual expansion to nation-wide representative government. The universities had restored to them that power of self-government that Alexander I had first given, then taken away, and lower schools benefited from the activities of local councils and *zemstva*.

The judicial reform of 1864 brought trial by jury, adequate pay and irremovability for judges. For a few brief years political crimes too were submitted to the jurisdiction of the reformed courts, but by 1874 they had been returned to the old evil of administrative judgment with little or no safeguard for the accused. This police system existed side by side with a regular judicial apparatus that compared respectably with the best legal structures of the West. But it was the political cases that drew most attention, and gave the whole Tsarist legal system a blacker character than it deserved.

Alexander had not persevered in his will to reform, and certain expressions of opposition to the regime were of a nature to encourage him in backsliding. Unrestrained by an organized mass of followers, or by the moderating influence of practical achievement, thus liberated from any necessity for compromise at the expense of purity of theory, Russian radicals were drawn to visionary programs and extremist acts. In the European revolutions of 1848 they heard, not the dominant note of middle-class liberalism, but the minor note of socialism. As Trotsky points out,

. . . in Russia the proletariat did not arise gradually through the ages, carrying with itself the burden of the past, as in England, but in leaps involving sharp changes of environment, ties, relations, and a sharp break with the past. It is just this fact—combined with the concentrated oppressions of tsarism—that made the Russian workers hospitable to the boldest conclusions of revolutionary thought—just as the backward industries of Russia were hospitable to the last word in capitalist organization.[7]

For essentially the same reasons, Russian intellectuals were also exceptionally hospitable to socialist ideas, and preceded Russian workers along this road by an even greater distance than did Western intellectuals their own proletariat.

The backwardness of the people and the government encouraged

[7] Leon Trotsky, *The History of the Russian Revolution*, Max Eastman, trans., New York, 1932, vol. 1, p. 11.

two different attitudes among Russian opponents of reaction. The gentler intellectual and lover of humanity as such could hope only in education and slow institutional growth toward the far distant goal. The impassioned type, certain of the truth and impatient of results, looked to violent revolution and even terrorism. These divergent attitudes and temperaments naturally found expression in the theoretical and ideological alternatives that were current in the Russian intellectual world.

From the time of Nicholas I, the moderates tended to follow the confused but democratically motivated thinking of the French Utopians. Extremists were entranced by German Idealistic philosophers, among whom Hegel came to predominate, proving deadly to the development of a workable reformist point of view. At the same time there began to develop a Slav-consciousness among the Russian intelligentsia, a tendency to assert a special mission and an inherent superiority in the Russian people. Since there was no objective evidence of such peculiar Slavic endowments, the latter had to be defined as spiritual. Right-wing Hegelians who were also Slavophils saw the Russian message in the Orthodox Church, the autocracy, the presumably devoted peasantry; left-wing Hegelians who were Slavophils saw Russia as the bearer of liberty and socialism through revolution, and found a model in the collectivism of the peasant village.

The followers of the French socialist tradition, among whom Alexander Herzen was outstanding, came to understand the hopelessness of perfectionist schemes for backward Russia, but their progress toward realism coincided with defeat in the contest for the souls of the ardent intelligentsia, who turned to the left and to Russified Hegelianism. The tragically limited vision of the Tsarist regime and its halting and reluctant action on what vision it had, demanded too much patience, too long a view, on the part of those who cried out for reform. At almost every decisive moment of historical turn, Tsarist ineptitude seemed to urge reformers to be more radical, more revolutionary. Even those with evolutionary, democratic points of view, like Herzen, experienced surges of anger and impatience which drove them at times to desire violent upheaval. And for those who had already foresworn waiting upon the slow movement of social and cultural progress, there was little in Tsarism to occasion second thoughts. Apart from a deviation into the anarchist extreme of Michael Bakunin, they came to adopt a revolutionary Utopianism, expressed most rigorously, perhaps, by Peter Tkachev.

Tkachev argued that a revolutionary minority, an elite, should lead the dissatisfied people in a violent overthrow of the government. This was only the beginning for the elite, but it was the end of an active role for the people:

> In its work of reformation, the revolutionary minority need not rely upon the active support of the people. The revolutionary role of the people ends the instant they have destroyed the institutions which oppressed them. . . . By utilizing the revolutionary destructive power of the people, . . . and by basing its constructive acts upon the character and urgency of the people's wants . . . the revolutionary minority will lay the foundation of a new and more sensible social order.[8]

This brave affirmation of the revolutionary's conceit was to be revived in 1917, with a certain amount of sugar coating, but in the 1870's another conception, reversing the roles of revolutionists and masses, captured the minds of the Russian intellectual rebels. It saw the Tsarist regime as so oppressive that it could be overthrown only by terror and violent destruction. But there would end the role of the revolutionaries, and begin that of the people, for after the elimination of the Tsarist barrier, the people, particularly the peasants, would establish socialism and would rule through the ordinary structures of political democracy. This was the view of the *Narodnaya Volya*, the *Narodniki*, the People's Will. There were some, however, who, while sharing the *Narodnik* belief in the peasant basis of socialism, rejected their recourse to terrorism. Revolutionists who held such humanitarian qualms joined another group, the Black Repartition. Among the latter was Plekhanov, who escaped with some comrades to Switzerland. They eventually judged the agrarian theory of revolution a failure, turned to Marx for guidance,[9] and founded the Russian Marxian Social Democratic Party in the early 1880's.[10]

[8] Quoted by David Shub, *Lenin, A Biography*, New York, 1948, p. 14.
[9] *Capital* had appeared in Russian in 1872, fifteen years before its translation into English. The Russian censors sadly misjudged the taste of the reading public, for they permitted publication of the translation of *Capital* on the ground that its style would prevent it from being widely read.
[10] In their search for forebears to lend historical sanction to their doctrine, Stalinists were to light on Belinski and Chernyshevsky who, being dead, could

In the meantime, the *Narodniki* had become increasingly active in their avocation of throwing bombs. The reforms of Alexander II had initially aroused great popular enthusiasm, but this had waned with the Tsar's reforming spirit and with his slow erosion of the judicial reform and of his original grants of power to the *zemstva.* Liberal elements whose hopes lay in progress through the existing regime were becoming disaffected. Their devotion to the throne was reinvigorated for a time by the successful Russian war against Turkey in 1877, but spirits sagged again when the international Congress of Berlin, in 1878, negated several Russian gains and brought the Tsar a diplomatic defeat. At this moment, when the Tsar's prestige was at low ebb, the terrorists intensified their activities, and made his royal person their declared principal target. The institution of military rule and courts martial failed to stop their attacks, and the Tsar wisely gave the task to a liberal, General Loris-Melikov. The General at once returned to the reforming path of the 1860's, and succeeded quickly in restoring public confidence and securing wide support. But this only hastened the terrorists, who had benefited from a tacit public sympathy that they were likely to lose because of Loris-Melikov's progressive administration. There is nothing the Utopian hates more than an amelioration of conditions that detracts from interest in his dream. The *Narodniki* redoubled their efforts, and met with success on March 13, 1881. Writes Pares, "The bomb that killed Alexander put an end to the faint beginnings of Russian constitutionalism."[11]

The regime of his son, Alexander III, was thoroughly reactionary, as was that of his grandson, Nicholas II, who became Tsar in 1894. The revolutionists continued active, although terrorism became less popular. The two wings of unrest, the *Narodniki* who idolized the peasants and planned the future in agrarian terms, and the Marxists who glorified the industrial proletariat and worked for a revolution

---

not protest. It is dubious whether Belinski, who ended his intellectual travels by denouncing Hegel and proclaiming the importance of the individual against the group, would appreciate the honor. Chernyshevsky might have approved of the Bolshevik Revolution as a way of ushering in a socialist Utopia, but a man with his predispositions toward political democracy, equalitarianism, and worker-run production could hardly have survived the purges of the 1930's. See Richard Hare, *Pioneers of Russian Social Thought,* London, 1951.

[11] *History of Russia,* p. 387.

to be born in the factories, gained new recruits from the rising commercial and professional classes. One family, of a provincial education official, contributed two sons to the cause. The elder, Alexander Ulianov, joined the People's Will, and was hanged in 1887 for plotting against the life of Alexander III; his devoted, and consequently embittered younger brother, Vladimir, became a Marxist, and under the name of Nikolai Lenin, was the founder of modern communism.

Lenin had already met his teacher in Marxism, Plekhanov, and had become recognized as one of the leaders of Russian socialism, when he was imprisoned as a revolutionary at the age of twenty-five, in 1895. But, despite their ill repute, Tsarist prisons and places of exile were not overly restrictive for some political inmates who had not yet made the leap from word to revolutionary deed. Two years of a St. Petersburg jail and three years of Siberia (where the river Lena gave him his *nom de plume et de guerre*), enabled him to pursue his Marxist studies with an undivided attention he could otherwise not have afforded. For one so dedicated to his cause as Lenin, it was as if he had been awarded a fellowship.

Lenin left for Europe in 1900, to work with Plekhanov and his group, and to infuse into the Russian Social Democratic movement both a new spirit and a new principle of close-knit and energetic organization. The focus of the organization was the editorial board and underground circulation system of *Iskra, The Spark*, edited by Lenin, Martov, Vera Zasulich, and others, with Plekhanov as the acknowledged master. The necessity for passing onionskin copies of *Iskra* under the eyes of the police of itself created a disciplined, secret network of small groups, and the dissemination of propaganda based on *Iskra* furthered the process. It was to this creation of a small body of what he called "professional revolutionists," and to securing their undivided leadership for himself, that Lenin devoted his particular attention. And it was out of Lenin's emendation of the Marxian theory of the revolution, and his tactics in the socialist movement, that a fundamental cleavage in the Russian Social Democratic Party arose and Bolshevism was born.

In *What Is To Be Done?* (1902), Lenin hammered home a basic and thoroughly valid proposition: of its own initiative, the working class was not revolutionary.

The history of all countries shows that the working class, exclusively by its own effort, is able to develop trade-union consciousness, i.e., it may itself realize the necessity for combining in unions, to fight against the employers and to strive to compel the government to pass necessary labor legislation, etc.

The theory of Socialism, however, grew out of the philosophic, historical and economic theories that were elaborated by the educated representatives of the propertied classes, the intellectuals.

The truth of this assertion is obvious in the American and British labor movements, but the conclusion Lenin drew from it is not easily acceptable to the non-Marxist mind:

Since the development of an independent ideology among the workers, as a result of their own struggle, is out of the question, there is thus possible either a bourgeois ideology or a Socialist ideology, and the question is: Which of the two shall it be? The blind unfolding of the labor movement can lead only to the permeation of that movement with a bourgeois ideology, because the unconscious growth of the labor movement takes the form of trade unionism, and trade unionism signifies the mental enslavement of the workers to the bourgeoisie. Therefore, our task as Social Democrats is to oppose this blind process, to divert the labor movement from the unconscious tendency of trade unionism to march under the protective wing of the bourgeoisie, and to bring it under the influence of Social Democracy instead.[12]

In other words, the workers had to be told that they were wrong as to both means and ends, that better brains than theirs had come to lead them. This arrogance was acceptable to good socialists because Marxism was scientifically, and absolutely correct, and the true interests of the working class could be properly understood and explained only by educated minds thoroughly steeped in this accurate science. As Lenin put it, "the theory of Marx is the objective truth. . . . Following in the direction of the Marxian theory, we shall draw nearer and nearer to the objective truth . . . following another path, we shall arrive at confusion and falsehood."[13]

But Lenin carried the doctrine of the "professional revolutionist"

[12] *Collected Works*, New York, 1929, vol. 4, pp. 114–115; Shub, *Lenin*, p. 54.
[13] *Materialism and Empirio-Criticism*, in E. Burns, *A Handbook of Marxism*, New York, 1935, p. 673.

even further. Taking off from Marx's vague and general references to the "dictatorship of the proletariat," Lenin argued (in the spirit of Tkachev) that his "professionals" should not only lead the revolution, but should remain in power after victory, to liquidate the remnants of capitalist opposition and establish the institutions needed to prepare the working class for socialism. This was more than many Russian socialists could stomach. Like their brethren in the German Social Democratic Party, they were accustomed to the use of revolutionary language, but rather hoped that their day might come without bloodshed. And even those who were reconciled to the inevitability of violence still expected that on the morrow of the seizure of power the truest political democracy could be instituted.

At a Russian Party Congress held at London in 1903, Lenin's views won out by a narrow margin. Leon Trotsky, who had risen rapidly in party councils, argued that the dictatorship of the proletariat was really a dictatorship only in a manner of speaking, since it meant the sovereignty of the overwhelming majority, the proletariat. But this euphemistic view was defeated, for Plekhanov laid down his interpretation and Lenin's in frank and brutal speech he was later to regret. He repeated the ancient dictum, *salus populi suprema lex*, which, he said, meant in revolutionary language that the success of the revolution was the supreme law. He argued that it was proper for the proletariat to curtail the rights of the middle class just as they had suffered at bourgeois hands. And if, after the revolution, the legislative elections turned out favorably for the revolutionists, there would be a long parliament; if unfavorably, the revolutionists should not hesitate to dissolve it in two weeks.[14] It was on this conception that Lenin and the majority (Bolsheviki) won, and Jules Martov and the minority (Mensheviki) lost. Lenin and Plekhanov now presumably dominated the party, which was committed to thoroughly centralized leadership. They had rejected love for democracy as such, and enshrined the principle of Tkachev, dictatorship by the revolutionists.[15] But the partnership soon broke up. Aside from the fact that Plekhanov began to swing back to his

[14] See Shub, *Lenin*, p. 62; B. D. Wolfe, *Three Who Made a Revolution*, New York, 1948, p. 236.

[15] On the relationship between Lenin and Tkachev see Shub, *Lenin*, pp. 54–55; Michael Karpovich, "A Forerunner of Lenin—P. N. Tkachev," *Review of Politics*, July, 1944, pp. 336 ff.

old democratic beliefs, he found Lenin intolerable, for the very good reason that Lenin thought himself the only fit judge of correct policy. Lenin resigned from *Iskra*, and established a new journal.

While Lenin was devoting himself to vitriolic and coarse criticism of his many opponents, and reading up on the tactics of street fighting, events in Russia were following their own dramatic course. As had happened before, the nation's misfortunes in international affairs had precipitated internal dissatisfaction, this time to the point of open revolution. The scandalous misconduct of the Russian war against Japan in 1904 and 1905 set off an explosion that almost brought Russia genuine constitutional government, and did make great progress toward this end.

Russia had been undergoing a major social and economic transformation. The statesmanship of Sergius Witte, Finance Minister from 1892 to 1903, had secured large foreign loans which, together with domestic investment and a governmental policy of aid and protection, had produced a rapid growth of industry.[16] This was naturally reflected in the rising numbers and social force of both middle class and proletariat. The old reactionary landed interests feared the newcomers' threat to their power, and were able to carry the Tsar with them in an effort, if not to turn the clock back, at least to stop it from running on.

The reactionaries had secured the dismissal of Witte, and embarked upon the war with Japan both to expand Russian power in Asia and to divert attention from ills at home. Russia's defeat was therefore their defeat, and the tide of protest had risen with news of each fresh debacle on the Japanese front. The reactionary Minister of the Interior, Plehve, master of repression and instigator of pogroms, was assassinated in 1904. As his successor the Tsar chose a moderate, Prince Svyatopolk-Mirsky, who returned to popular conciliation in the spirit of Loris-Melikov at the end of the reign of Alexander II. Mirsky encouraged responsible criticism in the press and the reformers in the *zemstva*. It was immediately evident that the ideologies of the extreme left and right had not monopolized Russian thinking, that between the revolutionary intelligentsia and the reactionaries stood a large body of responsible, thoughtful men, who were not far removed in their fundamental outlook from their

[16] See p. 407 ff.

contemporary Liberals and Conservatives in England. In November, 1904, a Congress of the *Zemstva* met and issued a program calling for all the political liberties of Western democracy. When the Tsar warned the *zemstva* not to discuss such matters, they were firmly supported by unions of professional men—doctors, lawyers, teachers, journalists—who met and resolved support for the *zemstva* program.[17]

This apparently sudden burgeoning of Western liberalism should sound a firm warning to those historians who see the Russian intellectual tradition as little more than a contest between revolutionaries and reactionaries. Perhaps it is not far from the mark to suggest that they have allowed the subsequent defeat of Russian democratic thought and the social forces behind it to distort their view. For it is obvious that the rapid flowering of a Western democratic outlook from 1904 on, its persistence against both the obstinacy of the Tsar and the siren calls of the revolutionists, could not have been a growth without roots. The truth is, rather, that this moderate outlook developed more or less quietly in the *zemstva,* in the law courts, in many sectors of an increasingly industrial and commercial society. Neither in itself nor in the temperaments of those who held it was it the kind of viewpoint that would play the hero against the political police, and thus easily catch the historian's eye. Its growth was quieter than that of revolutionary Marxism, but for all that more solid, and this is the likely explanation for the clear challenge to the Tsar, in 1904 and after, of the voice of Western liberalism.

The rougher native voices had not been stilled, however. The successors to the People's Will, the Social Revolutionaries, had continued preaching agrarian socialism as well as assassinating judiciously chosen subjects, such as the Grand Duke Sergius and Plehve. The Marxists had been making headway among the industrial workers, who numbered several million, concentrated in large centers.

To counteract the socialist influence, the government had adopted the devious tactic of having police agents take the lead in forming workers' organizations, keeping demands within safe limits and securing moderate benefits. One of these men was a priest, Father Gapon, in St. Petersburg, and on January 22, 1905, he led a proces-

---

[17] Many of these meetings took the form of banquets, somewhat reminiscent of middle-class agitation before the revolution of February, 1848, in France.

sion of workers and their families, carrying ikons and singing, to the Winter Palace, humbly to present a petition to the "little father," the Tsar, to redress their grievances. The huge crowd was met with gunfire.

The Tsar ordered liberals and radicals of all varieties to cease agitating for reform, and then made a few minor concessions, culminating with the promise, in August, 1905, of an indirectly elected consultative parliament (duma). This merely whetted the popular appetite for self-government. A wave of strikes rolled from St. Petersburg across the country, and in the capital itself a Soviet (or Council) of Workers' Deputies and socialists was established.[18] A Union of Unions of professional men and the *zemstva* members redoubled their pressure. The Tsar charged Witte with negotiating peace with Japan and then entrusted to him the task of turning back the revolutionary tide at home.

On October 30, 1905, on the advice of Witte and the Grand Duke Nicholas, the Tsar issued a manifesto promising a parliament, increased civil liberties, and a measure of constitutional and responsible government. No law was to take effect without the Duma's consent, but the cabinet would hold office not at its pleasure, but at that of the Tsar. Even in such half-measures were the makings of constitutionalism, and the people responded enthusiastically. Political parties organized openly: the Constitutional Democrats (Cadets), who wished to press for full ministerial responsibility on the British model; the Octobrists, who believed the needed reforms could be carried out within the more limited terms of the October Manifesto. In addition there were the Social Revolutionaries carrying on the *Narodnik* appeal to give all land to the peasants; the Social Democrats, whose Bolshevik and Menshevik wings had been partially, and temporarily, reunited; and not long before the Duma elections of 1906, the first nation-wide election in Russian history, there appeared the Labor group, radical but not Marxist. Aside from all these there was a faction, rather than a political party, that had less strength in the country than at court and in the bureaucracy— the reactionary defenders of absolutism.[19]

[18] The chairman was a Menshevik, Khrustalev-Nosar; Trotsky and a Social Revolutionary, Avksentiev, were vice-chairmen.

[19] The extremes of left and right were not led to inactivity by the October

It is a tribute to the sanity and wisdom of the unlettered and politically inexperienced Russian people that in the elections to the
first Duma, in March, 1906, they rejected the extremes of left and
right and yet gave the dishonest government no respite from their
insistence on progress toward democracy. Of 445 members, 190
were Cadets, 17 were Mensheviks, and there were no reactionaries.[20]
The Marxists were not quite so weak as their poor showing would
indicate: they had decided at first to boycott the elections, on the
ground that any imperial Duma represented a futile compromise
with Tsarism. Before the complex electoral system had run its
course,[21] some Social Democrats realized that the people had a very
different opinion of the worth of the Duma, and made a belated
entry into the campaign. By the time the Duma met, in May, 1906,
the Mensheviks led by Plekhanov had a complete change of heart,
for the Cadets asserted Parliament's independence from the throne.
Witte had been dismissed, and a bitter conflict immediately developed between the Duma and his reactionary successor, Goremykin.
The Mensheviks called upon their followers to support the Duma
liberals, but Lenin extended the original boycott into a campaign
to discredit Parliament. This was extremely convenient for the Tsar,
for he had determined to dissolve the Duma and yet could not risk
another revolutionary outbreak. Lenin's activities eliminated this

---

Manifesto. Reactionaries instigated pogroms, and punitive columns—the Black
Hundreds—visited bloody repression on towns and villages where dissidence
had been strong. In November and December, 1905, the St. Petersburg Soviet
called for a general strike, and although this met with an inadequate response
from a populace tiring of strife and disorder, a meeting at the Kronstadt naval
base and an uprising in Moscow bespoke the seriousness of discontent and the
survival of revolutionary sentiment.

[20] There were 100 nonparty men, including those of Octobrist outlook, 94 of
the Labor Party and 44 representing national minorities (G. Vernadsky, *Lenin,
Red Dictator*, New Haven, 1931, p. 83). Pares credits the Cadets with "over
150" seats (*Russia*, p. 437). A difficulty in determining party legislative
strength is frequently encountered with respect to Continental parliaments,
whose members are often elected as individuals and form groups with like-
minded deputies after the parliament meets. Another reason for the divergence
of estimates in the Russian case is that differences are possible in allocating
minorities representatives among the Russian parties.

[21] There were varying arrangements for town and country, for voting by
curiae or colleges based on residence and social status, and for preliminary
indirect balloting.

possibility, and the secret police, who had informers well posed in the Bolshevik councils, gave him an eloquent silent approval.

And so, on July 21, 1906, the Duma was dissolved, some ten weeks after it had assembled. While some two hundred of its members fled to Viborg in Finland and issued a vain appeal to the country for support, Lenin announced the time had come for renewed revolution. He was quite mistaken. The people did not respond, and the government did, with efficient repression of the few riots and local uprisings that occurred. A new hand was now at the helm, a former provincial governor, Peter Stolypin, who would suppress disorder with no qualms over cruelty, and yet keep alive the Duma within its limited role. More than this, he would initiate a program capable of transforming the social structure of Russia.

It was now Lenin's turn for a change of front, although never of heart. He urged socialist participation in the forthcoming elections for the second Duma, not because he had any interest in peaceful legislative reform, but because he now recognized that the Duma was an invaluable platform from which to attack his enemies. By the latter he meant primarily the Cadet party, for as liberal democrats they had secured a strong hold on the popular imagination, and were diverting even proletarian interest from eventual revolution to current issues.

The government exerted every kind of pressure to secure a friendly Duma, from barring the signers of the Viborg manifesto as candidates to simple police tactics at the polling places. "In face of these abuses of the administration," says Pares, "the attitude of the peasant electorate was very remarkable."

In one place they refused to elect because the presiding official persisted in refusing fair play; in another they watched the voting urns all night to see that there was no tampering with them; in another they three times reelected Aladin [leader of the Labor Party], excluded from the list of candidates by the Government.[22]

It was almost as if there were an innate sense for political democracy among these illiterate muzhiks, who had never had the opportunities of the British—or even the Germans—for political education. The

[22] Pares, *Russia*, p. 440.

election results therefore failed Stolypin's expectations, although Cadet representation declined.[23] The conservative constitutionalists, the Octobrists, gained, but among the winners were about one hundred sworn enemies of the regime, some two thirds of them Social Democrats and the rest Social Revolutionaries.

Stolypin wished to work with the moderate majority in the Duma, but the reactionaries made this impossible by disrupting its sessions and by incessant intrigues at Court. If they could not abolish the legislature, they would at least see to it that its composition was more congenial to the Tsar. The Social Democrats, meeting in London in May, 1907, issued a series of violent resolutions that furnished the government with an excellent pretext for forceful action. The Duma was dissolved as unrepresentative of the country and as containing men disloyal to the Tsar, which was, of course, correct. Thirty-one Social Democratic members of the Duma were packed off to Siberia, and a new electoral law was issued by decree, in plain violation of the Fundamental Laws the Tsar had granted to stop the revolution.[24] Representation of urban workers, of peasants, and of "unreliable" minorities such as the Poles was reduced, so that a strong bias was established in favor of the country gentry, who might be expected to show greater docility toward the imperial will.

Despite all this, the third Duma, which met in November, 1907, was no answer to an autocrat's prayers, for the autocracy's hold on the gentry had weakened. The Cadets, to be sure, were no longer the leading group: the new electoral arrangements had seen to that. But as against 50 tried and true reactionaries, there were half again as many Cadets and sympathizers, more than 30 Social Democrats and Laborites, and over 225 Octobrists.[25] The Duma had shifted to the right, but this did not mean that the Duma would be a rubber

[23] Vernadsky gives the following figures: extreme conservatives and Octobrists 54, Cadets 99, Labor 120, Social Revolutionaries 37, Social Democrats 65, national minority and other groups 40 (*Lenin*, p. 88). Pares differs, as follows: High Tories and "pure reactionaries" 46, Octobrists 32, Cadets 123, Labor 201, Social Revolutionaries 35, Social Democrats 54 (*Russia*, p. 441). Again, most of the differences may be accounted for by distribution of the minorities seats among the Russian parties in Pares' listing.

[24] It undoubtedly was unrepresentative, since straightforward and unmanipulated elections would have greatly strengthened the representation of those opposing the regime.

[25] Vernadsky, *Lenin*, p. 95.

stamp or that it would cease its call for reform. Its demands and its expectations would be more modest, it would accommodate itself to the necessity of working within the narrow confines of the authority the Tsar had left to it. Above all it would seek to gain prestige and to solidify its position as a leading institution in Russian government and society.

These objectives, which even the Cadets now came to share, were very largely achieved by 1914, owing to the dignity and competence with which the Duma pursued them, and to the fact that Stolypin and the more liberal members of the bureaucracy sought its alliance against the reactionary clique surrounding the Tsar. Since the Duma had to approve most financial measures, its support was valued by ministers, and it was therefore able to strengthen those who coöperated with it and make trouble for those who did not. If this seems a small matter, it should not be forgotten that it was precisely from the king's need for ministers who could secure support in Commons that the British system of genuine cabinet responsibility developed. Since foreign loans were always needed by the Russian government, the Duma's growing prestige in Europe reinforced its standing at home.

Among the important achievements of administrative coöperation with the third and fourth (1912) Dumas[26] were an increasing parliamentary voice in foreign policy, which helped range Russia on the side of the Allies in the First World War, an education program that made notable progress toward the goal of universal primary schooling by the mid-1920's, and the beginnings of social insurance for labor. But the most far-reaching change was the Stolypin land reform, whose aim was no less than the creation of a vast new class of independent farmers as a pillar of social order. The emancipation decrees of Alexander II had consolidated the position of the village commune. The Stolypin reform enabled the peasants to break away from communal land ownership,[27] to hold the soil as individual pro-

[26] The make-up of the fourth Duma was very much like that of the third, which had served its full five-year term. In the fourth Duma, the Cadets and their allies were somewhat stronger, the Octobrists, Laborites, and Marxists somewhat weaker.

[27] By 1916, about 6 million of the 16 million eligible peasant households had taken advantage of this opportunity to separate themselves from the communes or were in process of doing so. Some of them gained another important advan-

prietors.[28] It was hoped they would develop the celebrated industriousness, stability, and individualism of the free French peasant,
thereby undermining the dominance of the great landlords and the
appeal of Social Revolutionaries and Marxists.[29] Reactionaries and
radicals were therefore united in opposition to this agrarian transformation, the former because they valued the *mir* as a collective
means of controlling the peasantry and as a sanctuary of that mystic
entity, the "Russian soul"; the latter because as socialists they either
preferred communal landholding or favored outright nationalization
of the land. Each group was right, from its own standpoint: the
reform was a step toward capitalism, inimical to the interests of
both feudal landlords and socialists. Lenin saw this clearly. If
Stolypin's policy should persist, he wrote, the Bolsheviks might have
"to renounce any agrarian program at all," or, in other words, it
would be impossible for them to buy peasant support with promises
of confiscating the great estates.[30]

---

tage in the consolidation of strip holdings into unified farms. That this change
in the direction of individualism was more a matter of process than accomplished fact is brought out by G. T. Robinson, *Rural Russia Under the Old
Regime*, New York, 1932, pp. 208 ff., but its importance as a trend is not
denied.

[28] Witte had already terminated the land redemption payments the peasants
still owed under the emancipation laws of the 1860's.

[29] Hans von Eckhardt (*Russia*, C. A. Phillips, trans., New York, 1932, p. 273)
makes the following comment on the basis of his personal observations "as
temporary statistical official attached to a south Russian zemstvo in 1911": "The
peasants who possessed a homestead of their own, or had settled down on their
own parcels of land . . . produced quite a different impression from those
belonging to the *mir*. They approached questions affecting their own economic
interests in an independent spirit, knew how to stand up for their own ideas,
and displayed an astonishing eagerness to learn and thirst for knowledge:
whereas the representatives of the *mir* were in the habit of rejecting all technical
and economic suggestions with stolid indifference, out of a feeling that nothing
could be done to help them. This was also evident in politics. The villages belonging to the *mir* were for the most part openly hostile to the Government
. . . whereas the peasants on the newly-distributed settlements seemed politically more neutral, tried to set up coöperatives and land banks, and refused to
hear of fresh upheavals." The paradox that the growth of rural coöperatives did
not really get under way until the supposedly coöperative spirit of the commune
had been broken is explained by Pares in these words (*Russia*, p. 446): "Cooperation, which had remained a dream so long as the village community was
joint owner of all property, began to spring up of itself everywhere as soon as
the individual peasant had something of his own to coöperate with. . . ."

[30] Vernadsky, *Lenin*, pp. 102, 103. Lenin, still expecting Russia to develop a
higher bourgeois capitalism as a prelude to socialism, believed land nationaliza-

As stability returned to Russia, reinforced by a wave of prosperity and by Stolypin's severe police measures, the fortunes of the Marxists waned. Michael Tomsky, later the leader of the Soviet labor union movement until removed by Stalin, wrote in 1908:

The reaction has profoundly influenced the workers, especially those who have only superficial ties with political organizations, and even among the class conscious workers the effort to acquire knowledge has been turned under the direction of the reactionary forces frequently into undesirable and purely academic lines, that is to say into endeavors to prepare themselves to secure a high school diploma or to enter a university and so get out of the ranks of the proletariat, to become intellectuals . . . frequently with view of obtaining a purely professional education, as for example in such lines as sketching, drawing, and the like, which means an attempt to improve their economic situation by their individual efforts.[31]

From the Leninist viewpoint, such dissipation was positively sinful. It should not be imagined, however, that the twofold program of pacification and reform had succeeded in establishing anything resembling a whole-hearted acceptance of the status quo. It was true that "the Duma had plainly come to stay; it had become a habit; the country stood more and more behind it, and the bureaucracy and even the Court had reconciled themselves to its existence."[32] But this bespoke the vitality of the demand for further improvement, not complacency. The Duma itself grew restive in its limited role, and doubt rose concerning the value of the patient nagging after small improvements that had been pursued since 1908. In 1912, the distinguished historian and Cadet leader, Paul Miliukov, wrote bitterly: "The five years of the third Duma have sufficiently clarified the situation. In order to acquire one single right—to *exist*, the Duma had to become one of the wheels in the bureaucratic machine."[33]

---

tion to be compatible with a lower stage of capitalism. Once the bourgeoisie had settled firmly on the land—or genuine bourgeois had developed among the farmers—nationalization would be opposed by them, and the Marxists would lose their opportunity to use agriculture as a lever for advancing socialism. See Lenin, *Capitalism and Agriculture*, New York, 1946. Marxian theory was more than ordinarily confused with respect to agriculture.

[31] Quoted by Vernadsky, *Lenin*, p. 100.

[32] Pares, *Russia*, p. 448.

[33] In Alexander Kornilov, *Modern Russian History*, New York, 1917, vol. 2, p. 333.

The partial and uneven character of the various reforms brought full satisfaction to no one, and stimulated the appetite for more freedom and a greater measure of popular sovereignty. One victory of the Revolution of 1905 was that labor unions had been enabled to operate openly and lawfully, but this new power made the urban workers resent all the more administrative oppression and under-representation in the Duma and other bodies. The press was freer than before 1905, but liberals and radicals reacted all the more bit-terly to the restrictions that were still applied. And the caliber of the Tsarist government declined instead of improving. The iron hand of Stolypin had been removed by assassination in 1911,[34] and the Tsar never again appointed a man of like stature. The poisonous influ-ence of the incredible Rasputin, religious quack and master of de-pravity, continued to increase at Court. And the government, through a policy of surpassing stupidity, threw its weight behind Lenin in order to weaken the moderate opposition who were re-garded as more dangerous to Tsarism. The reactionaries could count on Lenin to attack the Cadets and annoy the Mensheviks, and if, perchance, the Bolsheviks produced a revolutionary outbreak, so much the better, for its suppression would strengthen the hand of autocracy and discredit all the Tsar's opponents. In the years im-mediately preceding the First World War, the reactionaries' im-mediate objective, which was also Lenin's, was to undermine the Mensheviks' position among the working class. Although "Bolshevik" signified majority, after 1905 Lenin's faction had consistently placed second to the Mensheviks among Russian workers and in the party organization. Plekhanov and his followers had lost some of their revolutionary fixation. By 1909 they had become interested in the possibilities of enacting social legislation, and had voted for the government's education measures in the Duma. By 1912 a good many of them wished to disband the underground organization that had been maintained beside the legal Social Democratic Party.

The underground was commanded by Lenin, who used it to gain control over the working class, and for a number of purposes inci-dental thereto, including fund raising. The latter was sometime accomplished by what the Bolsheviks called "expropriations," o

[34] By a Social Revolutionary "under circumstances which pointed strongly t the connivance of the reactionaries" (Pares, *Russia*, p. 448).

robberies.[35] Such operations rather upset the Mensheviks. Lenin was annoyed by their squeamishness: "When I see Social Democrats announcing with pride and self-satisfaction that 'we are no anarchists, no thieves, no brigands, we are above that, we reject the partisan struggle,' then I ask myself—do these people understand what they are saying?"[36]

The uneasy alliance between the two wings of Russian Marxism was finally broken completely in 1912, and Leninism was at a low ebb in Socialist party circles. But the very violence of his political line and management of the underground, which angered the Mensheviks, endeared him to the activist temperaments among the socialist workers. Lenin's strategy of intransigence, his insistence on the infallible correctness of whatever position he took, his casual dishonesty in maneuvering within the party for his own advantage, made him a person one could work for, if one chose, but never with. Any disagreement with him might bring forth the accusation of splitting the socialist ranks—it was always the other person or group that was guilty of splitting—and a stream of vituperation. It did not matter to Lenin that on the eve of the First World War he was probably the most hated man within the ranks of Russian socialism. For his behavior stemmed not from personal arrogance, but from intellectual conceit. His tactics of disruption[37] derived logically from

---

[35] The most famous of these was the Tiflis holdup, in June, 1907, when a consignment of cash for a bank, amounting to over 300,000 rubles, was seized by men under the overall command of Stalin, Lenin's deputy in the Caucasus. Several persons were killed and wounded in the process. Another celebrated instance of raising money by odd means was a strictly business deal by which the Bolsheviks undertook to sell a large quantity of arms to a well-known gang of ordinary nonpolitical bandits.

[36] Shub, *Lenin*, pp. 99 ff., 102. Stalin's field chieftain in the Tiflis robbery was a remarkable person named Ter-Petrosian, also known as Kamo. He escaped to Berlin, where he was arrested with bombs in his possession. On the advice of a prominent Bolshevik, Krassin, who had helped engineer the holdup, Kamo feigned insanity. "For the next four years, with incredible stamina and will power, he played the role of a violent maniac" (p. 101). Accounts of the "expropriation" campaign may be found in Wolfe, *Three Who Made a Revolution*, pp. 376 ff., and Boris Souvarine, *Stalin, A Critical Survey of Bolshevism*, New York, 1939, pp. 89 ff.

[37] Trotsky condemned "as a devilish brew the party squabble which is systematically fomented by the master of such affairs, Lenin, that professional exploiter of backwardness in the Russian workers' movement" (Shub, *Lenin*, p. 127).

his doctrine of an absolutely devoted and cohesive revolutionary elite that followed the uniquely correct political course. Since Lenin was always certain that he was right, splitting was merely a device to preserve uncontaminated that hard core of correct revolutionary leadership, a group, no matter how small, completely subservient to himself. This he was always able to do. Moreover, it is likely that his cocksure certainty, his readiness to employ any means whatever, his bold assertion that sometimes "a scoundrel is useful to our party precisely because he is a scoundrel,"[38] struck a responsive chord in the minds and hearts of less sophisticated and less Westernized Marxists, such as Stalin and his Caucasian strong-arm men.

The split in the Social Democratic Party, which met the desires of the Russian police, was naturally a matter of some concern to European socialists, and in the early summer of 1914 the Second International was preparing to give it formal consideration. This could have been disastrous to Lenin, for his uncomradely behavior and unsavory practices would undoubtedly have been condemned, forcing Lenin to choose between submission and being cast outside the pale of socialism to become the leader of an isolated and heretical splinter group. But luck was with him, as it had been before and would be time and again later on. He was now saved by the outbreak of the First World War; the scheduled Congress of the International did not meet.

For a time, the war united people and government, in Russia as elsewhere. In Russia it was even, in a sense, a continuation of the struggle for freedom and self-government, for the reactionary faction had been pro-German and the liberals and moderates pro-Ally. By the summer of 1915, the country, still eager to win the war, had become furious over disclosures of defeatism and failure to press arms production on the part of the War Minister. For once the Tsar agreed with the people, and by August, 1915, it seemed that not only would the war effort be placed under competent direction, but that all the political desires of the Duma liberals, short of full ministerial responsibility to parliament, would be met. The leading reactionaries were dismissed, and a war industries committee was established, including representatives from the legislature. The center groups in the Duma formed a progressive bloc which, with the

[38] Shub, *Lenin*, p. 105.

support of liberal ministers, requested the formation of a genuine cabinet, unified in outlook and program.

There was reason to hope that even this might be granted, but the Tsar had passed the peak of his coöperation with the representatives of the people. He was sliding swiftly into a depth of blundering reaction that exceeded anything in the checkered career of the three-century-old dynasty. The influence that overcame his better judgment was that of the Empress, who might well be recorded in history as Lenin's best friend. The spirit that moved her was that of Rasputin. It would be hard to conceive of a woman in high place who possessed the worst possible characteristics to a greater degree: bigotry, profound stupidity, the ability to nag her weak-willed husband into any course she chose, a limitless faith in a scoundrel who had captivated the neurotic mysticism in her.[39] Nor would it be easy to conceive of a more dangerous type of scoundrel in public life than Rasputin, for he did not run the risk of holding office and assuming responsibility. He was content with power, and used it to place grafters and incompetents in ministerial positions.

The terminal decay of Tsarism began on August 24, 1915, when the hopes engendered by the Tsar's coöperation with the Duma were still running strong. On that date, the Tsar, having been persuaded by his wife, replaced the Grand Duke Nicholas as Commander in Chief. The damage this did to the conduct of military operations was the least of its harm. With the Tsar at the front, the Empress took over the reins of government at home. In effect, although not in name, Rasputin became Prime Minister and whatever else he wished to be, issuing instructions and running the state through the scalawags appointed to office at his behest.

By the summer of 1916 nearly all the able ministers had been dismissed. By the fall serious discontent had spread through the country, and was particularly rife in the capital city of St. Petersburg.[40] In November the Duma met, and Cadets and reactionaries joined in denouncing the government. But the Tsar was incapable of any resolute action, along any course. He replaced Rasputin's pro-

---

[39] Rasputin's hold over the Empress arose from her belief that he had saved the life of her son, the heir apparent, who was afflicted with incurable hemophilia, by prayers that brought prompt divine intervention. In her letters to Nicholas, the Empress referred to Rasputin as "our Friend," or simply "He."

[40] Early in the war its name had been Russified to Petrograd.

German puppet Prime Minister with a pro-Allied bureaucrat, Trepov, but, when the Empress begged him to, he broke his promise to Trepov to dismiss the Minister of the Interior, Protopopov, who was known to have held unauthorized conversations with the Germans.

Various Grand Dukes and Duchesses now pleaded with the Tsar to grant a constitution, and fully responsible parliamentary government, as the only alternative to revolution. He was immovable, and the Empress inflexible. Amid this incredible decay, this distortion of human behavior into a flight from the very lowest level of common sense, several patriotic Russians struck down the one regarded by all to be the root of the evil, Rasputin.[41]

The assassination of "the Friend" galvanized Nicholas II into a state of complete inactivity, and the stricken Empress would consult only with Protopopov, who was having spiritualist conversations with the "martyred saint." Small wonder, then, that loyal supporters of the dynasty, reactionary believers in absolutism, Cadets and Octobrists, generals and Grand Dukes, plotted to force the Tsar from the throne. But in these days of the apogee of decadence, the process of secret consultation that was to produce a cure was outstripped by the advance of the disease. Riots and strikes began in the winter of 1917. In February, the breakdown of transport and governmental incompetence produced a bread shortage in Petrograd. Nicholas, away at the front, reacted to the consequent disturbances with the customary order to the military governor to repress them by force of arms. But now the soldiers joined the people. The Grand Duke Cyril telephoned the Duma President, Rodzianko, offering the allegiance of his regiment of Guards and asking that a Provisional Government be formed.

Here was revolution. But it was still revolution largely from above: the streets were seething, but had not replaced the parliament chamber. The Duma met against the Tsar's wishes. A Soviet of Workers' and Soldiers' Deputies was formed, under the leadership of a Menshevik and a Social Revolutionary member of the Duma, the

---

[41] He was murdered on December 30, 1916, in the home of Prince Yusopov, who was married to the Tsar's niece. The Prince was assisted by Purishkevitch, leader of the reactionary faction in the Duma. The Tsar's nephew, Grand Duke Dmitri, was in attendance.

latter Alexander Kerensky. And on March 15, 1917, the Duma created a Provisional Government. That day it secured the approval of both the Petrograd Soviet and the Tsar Nicholas II, who now courteously and coöperatively abdicated, on the advice of everyone but the Empress. The decree in which he renounced his imperial powers turned them over to his brother, Grand Duke Michael, and confirmed the Provisional Government that, for the first time in Russian history, had not been formed by the autocrat but by a Duma, and a Soviet.

To this point the revolution certainly betrayed nothing that could be explained by the economic interpretation of history. In the midst of a world war, there had been nothing to balance the destructive coincidence by which stupidity and stubbornness were united in the royal couple. This is not to explain the downfall of the regime exclusively in terms of a handful of personalities. The nature of Russia and of Russian history had made such an occurrence possible, but had not rendered it inevitable. Nor was there a fundamental inevitability to the partial but decisive turn to the left that the revolution now took, when Grand Duke Michael declined the throne. For the Provisional Government had no tradition behind it. It was the creation of a Duma which, although the best voice available to the country, was itself unrepresentative. And there was no liberal version of a Stolypin to provide firm and shrewd leadership. A bare seven months after the Provisional Government of March, 1917, was formed, it gave way to the iron dictatorship of the Bolsheviks under Lenin.

Nevertheless, when the Provisional Government was established under Prince Lvov, with Miliukov as Foreign Minister and Kerensky as Minister of Justice, there were few who would have predicted the rise of Lenin. He was then in neutral Switzerland, meeting with other Leninists, and analyzing the worldy Armageddon and Apocalypse according to the Leninist version of Marx. He had not been outstandingly successful in his vocation of revolutionist. His theory of the revolutionary elite had not replaced the gradualist and more democratic doctrines of the majority of socialists. He had been wrong in assessing the revolutionary tide of 1905, and right only in recognizing its defeat by Stolypin. It was the First World War which gave Lenin not only an opportunity for action, but the basis for a theory upon which to act. This doctrine he expounded in *Imperialism as the Highest Phase of Capitalism*, completed in 1916, a major addition to Marxism and the guidebook of international Communism after the war.[42]

Lenin argued that in advanced stages of capitalist development the concentration of ownership led to control of the means of production and distribution by a progressively smaller number of financier-monopolists. In accordance with the theory of immiserization,[43] domestic markets for the output of the monopolies would not keep pace with the growth of their productive forces, and the rate of profit would decline. To overcome falling profits, the monopolists would search for cheaper supplies of raw materials and for new fields in which to invest. This would involve them in the exploitation of backward areas and, in order to secure the social and political discipline necessary for efficient exploitation, the ruling monopolists would require their national governments (the political arm at their disposal, according to Marx and Lenin) to take over the colonial regions by force of arms. But, unlike the previous stage of competitive industrial capitalism, finance capitalism was capable of forced growth at the instance of governments and their financier rulers, so that instead of a relatively even spread of capitalist production from the more to the less advanced nations, an uneven development of capitalist powers was now possible. While imperialism tended to mask and even retard the immiserization of at least the higher ranks of the working class[44] by transferring the burden of exploitation to the shoulders of the backward people, the uneven development of the imperialist powers created friction among them, as they competed for the most advantageous colonial investment areas. Wars of imperialism were therefore inevitable, of progressively greater intensity and scope, producing revolutionary situations, not only in the advanced nations, but in the backward regions that imperialism

[42] The basic concepts of Lenin's theory of imperialism had been worked out by the Marxist Rudolf Hilferding in *Das Finanzkapital*, 1910, and by the non-Marxist J. A. Hobson, *Imperialism*, 1902. While in agreement on many points, Rosa Luxemburg's *Die Akkumulation des Kapitals*, 1913, had a different emphasis.

[43] See p. 212.

[44] This point ingeniously explained away the obvious improvement of living standards.

had drawn into the vortex of capitalist decay and conflict, and particularly in those countries that met defeat. Thus, even in a country like Russia, or in the Orient, an opportunity would be afforded the elite core of professional revolutionists. The dialectical mesh—monopolistic finance capitalism producing imperialist wars producing revolutionary situations—would shorten the duration of the highest phase of the capitalist system.

Even if it does not fit the facts,[45] Lenin's theory of imperialism does have a ring of plausibility, and would obviously strike most Marxists as a brilliant ray of light illuminating the complex events that followed 1914. Moreover, it afforded a convincing rationale for the position he took with respect to the Great War. While Plekhanov had urged support of the Allied war effort, and Trotsky had proclaimed an internationalist slogan of "peace without indemnities and annexation, peace without victors and vanquished," Lenin summoned the working class to "turn the imperialist war into a civil

[45] Like much Marxian interpretation, the theory of imperialism is more plausible than accurate, but, since it has been subjected to surprisingly little criticism, it has won great acceptance even among non-Marxists. As a matter of historical fact, there is little correlation between capital export and political imperialism and, contrary to Lenin's theory, capital-exporting nations directed their funds to other advanced countries to a far greater extent than to the colonies. A great many instances of colonialism, moreover, involved nations which had no capital to export, and great-power imperialism frequently ran counter to the desires of their leading capitalist groups. When we recall that political and military imperialism—the taking over by force of backward or relatively less advanced areas—is as old as recorded history, it is obvious that the Lenin theory is applicable only to those features of imperialism which are peculiar to imperialism in the era of advanced capitalism; these features are said to be capital export and (Rosa Luxemburg's emphasis) competition for markets. The latter is also an age-old phenomenon, and the former does not hold water when it is realized that the chief beneficiaries of European capital export in the late nineteenth and early twentieth centuries were such countries as the United States and Canada, Argentina, Austria-Hungary, and Russia.

Considering such imperialist efforts as the Italian campaign in Ethiopia in 1896 and French plantings of the tricolor as if *pour le sport*, while French capital was going to Russia, one would expect to find a clearer explanation of modern imperialism in the nature of modern, popular nationalism, in the social role of the military, in the psychology of national prestige. J. A. Schumpeter, *Imperialism and Social Classes*, New York, 1951, developed a sociological theory of imperialism which escapes the errors of the Hobson-Lenin approach, but which is itself rather narrow. There is a brilliant, brief discussion of imperialism and its interpreters in an article by William L. Langer, "A Critique of Imperialism," *Foreign Affairs*, 1935, conveniently reprinted in H. Ausubel, ed., *The Making of Modern Europe*, New York, 1951, vol. 2, pp. 918 ff.

war." The workers were now armed: let them shoot their officers and begin the proletarian revolution. As between the Central Powers and the Allies, two camps of "blackguards" as far as he was concerned, Lenin favored the Germans, for he remained primarily interested in a Russian revolution, and a Russian defeat would be a golden opportunity for the Bolsheviks.

Lenin's thesis on war, which he presented in numerous articles and pamphlets and before rump international socialist conferences in 1915 and 1916,[46] was of course adopted by his followers, although not without debate and hesitation. After the abdication of the Tsar, however, it was rather difficult for the Bolsheviks who were in Russia to preach the gospel of defeatism and civil war. The revolution of March, 1917, had not been a Bolshevik revolution. To a degree almost unique in history it had been an uprising of the will of all classes and parties. To be sure, old antagonisms and suspicions had not evaporated, or there would have been no opportunity at all for Lenin and his handful. But it was no longer a Romanov against whom Lenin's call to arms was directed, but a government in the name of the people that was preparing to hold elections for a constituent assembly. And even though war weariness had understandably grown, there was no general desire to submit to the Germans. Indeed, one of the principal factors leading to the March revolution had been the widespread and well-founded belief that the Empress and her coterie of malefactors were trying to carry out the Lenin strategy in reverse, to accept defeat at the hands of Germany in order to rescue the Tsarist autocracy.

While Lenin fumed in Switzerland, the Bolsheviks in Petrograd followed a very cautious line. The March revolution had freed the political prisoners and Siberian exiles, who immediately flocked to Petrograd. Lenin's old collaborator, Leon Kamenev (liquidated in 1936), and Stalin took over the direction of *Pravda,* the Bolshevik newspaper. Reversing the line Lenin had followed throughout the war, Stalin proclaimed that defeatism had died when the Tsar's troops had joined the people, and called for reunion with the Mensheviks and support of the Provisional Government insofar as it consolidated the revolution and worked toward objectives desired by the people.

[46] See p. 237.

But Lenin had to get back to Russia before he could overcome such apostasy, and while the Cadet leaders of the Provisional Government offered no objections, the Allies would not grant him the necessary visas. As a result, Lenin took the more direct route, through Germany, for the Germans realized that it would be very useful to them to have the defeatist Lenin in Petrograd. As the Kaiser's Chief of Staff on the Russian front put it,

We naturally tried, by means of propaganda, to increase the disintegration that the Russian Revolution had introduced into the Army. . . . In the same way as I send shells into the enemy trenches, as I discharge poison gas at him, I, as an enemy, have the right to employ the expedient of propaganda against his garrisons.[47]

It is not reported how Lenin liked being compared to poison gas, but the simile was to prove all too apt when the wind had shifted and Leninism had returned to plague the Germans who had expedited his passage.

Lenin's arrival in Petrograd soon brought about a sharp change in the situation. Just as the March revolution was not a socialist, much less a Bolshevik revolution, it may be said that the November coup that overthrew the Provisional Government was not so much a Bolshevik party undertaking as the work of this one man, Lenin. His first act on his native soil was to condemn the moderate course pursued by Kamenev and Stalin, to preach conflict with the bourgeoisie as represented by the Provisional Government. He changed the party name to "Communist," to emphasize the break with the old, and in his eyes decrepit, Social Democracy. At first his arguments met with a cool reception from the leading Bolsheviks, for no matter how logically derived from his theory of imperialism, which had been accepted by the party, they required a distinct change in the long-received Marxist doctrine on revolution in Russia.

The nature and timing of the proposed revolution had long been a subject for speculation and dispute, for Russia was not one of the industrially advanced nations to which the Marxian thesis particularly applied. Marx himself had left the door ajar for a socialist triumph in Russia with the statement that "the existing form of communal property in Russia can serve as the starting point of a com-

[47] Shub, *Lenin*, p. 182.

munist development," provided "the Russian revolution gives the signal for a workers' revolution in the west, so that both revolutions supplement each other."[48] But this obviously afforded no firm and definite guide and conflicting interpretations abounded. One group of Russian Marxists, the Economists, went so far as to urge that all agitation for socialism be dropped, and that all socialists should bend their efforts toward the establishment of a mature capitalist society as a necessary precondition for the sowing, let alone the achievement, of socialist ideas and objectives. This, of course, represented an extreme and even fatalistic sort of economic determinism which ill suited the violent and impatient spirit of the Russian revolutionary tradition. The position taken by Plekhanov and Lenin within the Social Democratic Party was not, however, diametrically opposite. In a famous writing of 1905, *Two Tactics*, Lenin declared:

Marxism has irrevocably broken with all the nonsense talked by the Narodniks and the Anarchists about Russia . . . being able to avoid capitalist development, jump out of capitalism, or skip over it, by some means other than the class struggle on the basis and within the limits of capitalism.

He went on to argue that a bourgeois revolution would be "more beneficial to the working class than to the bourgeoisie," for

. . . a socialist revolution is out of the question unless the masses become class-conscious, organized, trained and educated by open class struggle against the entire bourgeoisie. In answer to the anarchist objections . . . that we are delaying the socialist revolution, we shall say: we are not delaying it, but are taking the first step in its direction, using the only means that are possible along the only right path, namely, the path of a democratic republic.

A bourgeois democratic revolution would advance the cause of socialism through its ability to

. . . bring about a radical redistribution of the land to the advantage of the peasantry, establish consistent and full democracy including the republic, eliminate all the oppressive features of Asiatic bondage, not only of village but also of factory life, lay the foundation for thorough improvement in the position of the workers and raise their standard of living, and

[48] Mehring, *Marx*, p. 549.

last but not least—carry the revolutionary conflagration into Europe. Such a victory will by no means transform our bourgeois revolution into a socialist revolution; the democratic revolution will not extend beyond the scope of bourgeois social and economic relationships.[49]

Lenin differed from the fatalists not in his diagnosis of the economic and social development required to precede socialism but in the strategy to be adopted by Marxians. Whereas the former merely proposed to wait until capitalism should have developed through its own economic momentum, in effect allowing Marxism no political role, Lenin insisted that his party should actively foment and support a violent middle-class democratic revolution.[50]

He might have maintained this view in 1917 with perfect consistency, and supported the admittedly bourgeois Provisional Government while continuing to agitate for a more belligerently class-conscious proletariat. But the theory of imperialism opened more attractive vistas, and moreover, a new conception of revolution had come forth to gratify Lenin's activist spirit. This was Trotsky's theory of permanent revolution.[51] The middle-class challenge to autocracy was so late in maturing in Russia, the argument ran, that it would coincide with the rising of the proletariat. Furthermore, since the Russian middle class was incapable of vigorous action or leadership, the workers would be the chief actors in the revolutionary drama, and would accordingly assume command of the postrevolutionary government. In Russia, therefore, the bourgeois revolution (which took place in France in 1789) and the triumphant proletarian revolution (which had yet to occur in the West) would be fused into one continuous process. Even partial measures of socialization by

[49] *Two Tactics of Social Democracy in the Democratic Revolution*, New York, 1935, pp. 20, 38, 45.

[50] The principal difference between Lenin and Plekhanov was with respect to the role of the socialist party following the overthrow of the Tsar. The latter believed the party should neither enter into the postrevolutionary bourgeois government nor think in terms of governing alone until the proletariat had been brought to the proper degree of maturity. Lenin believed that, owing to the inertia of the middle class, the workers would have to take the leading part in the bourgeois revolution, and that the socialist party should join the government and try to direct its course, while continuing to prepare for the subsequent, proletarian revolution.

[51] Worked out in 1905 together with Parvus, who arranged with the Germans for Lenin's return to Russia in 1917.

the working-class government would lead to both resistance on the part of the bourgeoisie and to further progress toward socialism. The revolutionary flame from Russia would set off the conflagration for which Europe had been prepared by the slow development of the class struggle. Instead of a closed event, beginning and terminating, the revolution would be a process much more akin to a chain reaction.

This was Lenin's view when he called his errant followers to order in April, 1917. He had in large part become a Trotskyite, and the chief slogan in his forthcoming struggle for dictatorship was of Trotskyite inspiration, "All power to the Soviets!" The new Leninism was roundly condemned, on all sides, from the Bolshevik *Pravda* to soldiers' committees, not to speak of the Mensheviks and Cadets. But Lenin lost neither heart nor ground. Throughout April he devoted himself to organizational and propaganda activities among the factory workers and the garrison. In the meantime things were going badly for Russia at home and at the front, and peace sentiment was rising. Early in May the Provisional Government experienced a crisis, brought on by Foreign Minister Miliukov's pledge to continue the war at the side of the Allies. Miliukov, and the old Octobrist, Guchkov, who was War Minister, resigned. Although the reorganized government was much farther to the left, with Kerensky replacing Guchkov, Lenin redoubled his attacks, for the Mensheviks and Social Revolutionaries were the ones who most seriously threatened to split the working class—from Lenin's control. However the rest of the people might have felt, Lenin had regained complete authority within his own group: the All-Russian Bolshevik Congress early in May approved his course.

Had the Provisional Government surrendered its power to the Soviets, however, Lenin would not have profited. The first All-Russian Congress of Soviets, meeting at Petrograd in June, 1917, contained 285 Social Revolutionaries, 248 Mensheviks, and only 105 Bolsheviks.[52] And yet at least some of the tributaries to the turbulent stream of Russian history were running in his favor. Urban labor in particular was responding increasingly to the appeal of Bolshevik orators, as economic disintegration spread and neither the government nor the employers took adequate steps to conciliate the work-

[52] Trotsky, *History of the Russian Revolution*, vol. 3, p. 438.

ers. But Lenin overestimated this swing of opinion, and scheduled for June 23 a mass demonstration, including military units that supported the Bolsheviks, which he hoped would lead to the overthrow of the Provisional Government. Word of his plans reached the Soviet, however, and its disapproval forced their cancellation.

A few weeks later another opportunity presented itself that seemed altogether too good to let slip. The Cadet members of the Provisional Government resigned in protest against an agreement in respect of Ukranian autonomy concluded by several other ministers. The Bolsheviks, anticipating Adolf Hitler's favorite tactic, chose to strike in the midst of the enemy's cabinet crisis. On July 17, 1917, about twenty thousand pro-Bolshevik sailors from the nearby base at Kronstadt marched into Petrograd and moved on the palace where the Provisional Government was sitting. Army regiments followed, and then Bolshevik workers. For once, however, Lenin and his Central Committee failed to show decisive and well-organized leadership. The military had no specific orders, the Petrograd Soviet appealed to the workers to disband. There was a great deal of shooting and a good many deaths, but the day passed with the government still in power, and the final destruction of Bolshevism might well have been at hand.

On July 19 the government ordered the arrest of a number of leading Bolsheviks, on the charges of having plotted an insurrection and of having been financed by Germany. The first count of the indictment was not such as to shock the Leninist sense of propriety, but the second, for some strange reason, was taken as an offense against their honor. Not only did the Bolsheviks deny it at the time, which was the obvious thing to do, since the people were and continued to be bitterly anti-German, but they have denied it ever since.[53] After some heroic talk about standing trial and undoing the

[53] The evidence against the Bolsheviks is convincingly presented by David Shub, in his biography of Lenin (*Lenin*, pp. 211 ff.), and he points out that while they have attempted to shout the charges down with cries of "slander" and "base canard," they have never seriously tried to refute them. Once more, Lenin's superb luck softened the blow. The accusations and evidence were released by the Minister of Justice, who was unaware that a secret government committee had long been gathering data and were waiting to arrest a courier with documents before making any public announcements. As a result of the premature publication, the courier turned back to Sweden from the Russian border, and escaped. Lenin's—and the Kaiser's—useful Dr. Parvus, who had

slanderers, Lenin, together with Zinoviev, the future head of the Comintern (liquidated 1936) went into hiding in Finland. He had remarked to Trotsky, "Now they will shoot us," but, as Trotsky said, their "enemies at that time were not consistent enough and did not have the courage to do it."[54] Kerensky understood the character of his opponents, but among the Mensheviks and Social Revolutionaries there was too much comradely sentiment against shooting "fellow socialists." The Bolsheviks lived on, until luck turned their way.

The disclosures of Lenin's German associations sharply lowered the Bolsheviks' standing with the people. It was not, therefore, a "strong surge of proletarian will," nor anything else explicable in Marxian terms, that gave the Leninists the opportunity for a successful coup, but a fortuitous circumstance which, while quite consistent with the general state of disorganization in Russia, was in no way inevitable. At the very beginning of the revolution, in March, 1917, the Petrograd Soviet had issued Army Order No. 1 to the Petrograd garrison, instructing the ranks to form soldiers' committees and to obey only those orders which accorded with the orders of the Soviet. This order was not approved for general issue by the government, but word of it spread, contributing to the loosening of discipline and the demoralization of the Russian forces. Now, in July, 1917, to revitalize the army, Kerensky restored the death penalty for desertion and, from among the available generals, selected Lavr Kornilov as Commander in Chief. From the purely military standpoint, which seems to have monopolized Kerensky's mind at this time, this was neither an excellent nor an atrocious choice, but from the standpoint of the preservation of Russian democracy it proved to be catastrophic.

Kornilov had political ambitions, and early in September he marched on the capital. Kerensky had to appeal to the workers, who

---

arranged Lenin's trip from Switzerland to Russia, was the chief figure in the transactions, although Lenin denied having any dealings with him. Eduard Bernstein, the veteran German socialist, estimated that the Kaiser's government had invested over fifty million gold marks in the Bolshevik enterprise. It proved to be an extremely profitable German investment—from the short-run point of view. (p. 410).

[54] Shub, *Lenin*, p. 211.

took up arms and formed a militia that would soon be in Lenin's hands. Kornilov was defeated, but Kerensky was now indebted to the Petrograd Soviet and to the armed proletariat. The release of the imprisoned Bolsheviks followed, and although Lenin remained in Finland a while longer, he already knew that he had been rescued by the ill-conceived venture of an unintelligent general.

Lenin demanded that his group prepare an armed uprising. At the end of September, Kerensky, struggling to unite the country, summoned a conference of all parties, soviets, unions, etc., to organize a Preliminary Parliament, in order to fill the representational gap until the Constituent Assembly, whose election was scheduled for November 25, could meet. Fearing the conference would strengthen the government, Lenin instructed the Bolsheviks to boycott the meeting and seize its members. This one time they refused to obey, and his letter from Finland was burned by the unanimous decision of the Bolshevik Central Committee.[55] The all-party conference voted confidence in the Provisional Government and approved plans for the Preliminary Parliament. A few days later, on October 8, Kerensky became Prime Minister of a cabinet in which all liberal and socialist groups save the Bolsheviks were represented. Time was growing short for both sides.

Lenin soon regained control over the Bolshevik leadership, and when the Preliminary Parliament assembled, on October 20, the Bolsheviks withdrew. Several days later, Lenin was back in Petrograd, and in an all-night session persuaded a dubious and uncertain Bolshevik Central Committee to decide upon and prepare for armed revolt. A Military Revolutionary Committee was established, under Trotsky. On November 6, Kerensky demanded immediate military measures against the impending Bolshevik putsch, but his Menshevik colleagues opposed forceful repression as undemocratic, and accused Kerensky of exaggerating the danger. On the night of November 6-7, 1917,[56] Bolshevik soldiers, sailors, and armed militia seized the capital and the Provisional Government. Kerensky es-

---

[55] Shub, *Lenin*, p. 229.
[56] The revolution is celebrated in Communist lore as the October Revolution. Russia did not adopt the Gregorian calendar until 1918, and the Julian was thirteen days behind by the twentieth century.

caped, and made a futile effort to defeat the Bolsheviks by force of arms.[57]

Lenin was securely in power, at least for the time being, but there were not many in the first week of November, 1917, who gave the new Soviet of People's Commissars, as Lenin's government was called, a serious chance for survival.

The innumerable tasks and major policy decisions that faced the new regime would have shaken the confidence and staggered the imagination of anyone but a Lenin: the dictator oversimplified the problems in a characteristically Marxist way, and then proceeded to tackle them with skillful improvisation and an unequaled ruthless vigor. The simplest task was the creation of a government.[58] Bolshevik stalwarts were named Commissars and, backed up by trigger-happy militia and soldiers, secured control over the bureaucracy. Nor was it exceptionally difficult to formulate a program that would attract the peasants, the workers, and the soldiers, and would appear to usher in the new era of equalitarian socialism.

The first step was to support the demand of the peasants for land —and to detach them from the traditional party of the agrarian left, the Social Revolutionaries. Kerensky's postponement of land legislation until the Constituent Assembly should meet had aroused the peasants' suspicions. They had taken matters into their own hands and had been avidly seizing the land, and Bolshevik enactments legalizing their possession were consequently more of a bid for peasant support than a measure of generous policy. Expropriation without compensation was decreed for all large estates, which were

[57] Kerensky moved against Petrograd with a force under General Krasnov, and the Bolsheviks took the field to halt him. But the railroad workers intervened, insisting that the two forces negotiate. One of Lenin's deputies facetiously suggested a trade of Lenin for Kerensky, to save many lives at the cost of two heads. Krasnov's stupid Cossacks took him literally, and Kerensky was barely able to flee.

[58] This process was not without its amusing sides. The first act of more than one Commissar, or next in command, was to tack a penciled sign reading "People's Commissariat of———" over a table, or couch, in some corner of the Smolny Institute, the school for aristocratic young ladies the Bolsheviks had taken for their headquarters. Then followed a scramble for rubber stamps and similar appurtenances of office. When one comrade visited the office of the Commissar of Finance (a sofa), and happened to mention that he had taken some work at the University of London, including finance, he suddenly found himself appointed Director of the State Bank (Shub, *Lenin*, p. 269).

to be distributed among the peasants by local committees. All land was declared to be publicly owned, but the use of the soil was granted to the individual peasants. In this way were gratified both the simple peasant claim to possession and the intellectual's equalitarian opposition to private property. For the proletariat, a decree of November 28, 1917, established "workers' control bodies" in all enterprises employing wage or piecework labor, with full power over all business activities. The fiction of private ownership was, however, not disturbed for the time being.

For all the war-weary people of Russia, there was a proposal for an armistice, to be followed by a just peace. Negotiations with the Germans began late in November, and an armistice agreement was signed on December 15. To gain control of the levers of the economy, the banks were nationalized and uncoöperative bankers removed from authority. To gain control of the levers of public opinion, the activities of the Cadets and Mensheviks were curbed, and the press was subjected to a repression far more severe than anything seen in the last twelve years of Romanov rule. An even more effective measure for paralyzing the opposition was the reestablishment of a secret political police, triumphantly abolished in March as the very worst aspect of Tsarism, now recreated as the Bolshevik Extraordinary Commission (Cheka). The one goal that now motivated all of Lenin's strategy was the consolidation of Bolshevik power, upon which the establishment of a new society had to wait. And a dangerous moment was approaching. The Bolsheviks had made too much political capital of the delay in electing the Constituent Assembly for them to risk further postponement. They wished to set the elections back, to gain time to fix the results, but they did not dare do it when their authority was still shaky, and when the echoes of their strident appeals for democracy were still ringing in people's ears.

On November 25, therefore, for the first and only time in their history, the Russian people went to the polls in a simple and untrammeled direct election of their representatives. They voted in much the same spirit as in 1906, for those who, considering the state of the times, stood for moderation. In short, Lenin's worst fears were borne out. Over 36 million votes were cast. The Social Revolutionaries received about 21 million, the Cadets and other middle-class parties about 4.6 million, the Mensheviks and other moderate socialists about 1.7 million. Despite their pressure tactics, the Bolsheviks had only about 9 million, one quarter of the total, and won only 183 seats against the Social Revolutionaries' 412. The countryside had spoken, but even in the cities, the stronghold of the proletariat, Lenin's party did not win a majority: in Petrograd and Moscow they had 837,000 votes, against 928,000 for the other groups.[59] They did, however, hold a plurality in the strategic centers that had counted most, and would continue to do so, in any trial of strength.

Lenin was nevertheless disturbed. Agitation was begun against the Assembly upon whose election he had so strongly insisted. The Cadets were outlawed and several of their elected deputies were arrested. To protests against this Lenin replied:

We are being asked to summon the Constituent Assembly as it was planned. Begging your pardon——No. It was designed against the people. We overthrew the Government in order to have a guarantee that the Constituent Assembly would not be utilized against the people, and in order to hold this guarantee in the hands of the Government.[60]

Despite this warning, in plain Communist doubletalk, the Assembly majority patiently awaited the opening session, when they could take lawful parliamentary action against the dictator. But when the Assembly did meet on January 18, 1918, it found the palace swarming with Red troops and sailors, its supporters forced to disperse when they attempted to demonstrate in its favor, and the Bolsheviks in no mood to allow it to function. Nevertheless, above the shouts of Lenin's armed clique, it heroically carried through an all-night session under the guns of the Bolshevik soldiers in the galleries. The next day, the Assembly was dissolved, and its Bolshevik and allied[61] members were assimilated to a Central Executive Commit-

[59] W. H. Chamberlin, *The Russian Revolution 1917–1921*, New York, 1935, Vol. 2, pp. 365–366.

[60] Vernadsky, *Lenin*, p. 193. Lenin was willing to work with the Assembly provided it would allow recall of members when requested by local soviets, the new deputies to be named by the soviets, and if it would acknowledge the complete authority of his government. This resembled, although it was somewhat less generous, the Tsar's policy toward the Duma.

[61] A split had developed between the left and right wings of the Social Revolutionaries, and the left wing worked with the Bolsheviks for a relatively short period thereafter.

tee of Soviets, which would serve as a sounding board for the Communist high command, and as a transmission belt between the Communist Party and the people.

In destroying the Assembly, Lenin had not injected anything radically new into the doctrine of Russian Marxism. He had merely acted upon and extended somewhat the precept laid down by Plekhanov, at the London meeting of the Russian Social Democrats in 1903.[62] It must have been a bitter memory to the old teacher, who now lay dying, and a painful experience to realize that he had taught all too well. Plekhanov wrote:

By dissolving the Assembly, the People's Commissars fought not the enemies of the workers, but the enemies of the dictators of the Smolny Institute [Bolshevik headquarters]. . . . Their dictatorship is not one of the laboring people, but the dictatorship of a clique. And precisely for this reason they will have to resort more and more to terrorist methods.[63]

Plekhanov's most successful student was quite pleased with himself, however. "Naturally it was a great risk on our part that we did not postpone the convention," he explained to Trotsky. "Very, very unwise. But in the end it is best that it happened so. The breaking up of the Constituent Assembly by the Soviet power is the complete and public liquidation of formal democracy in the name of revolutionary dictatorship. It will be a good lesson."[64]

Back before the war, when there was no foreseeable chance for action, and theory was uppermost in the minds of Russian Marxists, Lenin had condemned Trotsky's proposal for an exclusively socialist revolutionary government, a proletarian dictatorship, with a keen and dire insight into his own future:

Whoever wants to approach socialism by any other path than that of political democracy, will inevitably arrive at the most absurd and reactionary conclusions both economic and political.[65]

Trotsky, for his part, had once shrewdly evaluated Lenin's belief in a rigorous, single-viewpoint party as "egocentralism," and had uttered an acute and fateful insight into their interwoven future:

[62] See p. 332.
[63] Shub, *Lenin*, p. 290.
[64] Trotsky, *Lenin*, London, 1925, pp. 149–150.
[65] *Two Tactics*, p. 20.

The organization of the party takes the place of the party itself; the Central Committee takes the place of the organization; and finally the dictator takes the place of the central committee.[66]

Now, however, when theory was rapidly becoming no more than rationalization for the deeds and misdeeds of power, the undemocratic in Lenin was reinforced by the undemocratic in Trotsky, and they rejoiced in the "dictatorship of the workers' and peasants' soviets." Soon this would be reformulated as the "dictatorship of the proletariat," exercised by the Communist Party, but the people of Russia would pass through three years of hell before a semblance of social order and productiveness could be restored. In the meantime, the Smolny Institute was the capital of Russia, and the only immediately important dissent was the kind with which Lenin could deal most effectively, disagreement within his own party.

Barely two weeks had passed since the Bolshevik revolution of November, when several Commissars resigned[67] in opposition to the abolition of democracy even within the ranks of socialism by excluding non-Bolsheviks from the government. Lenin held firm, of course, and the dissidents were not long in returning to the fold. A more serious controversy, at least in the short-run sense, arose over the acceptance of Germany's peace terms. Lenin was prepared to submit to the worst, for a number of reasons. First and foremost, peace, at whatever price in territorial cessions, would greatly ease the task of securing the Bolshevik regime. Second, Lenin was absolutely certain that revolution in one or more of the advanced nations, particularly Germany, would come to the aid of socialism in backward Russia.

The Germans, for their part, were more than anxious to end hostilities with Russia, but there was no pressure on them to be generous. They held nearly all the high cards and the Bolsheviks, by destroying the Russian General Staff organization, had just given them another. Trotsky was therefore unable to awe the German negotiators with a flighty harangue about the powers of the revolu-

---

[66] Wolfe, *Three Who Made a Revolution*, p. 253. Wolfe skillfully analyzes the way in which the acute but limited vision, and the limited but profound blindness of Lenin, Trotsky, and Plekhanov as well, paved the way for the regime of Stalin which none of them could long have approved.

[67] Including Kamenev, Zinoviev, and Rykov.

tionary proletariat.[68] Although the German terms remained severe as ever, Lenin insisted on accepting them. But only when the Germans had resumed their march did a majority of the Bolshevik government agree in March, 1918, to sign the Peace of Brest-Litovsk.[69] The Communists continued to fear the possibility of a German occupation of Petrograd, and the Russian capital was transferred to Moscow. Lenin had never hidden from his associates his intention of ignoring the treaty as soon as this was possible and, as had happened before, extraneous forces came to his assistance. A few days after the Allied victory in November, 1918, he was able to denounce Brest-Litovsk with no fear of German reprisal.

Peace with Germany ushered in the chaotic and catastrophic period of civil war, foreign intervention, "war communism," and the Red Terror. The organization of the Red Army, to replace the broken Russian Army, had begun in February, 1918. From the spring of that year until the fall of 1920 that army was almost steadily engaged against various White, or anti-Bolshevik, forces that were organized by Tsarist generals and admirals. The Whites were supported half-heartedly by the Allied powers, which also undertook minor occupations of Russian soil with their own troops.[70] But the activities of the Whites were poorly coördinated in space and time, and there was little effort on their part to formulate a program that could have appealed to the millions who were dissatisfied with the Bolshevik regime but who feared still more a return of the Romanovs. The net result of the civil war was immensely to strengthen the hold of the Bolsheviks on Russia. Their Red Army had become

[68] Before the negotiations had started, Trotsky had delivered himself of this gem: "I am convinced that if the Right Social Revolutionaries were miraculously to come to power once again, they would hurry to conclude a shameful peace in order to free their forces for the strengthening of the bourgeois order in Russia" (Shub, *Lenin*, p. 293).

[69] Brest-Litovsk cost Russia Latvia, Lithuania, Esthonia, Finland, and the Ukraine.

[70] The British and Americans moved into Murmansk and Archangel, the French and Greeks into Odessa, and the British, French, Americans, and Japanese into Russia's Pacific region. The Allied interventions were, of course, anti-Bolshevik, but ideological antipathy to Lenin's regime was not so important as the desire to replace it with a government which would resume the war against Germany. After the Armistice of November 11, 1918, the Allies naturally lost interest. Had the European war continued for another year, the civil struggle in Russia might well have had a rather different outcome.

a hard-fighting, fairly well organized force; the Red Terror could be readily justified by the needs of defense against the Whites; and Lenin's doctrine of the interfering hostility of the capitalist world was substantiated.

But Russia and the Russian people suffered horribly from the ravages of civil war and from the Bolshevik policies that make up what is known as "war communism." What was needed to strengthen his power, and what was required for the establishment of a socialist society, unfortunately coincided in Lenin's eyes. The very same measures, moreover, could be expected to overcome the progressive disorganization of the economy. There resulted an excess of oppression in accordance with the dogma of class struggle. Those who, for reasons of dogma, were not expected to coöperate with the Bolsheviks were penalized and terrorized. It would not be unfair to say that when war communism was finally abandoned, in 1921, only the first objective, the retention of power, had been met, and this owing to Bolshevik skill in the political and police art of dictatorship, not to the success or popularity of their policies.

The peasant seizure of the large estates had destroyed the efficiency of precisely those agricultural units which produced for the cities and this, together with the disruption of communications and commercial organizations, made the provision of food for the favored urban proletariat an extremely urgent task. Lenin attempted to meet it by introducing bread rationing and by summoning the workers to a crusade for grain. Requisitioning squads were sent into the countryside to seize grain from the more prosperous peasants for distribution in the towns and among the agricultural poor. But this naturally led to concealment of stocks and a decrease in production, and Lenin's answer was to organize in the villages Committees of the Poor (peasants) to assist the requisitioning squads in overcoming the resistance of those who held grain from the market. Again this amounted to an attack on the efficiency of those farmers whose coöperation was most needed, for while the poor peasants could in this way be integrated into the class struggle and the defense of the regime, they often did not have enough food for their own families, let alone for export to the cities. Economically, the policy was an utter failure; politically it was a success, since it split the peasantry, whose united opposition might well have overthrown the Bolsheviks.

The Communists held desperately to this system until 1921, with only half-hearted gestures toward common sense. City workers were allowed to bring in limited amounts of grain for their own use, which in effect legalized the illegal private market, and they were, moreover, given preferential rations.[71] There was some talk in the fall of 1918 of replacing the hated requisitioning system with a tax in kind, but the only concession to the peasantry was the substitution of village soviets for the Committees of the Poor. Since the latter controlled the composition of the soviets, the reform amounted to very little. In January, 1919, requisitioning was formalized, the peasant being allowed to retain only such grain and fodder as he needed for his family and livestock, and the following year new decrees made sowing and cultivation obligatory. None of these measures, however, was economically effective.

A good part of the difficulty was a disastrous fall in industrial output which left very little for the peasants to buy, and correspondingly little incentive to produce. Perhaps even more than in agriculture, Lenin's social and political objectives were incompatible with economic efficiency in the factories. Lenin had natural misgivings concerning the capacity of the workers to organize and operate industries, and he appealed to them for greater industriousness and honesty and, above all, for work discipline. But the disorder of war, long-ingrained habits of inefficiency, the failure to provide incentives other than "socialist zeal," and food shortages kept industry on a steep downward curve. Direction and discipline had therefore to be provided from above. Large-scale industries were nationalized in June, 1918. In October, work books were ordered for all city dwellers, on the principle that "Anyone who does not work should not eat."[72] In January, 1920, combat armies were transformed into labor armies, and in March labor unions and consumers' and producers' coöperatives became agencies for state control over production and

[71] Preferential rations became an important feature of Stalin's political and social system, as a means of furnishing incentives and securing loyalty. This could obviously be effective only in a country living close to the subsistence level.

[72] Vernadsky, *Lenin*, p. 172.

distribution. The Communist Party convention of that year resolved that

The trades-unions, in proportion as communistic consciousness and the creative power of the masses develop, must gradually be transformed into auxiliary agencies of the proletarian state. The tasks of the trades-unions lie chiefly in the field of economic organization and education.[73]

But the most far-reaching measure of war communism in the economic field came in November, 1920, as hostilities were drawing to a close. Industrial enterprises employing more than ten workers (more than five, when machinery was used) were nationalized, the war against private trade, outlawed in 1918, was intensified, and, to create a more effective incentive than Communist devotion, work was declared obligatory for all Russians, workers and peasants as well as the dying bourgeoisie. Forced labor was repeatedly and extensively used. Lenin had proclaimed that "Communism is the Soviet power plus the electrification of the whole country,"[74] an engaging and simple proposition, but it was much easier to organize soviets and electrify party workers with such slogans than to produce electricity when starvation was rife and industrial output dwindling to nothing.

The record of failures carried over into foreign policy. The Bolsheviks had been completely obsessed with the theory of proletarian revolutions in advanced countries, above all Germany, as a consequence of the war. Lenin realized that only a world war had made possible the Russian Revolution and had prevented a decisive foreign intervention against it, and fully accepted the modest view of his own achievements that doctrine required: "For us it is easy to begin a revolution and harder to continue it. In the west it is harder to begin a revolution but it will be easier to continue." On another occasion he said: "There is no island of Utopia. It is a question of creating a socialist state. . . . It isn't a question of Russia at all, gentlemen. I spit on Russia. This is merely one phase through which we must pass on the way to a world revolution."[75] And one could hardly find a clearer statement of Lenin's entire strategy than the following:

[73] Vernadsky, *Lenin*, p. 261.
[74] Vernadsky, *Lenin*, p. 270.
[75] Trotsky, *Russian Revolution*, vol. 3, p. 400; Shub, *Lenin*, p. 268.

When we began . . . the international revolution, we did this not with the conviction that we could anticipate its development, but because a whole series of circumstances impelled us to begin this revolution. Our thought was: either the international revolution will come to our aid, and in that case our victories are wholly assured, or we will do our modest revolutionary work in the consciousness that in case of defeat we have nevertheless served the cause of the revolution, and our experiment will be of help to other revolutions. It was clear to us that without the support of the international world revolution a victory of the proletarian overturn was impossible. Even before the revolution, and likewise after it, our thought was: immediately, or at any rate very quickly, a revolution will begin in the other countries, in capitalistically more developed countries—or in the contrary case we will have to perish. In spite of this consciousness we did everything to preserve the soviet system in all circumstances and at whatever cost, since we knew that we were working not only for ourselves, but for the international revolution.[76]

Given so deep an intellectual and political commitment, it was natural that every possible effort should have been directed toward the fomenting of revolution in Europe. From the very beginning of the Bolshevik regime, neither its own poverty nor that of Russia was allowed to stand in the way of the expenditure of large sums of money on organization and propaganda in Germany and other Western countries.[77] As soon as conditions permitted, Lenin returned to the project for a new International which he had urged while still in Switzerland, and the first congress of the Third, or Communist, International met in Moscow, in March, 1919. Some nations were represented by citizens who happened to be in Russia, others by prisoners of war, but that did not matter, for the organization got under way, and Lenin had an excellent forum from which to conduct his offensive against moderate socialists and capitalists everywhere, and to influence Allied opinion against intervention in the Russian civil war. A new theoretical tidbit was added to the Marxist

---

[76] Trotsky, *Russian Revolution*, vol. 3, p. 411.

[77] Some of this money was squandered with gay abandon. Two Italian war prisoners in Russia were entrusted with a good amount of cash and the task of setting things awry in Italy. They spent the money on high living in Milan (Shub, *Lenin*, p. 345, quoting Angelica Balabanoff). Benjamin Gitlow, *I Confess*, New York, 1939, p. 388, tells of one Lettish-American who was given $50,-000 while in Moscow for delivery to the American Communist Party. "He kept the money for himself and with it went into business in Chicago."

canons when Lenin redefined middle-class democracy as the dictatorship of the bourgeoisie over the working class, to be replaced by the dictatorship of the proletariat over the bourgeoisie.

Events in Europe, meanwhile, seemed to be bearing out Lenin's analysis. The Spartacist rising had been defeated in Berlin in January,[78] but Lenin never regarded a defeat as final. The revolutionary republic in Bavaria had several more weeks to live, and ten days after the Comintern met for the first time, the Hungarian Communist regime of Bela Kun began its brief existence. The failure of these ventures did not divert Lenin from his beliefs or his course, and 1920 witnessed the most overt effort in behalf of world Communism—and Soviet Russia—prior to the defeat of Hitler in 1945.

In the spring of 1920 Poland gave Lenin an opportunity to attempt the spread of Communism by force of arms. In April Poland invaded Russia, seizing Kiev, but aided by a surge of Russia patriotism which brought able Tsarist officers back to the colors, the Red Army threw the Poles back and marched on Warsaw. The Bolsheviks proclaimed:

> The war with Poland is a war of the workers and peasants for the independence of Socialistic Russia and for its union with a Socialistic Poland, as with the proletarians of Europe and the whole world.[79]

But the word "union" can attract or repel, and to many Poles union even with a professedly socialist Russia meant more of the same old tyranny they had so recently discarded. The Russian offensive ground on, but it was turned back from Warsaw and broken,[80] and once more Lenin had to conclude an unfavorable peace. As Trotsky wrote later on, the march on Warsaw had been a

> . . . bad mistake which not only led to the peace of Riga but . . . gave a powerful impulse to the consolidation of the bourgeoisie of Europe. The

[78] See p. 238.

[79] Vernadsky, *Lenin,* p. 264.

[80] One of the major factors in the Russian defeat was that the whiskered cavalry general, Budyenny, instead of attacking Warsaw from the south to coördinate with the offensive of General Tukhachevsky, moved west against Lwow in order to gain a feather for his cap and for that of his political commissar, J. V. Stalin. The Poles struck at the weak juncture of the two Russian armies and shattered the entire Russian operation. The resulting Peace of Riga set the Polish boundary much farther east than had been recommended by the impartial report of Lord Curzon.

counter-revolutionary significance of the Riga treaty . . . can best be understood if you picture the situation in 1923 [year of an abortive Communist rising in Germany], under the supposition that we had had a common frontier with Germany: everything seems to show that the development of events in Germany would have followed quite a different course. It is undoubtedly true that the revolutionary movement in Poland itself would have turned out more favorably without our military intervention and its failure.[81]

Before the conclusion of the Polish fiasco, the second Comintern congress met, and adopted the line elaborated by Lenin which has amounted to a basic creed for international Communism, to which it could always return with a feeling of confidence, as to a home port, when departures from it proved unprofitable. One principle was that Communists were to utilize the parliamentary and legal institutions of middle class democracy only to destroy them, that under no circumstances were they to look upon a parliament as "an arena of struggle for reforms, for betterment of the conditions of the working class." A second principle, drawn from Lenin's theory of imperialism, was that, since "European capitalism draws its chief strength not from industrial . . . Europe, but from its colonial possessions," Communists were to undertake a special effort to foment revolution in Asia and the Middle East, and were to devote particular attention to underprivileged minority groups, such as American Negroes, who were exploited by the domestic workings of imperialistic capitalism. A related point was the injunction to encourage nationalism among subject peoples, as a step toward liberation.[82]

A third principle, the most immediate and important in its practical implications, was the extension of "democratic centralism," the rigidly disciplined hierarchical structure of the Bolshevik Party, to international Communism. This principle was embodied in the famous Twenty-One Conditions for parties joining the Comintern, requiring them to accept "as binding . . . all decisions of the Congress of the Communist International, as well as the decisions of its executive committee . . ." and "to offer unqualified support to every

[81] Vernadsky, *Lenin*, pp. 140–141.

[82] This followed from the Soviet nationalities policy, worked out by Stalin at Lenin's behest. This policy was to encourage cultural nationalism and, theoretically, political autonomy. Only the cultural aspect ever had any practical significance, in a very limited way, and only for a time. See p. 454.

Soviet republic in its struggle against the counter-revolutionary forces."[83]

The conditions for admission into the privileged society of Communism were obviously a codification of Lenin's tactics and experience, and became a code of law for his, and later Stalin's followers. However the Communists might deviate in changing situations from the doctrines established in 1920, those provisions dealing with party organization and discipline remained rigidly fixed, and were even given an increasingly authoritarian interpretation. Since the Russian party remained the only one in power, it held both the purse strings and the greatest prestige. Democratic centralism therefore meant the total subordination of the Comintern to its Bolshevik unit, and therefore to the Soviet dictator. The chain of command ran all the way from the fraction constituted by five or six Communists working, let us say, for a steel company, to the local party executive and thence onward and upward through regional and national units and the Comintern, finally reaching the Politburo of the Soviet Russian Communist Party, and the person of the dictator. Here was organization for the skillful spreading of dissent among near-friends and total enemies, for the preparation of revolution. Underlying the entire structure and program of the Comintern was Lenin's proposition that

As long as capitalism and socialism remain, we cannot live in peace. In the end one or the other will triumph—a funeral requiem will be sung either over the Soviet Republic or over world capitalism. This is a respite in war.

To the moderates who felt that Russia should be thankful for the chance to create "an ordinary democratic republic," Lenin had replied:

In "ordinary" comparatively peaceful times such a "hope" would have sufficed for many a long decade.

But . . . the democratic republic is the bourgeois democratic republic, which has already become antiquated from the point of view of the problems which imperialism has placed on the agenda of history. . . . There is no other alternative: either the triumph of the Soviet regime in every

[83] O'Neal and Werner, *American Communism*, pp. 378 ff., gives the Twenty-One Conditions.

advanced country of the world, or the triumph of the most reactionary, the most savage imperialism, which is throttling all the small and weak nationalities and reinstating reaction all over the world—Anglo-American imperialism, which has perfectly mastered the art of using the form of a democratic republic.

One or the other.

There is no middle course.[84]

In strong and dedicated hands, such dogmatic certainty is capable of itself creating the situation it describes. Having forsworn peace as a good in itself, Communism also rejected the idea of genuine compromise. It would retreat only when compelled to, never out of respect for another's point of view. It would learn from mistakes, to be sure, but it would draw that moral which best seemed to accord with dogma. Communism would be ruled by a spirit of intransigence; its followers would take delight in picturing themselves as a Lenin, standing alone against the world, with naught but Objective Truth to support them. Even in the so-called self-criticism (brought on by the obstinacy of facts) in which they reveled, Communists would conceive only of an erroneous application of their doctrine; the doctrine itself could never be wrong.

In one respect, at least, the Soviet government proved an outstanding success, and that was in its ability to remain in power irrespective of its failures and of the number of enemies it made. It is no cause for surprise, therefore, that the one feature of war communism that contributed most heavily to the survival and strengthening of the dictatorship should have continued beyond the early years to become an enduring feature of the Soviet enterprise. This was the secret police, and the terror.

From the very beginning, Lenin had shown no disposition to underestimate the usefulness of the political police as a prop for his regime. Sudden arrests, trials by revolutionary tribunals—drumhead courts—sentences without trial, individual and mass executions, these ancient and proved procedures not only eliminated opponents, but tended to frighten the people at large into submissiveness. This was the essence of the early terror.[85]

[84] Shub, *Lenin*, p. 391; Lenin, *Collected Works*, New York, 1945, vol. 23, p. 309.

[85] Lenin had an ideal man to direct such operations, a quiet and ascetic Pole,

Opposition to Lenin rose rapidly in the spring of 1918, not only among army officers and the middle class, but among the Social Revolutionaries, who were too experienced with the Tsar's Okhrana to be cowed by the Bolshevik secret police. By the summer of 1918, even Left Social Revolutionaries, who alone had supported the Communists after the dissolution of the Constituent Assembly, were ready both to revolt and to resume the old Russian practice of assassination. One of the first to fall was the German Ambassador, whose government demanded punishment of the culprit. The latter had escaped, however, and, in order to satisfy Germany, Lenin ordered the execution of some twenty Left Social Revolutionaries held as hostages, saying, "We will make an internal loan from our 'comrades,' the Social Revolutionaries, and thus both preserve our 'innocence' and promote our interests."[86] On August 30, 1918, two events set off the formal opening of the Red Terror; the Cheka chief of Petrograd was assassinated, and Lenin was shot by a young woman who had served eleven years at hard labor under the Tsarist regime for her revolutionary activities, and who felt Lenin had betrayed the cause. His luck was with him once more, owing to her execrable marksmanship (she fired three times from but a few feet away) and to his own iron constitution. Lenin survived his wounds.

The terror was now directed against all his opponents under the slogan of "Death to the bourgeoisie," and anyone suspected of disloyalty to Bolshevism thereby automatically became a member of the middle class. The terror was portrayed as an act of supreme self-defense, forced upon the regime by foreign imperialists and

---

of a landed family, Felix Dzerzhinsky, who went about his business calmly, systematically, and efficiently, with the sense of doing an important job extremely well.

Of the many gruesome stories of his professional expertness, perhaps the following best reveals the spirit of this founding father of the Cheka, which was the ancestor of the OGPU, NKVD, and MVD. During a meeting, Lenin passed a note to Dzerzhinsky asking how many counterrevolutionaries were being held at the moment. The latter wrote, "About fifteen hundred," and handed the note back, whereat Lenin marked a cross beside the figure and returned the paper to his police chief. The latter left the room quietly, and it was soon learned that the luckless 1,500 had been shot. Dzerzhinsky had not realized that the cross was only Lenin's personal notation indicating he had read a report. It had not been intended as a sentence of death (Shub, *Lenin*, p. 308).

[86] Shub, *Lenin*, p. 317.

bourgeois traitors to Russia.[87] It was, indeed, an act of self-defense, but it was forced upon the regime by opponents who could still have commanded a large majority in any free election. But, like so many other measures of the war communism period, the terror advanced the bolshevization of Russia, in addition to consolidating Communist power. The Leninist viewpoint was well stated by one of the Cheka officers:

We are exterminating the bourgeoisie as a class. Don't look for evidence of proof showing that this or that person either by word or deed acted against the interests of the Soviet power. The first questions you should put to the arrested person are: To what class does he belong, what is his origin, what was his education, and what is his profession? These should determine the fate of the accused. This is the essence of the Red Terror.[88]

By this test, of course, nearly all the Bolshevik leaders, from Lenin down, should have been shot. In any case, Chamberlin estimates that about fifty thousand executions can be credited directly to the Cheka.[89] Against this, it should be noted that Russia was living through a particularly cruel civil war, and that the White Terror was no more gentle than the Red.

But even in purely Bolshevik terms the terror was not an unqualified success. Although it undoubtedly bolstered the dictatorship while the White armies were still in the field, the terror not only weakened Russia through its special victimization of the skilled and the educated, but, together with food shortages and general economic decay, it produced bitter resentment in groups which could not be passed off as vile bourgeois, Tsarist beasts, or foreign agents.

[87] Most of the foreign conspiracy charges centered around the British, and are still given currency. See M. Sayers and A. E. Kahn, *The Great Conspiracy*, Boston, 1946. W. H. Chamberlin, *Russian Revolution*, vol. 2, pp. 68 ff., suggests, from the evidence that a good deal of both the smoke and the fire resulted from a Cheka frame-up.

[88] Shub, *Lenin*, p. 325.

[89] *Russian Revolution*, vol. 2, p. 75. Lenin defended the terror as an act of a just war: "The bourgeoisie of international imperialism killed ten million and mutilated twenty million human beings in 'its' war, a war to decide whether British or German robbers should rule the whole world.

"If our war, the war of the oppressed and exploited against the oppressors and exploiters, will cost half a million or a million victims in all countries, the bourgeoisie will say that the former sacrifices were justified, the latter criminal.

"The proletariat will say something quite different" (p. 77).

In the fall of 1920 a peasant rebellion got under way, led by an indisputable peasant, Antonov, and by the following spring a separate army under General Tukhachevsky had to be sent against the embittered toilers of the soil. Even worse than this was the rebellion, early in March, 1921, of the sailors of Kronstadt. They had been the military heroes of the November Revolution. Without them it could hardly have been attempted. But the Red Sailors of Kronstadt had been more than an armed force, they had constituted one of the few really popular voices that had spoken for the Bolsheviks. And now they rose in revolt. Trotsky and Tukhachevsky (liquidated in 1937) were rushed to the scene, the troops in Petrograd were disarmed lest they join the rebellion. Naval officers advised the sailors to attack the city, but they would not be the first to shed blood. With a force of Cheka troops and other dependables Tukhachevsky stormed Kronstadt against the most tenacious and deadly opposition. The rebels were all but annihilated.

Fitting the uprising into his highly specialized Marxism, Lenin commented:

The most characteristic feature of the Kronstadt events was precisely the vacillation of the petty bourgeois element. There was very little . . . that was fully formed, clear and definite. We heard nebulous slogans about "liberty," "free trade," "emancipation from serfdom," "Soviets without the Bolsheviks" . . . or relief from "party dictatorship," and so on and so forth.

Perhaps the sailors had been confused, but it would have been hard for all but the narrowest sectarian to have called them counter-revolutionaries. The Kronstadt radio had proclaimed to the world that they had

. . . rebelled against the government of the Communists in order to re-establish the real power of the Soviets . . . for the bloodstained cause of the laboring people. Long live the power of the Soviets! Long live the world Socialist Revolution![90]

Having allowed, even encouraged, the social collapse and horror that had aroused the hatred and revulsion of once devoted followers, Lenin was quicker than most of his coworkers to grasp the meaning

[90] Shub, *Lenin,* pp. 359 ff.

of the Kronstadt and Antonov rebellions. Russia was once more at the breaking point, under the impact of a catastrophe such as no civilized country had ever borne before. Per capita national income had fallen from 100 in 1913 to 37 in 1921; coal production from 100 in 1916 to 63 in 1920, and the same years had seen a 28 percent drop in the number of horned cattle. The average real wage had dropped 62 percent and labor productivity 74 percent between 1913 and 1920. Over the same period acreage planted in grain and fodder crops had fallen by 37 percent, and the per acre yield on the reduced area was lower by 30 percent. A runaway inflation developed, for which Marxist economics offered no ingenious solution. Rolling stock was disappearing from the inadequate Russian railroads, the hungry population was fleeing the towns to search for food in the hungry villages, and the growing shortage of fuel was closing one factory after another.[91] In a Micawberish sort of way the Bolsheviks had hoped food supplies would rise, principally through their system of forced collections. But only the sailors and peasants rose, in arms, and this impelled Lenin to make one of those abrupt changes of policy which bring dictators a reputation for combining acute vision with decisive action.

While the battle of Kronstadt was still raging in March, 1921, Lenin announced the New Economic Policy (NEP). Since 1918 he had recognized some of the basic economic failings of his regime, but the pressure of events and of his sudden inclination to go as far to the left as he could, had produced war communism, which intensified old shortcomings and added new. He now admitted that some means had to be found to conciliate the peasantry, to encourage them to produce. Grain requisitions were replaced with a tax in kind, and private initiative was liberated so that there would be manufactured goods for the peasants to buy. By the end of the year capitalism had not only been restored in agriculture, small-scale manufacturing, and commerce, but Lenin was urging his startled comrades to become good businessmen. But the government retained the "heights" of the economy, the large industries, transport, the banks. Lenin called this compromise "state capitalism."

He blamed both the inefficiency of Communist bureaucrats and

---

[91] See Chamberlin, *Russian Revolution*, vol. 2, chap. 25; Lancelot Lawton, *An Economic History of Soviet Russia*, London, 1932, vol. 1, chaps. 16–22.

the social backwardness of the peasants for this enforced change of front, and he conceded that the world revolution which was to have enabled more advanced countries to help Russia's transformation, had not developed as rapidly as had been expected. In a word, his regime had made a number of mistakes:

Our New Economic Policy means that in applying our former methods we suffered defeat and had to begin a strategic retreat. . . . The defeat we suffered in the spring of 1921 on the economic front was more serious than any we had ever before suffered [in the war]. . . . The system of distribution in the villages and the immediate applications of Communist methods in the towns held back our productive forces and caused the great economic and political crisis we met in the spring of 1921.

Returning to earlier views, he declared that "a succession of transition periods such as State Capitalism and Socialism was required to prepare, through many years of preliminary work, the transition to Communism."[92] The Bolsheviks were shocked, and then quite unsettled, by the genuine economic recovery that ensued, despite the unbridled speculation, corruption, and debauchery that was set loose by four years of chaos and destructiveness. Lenin reassured them; the goal was unchanged and, moreover, his reversal of policy did not extend to the political sphere.

To those who called attention to the fact that he was now doing only what others had long been pleading for, Lenin declared:

When the Menshevik says, "You are now retreating, I was always in favor of retreat . . . let us retreat together," we say in reply that for the public advocacy of Menshevism our revolutionary courts must pass sentence of death.[93]

Communist Party discipline was tightened. A debate had been raging over Trotsky's proposal that labor unions become nothing more than the organizational units of a labor army. It was silenced with a compromise that left the unions some nominal independence, under Party control, and it was ordered that such intraparty discussions should cease.

The Communists dutifully swung into line behind their leader, and chanted his praises. But the gallant admission of error had

[92] Shub, *Lenin,* pp. 362, 363.
[93] Shub, *Lenin,* p. 364.

come too late to prevent the death of 5 million Russians in the famine of 1920 and 1921, or to forestall the descent into cannibalism that terrorized many a village and town. There is something disconcerting about the confessed bungler who will neither tolerate criticism nor yield one iota of his power. And that epitomizes the confidence, the arrogance, and the lust for power of Lenin, who was kindly, modest, and generous in his personal life, who loved to play with children and to chat with friends.

Institution of the NEP was Lenin's last major act. His health began to fail in 1921, and in the following May he suffered his first stroke. He recovered sufficiently to return to work, and continued to hold firmly to the line of NEP. His outlook seemed to be reverting more and more to earlier days, when he and Plekhanov had not been leagues apart. He said of the peasants and the Bolshevik desire to establish collective farms:

Peasants are not socialists. . . . The transformation of the peasant's psychology and habits is something that requires generations. The use of force will not help. The task before us is to influence the peasant morally. . . . The *efficient peasant* must be the *central figure* of our economic *recovery*.[94]

Where this kind of thinking might eventually have led, whether he ever began to speculate over his own statement—

Whoever wants to approach socialism by any other path than that of political democracy will inevitably arrive at the most absurd and reactionary conclusions both economic and political . . .

—whether, in short, this sincere fanatic and "dictator without vanity" might have forced the oligarchy beneath him to loosen its hold, no one can ever say. A second stroke came in December, 1922, and a third in March, 1923. His powers of speech and movement progressively declined, but his mind remained keen, and to his followers he was still the genius-leader.

Naturally enough, from the beginning of his sickness, speculation over the succession, and maneuvering to secure it, got under way. Trotsky, the second man of the regime, was unpopular in the Party, owing to his arrogance and theatrical manner. Zinoviev, the head of

[94] Shub, *Lenin*, pp. 379–380. Original italics.

the Comintern, was a very poor third indeed. The same congress that had followed Lenin into the NEP had elected Joseph Stalin General Secretary of the Communist Party, and he had carefully built a good political machine, naming his men to key positions, doing favors, placing adversaries where they could harm him least, conferring with Bolshevik politicos—in much the same way, of course, as any political machine is built. Stalin, however, did not have Trotsky's stature, or even Zinoviev's. Nevertheless, sick as he was, Lenin seems to have sensed the nature of the process that was going on: Stalin was combining with Zinoviev and Kamenev to block Trotsky's aspirations and to clear the path for himself. And Lenin disapproved.

On December 25, 1922, realizing he had not much longer to live, Lenin wrote a "political testament," giving his estimation of the party leadership:

Comrade Stalin, having become general secretary, has concentrated enormous power in his hands, and I am not sure that he always knows how to use that power with sufficient caution. On the other hand, Comrade Trotsky . . . is distinguished not only by his exceptional ability—he is, to be sure, the most able man in the present Central Committee—but also by his too far-reaching self-confidence and a disposition to be far too much attracted by the purely administrative side of affairs.

The two qualities of the two most able leaders of the present Central Committee might, quite innocently, lead to a split. If our Party does not take measures to prevent it, a split may occur unexpectedly.

Lenin then brushed lightly past Zinoviev and Kamenev, and had a mixture of praise and criticism for other leaders. Some ten days later, a postscript was added:

Stalin is too rude,[95] and this fault, entirely supportable in relation to us Communists, becomes insupportable in the office of general secretary. Therefore I propose to the comrades to find a way to remove Stalin from that position and appoint to it another man who in all respects differs from Stalin only in superiority—namely, more patient, more loyal, more polite, and more attentive to comrades, less capricious, etc. This circumstance may seem an insignificant trifle, but I think that from the point of view of

---

[95] The Russian word Lenin used carries the connotation of coarse, churlish, gross, rough, harsh, as well as lack of manners. "Churlish" is probably the most precise English equivalent.

preventing a split and from the point of view of the relation between Stalin and Trotsky, which I discussed above, it is not a trifle, or it is such a trifle as may acquire a decisive significance.[96]

Lenin, who was not one to stop with a mild recommendation such as this, devoted much of the brief active life remaining to him to an effort to destroy Stalin. The latter, in addition to being General Secretary, was Commissar of the Workers' and Peasants' Inspectorate, a strategic personnel and efficiency bureau which could investigate the functioning of the administrative agencies, and Commissar of Nationalities. Lenin, who had given Stalin these offices, now condemned the way in which they were managed.

Of the Inspectorate, he wrote:

Let us say frankly, that the . . . Inspectorate does not enjoy the slightest prestige. Everybody knows that a more badly organized institution than our . . . Inspectorate does not exist and that under present conditions nothing can be expected from this Commissariat.

He pointed to a lack of culture and proper manners as a source of weakness and, what must have seemed a personal insult to Stalin, who was always extremely sensitive about his lack of stature as a theorist, he added:

People dilate at too great length and too flippantly on "proletarian" culture. We would be satisfied with real bourgeois culture for a start, and we would be glad, for a start, to dispense with the cruder types of pre-bourgeois culture, i.e. bureaucratic or serf culture, etc.[97]

It was in connection with Stalin's other Commissariat, Nationalities, however, that a genuine and sharply defined issue arose. An autonomous Menshevik regime had been established in Stalin's native Georgia, and had been recognized by Moscow in 1920 in accordance with the Bolshevik doctrine on subject peoples which Stalin had played a large part in formulating. In 1921, however,

[96] The existence and nature of the document was naturally well known within the Communist hierarchy, but it was not published until Max Eastman, Trotsky's biographer, communicated it to the *New York Times*, October 18, 1926. Until the following year all good Stalinists denied its authenticity, but Stalin himself confirmed it in 1927. The text may be found conveniently in Julien Steinberg, ed., *Verdict of Three Decades*, New York, 1950, pp. 193 ff.

[97] Isaac Deutscher, *Stalin, A Political Biography*, New York, 1949, pp. 251–252.

Stalin, with his chief's approval, took advantage of Georgian peasant risings to send the Red Army in and Bolshevize Georgia. Then Stalin and his deputies proceeded to settle some prerevolutionary party feuds, to carry a party purge a bit too far, and to centralize control over Georgia in Moscow. Protests reached the capital and furnished Lenin with an excuse for another barrage. Such behavior toward a minority nationality, he said, showed that the Russian government was a "bourgeois and Tsarist mechanism," "barely touched by the Soviet world." Unless there were a distinct change, the Soviet Constitution and its nationalities guarantees would be "a scrap of paper, impotent to defend the races of Russia against these true Russians, chauvinist Great Russians, essentially cowardly and cruel like the typical Russian bureaucrat." He declared that "Stalin and [the Cheka chief] Dzerzhinsky must be held politically responsible for this nationalist Great Russian campaign," and wired support to Stalin's adversaries in Georgia. On March 6, 1923, his secretary remarked that Lenin was "preparing a bomb for Stalin at the Congress" of the Communist Party that was soon to meet.[98] The same day he dictated a note to Stalin breaking off "all personal and comradely relations."[99]

But now, when the master organizer was preparing Stalin's downfall, luck finally turned against him. On March 23 he suffered his severest stroke, and when the Communist Party Congress met in April, Stalin was in complete command of the situation, supported by Zinoviev and Kamenev. Lenin lingered on, and death came on January 21, 1924.

The Soviet Russia that Joseph Stalin took over was recovering from its horrifying travail, which would be written off to the world as the inevitable birthpangs of a new society. But the ordeal could as well have been merely the renewal under different forms of the essential inhumanity of authoritarianism. The Russian people had their soviets; but the Communist Party ruled the soviets, and one man had ruled and would continue to rule the Party. The teaching of Lenin, after all, was that the new, proletarian democracy ex-

[98] Souvarine, *Stalin*, pp. 307 ff.

[99] Krupskaya, Lenin's wife, had been insulted by Stalin but, she told Kamenev, Lenin "would never have ventured to break off personal relations, if he had not thought it necessary to crush Stalin politically" (Trotsky, *Stalin, An Appraisal of the Man and his Influence*, New York, 1941, p. 374).

cluded the middle class, that its will was expressed through the soviets and the only true party of the working class, the Communist Party. And Lenin had written:

> The Soviet Socialist Democracy is in no way inconsistent with the rule of one person: . . . the will of a class is at times best realized by a dictator who sometimes will accomplish more by himself and is frequently more needed.[100]

Lenin's followers and critics alike have agreed that his genius lay in his ability to relate theory and action. Trotsky put it this way:

> Nature produced a masterpiece when she created in a single figure an embodiment of the revolutionary thinking and the unbending energy of the workmen's class.[101]

Or one might say that Lenin embodied an unusually successful combination of the German, Marxian capacity for theorizing with the daring and violent spirit of the Russian revolutionary tradition. Perhaps even more important was his politician's flair for sizing up a situation, and fanatic's willingness to force events and circumstances into his preconceived pattern. But, unless it came to him in those last dark and silent months, one ingredient for greatness was missing, a principle which might have compelled a less dazzling pace, but would have enabled him to face the judgment of history with fewer blemishes. And, if his aversion to Stalin was ideological rather than personal, this principle would have made it impossible for Stalinism to be the direct and logical issue of Leninism. It was well stated by a Russian revolutionary of an older generation, Peter Lavrov:

> Falsehood can never be the means for spreading truth. Exploitation or the authoritarian rule of individuals can never be the means for the realization of justice. Triumph over idle pleasure cannot be attained by the forcible seizure of unearned wealth. . . . People who assert that the *end justifies the means* should keep in mind the limitation of their rule by the rather simple truism: *except those means which undermine the goal itself.*[102]

[100] Shub, *Lenin*, p. 389.
[101] Trotsky, *Lenin*, p. 227.
[102] Shub, *Lenin*, p. 15. Original italics.

II. *The Shaping of Stalinism*

It was not generally expected, when Lenin died, that Joseph Stalin would become the sole heir to his power, and would go on to establish a more intensified dictatorship than Lenin had ever conceived or desired. Lenin, like most imaginative and innovating statesmen, believed the highest ranks of political leadership should be occupied by policy makers, whose capacity for executive efficiency need not extend beyond the ability to choose the right men to carry out their decisions. Stalin was a ruthless driver who got things done, and this had induced Lenin to bring him to the fore. But administrative skill was precisely not what Lenin sought in his successor. He was altogether too intelligent and realistic not to be aware of the stultifying effects of bureaucracy, which he saw as a failing in Trotsky and others, but as a major defect in Stalin's "hastiness and bureaucratic enthusiasm."

The relative relaxation of social tension that came with peace and the NEP undoubtedly led Lenin to search for some way of relating government more directly to the people, in some artful combination of a centralized dictatorship with greater popular participation in administering the Party's and the dictator's policies. But any such democratization would inevitably diminish centralized power, an act for which even the most enlightened of despots is ill suited by the very nature of his position. Lenin himself was not one who could relinquish power at the price of seeing some of his short-run objectives undermined or even diluted, and the lesser people about him were, as he saw, addicted to the ways and thinking of the bureaucrat. They had already acquired the habit to which bureaucrats of an authoritarian system are so prone and which was to gain the standing of an institution under Stalin: they tended to confuse, and hence to substitute, bombastic proclamations of success for achievement itself. Lenin had castigated this tendency, the boasts and the lies of Communist officials, which he called "com-boasts" and "com-lies."[103] But even had he been capable of discovering a miraculously viable solution to the problem of dictatorship without bureaucracy, which is rather more than doubtful, illness and death

---

[103] Souvarine, *Stalin,* pp. 302, 308.

denied him the opportunity. As it was, he bequeathed to his successors bureaucracy, "com-lies," and "com-boasts."

Stalin's method for securing power was simple although characteristically devious. What he did, starting in 1923, was to adapt to intraparty struggles Lenin's splitting technique, which had been intended to induce the working class to turn, in desperation, to the Bolsheviks for strong leadership. Throughout these factional struggles, Stalin frequently shifted his policies, more often than not adopting the program of the group he had just routed. He played one faction against the other, and then was able to condemn them all out of their own mouths. All were obsessed with the Leninist dogma of party solidarity, designed to present a hard, impervious front to the non-Bolshevik world. Carried over into the Soviet era, this dogma meant that intraparty disputes had to be kept from the public as long as possible, and that, even after they had been aired, there could be no appeal to the people, for this would have been to commit the major sin of splitting, if not the ultimate sin of counter-revolution. Stalin took the fullest possible advantage of this over-riding belief in Party regularity. Had he attempted to establish his dictatorship in one swift coup he would unquestionably have been defeated. But Stalin was a very patient man. In most of the disputes over policy which served as the medium for the battle for power, he managed to appear as the man of moderation, trying to hold the Party together against the selfish desires of extremist factionalism. He usually allowed his allies of the moment to make the bitterest attacks on the foe and, when the particular campaign had been won, would encourage members of the defeated faction to rejoin the fold. They had to pay a price, however; for the sake of Party solidarity they had to confess their error in the dispute, to demonstrate their complete devotion to the Party by admitting that they had been wrong. As a result, they were thoroughly discredited. In time, Stalin began to stand out as the only one who could provide firm leadership, and many who hated him rallied to his side in order to preserve the Party. And, over the years, Stalin was able to remodel both the government and the Party to his liking.

In the long list of adulatory titles that Stalin later encouraged official sycophants to bestow on him, ranging from the simple *vozhd* (Russian for führer, duce, or leader) to "father of the peoples," it is quite understandable that there should not appear the one that he really earned: "greatest of machine politicians." One is at a loss to think of another virtuoso who might challenge Stalin's preëminence in this art. His skill was such that on more than one occasion he was able to take credit for correcting blunders that he had himself committed. In all these achievements, however, he had the inestimable assistance of his secret political police.

The first phase of Stalin's campaign saw the triumvirate of Stalin, Zinoviev, and Kamenev battle Trotsky, three lesser men combining to outweigh the organizer of the Red Army, the most eloquent of all the revolutionary orators.[104] Even the purest politician has to deal with issues of policy, however, so that although the triumvirs could force Trotsky to meet them on their ground of machine politics, they had also to meet him on his. An ideological debate therefore ensued, liberally cluttered with "as Comrade Lenin said." In the process Lenin's thought was as thoroughly embalmed as his body, and the whole dispute has an air of unreality. But the quarreling over a theoretical line also could not help but influence future policy. Since all the disputants were professional Marxists, both their programs and their doctrinal justifications had to be elaborated in Marxian-sounding phraseology.

In searching for a weak point in Trotsky's armor, the triumvirs naturally seized upon Lenin's polemics against the theory of per-

[104] Although it is not likely, as has often been said, that Trotsky lost the fight by failing to appear at Lenin's funeral, he may well have missed an opportunity to win it. An electrifying address in the Red Square might have resulted in one of those elections without balloting, a general acknowledgment that he stood above the rest. Trotsky accuses Stalin of having deliberately misinformed him as to the date of Lenin's funeral, so that he continued his rest at the Black Sea. A few days after Lenin's death, Stalin delivered himself of a speech before the Congress of Soviets the peroration of which was an utterly bizarre combination of revolutionary ideas and liturgical phrasing. For example:

> In leaving us, Comrade Lenin ordained us to hold high and keep pure the great title of member of the party. We vow to thee, Comrade Lenin, that we shall honorably fulfill this thy commandment. . . . In leaving us, Comrade Lenin ordained us to guard the unity of our party like the apple of our eye. We vow to thee, Comrade Lenin, that we shall fulfill honorably this thy commandment, too (as translated by Deutscher, *Stalin*, p. 270).

This shows that Stalin had not forgotten everything he had learned at the theological seminary in Tiflis where his education and revolutionary career had both begun. It also suggests that if Lenin had been alive to hear it it would certainly have hastened his demise.

manent revolution, dating from 1905. Lenin, of course, had not permitted his earlier views to prevent him from adopting Trotsky's
outlook in 1917. But, to a country that was physically and emotion-
ally tired of war and struggle, the idea of permanent revolution, in
1923, tended to reinforce the feeling that Trotsky was something of a
wild man. Zinoviev and Kamenev blasted away on this theme,
charging that Trotsky was guilty of heresy against Marxism-Leninism. Stalin, however, managed to dissociate himself from the rather
negative impression given by his colleagues, by proposing a new,
positive doctrine. This was the idea of "socialism in one country,"
which he worked up from hesitant beginnings over the course of
the debate.

Trotsky had never denied that a socialist revolution could start
in Russia without the aid of the advanced Western proletariat. But
Trotsky did hold, in accordance with the overwhelming weight of
Marxian and Leninist thinking, that the erection of a socialist society
in Russia could not be completed without help from a revolutionary,
industrialized Europe. Stalin's theory of "socialism in one country"
differed from Trotsky's chiefly in the proposition that socialism
could be fully established in Russia. Practically speaking, Stalin's
innovation did not imply any greater or lesser militancy, any different policies, than Trotsky's. Indeed, the triumvirate attacked Trotsky
as a "superindustrializer." But Stalin's new line, in addition to
assuaging his own sense of inferiority as a theoretician, responded
to the mood of the Russian Communists. Since the mid-nineteenth
century, the Russian intelligentsia had oscillated between self-abasement before the civilized West and a frenetic assertion of the innate
superiority of their own culture. Now the Marxist intelligentsia—
who alone were allowed to be vocal—were sadly disillusioned with
the West; after all, no matter how culturally and industrially advanced Europe was, only Russia had carried through a socialist
revolution.

Moreover, the time was ripe for the proclamation of something
positive as a driving motivation for Soviet policy and what was
really novel and captivating in Stalin's thesis was its "assertion of
the self-sufficiency of the Russian revolution."[105] Stalin's position
therefore had a double advantage; for the short run he proposed

[105] Deutscher, *Stalin*, p. 288. This interpretation closely follows Deutscher's
skillful dissection of the controversy.

moderation, as against Trotsky's forced pace of industrialization, and this met the Communists' and also the people's desire for stability; for the long run he offered a dazzling goal of a rich socialist society, whose construction did not depend on the fading hope of revolution in Europe.[106]

In defeating Trotsky, the triumvirate had undermined his influence in the Party by admitting about 250,000 new members, by progressively reducing his press facilities, and by organizing "spontaneous" condemnations of "Trotskyism" on the part of Communist and other local organizations. In this whole process, the hand of the General Secretary of the Party, as the one principally concerned with matters of organization, was immeasurably strengthened, even in Leningrad and Moscow, where Zinoviev and Kamenev were the respective bosses. As a result, Stalin was in an excellent position for the second phase of his campaign for the dictatorship which opened in 1925. Now it was the turn of Zinoviev and Kamenev to feel the grinding force of Stalin's machine press. His new allies consisted of Premier Rykov, trade-union leader Tomsky, and the number one theoretician, Bukharin, amounting to four of the seven votes in the Politburo, the highest executive committee of the Communist Party. The other three were Zinoviev, Kamenev, and still the weakened Trotsky, for the pace of Stalin's ascent was slow, and the day of violent purges and executions was yet to come.

The first phase of the struggle for power had aroused a policy dispute to which the triumvirs had managed to give the appearance of Leninist orthodoxy vs. Trotskyism. The second phase, too, naturally held implications for the course of the Soviet government, and appeared before Party and public as a battle of the right vs. the left wing of communism. As before, Stalin let the other members of his faction, particularly Bukharin, make the extreme rightist statements, while he combined support of their immediate position with a somewhat muddled reassertion of what passed for orthodox Bolshevism. The real issue concerned the dissatisfaction of the peasantry with a drop in income brought on in part by poor harvests but largely by a

---

[106] The sound Marxist criticism of the theory was that full socialism was conceivable only in a very high-surplus economy; that the effort to establish it in an economy of scarcity would not only fail to achieve the productivity of capitalism but would lead to new forms of class inequality.

sharp fall of the price of agricultural relative to industrial commodities. This was the famous "scissors" crisis, in which not only agrarian and industrial prices, but more importantly, peasants and workers, moved farther and farther apart.[107] As all Communists agreed the regime depended upon harmony between these classes, a solution had to be found to a situation in which peasant bitterness led them to withhold food supplies, a solution which would not yield so much to the peasants as to raise unduly the cost of urban living or of industrial raw materials. The general policy of the ruling faction was to force the prices of manufactured goods downward, to make more generous payments for grain, and to encourage production by the small and middle peasants. Stalin, at least, had drawn the proper moral from a new uprising in Georgia in 1924:

Either non-party peasants and workers must be able to criticize us, or we shall be subjected to criticism in the form of insurrection. The Georgian insurrection was such a criticism.

Individual peasants were given greater freedom to lease land and hire laborers. The spirit of NEP was confirmed and extended, Bukharin declaring, "We must tell the peasants, all the peasants, to enrich themselves, to develop their business and not fear spoliation."[108]

Moderation, which harmonized with "socialism in one country" as easily as did the most extreme militancy, carried over into foreign affairs: capitalists were invited to do business with Russia, and make good profits helping Bolshevism. Zinoviev, Kamenev, and the beaten but still dangerous Trotsky counterattacked on several fronts: international revolution was being betrayed; the industrialization of Russia was being neglected; the *kulak*, the rich peasant, was being favored at the expense of the poor peasant. They suggested more

[107] The scissors, of course, did not remain at a fixed angle. At its widest, and worst, in the late summer and early fall of 1923, industrial prices were about 276 and agricultural 89, with both at 100 for 1913. Even these figures underestimate the peasants' difficulties, for they are based on wholesale prices, whereas the farmer receives wholesale prices but pays retail. See A. Baykov, *The Development of the Soviet Economic System*, New York, 1947, p. 56; Maurice Dobb, *Russian Economic Development Since the Revolution*, London, 2d ed., 1929, chaps. 8, 9. As late as 1927 peasant ability to purchase industrial goods was 50 percent lower than in 1913.

[108] Souvarine, *Stalin*, pp. 373, 390.

intensive industrialization, stepping up agricultural production, and attacking poverty in the countryside by bringing the poor peasants together in collective farms. These larger and more efficient farming units would obviously be based on the socialist rather than the capitalist principle but, in line with Lenin's thinking, they were to be voluntary groupings.

Both criticisms and proposals were well taken, but had nothing whatever to do with the outcome of the factional struggle. The Communist Party Congress of December, 1925, had been well packed, and the efforts of Zinoviev and Kamenev to fight the real battle on the floor only brought them a less dignified downfall than that reserved for Trotsky. Kamenev did at least manage to cut through what one might term, in imitation of Lenin, the "com-cant":

> We object to the creation of a headship theory; to the setting up of a "head." We object to the Secretariat, uniting policy and organization in itself, being placed above the political organism. *We stand for an internal organization of the supreme power so as to assure full power to the Political Bureau, which contains all the political brains of our Party,* and subordinate the Secretariat to it as the technical executant of its decisions. . . . I have become convinced that Comrade Stalin cannot play the part of coordinator of the Bolshevik general staff.[109]

And then there descended a deluge of cheers for Stalin.

The General Secretary accused his enemies of being "splitters," and turned their own words and deeds against them. Loyal to his friends, and, as always, moderate, Stalin recounted how Zinoviev and Kamenev had wished to expel Trotsky from the Party and even imprison him:

> We did not agree with Zinoviev and Kamenev, being fully aware that an amputation policy is full of dangers to the Party . . . ; today, one is amputated, another tomorrow, a third the day after. What will be left of the Party in the end?[110]

And now Zinoviev and Kamenev were thirsting for Bukharin's blood, said Stalin, and "We will not let you have it; be sure of that."

---

[109] Italics have been supplied to call attention to the fact that neither faction was interested in anything more than "democratic centralism," which would have given the opposition at least a talking chance, but would in no way have broken the exclusiveness of "Soviet democracy."

[110] Souvarine, *Stalin,* pp. 404, 406.

Having won the planned support of the Congress, Stalin proceeded to replace Zinoviev with one of his own men, Kirov, as boss of Leningrad, and to prepare the finishing touches of the second phase of his campaign. An abortive conspiracy in the army gave him the pretext to remove Trotsky and Zinoviev from the Politburo, and the latter from the presidency of the Comintern.[111] Zinoviev, Kamenev, and Trotsky had joined forces too late, after they had been discredited by Stalin.

Aside from their own ineptitude, the opposition had been hamstrung by the fetish of Party loyalty, which forbade an effective appeal to the people. Only in 1927 did they openly raise the matter of Lenin's Testament and its denunciation of Stalin's bureaucratic "rudeness," after a year in which they had shamefacedly and half-heartedly denied its authenticity as published abroad. The Testament was, of course, well known among the higher Bolshevik echelons. It was read to the Central Committee of the Communist Party in May, 1924, and, at the suggestion of the then triumvirate of Stalin, Zinoviev, and Kamenev, knowledge of it was restricted to inner Party circles and all discussion of it was prohibited. When he was forced to speak of the Testament, in 1927, Stalin was therefore able to claim that he had not concealed it; the all-wise Party had. The suppression of the document during the two years when it might have tipped the scales against Stalin testifies to the amazing Party discipline, not only of his outspoken opponents, but of Lenin's widow, Krupskaya, who had protested bitterly against the decision to withhold from the Party as a whole her husband's last advice. When they at last tried to make use of the document, Stalin, in complete control, was able to say:

Yes, Comrades, I am rude toward those who rudely and traitorously break their word, who split and destroy the Party. I have never concealed it and I do not conceal it now.[112]

---

[111] When Trotsky resigned as War Commissar, he was replaced by Frunze, with one of Zinoviev's followers as deputy. Frunze, who was not as "reliable" as Stalin would have wished, died early in 1926 under the most unusual circumstances. He was ill and in need of an operation, but he and his doctors thought him too weak for the ordeal. On the order of the Politburo, however, he submitted to surgery and died. His successor was Stalin's old friend Voroshilov.

[112] Souvarine, *Stalin*, p. 458.

Exile, imprisonment, simple unemployment, or at best degrading jobs were the lot of the opposition. A few of these dispositions were announced; many more were not.

A third phase began almost immediately, and was the easiest of Stalin's victories. He no longer had to league with the leaders of other groups. This time it was the Stalin faction, with Molotov as chief lieutenant, against Bukharin, Rykov, Tomsky, and the right. The campaign opened on the bureaucratic front, with the usual displacement of Bukharin's friends from influential positions, and was speedily dissolved in a genuine economic and political crisis. Early in 1928 it was apparent that grain deliveries were falling far short of the needs of basic subsistence. The peasants had either to be induced or forced to hand over more food to the state purchasing agencies. Since the more prosperous peasants, the *kulaks,* had the largest quantities for disposal, the question was whether to appease or to fight the *kulaks.* During the second phase, Stalin and the right wing had been correctly called appeasers. In 1925, he had replied to the question, "How can one fight against the *kulaks* without fanning the class struggle?" with a condemnation of "fanning class struggle" in agriculture. As late as June, 1928, he declared, "Dekulakization under our conditions is lunacy."[113] By this criterion he was shortly to become a raving lunatic, but his most recent allies and scheduled victims did not need any alarming overt signs to know what he had in store for them. In July, 1928, Bukharin went hysterically to Kamenev to urge a coalition of all opponents of the dictatorship, of the beaten left and the still-to-be-whipped right.

He called Stalin an "unprincipled intriguer who subordinates everything to his appetite for power. At any given moment he will change his theories in order to get rid of someone."[114] Now he changed his theories in a masterstroke that kept left and right apart. All that united them was hatred for Stalin and his methods, but they were not permitted adequately to communicate this hatred to their followers, and Stalin's new policies brought many an exiled leftist back to Moscow to beg forgiveness and to be permitted to work for the man who now adopted the left's point of view. This was, to be sure, more than just a political maneuver on Stalin's part. Grain had

[113] Souvarine, *Stalin,* p. 481.
[114] Souvarine, *Stalin,* p. 482.

to be found, and Stalin chose the means most congenial to his nature, the administrative, bureaucratic method of force, rather than concession and persuasion. By the summer of 1928 grain requisitioning squads were again working through the countryside; by the following year Stalin had cloaked the campaign to get more grain from the peasants in the garb of a rather spurious class struggle:

We have tolerated these bloodsuckers, spiders and vampires [the *kulaks*, that is] . . . because there was nothing to replace *kulak* farms . . . *kulak* production. We are now in a position to replace and more than replace their farms by collective and Soviet farms. . . . Hence the policy of liquidating the *kulaks* as a class must be pursued with all the firmness and consistency of which Bolsheviks are capable.[115]

This was to the left of Trotskyism, as was Stalin's swift conversion to the industrialization madness, which came in 1929. Collectivization and the First Five-Year Plan—the Stalin Revolution—were under way. But his political revolution was not quite complete, for he would be satisfied with nothing less than an absolutely unimpeded and unchallenged dictatorship. Closing the conquest of the right opposition in 1929, Rykov was replaced with Molotov as Premier, while Bukharin and Tomsky lost their jobs and were condemned by the general state of terror to live as lepers in Moscow.[116] The second red dictator may be said to have been officially installed on the occasion of his fiftieth birthday, December 21, 1929, when he was hailed as "the Lenin of today."

The fourth phase of Stalin's campaign, the most dramatic of all, was actually by way of a bloody postscript to his earlier triumphs as a machine politician. Stalin now assumed his role of the Greatest of Liquidators vs. the Old Bolsheviks and other leaders of Soviet society. The purges of 1936–1938 and the public trials which played so prominent a part in them took place against a background of genuine social problems. But now there was no issue of a Stalinist vs. an opposition program. There was only the question of what

---

[115] J. Stalin, *Building Collective Farms*, London, 1931, p. 141.
[116] Trotsky was exiled, in January, 1929, to the Turkish island of Prinkipo, whence the founder of the Red Army made his way to Norway and thereafter to Mexico where, in 1940, he was murdered by a mysterious individual whose sponsors were not hard to guess. He had at least outlived most of the Old Bolsheviks.

Stalin would do to strengthen his hold in the face of a rising mood of despair, disgust, and anger. The boasts of the regime were belied by daily life. To both devout Communists and ordinary people, the sacrifices and suffering of millions, the deaths and destitution, showed no prospect of being recompensed by the advent of socialist peace and plenty. Stalin shifted back and forth between tyrannical application of his program and grudging gestures of "liberalization," such as making OGPU activities (theoretically) reviewable by the Attorney General.

During 1932 and most of the following year he withdrew from the public eye.[117] He had already had to imprison high Communist officials who were quietly circulating petitions to the Central Committee of the Party to carry out Lenin's advice and find another Secretary. Even in the subservient Politburo there were voices raised in favor of liberalization, among them that of Kirov, Zinoviev's successor as satrap of Leningrad. So Stalin vacillated between repression and liberalization, never, of course, relaxing his grip on the police or their grip on the country.

But on December 1, 1934, occurred an event which ended his hesitation and opened the most violent phase of the Stalin terror, the assassination of Kirov by a young Communist.[118] The murderer, of course, was executed, along with sixteen other young Party mem-

[117] His second wife committed suicide in 1932. Stalin's iron will may have weakened under this blow: it is reported that he offered the Politburo his resignation, if they thought it best. Molotov said, "Stop it, stop it. You have got the party's confidence." And Stalin's excellent suggestion was dropped (Deutscher, *Stalin*, p. 334).

[118] There are grounds for at least suspecting that Stalin was an accessory before the fact to Kirov's murder. Two months earlier the assassin had been arrested by the OGPU with a revolver in his possession, and his intentions known. He was released, however, after clearance with Moscow headquarters. After the success of the second attempt, Stalin himself rushed to Leningrad to conduct the investigation, but it was never given any publicity, and the murderer's letter was never released. Although Stalin punished thousands of "Kirov's murderers," the Leningrad OGPU chiefs, who were held guilty of negligence, received extremely light prison sentences, and did not serve them in full. Stalin—and Stalin alone—benefited from Kirov's death in three ways: Kirov was becoming extremely popular, especially with the younger element, and might have appeared to the dictator as a possible rival; his advocacy of the relaxation of tyranny was an obstacle to its intensification; his death itself was a splendid excuse to wipe out all possibility of organized dissent. See W. G. Krivitsky, *In Stalin's Secret Service*, New York, 1939, pp. 184 ff.; Souvarine, *Stalin*, pp. 593 ff.

bers held to have been associated with him. But this was barely a beginning. Close to two hundred more were shot as accomplices, some of whom had been in prison for several years. Young Communists had obviously been acquiring some improper habits of thought and action; ten thousand or more were committed to forced labor. Leningrad had always been a nuisance to Stalin through its years under Zinoviev, and even later under Kirov (perhaps because it was Russia's "window to the West"); up to one hundred thousand of its residents were "relocated." Zinoviev and Kamenev, who had already established a record for recantations and confessions of error, were trotted out once more, to answer to the charge of having inspired the murder of Kirov. They were tried in secret and sentenced to prison, but the important thing for Stalin was to secure from them an admission of guilt: the condition of Russia meant that any living major opponent was dangerous to Stalin, but he was not yet ready for more than character assassination with respect to the leaders. A bargain was finally struck between the dictator and his captives, whereby they were exonerated of any direct connection with the deed, which was self-evident, and they accepted what might be called a moral responsibility, if morality were at all relevant. Zinoviev's public statement of his part in the crime was a masterpiece of diplomatic phrasing:

The former activity of the former opposition could not, by the force of objective circumstances, but stimulate the degeneration of those criminals. . . .[119]

What this meant was that the ideas of the now inactive opposition had been sound, that young Communists had come to perceive their soundness, and were being driven by the "objective circumstances" of Stalin's misrule to acts of terrorism.

Stalin knew only too well that similar sentiments pervaded the entire structure of the Soviet state. Krivitsky wrote:

I should say that, at this time, not only the immense mass of the peasants but the majority of the army, including its best generals, a majority of the commissars, 90 percent of the directors of factories, 90 percent of the party machine, were in more or less extreme degree opposed to Stalin's dictatorship.[120]

[119] Deutscher, *Stalin*, p. 357.
[120] *In Stalin's Secret Service*, New York, 1939, p. 187.

Even if this be exaggerated, unrest had evidently grown far beyond the point where the dictator could be reassured by the votes of party congresses and the insincere apologies of prominent enemies. But stronger measures required preparation. A lulling calm was created by a slow improvement in economic conditions, and by the decision, in February, 1935, to write a new and democratic constitution. Stalin himself headed the drafting committee, and appointed to it representatives of both the right and left opposition factions. On the other hand, no longer trusting even the OGPU, Stalin had been organizing a separate secret police of his own.

Lightning finally struck in August, 1936, with the first of the great "show trials," the trial of the "Sixteen," headed by Zinoviev and Kamenev. All were shot. In January, 1937, came the public trial of the "Seventeen." Thirteen were shot, while four received prison terms. The alleged or at least secret trial of eight marshals and generals, headed by Tukhachevsky, resulted in death for all in June, 1937. The last great show trial of the "Twenty-One," including Bukharin, Rykov, and the OGPU chief Yagoda, took place in March, 1938, and eighteen were shot. In addition there were notable suicides, such as trade-union leader Tomsky. The show trials were a very small proportion of the total: they were only for men who would agree to confess, and who were prominent enough to make their confessions worth publicizing. Most numerous were the administrative sentences without the formality of a hearing before a rigged court.

In the public trials Stalin proved himself as an architect of law. Not only was the principle of guilt by association[121] brilliantly extended, but a new and highly original legal concept was perfected. This may be called the doctrine of "What might conceivably have been therefore actually was." A man was to be deemed guilty of an act he might have wished to commit, or one that would have been a possible logical consequence of a position he had once taken. This was extremely comprehensive, since few good Communists had not disagreed with Stalin at least once in the preceding twelve years. An ingenious corollary of this principle was retroactive criminality.

---

[121] Stalin had made this a part of Soviet law in 1935, when it was provided that families of traitors, of persons who fled Russia, or of those who refused to return from missions abroad were to be deemed accomplices.

If a person were now "proved" to be, let us say, a German spy, it would be declared that, as it was logical to assume, he had always been a German spy. For example, police chief Yagoda, whose glories had been sung as "the flaming sword of the revolution," was now declared to have been a Tsarist agent from the age of ten, and a German agent since the birth of the Cheka.

The purges and trials also provided Stalin with the opportunity to develop a genuine innovation in Marxist doctrine. Yagoda, accused of having poisoned his predecessor, liquidated a goodly number in his days of being a "flaming sword"; then he was liquidated by his successor, Yezhov, who liquidated so vast a number that he was liquidated by his successor, Beria. Marx had described the overthrow of the bourgeoisie as the "expropriation of the expropriators"; in the higher plane of a socialist and Stalinist society we behold the "liquidation of the liquidators."

The public affairs were trials only in a topsy-turvy, black-is-white sense of the word. The accused treated these spectacles not as opportunities for defense but for self-vilification. "We were bandits, assassins, fascists, agents of the Gestapo. I thank the prosecutor for having demanded for us the only penalty that we deserve." In each case there were several suspiciously obscure defendants sprinkled among the celebrities, to supply the occasional bits of factual reporting offered. It does not tax the imagination to recognize them as police agents. The charges comprised all or part of the following: plotting or attempting to assassinate Stalin or a leading Stalinist; plotting or organizing subversive groups which entered into the service of Germany, France, England, Japan, Italy, etc., or any combination thereof; economic sabotage, or wrecking, in order to frustrate the invincible progress of Stalinist socialist construction. All of this led the prosecutor, the Menshevik lawyer Vyshinsky who climbed to success through the confessions of lifelong Bolsheviks, to a brilliant and moving peroration: "Shoot the mad dogs!"

As a whole and in detail, accusations, evidence, and confessions were manifestly absurd. Occasionally a defendant would deviate from the agreed line of his testimony and betray its falseness.[122] But

[122] For example, I. N. Smirnov, a very prominent Old Bolshevik, had confessed belonging to a "Trotskyite center," whose purpose was murder, treason, and sabotage. At his trial, however, he so far forgot himself as to reply to the

the most convincing demonstration of the utter preposterousness of
the proceedings is in the nature of the charges themselves. After all,
it matters little whether Trotsky met Zinoviev's courier on the Moon
or Mars, when the falsity of the entire tale is self-evident. Among
the accused were many who had had numberless opportunities to
kill Stalin or any of his bigwigs. A vast number of the top functionaries of the Soviet government and the Communist Party were
alleged to have organized secretly and systematically to overthrow
him, and yet had accomplished absolutely nothing. "It was," says
Deutscher, "as if the whole power of Niagara Falls had been harnessed in order to move a toy boat."[123]

Stalin himself gave the game away. When in 1939 he finally announced to a genuinely relieved and possibly even grateful public
that the purges had come to an end, he claimed that the activities
of the assassins-traitors-saboteurs proved the need for ceaseless
vigilance:

> Is it not surprising that we learned about the espionage and conspira-
> torial activities of the Trotskyist and Bukharinist leaders only quite re-
> cently, in 1937 and 1938, although, as the evidence shows, these gentry
> were in the service of foreign espionage organizations and carried on
> conspiratorial activities from the very first days of the October revolution?
> How could we have failed to notice so grave a matter? How are we to
> explain this blunder?[124]

Very simply: it had never happened, save as he deliberately imagined it. This query of Stalin's must be put down to "com-hy-
pocrisy."

And yet, the bourgeois Western mind, confused by words such as
"trial" and "confession," which have acquired precise legal connotations over the centuries, remains uneasy and puzzled. Why

---

question, "When did you leave the center?" with an impudence of which only
a mad dog is capable, saying, "I didn't think of leaving it because there was
nothing to leave." All the defendants were linked with Trotsky (the chief but
absent accused), bitter enemies as well as friends, but the evidence had been
fabricated very carelessly. Meetings were reported in a hotel that had long
ceased to exist, and there were airplane flights of which the airports in question
had no record (Max Shachtman, *Behind the Moscow Trial*, New York, 1936;
investigation by an impartial committee headed by John Dewey, *The Case of
Leon Trotsky*, report of Preliminary Commission of Inquiry, London, 1937).

[123] *Stalin*, p. 373.
[124] *Problems of Leninism*, Moscow, 1945, p. 625.

should fanatically devoted Bolsheviks, many of a stoic cast, outdo the prosecutor in slandering themselves? And why should the dictator, working around the clock to construct a socialist society, wipe out the country's best and most experienced builders?

There is actually very little mystery to the confessions. The relatively small number of leading Bolsheviks who complied had been worn down by a process of mental and physical torture that depended upon the debilitating effect of prolonged strain rather than acute agony. Prisoners were encouraged to think that by confessing they might save their families from destruction, and actual deals of this sort were concluded directly between Stalin and some of his captives.[125] They were confronted with confessions previously extorted from friends and associates, and with the interminable dossiers containing every damaging scrap of fact or fancy that Stalin had assiduously collected over the years. By promises of reward or threats of punishment, Stalin had been corrupting Soviet politicians into denouncing each other, and now their own words were used against them. The false testimony of police agents was thrust before them, and they knew there would be no chance to disprove it in open court.

In a word, they were compelled to balance the alternative of a silent death against the iota of hope for themselves or their families that was associated with public self-abasement. They had nothing to lose save honor, and most of them were old, tired, and had become cynical after years of bland acceptance of lesser falsehoods, confessions, and chicanery. A few saw an opportunity in the very exaggeration and ridiculousness of their confessions to absolve themselves and condemn Stalin before their comrades and the world.

There was one more lever with which the dictator could move them, possibly the most effective of all. These men were fanatical Bolsheviks. They saw a situation in which mass opposition to the regime, however justified in their eyes, might eventuate in the over-

[125] Krivitsky writes: "It may seem surprising to the western mind that there should be barters in human lives between a lord high executioner and his trapped victims. We of the inner Bolshevik circle always took such negotiations as a matter of course. Certain of the family, the friends, even the less conspicuous political followers, of the victims would be spared, if they would through their 'confessions' help to implicate the key men, and make a general clean-up possible." In Stalin's Secret Service, p. 192.

throw of the Communist Party and the revolution itself. Stalin, who used all of Lenin's stock words and phrases—Soviet, socialist, revolutionary, vanguard of the proletariat, workers and peasants, etc.— at least offered the hope of perpetuating Communist rule. Some day, it was suggested to the doomed men, the Party might return to the true Leninist course of their imagination. As long ago as 1928, Piatakov, a bitter opponent, had said:

> Stalin is the only man we must obey, for fear of getting worse. Bukharin and Rykov deceive themselves in thinking they would govern in Stalin's place. Kaganovich and such would succeed him, and I cannot and will not obey a Kaganovich.[126]

In 1933 a Trotskyite in Russia wrote of the opposition: "They all speak about Stalin's isolation and the general hatred of him. . . . But they often add: 'If it were not for that . . . [obscenity] . . . everything would have fallen into pieces by now. It is he who keeps everything together.' "[127] Now, in 1936 and after, it seemed to be Stalin or no one, and he played upon this feeling. However his victims blamed him for the failures of the regime, they had to recognize that only he could maintain the unitary power of the Communist Party. So long as they continued to be obsessed by the belief that only the Communist Party could create socialism, they had not merely to accept but to support the man they loathed. For him to succeed in this task, however, it was necessary that the lower ranks of the Party and the masses at large look upon him as the only leader who was right and just. Otherwise popular unrest might sweep him out, and all Communism with him. The victims were therefore in a position to perform one last heroic service to their beloved Party. By publicly assuming responsibility for all that had gone wrong, by so degrading themselves that no prestige or respect could remain attached to their names or memory, they would strengthen Stalin, now standing alone as the guardian of Russia and of socialism. They would help him keep alive, after they had died, the thread of the Marxist dream and hope that had motivated their entire existence.[128]

[126] Souvarine, *Stalin*, p. 489. Kaganovich was Stalin's brother-in-law.
[127] Deutscher, *Stalin*, p. 352.
[128] The breaking down of an outstanding Old Bolshevik, Mrachkovsky, is described by Krivitsky, *In Stalin's Secret Service*, pp. 198 ff. See also the remark-

But why did Stalin destroy the elite of Soviet Russia, why did he execute former Premiers and Commissars, Generals and Ambassadors, up to 35,000 of the officer corps of the Red Army? Why did political arrests in the years of the purges run to perhaps 500,000, ending in death, forced labor, or perhaps, in cases of Stalinist generosity, in minor jobs in Siberia? Aside from leading figures, why did Stalin foster a tide of terror, with many thousands of arrests in the dead of night, with hundreds of man-years wasted on inquisitions, interrupting and often halting the work of ordinary technicians, managers, office personnel, and laborers, the friends, relatives, or protégés of men already arrested, the victims of gossip and slander or of the arrest quotas of the OGPU? A number of motives mingled in the dictator's strange mind. For one, he found vengeance sweet. He had once said:

> To choose the victim, to prepare the blow with care, to sate an implacable vengeance, and then to go to bed. . . . There is nothing sweeter in the world![129]

This might help to explain the fate of a Zinoviev, or the pursuit and murder of Trotsky. Others, like the executioners Yagoda and Yezhov, perhaps too some of his oldest friends, knew too much, however loyal they had been to him. He did, of course, stand in dire need of scapegoats, on whom to pin the blame for the inefficiency of industry and agriculture. Purges and show trials to provide whipping boys had been employed as far back as 1928, and the liquidation of the Old Bolsheviks served this among other purposes.

---

able Shipkov letter, a report on his own experiences by a Bulgarian employee of the American Embassy in Sofia, *New York Times*, March 5, 1950. As is often the case, the pen of a discerning and well-informed artist has produced one of the most revealing descriptions of the process: Arthur Koestler's *Darkness at Noon*. The analysis by F. Beck and W. Godin, *Russian Purge and the Extraction of Confession*, New York, 1951, is thoughtful and penetrating.

[129] Souvarine, *Stalin*, p. 659. Max Eastman quotes Serebryakov, an outstanding economic official, as saying, in New York in 1929: "If he lives long enough he will get every single one of us who has ever injured him in speech or action. That is his principal aim in life. He is completely dominated by vindictive passion. He will lie back and wait ten, twenty, thirty years, secretly plotting to achieve an exquisitely appropriate revenge upon an enemy, and then, when everything is ready, he will spring. Believe me, I am not telling fairy stories. I have lived with him, roomed with him, camped with him on the battlefield. He is the most vindictive man on earth" (*Stalin's Russia and the Crisis in Socialism*, New York, 1940, p. 78).

There may have been more compelling reasons, however. Adolf Hitler had come to power in 1933, and his anti-Bolshevism and anti-Slavism apparently ran deep. The Russian regime dreaded the possibility of a war which might threaten Stalin's dictatorship, if not the Soviet Union itself. In 1927 Trotsky had said that in the event of war he would do what Clemenceau had done in France in World War I: he would strive to combine with all loyal Bolsheviks to get rid of the incompetent Stalin faction and form a government capable of leading the Soviet Union to victory. The scope of the liquidations therefore becomes quite understandable. Stalin

. . . had set out to destroy the men capable of forming an alternative government. But each of these men had behind him long years of service, in the course of which he had trained and promoted administrators and officers and made many friends. Stalin could not be sure that avengers of his victims would not arise from the ranks of their followers. Having destroyed the first team of potential leaders of an alternative government, he could not spare the second, the third, the fourth and the nth teams.[130]

Once loosed, the terror snowballed and encompassed thousands who were harmless even by Stalin's standards.

As for the Red Army command, it had always maintained some degree of independence of the political arm. Stalin's system of sowing suspicion and rivalry, which disrupted the unity of potential enemies, had not been as pervasive or effective among the professional corps of officers. It would not have been strange for the Red Marshals and General Staff to have shared the wave of disgust with Stalin of the early 1930's, and to have thought in terms of a military coup in which, after all, they would have had the support of most of the Old Bolsheviks. In short, Stalin had a great deal to fear from the army, and in a time of war would be helpless against them. In 1937, therefore, making use of "evidence" faked by the Nazi Gestapo, he accused them of the very crime of coöperation with Germany which he himself was soon to commit.[131] The charges, naturally, were made as lurid as possible to convince the masses.

Even before the purges, Stalin had triumphed over all the different oppositions, but *that* victory could endure only so long as the

---

[130] Deutscher, *Stalin*, p. 380.
[131] See Krivitsky, *In Stalin's Secret Service*, ch. 7.

condition of Russia was generally satisfactory, and so long as peace obtained. After the purges, the only danger he faced was outright military conquest by a foreign power. Russia suffered the loss of her ablest officials and soldiers, but there were many young aspirants to grow into their jobs. The new generation of subleaders consisted in fair part of men who had reached maturity under Stalin. They were eager to profit by the opportunity for rapid advancement created by the destruction of their superiors. Their promotion depended exclusively upon Stalin and his machine, their loyalty was entirely his. As a precautionary measure, moreover, he pursued a policy of reshuffling positions at irregular intervals and for no apparent reason. This prevented the formation of solid associations from which new oppositions might arise.

Following his customary tactic of throwing a sop of superficial liberalization to the masses when his tyranny was at its harshest, in 1936 the dictator secured the official adoption of the Stalin Constitution, "the most democratic in the world."[132] In the spurious debates that preceded its ratification, Stalin opposed the suggestion that only Communist Party members be allowed to run for the Supreme Soviet, and condemned the proposal that sovereignty be vested in the President of the USSR rather than in the three-man Presidium of the Supreme Soviet on the ground that the President might become a dictator! There was not a little brass in the Man of Steel. The Constitution itself showed a similar concern for the appearances of ordinary, Western democracy. It guaranteed freedom of speech, the press, assembly, and processions, including street demonstrations. It "recognized for all citizens . . . freedom of religious worship and freedom of anti-religious propaganda." To the member republics of the Soviet Union was "reserved the right freely to secede from the USSR." All citizens aged eighteen or over were given the right to vote and to be elected deputies to the Supreme Soviet. Citizens were guaranteed "inviolability of the person. No person may be placed under arrest except by decision of a court or with the sanction of a procurator. The inviolability of the homes of citizens and privacy of correspondence are protected by law."

If all of this, and some other fine clauses, meant anything in actu-

[132] The Constitution, written largely by Bukharin and Radek, also had an important role to play in his foreign policy. See p. 477.

ality, it would be very democratic indeed. The Constitution itself diminished the supremacy of the Supreme Soviet by its failure to provide for regular meetings. Everyone had the right to vote, but for whom? Article 126 refers to the Communist Party merely as "the vanguard of the working people . . . and . . . the leading core of all organizations of the working people, both public and state." In explaining the Constitution, however, Stalin hastened to remove any possible misunderstanding. To critics who believed that "the absence of freedom for parties in the USSR is an indication of the violation of the fundamental principles of democracy," he had this to say:

. . . the new Constitution really does leave in force the regime of the dictatorship of the working class, and also leaves unchanged the present leading position of the Communist Party of the USSR. . . . The party is part of the class, its vanguard section. Several parties and consequently freedom of parties can only exist in a society where antagonistic classes exist whose interests are hostile and irreconcilable, where there are capitalists and workers, landlords and peasants, kulaks and poor peasants. But in the USSR there are . . . only two classes, workers and peasants, whose interests not only are not antagonistic but, on the contrary, amicable. Consequently there are no grounds for the existence of several parties, and therefore for the existence of freedom of such parties in the USSR. There are grounds for the existence of only one party, the Communist Party, in the USSR. . . . Democracy in capitalist countries where there are antagonistic classes is in the last analysis the democracy for the strong, democracy for the propertied minority. Democracy in the USSR, on the contrary, is democracy for all. . . . That is why I think that the Constitution of the USSR is the only thoroughly democratic constitution in the world.

It must be pointed out that this is rather bad Marxism. From the Marxian standpoint both Democrats and Republicans in the United States must be regarded as representatives of the ruling bourgeoisie; why not have more than one party to represent the ruling "working class" in Russia, which is what Lenin at one time envisaged?[133]

Lastly, regarding the inviolability of the person, perhaps the most

---

[133] Deutscher, *Stalin*, p. 381. The Constitution and Stalin's explanatory address may be found conveniently in *Introduction to Contemporary Civilization in the West*, vol. II, pp. 1077 ff.

fundamental test of political democracy, Vyshinsky, who is one of the outstanding Soviet jurists, explains that

The court and the Public Prosecutor, in issuing a warrant for arrest, verify the necessity and legality of the application of this measure. Having in view that the Soviet Court and the Soviet prosecutor represent the authority of the socialist state and express and defend the interest of all toilers, their verification of the correctness of the arrest is a true and real guarantee that citizens are not being deprived of their freedom illegally and without adequate foundation.

He then goes on to say, and there are very few indeed who would disagree with him, that

The reality and the scope of the guarantees against unfounded arrests are always defined by the political regime of the state proclaiming them. The degree and the reality of guarantees against unjustified arrest depend directly upon the degree to which democracy has developed.[134]

Stalin, Vyshinsky, *et al.* undoubtedly appreciated the difference between a police tyranny and a democracy. But in the meantime, Stalinism needed friends and support at home and abroad, and in the twentieth century no word is more potent in making friends than *democracy*. It is especially efficacious among the "toiling masses" and their intellectual spokesmen to whom the Stalinists wished to appeal.

According to their lights, moreover, there is a sense in which the Soviet Union is democratic and the West is not, a criterion which lends a slight degree of Marxian plausibility to their claim. We have already had occasion to refer to this criterion, which is not only Stalinist but Leninist and Marxist, not only Marxist but shared by most non-Marxian socialists as well—the legal fiction of public ownership of the means of production and distribution. This fiction holds that when title to productive enterprise is vested in the people as a whole, exploitation of man by man disappears, caste and class distinctions vanish, and society is genuinely democratic, socially and economically. The special Stalinist extension carries this to a logical conclusion: since politics express only class interests, public ownership, by eliminating the economic foundations on which alone class structures rest, also yields political democracy. The legal fiction of

[134] *The Law of the Soviet State*, H. W. Babb, trans., New York, 1948, p. 630.

public ownership is of precisely the same logical character as the fiction by which Western law deems corporations to be persons. Both ignore the essentially political question of control. Like all fictions, they can be useful or dangerous, depending on how much is built upon them, and on how clearly their fictional nature is recognized. We all know that a corporation is not a person, save for limited purposes of law, but all too many forget that in itself the public title to property guarantees absolutely nothing save that the property will be managed by the political arm of society, by the state. The most important condition is missing from the Stalinist logic: the citizens must have the opportunity to approve or disapprove of what the state does, and to change the personnel of government if they wish.

Here is an obvious and glaring deficiency, and yet the entire Soviet apologia is built upon the legal fiction taken as if it were a fact. In order to make the resultant conception óf "Soviet democracy" consistent with Marxism, and to give the people a feeling of progress, Stalin linked the new Constitution with the announcement that socialism had come into existence in Russia. Not communism, of course, for that bespeaks a surplus of abundance, whereas socialism bespeaks mere abundance. An unsupported proclamation of abundance would not be persuasive, however: it had to be buttressed with tangible achievements to which Stalin could point with pride while reiterating the assertion that Russia alone of the leading nations had escaped the Great Depression.[135] And the dictator himself had already issued the most fatuous of all Communist slogans: "Life has become better, comrades. Life has become more joyful."

There were nevertheless many concrete achievements of which Stalin could boast, a more effective advertisement for his regime than the Constitution, if almost as superficial. Summing up the results of the First Five-Year Plan, which began in 1928, Stalin declared, in the sparse language of the man of action:

Formerly we did not have an iron and steel industry, the basis of the industrialization of the country. Now we have such an industry.

[135] Aside from the fact that depression is inconsistent with a subsistence economy, this particular Soviet "accomplishment" is rendered questionable, to say the least, by the fact that millions of potential unemployed were wiped out in the famines of the early thirties, and that the Russian economy is one of disguised unemployment, i.e., uneconomic use of manpower.

We did not have a tractor industry. Now we have one.

We did not have an automobile industry. Now we have one.

We did not have an engineering industry. Now we have one.

We did not have an important and modern chemical industry. Now we have one. . . .

And we have not only created these new enormous branches of industry, but we have created them on such a scale and of such dimensions that they make the scale and dimensions of European industry pale into insignificance.[136]

Some of these assertions are unquestionably correct, others call for critical examination, but such a recital tells little about the real level of accomplishment.

Russia had not only hired technicians and tried to imitate the latest methods of American industry, but had imported a rather unfortunate Americanism, the notion of a passing phase of American culture, that "biggest" somehow equals "best." The great Dnieperstroy dam, the tractor works at Stalingrad, the Baltic–White Sea canal, these were the pride of Stalin, together with the Moscow subway and its marble- and statuary-lined stations in which workers rode to and from their beehive homes, and a projected but unbuilt Palace of the Soviets whose sole virtue was that it would have been higher than the Empire State building. But engineering triumphs do not of themselves solve social problems, and there is a suggestion of Hollywood to "big" economic ventures that are out of proportion to their economic environment. The dictator himself is reported to have likened the Dnieperstroy dam project to a muzhik's buying a phonograph instead of a cow, which implies that the peasant would not only lack an economic resource he knew how to handle, but would acquire one he would misuse.[137]

From the Marxian, as from any human standpoint, the purges, famines, and exiles had to be charged as costs against Stalin's engineering works. Were the latter so very extraordinary, then, as to justify these costs? Did Soviet Russia advance more rapidly than the West? Were her toiling masses subjected to no exploitation, or to less than in the capitalist world? An affirmative answer to these questions would be far more eloquent propaganda than photo-

[136] Souvarine, *Stalin*, pp. 539–540.
[137] Deutscher, *Stalin*, p. 320.

graphs of the dictator with an Uzbek child on his knee, or the wearisome reports of the exploits of "heroes of labor." To each question, Stalin and his propagandists shouted "Yes!" But as the years went by, and the labor of a numerous and hard-working people should have brought actual achievements in ever closer correspondence to "com-boasts," one would have expected a lessening of secrecy, a heartier invitation to make comparisons. Instead, the Iron Curtain was made to cover more and more of Soviet life. The global quantity data in which Soviet statisticians and publicists used to delight gave way to statements that, let us say, caviar production had risen 23 percent since 1935, which tells very little when one is not permitted to know how much was produced in the base year. Parts of this statistical smokescreen have been pierced by patient Western scholars, who piece together scraps of pertinent information and eventually make the Soviet percentages more or less meaningful. But why all the obfuscation? The usual explanation on grounds of security does not hold. Concealment of retail prices or of the production figures of nonessential commodities will be annoying to a hostile analyst, but will not seriously hamper him. Nor is it an adequate explanation that the Russians have always been given to secrecy. Thirty years are long enough to shake a bad habit, unless there are convincing reasons to perpetuate it, and it cannot be said that the Stalinist leaders have ever shown any disposition to hide or belittle their own accomplishments.

It is not amiss to suggest that the purpose of this, as of every smokescreen, is to deny the enemy a clear view of a vulnerable target; in this instance the social and economic record of the Stalin regime. Fortunately, however, smoke is not absolutely impenetrable. The policy of concealment was slow and uneven in development, and, by the very nature of the case, it could never be applied totally. A good many of the smoke particles, moreover, are lodged in Western rather than Russian eyes, and, as a first step, some of these can be removed. Both common and erroneous is the conception of prerevolutionary Russia as backward and stagnant, a China without a rich past. To the contrary, although backward, Russia was dynamic, socially and economically as well as culturally. The age of Chekhov, Diaghilev, and Scriabin was equally productive of a vigorous social and economic progress in the direction of Western capitalist civilization. This advance was especially marked in the years of the twentieth century before the First World War.[138]

The rapid growth of Russian industry had got under way in the closing decades of the preceding century, and had gained astonishing momentum. For example, with 1890 = 100, the following approximate figures appear for 1900 and 1913:

	1900	1913
	(1890 = 100)	
Petroleum[139]	275	205
Coal	270	605
Pig iron	320	510
Steel	240	450
Cotton cloth	300	500
New railroad mileage	175	225
Industrial workers[a]	220	550

  [a] In large establishments.

With 1900 = 100, sugar production moved to 218 in 1913; with 1908 = 100, electric power output advanced to 640 in 1913. "Production of agricultural machinery . . . increased 15 times over a period of 15 years in response to the capitalist reconstitution of the Russian village after 1900."[140] This industrial revolution, like Stalin's a generation later, centered in producers' goods; consumers' goods were still largely provided by peasant or city craftsmen, working as individuals or in coöperatives. Large industry, on the other hand, true to the pattern of importing the latest phase of Western development, was extremely concentrated.[141]

The foregoing data unquestionably indicate a progressing economy, but this in itself should be a warning of the need for caution in dealing with the later Soviet claims. When percentages are aban-

[138] See N. S. Timasheff, *The Great Retreat: the Growth and Decline of Communism in Soviet Russia,* New York, 1946, ch. 2.

[139] The 1905 revolution and other factors leveled the Russian oil industry below its 1900 peak, at which it was ahead of the American.

[140] P. I. Lyashchenko, *History of the National Economy of Russia to the 1917 Revolution,* L. M. Herman, trans., New York, 1949, p. 690.

[141] In 1895, 42 percent of all Russian workers were employed by factories with 500 or more employees as against 15 percent for Germany. In 1910 such factories, only 5 percent of the total, accounted for 53.5 percent of industrial labor. And combines, cartels and syndicates, with foreign capital and direction heavily involved, abounded. Manya Gordon, *Workers Before and After Lenin,* New York, 1941, p. 354; Lyashchenko, *National Economy,* p. 669.

doned for physical quantities, it can be seen that Russian industrialization had started from a very low level indeed, which would partly account for its rapid advance. In 1913, for example, "the total volume of industrial production in France was 2.5 times as much, England 4.6 times, Germany 6 times, and the United States 14.3 times as much as in Russia." Against Russia's 36 million tons of coal in 1913, Germany produced 190 million and the United States 517 million. The disparities were even greater, of course, on a per capita basis, for the population of the Tsar's empire stood at 167 million at the outbreak of the First World War, having risen 31 percent since 1897. Per capita national income is estimated at $50 as of 1914, compared with $154 for Germany, $232 for Great Britain, and $351 for the United States.

Where did so backward a nation find the means for a surge of investment which provided it with the bases for a modern industrial system? There were two principal sources, agriculture and foreign loans. Russian farming was not merely backward but primitive. Machinery and artificial fertilizers were used in increasing amounts, but by the larger farmers, and for specialized crops. The mass of the peasants still rotated a third of the land in fallow, and tilled with wooden implements. Nevertheless, between 1895 and 1913 the value of agricultural exports rose almost two and one-half times, in accordance with the principle stated years earlier by a Tsarist minister, Vyshnegradsky: "We shall eat a little less but we shall export"—and industrialize. Foreign capital, however, was the greatest single factor in industrializing and generally awakening the Russian economy. In 1914, the foreign share in total corporate capital in Russia was about one third, of which one third was held by French interests. But the foreign holdings amounted to 60 percent in oil, 70 percent in coal mining, and 67 percent in the cotton textile industry.[142] The Bolsheviks loved to denounce this huge Western investment as the reduction of Russia to the status of a colonial possession of the advanced nations. But it was impossible to deny that European investment had been the key to the economic expansion of the period before the First World War.

This picture of the Russian economy of 1913, somber but with a

[142] Lyashchenko, *National Economy*, pp. 674, 716, 735; Gordon, *Workers*, pp. 343, 350.

bright ray of hope, does more than raise to a higher level one of the standards against which Soviet achievements must be judged. In more ways than one it affords a preview of Bolshevik policies and programs. Under Stalin as under Nicholas, the emphasis would be placed upon heavy industry at the expense of the output of consumers' goods, but to a more marked degree. Under the dictatorship of the proletariat as under the Tsar, peasant income would be low, and peasant output would provide funds for industrial investment, again, to a much greater extent; factory wages too would remain low, and food that would eagerly have been consumed in Russian cities and villages would be exported to pay for Western machinery. As striking as are the similarities, however, there are differences which added up to a heavier burden for the Russian people. The socialist society would do without the services of the small craftsmen who had provided most of the articles of common consumption, such as footwear and household utensils. They would be replaced with the presumably more efficient large-scale, state-owned factories; but these belonged to light rather than heavy industry, and when the inevitable choice had to be made between, on the one hand, building foundations for both future consumers' industries and immediate war production, and, on the other hand, a higher standard of living, heavy industry would be favored to the detriment of light. Nor would there be the strong leaven of foreign investment. In the early years of NEP, Western capitalists were encouraged to put their money to work in Soviet Russia. But even while NEP was still the official program, foreign investors were being frightened away, and with Stalin's swing to the left in 1928, the die was cast: Russia would industrialize herself at the most rapid rate in human history, agriculture would be rationalized through collective farming, and no obstacle would be left standing.

When the First Five-Year Plan got under way in 1928, the Russian economy had approximately recovered its 1913 level, as a result of NEP.[143] But there had been no net progress over these fifteen years,

[143] The extent of decline and recovery is suggested by the following index numbers of the gross value of output of large-scale industry at 1926–1927 prices: 1913, 100; 1920, 13.75; 1928, 154.31. In 1928 the index of gross value of output of all industry stood at 110.8, with 1913 = 100 (A. Gerschenkron, "The Rate of Growth in Russia," *Journal of Economic History*, Supp. VII, 1947, p. 161).

and it was now proposed to make up this loss in one five-year leap. This objective was achieved, but in a limited sense only, and in longer than five years.

	1913	1928	1932	1940
Pig iron[a]	4.2	3.3	6.2	14.9
Steel	4.2	4.3	5.9	19.4
Coal	29.1	35.5	64.7	164.7
Petroleum	9.2	12.3	22.3	31.0
Motor vehicles and tractors	—	2.0	74.5	242.4
Electric power	1.9	5.0	13.5	40.8

[a] Million tons; motor vehicles and tractors in thousands; electric power in billion kwh.

There can be no question of the great surge of Russian heavy industry under Stalinism, nor of the part played by the burst of popular enthusiasm that accompanied the First Five-Year Plan. Workers were inspired by the promise of socialist plenty to follow a few years of struggle, and it was this hope that failed them.[144]

A very rough idea of the degree of accomplishment is given by these figures: the First Plan (1928–1932) called for a median increase of 264 percent in the output of twelve major items, but the median fulfillment of the plan was 61 percent, and the median increase for these items was 80 percent; the Second Plan (1932–1937) required a median rise of 260 percent for nineteen major items, and median fulfillment was 68 percent and increase 76 percent; the Third Plan (1937–1942) was, of course, interrupted by mobilization and war, and the Soviet government had become much less generous in the information it bestowed upon the world. In 1940, nine items for which a median increase of 167 percent was planned showed a median fulfillment of quotas of 67 percent, with a median increase of 3.4 percent over 1937.[145]

[144] Much of the enthusiasm and, in the earlier years, possibly most of it was a genuine mixture of socialist zeal and the old bourgeois team spirit. Some, however, had a false and nonsensical ring, like the demand of a leading politician, Krylenko, for a Five-Year Plan for chess: "We must condemn once and for all the formula 'chess for the sake of chess,' like the formula 'art for art's sake.' We must organize shock-brigades of chess players and begin the immediate realization of a Five-Year Plan for chess" (Souvarine, *Stalin*, p. 575).

[145] First Plan average increase goal for these items was 258 percent, average fulfillment 68 percent, average increase 91 percent; Second Plan, 312 percent, 73 percent, 105 percent; Third Plan to 1940, 171 percent, 64 percent, 7 percent. The averages reflect rapid progress in new industries such as motor vehicles and failures in consumers' goods.

These figures do little more than indicate that while Russia made distinct and rapid progress in a good many lines, the plans proved quite unreliable as forecasts—hence as plans. It is also evident that the breakneck pace of industrialization had to slow down. Much of the initial spurt was accounted for by fuller utilization of old plant, and to a significant degree by the introduction of new industries, such as tractors and automobiles. Once they had been well established, their rate of advance was necessarily slower. The annual average percentage rate of industrial growth indicated by Soviet data was 20.35 for the First Plan, 17.24 for the Second, 13.12 for the Third, and 10.00 for the Fourth (1946–1950).[146] Furthermore, such overall averages can conceal extreme variations in growth from one field to another and, therefore, a lack of balance which would be nothing short of disastrous in a freer society. For example, the Second Five-Year Plan reported 100 percent fulfillment for steel, rolled metal, and automobiles, but 48 percent for tractors, 57 percent for locomotives, 65 percent for petroleum, 73 percent for cement, and 83 percent for coal. Rail transport was not expanded at a rate commensurate with the new industrialization: the 58,500 kilometers of 1913 had risen to 76,500 in 1928, 86,400 in 1937, and 100,000 in 1940, a lower rate of increase than in the last decades of the Tsarist regime. As a result the roads had to be overworked.

The unbalance is more extreme from another standpoint, for the consumers were given a decreasing portion of the bigger pie baked in bigger and better ovens. Cotton goods output in 1940 was less than projected (but not produced) for 1932, and the planned figure for 1950 (the end of the Fourth Plan) was the same as that for the First. The planned quotas of woolen fabrics fell from 270,000 square meters in 1932 to 159,400 for 1950, having actually amounted to 123,000 in 1940.

[146] *Journal of Economic History,* Supp. VII, 1947, p. 170. Jasny believes Gerschenkron's index exaggerates Soviet progress by starting from underestimations of the level in 1913 and 1928. The objection appears to be well taken (N. Jasny, *The Soviet Price System,* Stanford, Cal., 1951, p. 127). The nine items under the Third Plan were pig iron, steel, rolled metal, coal, petroleum, electric power, automobiles, cotton, and woolen cloth. In addition, under the First Plan were tractors, lumber, leather footwear, and sugar (automobiles omitted). For the Second Plan, in addition to all items just mentioned, there were locomotives, passenger and freight cars, paper, cement, lumber, and soap (W. W. Leontief, Sr., "Soviet Planning: The Problem of Economic Balance," *Russian Review,* Autumn, 1946, pp. 28–29, 32).

The absolute rise in quantities produced, especially in the basic heavy industries which provide the sinews for modern war, is unquestionably impressive. But, after all, Russia is a vast, heavily populated, and in some respects richly endowed nation, and her workers have assuredly not been encouraged to relax on the job. It is consequently rather disillusioning to find that if the index number for output of all industries was roughly 445 for 1938, with 1913 = 100, a continuation of the Tsarist rate of growth would have yielded a figure of 409 by 1938, about a year and one half behind the Stalinist pace—without Five-Year Plans and industrial heroics, not to mention the social costs of tyranny.[147] This reasoning, it is true, ignores the castastrophic losses of the wars and revolution, but if, as the very successes of the First and Second Plans suggest, the Russian economy had just reached the stage where it was ready to leap ahead, there is good reason to surmise that Russian capitalism might likewise have experienced a decade or more of unprecedented growth and outstripped the Soviet mark.

It is, of course, invidious to compare formerly backward Russia with the United States, but the Stalin regime claimed that, as of 1938, Russian industrial output had risen to 45 percent of American, from less than 7 percent in 1913 and 1928. This would indeed represent remarkable progress in overtaking the enemy of socialism. In 1946, however, Stalin indicated a number of his goals for a more distant future, following a Fifth, Sixth, and Seventh Five-Year Plan. According to these long-range objectives, Russia, by 1960–1965, would produce crude oil amounting to 43.6 percent of American output, coal to 90.6 percent, pig iron to 117.8 percent, and steel to 104.7 percent—of American output in 1929![148]

[147] The figure 445 is Gerschenkron's adjusted index number, offered only as an approximation. The figure 409 results from compounding progress at the rate of 5.83 annually he gives for 1885–1913 (6.10 for 1885–1889; 8.03 for 1890–1899; 6.25 for 1907–1913; the average for 1885–1913 was held down by disorder and depression during 1900–1906) (*Journal of Economic History*, Supp. VII, 1947, pp. 156, 168).

[148] Gerschenkron, *Journal of Economic History*, Supp. VII, 1947, pp. 171–172. As Gerschenkron points out, if Russia were to progress for twelve years from 1951 at the 10 percent annual rate of industrial growth planned for 1946–1950, "the value of output should be about 180 percent of the 1937 value of output in the United States. But the production of steel in Russia would be only 117 percent of the 1937 steel output in the United States." Recognizing that as industry advances in complexity "the spread between physical out-

This hasty glance at the vaunted miracle of Russian socialist industrialization arouses increased interest in the costs. If it be argued that a miracle of industrialization is sufficient unto the pains therefrom, a rather dubious proposition, it must be said that no miracle was performed, while the pains were severe.

In the absence of foreign loans, investment had to be financed entirely at the expense of domestic consumption. Dignified by a Soviet economist as "asceticism of consumption,"[149] in plain language the policy amounted to "starve and save for the state." In 1937, for example, 25.2 percent of gross national product entered into investment (and another 7.4 percent into defense). In 1869–1878, when the American per capita national product was comparable to that of Russia in 1937, the United States allocated 18.9 percent to investment (and only 1 percent to defense)[150] The process of enforced belt tightening stopped just short of strangulation. In ordinary circumstances this could be roughly measured by dividing an index of money wages by a cost of living index, but the Soviet government is annoyingly secretive about what it calls "the best statistics in the world." Several efforts have been made to piece together a puny counterpart to the indexes of the American Bureau of Labor Statistics, and they suggest a good reason why Moscow would consider fuller price-wage information as offering aid and comfort to the enemy.[151]

For example, the following table shows five different sets of index numbers, each of which indicates the purchasing power of average wages in terms of food, and a sixth indicating their purchasing power in an overall urban worker's budget.[152]

put of basic industrial materials and the value of total industrial production" will increase, "the discrepancy is very large. . . ." And, of course, capitalist economies are hardly likely to stand still.

[149] Gordon, *Workers*, p. 346.

[150] A. Bergson, "Soviet National Income and Product in 1937," Part II, *Quarterly Journal of Economics*, August, 1950, p. 440.

[151] Russia ceased publishing a price index after 1931, and has not revealed the number of workers in the various wage groups.

[152] Column I is based on weights given in N. Filippova, "Changes in the Budget of a Worker's Family in the Year 1928 (Nov. 1927–Nov. 1928)," *Statistical Review* (Central Statistical Administration of the USSR) December 1929, p. 43; 1913 prices are from *Economic Bulletin of the Conjuncture Institute* (Moscow), June, 1922, p. 4; prices for 1928 in Filippova, *op. cit.*; for 1936 and 1939 in *Monthly Labor Review*, May, 1940, pp. 1273 ff. and May, 1941,

There are differences owing to variation in original data, weights, and base years. But all six series tell the same general story: from the standpoint of the well-being of the Russian masses, as represented by their ability to purchase food (from about half to two-thirds of typical working class expenditures), the high point of the Soviet era was at the close of NEP. Thereafter, along with collectivization and industrialization, came a decline in real wages, so that on the eve of World War II, the average Russian worker's ability to purchase food was about 40 percent lower than in 1913.

	I	II	III	IV	V	VI
	(base)	(base)	(base)	—	—	—
1913	100	100	100			
	—	—	—	(base)	(base)	(base)
1928	118		125	100	100	100
1929		154				
1932				101		
1933					52	
1936	43			49	51	
1937		68		52		57.6
1938				57		
1939	61					
1940			62.4	49		52.5

It is quite unnecessary to take such data literally, or cavil over the precise margin of error; Soviet published statistics do not afford the capitalist luxury of precision. The all-important conclusion is that, whatever else one may wish to deduce, it cannot be claimed that

pp. 1294 ff. (also July, 1947, pp. 28 ff.); for 1948 and 1949 in Kravis and Mintzes, "Food Prices in the Soviet Union," *Review of Economics and Statistics,* May, 1950, pp. 166, 167. See also budgets in *International Labor Review,* 1928, p. 659 and 1929, p. 573. Columns II and III: Peter Meyer, "The Soviet Union: a New Class Society," in Steinberg, *Verdict of Three Decades,* pp. 482–483. Column IV: Harry Schwartz, *Russia's Soviet Economy,* New York, 1950, linking the indexes of Prokopovicz, in *Russlands Volkswirtschaft unter den Sowjets,* Zurich, 1944, p. 306, and of Kravis and Mintzes, *op. cit.,* p. 167; Schwartz's figures have been converted to 1928 = 100 for easier comparability with the others here given. Column V: L. E. Hubbard, *Soviet Trade and Distribution,* London, 1938, p. 278; *Soviet Labour and Industry,* London, 1942, pp. 162 ff.; *Soviet Money and Finance,* London, 1936, pp. 331 ff. Column VI: N. Jasny, *The Soviet Economy During the Plan Era,* Stanford, Cal., 1951, p. 69. See also Solomon M. Schwarz, "The Living Standard of the Soviet Worker, 1928–1938–1948," *Modern Review,* June, 1948, pp. 272–286; A. Yugow, *Russia's Economic Front for War and Peace,* New York, 1942, pp. 204–210.

the available evidence reveals a notable improvement in the Russian worker's diet. If, however, one were to find a relative decline in the prices of clothing and other items of convenience, one might be tempted to conclude that the state of the peasantry had been the one serious blot—albeit a majority blot—on the Stalin economic record. But, as series VI suggests, this rescue does not come off. Setting 1913 average wages and the prices of boots, cotton, and woolen cloth at 100, they had risen as follows:[153]

	Wages	Boots	Cotton Cloth	Woolen Cloth
1926–1927	208	180	332	228
1937	1016	1600	1500	5950

In 1936 a Soviet average wage earner would have needed almost six weeks to earn the price of a man's suit of common quality, about three weeks to earn the price of lower grade leather shoes, and a week to be able to buy a shirt. By 1940 he would have had to work eight weeks for the suit, between three and four for the shoes, and between one and two for the shirt. There was, in addition, a more or less concealed further increase in these prices by virtue of the poor quality of the goods. The veteran Soviet foreign trade chief, Mikoyan, complained

Are not the leaders of light industry ashamed when, for instance, a woman cannot wear a good pair of stockings without people saying they must be imported? Why can't we produce more good stockings? Or take ties—if they are attractive, people say they must be imported.[154]

But that is not all; high prices and low quality are minor hazards to the Soviet consumer compared to the plain unavailability of goods. And such was the case for many items from time to time. As the *Monthly Labor Review* commented in 1941 about clothing prices, "No comparison can be made with the price level of January 1, 1940, since on that date practically no clothing was available for sale." In 1933, small independent industry having been success-

[153] Hubbard, *Trade and Distribution*, p. 270; *Labour and Industry*, p. 164; Gordon, *Workers*, p. 140. Soviet data on prices of consumers' goods are even scarcer than the goods themselves. The 1913 wool cloth price is based on the price to peasants as given by Gordon, and adjusted by the urban-rural ratio for cotton cloth.

[154] Quoted by Schwartz, *Soviet Economy*, p. 253.

fully liquidated, the new-era government knitting plants produced 1.6 pair of hose per person, 1 piece of underwear per 5.5 persons, 1 pair of gloves per 10 persons.[155]

If ill fed and ill clothed, perhaps the Russian workers might at least have been well housed, for the archaically organized construction industry of the capitalist world must have been an inviting target for socialist production. But all the Soviet government was able to accomplish was a selective redistribution of misery. The homes of aristocrats and bourgeois were confiscated and filled to overflowing. Only when a new Soviet wealthy class arose was the distinction between human housing and a rabbit warren restored, for a few. Soviet law provided that the minimum floor space per person should be 6 square meters, or about 8' × 8'. In Moscow, in 1928, there were actually 4.3 square meters per person, or about 7' × 6'6". This was to rise by 1937, at the close of the Second Five-Year Plan, whose housing program had been hailed as "unprecedented in the history of man," to about 4.4 square meters or 7' × 6'9".

> Only in our country, where the proletariat holds the power in its own hands, has there ever evolved such a grandiose housing program. Workers' home construction in the Soviet Union has attained proportions never seen in history and it grows bigger with each day. During the First Five Year Plan we built 27 million square meters, and during the Second we will build 65 million meters.

This "unprecedented achievement" would have amounted, had it occurred, to the annual provision of the equivalent of about 380,000 very tiny apartments (360 square feet), without private baths or kitchens, for a populous nation whose housing had always been less than adequate. In the large cities of Russia in 1935, not more than one family in four had more than one room to itself, and in the provincial towns not more than one in 3.7. As a postscript to the "grandiose" plans, *Pravda* reported that in the entire Soviet era up to 1937 there had been constructed 54 million square meters of living space. Of new urban housing built in 1935, "32 percent had no water supply, 38 percent had no sewage facilities, 92.7 percent had no gas supply, and 54.7 percent had no central heating."[156]

[155] May, 1941, p. 1293; Gordon, *Workers*, p. 230.
[156] Gordon, *Workers*, pp. 190, 201 ff. Quotation from the Moscow Architectural Magazine; Schwartz, *Soviet Economy*, p. 390.

The rewards to the Russian working class in terms of the first desiderata of Marxian materialism—food, clothing, and shelter—are not only utterly inadequate to justify the costs of Soviet rule but constitute a most severe indictment of it. Even more than Soviet factories and Stalin's Constitution, labor's standard of living gives the lie to boasts about the "workers' paradise."

There do remain a number of possibilities for relieving the dismal picture. Perhaps the costs of Stalinism were significantly balanced by social services and cultural advantages, by increased and more fruitful leisure and better health. Here, if anywhere, the contrast between Soviet and Tsarist eras should be most flattering to the Communists. But once again, the most that can be said is that progress has been partial, slow, and uneven, the propaganda misleading, and the losses severe.

In the early days of Bolshevik rule, the workers' movement to take over the factories was encouraged. Under the exigencies of the civil war, however, the new regime found it necessary not only to appeal for worker discipline but to employ militarized labor, and Trotsky urged that this practice be made universal. This, of course, challenged the basic function of unions as spokesmen for the rights of labor, and was bitterly opposed by men who had struggled for mere recognition before 1905 and to build a genuine, independent labor movement thereafter. Trotsky's extreme suggestion of merging the unions with the state, his argument that since the Communist Party represented the working class there was no need for the unions to be independent of the state in order to defend labor's interests, promised to erase the hard-won victories over Tsarist reaction. Lenin had to settle the dispute that arose and, in effect, gave the substance to the Party officials and to the Trotsky point of view. Strikes were explicitly condemned and tacitly prohibited; it was made abundantly clear that the unions' first duty was to spur production. But, as was so often the case, in one of those flashes of clarity which indicted his own actions, Lenin gave the theoretical victory to the trade unionists proper.

Ours is a workers' government with a bureaucratic twist. Our present government is such that the proletariat, organized to the last man, must protect itself against it. And we must use the workers' organizations for the protection of the workers against their government.

The unions, he held, must not only defend their members' interests, but strive to improve material conditions, and

. . . continually correct the mistakes and excesses of the administrative departments in so far as they are the result of bureaucratic perversion of the government apparatus. Under no circumstances is it advisable to demand of the trade union members a specific political view point. In this matter just as on the question of religion the trade unions must be nonpartisan.

This, of course, was quite forgotten by his successor, having been ignored in practice by himself. During what has since been called the golden age of Soviet labor unions, the NEP, they acted as junior partners of the Communist Party and its state. Nevertheless, they had a certain degree of autonomy, serving as collective bargaining agencies with respect to wages and working conditions, and as administrators of welfare activities. The plant union leader was a member of the factory's high command of three, the *troika*, along with the manager and plant Communist chairman. But with the beginning of the First Five-Year Plan, the "merging" of the unions with the state was made complete, and Trotskyism again triumphed in the hands of Stalin. The prime function of the unions became the organization of shock brigades of especially zealous workers devoting extra hours and effort to speeding up production. The unions ceased to act as collective bargaining agencies, since wages, output quotas, and work organization became the exclusive concern of management (and, of course, of the Communist Party). The unions became no more than one of the state's means of maintaining labor discipline, and Lenin's theoretical point of view was thoroughly rejected. In the words of one of the new labor leaders who came to the fore after the purge of the Tomsky group, the workers

. . . must not defend themselves against their government. That is absolutely wrong. That is supplanting the administrative organs. That is Left opportunistic perversion, the annihilation of individual authority and interference in the administrative departments. It is imperative that it be liquidated.[157]

And so, indeed, it was. The unions still acted as the workers' welfare agencies, but here too they were so completely subjected to the

[157] Gordon, *Workers*, pp. 88, 89, 104.

state and Party that even their limited usefulness to the rulers was diminished by the deepening apathy of the union members. As this was an unplanned reaction, it had to be corrected. Furthermore, Stalin found additional reason for re-creating at least the appearances of a democratic and vigorous union movement in the switch of Russian foreign policy in the mid-1930's from truculent isolation to coöperation with the League of Nations and the Western democracies. Still more reason was to be found at home, for "liberalization" in the unions would have the same effect as the Constitution of 1936, mitigating the blow of the purges that were getting under way and helping to convince the people that "life is better." In 1935, therefore, the regime began railing against evils in the unions of which it had been aware for some time, and for most of which it was directly responsible. It was suddenly discovered that there had been no elections of union officials in several years, that the members took no interest in their organizations, and that union and welfare funds had been misappropriated. The blame for these sins was properly ascribed to bureaucratism, of which Stalin was a learned judge. Elections by secret ballot were ordered (the candidates having been nominated in open meetings controlled by the Communist Party). But no general trade-union congress met between 1932 and 1949.

The chief concern of the regime, however, remained increased labor productivity, and steps were taken to reduce the exceptionally high labor turnover, absenteeism, and poor discipline that prevailed as a result of the shortage of industrial labor, itself the consequence of forced industrialization. Early in 1939, in response to an exceptionally brazen synthetic "spontaneous" demand of the people, labor books where introduced, in which breaches of discipline, tardiness (originally up to fifteen minutes, later up to twenty, after which an absence was recorded), and reasons for dismissal were entered. Since a worker had to present his book when applying for a job, managers were given an unrivaled opportunity for both blackmail and blacklisting. The supreme penalty, dismissal, included eviction from factory housing and loss of cafeteria and factory store privileges. The art of labor control was carried a step closer to perfection by a decree of 1940 which froze workers in their jobs by making it a crime (punishable by imprisonment following a court trial) to leave a post without authorization. There was a slight loophole in the law, however, for a man could deliberately be more than twenty minutes late, incur dismissal (mandatory upon the employer in such cases), and get a chance to look for another job. This defect was soon remedied by a provision making tardiness or loitering on the job subject to disciplinary penalties imposed by management, while absenteeism was distinguished as an offense calling for trial. Another edict of 1940 authorized the transfer of technical and supervisory employees to other jobs at the discretion of the government. An order of 1943 made railroad workers subject to twenty days in jail merely at the instance of a superior, and this was extended to utilities employees and watchmen in defense industries.[158] All in all, the spirit of the Stalinist attitude toward labor was neatly summarized by the dictator's retort to Harry Hopkins, who had explained that delays in Lend-Lease deliveries had been caused by strikes in the United States: "Strikes? Don't you have police?"[159]

It should not be thought, however, that labor was entirely defenseless. The old capitalist principle of supply and demand made their scarce services valuable to plant managers, gave them a degree of security against employer caprice, and encouraged employers to wink at the labor book requirement. Furthermore, the regime was at any moment liable to turn from scathing denunciations of its toilers as "tramps and loafers" to one of its periodic moods of mollifying the masses (either was called "self-criticism"). Just as it was suddenly learned that the unions were rapidly becoming atrophied owing to "bureaucratism," it occurred to the government to attack excessive requirements of overtime, withholding of wages, and child labor, as if it had been totally unaware that these abuses—which were necessarily known to millions of Russians—existed. A storm would descend upon the heads of intermediate and lower bureaucrats, who were punished severely for following orders that were

[158] See V. Gsovski, "Elements of Soviet Labor Law," *Monthly Labor Review*, March and April, 1951. Tsarist law had permitted an employer to dismiss a worker absent without reason 3 consecutive days, or 6 days in a given month. This was maintained by the Soviet code of 1922, but changed, in 1927, to dismissal for any 3 days' absence in a month, and, in 1932, to mandatory dismissal for a single day's unexcused absence (April, p. 385).

[159] Walter Bedell Smith, *My Three Years in Moscow*, Philadelphia, 1950, p. 123.

now to be changed. Workers were encouraged to write protest letters to the papers which, if they coincided with a wave of "self-criticism," could produce tragedy for the managers.

In this way the top leadership induced a class struggle from which it alone could gain. The managerial group was dependent on the Kremlin for its authority over labor as, indeed, for its very existence. It was itself effectively disciplined by the threat of "self-criticism," and the repeated milder variety of purges became a normal Soviet process of promotion and demotion, restricting the upward avenues to those who were politically most reliable. Labor, otherwise largely at the mercy of management, could look only to Stalin for relief. When difficulties arose, the blame could be pinned, at choice and according to the swing of the pendulum between crackdown and letup, either upon the slothfulness of labor or the tyranny of management. In either event, the halo of the Kremlin remained untarnished, unless one were so careless of life as to suggest that Stalin was somehow really responsible for the policies generally pursued in the Soviet Union.

It is true that Soviet workers had wider insurance coverage than Americans before 1935, for the Soviet regime was naturally quick to institute a social insurance system on the model long since established by Bismarck in Germany and Lloyd George in England, vastly expanding the hesitant beginnings in Russia under Nicholas II. But, as was so often the case, generous laws were more effective as advertising at home and abroad than in changing material conditions.

In 1928 it was provided that old age pensions should equal 44 percent of wages at retirement, age sixty. In 1938 a monthly pension of sixty rubles was ordered for workers of this age without dependents. This amounted to 21 percent of the 1938 average wage of 289 rubles. About 40 of the 60 rubles would have gone into the basic elements of a minimum diet; the remainder would have bought about half a shirt. Small wonder, then, that a good many elderly people were eager to comply with the regime's desire that they continue to work, in lower-paid jobs, with a very small pension. State old-age pensions were advertised to the workers as a free gift from their government, as if the pension fund did not come from the profits of their own labor by way of payroll deduction.

It would be tedious to go through the entire Soviet welfare program. Suffice it to say that it did constitute progress, but to a degree that was far from remarkable. Paid maternity leaves, which had started out as an ambitious sixteen weeks after the revolution, compared to six under the Tsar, eventually fell to twelve, and maternal and child care allowances were sharply reduced. In 1937, the planned capacity of the vaunted resorts, rest homes, and sanatoria was only for 9 percent of the eligible workers, so that the right of a country vacation—in barracks, at that—was the privilege of the favored, loyal few. In 1951, only 2,700,000 of about 39,000,000 workers and employees, some 7 percent, were able to spend vacations, or receive treatment at Soviet health resorts, most of them paying 30 percent of the cost. Medical services increased at a moderate rate: in 1913 there had been roughly one hospital bed per 975 persons, and one doctor per 8600; in 1938 there was one hospital bed for about 275 persons, and one doctor for 1500 (in the United States, around 1940, the figures were approximately 98 and 750, respectively). But the quality of service for the many was another matter. There were frequent press complaints about unsanitary and archaic hospital and infirmary conditions, and a "bureaucratic" attitude on the part of medical personnel. The Hippocratic oath had been modified by the peculiar nature of Stalin's love for the toiling masses, his desire to keep them toiling: the rights of physicians to prescribe hospitalization or absence from work were limited by regulation. Of course, an avalanche of "spontaneous" letters had appeared in the press demanding a drive against "invalidism."[160]

While boasting of the vast new cultural opportunities it had created, Stalinist socialism clearly was not concerned to provide the leisure in which to enjoy them. The basic work week in industry (before overtime), which had been set at five seven-hour days in 1931, was restored to six eight-hour days in 1940. The hours worked per month increased, of course, so that piecework rates had to be lowered to prevent wages from rising.

But there was another, more drastic way in which leisure was prevented from interfering with socialist production. In 1924, when NEP was beginning to hit its stride, the government boasted that

[160] Gordon, *Workers*, pp. 300 ff., 311; *Trud*, March 20, 1952, cited in U.S. Department of State, *Notes on Soviet Affairs*, January 12, 1953.

wages were so high that wives and children did not have to work. At that time there were 3.34 dependents per heavy industry worker, falling to 2.28 dependents in 1927, toward the close of NEP, and to 2.05 in 1930, as the First Five-Year Plan got under way. In the latter year, the average family of such workers consisted of 4.02 persons, so that two of the four had to work. In 1935, the average number of dependents was 1.59, and the average family 3.80, so that 2.4 members had to work.[161] This tendency for more and more members of a family to seek gainful employment helps explain how the Russian people existed on inadequate wages, and also illuminates an interesting contradiction in Bolshevik policy.

The early years of the regime, as all "forward-looking modernists" will remember, was characterized by opposition to the bourgeois tradition of the family, which Engels had shown to be derived from the twin evils, brute force and private property. Marriage and divorce were equally easy to accomplish, and abortion was legalized. The birth rate rose until the First Five-Year Plan, which called for an increase in population of about three million a year. The planned production was not forthcoming, however, and Stalin turned to bourgeois morality to get results that Communist morality had failed to achieve. In 1936, abortion was outlawed, divorce was made extremely difficult, and, following the Hitler-Mussolini pattern, bounties were provided for large families. This is a strictly economic inducement, however, merely lowering the monetary penalty for having children. A more truly socialist recognition of productivity was therefore created, a series of decorations for childbearing.[162]

How such inducements would have operated had all other things been equal is quite impossible to estimate, for low wages continued to discourage the raising of large families, and the child-care sub-

[161] Lorimer's objection to these data, taken from the Soviet labor publication, *Trud*, does not apply to the manner in which they are used here (*The Population of the Soviet Union: History and Prospects*, Geneva, 1946, p. 226). Lorimer (p. 225) reaches the following estimates of dependents per gainfully employed worker: 1926, 1.71; 1939, 1.62 or 1.41 as adjusted according to his analysis. See Gordon, *Workers*, p. 169.

[162] They ranged from the Motherhood Medal, Second Class, for the fifth child (provided it reached the age of one year), to the Order of Glory of Motherhood for the seventh, eighth, and ninth children and, with the tenth, the "Order of Mother Heroine (Gold Star), with Scroll from the Presidium of the Supreme Soviet of the USSR."

sidies were entirely inadequate. The economic pressure of low individual earnings forced women into the factories, as desired, but this had the undesired effect of adversely affecting family life, and therefore the birth rate. Of the two conflicting aims, the proletarianization of women was obviously the more easily accomplished. This was naturally hailed as their advent to full equality with men and as evidence that yet another facet of capitalist tyranny had been discarded.[163]

Whether owing to an outmoded sense of chivalry, or to a recognition of physiological difference, the old regime had limited woman labor in mines and factories, but enforcement was lax. Soviet laws were even more beneficent, in the early years, and enforcement even more lax. This was all cast aside under the banner of Stalinist equality of the sexes, however; the proportion of women among workers and employees was 27.2 percent in 1929, and rose to 35.4 percent in 1937 and 37 percent in 1940. In 1927, 8.2 percent of coal mine workers were women, by 1932 the percentage had risen to 23.7, and this progression was rather characteristic; the percentage of women in cast iron and steel mills rose from 6.9 to 23 between 1927 and 1932.[164] There is some question as to whether or not even the Soviet regime is genuinely persuaded that the influx of women into heavy industry results merely from the modernization of Russian society. The Communist Party itself had occasion to observe that to restrict industrial employment of women is "to swell the ranks of prostitution."[165]

For the masses of laborers, wages and working conditions would appear to be governed by an artificial version of the iron law of wages, but the most effective defense of the position of labor under the proletarian dictatorship has been the doctrine of the "socialized wage." It has, at least, been undoubtedly persuasive not only to a great many Russians but to sympathizers and apologists in the West. "Socialized wages," according to the Soviet regime, include

[163] It should be recognized, however, that the entry of women into professional and administrative careers greatly accelerated under the Soviet regime, probably outstripping the similar trend in capitalist countries, where the economic pressure on women was less.

[164] Lorimer, *Population of the Soviet Union,* pp. 180, 226; Gordon, *Workers,* pp. 169, 275.

[165] Gordon, *Workers,* p. 275.

free medical care, the noncontributory part of social insurance, free education, cultural services, vocational training, recreation, parks, etc. Expenditures on education, insurance and health had grown rapidly under the old regime, more than doubling between 1908 and 1913, and it would be surprising if Communism had not continued this progress. Yet, even if it be conceded that the Soviet worker receives a higher proportion of total income in "free" services (that is, paid for indirectly through taxation rather than directly out of pocket) than the Western laborer, the achievements of the regime are not impressive. At the close of NEP the Soviet government claimed that "socialized wages" amounted to 27 percent of average individual wages. They claimed 38 percent after the Second World War. A considerable part of such expenditures is of course taken for granted as society's collective contribution to living in progressive capitalist countries. To render Russian claims comparable to American conditions would require a complex calculation of how public and endowed expenditures are to be allocated to the real income of various social groups. But it is most likely that the Communists have done much less along this line than the Coalition and Labour governments in England.

In England, as in the United States, labor demands and receives "socialized wages" from the government budget, paying a good share thereof in taxes, of course. In addition, however, it demands and receives higher real individual wages, and what a howl would arise if, for example, General Motors were to argue that part of the city of Detroit's education and health expenditures should be credited as earnings of the auto workers. In Russia, as of 1948,

Close study reveals that during the last two decades practically no change has taken place in the proportion of free services in the average worker's total budget. No increase in the ratio of social services to wage income has come to offset the heavy actual decline in real wages.[166]

It should be noted, too, that the impressive figures of, for example, the Soviet education budget include the vast expenditures on propaganda and political agitation. In short, even if the principle of "socialized wages" be granted, despite the fact that it affords the best excuse since Malthus for the exploitation of labor, "socialized wages"

[166] S. M. Schwarz, "The Living Standard of the Soviet Worker, 1928–1938–1948," *Modern Review*, June, 1948, p. 283.

have been too skimpy to compensate for the even skimpier individual earnings. The Soviet worker has been at the mercy of his employer (the Soviet state), and the Soviet employer-dictatorship—a despotic "Investment Party" in our earlier terms (see p. 255)—has followed a policy of rigorous exploitation of its hired hands, limited by the workers' needs if they were to be able to meet, if only in part, the demands of management.

It should not be forgotten that the working class was the beloved of the revolution, the group in whose name and for whose sake the Bolsheviks fought, and then presumably governed. Viewing the status of this favored rank, one is led to expect an even sorrier condition for the peasantry, children of the Communist fathers only by a late marriage of convenience. The Russian peasantry had long held two ideals common among depressed agrarian groups, but which were by no means quite compatible. One was the desire of each peasant to own his own land, upon which Stolypin had based his wager. The other was an ingrained feeling that the land belonged to all and that control of the soil should be governed by need rather than property rights. This belief had been encouraged by the Social Revolutionaries. Lenin's politically successful opportunist compromise had been to recognize peasant seizure of agrarian property in fact, and public ownership of all the land in law. The underlying Marxist attitude toward agriculture called for its reorganization along the lines proved successful in industry. The small-family-run farm would have to yield to large mechanized units. But Lenin, it will be remembered, had warned against the use of force in converting the muzhiks, and Stalin echoed him.[167]

However, once Stalin, in 1928, had decided upon rapid planned industrialization, there was no alternative to compelling the peasantry to increase their deliveries of agricultural products. And there could be no better means to this end than the organization of the agrarian population into collective farms, which had the added virtue of extending the postcapitalist Marxian pattern of organization into the countryside. In 1928, therefore, Stalin announced a campaign for the voluntary formation of collective farms, *kolkhozy*, and for class war against the *kulaks*. He declared, in December, 1929:

[167] Souvarine, *Stalin*, p. 464; Deutscher, *Stalin*, p. 319.

We have passed from the policy of restricting the exploiting propensities of the kulaki to the policy of liquidating the kulaki as a class.[168]

This was correctly interpreted by the Communist Party as an order to herd the peasants into the collectives willy-nilly, and the original schedules for collectivization under the Five-Year Plan were speedily surpassed. Stalin and the ruling clique were delighted, and the goal was revised upward.

The only trouble was that the liquidation of the *kulaks* meant the deportation and, in many cases, death of the most efficient individual farmers. The compulsory "voluntary" collectivization of the rank and file muzhiks produced chaos. The zealous Communists socialized (confiscated) peasant property, down to small hand implements, and all livestock, although this exceeded the official instructions. By March, 1930, Stalin realized the process had gone too far, and wrote a celebrated article called "Dizziness from Success," in which he said that some Party officials had actually used force upon the peasants and had let their achievements carry them into deviationist heresy. Once more, the blame for excesses was pinned upon lesser functionaries, and Stalin appeared in the role of protector of the toilers from zealots.[169] A good many peasants, however, made the mistake of taking him at his word, and in two months the proportion of collectivized households in the Russian Republic had fallen from 60 to 23.4 percent. The error was quickly corrected. That voluntary collectivization was compulsory was made clear by Stalin in June, 1930, and by 1936 over 90 percent of the peasant households were safely enclosed in *kolkhozy*, covering 98 percent of the cropped plowland of Russia.[170]

[168] V. Gsovski, *Soviet Civil Law*, Ann Arbor, Mich., 1948, vol. 1, p. 709.

[169] It is not certain that this maneuver was entirely successful. Deutscher reports that an old peasant said to him: "Things were very bad in our collective farm, but have been easier since *Stalin* got over *his* dizziness from success" (*Stalin*, p. 330).

[170] Naum Jasny, *The Socialized Agriculture of the USSR: Plans and Performance*, Stanford, Cal., 1949, pp. 304 ff. The *sovkhoz*, or state farm, in which peasants worked purely as employees, was not destined to play an important part in Soviet agriculture, despite huge government investments. They were the outstanding instances of the mania for industrializing agriculture, since it was intended that each farm would specialize in a single product. Land and weather are, unfortunately, subject to wider variation even than Stalinist policy, as the government eventually discovered. In the face of facts, however assiduously

No vast social experiment has ever been conducted under more adverse circumstances than Soviet collective farming. The initial chaos of organizing the *kolkhozy* was a severe setback, and many of the city Communists who assumed the leadership of the collectives hardly knew a barn from a haystack. The peasants, confronted with the prospect of losing their property as well as their freedom, slaughtered their livestock, and in this respect Russian agriculture had not recovered at the outbreak of World War II, despite the Five-Year Plans.[171] Perhaps an even greater handicap than the regime's inability to manage the human nature of the peasant was a fundamental misconception of the potential of Russian agriculture, which the Stalinist leaders shared with most of the outside world.

The vast area of Russia, and the celebrated richness of its black-soil belt, have created a picture of an almost infinite wealth of agricultural resources, waiting only to be exploited and harnessed by scientific farming and efficient organization. But of the three principal natural factors in agriculture, quality of soil, temperature, and moisture, the Soviet Union is well endowed only with respect to the first. The Russian black-soil belt is the largest rich land area in the world, and it accounts for three-fourths of the cropped plowland of the USSR. But the success with which this soil can be exploited is limited by the other two factors, temperature and rainfall, in respect of which nature has been harsh with Russia. Only a small part of the black-soil belt lies within the area of high annual average precipitation, about 26 inches in the USSR. The overwhelming proportion receives less than 20 inches, and the greater part of this less than 16. By way of contrast, Indiana averages about 38 inches, Pennsylvania 42, and some of the Mississippi valley states range into the 50-inch zone. As for temperature, most of the Soviet Union, and almost all of its good land, lies above the 45th parallel (Minneapolis: Simferopol in the Crimea), the greater part lies above the

---

concealed, such as that "the average grain yield in sovkhozy in 1938–1940 was about 10 percent below that obtained by large producers before World War I" (p. 263), the *sovkhozy* were relegated to a back seat in Soviet planning, billions of rubles having been invested.

[171] From 1927 to 1932, the number of horses fell from 30.8 million to 19.6 million, of cattle from 66.4 million to 40.7 million, of hogs from 22.6 million to 11.6 million, of sheep and goats from 132.1 million to 52.1 million (Jasny, *Socialized Agriculture*, p. 797).

50th (Winnipeg: Kharkov), and a good deal above the 60th (Seward, Alaska: Leningrad). Russia does not receive the moderating benefit of ocean climate.

In a word, the expanse of the USSR across the map and the fame of its black soil are deceptive. While American land of moderate richness can grow fifty bushels of corn per acre, equivalent Russian soil is too cold for this crop, a chief basis of animal husbandry. Low temperatures limit the east Ukrainian and Siberian black-soil regions to the less desirable spring wheat. Nor are there ready reserves of unused arable land. In many cases submarginal lands are under cultivation, and in others huge and possibly uneconomic investment would be necessary to secure at best moderate yields. "For its tremendous population (170.5 million in 1939)," writes Jasny,

. . . the Union in 1938 harvested, aside from natural hay, only . . . 338 million acres . . . that returned yields ranking among the lowest in the world. Two acres of such land per capita is all that the USSR could boast in that year. . . . When the proper yardstick is applied, Russia can only be recognized as a country very poorly endowed with land resources.[172]

While at least part of this picture was grasped by Soviet economists in the early 1920's,[173] the lesson had been quite forgotten by the time the collectivization drive was launched. Bolshevik eyes saw only limitless horizons to an agriculture organized on socialist principles around the tractor and the combine. But, as with most rationalist visions imposed upon unruly fact, it proved a mirage. Some progress indeed occurred in certain aspects of agricultural performance, but necessarily less than in industry and—here is the crucial and tragic fact—less than required by the rise in population, which outstripped the advance of food supply and forced a Marxian regime

[172] Jasny, *Socialized Agriculture*, pp. 108, 115. "Annual temperature ranges as great as those in eastern European Russia . . . and western Asiatic Russia . . . are normal in North America only in the severe eastern part of the Canadian Prairie Provinces."

[173] For example, Bolshakov wrote in 1923: "Russia's land reserves for colonization have been reduced greatly and have also sharply deteriorated in quality. The chernozem [black soil] zone . . . must be accepted as exhausted. Since as early as 1910 or 1911 colonization has had to be directed to areas located either north or south of the chernozem zone with substantially poorer natural conditions" Jasny, *Socialized Agriculture*, p. 119).

to face Malthusian consequences that the leading capitalist nations had succeeded in escaping. Grain acreage rose by about 9 percent from NEP to the beginning of the Second World War, potato acreage by about 21 percent; sugar beet and cotton acreage rose by 46 percent and 63 percent respectively; sunflower plantings fell by 5 percent. But, owing to the nature of the land, improvement in Russian agriculture had to be not so much a matter of increasing plantings, as of increasing yields, and here the results were little short of distressing.[174]

	Yields in Quintals per Hectare	
	1909–1913	1935–1939
Grain	8	7.7
Sugar beets	155	153.4
Potatoes	76.5	79.7 (1934–8)
Sunflower seeds	7.5	5.4 (1934–8)
Cotton	11.7	14.7 (1936–9)

Only in cotton, a nonfood crop to which the regime had devoted a great deal of effort, was there any noteworthy gain. In animal husbandry, as we have seen, Russia failed to recover from the slaughter of stock that attended the collectivization drive. Nor did an improvement in quality compensate for the loss of numbers. Average slaughter weights of cattle, hogs, and sheep in 1928–1929 were 334, 103, and 44 kilograms, respectively, and in 1938 they were 275, 89, and 36. Small wonder then, that per capita meat and milk consumption fell.

	Meat (kg. per capita per year)	Milk and Milk Products (kg. per capita per year in terms of milk)
1928–1929	27.5	189
1937	14	132
1937 (goal)	28.4	169

The decline of food supply relative to population is even more dramatically illustrated by the following figures, which show prob-

[174] Jasny, *Socialized Agriculture*, pp. 790, 791. NEP averages 1926–1928. Sunflower seed oil is the principal shortening in use in Russia.

able growth to January 1, 1941, had no war preparations intervened (1928 = 100):[175]

Population	120
Hogs	110
Poultry	110–115
Cattle	85–90
Sheep, goats	100
Horses	60

And grain, as of 1939, was at 112.

The relative failure of Soviet agriculture was, of course, officially blamed on everything but the real reason, mismanagement of limited resources, and the actual question before the Stalin regime was not so much how to reform and improve, but where this Malthusian pressure should be applied. As was to be expected, the government chose to make the food producers eat less in order that industrial producers might eat somewhat more. For example:

Per Capita Meat Consumption (kg. per year)

	Urban	Percent of 1927–1928	Rural	Percent of 1927–1928
1927–1928	49.1	100	22.6	100
1937	25.5	52	8.5	38
1942 (goal)	50.0	102	20.5	88

The immediate purpose of collectivization, to provide investment and food for the industrialization program, was clearly indicated by what was called, literally, the First Commandment: the first obligation of the *kolkhozy* was to meet in full the delivery quotas set by the state. And there was a Second Commandment: having delivered unto Stalin that which is Stalin's, then lay away seed for future years. There was, presumably, no need for a Third Commandment, which might have been phrased: "Thou shalt eat what happens to be left over." The Communist Party naturally found great satisfaction in the fact that "Soviet agriculture became the one with the highest proportion of marketings in the world."[176]

There is no question that the regime would have been immensely

[175] Jasny, *Socialized Agriculture*, pp. 629, 778.
[176] Jasny, *Socialized Agriculture*, p. 35.

gratified had socialized agriculture been able to provide a better diet for both city and country people. The peasants were in fact proclaimed to have prospered magnificently: there had occurred an "immense growth of well-to-do life and culture of the *kolkhozy* and *kolkhozniki*," certified an important official in 1939. Most unfortunately for the peasants, the facts were not equal to the certification. Per capita income of rank and file peasants fell by about 20 percent in the decade 1928–1938, and prices of manufactured goods continued to rise more rapidly than prices paid the farmers. But procurement of crops remained constant, or rose, in obedience to the First Commandment, with the result that peasant food consumption was at the mercy of the weather and of the uncertainty of yields.

The Second Commandment was more difficult to enforce. Jasny estimates that 6.5 percent of *kolkhoz* members' income in the exceptional year 1937, and 9 percent in the more normal year 1938, consisted of thefts from produce belonging to the *kolkhoz*.[177] The regime took this very seriously, for robbing the state—the people as a whole in legal theory—was regarded as a far more serious crime than murder. As a result, guards were assigned to the barns, and even the fields.

This was a shockingly wasteful utilization of manpower, but it was rather characteristic of *kolkhoz* inefficiency. Labor alone was cheap. As a Soviet journalist had once observed, "We are not in the habit of worrying about people. Rather we feel that of that bounty —people—we have more than enough."[178] The most original and highly special crop of Soviet agriculture was bureaucrats and supervisory workers. For the sake of efficiency and control, tractors and combines were operated by Machine Tractor Stations, but it hardly appears that a saving of labor resulted.[179]

The operational unit of the MTS is a brigade built around a few tractors. The brigade personnel includes a brigadier, his assistant, fuel controller, guard, cook, and possibly another general worker in addition to the machine operators. Each tractor is served by two drivers, two to four

[177] Jasny, *Socialized Agriculture*, pp. 75, 76, 693.
[178] Gordon, *Workers*, p. 326.
[179] Originally owned by the collective farms, and then by a coöperative organization, tractors and combines as well as other agricultural implements were made state property in 1934.

assistants (hitchmen), and sometimes another man with a horse and wagon.[180]

Nor was wasteful employment restricted to the mechanical side of agriculture. One dairy *sovkhoz* in the Moscow region, in 1939, had 18 administrative and supervisory persons directing the efforts of 73 milkmaids, barn workers, and transport workers who managed the efforts of 147 cows. The *sovkhoz* as a whole had 680 permanent and seasonal employees concerned with 970 cows operating on a farm of about 1400 acres. "A manager of a *kolkhoz* dairy with twenty or more cows does no manual work." Eventually, in 1946, there was ordered a weeding out of "un-needed and invented jobs in *kolkhozy* in which rascals and idlers who avoid productive work conceal themselves."[181] As a result, 600,000 persons were cut from *kolkhoz* overhead. But it was not merely their desire to avoid hard work that had brought them to their desks. Centralized planning and control demanded close supervision. The failings of bureaucratic management tend to be met with the creation of more bureaus. Very little discretion is permitted to the *kolkhoz,* or its manager. Acreage and production quotas are laid down in Moscow, and filtered to individual collective farms through lower echelons of officialdom. Increasingly detailed regulation and accounting were the necessary consequence. Piecework had been the normal basis of earnings almost from the beginning of collectivization, and when, in 1941, a system of premiums was instituted, a further bureaucratic inflation took place. The official Soviet spokesman on the subject declared:

In 1942 all kolkhozy are to apply the law regarding premiums for kolkhozniki, which is a powerful means of raising the productivity of kolkhoz labor. For this it is necessary that the squads and brigades be firmly organized, that the work of each kolkhoznik be strictly counted, and that the harvests of the brigades and squads be ascertained separately.[182]

The old problem of collective systems, finding effective incentives for work, had produced bureaucratic overhead which reduced ef-

---

[180] Jasny, *Socialized Agriculture,* p. 283.
[181] Jasny, *Socialized Agriculture,* pp. 333, 424, 437.
[182] Quoted, Jasny, *Socialized Agriculture,* p. 409.

ficiency, which required further individual incentives, which required more bureaucracy, etc.

Collectivization not only failed to revolutionize Russian food supply, but brought about one of the most sweeping and drastic counterrevolutions in history: functionally and sociologically the peasants were returned to the serfdom from which they had been emancipated in 1861.

The serfs of old Russia had to put in three days a week on the lord's land under the worst degree of servile status; in actual fact, however, many were no better than full-time slaves. But many others did have opportunities to acquire property and become fully independent. Whatever its shortcomings, the emancipation program of Alexander II succeeded in eliminating serfdom as the organizing principle of agrarian society, and subsequent developments, especially the Stolypin reform, advanced the peasantry toward the status of completely independent farmers. On the eve of the First World War, 85–90 percent of cropped plowland was in peasant hands, and large landlords accounted for only 12 percent of grain production and 5–6 percent of livestock. To be sure, much of the peasant land remained subject to communal regulation, from which Stolypin had desired to liberate the energies of the abler peasants. But even within the structure of the economically inefficient peasant-controlled commune, the individual peasant was free to be as vigorous or as indolent a farmer as he chose. He was always certain of one thing however: he had first call on what he produced. If the prewar peasant was, by and large, extremely poor, he was at least as free as his poverty permitted him to be. A generation later, the collective farmer was equally poor and was more of a serf, practically speaking, than his grandfather had been.

The fact that the peasants' share of *kolkhoz* income had the lowest priority drove the *kolkhozniki* to devote their greatest efforts to the small plots they were allowed to own and work as individuals. Despite the fact that individual household lands were generally limited to from about 0.6 to 1.2 acres, and stock holdings to one cow and one sow with young,[183] the peasants' own production amounted, in 1937, to about 21.5 percent of Russian gross agricultural output.

[183] Also ten sheep and/or goats; unlimited poultry and rabbits; twenty beehives.

Here seemed to lie a challenge to the Stalinist system that could not be ignored. In 1939 a decree set forth minimum numbers of days to be worked for the *kolkhoz*. But such measures, characteristic of serf-labor subsistence agriculture, were apparently insufficient to raise *kolkhoz* deliveries and an additional direct attack was made against the peasants' individual efforts, the pressure being greatest in meat and dairy product deliveries. Despite a successful campaign to increase collective herds at the expense of individually owned stock, members were required to provide meat whether or not they owned animals, and milk whether or not the one cow permitted to them was producing. Penalties for nonfulfillment were extremely severe. Jasny remarks: "No private usurer would dream of gathering his due twice and putting the debtor in jail as well."[184]

With agricultural productivity rising so slowly relative to need, and under Stalin's authoritative—

. . . assumption that there is a kolkhoz economy . . . for the satisfaction of social needs . . . a small individual economy . . . for the satisfaction of the personal needs of the kolkhozniki

—it is small wonder that the condition of the farm population remained depressed. As calculated by Jasny, total Russian income from agriculture amounted to 9.2 billion rubles in 1928, but only 10.5 billion in the exceptional year 1937, 9.5 billion in 1938, 9.7 billion in 1943.[185] The relative fixity of agricultural output, taken with rising needs of the urban population, made the scissors an enduring feature of Soviet society. Economic pressure and the bureaucratic propensities of the regime created a twentieth-century variety of serfdom. It was shorn, of course, of some of the worst abuses of the preëmancipation form, but in some respects made even more severe by the tensions and exigencies of Soviet life. There were arbitrary expulsions from collective farms, on the charge of indolence or insubordination, with all the tragedy that this entailed for a property-less muzhik household. Just as the landlords and, after emancipation, the *mir*, was responsible for providing quotas of peasants for the Tsar's army, so the *kolkhoz* was required to deliver a quota of young males for Stalin's labor force. This usually meant that the

---

[184] *Socialized Agriculture*, pp. 370, 371.
[185] *Socialized Agriculture*, pp. 32, 682.

kolkhoz chairman, like the landlord of old, made the assignments.

The original vision of a close-knit agricultural coöperative, run democratically by its members, disappeared into one of the deep ruts of Communist practice. The assembly of all collective farm members was to elect the *kolkhoz* chairman, and decide major farm policy, but the chairmen were ordinarily appointed from above and from the outside. On many farms, as the regime complained in more than one of its periodic denunciations of the practices it had established, the assemblies never met, or gathered only to apply the collective rubber stamp and to sing the praises of Stalin.

In agriculture as elsewhere, the Soviet regime had to take refuge behind "com-boasts" and "com-lies." In 1933 the method of estimating grain crops was changed from an assessment of crops actually harvested to a judgment, based on a sample, of what the harvest should be. The purpose was to discourage wasteful harvesting and theft of grain before it could be weighed. In 1942, crop estimating was strictly limited to sight appraisal only. This was called the "factual harvest," and officials were forbidden "to collect data on the threshing results in *kolkhozy*, as distorting the factual situation of the harvest."[186]

Such drastic tactics have not been necessary with respect to mechanization. The rapid increase of Soviet tractor and combine production has enabled Stalin's boast that Soviet agriculture was the most mechanized in the world to strike the unsuspecting as quite legitimate. Stalin proclaimed in 1939:

Our agriculture is . . . not only the largest-scale and most mechanized . . . but also is equipped with more modern techniques than the agriculture of any other country.

As it happens, this is false. On the eve of World War II, Russian agriculture exceeded American only in the horsepower of combines, and approached it only in numbers of tractors and combines, but America had about six times as much draft power per person engaged in agriculture as Russia. The fact that a Russian tractor averaged 4.7 times as many acres plowed as an American reveals only the general poverty of Soviet agriculture and the curious eco-

---

[186] Jasny, *Socialized Agriculture*, p. 735.

nomics of the Communist mechanization program. Mechanization is economically advantageous only when it saves high-wage labor. Its human justification is that it can release people from arduous toil. There has been relatively little saving of the pitifully low-wage Russian labor, and no reduction in the peasants' time or severity of work. "Everything," writes Jasny, "can be summed up in the saying, 'A mountain yielded a mouse.'"

At first glance, when one thinks of the huge farms and the large tractors and combines which have replaced the peasants' tiny strips, small horses, and scythes and sickles, such a conclusion seems incredible. On second thought, however, about one quarter of the total farm output in 1938 was produced in the tiny enterprises of kolkhozniki, individual peasants, and rural and city workers, with a labor productivity certainly lower than the pre-collectivization average. The kolkhozy used vast amounts of labor in their livestock enterprises, and the sovkhozy were little more effective in these. Little or no saving in labor was attained by the kolkhozy and sovkhozy in fibers, sugar beets, potatoes, and vegetables, and these crops are the ones that require large labor inputs per hectare. The gains in labor productivity were more or less confined to those attained in growing . . . wheat, rye, barley and oats, sunflower seed, and similar crops that are harvested with the combine. Under the peculiar Soviet conditions, even these gains were not very large.[187]

Rationalization did succeed in increasing the average number of work-days, and Soviet discipline strove to keep the days as long as before. But the productiveness of socialized labor was not notably increased.

Soviet labor input on the major grains and potatoes was about four times that of the United States, between three and four times as great on cotton, almost six times as great on sugar beets. Between three and four days were expended on each cow in Russia for a single day in America, and six times as many for a given quantity of milk, six and one-half times per sheep. The Soviet government did not make the wisest possible use of its farm machinery. Combines—which are very wasteful of straw, a more important commodity to Russia than America—were used in areas of unstable weather. This made it necessary often to dry combine-harvested

[187] *Socialized Agriculture,* pp. 63, 441, 456.

grain before storing, either by the age-old hand methods or by drying machinery with which Russia is inadequately equipped. But the tractor and the combine shared with Stalin himself the status of agricultural divinities.

The spirit of collectivization is superbly summarized in a midnight conversation between Winston Churchill and Stalin, in which the former suggested that the struggle against millions of peasants must have been a greater strain to Stalin than the war itself.

"Ten millions," he said, holding up his hands. "It was fearful. Four years it lasted. It was absolutely necessary for Russia, if we were to avoid periodic famines, to plough the land with tractors. . . . When we gave tractors to the peasants they were all spoiled in a few months. After you have said all you can to a peasant he . . . answers that he does not want the Collective Farm and he would rather do without the tractors."

"These were what you call kulaks?"

"Yes," he said, . . . "It was all very bad and difficult—but necessary."

"What happened?" I asked.

"Oh, well," he said, "many of them agreed to come in with us. Some of them were given land of their own to cultivate in the province of Tomsk or the province of Irkutsk [both in Siberia] or farther north, but the great bulk were unpopular and were wiped out by their laborers. . . .

Not only have we vastly increased the food supply, but we have improved the quality of the grain beyond all measure."[188]

Here, in a few brief paragraphs, are eloquently revealed the demonic and the distortions of Stalinism. True, the basic motive is not stated—superrapid industrialization to carry out the dictator's politics and his theory of socialism in one country. But the maddening inevitability of the dictatorial process is thereafter clearly bespoken. Once the decision had been taken to industrialize, it was absolutely essential to secure higher agricultural marketings to provide food for the growing cities and, by paying the peasants low prices, to secure funds for investment in factories; at the same time, by mechanizing agriculture, labor would supposedly be released for industrial work and a class inimical to Bolshevism, the peasantry, would be reduced in strength and brought under stricter control. The machine mania and worship of large organizations that came from looking at agriculture with Marxian eyes made the *kolkhoz*

[188] *The Hinge of Fate*, Boston, 1950, p. 498.

seem an ideal step along the road to Utopia. And when the peasants, with their lack of Marxian understanding, declined to take this step, they had to be forced, for their own as well as the country's good, to be sure. Stalin may perhaps be pardoned, in explaining the sad affair to one of Communism's earliest and most redoubtable enemies, for casting his explanation in Marxian terms, and having the "unpopular" *kulaks* "wiped out by their laborers." Why, after all, speak of a family skeleton—the GPU—to an arch-imperialist? The dictator may also be forgiven, perhaps, for speaking of vastly increased food supply. He could hardly be expected to concede, to Churchill, that his collectivist fireworks had fizzled.

There is, however, a rather strong likelihood that Stalin knew the truth. Years earlier, when he was attacking the "left deviationists," Zinoviev and his coterie, he had shown a good deal of understanding of the basic and ineluctable dilemma.

In manufacturing industry . . . we, who have to live upon the means we can heap up here at home, must . . . devote our resources only to those enterprises which are absolutely indispensable at the moment under consideration. . . . Of course we can double the sums allotted to furnishing agricultural credits; but if we were to do this, we would not have the necessary reserves for the financing of industry. . . . We might devote double the present sum to the development of industry. But this would bring about an unduly rapid tempo in the development of industry. . . . We might greatly increase exports, without paying heed to any other of the main constituents of our economic life. We might do this regardless of the condition of the home market. The consequence of such a policy would inevitably be to produce great complications in the towns, owing to an enormous increase in the prices of agricultural produce, this meaning a decline in real wages and a sort of artificially organized famine with all its disastrous consequences.[189]

And yet industrial investment was more than doubled, agricultural exports actually increased in the famine year, and the city folk did not quite starve. Stalin's ingenious solution was to take his resources from the hides of the recalcitrant peasantry, and the "artificially organized famine" resulted in the death of about 5½ million persons, mostly muzhiks. And, despite collectivization and mechanization, in 1946, about three-fifths of the 30 million Soviet wage and

[189] Stalin, *Leninism,* New York, 1928, pp. 385–386.

salary earners worked after hours on subsistence allotments—a far cry from postcapitalist division of labor.[190]

The benefits of collectivization went to the government and, in a sense, to the urban population in the form of assured subsistence. But the *kolkhozy* bore far closer resemblance to the military colonies established by Arakcheev under Alexander I, where serf-soldiers were to farm and train more efficiently for the service of the Tsar, than to pastoral Utopias. Even social equality had been sacrificed to the steel god with a Fordson motor. Equality of income, or condition, was not required by the Marxian definition of socialism, but the Soviet agrarian system, while destroying the supposedly rich *kulaks,* had established a new and stricter stratification, a new order of classes.

The degree of stratification in the agrarian population, before both the Revolution and collectivization, was greatly exaggerated by the Stalin regime. In respect of income as well as status (owner, owner and renter, tenant, hired hand, etc.) there was a strong tendency toward equality at a low level. The Stolypin reform, after all, had not the opportunity to work itself out.

Before World War I, Russia had been a land of large estates and small peasant farms. The share of the latter had been gaining rapidly,[191] and the Revolution naturally accentuated this process. A survey of the rural economy in 1927 showed that 6.3 percent of the peasant households had less than one-quarter acre of land, that 77.2 percent had between one-quarter and sixteen acres, and 16.5

[190] Grain exports were 0.4 million tons of a total production of 73.9 million tons in 1927–1928; 1.4 million of a total of 64.5 million in 1932; averaged 1.3 million of a total of 69.5 million in 1933–1934 to 1936–1937 (Jasny, *Socialized Agriculture,* p. 794; S. M. Schwarz, in *Modern Review,* June, 1948, p. 286).

[191]

	Privately Owned Land		
	1862	1905	1911
Nobles and officials	89%	51%	44%
Peasant individuals and coöperatives	6%	25%	31%

In addition, of course, there was the allotment land, held by the peasant communes, which exceeded the area of privately owned land by about one-third. A further large area, estimated at about 20 percent of the allotment land, was leased by peasants from noble or other owners at the beginning of World War I. Peasant holdings were, for the most part, very small—about 15–20 acres is Jasny's estimated average—although some were of estate size. See *Socialized Agriculture,* pp. 143 ff.

percent had over sixteen acres. Only 3.9 percent of the peasant households were classed by the Soviet regime as "entrepreneur" or *kulak*.[192] In a word, there was substantial equality in poverty, although some peasant families were improving their condition through superior effort or fortune.

The picture after collectivization was rather different, as a class of "wage *kulaks*" had come into being. Even some of the small number of uncollectivized peasants, who had to pay higher taxes and were discriminated against in other ways, were better off than many *kolkhoz* members, owing to the contradictory and irrational aspects of the *kolkhoz* system: despite the law against middlemen, free peasants were able to earn money as market agents for *kolkhozniki*. Wage differentiation in the collectives gave the advantage to farm administrators, with the result that able-bodied peasants tried for the all too numerous desk jobs. In some farms this had the fantastic consequence of a field-labor shortage, which the *kolkhoz* met by hiring outside hands at higher rates than the ordinary members could receive. Of far greater importance, however, was a new class stratification, both as to function and income; administrators and tractor drivers were constituted an agrarian elite. "The former kulaki," writes Jasny,

. . . actually the more energetic, hard-working peasants, are now replaced by the army of chairmen of the kolkhozy, tractor drivers, combine operators, and the like. These workers both number and earn relatively more than did the kulaki. The increase was particularly large in the number of persons with incomes several times that of an ordinary kolkhoz peasant. The directors, assistant directors (those representing the political police and others), and high officials of the MTS and sovkhozy, including the trained technicians, add up to quite a number. The computations . . . indicate that *the incomes of the rank-and-file peasants were below the average by only 3 percent before collectivization and by about 15 percent around 1938.*[193]

[192] These tycoons owned means of production valued at more than 1,600 rubles (about $800 at the time, according to Jasny) and leased equipment or hired labor for over 50 days a year; or owned more than 800 rubles worth of equipment and hired labor more than 75 days a year; or had means of production worth over 400 rubles and hired labor more than 150 days a year (*Socialized Agriculture*, pp. 161 ff.).

[193] *Socialized Agriculture*, pp. 75, 702; see also pp. 285 ff., 400 ff., 695. Italics added.

Restratification was neither an incidental phenomenon nor confined to the countryside. Since the state or its agencies and hence, theoretically, the people owned all productive property, Stalinists were able to declare with strict Marxian consistency that Soviet society was classless.[194] But the Marxian conception of classes is neither uniquely nor eternally valid. As capitalism has developed, income, rather than ownership or nonownership, has increasingly become the most important criterion for drawing class lines. The Soviet economic program, especially the hothouse industrialization, had in fact created a class system based, as in modern capitalism, on wide variations in income attaching to different social functions.

The most important difference between the Stalinist and capitalist class structures lay in the intimate relationship between class status and participation in state or Communist Party activity. All paths to advancement converged when a high level was reached into the narrow and strictly policed road of government and Party. In Russia, in sharp distinction to the United States, high real incomes and high political positions were uniformly linked. This is not to say that only state and Party officialdom had a chance for wealth in Russia. Soviet artists, writers, musicians, etc., were very much favored. But however comfortably they lived, they were a distinctly subservient group, and their artistic prominence and comfort were dependent on political favor. Nor could it be said that, for example, non-Party plant managers belonged to the lower order; their position was similar to that of non-Party artists, although at a lower income level than the most prominent of these. As it took shape in the 1930's and 1940's, the Soviet class structure comprised a ruling and privileged class, enjoying the power, prestige, and the best in living that Russia had to offer; a middle class, including the intelligentsia, the lower echelons of the bureaucracy, business management, white-collar employees, especially successful workers; and the lower class, the

[194] The Soviet regime, to be sure, did not consistently proclaim the arrival of a classless society, for a number of very good reasons. In Marxian terms, this would suggest a higher state of productivity than had been achieved, or even foreseen. It would invite renewed attention to the failure of the state to wither away. Lastly, it would have been too blatant a denial of evident fact. Stalin and his aides therefore usually argued that the Soviet Union had accomplished a unique harmony among three classes, intellectuals, workers, and peasants—workers by brain and workers by hand in industry and agriculture.

overwhelming majority, the toiling masses in field and factory, for whose sake the Revolution was carried out and whose condition is reflected by the depressing statistics of Soviet life.

None of this was foreshadowed or intended in the early days of the regime. Then the leaders were moved by the emotional equalitarianism that runs so deep in all brands of socialist thinking. They were influenced by the need for outbidding the Mensheviks and Social Revolutionaries. They were compelled, above all, by the simple equalitarianism of the workers, to whom equality of condition was perhaps the best index of progress toward socialism. Equalization consequently exceeded the limits of common sense, although, to be sure, there were always wage distinctions. Equalitarianism dominated until 1921, when a system of seventeen grades was introduced, from apprentices at the lowest to managerial and technical personnel at the higher ranks. The salary of the seventeenth grade was eight times as large as that of the lowest.[195] Lenin laid down the rule that government officials, and all Communist Party members, were to be paid no more than the highest category of workers. Equalitarianism came to the fore again in 1927 in part as a Communist response to the relative prosperity of NEP. With collectivization and the Five-Year Plans, however, the tendency toward equality of incomes was doomed, seemingly forever. A fatal weakness had been working against the Soviet experiment from the very beginning, the inevitable contradiction, as the Marxists call it, that had to develop when socialism, the Utopia of plenty, was introduced in a condition of chaotic poverty. Political wages were more decisive than money wages, real income became a variant of political status. During war communism, when wages had to be paid in kind to be meaningful, loyal followers had first call. During the periods of general rationing, 1930–1935 and the war and postwar years 1941–1947, favored employments and political status had favored, restricted stores. Since even goods on the ration list were scarce, to say nothing of "luxuries," the right to purchase at a shop which actually stocked them was the only catalyst which could turn money wages into real income. The unprivileged, on the other hand, had to supplement inadequate or unavailable rations in so-

[195] Alexander Baykov, *The Development of the Soviet Economic System*, New York, 1947, p. 145.

called commercial stores and free markets, where prices, at times, ranged as high as five and fifteen times, respectively, the regular prices.

The link between political and economic privilege was accordingly being forged even in the earliest days of vague equalitarianism, strengthened by the heightened attractiveness of material goods in a condition of extreme scarcity. But the real formation of the Soviet class structure awaited the completion of Stalin's political victory and the purges. For the highest class was destined to consist mostly of intellectuals—paper workers—and this group, which is always the source of really dangerous organized opposition, Stalin regarded as untrustworthy. In the early days of Bolshevik rule, it was inevitable that the old Tsarist intelligentsia should first be cast down and then restored to positions of command, as Lenin discovered that Marxian conviction was no substitute for education and training. Sympathy for the Soviet experiment, the desire to eat, and the Cheka kept them sufficiently docile. During the NEP the intelligentsia had its greatest and freest day under Communism. Starting in 1928, however, Stalin aimed his guns at the intellectual-technician group: the old "bourgeois intelligentsia" was accused of deliberate "wrecking" of Soviet plant and plans. This lasted until 1931, when Stalin announced, "Even the confirmed wreckers of yesterday are beginning to coöperate with the working class"—that is, the government. But they were the obvious source for Communist opposition recruits. Hence, and still in 1931, new accusations of "wrecking" came forth, including "infecting cattle in collectives with plague germs and the Siberian anthrax, spreading meningitis among horses," and other wondrous accomplishments. In a word, they were accused of modernized witchcraft. The official mind was not fully decided during the years of the great purges, 1936–1938, although the intelligentsia provided a good share of the victims and most of the actors for the show trials. In 1939, however, Stalin decided that the war against the intelligentsia had become infected with some sort of "dizziness from success." Reiterating his inspiring slogan of 1935, "Cadres [skilled leaders] decided everything," Stalin pointed out that, together with the dissolution of the old, "a new Soviet intelligentsia, closely bound to the people, was . . . created."[196] And

[196] D. J. Dallin, *The Real Soviet Russia*, New Haven, 1944, p. 120.

he called off his dogs. While the beginning of World War II saw a moderate renewal of terror for the purpose of insuring loyalty, the reliability and respectability of the intelligentsia had been certified by the dictator, and since the purges their privileged position had been strengthened and enhanced.

The road to the upper class was relatively easy of access through the 1930's. The Communist Party and its youth organization, the Komsomol, were the natural channel, and the mushrooming educational system was turning out potential leaders for the party to develop. Another avenue developed as a by-product of productivity incentives in industry. This was the celebrated Stakhanov movement, named for a coal miner who, in 1935, cut fourteen times as much coal as the official norm. Stakhanovism was in part simple rationalization of work methods, following long-established practices of division of labor in capitalist countries.[197] In part it was the speed-up so bitterly hated by union labor in the capitalist world, since ordinary norms would be advanced toward the Stakhanov record-breaking achievements.[198] In part, Stakhanovism was merely the Soviet materialist equivalent of Paul Bunyan and his ox. But the approved Stakhanovite could earn as much as almost thirteen times the average wage, and one heroine of labor was able to report, "I bought myself cream-colored slippers for 180 rubles, a crepe de chine dress for 200 rubles and a coat for 700 rubles."[199] This was in 1936 when the average monthly wage was 238 rubles.

That the ordinary worker often regarded the Stakhanovite as a

[197] Stakhanov's own startling discovery was that if he concentrated on coal cutting while his assistants attended to preparation and removal, he could accomplish a great deal more than usual. Most Stakhanovite efforts, and their companion "socialist competitions" between producing teams, were preceded by practice, careful stocking of parts and materials, and then herculean speed-up for the shift during which the record was to be made—very similar to American efforts in track and field sports, and proving just about as much. Some Stakhanovite records were truly astonishing, even so. One miner split off 981 tons in a shift, 9 times faster than the great Stakhanov and 58 times as much as the average German miner. For some strange reason, the German coal mines continued to be more efficient than the Soviet, however.

[198] Marx himself had pointed to the dirty trick of British capitalist exploiters, inducing superior workers to lead the rest to higher outputs.

[199] Gordon, *Workers*, pp. 173 ff.; see Merle Fainsod, "The Komsomols—A Study of Youth Under Dictatorship," *American Political Science Review*, March, 1951, pp. 18 ff.

scab is attested to by the fact that a number of them were murdered, and the machines of others were sabotaged. But the Stakhanovite movement was a way for the ambitious worker to rise toward the upper class, and many Stakhanovites, including the originator himself, gravitated toward the less arduous jobs of the paper workers.

It must be said that the differential in favor of paper work over manual labor appears to be greater in the Soviet Union than under advanced, unionized capitalism. In 1934, technical staff in large-scale industry averaged 380 rubles a month, when the national average wage was 155. In 1933 chief mine engineers received up to 1500 rubles a month, when the national average was 131. After the Second World War, in 1948, when the average monthly wage was about 600 rubles, college teachers received between 4000 and 5000, the heads of research institutes 8000, members of the Academy of Sciences 5000 by virtue of their membership (so that an Academician who directed a research institute would get 13,000). Regular wage scales could be raised by as much as 50 percent by personal negotiation, approved by high officials, for outstanding experts. In addition there were bonuses, prizes, royalties, etc., with Stalin Prize winners receiving as much as 200,000 tax-exempt rubles, "at least 100 times as much as the annual income of the lowest paid Soviet workers." The wage ratio between highest- and lowest-paid *workers* has been variously calculated as 28:1 during the First Five-Year Plan (and with a pattern essentially like that of American industry before the First World War), and "50:1 or even higher" after World War II.[200] Considering money income alone—and by-passing the question whether Soviet bond issues at high rates of interest, exempt from income and inheritance taxes, tend further to exaggerate inequalities—Max Eastman's conclusion, over a decade ago, seems justified: "A large proportion of the capitalists of America could profitably change places with them [the Soviet upper class], *if the general level of wealth in the two countries were equal.*"[201]

But, in a country where all roads to advancement become politi-

[200] Schwartz, *Soviet Economy*, pp. 466–467 (see also pp. 457 ff.); G. Bienstock, S. M. Schwarz, and A. Yugow, *Management in Russian Industry and Agriculture*, London, 1944, pp. 91 ff.; A. Bergson, *The Structure of Soviet Wages*, Cambridge, 1944, pp. 120 ff.

[201] *Stalin's Russia and the Crisis in Socialism*, New York, 1940, p. 45. His italics.

cal, money earnings tell only part of the story about real income. A good deal of the high standard of living of the ruling and privileged class comes to them as perquisites of office. "As a rule, a successful manager or chief engineer enjoys personal use of a car and chauffeur; free family vacations in a rest home, including transportation; or perhaps a factory apartment or cottage—of special value in a country with an acute housing shortage." A high officer of the automobile industry had "a fine home with two servants, two official cars at his disposal, and a Packard of his own bought in America." At the top of the ladder luxury abounded: villas built to order, furnished with non-Marxian museum pieces, staffed at state expense; vacation palaces, rare foods flown in on demand, private railroad cars. How important is it that the salary may actually be moderate, perhaps only twenty or twenty-five times the average! For Kremlin occupants there are private physicians, a model hospital, special stores. And for the wealthy lacking sufficient perquisites of office, money can buy a house and car. Domestic servants are plentiful and inexpensive in Russia, and let the American bourgeois housewife eying her all-electric kitchen remember that one husky Katya, working a fourteen-hour day, demands even less effort from her mistress than the latest shining gadget.[202]

A class, however, is not constituted by differences in income and privilege alone. It calls for a certain degree of continuity, of transmission of status from generation to generation. This, surely, was neither intended by Marxism nor required by any exigencies of Soviet economics. And the Soviet educational system, perhaps the proudest boast of the regime, should have been a guarantee of adequate class fluidity. Illiteracy was wiped out, thousands of new schools were built, thousands of new teachers were trained. Elementary education was, at least in theory, universal.[203] The higher

[202] D. J. Dallin, *The New Soviet Empire*, New Haven, 1951, pp. 139 ff.

[203] In education, too, Soviet achievements have been vastly exaggerated, both in themselves and by comparison with the Tsarist regime. Rather fortunately, education had been one of the few areas where local initiative had been given some latitude under the empire, and the *zemstva* had made it their chief concern. After the Revolution of 1905, the central government was slowly brought around and, had war and revolution not intervened, universal compulsory elementary education would have been established by about 1925. Illiteracy was declining, although the rate of progress appeared slow because no great effort was made to educate the older generations. In 1914, however, 92 percent of

branches were permeated by the Bolshevik conception of democracy, an inequality favoring the working class. In 1930, for example, minimum quotas for admission of children of workers and/or peasants ranged from 50 percent for art schools to 70 percent for higher technical schools and 75 percent for higher agricultural schools.[204]

But this proletarian favoritism did not long endure. The percentage of ex-manual workers and their children in all higher institutions fell from a peak of 50.3 in 1933 to 33.9 in 1938; the percentage of such proletarian students in higher institutions training for industry fell from 61.2 in 1934 to 43.5 in 1938, while the percentage of salaried employees, specialists, and their children—upper and middle class—rose from 31.1 in 1934 to 42.2 in 1938. It was merely in recognition and furtherance of an established trend, therefore, that the regime took a major step toward class formation in 1940. Tuition fees were established from the eighth grade up, on the official ground that "in conditions of increasing welfare, the interests of the socialist state and society demand that part of the expenses of public education be borne by the toilers themselves."[205] Fees for the eighth through tenth grades (secondary school) were set at 200 rubles a year in major cities, and 150 in the towns; college fees were 400 a year and 300; art, drama, and music schools were to charge 500 rubles. The average monthly wage in 1940 was 343

---

the urban army recruits were literate, and 68 percent of all recruits. While the Soviet government officially succeeded in stamping out illiteracy, the nature of this operation was for a time somewhat dubious, as is brought out by a Soviet complaint, in 1938: "In a number of schools there are a considerable amount of semi-literate children. Even in Moscow many children do not have a command of the Russian language" (N. S. Timasheff, *The Great Retreat*, New York, 1946, p. 212). A hint as to the nature of the literacy induced by adult education is given in Zoshchenko's delightful satire, "A Slight Mistake," in *Russia Laughs*, Boston, 1935.

Compulsory education for all children was not instituted until 1931, and then only for a four-year course. The annual rate of increase in schools and teachers had previously been lower than before the Revolution, and a rapid rise in the birth rate made the task of catching up even more difficult (N. De Basily, *Russia Under Soviet Rule*, London, 1938, pp. 452–453). "It is reported that nineteen out of every twenty children in the USSR leave school before the tenth grade. The major reason appears to be about the same as in capitalist societies: poor people need to have children earning as soon as possible" (Barrington Moore, Jr., *Soviet Politics—The Dilemma of Power*, Cambridge, 1950, p. 237).

[204] De Basily, *Russia Under Soviet Rule*, p. 451.

[205] Bienstock, Schwarz, and Yugow, *Management*, pp. 111–112; Timasheff, *Great Retreat*, p. 223.

rubles. Scholarships were available, of course, for students receiving the grade "excellent" in two-thirds of their work and "good" in the remainder. The gateway to the universities, and to positions of leadership, had not been closed to the children of the vast lower class, but it had been severely narrowed.

That fees were established for deeper reasons than lightening the state's educational bill, is borne out by another measure of the year 1940, establishing the State Labor Reserves. This decree provided for the drafting each year of between 800,000 and 1,000,000 boys aged 14–17, the 14- and 15-year-olds to attend two-year technical or railroad schools and be subject to a four-year work assignment, at any place in the country, on graduation. The 15- and 16-year olds were to attend a six months' factory training school, acquiring a lower grade of skills. In 1947 the program was extended to cover boys up to 18 and girls 15–18, and boys up to 19 were made subject to draft for key industries, such as mining, metals, petroleum. These youngsters would certainly help meet the country's need for skilled laborers; technical high schools would turn out the lower grades of technical and supervisory personnel, and the universities would prepare the "cadres" who "decide everything." In a word, the institutional arrangement was such that, if fluidity in income levels were inadequate, the lower class would be more clearly divided into skilled and unskilled laborers, the middle class would be expanded and divided into technicians and clerical workers, the upper class would strengthen a quasi-monopoly of privilege. And the labor trainees were indoctrinated with a spirit of disciplined, respectful obedience toward their betters. They wore a special uniform, and their schools operated in military fashion. A rule of 1947 prescribed:

When the instructor approaches the trainee must get up and he may not sit down until the instructor passes by or gives him permission to it. When the instructor addresses him the trainee must stand at attention. If the trainee has to pass by the instructor, he must ask permission to do so, e.g., "Allow me to pass by."[206]

The trainees were to be molded into docile workers, for whom the nagging problem of incentives would presumably have been solved

[206] Gsovski, "Elements of Soviet Labor Law," *Monthly Labor Review*, April, 1951, p. 389; Schwartz, *Soviet Economy*, p. 449.

by prior discipline. Even the educated elite were not free to choose employment, but were assigned to jobs on graduation for periods of three to five years. From the beginning, however, they entered into managerial and supervisory careers.

Perpetuation of inequality of opportunity is, furthermore, strongly suggested by a sample investigation of savings deposits in 1938: 10 percent of the depositors held two-thirds of the deposits; two-thirds of the depositors held 5 percent of the savings.[207] There is another approach to the question of class structure, however. In 1939 Molotov declared that the Soviet intelligentsia numbered almost 9,600,-000. Since this included 1,617,000 "bookkeepers, accountants," and 810,000 "engineering aides, foresters, station masters, etc.," it would seem fair to accept the judgment of a distinguished expert on Soviet affairs that higher-salaried employees and specialists numbered 2,500,000 to 3,000,000, whose top ranks numbered 800,000 to 1,000,-000.[208] With their families, therefore, the ruling and privileged class would range about 2,100,000 (1.2 percent of the population); the upper and lower middle class about 21,000,000 (12.8 percent of the population); the lower class would consequently account for about 86 percent of the population of the USSR.[209] Education-wise, 14 percent of the population provided 42.2 percent of the students in higher education, and few of these could have come from the lower strata of Molotov's "intelligentsia."[210]

---

[207] Schwartz, *Soviet Economy*, p. 435. Monetary conversion in 1947 indicated that 80 percent of the savings accounts consisted of less than 3,000 rubles, whereas in the 1938 study the high group of 10 percent comprised accounts exceeding 1,000 rubles. Since total savings deposits had almost doubled between the middle of 1941 and mid-1947, and by mid-1950 had risen to 2.5 times the 1941 level, the fact that 80 percent were below 3,000 rubles in 1947 does not indicate equalization.

[208] Bienstock, Schwarz, and Yugow, *Management*, p. 112; Timasheff, *Great Retreat*, pp. 305 ff.; Moore, *Soviet Politics*, pp. 236 ff., 280 ff.; Yugow, *Russia's Economic Front*, pp. 227 ff.; Julian Towster, *Political Power in the USSR, 1917–1947*, New York, 1948, pp. 325 ff.

[209] The workers constitute the upper stratum of the lower class, the peasants the lower. Slave laborers, of course, are a completely submerged but by no means insignificant group. See below, p. 492.

[210] Amusingly, Molotov's analysis seems to have been based on the 1937 census, suppressed because its results were below the anticipations (Gordon, *Workers*, pp. 327 ff.). The total population in 1937 is stated variously to have been 154.7, 156.8, 157.5, 164.2 million. The last figure was used in the foregoing discussion, as being closest to the 1939 census figure of 170.5 million.

All of this, of course, would prove little if unrelated to political power, the dominant factor in the land of economic determinism. But the social composition of the political ruling group, the Communist Party, demonstrates that the ruling and privileged class was being drawn into a tighter, more cohesive knot. The Party was itself an oligarchy—about 2 percent of the population in 1940—and was in turn ruled by its elite. Stalin, who loved military terminology, put it this way, that the leadership of the Party was composed of

. . . three or four thousand men of the high command—the generals of our party. Then thirty to forty thousand intermediate commanders: these constitute the officers' corps of our party. And further, one hundred to one hundred fifty thousand of the leading elements of our party—these are, so to speak, the subaltern officers of the party.[211]

Until 1939, it was officially advantageous to be of proletarian origin in gaining admittance to the Party, but years earlier the proportion of actual workers had declined. In 1930, 48.6 percent of the Party members were workers; in 1934, this was true of only 9.3 percent of the delegates to the Party Congress (where the proportion of intelligentsia always exceeded that in the Party as a whole). No social breakdown has since been revealed, but in 1941 new membership in the province of Chelyabinsk (Ural region) comprised 909 workers, 399 farmers, and 3515 paper workers. And it goes without saying that the Party is well represented in positions of practical importance. In 1923, 29 percent of factory directors were members, but this had risen to about 98 percent by 1936. At the Tenth Trade Union Congress held in 1949, 72 percent were Party members or applicants for admission (only 23.5 percent of the delegates were actual workers; 43 percent were full-time union officers; 71 percent had secondary or higher education). As a result of the 1946 elections of the Soviet parliament, 84.4 percent of the members of the Soviet of the Union and 77.4 percent of those of the Soviet of Nationalities were Party members.[212]

---

[211] Dallin, *Real Soviet Russia*, p. 226.
[212] Moore, *Soviet Politics*, p. 258; Isaac Deutscher, *Soviet Trade Unions: Their Place in Soviet Labour Policy*, London, 1950, pp. 128–129; Merle Fainsod, "Postwar Role of the Communist Party," *The Soviet Union Since World War II*, Annals of the American Academy of Political and Social Science, May, 1949, p. 21.

In a word, the Communist Party ran Russia, the paper workers ran the Party, and Stalin and his clique ran the paper workers. Wealth, education, power, and prestige were being concentrated in one small group, and the eternal factor of family influence would weave the thread into an even tighter fabric. Of equal importance was the fact that Stalin had effectively eliminated the elective principle from Soviet and Communist Party life. From the Soviet parliament and leading Party committees down to union and collective farm chairmanships, elections, when and where they occurred, were merely open ratifications of candidates selected from above. The periodic complaints that democracy was being ignored in elections to soviets and representative and governing committees of all sorts only served as proof of the appointive process, and appointments were made increasingly from the class of paper workers. The actually administering bureaucracy, of course, was not even elective in theory.

There was even a tendency to go beyond class to the formation of caste—a strictly hereditary grouping—most evident in the army. The old revolutionary democracy of ranks was discarded in 1935, when "comrade commander" was replaced with the formal ranks of the Tsarist army. The chest of a Soviet field marshal came to look like a padded display rack for medals. Pay and privilege differentials were much greater in the Russian than the American army. But the crowning step, which came after the restoration of hereditary Cossack formations and of Guard regiments, was the establishment in 1943 of special military academies, named after the imperial Marshal Suvorov,[213] for the sons of fallen Russian soldiers, and with the sons of army officers given preference in admission. Perhaps it is not too fanciful to perceive a tendency of social history in what may have been an idyllic love affair: the reported marriage of Svetlana, Stalin's daughter, to the son of Lazar Kaganovich, Stalin's brother-in-law.[214]

---

[213] A. V. Suvorov, 1729–1800, was probably the greatest of all Russian military commanders. Among his feats was driving the French revolutionary army out of Italy and then withdrawing through the Alps (1798–1799). An earlier, important domestic success was his defeat of the rebellion of Pugachev in 1774, which most properly made him eligible as a proletarian hero a century and a half later.

[214] *Time*, July 23, 1951, p. 18. Svetlana was the daughter of Stalin's second wife; Lazar Kaganovich the brother of Stalin's third wife.

Of course, under the Marxian definition of classes in terms of legal ownership of productive property, the most that could properly be said was that the basis for new classes had been established. But if the rigorously limited Marxian conception be discarded as begging reality, then Soviet Russia has classes. That they are, in fact, more clearly drawn than in advanced capitalist nations, arouses the impression that in one respect after another Russian society has been coming increasingly and tragically to resemble the structure of Peter the Great: a service caste has been taking shape. The degree of rigidity should not be exaggerated, however. Limitation of access to the higher level, reinforced by a constitutional guarantee of untaxed inheritance of personal property, did not go to the absolute extent practiced in Oriental countries. There were no untouchables, no true priestly, scholarly, or warrior caste. But it was manifestly far easier for the son of an officer to become an officer, for the child of educated parents to receive higher education, for a well-to-do youngster to win a well-paying position, than for the son or daughter of the ordinary worker or peasant. If class rigidity did not go to Oriental or even medieval European extremes, it did nevertheless appear to be more intense than in progressive capitalist areas. The least that can be said is that opportunity was more equal in the Midwestern and Pacific Coast states of America, where free education had been furthest developed. And there is reason to suspect that if published Soviet social statistics were as abundant as American, the opportunities of the lower class as a whole in Russia would be comparable to those of the lowest groups in the least advanced areas of the United States. The latter, indeed, would have greater cause for hope, for their condition is universally conceded to be the shame of their nation. The Russians, on the contrary, were required to relax in the assurance that a perfection of social justice had been achieved.

III. *The Nature and Prospects of Stalinism*

The retrograde character of so much that occurred under Stalin has given support to the view that old Russia has risen from its ashes to stand anew, only wearing a Marxian rather than a Tsarist cloak. This view appears, in the end, to be a dangerous oversimplification, but its attractiveness is easy to understand. Stalin achieved control to which the Tsars could only aspire, and the hope for Western, liberal reform, always latent under the old regime, is consequently weaker than in centuries. Serfdom has reappeared, in a collectivized form; a service caste has begun to take shape; the overwhelming majority are held to a subsistence standard of living; initiative and control are remarkably centralized.

Moreover, one of the saddest instances of retrogression has been the revival of Great Russian nationalism.[215] It had long been the special pride of the Soviet Union that it alone had been able to solve the problem of nationalism. Here, if nowhere else, the ideal might have been expected to triumph, for it was Stalin, at Lenin's behest, who in 1913 worked out the Bolshevik theory of nationalities. In essence this doctrine called for the sublimation of the explosive sentiment of nationalism by restricting its expression to the cultural level, and there giving it every encouragement. Political nationalism was regarded as proper for oppressed or subject peoples, but as improper for ruling peoples, including the Great Russians. In a characteristic vein, Lenin once wrote to Stalin: "As soon as I have got rid of this damned bad tooth I will start a life-and-death struggle against Great Russian chauvinism. I will devour it with all my sound teeth." Lenin was quite prepared to use force against weaker national groups to Bolshevize them, but thereafter he did expect to rely to a large degree on local talent.

But political autonomy had become a mockery even before Lenin's death, with the crushing of the Bashkir republic and with Stalin's forcible assimilation of his native Georgia. As Lenin had observed, "a Russified non-Russian always shoots beyond the mark in his true-Russian moods."[216] Cultural autonomy, however, continued to be the policy of the Soviet regime. National theaters and universities, a press and literature, in Ukrainian, or Tartar, or Chechen-Ingush, or Kalmyk, were fostered. In some cases an alphabet was created in order to transform native dialect into a literary tongue. This wine eventually turned to vinegar. The very nature of the Soviet regime and the exigencies of planning and police control called for centralized management from Moscow.

[215] "Great Russian" refers to the largest ethnic Russian group, as distinct from the White Russians of the Minsk region and the Little Russians or Ukrainians.
[216] Shub, *Lenin*, p. 373; Dallin, *New Soviet Empire*, pp. 107, 108.

And, when individual intellectual autonomy was itself everywhere frowned upon, cultural autonomy could mean little more than the right to translate the unitary truth from the original Russian into a lesser language.

The failure of the Soviet answer to the problem of nationalism became apparent during the Second World War, when the Chechen-Ingush, Kalmyk, Volga German, and Crimean Tartar Autonomous Republics were dissolved, and their populations transported wholesale to distant regions because of disloyalty, real or suspected, to the Kremlin.[217] A natural counterpart to the oppression of lesser nationalities was a sharp revival of Great Russian nationalism. During the Second World War, Tsarist heroes were restored to their pedestals, and the war fought in the name of beloved Russia, rather than socialism. The new Soviet anthem which replaced the *Internationale* in 1943 opens with the proposition that "Great Russia has forever consolidated the inviolable union of free republics."[218] In 1945, Stalin toasted the Great Russians as the leading people of the country—quite true, of course, but a sharp break with Bolshevik tradition. One hesitates to speak of high-water marks in connection with Stalinist trends, but it is difficult to conceive of their surpassing the Russomania that followed victory over Hitler. It was discovered that Russians had invented practically everything worth inventing. Popov invented radio, Lodygin the electric light, another penicillin, a fourth steel girders, a fifth the airplane. Even baseball was not spared Russian paternity.

This explosion of nationalist bombast was not merely the whim of the "Russified non-Russian," Stalin. There was more than a grain of truth to Stalin's observation that "the confidence of the *Russian* people in the *Soviet* government proved to be the decisive force which insured" victory over Germany.[219] In other words, he saw the key to victory in the association of Russian nationalism with Soviet patriot-

[217] If, as Stalin is reported to have said, the Ukraine and White Russia had to be given independent membership in the United Nations to appease their national opinion, and not just to gain two rather meaningless additional votes in the Assembly, it would further support the suggestion that folk songs and translations of *Pravda* were not enough to satisfy a desire for genuine national self-expression.

[218] Dallin, *New Soviet Empire*, pp. 104, 105.

[219] Dallin, *New Soviet Empire*, p. 105. Italics added.

ism. The revival of Russian nationalism was in part an effort to consolidate that relationship. Coupled with perfervid attacks on the West, it was a defensive assertion of Russian, and consequently Soviet, superiority, an effort to destroy the old Russian admiration for the progressive West, enhanced by the war and by the observations of Russian soldiers in Europe. At the same time it actually assisted Russian-Soviet imperialism by making it easier to assert, at least in the initial stages of expansion, that Russia had abandoned world revolution along with the Comintern (1943) for a self-sufficient nationalism. Lastly, the campaign of nationalism undoubtedly responded to a genuine popular demand.

But it is precisely this that mystifies the Westerner—the patriotism of the Russians, their magnificent struggle against Germany—if the economic and social data can be trusted in their revelation of meager successes and gigantic failures. The apparent paradox of World War II, the heroic combat of a presumably miserable people, results from forgetfulness, and from a gloss. The same miserable people fought superbly under Alexander I and Nicholas II, and the final triumph over Hitler has diverted attention from prior events that are extremely revealing. The Kremlin told the truth at the outbreak of war, even at the risk of undermining the doctrine of its infallibility, when Molotov glumly admitted that his government had been double-crossed by the Nazis. It was several weeks later that Stalin himself, on July 3, 1941, finally came through with the explanation of the Nazi-Bolshevik pact of 1939, which would retouch the picture of infallibility: "We secured our country peace for a year and a half and the opportunity of preparing its forces."[220] Actually, however, this was an even more damaging admission of incompetence than an outright confession that Russia had been swindled, for Russian preparations did not prevent the initial German thrust from being completely successful.

The Russian recovery was equally remarkable, however. Having traded space and lives for time, the Soviet forces first held and then drove the enemy back. It is unquestionable that the people rallied around their government, but there was no alternative, no matter how dissatisfied they were with Stalinist rule. As in his factional struggles, Stalin profited from the simple fact of his incumbency in

[220] *The Great Patriotic War of the Soviet Union*, New York, 1945, p. 11.

office. His government constituted the only possible marshaling center for Russian resistance and survival, for organizing the hatred aroused by the outrageous behavior of the German invaders. And his government, unlike the Tsar's, successfully provisioned the fighting armies, which was important not only at the front, but in boosting morale behind the lines. And for once the dictator met the people part way. The old Bolshevik war horses, Voroshilov and Budenny, were retired to pasture, and new commanders were allowed to rise to the top. Political commissars with the fighting forces lost their power to veto or even supersede the orders of commanders. Police state control was relaxed, and the people were allowed to become conscious of their own strength and initiative. Allied material aid was extremely important. The Soviet regime did an effective job of relocating industries, and organizing guerrilla warfare. The very low standard of living of the Russians was in itself a tremendous wartime asset, since it enabled the government immediately to concentrate resources on the war effort to a degree impossible in the West. Above all, however, the Russian people rose in wrath and fury. And they fought not only for the sake of vengeance, but with hope, for there seems to have been a feeling that victory would consolidate the wartime gains in moderation of tyranny, that Stalin might at last be willing and able to relax his dictatorship once the Nazi menace had been overthrown.

Never was there a hope more forlorn. Even before the Russians entered Berlin the Communist Party began to reaffirm its control by restoring the authority of its political officers in the army. In 1946 Stalin attributed victory not so much to Great Russian valor (and help from abroad) as to "our Soviet order, our state, our government, and our Communist Party," and declared the war had proved that

. . . the Soviet social order has shown itself to be more vigorous and stable than the non-Soviet social order, that the Soviet social order is a better form of social organization than any non-Soviet social order.[221]

Great Russian and Soviet nationalism were thereafter extravagantly combined, but the heroic past was relegated to the shadows, and the

[221] G. S. Counts and N. Lodge, *The Country of the Blind,* Boston, 1949, p. 59.

Communist Party and Leninism-Stalinism once more received the spotlight. The weaving of the postwar Iron Curtain got under way with a concentrated effort to repatriate Russian laborers and prisoners in German hands, subjecting them to a political decontamination treatment before they were released to their homes. The military heroes about whom the country had rallied with voluntary enthusiasm were no longer publicized.[222] World tension, which constituted the best theoretical justification for perpetuating the dictatorship, was heightened by Soviet foreign policy, and the degree of tension was even exaggerated for domestic consumption. Thus it could be repeated that Soviet Russia, alone in a hostile world save for such accretions as could be won by the Red Army and the Communist parties, had to see to its defenses, first among which was the iron spirited Soviet state. The dictatorship remained necessary for survival. Only now it was the most democratic country in the world, and there was no talk of "asceticism of consumption," but of ever-increasing material welfare which outstripped the achievements of capitalism.

The surprising thing, indeed, is how little change the Second World War brought about in Soviet internal conditions and policies. The old pattern was reproduced, the use of old remedies for old problems. Russia's war losses were enormous. The receipt of German reparations and the "expropriations" of enemy and satellite properties still left the major task of reconstruction and development for Russian energies. The Fourth Five-Year Plan, announced in 1946, accordingly set goals for 1950 which required not only the complete restoration of devastated areas but a moderate increase in their output above 1940, and a vast rise in the output of newer industrial centers, particularly the Ural region, whose development had been hastened by the war. Great success was recorded for basic industrial commodities, such as coal, oil, steel, and electricity, all of which met or exceeded 1950 goals. Tractor and motor vehicle production rose to about 275 percent of 1940, although it fell short of its goal. But the production of cotton cloth was not only below plan

---

[222] The outstanding Russian commander, Marshal Zhukov, conqueror of Berlin, was sent to a minor command in the Crimea, and new, revised accounts of the capture of Berlin omitted his name. He returned to the light of publicity in the summer of 1951.

but below 1940; the same held true for leather shoes, revealing an absolute decline in the Russian standard of clothing.[223] Housing, of course, had been very severely affected by war destruction and the postponement of new buildings and maintenance work. The goal of the Fourth Five-Year Plan for new construction and restoration was declared to have been exceeded by about 7 percent, for a total of under a billion square feet.[224] But one room per family remained the norm: in Leningrad in 1950 the average was twelve persons per apartment, in Moscow per capita area dropped from 47 square feet in 1937 to 38 square feet in 1950. Quality of both materials and construction was, if anything, poorer than before the war.

In announcing the success of the Fourth Five-Year Plan, Vice-Premier Marshal Bulganin indicated that the Russian people would have much more food than in 1940. If this were so it could be explained only by efficient milking of the satellites, for Soviet agricultural production fell short of the plan. Grain production rose in 1950 to 124 million metric tons, as against 119 million in 1940, but was still 3 million short of the goal. The numbers of horses, cattle, sheep, and goats remained not only below plan but below 1940 and 1916. There were in 1950 a third fewer hogs than in 1940, although more than in 1916. A real advance was registered only with respect to sugar beets and cotton.

The relative moderation of the goals of the Fourth Five-Year Plan and the continued heavy emphasis upon producers' rather than consumers' goods did not mean that the Soviet regime was abandoning all hope of realizing its boasts about a more plentiful life. There were vast new resources—those of the satellite states of eastern Europe—to be integrated into the Soviet national plan, and for a time, indeed, it appeared that a new pattern was developing in which Poland, Czechoslovakia, and the rest would provide consumers' goods against Russian raw materials, at a rate of exchange favorable to the Russians. But, whether owing to a desire to increase war potential still further, or for a greater degree of uniformity throughout the new Soviet empire, the satellite economies too began

[223] This was partly relieved by imports from the satellites.

[224] But Jasny writes, "Data for new housing in Moscow . . . indicate that the goal of the fourth FYP was less than 50 percent fulfilled" ("A Close-Up of the Soviet Fourth Five-Year Plan," *Quarterly Journal of Economics,* May, 1952, p. 166.

to stress heavy industry, and their standards of living sank toward the Soviet level.[225]

The satellites aside, however, there was evidence that the Soviet regime had determined to tackle its basic difficulties—as it saw them: more manpower was required for industry and more food was needed. Two great schemes were undertaken with a sense of urgency and a touch of gigantomania that recalled the days of the First Five-Year Plan and collectivization. The prewar emphasis on individual output in the collective farms was reversed, along with the preference for the smaller work squad to the brigade. More important (and surprising, in view of earlier experience with the *sovkhozy*) was a campaign to amalgamate collective farms into larger units. This started in the spring of 1950, and by the end of the year the number of collective farms had fallen from 252,000 to 123,000 and the average *kolkhoz* had risen from some 80 families working 1200 acres to about 200 families working 2500 acres or more. Many advantages were claimed for this reform: it would enable the more efficient use of more machinery on larger-scale farm enterprises; it would make possible economies in labor and even more in administrative overhead, thus releasing workers for industry. An added, and unquestionably valid reason, was that it would greatly enhance Communist Party control over the countryside. Where before Party members had been scattered among many small *kolkhozy*, in the enlarged communities it would be much easier to establish strong ruling cells. Furthermore, since the new huge farms required highly skilled management, the government could easily erase a slight twinge of conscience over the lack of *kolkhoz* democracy, for since the farmers lacked the requisite training, it became necessary to provide agronomists through normal Party and state channels.

Marxian doctrine endowed the reform with a greater promise for the future, the full industrialization of agriculture. It was accordingly decided that the small villages would, like the *kolkhozy*, be

[225] For material on postwar Soviet economic policy and results see Harry Schwartz, *Russia's Postwar Economy*, Syracuse, 1947; *Soviet Economy*, chap. 25 and elsewhere; and articles in the *New York Times*, especially August 6, 1950, October 24, 1950, November 19, 1950, January 3, 1951, April 22, 1951, November 10 and 15, 1951; *The Economist*, February 24, March 3, March 10, April 7, and October 20, 1951.

amalgamated into large agrotowns. The farmer, like the factory hand, would live in the city and go to his field or barn like any other worker to his bench. A Party handbook explained:

The agrogorods are a new and admirable phenomenon of rural construction such as history never knew until our day. The creation of these towns is an important step toward destruction of the contrast between town and country.

The Utopianism lingering just beneath the Marxian surface came to the fore with a lyrical picture of the future:

Two thousand beautiful homes along asphalted streets and avenues with lawns. Two thousand two-, three- and four-storey houses with electricity, radio, water supplies and bathrooms. A central square with a statue of Stalin. Next to each house a fruit garden.

This was less lush than Fourier's phalanstery but, under the immediate economic circumstances, no more feasible (save, perhaps, for the statue of Stalin). One obvious trouble with the scheme was that it implied the end of the peasants' individual holdings, for which unplanted apartment house orchards in unbuilt cities were an unattractive substitute. Then, of course, the resources with which to build these towns were utterly lacking. The government soon retreated. What remained of the vast project was the original administrative reform: the amalgamation of collective farms with its attendant benefits of greater centralization of authority and Communist Party control.[226]

But the Soviet regime had also embarked upon another scheme, more material, yet more grandiose in character. Possibly recalling the discouraging estimates of land potential that had been ignored through the exhilarating 1930's, the government, in 1948, announced "Stalin's Plan for Changing Nature"—in which, to be sure, the collective farmers had their work cut out for them. To prevent drought, curb erosion, and increase soil fertility, the state proposed to build eight forest shelter belts, running over 3000 miles and covering almost 300,000 acres. The kolkhozy, with financial assistance, were to plant 14 million acres with trees. In 1950 a vast new water development program was announced, calling for 1000 miles of

[226] New York Times, October 8, 1950, August 13, 1950, March 19, 1951, April 2, 1951, April 12, 1951; The Economist, January 27, 1951.

new canals and huge new power stations, and the irrigation of about 60 million acres, much of it previously desert or waste. Should these monumental projects succeed—forestation in fifteen years and water development in less—Russian agriculture and industry would without question benefit enormously. Promising as they were, however, these schemes were not without difficulties other than those of mere scale. Trees, like other vegetation, need water; nor can they add to water supply, for they merely work to diminish evaporation and run-off of such water as is present, and will impede drying winds only over a narrow range. And too much of the shelter belt area receives less than 15 inches of annual precipitation, the minimum regarded as necessary for forest growth. The required types of soil are also lacking. Indeed, the canal and irrigation scheme, which appears to be more practicable, covers much of the same region, casting doubt upon Soviet confidence in the shelter belt project.

The technical difficulties of all these schemes for changing fundamental climate greatly illuminate Soviet social policy. For, Jasny argues, a much more promising program would be the slow enriching of the thin and acid soils of northwestern European Russia, with successful German experience as a guide. But this would require a heavy investment *in* agriculture, from the industrial sector of the Russian economy. The shelter belt project and much of the irrigation program, to the contrary, call primarily for investment *from* agriculture, through the labor of collective farmers. The latter course, whatever its natural obstacles, was in much closer harmony with Stalinist policy.[227]

At best, gigantomania postponed to a still more distant future any significant improvement in the condition of the lower classes. Dur-

[227] Schwartz, *Soviet Economy*, pp. 298 ff.; Jasny, *Socialized Agriculture*, pp. 121–122; "Soil Conservation in the USSR," Symposium, *Land Economics*, November, 1949, pp. 333–364. An amusing by-product of the Stalinist transformation of nature was the greatest of all "com-boasts," the then Foreign Minister Vyshinsky's celebrated gaff before the United Nations, when he proclaimed: "Right now we are utilizing atomic energy for our economic needs in our economic interests. We are razing mountains; we are irrigating deserts; we are cutting through the jungle and the tundra; we are spreading life, happiness, prosperity and welfare in places where the human footstep has not been seen for a thousand years." Even the Soviet government realized this whopper had to be cut down to size and issued a "corrected" version of Vyshinsky's public statement (*New York Times*, November 11 and 30, 1949).

ing the war Stalin had used time-tested incentives to spur his people on to greater efforts: quick promotions, a profusion of medals and preferential treatment for the military; rising incomes and an appeal to patriotism for civilians (the wartime 48-hour week, which became permanent, brought only 40 hours' pay, however). The latter earned too much for the Soviet economy to bear without riotous inflation. The peasants, especially, had stored up great quantities of rubles, being less prone than city people to invest in government bonds. The Soviet government met this threat with characteristic forthrightness in December, 1947. Old cash currency was canceled, to be exchanged for new at the rate of 10:1, and savings deposits at more generous rates. Excess purchasing power was thus sharply decreased, the most numerous and least favored element of the lower class, the peasantry, being squeezed hardest. At the same time rationing was abolished and prices were raised (there were several reductions later, notably in the spring of 1950 and 1952). Investment capital was once again raised by reducing consumption. Schwartz's index of earnings in terms of "food rubles," which stood at 49 for 1940 (1928 = 100), had fallen to 36 by 1948. The "standard of eating" index number (column I in table on p. 414, 1913 = 100), which stood at 61 in 1939, was 33 for 1948, and 36 for 1949. Jasny's general purchasing power index (column VI in table on p. 414, 1928 = 100), which stood at 52.5 for 1940, was 44.3 in 1948. He writes, "The consumption levels after March 1, 1950 were considerably worse than in the first half of 1939 [which he regards as the high point of the Soviet planning era, with a level over two-thirds of 1928], even if computed on an annual basis, disregarding the substantial increase in the number of hours worked."[228] The standard of living in general was brought out clearly enough by a comparison of Russian and American commodity costs calculated in terms of the hours of work required to obtain various items.[229] The disparity is tremendous.

[228] Schwartz, *Soviet Economy*, p. 461; Jasny, *Soviet Economy During the Plan Era*, p. 71.

[229] Will Lissner, *New York Times*, July 4, 1950. Russian prices used were state store prices (lowest type); American prices were Sears, Roebuck, highest quality in each category. The average Soviet wage was taken as 500 rubles monthly in 1947 and 600 in 1950. Soviet critics objected that the 1947 wage should also have been 600, but the difference is not enough to affect significantly

	USSR				USA			
	1947		1950		1947		1950	
	Hrs.	Mins.	Hrs.	Mins.	Hrs.	Mins.	Hrs.	Mins.
Soap (one bar)	1	39	0	41	0	6	0	3
Woman's cotton dress	31	51	23	0	2	22	1	57
Woman's shoes (pair)	107	30	72	0	5	32	3	30
Man's leather shoes	104	30	112	0	7	15	5	20
Man's wool suit	580	15	376	0	28	4	24	24
Woman's wool suit	252	0	176	0	12	54	11	31

A computation on the same basis of labor hours per commodity, covering most foodstuffs, reveals the food purchasing power of Russian hourly earnings to have been 24 percent of American in 1936, 13 in 1949, 14 in 1950. Russia had the poorest comparative rating among nineteen nations (including Chile, Italy, and Hungary) in each of the three years and one of the sharpest declines from pre- to postwar. Italy, her closest rival in poverty, fell from 26 percent of the American standard before the war to 24 in 1950; Russia from 24 to 14.[230]

The Soviet economic system has been called "state capitalism," since the state owns or controls all productive enterprise, makes or supervises all economic decisions. A more accurate description might be "state monopoly capitalism," since the economic position of the state is very suggestive of what would occur under capitalism if all enterprise were in the hands of one overgrown monopoly, with subsidiaries and subcontractors, but no competitors. Decisions filter down from the Politburo,[231] and its technical planning agencies through economic ministries, trusts, regional organizations, and, eventually, the individual plant. There the director, who has reigned supreme since the decline of the *troika* during the First Five-Year Plan, is responsible for meeting or exceeding the production quotas given him, although the Secretary of the organiza-

the very great gap between Russian and American purchasing power per labor hour. Revision of the 1947 estimates on the basis of a 600 ruble wage would merely diminish the degree of real price reduction between 1947 and 1950. See also *New York Times*, December 21, 1947, January 11, 1948.

[230] I. B. Kravis, "Work Time Required to Buy Food, 1937–1950," *Monthly Labor Review*, February, 1951, pp. 143 ff., 195 ff.

[231] After October, 1952, the Presidium of the Central Committee of the Communist Party combined the functions of the Political Bureau and the Organization Bureau.

tion's Communist Party cell is never without influence. While the director has received increasing authority and responsibility, the scope thereof has narrowed. Given the perpetual shortages of the Soviet economy, competition for materials has developed among plant managements desirous of fulfilling their plans at whatever cost. It became necessary, if planning were to have any meaning, to prescribe both sources of supply and markets for finished goods. Prices were set from above, calculated to yield a planned profit which accrued to the state and could be devoted in whole or part to further investment. The plant's operations were financed by the state bank, whose functions became similar to those of an American budget or audit bureau, checking on performance and plan fulfillment. The director's initiative, in a word, was restricted to securing increased efficiency. His path to promotion was overfulfillment of the plan, or major reductions in cost. In addition to all the measures of coercion at his disposal, he was enabled to use the incentive of higher earnings, for a small percentage of planned profits and a much higher proportion of surplus profits went into the Director's Fund. Of the latter, 50 percent was devoted to increasing productive capacity and workers' housing in excess of plan. The rest was to be used for employee welfare activities and for distribution as bonuses to workers the director considered deserving. Since the unions were so ineffectual in defending their members' interests, even the incentives were capable of degenerating into disciplinary measures.

Although it would be theoretically possible for profits to be planned at a sufficiently high rate to pay for all government expenditures, including investment, the Soviet state made use of taxation, especially the turnover or sales tax, and of bond issues to which subscription was voluntary only in the Stalinist meaning of the word. The income tax, which yielded only 5–6 percent of government revenues, was very moderately progressive by capitalist standards. An annual income of 2400 rubles paid 2.5 percent; an income of 6000 paid 5.2 percent; the rate remained at 13 percent on incomes in excess of 12,000 rubles.[232]

The turnover tax was employed as a method of rationing as well

[232] Schwartz, *Soviet Economy*, p. 419. There are special surtax rates for writers, artists, etc., which, writes Yugow are lower than "those applicable to persons who do not earn their living through personal efforts": 12 percent on 50,000 rubles, 25 percent on 100,000 rubles, 50 percent on 300,000 rubles and over (*Russia's Economic Front*, p. 137).

as the major revenue producer (about 60 percent of all government receipts) and afforded no trace of Western "petit bourgeois equalitarianism." The rates were highest on items of general consumption, and lower on what might be classed as luxuries In 1939, for example, the sales tax on calico was 48 percent, the rates on silk ran from 21 to 37 percent, and woolen goods were taxed at 13 percent. One quarter of the retail price of bread was sufficient to cover all costs of production and distribution; three-quarters went into the turnover tax.

Out of 108.3 billion rubles of revenue derived from the turnover tax in 1940, 73.8 billion rubles came from food products; 13.3 billion from textile products; 7 billion from petroleum products, while the remaining 13.7 billion came from the turnover tax on all other commodities.[233]

The tax on profits, second only to the sales tax as a revenue producer, was also regressive. It bore most heavily on food industries, with transportation, housing and light industries following, and heavy industry bringing up the rear. This restriction of mass consumption reflected both the shortage of goods and the high investment policy; the antiequalitarian features of Russian taxation also reflected the need of the state to provide rewards for the loyalty of the privileged and upper-middle classes. In both aspects, moreover, the supremacy of the state, and of the group that controls it, was reasserted.

Indeed, if one were to name a single principle as the most pervasive in Soviet life, it would be: The interests of the state, as conceived by its leaders, are sacrosanct. The latter word should be taken in its strict meaning. This ruling precept was evident in the economic system that established excessive inequalities; in the political system in which appointment and hierarchy replaced election from below, and which forbade any possibility of censure or recall of the Kremlin clique; in the educational system that reinforced political and economic privilege, and promoted the kind of literacy that makes useful technicians while prohibiting the learning that produces questioning minds. The principle was, of course, most clearly displayed in Soviet law, for as in any ordered society, the law is ultimately the sharpest mirror of the values, standards,

[233] Yugow, *Russia's Economic Front,* pp. 132, 133.

and abstractions (not always the realities, however) by which the society lives.

From the beginning, administrative justice—judgment, sentence, and execution of sentence without due judicial process—was dispensed by the Cheka and in its various alphabetical replacements (GPU, NKVD, MVD). Soviet, like Tsarist, law distinguished between ordinary civil and criminal actions and political offenses, providing a genuine legal and court system for the first and bureaucratic dispensation for the second. When charged with a political crime—such as counterrevolutionary conspiracy, betrayal of state secrets, lese majesty, or a hostile social viewpoint—the accused need be given no opportunity for defense. Confession was part of the bureaucratic process of conviction.

The particular severity and rigidity of Stalinism was not without its effect on ordinary law, however, overthrowing some reforms introduced under Lenin. For a number of years prior to the pure Stalinist era, Russian penology carried almost to a logical conclusion the belief that criminals (in the usual, nonpolitical sense) were to be regarded as sick and curable. This was certainly in accord with the Marxian emphasis on the determining influence of environment. But so charitable an outlook could hardly be applied to the criminal products of the Soviet society without indicting the Soviet environment. The problem was incapable of a satisfactory solution in terms of Marxian theory, especially since there were unprecedented waves of juvenile crime, and since ideologically sound workers and peasants provided the greatest proportion of common criminals. During the 1930's, the words *crime, guilt, punishment,* and *prison* returned to Soviet usage, whence the great reform had banished them. Children over twelve were made subject to adult penalties, including death, and special juvenile courts were abolished. The leaders of the reformed penology were discovered by Vyshinsky, who had been among their lesser lights, to have been "deviationists" and "wreckers."

But the Stalin regime was unable to offer a consistent explanation of its penology. On the one hand, in 1937, an official law journal condemned the "reform school" approach and asserted, "We must overcome the sugary liberalism, the compassionate attitude toward the offender." And Vyshinsky observed that "punishment cannot be reduced to education and let us not pretend that prisons are no different from schools." In 1949, on the other hand, the Soviet government, denying Western accusations of employing slave labor, insisted that Russian criminals were reëducated to a useful and dignified place in society, and that they labored under beneficent conditions—a reversion to "sugary liberalism" and the education pretense.[234]

Not that the Tsarist-Stalinist distinction between ordinary and political offenses was lost sight of even after conviction. The ordinary criminal received better treatment than political offenders, and was apt to be given lighter and more definite sentences. And, among the refinements Stalin bestowed upon Tsarist practice was an unprecedented extension of the concept of political crime. To steal, let us say, a neighbor's samovar, was theft, punishable by no more than two years in prison, following a public trial before a mixed professional and lay court, with prosecuting and defense attorneys and definite rules of procedure. To steal an identical samovar, or even the teapot, from a government establishment was as serious as stealing the winnowings of grain from the field of a *kolkhoz,* a crime against the state. "Misappropriation, embezzlement, or any kind of theft" of government property (including industrial property) was punishable by death.[235] A law of 1932 ruled that

Socialist property (state, kolkhoz and coöperative) is the basis of the Soviet social order, sanctified and inviolable. Persons making an attempt upon it must be deemed enemies of the people.

Six years earlier, Stalin had made the same point in less restrained language:

[234] They even had showplaces to prove their point, such as the town of Bolshevo, inhabited by convicts working their way back toward freedom and equality of status. The great French writer André Gide was much impressed by Bolshevo, until he learned that it was peopled by convict stool pigeons and informers as a reward for their services. (R. Crossman, ed., *The God That Failed,* New York, 1949, p. 185). On several occasions in the thirties, traces of certain prison camps were obliterated when it was thought a foreign investigating commission might arrive.

[235] In 1946 the highest penalty was reduced to twenty-five years in a forced labor camp—death drawn out—but the simple death penalty was reinstituted in 1950 for treason and subversion.

When a spy or a traitor is caught, the indignation of the people knows no bounds. It demands that he be shot. When, however, a thief operates before the eyes of all, pillaging state property, the public around merely laughs good-humoredly and claps him on the shoulder. Yet it is clear that the thief, who pillages the people's property and undermines the interests of the people's economy, is just as much a spy and a traitor, if not worse.[236]

By a simple logical extension, moreover, failure to fulfill a production norm might be construed, were it so desired, as constructive evidence of sabotage, and industrial accidents as "wrecking." Nor was it surprising that lese majesty should be regarded seriously, which made a little humor a dangerous thing. The citizen had no defense against "his" state because the state, being run by perfect leaders perfectly versed in a perfect science must be presumed to be perfect. Hence the severity of Soviet law against acts that detracted from perfection, and the political show trial whose function was to display that perfection.

Since the Soviet state was essentially bureaucratic with legislature and judiciary occupying strictly subordinate positions, the law itself displayed the unchallenged sovereignty of the administrative organs. Orders or rulings of bureaus, ministries or other agencies were binding *as law*, unless and until reversed, not by a court, but by a higher administrative agency. If such edicts conflicted with statutes or even with the Constitution, they were nonetheless binding, and either statute or Constitution would eventually be revised to correspond to administrative practice. A Soviet Constitution, Vyshinsky aptly observes (quoting Stalin) is not a document limiting and controlling future governmental action, but is rather a "formal record and legal confirmation of socialist conquests," that is, of state policy and practice. In short, the Constitution, even in Soviet law, could never inhibit the will of the Soviet rulers.[237]

The Stalinist preoccupation with power is well brought out by the nature and intent of Soviet policy toward other nations, toward the other Communist parties, toward the advancement of world socialism. In its dealings with foreign countries, friendly or hostile,

[236] Gsovski, "Elements of Soviet Labor Law," *Monthly Labor Review*, March, 1951, p. 258; Vyshinsky, *Law of the Soviet State*, pp. 647, 648.
[237] Gsovski, *Monthly Labor Review*, March, 1951, pp. 261, 262; Vyshinsky, *Law of the Soviet State*, p. 87.

the Kremlin has always behaved precisely like any other national power, seeking profitable transactions, striving to advance its own interests. Soviet foreign policy showed no trace of sentimentality and, until the end of the Second World War, little evidence of ideological influence or preference. There is, however, no parallel for Russia's dealings with the outside Communist parties. The latter had, to begin with renounced independence by accepting the Twenty-One Conditions for membership in the Third International. Purges were carried out wherever a Communist organization existed, although the anti-Stalin Communist abroad ordinarily suffered no more than expulsion from the Party.[238] Many of the most prominent foreign leaders joined the units of the weak and stunted Trotsky Fourth International, or various splinter groups which specialized in intra-Marxist recriminations. Some eventually drifted back toward democratic capitalism, some into the arms of the Catholic Church, and others, impelled by the same psychological motives that led them to accept a red dictatorship, made the relatively easy adjustment to the black, brown, or blue dictatorship of fascism. The remaining core of the Communist organizations was more rigid than ever before, hardening to the point of mental calcification, and responding to the guide wires from Moscow with the jerky and often ludicrous motions of a puppet.

One doctrine—together with self-hypnosis and, in many instances, very real self-interest—enabled foreign Communists to remain faithful to the *vozhd* through all his vagaries. It was a doctrine that played the same basic role in Stalinist Comintern policy as did the legal fiction of public ownership in Russia. This was the meticulously logical proposition that since the USSR was the home of socialism, and since world socialism depended on its success at home, the first duty of every socialist outside Russia was to defend that home, and place its interests above all others. Of course, a

[238] The arm of the GPU did nevertheless extend far beyond Russian boundaries. Prominent dissidents were very poor insurance risks. Russian rebels like the espionage expert Ignacz Reisz, Trotsky, and his son Sedov were either clearly murdered by Stalin's agents or, like General Krivitsky, "died in mysterious circumstances." Juliet Stuart Poyntz, a woman of good family who had become a high functionary in the American Communist Party, was taken for a ride that began in Manhattan's Central Park and ended in a lined grave near Hyde Park (Benjamin Gitlow, *The Whole of Their Lives*, New York, 1948, pp. 331 ff.).

devoted Sovietist could accept this reasoning and still argue that Stalin was harming Russia. Such, essentially, was the view of Trotsky and his followers after his exile. But those who were reconciled to Stalin's rule over Russia were to accept its corollary, that he knew best what was to the interest of the USSR, and therefore were prepared not only to support Russian foreign policy but to let it determine the programs of their own Communist parties.

It is not especially illuminating to say that, from the first, Soviet foreign policy and its Comintern adjunct were directed to increasing the security of the Soviet state. This objective is an important aspect of any nation's foreign policy, and the question is how security was understood, and what methods were employed in seeking it. A consideration of these questions shows that Russian policy was more stable over the years than it has often been regarded, for the following elements have been regularly present from 1918 to 1953:

While never pacifist in the sense that she believed war an evil in itself, Russia sought peace and isolation from the wars among capitalist nations which Leninism held to be inevitable. Should such wars occur, she would hope to stand aside unless and until she could profit by entering them.

Security could best be accomplished by extending the Soviet frontier westward, through Communist revolutions and/or Red Army intervention, but the latter would not be attempted if it risked involvement in general war.

Security would next best be enhanced by establishing friendly relations with other states, particularly those bordering the Soviet Union, by any of the following means that seemed most propitious at the moment, and in the following order of preference: (1) imperialist expansion; (2) coöperation or purely *tactical* alliances with existing bourgeois states; (3) pressure by non-Russian Communist parties against governments hostile to the USSR.

International organizations, such as the League of Nations, were not a good in themselves, but could be dangerous to or useful to Soviet security, depending upon circumstances.

Russia must at all times seek to divide the capitalist nations, since their unity constituted, by definition, a threat to her existence. She would therefore also stimulate dissension within each of these nations through the various Communist parties.

As a consequence of these beliefs, the Soviet leaders could at any time proclaim either of the following propositions, depending on their analysis of the existing situation in the capitalist world and on their tactical judgment. They could affirm their belief in "the peaceful coexistence of different social-political systems at a given historical stage," or revert to Lenin's judgment that

We are living not only in a state, but in a system of states, and the existence of the Soviet Republic side by side with imperialist states for a long time is unthinkable. One or the other must triumph in the end. And before that end comes, a series of frightful clashes between the Soviet Republic and the bourgeois states is inevitable.[239]

It is not too much to suggest that the foregoing principles, presuppositions and corollaries make it possible to see Soviet foreign policy as a consistent whole, not in the sense of an elaborate and devious plot, but as a set of constant and consistent objectives and as a group of attitudes by which the most appropriate means were chosen. On this basis, too, the query as to whether Soviet expansion is merely old-Russian imperialism reborn, or a Trotskyite international revolution, becomes rather meaningless. There is no more inconsistency between renewed old-Russian expansion and renewed Communist expansion than between Russia and the Soviet state. The author of "socialism in one country" explained that while "our bourgeoisie has already been liquidated and socialism has already been built in essentials," this victory could be regarded as final only "if our country were situated on an island and had not been surrounded by a number of other, capitalist, states." Final victory, Stalin went on, could be achieved

. . . only by combining a serious effort of the international proletariat with a still more serious effort of the whole of our Soviet people. It is necessary to strengthen and consolidate the international proletarian ties between the working class of the USSR and the working class of the bourgeois countries; it is necessary to organize the political aid of the working class of the bourgeois countries to the working class of our country in the event of military aggression against our country, just as to organize all kinds of help on the part of the working class of our country to the working class of the bourgeois countries.[240]

[239] Foreign Commissar Litvinov before the League of Nations, a statement repeated on many occasions. Lenin quotation from Shub, *Lenin*, p. 394.
[240] "Letter to Comrade Ivanov, February 12, 1938," reprinted in *The Strategy and Tactics of World Communism*, 80th Congress, 2d Session, H.R. Doc. 619, Supp. I, p. 151.

"Peaceful coexistence" of capitalism and Stalinism could occur from time to time, but during such periods Soviet Russia must secure herself against the next inevitable crisis.

Through 1924 or 1925, Russia attempted to extend her European borders and Bolshevik influence. These attempts all failed: the 1920 campaign in Poland, the 1923 uprising in Germany, the 1924 revolt in Estonia, and, although this is shrouded in mystery, an attempted coup in Bulgaria in 1925.[241] These defeats did not bring a halt to direct Russian efforts at expansion of territory or influence, but only a shift of attention to Asia.[242] From the beginning, the Bolsheviks had been deeply interested in Asiatic affairs, Chinese in particular, and had encouraged the Chinese Nationalist movement of Sun Yat Sen. As Lenin saw it, in a country so backward as China there was no likelihood of establishing socialism. The necessary preliminary step to socialism was the expulsion of Western imperialism and the formation of a bourgeois, democratic nationalist republic (Menshevism!). The Soviet Union showed respect and generosity toward the Chinese and finally, in 1923, Chiang Kai-Shek was sent to Moscow to arrange for Soviet aid to the Kuomintang. But in 1927 Chiang turned to the right, dismissed the Russians, and broke with the Chinese Communists. An uprising in Canton, in that year, stupidly ordered by Moscow, was vigorously repressed, and it was this defeat that called a temporary halt to Soviet efforts through violence.

Back in Europe, Russia had pursued a dual and contradictory course since even before the German Communist debacle of 1923. On the one hand, she was eager to achieve normal diplomatic and economic relations with all powers; on the other hand, the Comintern screamed for revolution and repeatedly compromised the Soviet state with abortive plans and intrigues. A similar duality existed in Communist relations with other left-wing political and labor groups. The latter were invited to form united fronts with the Communists *from above*, that is, economic and political coalitions or alliances; their members were summoned to a united front *from below*, that is, to desert their own leaders, usually socialist, and

[241] R. Fischer, *Stalin and German Communism*, Cambridge, 1948, pp. 291 ff., 456 ff.

[242] A by-product of the European failures was a lowering of the prestige of Zinoviev, head of the Comintern, which suited Stalin's domestic needs.

come under Communist command. This policy produced even less harmony with non-Communist left-wing groups than did the foreign office–Comintern duality with other nations. Like the latter, it was in large part a reflection of the domestic battle between Stalin and the "left opposition" of Zinoviev and Kamenev. International Communism, moreover, was warned not to take the "united front" too seriously:

> Comrades of the Third International: There is a movement on foot in Europe for a united front. It does not matter whether we are in favor of it or not; our tactics compel us to appear to be in favor of it; but we ask the Communist sections all over Europe to take part in the creation of the united front, not for the purpose of making it effective, but for the purpose of strengthening the Communists through direct propaganda inside the organizations taking part in the movement.[243]

Stalin's victory in the war of factions led to the purging and tightening of Communist parties abroad. As this was carried through, the "united front" line was dropped, and the socialists became "social fascists" in Stalinist lingo. While the foreign Communist parties were thus being reforged into a strictly Stalinist agency, Soviet foreign policy was even more sharply focused on securing peace for Russia, so that the Five-Year Plan might proceed unhindered. The USSR, therefore, began to negotiate nonaggression pacts with many countries, and to reiterate an oft-expressed desire for disarmament. Throughout the period from 1918 to 1934, however, the keystone of Soviet foreign policy was relations with Germany. The Kremlin regarded England, and secondarily France, as its worst enemies—the citadels of capitalist imperialism—and avowed its sympathies for the victims of Versailles, "the most shameless robber treaty," and its hatred for the League of Nations, the "Holy Alliance of the bourgeoisie for the suppression of the proletarian revolution."

Friendship between Russian and German governments had long run deep, interrupted by intense conflict. It was resumed in 1922 and reinforced by further agreements in 1925, 1926, and 1931. It was

---

[243] O'Neal and Werner, *American Communism*, p. 141.

given substance by a huge volume of trade between the two nations, by German loans and technical assistance, by Russian facilities for German military work prohibited by the Versailles treaty, by German help in developing the Red Army and Air Force. To Russia, this was not only a counterweight to Anglo-French animosity, but a highly profitable relationship with the one country on which the Bolsheviks had set their sights from the time of Lenin on. When asked, in 1931, if it were true that the Russians greatly admired America, Stalin replied:

> If one is to speak about our sympathies for any nation, or, to be more correct, for the majority of any nation, one would, of course, speak of our sympathies for the Germans. There can be no comparison between these sympathies and our feelings for the Americans.[244]

And the Russians, as Marxists, saw an additional reason to focus on Germany, for according to their doctrine the German Communist revolution was an inevitability. This last point aside, the nationalistic Germans—bourgeois, socialist, or military—found the relationship valuable for precisely the same reasons as the Russians, and balanced each step of reconciliation with the West with a corresponding tightening of bonds with the USSR.

So things might have continued for an indeterminate number of years, had not Hitler risen to power. Stalin had correctly assessed the Great Depression as a bearer of revolution for the capitalist world. But Marxian theory distorted his otherwise accurate view. No more than his wool-brained contemporaries in the west European governments did Stalin take Hitler's frankness for what it was, but deluded himself with the favorite Marxist thesis of the day, that fascism was the very last stage of decaying capitalism. There was superficial justification for it in that when some capitalists persuaded themselves their only choice was between fascism and the left, they chose the former. There was further apparent justification in the fact that fascism did prosper in the most severe depression in the history of modern capitalism, that the lower middle class were its easiest recruits and some big businessmen its financiers.

---

[244] To Emil Ludwig, quoted by Dallin, *Russia and Postwar Europe*, New Haven, 1943, p. 79.

The explanation was at least plausible, and fitted extremely well with Marxian generalized thinking.[245] And it must be said for Stalin that he followed out the logic of this theory of fascism, a course made easier for him by Communist hatred for the socialists. For, if fascism was the last phase of dying capitalism, it could not be other than transitory. A few days before Hitler became Chancellor, the Soviet attaché in Berlin told a German socialist seeking German Communist help against the Nazis, "Moscow is convinced that the road to Soviet Germany leads through Hitler."[246] A more serious enemy of Communism were therefore the moderate, well organized Social Democrats whose hold on the working class was a major obstacle to a future Communist revolt. It was accordingly the duty of the Communists to concentrate on winning the proletariat away from the socialists while, at the same time, going on record in opposition to fascism.

Such was the course resolutely followed by Germany's Communists, at Stalin's direction, unto their own destruction. Only some time after Hitler had wrecked the strongest Communist Party outside Russia, did the Soviet Union, beginning in 1934, attempt to mend her diplomatic fences and correct her Comintern mistakes, opening the most tortuous and mysterious phase of her foreign policy.

There was issued a tremendously appealing call for a popular front *from above*, a coalition against fascism of Communists, socialists and liberal democratic bourgeois groups. The old hatreds were suddenly to be submerged, the tirades and zoological epithets were to be reserved for the common enemy at the extreme right. The old slogan of French republicanism, "no enemies on the left," was successfully invoked in a new cause. Humanitarian idealism, the belief in the rights and liberty of man from which Marxism had distantly sprung, resumed its place in Communist slogans. The new tactic

[245] An alternative view was that the strength of fascism came from its appeal to the emotion of nationalism and to a fierce desire to escape from the frustrations of economic and ideological disintegration through a dynamic and strictly ordered movement. In a word, fascism was a nationalist and revolutionary response to the troubles of Western capitalist civilization, and fully antithetical to the bases on which that civilization rested.

[246] Dallin, *Russia and Postwar Europe*, pp. 61, 62.

drew a natural and favorable response from the Western world, addicted as it was to common sense and democratic coöperativeness. Under the name of the Popular Front it swept to victory in France and Spain in 1936, and even dented the hard shell of bitter anti-communism that prevailed in American labor and politics. Soviet Russia, where the working class had been spared the ravages of depression, where a new democratic Constitution was being enacted, was summoning the Western world to follow her in steadfast opposition to fascism and to war.

The Popular Front, in a word, was one facet of an adroitly polished gem of propaganda. It proclaimed the Soviet appeal to the brotherhood of man, and reinforced the Soviet appeal to the human love of peace. The Russian peace campaign of previous years had emphasized disarmament, in a manner somewhat reminiscent of the Tsarist effort of 1899, when Russia also feared the costs and risks of an arms race. Russian emphasis now switched in 1933 from disarmament to collective security, and in 1934 the Soviet Union entered the League of Nations. Having won the mantle of peace in the popular mind, the USSR turned to the practical method of pacts and alliances to erect a defense against the threat of German aggression.

From 1934 on, most of the basic facts are quite clear, but they are subject to strikingly contradictory interpretations. The Soviet government initialed an alliance with France, which the French were loath to implement. It signed nonaggression pacts with all who would sign, supported the League of Nations, and backed the legal Spanish Republican government against the German-Italian supported Franco rebellion. It proposed to support Czechoslovakia against Hitler in 1938, if France honored her alliance with the Czechs. Even after the disastrous Munich conference excluded Russia from the concert of powers, she remained loyal to the principle of collective security of nations. In the spring of 1939, after Hitler's seizure of Prague, Russia offered to enter into a firm alliance with England and France for the defense of Poland, marked next on Hitler's list. Only when this was rejected, and when the Western powers grudgingly sent an undistinguished military mission to Moscow, did the Kremlin decide that France and England were insincere and were hoping for a Russo-German war that would ruin both nations.[247] Only then did Russia turn toward Germany and negotiate the Molotov-Ribbentrop Pact that ushered in World War II.

So runs the account most favorable to the Soviets. The subsequent partition of Poland, the seizure of Latvia, Lithuania, and Esthonia, the Russian attack on Finland in the winter of 1939–1940, are all represented by this view as defensive measures necessitated by the German blitz in Poland. Stalin, it is said, understood that Hitler's rage would turn to the East, and was compelled to prepare his defense.

This account is quite plausible, and is, for the most part, in accord with generally known fact. But there are other well-known facts that do not fit at all well with this picture. An alternative interpretation is that from the moment Hitler had consolidated his power after the purge of June, 1934, Stalin determined to come to terms with him, and, even while waging the popular front and collective security campaigns, pursued a second, concealed diplomacy with contrary objectives. According to this view, Stalin's flirtations with the West were intended primarily to strengthen his hand in bargaining with Hitler and, at most, to prepare another course should Hitler prove obdurate. The purpose of intervening in Spain, as is rather well substantiated by recorded Soviet behavior, was to take over the country to increase Russian pressure on both Hitler and the West. The partition of Poland, and the Soviet seizure of the Baltic states, were merely part of the Russo-German deal.

The evidence for this interpretation consists not so much of large actions that captured headlines as of insinuations and bits of secret negotiations that have become known through the statements of informed individuals, and through Nazi documents seized by the American Army during World War II. Shortly after the Nazi assumption of power, Germany and Russia carried the same tune. Hitler announced, in 1933, "The battle with Communism in Germany is our internal affair. . . . Our diplomatic connections with other powers are not affected thereby." Litvinov declared for Russia, in September of the same year:

---

[247] This was the avowed objective of influential sectors of British and French opinion.

We of course sympathize with the sufferings of our German comrades, but we Marxists are the last who can be reproached with allowing our feelings to dictate our policy.

The whole world knows that we can and do maintain good relations with capitalist states of any regime including the Fascist. We do not interfere in the internal affairs of Germany, as we do not interfere in that of other countries, and our relations with her are conditioned not by her internal but by her external policy.[248]

This theme was repeated on many occasions thereafter by the Russians. It was Germany that tended to hold back. The German military leadership and a good many industrialists were anxious to continue their close and mutually profitable coöperation with the USSR, which had been in accord with the principles for German foreign policy laid down by Bismarck in the nineteenth century. The outstanding Nazis, on the other hand, were ideological fanatics, and for Hitler especially a good deal of emotional opposition had to be overcome in order to make a deal with the hated Bolsheviks palatable on practical grounds. There was an even more convincing reason for German hesitation, however. The longer it was possible to convince right-wing statesmen in western Europe that Germany was primarily anticommunist, the easier it would be for Hitler to carry out his plans on the Rhine, in Austria, and in Czechoslovakia, and his program for German rearmament. Until the spring of 1939, therefore, Russia was the anxious suitor, and Germany was rather coy.

The USSR began to divert trade from Germany to Great Britain and the United States, with the result that Germany took the lead in commercial negotiations and extended credits to the amount of several hundred million marks. While Russo-German commerce never returned to its high point of 1932, its fluctuations reflected Stalin's estimate that German finance capitalists would not wish to lose their Soviet customer, and would influence Hitler in the Russian direction. Simultaneously, from 1935, Stalin pursued his policy of collective security, and Hitler his program of expansion in western and central Europe and of anti-Bolshevik fulminations. Neverthe-

[248] Dallin, *Russia and Postwar Europe*, p. 102; M. Beloff, *The Foreign Policy of Soviet Russia*, vol. 1, London, 1947, p. 98.

less, late in 1936 and in the spring of 1937, there were recurrent reports of Russo-German negotiations.[249]

Shortly after the Munich agreement of September, 1938, Germany and the USSR agreed to reduce the intensity of the campaign of hate which the controlled press of each country had been waging against the other. In an important development in February, 1939, Russia agreed to sell oil exclusively to Germany and Italy. After Hitler had seized Prague, in March, 1939, in violation of the Munich pact, the USSR suggested that England and France join her in a guarantee of the borders of Poland and Rumania. The very same day, however, on April 17, 1939, the Soviet ambassador in Berlin gave the Germans to understand that Russia was still interested in an agreement with the Nazi Reich.

The distribution of needs and power between Russia and Germany had now changed. Hitler's next scheduled victim was Poland, and it was increasingly apparent that this time France and England would fight instead of appease. Germany therefore needed Russia's benevolent neutrality. Russo-German negotiations consequently got under way, ostensibly over a commercial pact, but soon ran into a Soviet demand that a political understanding be reached prior to the economic; a reversal of policy which showed the USSR was aiming not only at securing peace for herself in the probable event of a European war, but further specific advantages. Simultaneously with these Russo-German discussions, which the Kremlin held to a very, very slow pace, the USSR engaged in military and political conversations with England and France. Here Russia insisted on a military convention preceding any political agreement, obviously fearing the Western powers would leave her in the lurch after war had broken out. The Russians also demanded a free hand in the Baltic states of Latvia, Lithuania, and Esthonia, which the Westerners did not wish to concede. A second obstacle to Russian agreement with the West was the paradoxical position taken by Poland and Rumania: they were willing to accept Russian aid and guarantees, but would not permit the Red Army to enter their territory. While this was quite comprehensible in view of these nations' past relations with the USSR and their not unjustifiable fear of Bolshevi-

---

[249] Krivitsky, *In Stalin's Secret Service*, pp. 4, 14 ff.; Dallin, *Russia and Postwar Europe*, p. 108.

zation, it was an obvious block to a serious military agreement. A third obstacle may have been the drab character of the Anglo-French military mission.

The Russians skillfully dragged out negotiations with both sides. The Germans, with a deadline for war with Poland of September 1, 1939, had become the increasingly assiduous pleaders and pointed out to the Russians that England and France had little that was concrete to offer the USSR in exchange for her risks, while Germany would make a mutually profitable deal. This was obviously correct and finally, on August 23, 1939, the Soviet-Nazi pact was concluded, the go-ahead was given for World War II.[250]

The Russian choice would seem to have been based on the following factors, all of which, it will be seen, harmonize closely with the essential character of Soviet foreign and Comintern policy:

Russia did not wish to become embroiled in a general European war if she could help it. Russia hoped rather "to play, as did the United States in 1918, the role of arbiter in a Europe exhausted by a merciless war."

Should war break out, Russia would seek to profit by it, expanding Russian and Communist borders, power, and influence. Early in 1939, the head of the army's political department had stated to the Communist Party Congress that, in the event of war, "military operations must be transferred to the territory of the enemy: we must fulfill our internationalist obligations and increase the number of Soviet republics."

Russia tended to prefer Germany to the Allies. Molotov said: "It is the fear of losing world supremacy that dictates to the ruling circles of Great Britain and France the policy of fomenting war against Germany."[251]

Nazi-Soviet collaboration, then, constituted a link, rather than a break between Soviet and Comintern policy before and after World War II. From her deal with Germany, Russia secured a free hand in the Baltic region, and recovered territory lost to Rumania at the end of the First World War. That the treaty with Germany was not,

[250] See R. J. Sontag and J. S. Beddie, eds., *Nazi-Soviet Relations, 1939–1941*, New York, 1948; D. J. Dallin, *Soviet Russia's Foreign Policy, 1939–1942*, New Haven, 1942; A. Rossi, *Russo-German Alliance August 1939–June 1941*, London, 1950.

[251] General Schweisguth, quoted by G. Bonnet, *Défense de la Paix: De Washington au Quai d'Orsay*, Geneva, 1946, p. 124; Dallin, *Russia and Postwar Europe*, p. 74; *New Soviet Empire*, p. 79; P. Viereck, *Conservatism Revisited*, New York, 1949, p. 164.

as Stalin later professed, merely a device to gain time and space, is borne out by a good deal of evidence. Molotov's radio address announcing the Nazi attack in June, 1941, lamely protested:

> The attack on our country was perpetrated despite the fact that a treaty of non-aggression had been signed between the USSR and Germany and that the Soviet Government most faithfully abided by all provisions of this treaty. . . . Until the very last moment the German Government had not presented any claims to the Soviet Government. . . .[252]

Molotov was quite right. Russia had faithfully observed her political and economic obligations, as captured Nazi documents were to testify. Nor had she properly prepared for war.[253] Her army had not been fully mobilized or aligned against attack. Her economy had not been geared to war, and it was only after the German invasion that a Soviet economic plan for war was elaborated.[254] Until the very last moment Stalin continued to condemn the British and praise Germany.[255]

The very issue over which Russia and Germany fell out further supports the view that the Nazi-Soviet agreement was an integral phase of Kremlin foreign policy, rather than an expedient forced upon Stalin by Western blunders. At a conference with Hitler and Ribbentrop in November, 1940, Molotov indicated Russia wished the Balkans and the Straits as her sphere of influence and expansion. The Germans suggested Persia and India instead and, when Russia persisted in her Balkan desires, Hitler ordered his army to prepare for the attack. Obviously, the Soviet Union was seeking to take advantage of the opportunity afforded by war to create more "Soviet republics"; here was the real profit to be gained from coöperation with the Nazis. The only difficulty was that Stalin, like the

[252] *New York Times,* June 23, 1941.

[253] Stalin made two important miscalculations: he overestimated the power of the French Army and apparently expected Hitler, if he were to turn against Russia, to spend several months, in accordance with previous Nazi practice, trumping up claims which would allow for negotiation—and give warning.

[254] Deutscher, *Stalin,* pp. 457–458.

[255] There is, of course, evidence of Soviet suspicion of Germany, and of some preparation on Russia's part. On the whole, however, this would seem to reveal little more than what is already known of the leading personalities in both countries. None of them was what might be called a "trusting" type.

Tsars before him, found Germany a competitor in the Balkans. Russian actions from the time the defeat of Germany was reasonably certain were a continuation of the expansionist program of 1939–1941 and of the aggressive Balkan policy rather than of the era of the popular front and collective security; if Russia had actually desired to establish honest relations with the West between 1934 and 1939, why should she have abandoned this course just when it had at last proved profitable to her? If, on the other hand, the expansionist possibilities inherent in a Russo-German agreement had been the real objective in 1934–1939, what better time to carry them forward than at the close of World War II, when German opposition was removed and the West was anxious only to return to its peaceful bourgeois ways? Nor was the possibility of coöperation with the Germans ever completely discarded by Stalin, who personally held aloof from the "hate the Germans" campaign in which his journalists engaged. An early start was made toward renewing the old Reichswehr–Red Army coöperation, when German officers who were prisoners in Russia were formed into a political league. This step had its counterpart in Germany, for many of the military involved in the attempted assassination of Hitler in 1944 had a pro-Soviet rather than pro-Western orientation. Indeed, much of Stalin's policy after World War II can be understood in terms of his greatest hope, a Soviet Germany, and his greatest fear, a Germany securely in the Western camp.

The Soviet decision to abandon coöperation with the West was not taken only after the end of World War II, nor was it implemented in a single dramatic step. It was foreshadowed in the very first year of the Russo-German war, when Stalin first started pressing for postwar political agreements with the Western powers. Kravchenko reports that even before the tide had turned at Stalingrad, in 1942, a high Party theoretician warned an indoctrination meeting of Kremlin officials that

. . . our war partnership with the capitalist nations must not breed illusions. We must hold fast to fundamentals. There are two worlds. Now and then it is possible to throw a bridge across the gulf that divides them, as we have done in this war. But we know that the bridge must collapse sooner or later. The two worlds of capitalism and Communism cannot forever exist side by side. *Kto kovo?*—who will conquer whom?—remains the great question, now as always.[256]

All through the war the Soviet government carefully played down the importance of Allied material aid to Russia, guarding against the day when Stalin's public policy would be openly anti-Western. That Stalin tried to play with the Western powers the game he had tried to play with Hitler is indicated by the very precise division—percentages being given—of British and Russian spheres of influence in the Balkans. And, in 1945, he raised the old question of the Dardanelles and asked for a Soviet mandate over part of the Italian North African territory.

Russia had been interested in coöperation with the West only when she had deemed this necessary for her security or for her economic advancement. After World War II, neither security nor economic progress depended upon aid from the capitalist countries. Her own military power adequately guaranteed the first; a new string of Five-Year Plans and the resources of the satellites seemed to give adequate promise of the second. Marxian belief in the inevitability of capitalist economic crises and collapse undoubtedly stimulated Russian aggressiveness.

There was, moreover, a very strong affirmative reason for avoiding coöperation with the capitalist powers. The Stalin system rested in fair part on its claims to infallibility, and its assertion that Soviet socialism produced a higher degree of welfare than capitalism. The Stalin system also required rigorous control. Contact between Russians and foreigners therefore had to be kept to the barest minimum. The Iron Curtain, which began to fall during the First Five-Year Plan, was not a whim. Nor was it designed so much to keep Soviet conditions secret from foreigners as to keep foreign conditions secret from the Russian people. After World War II, the need for secrecy was greater than ever. Not only had too many Russians seen

---

[256] Victor Kravchenko, *I Chose Freedom*, New York, 1946, p. 424. Professor Barghoorn regards this account as confirmed by other evidence which has come his way, and, indeed, it certainly fits the general picture (*The Soviet Image of the United States, A Study in Distortion*, New York, 1950, p. 45). Kravchenko observes: "No properly indoctrinated Communist felt that the Party was 'lying' in professing one set of policies in public and its very opposite in private. He had no more conscience about it than a general in the field who misleads and disorients the enemy."

Europe and talked with Europeans, but too many Europeans—in the satellites—had come within the Soviet empire. There had, therefore, to be two Iron Curtains, one at the Soviet border proper, the other at the frontiers between the satellites and the world of capitalism. Had the Czechs and the other east European satellites been permitted to enter into the Marshall Plan, their economies, and consequently that of Russia herself, would have benefited. But this would necessarily have been at the expense of the sacrosanct principle of Soviet state power, for the sake of which the Iron Curtain had been created, and the Marshall Plan was therefore castigated as an American imperialist trick to gain control over Europe, and also to forestall the "inevitable" postwar depression in the United States.

The very slight possibility that Soviet imperialism might follow a more flexible and gentle course was destroyed in Yugoslavia. Russian troops had been withdrawn from that country at the close of the war, and Stalin was therefore unable to exert military pressure on its ruler, Marshal Tito, a self-made dictator. Tito began to grow restive under the burdens of close coöperation with Soviet Russia, for the logic of Stalinism, that the USSR was the first concern of *all* Communists, inevitably dictated terms of trade that were unfavorable to Yugoslavia. By 1947, the friction between Tito and the Kremlin had led Stalin to resurrect the Comintern (only formally buried in 1943) as the Cominform. In 1948, Tito was expelled from the Stalinist fraternity with the most violent imprecations of which its shamans were capable. And the Tito "heresy" continued to be a torturing sore to the Stalinists. For the first time since the crushing of the various Russian oppositions, a noted Communist official with strong public support repeatedly condemned Stalin as a deviationist from Marxism-Leninism, in the familiar Marxian language that would appeal most strongly to Communists everywhere. Tito proved, if proof were needed, that Stalinism as a world movement was incompatible not only with non-Russian nationalism, but even with the genuinely socialist interests of non-Russian Communists. It was abundantly clear that Stalinism could expand and remain in power only through the force of the Russian army.

In a word, the logic and pattern of Stalinist domestic policy— direction, control, and compulsion from above, secured by police measures and by relentless propagation of the myth of infallibility and perfection—literally necessitated the transfer of domestic policy abroad in the shape of the outward pressure of Soviet imperial frontiers, of noncoöperation with the West and of Iron Curtains, of a recasting of satellite life according to the Soviet forms. Because the other alternative would have entailed increased contact with the capitalist world and relatively greater flexibility in the domestic patterns of any nation engaging in coöperative measures with it, it was not even a real possibility for Russia. Once the Nazi attack, the external factor that had compelled a deviation from this course, had been thrown back, the Soviet Union returned to its old ways, extending them to its new territorial acquisitions.

The spirit of Russian world policy throughout the Soviet era is clearly indicated by Lenin's statement, while World War I still raged:

We are at present between two foes. If we are unable to defeat them both, we must know how to dispose of our forces in such a way that they fall out among themselves, because, as is always the case, when thieves fall out honest men come into their own; but, as soon as we are strong enough to defeat capitalism as a whole, we shall immediately take it by the scruff of the neck.

In a sense, therefore, the USSR, mightier than ever, was more vulnerable than before World War II. Then she had been protected by conflict within the capitalist world. Now, according to Marxian logic, one power, the United States, had in effect absorbed all that was not in Soviet hands, and the Soviet Union stood face to face with a mighty America that was, by Marxian definition, hostile and predatory. Said Politburo member Malenkov, in 1947, "The center of class struggle has shifted to the international arena." And, Zhdanov observed, "The principal leading force of the imperialist camp is the United States of America." Russian diplomacy, therefore, had to be directed to sowing discord between the United States and the other non-Soviet nations, and within the Soviet empire the measures for state security had to be brought to the highest possible effectiveness. That is why the ideological purge that got under way shortly after World War II was more extreme and, by Western standards, more bizarre than anything previously recorded.

This campaign for ideological rigidity and uniformity, Soviet foreign and Comintern (or Cominform) policy, the relatively minor changes in Russian domestic patterns and programs, are among the elements most helpful in reaching a judgment concerning the nature and prospects of Stalinist society. The observer will perhaps experience some slight satisfaction in turning on Stalinism the favorite Marxian tool of analysis, dialectical contradictions. Tactical lies need occasion no delay; the contradictions that do demand attention are those situations in which a policy engenders the opposite effect from that desired.

Some of these we have already had occasion to note: enforced socialization ending in the creation of a class structure more rigid, if anything, than that which the revolution had destroyed; a campaign against the small peasant landholder from which emerged a more severe form of the serfdom which had been the shame of the old empire. In both these instances the compelling motive behind measures which produced undesired (and unadmitted) results was to strengthen the power of the state, in order that the state might speed the industrial development from which it would derive further power.

The same power factor was of course evident in one of the most absurd traits of the Soviet system, one particularly ill suited to a Marxian society believing in economic determinism. This was the worship of individual heroes. Stalin was hailed as the greatest of philosophers, writers, aesthetes, scientists, warriors, and everything else. Alexis Tolstoy, one of the first Soviet millionaires, expressed his admiration, and appreciation, in the following gem of understatement:

I want to howl, roar, shriek, bawl with rapture at the thought that we are living in the days of the most glorious, one and only, incomparable Stalin! Our breath, our blood, our life—here take it, O great Stalin!

The following "poem" swept the broad Soviet land and brought its author fame and fortune:

> When Budyenny smiles,
> The ice breaks on the Don;
> When Budyenny smiles,
> The maple's bloom is on.

> When Voroshilov smiles,
> The sun begins to shine;
> When Voroshilov smiles,
> Then spring falls into line.
>
> When Stalin smiles,
> What might a poet dare?
> When Stalin smiles,
> It is beyond compare![257]

The hierarchy of heroes, it will be noted, is carefully preserved, for Stalin's smile accomplishes the greatest possible good in the immediate circumstance by stopping the poet. Such inanities, if they did not nauseate, must surely have amused the brooding "realist" in the Kremlin. They are not only uncivilized but un-Marxian, as Stalin himself indicated in a number of mildly critical comments. But they did add to the perpetual repetition of the dictator's greatness and thereby justify his power, and he assuredly did not exert himself to halt them.

Such stress on individuals was naturally limited to the oligarchy and its chosen symbols, while the ordinary man was submerged in aggregates.[258] The individual, whose total liberation is the ultimate goal of Marxism, was transformed into a cog. Marx had argued that capitalism enslaved man through "commodity fetishism"; it is much more correct to say that Stalinism has enslaved man through "production fetishism." Marxian materialism had been converted, in practice, to abstract, unmaterial generalizations. Classes and systems exist for the Stalinist, but no individual man. And, as it moves from

[257] Quoted by Alexander Barmine, *One Who Survived*, New York, 1945, p. 299. When the French writer André Gide was so moved by the hospitality he received in Russia and by what he had been shown as to wish to express his appreciation to Stalin, he was told he could not telegraph "I feel the impulse to send you . . ." but would have to say "you, leader of the workers," or "you, Lord of the people." Other excellent examples of adulation for Stalin are given by Y. Gluckstein, *Stalin's Satellites in Europe*, London, 1952, pp. 318 ff.

[258] The practice of personalization, as distinct from glorification, was not, however, restricted only to Stalin and his immediate clique. Partly as a heritage from Marxian factional squabbles, the Soviet tendency was to name ideas and movements after individuals, rather than attempt to find a few aptly descriptive words. The correct line in biology after World War II, for example, was Michurinism; zealous workers were Stakhanovites; the greatest of heresies was Trotskyism.

the specific to the general, from the concrete to the abstract, practical Marxism becomes Hegelian. Hegel has now stood Marx on his head. The legal fiction of public ownership substitutes for the reality of individual option. Freedom, which Marx seems to have envisaged as bourgeois democracy without any trace of economic exploitation, has become the Hegelian "freedom" of the society ordered from above, without the charitable influence of Christianity and monarchical tradition. In the process of removing the Western abstraction of "freedom," Stalinism has dialectically created its opposite.

The validity of this proposition is most strikingly demonstrated by the Soviet use of forced, or slave labor. Nothing is so quick to arouse the ire of Soviet spokesmen and their sympathizers as the merest mention of forced labor in Russia, for not even the ablest casuist in the Communist organization can rationalize this into an acceptable aspect of contemporary civilization. It is either denied outright, whitewashed with talk of reeducation, or parried with the classic Stalinist tactic of *tu quoque*.

Unfortunately for the millions involved, there can be little question concerning the existence, extent or nature of slave labor in the USSR. The testimony of early escaped prisoners had little influence in the Western world, conditioned as it was to disbelief in inhuman practices and in slanders against the Soviet Union. But the Nazis educated the West concerning the modern capacity for barbarism, and, instead of an occasional lucky soul who escaped to Finland, the testimony of hundreds of former inmates had become available. Among the latter were Poles imprisoned as "socially undesirable elements" after the Russian seizure of eastern Poland in 1939 and released by Soviet agreement with the wartime Polish government-in-exile, and ordinary Soviet citizens caught up in the German forced labor net who refused to return to Russia after the war. In a word, this most carefully attended part of the Iron Curtain was one of the most thoroughly breached.

This is not the place to dwell on the nature of existence in Soviet forced labor camps. Suffice it to say that inmates worked for mere subsistence, and not all succeeded in obtaining it; that they were subject to severe summary discipline without appeal; that they worked twelve or more hours a day with about three free days a month; that clothing, shelter, and work tools were as inadequate as diet; that common criminals received preferred treatment and were permitted to tyrannize over political convicts; that women prisoners were almost inevitably driven to prostitution to keep alive; that among the inmates were children twelve to fifteen years old, who were ruined for life; that sentences could be extended by administrative decision. The picture has been well drawn by many witnesses. Perhaps the best summary is that those particularly tormented sufferers who were in a position to compare Nazi and Soviet camps found little to choose between the efficient brutality of the Germans and the sloppier brutality of the Russians.[259]

Slave labor did not come into use in the early days of the Soviet regime and, indeed, it would have been unthinkable to most of the old Bolsheviks, whatever their faults, to restore the hated hard labor punishment, the *katorga,* of the Tsarist regime. The latter had grown to a peak of 32,000 inmates in the year 1912, so that this was one sphere in which the Soviet regime easily surpassed Tsarism. Increase in both supply and demand for forced labor came simultaneously, in the era of the First Five-Year Plan. When labor for industrialization proved scarce, particularly for such activities as canal building and forestry, it was found extremely practical to put prisoners on the job and then arrest people to make them eligible for such assignment. The collectivization drive and the many purges provided a bonanza of socially undesirable elements and wreckers. The mortality among prisoners was very high, however, for despite the fact that forced labor was rapidly becoming an economic as well as a punitive activity, the element of severity could never be removed. Demand, at times, threatened to outrun supply and, since the Soviet Union operated as a planned rather than a free market economy, measures were taken to increase the supply. In at least one year, 1937, it is reported, quotas for arrests were actually established.

Such problems of equilibrium economics were apparently solved, however, for the role of forced labor in the socialist economy con-

[259] See D. J. Dallin and B. L. Nicolaevsky, *Forced Labor in Soviet Russia,* New Haven, 1947; Dallin, *Real Soviet Russia,* chap. 11; American Federation of Labor, *Slave Labor in Russia,* 1949; Anonymous, *The Dark Side of the Moon,* New York, 1947; S. Mora and P. Zwierniak, *La Justice Soviétique,* Rome, 1945; J. Gliksman, *Tell the West,* New York, 1948; M. Buber, *Under Two Dictators,* New York, 1951.

tinued to grow. It was particularly suited to vast undertakings. The government explained, in 1934:

> The following should be chosen as objects of mass labor best fitted for the realization of the purposes of corrective labor; large scale industrial construction (factories, dams, blast-furnaces, railroads, etc.) . . . irrigation work; highway construction.[260]

Forced labor was particularly desirable where the work was arduous and the climate severe, so that extra attractions would have been needed to secure free workers; the Baltic–White Sea Canal and the Kolyma gold mines are two outstanding examples. Other advantages were lower cost of maintenance, since prisoners did not have to be fed as well as free men, and lower overhead costs, since prisoners could be made to work for longer hours with much less mechanical equipment. By appropriating this extra measure of surplus value, the GPU (and its successors) was able to record much higher profits than Soviet organizations employing wage workers, and was also able to force through an outstanding degree of achievement of goals. As a result, its activities as a supplier of slaves on contract with other agencies appear to have declined, and it struck out increasingly on its own, to become the world's largest employer.

Precisely how many souls are in the possession of the GPU is known only to the executives of that firm. Guesses run all the way to well over 30 million. Dallin and Nicolaevsky, the authors of the outstanding work on this subject, suggest that there were from 8 to 12 million forced laborers in Russia at the time of her entry into the Second World War. Women accounted for no more than 10–15 percent of the total, so that the male prisoners were from 15 to 23 percent of the adult male population of the USSR. This naturally seems fantastic, but the figures are in accord with the estimates of other students and of released Polish prisoners, and tend to be confirmed by rather convincing indirect evidence. Dallin points out that the transfer of some 23 million persons from the rural to the urban classification between the censuses of 1926 and 1939 actually reflected the growth of the forced labor camps, since the largest camps were classed as towns in the census.

[260] Dallin and Nicolaevsky, *Forced Labor*, p. 90.

While the urban population increased by 100 percent in the period between 1926 and 1939, the greatest increase—558 percent—was in the Karelo-Murmansk region (between the Arctic Ocean and the Gulf of Finland); in the northeastern regions (which include a number of great camps) the urban population increased by 335 percent; in eastern Siberia by 384 percent; and in the Far East by 329 percent.[261]

It is revealing, in short, that the greatest urbanization should have occurred not in the new industrial centers of the Urals, but in the inhospitable lumbering and mining areas which are favorite regions for prison camps.

Statistical detection in another area was made to yield other indirect evidence. Schwartz noted that a study of the Soviet national wage bill revealed a discrepancy of 37 billion rubles for 1940 and of 51 billion rubles for 1950 between wages paid to all employees and the total national outlay on wages. On the assumption that soldiers and forced laborers were paid about half the average free worker's wage—which errs, if anywhere, on the side of generosity—Schwartz was able to suggest that the number of forced laborers in 1940, and planned for 1950, was in the neighborhood of 13.5 million which, he observed, was close to Dallin's estimate.[262]

Further evidence, of still another type, is offered by Soviet planning data. Russian 1941 plan documents seized by the Germans which later fell into Western possession revealed that for 1941 the NKVD (GPU) was responsible for 18 percent of all new construction in the USSR, 12 percent of all timber, 20 percent of railroad ties, 5 percent of coal, 40 percent of chromium ore. Estimating from such data, Naum Jasny arrived at a figure of about 3.5 million forced laborers; a critic argued the same data would support a range running from as low as 500,000 to as high as 15 million; another scholar, interpreting the same fragmentary evidence, reached a figure of about 10 million.[263] The principal argument against the higher esti-

---

[261] *Forced Labor*, p. 51; Dallin, *Real Soviet Russia*, pp. 186 ff.

[262] Abram Bergson, "A Problem in Soviet Statistics," *Review of Economic Statistics*, 1947, pp. 234 ff.; Harry Schwartz, "A Critique of 'Appraisals of Russian Economic Statistics,'" *Review of Economics and Statistics*, 1948, pp. 38 ff.

[263] *New York Times*, February 28, 1950, December 17, 1950; Naum Jasny, "Labor and Output in Soviet Concentration Camps"; A. D. Redding, "Reliability of Estimates of Unfree Labor in the USSR"; and Jasny's "Comment," *Journal of Political Economy*, October, 1951, pp. 405 ff., August 1952, pp.

mates is that they engulf an outrageous proportion of the Soviet population; against the lower estimates, it can be argued that they contradict the consensus of direct testimony. Since the Soviet regime does not choose to air its accomplishments in this area it is unlikely to offer any assistance in settling this controversy among Western scholars.

Forced labor, it must be remembered, was but the most severe of the various forms of compulsion practiced by the Soviet regime. The others, in order of descending severity, were exile combined with corrective labor, corrective labor in locality of residence, and "free labor" of the ordinary citizen, who could not leave his job without permission. That the distinction was largely one of degree rather than kind was recognized by a Soviet scholar, writing in 1949:

In the socialist society there is no difference in principle and quality between drafted labor and labor performed by voluntary entering into labor relations by taking employment. When we are saying that in the socialist society the principle of voluntary labor is recognized we are not speaking of recognition of some kind of abstract principle of free labor and trade in a liberal and bourgeois sense, a principle which would be treated as a value per se.

Under the conditions of socialist society . . . it is impossible to secure the principle "from each according to his ability" without a pressure by the state and law regarding the universal duty to work.

In short, it was in the nature of Soviet socialism to employ administrative compulsion as the only alternative to the capitalist labor market, which is so readily influenced by trade unions. This viewpoint was in all essentials the same as that of Trotsky, in the early days of the USSR, and was a natural outlook for Soviet leadership.[264]

Forced labor was perhaps the most glaring and outrageous of

---

337 ff. The Soviet forced labor code, released to the world by the British government, is reprinted in the AFL volume, *Slave Labor in Russia*, which also contains affidavits of former prisoners and the debates in the United Nations (1949). See also Y. Gluckstein, *Stalin's Satellites in Europe*, pp. 93 ff., for confirming data from *Pravda*, and an estimate of 11 million.

[264] Quoted by Gsovski from a treatise on Soviet labor law by Dogadov in *Uchenye Zapiski* of Leningrad University; *Monthly Labor Review*, April, 1951, p. 390; Trotsky's remarks to the Third Trade Union Congress in Deutscher, *Soviet Trade Unions*, p. 37.

Soviet socialist contradictions; a subsidiary contradiction reveals the greater emphasis placed upon power than economic efficiency: despite the fact that the USSR was always short of trained personnel, such people, the intelligentsia, were disproportionately represented among the forced laborers. Some were able to work at their skills, as doctors or engineers, others as desk workers in the camp administration, but many were assigned to common labor, and their costly training wasted.

Second only to forced labor in the depth of its irony was the relationship of the Soviet imperium to its satellites or, in Stalinist terms, the "people's democracies." Even immediately after World War II, when socialists and agrarians were allowed to participate in satellite governments, Russia took full advantage of her opportunity for seizing important capital assets. German-owned properties—which the Nazis had confiscated from Western capitalists or domestic Jewish holders—were taken over by the USSR. A great deal of plant was dismantled and shipped to Russia for reparations. This rich vein of treasure was soon exhausted, however, and the Soviet government had to develop more orderly methods of exploitation for the long run. These included the formation of Russo-satellite corporations, frequently exempted from normal satellite taxes, in which the stock was divided on a 50–50 or 51–49 basis, with the Russians in control; trade agreements in which Russian export prices were higher and satellite export prices lower than the world market level; and a highly profitable trade as middleman in the exchange of goods between two satellites. In one instance, in 1948, Poland sold Russia coal at $1.20 a ton, when the world price ranged between $14 and $20, at which Russia sold Polish coal to other nations, such as Sweden. In another case, when Bulgaria was negotiating a sale of zinc concentrate with Czechoslovakia, Russia undersold her with supplies previously purchased from the very same Bulgarian source at a much lower price. Another device for milking the satellites, although of less quantitative importance, was the upkeep of Soviet advisors and technicians who carried out the process of Russian imperial control. In Yugoslavia, for example, before Marshal Tito's split with the Kremlin, the Yugoslav government paid the Russian manager of a bridge construction project 50,000 dinars a month, in addition to residence, service, and automobile, while a Yugoslav minister of state received 12,000 dinars.[265]

Nor was the Soviet regime content to exercise its command through native satellite Communists, particularly after the Tito heresy. The hand of Moscow became less and less concealed. In 1949, Polish-born Soviet Marshal Rokossovsky was made head of the Polish armed forces, at the request of the Polish government, of course, and Russian officers with Polonized names began to take over key commands. At a time when many colonies had become independent, when bourgeois finance capitalists were praying only to retain their investments under soverign laws of ex-colonial states, Russia was unique in fulfilling to the letter all the horrible aspects of imperialist exploitation. However, one of the most salutary aspects of imperialism, capital investment which would raise the social level of the backward nation was not present to any significant degree.[266] The economic level of several of the European satellites was actually higher than the Russian, to begin with, and had to be brought to the Soviet level for the security of the Soviet state. Exploitation of satellites enabled the Stalin government to fill Moscow shop windows after World War II, and to achieve greater success with the Fourth Five-Year Plan than would otherwise have been possible. Increasingly strict political control, repeated purges and show trials, the introduction of Russian as a second language, were all forced upon the satellites in order to bring them into closer harmony with the

[265] Dallin, *New Soviet Empire*, pp. 20 ff. Soviet acquisitions in the form of reparations are conservatively estimated to have been between $4 billion and $5 billion by the end of 1950 (Schwartz, *Soviet Economy*, p. 517). See Gluckstein, *Stalin's Satellites*, pp. 62 ff.

[266] The Black Sea coast of Rumania and Bulgaria may have been an instance of major capital investment by the Russians, who were reported to have combined Russian material, equipment, and technical direction with satellite forced labor in a "transformation of nature" described as the "personal idea of the great Stalin." This involved building a Danube–Black Sea canal, development of the Bulgarian port of Varna (renamed Stalin), and construction of a new port at a village just north of Constanta in Rumania. These projects, reminiscent of capitalist imperialism in its most useful aspects, were moreover accompanied with a socialized version of old-time Western colonialism; Russian settlers were moved into the region in wholesale, collectivized fashion, displacing the native Balkan peasantry, who were collectively resettled elsewhere (*Economist*, February 9, 1952, pp. 315 ff.). The USSR has, however, contributed to the expansion of satellite war industries.

Soviet way of existence and to diminish disparities behind the outer
Iron Curtain that might detract from the perfection of Stalinist rule.
And, if the record of Soviet experience with minor nationalities
within the USSR left any doubt as to the disintegration of the old
Leninist-Stalinist nationalities policy, the experience of the satellites
dispelled it and proved the continuing integration of Great Russian
and Soviet nationalism and imperialism.

Unlike the Stalin cult, forced labor, and imperialist exploitation,
certain characteristics of Soviet society do not appear to be the result of deliberate policy decisions, and therefore take the form of
contradictions between the ordinary procedures of the regime and
the habitual ways of man. We have had occasion to observe that
disproportions in the results of planned economic activity made a
mockery of planning as such.[267] But uneven economic development
might represent no more than "growing pains," were it not to a very
great extent the outcome of a preposterous degree of centralization
of command. Alexander Barmine, an intelligent and convincing witness of the workings of the upper Soviet bureaucracy, reports that
quantities, prices, and even freight plans for goods in foreign trade
required a Politburo order and Stalin's signature.[268] An emmense
amount of detail therefore had to be handled by a very small number of hard-working men, and ultimately, by one man alone. Coördinated operations were broken up repeatedly when approval for part
of the project was delayed in the bureaucratic machinery. Another
serious consequence of overcentralization was that subordinate
officials who were actually responsible for carrying out instructions

---

[267] Inflation, which has characterized Soviet socialism to an even greater
extent than it has the better regulated capitalist countries, is not necessarily
an indication of the unreality of Russian planning. Disregarding the runaway
inflation down to 1924, subsequent monetary developments which moved up
consumer prices more rapidly than wages may have amounted to an indirect
way of financing industrialization. Or, on the other hand, the inflation may have
been an unwanted but not especially disturbing result of channeling the economy into producers' rather than consumers' goods. In either case, the basic
reason was that money wages had to be raised to provide incentives, while the
regime concentrated increased production in the heavy industries and military
lines, thus failing to soak up enlarged money incomes with more goods for the
wage earners to buy. Whereas the price of bread increased almost fortyfold between 1926–1927 and 1948, the price of steel rose less than threefold during
the same period (N. Jasny, *The Soviet Price System*, Stanford, 1951, p. 18).

[268] *One Who Survived*, pp. 217 ff.

were impelled to concentrate on quantity rather than quality. The following official Soviet complaints are typical:

Rejects in steel and machine-making plants amounted to 2 billion rubles in 1940. In the metal working plants of Moscow alone, rejects reach 200 million rubles a year. . . .

In so important and large a plant as the Stalingrad tractor plant the carelessness of the workers in the foundry department caused the rejection of 16,000 tons of metal. Enough metal to make 3,500 tractors. . . .

In the Mayakeva Industrial Combine, Stalin Province, out of 7,770 cultivator wheels . . . all save 217 were defective. Chief Engineer Chrdakov and chief of the technical control department, Radchemko, have been sentenced to five years loss of liberty.

One is inclined to doubt that the "carelessness" of workers was the cause rather than faulty organization of work and hurried and improper use of machinery. The official press protested, in 1951, that the output of the great Ukranian iron mines at Krivoi Rog could be raised by more than 40 percent without additional equipment if existing machinery were fully utilized. But much was kept idle, owing to poor organization, some being employed to only 25 percent of capacity.[269]

Deficient utilization of human resources constituted a widespread form of waste. The Soviet Union had long boasted that it alone knew no unemployment. Forced labor and a large army are partial explanations, but the key to the Soviet solution is *disguised* unemployment on a vast scale, that is, utterly wasteful employment. For example, a Russian electric power plant employed 480 men, while a comparable American installation employed 51; a Soviet steel mill with 20,000 workers produced 1,200,000 tons a year, while an American firm produced 1,500,000 tons with 9,200 workers. In part this reflects lower Russian mechanization, but probably to a much more significant degree it results from inflated office staffs and poor shop organization. A comparison between a Russian and an American coal mine showed that the latter produced three times as much coal,

[269] Yugow, *Russia's Economic Front*, pp. 21, 22; Smith, *Three Years in Moscow*, p. 140; *New York Times*, May 13, 1951. Jasny believes that Soviet planning has become less inclusive and less effective as planning, owing to a failure or inability to work out the manifold tie-ins a genuine comprehensive plan would require ("A Close-Up of the Soviet Fourth Five-Year Plan," *Quarterly Journal of Economics*, May, 1952, pp. 139 ff.).

but the former had two miners for each American, three surface workers, eight office workers, eleven technicians, and twelve supervisory persons for each American.[270] And while it is true that the Soviet Union had a plenty of "that bounty—people," there was at the same time a perpetual shortage of labor. One can only conclude that the Stalinist system of social organization was incapable of a highly rational allocation of manpower, despite the complex planning and the all-pervasive coercion.

Excessive centralization led to the absurd situation, reported in the Leningrad *Pravda*, in which a factory had to make its own electrical and optical equipment, while other Leningrad factories specializing in such goods were operating below capacity. The main reason for this double wastage was that plants belonging to different ministries could not negotiate directly with each other. And despite the fact that the government employed thousands of negotiators and expediters to arrange the orderly flow of raw, component, and finished goods, the system worked so poorly that the factories themselves hired middlemen to search out surpluses and deficits in order to arrange illegal interplant barter.[271]

It would appear that a form of private enterprise was rearing its head, and certainly not the best features thereof. It could have been effectively eliminated only by drastic decentralization of authority, but that would have meant loosening the dictatorship, which was not to be considered. The alternative, which was followed, was to allow illegal enterprise to exist, provided it was kept within the customary limits that developed, and subjected to occasional exemplary arrests and punishments which prevented any doubts from arising concerning the ultimate authority and power of the state.

Physicians of the state medical service engaged in private practice and patients who could afford it preferred to deal with the very same doctor on a private rather than socialized basis.[272] The greatest illustration of under-the-counter capitalism, however, was *"blat,"* Russian slang for illegal business and for the profitable use of influence. What *blat* amounted to was a system of keeping the books in order while the goods went astray. A tailoring coöperative needed

[270] Yugow, *Russia's Economic Front*, p. 180.
[271] *New York Times*, June 11, 1950.
[272] *New York Times*, Aug. 20, 1950.

cloth to work up. The director of a textile mill was delighted to provide all the material at a ruble per meter above the government price. The books of both buyer and seller, of course, showed a transaction at the lawful price. The mill manager shared the surplus with those members of his staff who would necessarily know of the deal. The coöp recouped its overpayment by selling part of its output in the free market at free market prices; part was sold to state market stalls, again above the legal price, and the stallkeeper then sold a fraction of his supply to the people waiting in the regular line, at the official rate, and the greater part illegally, in private transactions of his own. In this magic way, production and distribution increased. Actual prices were higher, of course; but deflation by bureaucracy was overcome to some extent.

Another type of *blat*, reported by *Pravda* in 1950, suggests the beginnings of an illegally free labor market. A construction superintendent relieved four carpenters from the job and sent them to work for a prosperous-looking citizen. They were continued on the construction payroll, of course, and the extra money paid by the private employer was split between the carpenters and their superintendent.[273] The Soviet press indicated that *blat* too had been collectivized, when it reported in 1939 that visitors to *kolkhozy* saw peasants lining up at a cashier's window to buy *kolkhoz* work-day certificates from the farm chairman, so that the books would show they had met their collective obligations, while they would actually be able to put in the time on their own plots.[274]

Naturally enough, *blat* succeeded best when all knowledgeable parties were involved as accomplices including, in certain circumstances, members of the police, who appeared to be incorruptible only in political cases. *Blat* appears to have been a compensatory device on the part of human nature, evading unpalatable regulations without directly challenging the regulating authority.[275]

A similar type of compensation appeared in another area of Soviet life. The Stalinist bureaucracy, monolithic though it be, was de-

---

[273] Dallin, *New Soviet Empire*, pp. 180 ff.; see also Hubbard, *Soviet Labour and Industry*, London, 1942, pp. 239 ff.

[274] Timasheff, *Great Retreat*, p. 142.

[275] Since outcroppings of the capitalist spirit were illegal, they were apt to be of a character that would place them beyond bourgeois as well as socialist law. The government itself was not above watering bread and sausage improperly,

signed to work through a system of checks and balances—not, to be sure, to prevent overhasty exercise of the will of the people, but to forestall any possibility of the growth of faction or opposition in the ranks of officialdom. The state bureaucracy and the economic bureaucracies were set to watching each other and the Communist Party bureaucracy which overlapped both, watched both. The Party, however, was ever subject to the charge of excessive meddling in administrative affairs, and every lower-echelon Party group had to watch its step lest it be compelled to go through a "democratic" reorganization. Peering from behind the filing cabinets at all three bureaucracies, moreover, was the secret police. The regime had a "vested interest in confusion," and, one is tempted to add, the elaborate checks were designed to perpetuate a state of imbalance among its servants.[276] But the bourgeois devil who apparently lurks in the soul of every Soviet official has developed a method of evasion akin to *blat*. State, Party, and economic officials with common concerns frequently discovered that it paid to coöperate rather than inform. The regime decried such occurrences as denoting a lack of Bolshevik vigilance, as evidence of a clique—"familyness" was the term used. So the families were broken up, until new ones formed.

The workings of human nature in the fields of the arts and sciences caused Stalin untold trouble. Every artist and every scientist worth his salt must have a certain conceit that his work is a contribution to the progress of his field. In a word, creative work is likely to go hand in hand with, and to breed, individualism. And individualism, in the words of Fadeev, who became chief literary factotum

---

and private citizens showed no lack of ingenuity in practicing several common forms of dishonesty (Jasny, *Socialized Agriculture,* pp. 558, 643).

In February, 1951, twenty-five men were convicted of having organized a ring that swindled the national economy to the tune of 4 million rubles by operating a string of fake coöperatives. The "workers" they hired took a cut of the money received by the swindlers in order to pay "wages," and a good many Soviet economic organizations were involved in fraudulent contracts (*New York Times,* February 5, 1951, from *Pravda*).

An even seamier side of capitalist life was revealed by the case of a sports official who, with a crudity that would astound an American gambler, attempted to fix a soccer game. This official, it was discovered, had become Director of a Physical Culture Institute, although his only qualifications were two degrees he had awarded himself (*New York Times,* April 8, 1951, from *Pravda*).

[276] Moore, *Soviet Politics,* pp. 286 ff.

after World War II, "is profoundly alien to the spirit of our [Soviet] society." Furthermore, there had never been any ideological uncertainty as to the function of art in the Soviet scheme of things. As early as 1905, Lenin had written:

> Literature must become Party. As a counterpoise to bourgeois literary careerism and individualism . . . the socialist proletariat must promote and develop the principle of *Party literature*. . . . The literary cause must become *part* of the general proletarian cause.[277]

And it was Stalin who called writers "engineers of human souls."

It was not until the campaign for ideological purity that followed World War II, however, that the straitjacket was fully applied. Nothing frankly hostile to the Communist regime had ever been published, of course, but during the first decade of Soviet rule there was sufficient uncertainty as to whether or not there was such a thing as "proletarian art" to permit a rather wide variety of artistic expression within the Communist framework. There was still place in Russia for satirists such as Bulgakov and Ilf and Petrov. The relative freedom allowed Russian literary people was sharply reduced, along with that of workers and peasants, when the Stalinist dictatorship was set on its steady course in 1929. An organization called the Russian Association of Proletarian Writers (RAPP), which had previously been badgering all it deemed unorthodox, was now endowed with authorilty to carry out a dictatorship over letters. Authors had to write about the success of the Five-Year Plan, show how devoted members of the Komsomol and the local Party secretary overcame wrecking, timidity, and individualism. It was, on the whole, extremely stultifying and Stalin apparently decided that this campaign too had suffered from a "dizziness from success." In 1932 RAPP and its dictatorship were abolished, all literary organizations were amalgamated into one Union of Soviet Writers, which became the exclusive road to a literary career. At the first congress of this body, in 1934, Zhdanov, who followed Kirov as leader of Leningrad, laid down the new party line. It was essentially the same as the old, merely replacing control by one narrow literary cult with a universal decree that "socialist realism" was to be followed. Zhdanov declared:

[277] Counts and Lodge, *Country of the Blind*, p. 89. Original italics.

Our Soviet literature is not afraid of being accused of tendentiousness. Yes, Soviet literature *is* tendentious, for in the age of class struggle a non-class, non-tendentious, would-be apolitical literature does not and cannot exist.

As for "socialist realism," the clearest explanation Zhdanov could offer was that writers had to "depict real life in its revolutionary development," not "just as 'objective reality.' "[278] In short, if writers were engineers of human souls or minds, their writings had to be Stalinist propaganda. There followed, naturally, a flood of writings about triumphs of the Five-Year Plans and glorious successes in factory construction and *kolkhoz* management, and contributions to the mythology of Stalin the Lord of the Soviet peoples. The latter operation called for historical novels, revising history to exaggerate Stalin's role in the early Bolshevik movement and the Civil War, and reviving great figures of old Russia as a spur to renewed nationalism.

It was only in August, 1946, however, that the great Zhdanov bombshell exploded. Zhdanov, who had become the leading official ideologist, reiterated and called for the most thorough carrying out of the policy he had laid down in 1934. The extremely popular and skillful short story writer Zoshchenko, and a poetess, Anna Akhmatova, were singled out for particular attention by a resolution of the Central Committee of the Communist Party and by its spokesman, Zhdanov. Said he:

It is not for us to reform our life and our social order according to Zoshchenko.[279] Let him reform. But he does not want to reform. Let him get out of Soviet literature. . . . In his "The Adventures of a Monkey" [which escaped from the zoo and got caught in the toils of Soviet red tape] he gives a deliberately deformed and vulgar caricature of the life of the Soviet people in order to insert into the mouth of a monkey the vile, poisonous, anti-Soviet maxim that it is better to live in a zoo than at

[278] Gleb Struve, *Soviet Russian Literature, 1917–1950,* Norman, Okla., 1951, pp. 244, 246.

[279] One reason Zoshchenko may have been able to get away with his satires of Soviet shortcomings for so many years was that his usual protagonist was a Soviet citizen with vestiges of bourgeois psychology. Thus the fire could be taken as directed against bourgeois elements. It would hardly occur to an orthodox Communist critic that this was another way of saying that the bourgeois spirit appeared to be ineradicable, so that Soviet institutions were in perpetual conflict with the Russian people.

liberty, and that it is easier to breathe in a cage than among Soviet people.

As for Akhmatova, Zhdanov commented:

Basic with her are amorous-erotic motifs, interlaced with motifs of sadness, anguish, death, mysticism and doom. . . . Not quite a nun and not quite a fornicatrix, but rather a fornicatrix and a nun in whom fornication is mingled with prayer.

Neither satire of the outer world nor preoccupation with the world of inner thoughts was permissible. "Soviet writers," declared Zhdanov, "must assist the people, the State and the Party in the education of our youth to be cheerful, confident of their own strength, and fearful of no difficulties."[280]

The literary bureaucrats and editors who had published the works of these and other sinners tearfully confessed, and asked the question, "How could we have made such mistakes?" And the answer was, through ideological negligence. The Union of Soviet Writers, having been duly purged, summed up the Party line.

The Central Committee of the Party pointed out that the strength of Soviet literature, the most advanced literature in the world, consists in the fact that it is a literature which has and can have no interests except the interests of the people and the interests of the state [by definition identical]. The task of Soviet literature is to aid the state to educate youth correctly, to meet their needs, to rear a new generation which is hale and hearty, which has faith in its own cause, which fears no obstacles, which is prepared to overcome all obstacles. . . .

It is necessary to saturate all this work with the militant spirit of the active and aggressive ideology of Communism.

Soviet writers must lash those works which express any manifestation of servility before the bourgeois west, so foreign to Soviet people.[281]

The new-old line, it is clear, was to prevent a sense of relaxation after the war, to fight any growth of individualism with its attendant stress on personal reactions and therefore on doubt, to spur nationalism and condemn the West. Well and good. But if Zoshchenko had been popular, would the suppression of Zoshchenko eliminate those feelings and thoughts in his readers which constituted the basis for

---

[280] Counts and Lodge, *Country of the Blind,* pp. 85, 96.
[281] Counts and Lodge, *Country of the Blind,* p. 115.

his popularity? Thoughts could be forced underground, in accordance with the well-known underground Soviet adage: "If you think, don't speak! If you speak, don't write! If you write, don't publish! If you publish, recant immediately!" But it was not quite so certain that thoughts could be changed, and there was no way to guarantee that the literary containers for the new, approved thoughts, would be liked by the people. The stereotypes of postwar Soviet literature —the Western spy, the heroic Communist—spread a cover of repellent dullness over Russian literary genius. Back in the 1930's, Zoshchenko had satirized the Party version of a healthy romance; the loyal Communist lovers would live separately, because of their work, and would meet once in five days:

Lida, feeling a little sorry at heart, and at the same time surprised by the haste with which he had married, consented to wait a little, agreeing that the search for an apartment, the removal, and various domestic affairs and cares might unfavorably effect the course of his work. He praised her for her common sense and political maturity, saying that he now realized quite well that he had made no mistake in choosing her and that, indeed, he would perhaps be unable to find at present a better wife. And Lida, pleased with his praises, looked at him with admiring eyes and said that, maybe, she too could not have a better husband. They were happy in their own way, and in no hurry to disturb their happiness with kisses and embraces.[282]

The very slowness with which the Zhdanov principles of 1934 were fully implemented was left-handed admission that such biting criticism was valid. But the political requirements of the regime demanded the imposition of thought control, and the government had nothing to lose, from its standpoint, save good literature, for even enforced hypocrisy was less risky to the state than writing that might stir dangerous thoughts.[283]

The confessions and recantations of the pilloried artists, as stereo-

[282] Quoted by Struve, *Soviet Literature*, p. 152.

[283] Not that the regime found reason for contentment. Playwrights and other authors were as likely to be attacked for dullness as for deviations from the party line, and there was a tendency among writers to seek refuge in grandiose projects requiring years of work and affording time for revision in the interest of personal safety. (See H. E. Salisbury, "Moscow Season Opens," *New York Times*, September 21, 1952, sec. II; "Problems and Projects of Soviet Writers," *Times Literary Supplement*, February 8, 1952.)

typed as politically acceptable literature, revealed a sincere and completely understandable desire to escape more severe punishment, but not a change of heart. The great movie director, Eisenstein, apologizing for having depicted the bodyguard of Ivan the Terrible as a bloodthirsty and cruel crew, which it was, and for having shown the Tsar as troubled over his misdeeds, confessed, "The sense of historical truth betrayed me." He had failed to realize that Ivan and his strong-arm men were a progressive force—like Stalin and the GPU.[284] That even music came under the Party hammer may be attributed to the whims of Stalin's personal taste and to the inbred insistence on uniformity. Surely, if Stalin's subjects did not like Shostakovitch, they had only to refrain from listening. And if they did hear some of his most "deviationist" music, it would be most unlikely to contain any tunes that might subvert their loyalty to the state. Here was one instance, however, in which Stalin may well have had the genuine sympathy of the Russian masses, for they, like him, preferred melodies that could be hummed to the highly intellectual and rather dry modern music. The composers, therefore, were not serving the people when they wrote difficult music. They must swing about and write melodies the people could whistle. Yet it is to be doubted that the Politburo was really so very concerned over the output of music to delight the humblest muzhik. The attack on music, the least topical of the arts, had to be made as part of the war against "art for art's sake," for this heresy if tolerated only in music would undermine the purity of political conformity in literature and theater, and from the arts might arise that dread contagion of questioning that could infect the entire Soviet intelligentsia.

This would also appear to have been the central reason behind the drive against the scientists, although there were related subsidiary factors. The Bolsheviks, as Marxian materialists, had always boasted of their devotion to science, and had poured money and equipment into scientific research even during the worst periods of shortage. The fact that the leaders of society, including most scientific organizations, were Marxists, made it inevitable that Soviet science would always be in danger of crossing the low barrier that separates a Marxian materialism which need not overly interfere with scentific

[284] Counts and Lodge, *Country of the Blind*, p. 148.

inquiry from the crude mechanism that would certainly ruin it. So long as scientists were not excessively regimented, the danger would not be too great, and this in a general way was the status of Soviet science down to the great Zhdanov purge. Many scientists were naturally victimized during the purges, but this was because, as intellectuals, they belonged to the group that offered the greatest potential threat to a dictatorship. The postwar struggle for ideological purity struck science itself, however, and left little undisturbed.

The first branch of science to suffer, and in the most spectacular fashion, was genetics. This is not surprising, for this particular field of biology touches closest the problem of environmental-or-hereditary determination of characteristics in living organisms, and therefore affects the most fundamental scientific and political presuppositions of Marxism. As a matter of fact, Marxism or, at the very least, a favorable attitude toward Soviet Russia, had made a good deal of headway among Western geneticists. This was partly because Soviet researchers had always rejected the approach generally described by the word "vitalism," which, postulating such concepts as a "life force," smacked of mysticism to many laboratory researchers. Another reason was simply the attraction of genuine achievement, for Soviet genetics, amply financed, and led by a great scientist, I. N. Vavilov, had established a world-wide reputation for advances in pure science.

This very fact was one of the causes of its downfall, for the charge often leveled against Americans, that they neglect pure science in the interest of applied, holds far more true of Russia. And, considering the Soviet need for a vast expansion of agricultural output, it is logical that the Stalinist rulers should have been particularly impatient with the slow and tortuous progress of pure science in fields related to plant and animal growth. Their impatience might have been limited to a diversion of funds from pure to applied research, had not a seemingly practical alternative presented itself. This alternative first appeared on the brilliantly lighted stage of Soviet politico-scientific dispute in 1935, when a geneticist-politician, Lysenko, allied with a Marxist-philosopher-politician, Prezent, publicly attacked genetics as it was understood throughout the world, and campaigned for government and Party support for their own conception of the science.

Lysenko and Prezent were excellent examples of what Stalin

called "careerists," men unable to win prominence through solid work who attempted to do so by taking advantage of shifts in the Party line and of the practices of Soviet bureaucracy. But, since a careerist was a careerist only when Stalin disapproved of him, the two rebels were able to triumph. The scientific dispute itself was carried out in an atmosphere of striking unreality. Orthodox genetics (neo-Mendelian or neo-Darwinian) holds that heredity is governed specifically by genes and chromosomes. Inheritable changes therefore can come about only through a natural mutation of these factors or artificially as, for example, through x-radiation. Adaptation of a species to environment is explained on the principle of natural selection: for example, animals inheriting a physique highly resistant to cold will live and reproduce, and those with a low resistance will die out, in arctic regions.

Lysenko's alternative doctrine was very similar to the pre-Darwinian theory of Lamarck. Its essential difference from orthodox genetics was the proposition that acquired characteristics could be inherited, with the corollary that the whole organism, not merely the germ cells, governed heredity.[285] This doctrine was popularized among the Soviet hierarchy by a practical horticulturist, Michurin—the Russian Burbank, he has been called. Genetics, according to Michurin, was not primarily to be a study of the natural laws governing heredity, but rather a technique for transforming species. The promise to remake nature naturally gave hope to the Kremlin.

It is not within our province to analyze the actual results of Lysenko's experiments, so far as they are known,[286] but it would

[285] This would suggest, for example, that children might inherit their parents' suntan.

[286] It is worth noting, nevertheless, that his principal claim to fame, vernalization—the treatment of winter strains of rye and wheat (sown in the fall) so that they can be sown in the spring, like spring strains—was known in the United States before the Civil War. It has not had much practical success, here or in Russia, and Soviet orders to vernalize as routine procedure turn out, on inspection, to be nothing more than a requirement for a standard germination test that has nothing to do with vernalization. His other claims—that winter wheat actually can be changed into hereditary spring wheat, that hereditary changes can be induced by grafting, that wheat can actually be turned into rye—are, depending upon their nature, (1) more easily explained by orthodox than Michurinist genetics, (2) explicable in terms of absence of controls, pure strains, and statistical verification, or (3) incapable of demonstration or explanation by scientists outside the USSR who have made careful efforts to do so. (J. Huxley, *Soviet Genetics and World Science*, London, 1948, p. 70 and esp. chap. 3; *New York Times*, Dec. 16, 1949.)

appear that Stalin bought a scientific absurdity, an impression enhanced by the quality of the arguments offered by some of Lysenko's followers in the great public disputation held in 1948. One, a cattle breeding official named Shaumyan, announced that the nature of a cow's udder is governed by the exercise it is given in the process of milking!

> The development of the cow's udder is a most characteristic and irrefutable example of the inheritance of characteristics arising under the influence of the action of external factors.[287]

But Lysenko triumphed, and those of his adversaries who desired to survive had to submit. The scientific issue was settled, not by a public laboratory demonstration, but by the following statement by Lysenko:

> I have been asked . . . as to the attitude of the Central Committee concerning my paper. I answer: the Central Committee of the Party has examined my report and approved it. (*Tremendous applause, passing into an ovation. All rise.*)[288]

This dramatic conclusion to the debate had been decided years before, for Vavilov, whose views were now rejected, whose students and followers were now forced to yield, had been arrested in 1940 and had died in a prison camp in 1942. There is a suggestion, in this, that the campaign for ideological purification had been scheduled for an earlier start than fourteen years after Zhdanov's 1934 blast at the writers, and had been postponed by the war. It is, of course, possible that Stalin hoped for quicker practical results in the form of improved crops from Lysenko's work. But the ideological reasons would seem to carry greater weight. Orthodox genetics depends heavily on probability theory and statistics, and, understood in a mechanical fashion, this suggests that *certainty* is not to be had, and that there is room for chance in nature. While such implications need not be drawn from genetics, they would occur to

---

[287] Zirkle, *Death of a Science*, p. 148.

[288] *Pravda*, from which this pronouncement was translated, described the audience's reaction more fully. "As if moved by a single impulse, all those present arose from their seats and started a stormy, prolonged ovation in honor of the Central Committee of the Lenin-Stalin Party, in honor of the wise leader and teacher of the Soviet people, the greatest scientist of our era, Comrade Stalin" (Zirkle, *Death of a Science*, p. 249).

a Marxist, and he would find them unacceptable, particularly if, in their turn, they carried corollary implications of uncertainty for politics. Further, as suggested by the distinguished American geneticist, H. J. Muller, the Lysenko doctrine actually supports a new, Soviet type of racialism: if acquired characteristics can be inherited, Soviet people, living, by definition, in a higher type of environment, should eventually prove racially superior to all others. In a word, genetics, like history, could be made to further the cause of the new Soviet and Russian nationalism.[289] Add to all this the fact that in a dictatorship it is a sound precaution to keep the intelligentsia from feeling too secure, and it is not impossible to understand why the Central Committee should have chosen to add to its laurels the title of supreme court of biological truth, as it had previously become the final arbiter of literary and musical worth. Lastly, it should not be forgotten that scientific quacks can sell their wares more easily to scientifically ignorant politicians than to scholars, and that they can cut their goods so as to make the sale. This is especially the case when the politicians, as in Russia, claim to be savants of an overall, master science, Marxism.

Other fields of science, physics, chemistry, astronomy, were subjected to the ideological purge, although not so dramatically as genetics. The attacks were aimed against what was called "idealism" or even mysticism in modern science and in general reduced to a refusal to admit the possibility of indefinite uncertainty. What the Stalinist authorities particularly objected to was the scientific practice of positing components of matter whose existence could only be inferred, and the tendency, particularly in nuclear physics, to detract from the crude material solidity of matter. The fact is that a good many of the Western conceptions, from relativity and the positron to the chemical theory of resonance, are regarded not so much as statements of material conditions as analytical tools or constructs, to be held as valid so long as they prove fruitful in scientific investigations. The philosophical viewpoint which is willing to work along with usable hypotheses and constructs, without insisting on immediately absolute and material truth, pervades modern science, of course. But it has never been acceptable to good Bolsheviks. Relativity theory was denounced in 1938 (again suggesting that the

[289] See Muller's comments, Zirkle, *Death of a Science,* pp. 89 ff.

full-scale ideological purge was delayed by the war), and in 1949 a Soviet astronomer condemned it as a "cancerous tumor that gnaws through modern astronomical theory and is the main ideological enemy of materialist [Marxist] astronomy."[290] He was probably right. As long ago as 1909, Lenin devoted much of his major philosophical work, *Materialism and Empirio-Criticism*, to an attack on Ernst Mach, the physicist and philosopher of science who was probably the late nineteenth century's best known exponent of the intellectual outlook that threads through nearly all contemporary science. The Zhdanov purge and its consequences were, to this extent, nothing more than a higher stage of the enactment of Marxism-Leninism-Stalinism into social practice. And yet the policy necessarily forced the regime into several serious contradictions. As with the artists, a great many extremely able men, whose skills were expensively acquired, scarce and valuable to the state, were compelled to choose between hypocrisy and social extinction. An example of their cynicism was revealed by Lysenko's partner Prezent, when he described a biological museum in which

. . . on one side of exhibition boards were mounted exhibits propagandizing the Michurinist trends, while on the reverse side of these movable boards were mounted exhibits propagandizing Morgan's [Western] views. So that, depending on the composition of the visiting group, it was possible to turn these exhibits any way you chose.[291]

In the process of enforcing ideological loyalty, loyalty to Stalinism was dissipated. And, in compelling science to turn from the paths worked out by thousands of men over many years in many places, Soviet science was forced into that terrible descent which ends in contradiction with nature.

The very internal logic of Stalinism compelled it to seek to enforce a rigid ideological uniformity, pretending to infallibility, but correctly insisting upon its flexibility of view and practice. And these

[290] *New York Times*, July 17, 1949; see also July 13, 1949, July 15, 1951; Counts and Lodge, *Country of the Blind*, pp. 233 ff. The core of modern philosophy of science is superbly and simply stated by Einstein in a letter to Viscount Samuel (*New York Times*, August 13, 1951). To the Stalinist it is offensive because it is hostile to dogma.

[291] Zirkle, *Death of a Science*, p. 244.

do not go well together. It is perhaps possible to persuade a population and even its most intelligent and discriminating elements that the most abrupt political reversals are sound, on the ground that the rulers, alone in possession of full knowledge, can best decide for the people. But it is quite a different matter to convince a scientist that ice is hot, or a writer that drivel is art, and it is even more difficult to do this when, but a short time before, they were assured by the highest political agencies that ice was cold and drivel was drivel. The average Russian may be uninformed, and possibly naïve, but it takes little sophistication for people who are barely subsisting to perceive that there is something wrong with the explanation that academic fees have been introduced because the masses are now so well-to-do. History, that foundation of Marxism, can be falsified, but not too often. There will soon be relatively few Russians alive to remember that Trotsky organized the Red Army and led it to victory; the early history of Bolshevism has been rewritten to show that Trotsky was even then an enemy of the people, and that Stalin was the organizer of all good (with Lenin's blessing). For, as Stalin said, "Paper will put up with anything that is written on it."[292] But there are many who recall when the Western powers were beloved allies, when Shostakovich was terrible, good, terrible, and perhaps good again, when Zoshchenko was everyone's favorite. And after the Zhdanov purge is ruled to have suffered from vertigo there will be many who will recall the immutable line as he uttered it. The bureaucrats and higher intelligentsia may become inured to purges, provided they are not too severe. The purge has been a means of securing rotation in office, and a vent for popular dissatisfaction with the ranks of the bureaucracy. But while the purges can inspire fear, they can hardly instill love or loyalty in their victims, or anything but distrust and cynicism in the masses. Stalin had given the impression, before his dictatorship was absolute, that he was aware of this fact, and that he realized that fear was a poor foundation on which to build. Purges, he once wrote,

[292] See Wolfe, *Three Who Made a Revolution*, pp. 437 ff., on the rewriting of history. The famous *History of the Communist Party of the Soviet Union (Bolsheviks)* prepared under Stalin's personal editorship and published in 1938 makes wonderful reading for anyone familiar with the course of events. It is, of course, the model for part of the nightmare that is George Orwell's *1984*.

. . . would produce a regime of intimidation in the Party, a regime of fear, a regime that would not foster a spirit of self-criticism and initiative. The leaders of the Party can be real leaders only if the Party does not fear them but honors them and recognizes their authority.[293]

But perhaps Stalin never understood that what was true for the Party was also true for the people.

What could people think, moreover, when Stalin, who had not openly participated in the intellectual purges, suddenly joined in and, with a single letter to *Pravda*, exploded what had been accepted Soviet doctrine in philology since the revolution? The theory he attacked, propounded by Professor N. Y. Marr (who had, luckily for himself, died in 1934), held that language was part of the superstructure of class society. Stalin pointed out that it was as absurd to speak of a bourgeois and a proletarian language as to speak of bourgeois and proletarian railways. Languages developed slowly, he argued, and survived revolutions, so that classical Russian was the language of socialist Russia. The reader, at this point, might wonder why, if Marr had been such a poor Marxist, Stalin had waited all these years to call attention to the fact. But even more disturbing thoughts would be occasioned by Stalin's comments on the professional state of Soviet philology:

> The slightest criticism of the prevailing state of affairs in Soviet philology, even timid attempts to question the so-called "new doctrine" [of Marr], have been suppressed and persecuted by leading philological circles. Valuable men, explorers in the field of linguistics, have been removed from their posts or lowered in rank in reprisal for a critical attitude toward the legacy of N. Y. Marr or for the slightest disapproval of Marr's doctrine. Leaders in the field of linguistics were appointed to their responsible posts not because of their capacities but for unreserved recognition of Marr's teaching.[294]

Could this tyranny have occurred without Stalin's knowledge? Was linguistics more severely oppressed than any other field of Soviet life? And, if Stalin, as it was officially proclaimed, was always right, did it not mean that he was also always wrong? It was a very cruel blow to the professors of philology who had faithfully followed the

[293] In a letter to Maslow, whom Stalin thereupon purged as leader of the German Communist Party (Fischer, *Stalin and German Communism*, p. 437).
[294] Dallin, *New Soviet Empire*, p. 126.

Party line for thirty years, and who now had to confess that they had failed to understand their specialty until it was explained to them by the scholarly genius of Premier Stalin. To all intelligent Russians the incident must at the very least have cast some light on the inner contradiction of the system in which they lived.[295]

It is apparent that the key to both the real nature and the prospects of the Stalinist system lies in the attitudes of the Russian people. Without public opinion polls or a free press, with a protective private Iron Curtain screening every Soviet citizen from his compatriots and isolating him from the occasional foreigners he may meet, one is reduced to inference and guesswork and the scattering reports of refugees and Western observers in seeking to gauge the reactions of the people to the words and doings of their masters. And yet the effort must be made, with an added cause for complaint against Stalinism that it should have forced bourgeois, fact-objective social scientists to undertake an analysis that is rather unscientific. For otherwise we can only assume that the people accept as accurate the official explanations of poverty, spurious elections, mangled history, reversals of line, and tyranny. There is a tendency among Western observers to make this mistake, and explain Stalinism as a response to a deep psychological need for firm leadership, to assert that the Russians have always accepted tyranny and poverty and, finding it quite normal, are willing to have it go under the name of socialism and democracy.[296] Such assumptions concerning the attitudes of the Russian masses underlie the oversimplified historical explanations of Stalinism as essentially no more than a revival of Tsarist autocracy and imperialism under a Marxian veneer. However unscientific it be, therefore, it is less so to pick up the crumbs

[295] An embarrassing dead end had been reached in this field, in that the Russian language was, of course, essentially the same as it had long been. Under a class theory of language this would imply the failure of the revolution. A further point was that Marr, like all Old Bolsheviks, had regarded Russia as backward relative to the West, and the Russian language as in an immature state compared to French and English, which is philologically correct. This, however, could not be admitted when Soviet Russian culture was being proclaimed as the world's highest. The glorification of the Russian language also fitted well with Great Russian nationalism, and the campaign for Russification of subject peoples.

[296] D. J. Dallin has competently dissected this view under the heading "Diaperology and Racism," *New Soviet Empire*, pp. 62 ff.

of knowledge that have fallen our way, and try to see what they mean, than to take refuge in sweeping generalizations based on unproved psychological postulates and inaccurate readings of pre-revolutionary Russian history.

Some of the most suggestive glimpses into the thinking of the ordinary Soviet citizen come from Russian propaganda about the United States, for "it is a safe rule in evaluating Soviet propaganda to assume that the volume devoted to a particular theme is a key to the resistance which it encounters among the Soviet public."[297] Aside from the expected Marxian analysis, the Soviet regime reveals the things that disturb its own subjects by its effort to reassure them that Americans are even worse off than they in precisely the same respects. For example, the Russian publication *New Times* attacked the Voice of America for trying to make the Russians believe "that Americans—all Americans!—live like princes." The following comprised the Voice's exaggerations: American workers were said to live either in separate houses or separate apartments with kitchen and bathroom, and many were said to prefer a suburban cottage with a garden. But this was not all; the Voice referred to carpet cleaning! "Carpets, of course, are mentioned here not by chance," commented *New Times.* "The Voice of America wants to insinuate that carpets are as common a thing in America as gas rings."[298] We learn from the Russian press that 500,000 Americans are "reduced to such a stage that they have to live in trailers"; that the average automobile worker is invalided after five years; that of our 30 million rural population in 1949 one-third were in hopeless poverty and the rest below the minimum standard of decency. We learn that

The simple man in the United States is completely unprotected from arbitrary action by police, Federal organs and reactional organizations. The FBI creates an atmosphere of fear and oppression.[299]

A Soviet *Handbook for Elementary School Teachers* announces that "in elementary school, children are taught only reading, writing and arithmetic because in the opinion of the American bourgeoisie this is enough for the children of the toilers." America, Soviet commenta-

[297] Barghoorn, *Soviet Image of the United States,* p. 262.
[298] *New York Times,* December 24, 1950.
[299] *New York Times,* July 16, 1949.

tors are fond of repeating, is a land of extremes, a land of wealth for a handful and of abject poverty for the millions. The Moscow radio brought this point home to its listeners:

> The streets of New York are full of the children of the workers, dressed in tatters, with pale, thin faces. They stand for ages at the doors of luxurious hotels and restaurants, begging. . . . They often appear on Fifth Avenue in search of something to eat in the rubbish. . . . [On this avenue] is a very beautiful . . . house. . . . This is the house of the little dog Toby, whose mistress, a mad American woman, left it $75,000,000. The dog sleeps on a golden bed; it is attended by a staff of forty-five servants and six lawyers. . . . This picture gives one a good idea of the American way of life.[300]

And we may top it off with a shocking revelation concerning American penology: a Russian who had once experienced the rigors of Sing Sing and was now working under the beneficent eye of the GPU recalled New York's prison as "that devilish island. . . . And the soup—five spoonfuls to a person." Sing Sing must indeed be a horrible place, for "even the solitary confinement cells have steam. . . . They lock you in and smother you with steam, like a rat."[301]

These and thousands of other Russian commentaries on the sadness of American life do, of course, give us a kind of information that we on the scene are literally unable to get. But they also tell us two things about Russia: first, that the Soviet people are aware of and do not accept as normal and proper such things as poverty, the police state and police cruelty, overwork, lack of housing, education sufficient only to make them useful servants of their masters, the vast gap between their poor lives and the luxury of the rulers; second, that the regime is aware of their feelings and tries to counter them by saying in effect, "Things are just the same or worse the world over, even in your vaunted America where the streets are supposed to be paved with gold. And here, in Russia, we are at least building socialism, so that you will eventually be better off."

Do the Russians swallow this propaganda? Many undoubtedly do.

[300] This delightful fantasy contains reference to two specific Soviet problems: poor children and wandering waifs who beg from the wealthy (to whom nearly all nonreturners and refugees from Russia refer); and rubbish removal, which apparently causes great difficulty in Russian cities and towns. The tale of Toby appeared in the *New York Times*, July 14, 1951.

[301] Barghoorn, *Soviet Image of the United States*, pp. 25–26.

But some, particularly among the Soviet intelligentsia, do not. Many Russians are sent abroad, see with their own eyes, and on returning talk, however discreetly, with their friends. And, as for those not fortunate enough to be assigned to foreign work, General Smith reports that showings of an anti-American film had to be stopped because the audience reaction to actual newsreel shots of the slums of New York with their backyard clotheslines was "gasps and exclamations of 'How many clothes they have!'" The American Embassy's Russian-language magazine, *Amerika*, though subject to Soviet censorship and to obstacles in distribution that led to its eventual abandonment, was widely read, passed from hand to hand and, "incredible though it may seem, *single sheets* of the magazine are sometimes sold on the black market." The Voice of America had so good a reception that outstanding propagandists were assigned to attack it, and jamming was finally resorted to at great expense. When a Soviet school teacher, Mme. Kosankina, jumped from a Russian consulate window in New York to escape being returned to the USSR, the Voice's version of the story was as quickly current in Moscow as that of the official Soviet propaganda.[302] And a great compliment to the effectiveness of the radio assault against Stalinism was paid by a Soviet propaganda official when he indicated that since the Voice and BBC had started beaming programs to Russia in Russian, indoctrination in Marxism had become a much more difficult task.[303]

America was singled out for special attack, because the Soviet regime regarded the United States as the leading representative of Western civilization. The Russian feeling of inferiority with respect to the West had always been associated with Russian opposition to autocracy. It had endangered the Tsars, it might embarrass Stalin. It was both offensive and defensive, therefore, for the Soviet regime to condemn Western culture and civilization wholesale, after a war in which Russian self-confidence and admiration for the West had both grown; to condemn cosmopolitanism (which permeated the very soul of Marx) as a "bourgeois ideology denying the right of nations to national existence and state sovereignty";[304] to attack

---

[302] Smith, *Three Years in Moscow*, pp. 177 ff., 302.
[303] Barghoorn, *Soviet Image of the United States*, p. 287.
[304] "Humpty Dumpski," *The Economist*, November 11, 1950, p. 723.

Jewish Soviet intellectuals as "rootless cosmopolitans."[305] But the attraction exercised by the West upon the Russians, measured by the anti-West campaign, was largely "the result of discontent among Soviet people with the conditions of life in the USSR."[306]

There is other rather convincing evidence that the Russian people have had their fill of the Party line. Theater attendance is a rough mirror of public opinion in Russia, especially since the elimination of state subsidies in 1948 made the consumer king again in this restricted sphere. Western comedies and prerevolutionary Russian classics of the stage came off best; contemporary Soviet productions hewing to the Party line were least successful.[307] And the history of religion is more persuasive. From the very beginning the Soviet regime had fought the Orthodox Church, not only because religion, to any Marxist, was the "opiate for the masses," but because the church might become a center for opposition, particularly among the peasantry. The various shifts in religious policy for both foreign and domestic reasons, including the wartime restoration of the Patriarchate, amounted to little more than an increase or a relaxation of persecution. Considering the many years of antireligious propaganda, the exile and execution of clergy, the closing of churches, above all, the heavy pall of official disapproval that hung over all religious activity, particularly on the part of or among the young, it is little short of a miracle that the Orthodox Church should have survived.[308] It did so in sufficient strength to be worth Stalin's gestures of appeasement. When General Smith, as American Ambassador to Russia, was invited to attend midnight Easter Service in

[305] There was a revival of anti-Semitism in Russia after the war, the Jews being used as scapegoats in the anti-Western crusade, as they had been used as scapegoats for a variety of reasons under the Tsars. The crude pogroms of the old days were not repeated, however, if only for the reason that so lusty a degree of popular expression could not be tolerated under Stalinism. See Viereck, *Conservatism Revisited*, pp. 157 ff.; Dallin, *New Soviet Empire*, pp. 110 ff.; S. M. Schwarz, *The Jews in the Soviet Union*, Syracuse, 1951.

[306] Barghoorn, *Soviet Image of the United States*, p. 272.

[307] Dallin, *New Soviet Empire*, p. 174.

[308] In 1900 there were 351 churches in Moscow; in 1934, 40; in 1939, 15; spring of 1943, 30; end of 1943, about 50 (Dallin, *Real Soviet Russia*, p. 69). Chapter 4 of this book, "The New Religious Policy," is an admirable outline of the subject. See also N. S. Timasheff, *Religion in Soviet Russia*, New York, 1942, and *The Great Retreat*, pp. 225 ff.

Moscow Cathedral, he found so dense a crowd—"The great square was a solid mass of people—thousands and thousands of them"— that a wedge of twenty-five police was necessary to open a path to the church door.

> The interior of the vast building was a solid mass of humanity, packed together even closer, if possible, than the crowd outside. The congregation seemed to represent every stratum of Soviet society, with the important exceptions of the political and military. Men and women, divided about equally, had been in the church since early afternoon to hold their places.[309]

Five years later, in 1951, the *New York Times* correspondent Harrison Salisbury described much the same scene at the Troitski Monastery, forty miles outside Moscow, and in the villages in between: "congregations that packed the chapels tighter than a subway rush hour crush."[310] It would certainly seem that Leninist-Stalinist propaganda has not been an overwhelming success in this crucial field directly related to the most basic aspects of ideology.

While it is probably true that most Russians have lost any genuine recollection and understanding of a multiparty political system, it is equally doubtful that they take the rigged Soviet "elections" at face value, as a form of political democracy, or that they believe that the Supreme Soviet of the USSR is actually a law-making body. F. C. Barghoorn found intelligent young Russians "highly cynical" about the elections. A Soviet friend remarked to Edmund Stevens of the *Christian Science Monitor*, "We Russians can claim one priority that nobody ever will challenge. We have invented the world's dullest Parliament."[311]

There is, after all, a flaw in the argument that endless repetition of a lie or endless misuse of a word can transform the lie into truth in the popular mind and can change the meaning of the word. This can hold in the long run only when the lie contradicts neither common sense nor evident fact and when there is no test by which the misuse can be judged. These favorable conditions do not surround much of the basic Stalinist propaganda. Vyshinsky writes:

[309] *Three Years in Moscow*, pp. 262–263.
[310] *New York Times*, April 30, 1951.
[311] Barghoorn, *Soviet Image of the United States*, p. 246; Stevens, *This is Russia—Uncensored*, New York, 1951, p. 17.

The democracy of a state is expressed with particular clarity in its elective system. The democracy of an elective system is measured by the degree to which it is actually possible for the people to elect their representatives, those who enjoy the people's confidence, whom the people themselves freely nominate.[312]

But the Russian intelligentsia are in a position to see very clearly that the elections are merely a complex way of appointment, that the Supreme Soviet is a rather useless registrar of Politburo decisions. And they have the writings of Marx, Lenin, Russian revolutionaries of the nineteenth century, and the political philosophers of the West to give them the traditional definitions of the key words of political democracy which reveal Stalinist usage as distortion. Once it has got under way, the autonomous process of reasoning cannot be interrupted or reversed, save by terror or extinction of the thinking mind. So far as the nonintelligentsia are concerned, even if the majority can be persuaded that the Stalinist system is democracy, there is enough contact between them and the educated, and sufficient participation in the complex life of an industrial society for them to feel that, if Stalinism is democracy, they would like something not called democracy—perhaps freedom. Nearly all Soviet contradictions are thus reducible to the patent conflict between the ideals constantly propounded by Stalinism and the realities it enforces.

Perhaps the matter is best summarized by the Komsomol girl who told a Westener that she was not a Marxist but a democrat. Asked how one trained, indoctrinated, fed with Marxism, had reached such a position, she replied, "From life."[313]

The misfortunes of war and history enabled thousands of Russians to express their feelings toward Stalinism concretely. During World War II, Soviet General Vlasov, captured by the Nazis, recruited a force among Russian prisoners of war, to fight the government and armies of Stalin. Vlasov was thus a traitor to his state, and, having been associated with the Germans, has been described as a fascist and Ukrainian separatist. Neither appears to have been true. Vlasov, like most of his officers, was a Great Russian, and a Communist with

---

[312] *Law of the Soviet State*, p. 665.
[313] Barghoorn, *Soviet Image of the United States*, p. 274.

an excellent record. A German Propaganda Ministry memorandum gives the following picture of his ideological outlook:

> The Vlasov movement does not consider itself linked with Germany to the bitter end. It has strong Anglophile sympathies and entertains the idea of some day changing its course. The Vlasov movement is not National Socialist. . . . [It] is a diluted fusion of liberal and Bolshevik ideologies. The essential fact is that they do not fight the Jews; they fail to consider the Jewish question at all. The Vlasov movement thinks it can laugh off the National Socialist ideology. It does not represent a great Russian national renaissance, like Fascism in Italy and National Socialism in Germany.[314]

The word "liberal" expresses the hopes that led these Russians to war against Stalin; the word "Bolshevik" reveals the long conditioning, the continued desire for socialism vaguely understood (the tactic of treason, after all, might have been suggested to Vlasov and his followers by a reading of Lenin). The striking thing is that, however mistakenly, a number of patriotic Russians who had achieved success in Stalinist society felt it worth joining the Nazis they had hated in order to liberate their country from the dictatorship they had grown to hate even more.

Thousands of other Russians expressed their revulsion against Stalinism in less organized fashion: the nonreturners and the refugees. The former were Russian prisoners of war and workers conscripted by the Nazis. Neither cajoling by propagandists nor the threats of the NKVD (GPU) could induce them to return to their homeland, despite the terror of beginning anew in a strange world that was shamefully slow to awake to its moral obligations toward these people. Over 2 million were repatriated, no one knows how many willingly and how many by force;[315] about 500,000 managed to remain behind the Allied lines. There is no parallel for such an occurrence in modern times.[316]

---

[314] Quoted by Dallin, *New Soviet Empire*, p. 67. The general conclusions are borne out by the detailed study by George Fischer, *Soviet Opposition to Stalin, A Case Study in World War II*, Cambridge, 1952.

[315] Many, in fact, were forcibly taken by the NKVD. It was not until after there had been suicides in anticipation of being returned that the American Army stopped handing them over to Soviet authorities.

[316] See Louis Fischer, ed., *Thirteen Who Fled*, New York, 1949, for a most valuable introductory discussion of the nonreturners and their significance and

Our evidence is admittedly not as good as one would wish, but it appears to argue rather convincingly that very many Soviet subjects are resentful of and inwardly disloyal to the Stalinist regime. Under the conditions of the Soviet order, they are able neither to express their views nor to formulate their desires for change. It would be a reasonable guess that if the Russians were given the opportunity they would vote for a greater degree of freedom and welfare but that they would be unlikely to have developed any clear ideas as to what institutional arrangements were most conducive to freedom and welfare.

Even the question, how seriously does the leadership take its own propaganda, is not completely sealed off from reasonable speculation, although this is one of the most mysterious aspects of the Stalinist as of any totalitarian system. There is a hint of their attitude in the increasing secrecy about Soviet social and economic affairs: statistics were a major Soviet output in the early years when there was passionate belief in the intrinsic superiority of socialist production. The statistical blackout may reflect disillusionment with this belief, or at least awareness that it would be unwise to base a propaganda wager upon it. We may be fairly sure that the Kremlin clique, like their top emissaries abroad, are fully aware of the real difference between the Western and Soviet standards of living and freedom. Their cynicism in blandly inverting these differences is probably a minor matter in their eyes, for, as Marxists, they are most likely to believe in all sincerity that capitalism is doomed to decadence while Soviet socialism is certain to advance.[317] If their cynicism actually runs deep enough to encompass Stalinism and Marx-

---

thirteen biographical explanations of their action. Merle Fainsod, "Controls and Tensions in the Soviet System," *American Political Science Review,* June, 1950, pp. 266 ff., employs interviews with nonreturners as a rich source for social analysis. See also Boris Shub, *The Choice,* New York, 1950. A preliminary report on the Harvard Russian Research Center's project, interviewing thousands of nonreturners, is given by A. Inkeles and R. A. Bauer, "Portrait of Russia by Russians," *New York Times Magazine,* November 25, 1951.

[317] That they are cynical in the immediate present is suggested by the purchasing habits of Russian officials abroad, who return home with vast amounts of clothing and appliances. That irrepressible wit Gubitchev, the Russian UN employee convicted of espionage and deported in 1950, explained his departure with a television set by saying, somewhat illogically, "We invented television. That's why I'm taking this set home" (*New York Times,* March 20, 1950).

ism, it would only serve to reinforce a most corrosive characteristic of any dictatorship: the tendency of officials to present inaccurate reports of fact in order to conform to the prejudgments of higher bureaucrats.

Once one has overcome the defeatism inherent in regarding Russia as a "riddle wrapped . . . inside an enigma," it is possible to arrive at a reasonable evaluation of the nature and prospects of Stalinism. The Phoenix theory—old Russia rising from its ashes—will have to go by the board. The superficial evidence for it is plentiful, but it is quite superficial or superficially interpreted. Stalin, to be sure, was strongly reminiscent of three Tsars, Ivan the Terrible, Peter the Great, and Nicholas I, the policeman. There is reënserfment, the organized class structure and the beginnings of caste, the police state, Siberia and the suppression of freedom of thought, the military emphasis and aggressiveness, expansion toward traditional objectives of Russian imperialism, the show and extravagance of the Russian court and of Russian missions abroad, the intrigues of Russian agents. All of this and more seems to argue that what the world has witnessed and suffered is a recrudescence of the aggressive expansion of autocratic Russia, different only in its Marxian guise. This, of course, is obviously true to the extent that one speaks of the Russian *state*, but one should never forget that the history of Russia has been aptly described as consisting of two elements, strangely divorced: the history of a government and the history of a people. And the history of the people consists in great part of its struggle against that government, a struggle for freedom. This, after all, is the meaning of the peasant uprisings against the Tsars, without which scarcely a year went by, and of the revolutionary tradition of the Russian intelligentsia. This struggle was beginning to bear visible fruits of success in the twentieth century, until the progress of freedom was halted by the second revolution of 1917, the Bolshevik coup d'état. It is this historical choice of the path of tyranny that has given substance to de Tocqueville's prediction that the Russian, whose "adversaries . . . are men," whose "conquests . . . are gained . . . by the sword," who "centers all the authority of society in a single arm," and whose "principle instrument . . . is . . . servitude"; that this dark figure should have come "to sway the destinies of half the globe" constitutes a recapitulation on the world stage of the history of Russia itself.[318] The state has triumphed over the people, whom it exploits for its own forceful ends. At each of the decisive periods of turn in modern Russian history, during the reigns of Alexander I, Alexander II, and Nicholas II, Russian society was sufficiently flexible and dynamic to have been directed firmly toward progress in the Western sense. This was especially true of the era of the last Romanov Tsar. But in each of these periods of turn the scales were delicately balanced between an increase of freedom and a reiteration of depotism. The failures of the Cadets, the Octobrists, and the Kerenskys were the failures, in a general sense, of the half-measures of moderate democracy turned into disasters by a war that isolated Russian liberalism from its friends in the West. The successes of Lenin were the successes of a skillful politician who made Machiavelli sit with Marx, and his successes were built into triumphs by the circumstances of world war. Thus it was that Russia "chose" tyranny over freedom and the Russian people sank again behind the stone edifice of the state after a fleeting moment in the light.

The argument of history is not, therefore, that a civilization of despotism has recovered from its momentary eclipse by a liberating revolution. To the contrary, what history argues is that the nature of Bolshevism was such as to turn its back on the liberating forces in Russian culture (of which Bolshevism itself was a perverted offspring) and to revive wholesale the tyranny which these forces were slowly overcoming. It did this, let it be reiterated, not as a matter of conscious, rational choice, but because the very nature of Bolshevism forced it to do so. It is indeed an interesting speculation that Lenin, in his lingering death, may have realized that his grim warning of 1905 had been borne out by the degeneration of his own policies, by his own revolution:

Without political freedom all forms of workers' representation will continue to be a fraud. The proletariat will remain as heretofore in prison.

But, practically speaking, Lenin left his successors with but one choice, to reinforce tyranny to secure their objectives rapidly. It is a mistake, therefore, to regard Stalinism as a right-wing (or a left-wing) distortion of Lenin's revolution. It is a mistake to equate

[318] See p. 320.

Stalinism with the Thermidorian reaction and Bonapartism, the swing to a right-wing dictatorship after the reign of terror in the French Revolution of the eighteenth century. The historically logical consequence to what Lenin had done, as against what he might possibly have wished he had done, was Stalinism. The conflicts between Stalin and the left and right opposition factions within the Communist Party were primarily contests for power. Issues of policy, insofar as they were real, involved disagreements over pace and timing, not objectives. The right opposition of Bukharin, Rykov, and Tomsky wished temporarily to hold the process of social change in a state of suspended animation, without in any way weakening the power of the Communist party. Nor would a Trotskyite victory have made much difference, for Stalin was a Trotskyite. Militarization of labor, rapid industrialization, collectivization of agriculture, all were part of Trotsky's platform before Stalin adopted them. Trotsky's—and other opposition leaders'—pleas for intraparty democracy were the characteristic cry of the "outs." Had they, in power, remained true to their program, they could hardly have been more democratic than Stalin.

In its broad outlines, in its essentials, Stalinism is Leninism and Trotskyism. Fundamentally they are one, as they were in 1917. Perhaps another dictatorship might have managed with a little less ostentation, and a little less exaggerated worship of the *vozhd*. Perhaps these accidental traits derived from Stalin's own Asiatic character, to which he was fond of referring. But they were indeed no more than superstructure. The dictatorship as such rests upon an ideological, economic, and social basis which it created, and of which it is now a logical resultant.

Nor may we forget that Leninism-Stalinism is also Marxism, so that anyone who rejects the former must at least question the latter. Those among us who are still overawed by the towering reputation of Marx will protest that the failures and contradictions of socialism in Russia stem from its introduction in so backward a country. They are right, to a degree, but if we have learned anything from the events of the last thirty-five years it should be that it is precisely in backward countries that Marxism is most readily introduced, and by force. We should also recognize that it is the combination not only of Marxism and backwardness that produces tyranny, but of Marxism and revolutionary impatience. We can say, at the least, that we are now in a position to recognize the dangers attendant upon revolutionary Marxism, and there is as yet little or no evidence regarding the nature of a nonrevolutionary Marxian regime.[319]

Stalinism would appear to be an ideology and program devoted in the immediate to power, not as an absolute end for its own sake, but for reasons that are ultimately Marxist and Leninist. It is also devoted to the eventual achievement of socialism, in any traditional sense a hardly less distant and Utopian goal today than when Marx first wrote. The Stalin regime was always moved by a sense of urgency, it was always impatient of obstacles and supremely jealous of its monopoly of power. The sense of urgency, the will for power, the hindrances to sensible judgments that the system itself created, these combined with poverty to induce a search for and adoption of varying expedients, a process that at times seemed aimless. But both power and expediency were seen through Marxian and Leninist eyes. The pendulum swings between oppressive regulation and partial relaxation, almost always ending in a hardening of controls, derived from a conflict between the innermost conviction of the rulers and the common sense of human nature. This conviction is that the power of the Soviet state is a good, because the system on which it rests and which it invigorates is, by definition, itself good. That is why, in the end, the shifts and changes of wind settle into a reassertion of the essential sanctity of the Soviet order, and force is summoned to compel the recalcitrant human subjects to live their lives and cut their ways within the rules of that system.

The Soviet regime has neatly summarized its own nature. Stalin repeatedly condemned "careerism," "bureaucratism," and "undemocratic practices." And they do indeed abound. In a note to Yugoslavia after the break with Tito, Russia protested against police brutality and lack of civil liberties and genuine judicial protection under Tito's rule. "Can a regime that practices such outrages and gives people such inhuman treatment be called a democratic peo-

[319] There are even grounds for fearing that this moderate and presumably democratic type might degenerate of its own nature into a bureaucratic totalitarianism. See p. 253 ff.

ple's regime?" the Soviet government asked. And the note continued, "Would it not be more true to say that a regime that permits such abuse of people is a Fascist Gestapo regime?"[320]

What was true of Yugoslavia has long been and remains true of Soviet Russia, and the prospects are that so long as the sheer force of the Kremlin remains intact, Russia will continue to be an exploiting, oppressive, aggressive totalitarian despotism. If it be granted that immanent espionage, a large and loyal police force, repeated purges, and relocation of bureaucratic personnel will prevent the formation of any organized knots of opposition, what factors or processes in Soviet life are there that do make for change?

The Soviet economy will continue to progress, and even to diminish still further the gap between itself and the advanced West, although at a reduced rate. But this circumstance offers little hope for any genuine moderation of Stalinist oppression, for the system has not so far shown any capacity or disposition to organize its human subjects in a way to better their condition.

An analysis of productivity—conceived as real national product per hour of man work—by the distinguished Australian economist Colin Clark showed that Russia, in 1940, had been only slightly above her productivity level of 1900, and was slightly below in 1947, at least partly because of the war. Over the same period the productivity of the United States had tripled, reaching in 1947 a level over six and one-half times higher than the Soviet Union's peak of 1940. These figures, of course, are very rough approximations, and in no way deny the absolute increases in national productive capacity that Russia achieved in the first half of the twentieth century.[321] They merely record the fact that the lag in agriculture has roughly equaled the advance in industry and reflect the tremendous disguised unemployment that characterized the Soviet economy.

The pessimistic conclusions suggested by Clark's study are fully borne out by a projection of the Soviet economy under the most favorable assumptions. As Harry Schwartz points out, even if American per capita production in 1948 be regarded as adequate for a

---

[320] *New York Times*, August 11, 1949.

[321] Clark's analysis, based on material prepared for the second edition of his famous *Conditions of Economic Progress*, London, 1951, is conveniently summarized in an article in the *New York Times*, August 21, 1949.

state of communism (literally one in which no goods are scarce relative to needs), for the Russian economy to reach this per capita level over the years 1950–1970 with which Russian speculation over the declaration of communism is concerned, it would be necessary that

. . . steel production be increased over five times, pig iron output over four times, petroleum over eleven times, electric power over six times, shoes as much as four times, hosiery about seven times, cotton cloth almost four times, and woollen cloth over four times.

The goals of the Fifth Five-Year Plan, announced in August, 1952, to run through 1955, revealed no basic change in the Soviet emphasis on producers' goods and war industries at the expense of consumption. The targets, if fulfilled, would bring the USSR's output of basic materials to the level of the United States in 1934 or 1935; on a per capita basis they would afford about a third of American output in 1951.

There remain, moreover, the vast areas of consumer services, which presumably would be required for felicitous communism, and in which Russia's lag is most extreme. And the agricultural requirements would be more difficult to meet than the industrial. If the communist citizens of the USSR are to have a distinctly better diet than their socialist fathers, they must eat much more meat and dairy food and depend less on grain. But such a shift to an indirect consumption of grain by the people would require a vastly larger rise in grain output than an increase in direct grain consumption, for one pound of meat calls for five to ten pounds of grain as livestock feed. For Russia to reach, by 1970, America's per capita meat consumption as of 1948 would necessitate more than a doubling of Russian grain production, which, given the basic conditions of Soviet agricultural resources, would seem to lie beyond the limits of possibility.[322]

The danger, therefore, is that the advance of the Russian economy will lag behind the rise in population and fall far short of a condition of plenty. The Soviet system practically forbids that kind

[322] Schwartz, *Soviet Economy*, pp. 558 ff.; Schwartz article and summary of Plan, *New York Times*, August 23, 1952; *Current Digest of the Soviet Press*, September 13 and 20, 1952.

of industrial specialization and achievement of qualitative superiority in particular lines which would enable Russia to acquire food abroad through relatively free trade with the outside world. And the new Russian empire does not give promise of fulfilling this role. The conditions of the economy will probably tend to reinforce those social and political factors that make for the perpetuation of totalitarian despotism, for only through stringent controls will the regime be able to devote a sufficient proportion of relatively inadequate output to military purposes. And so long as the Soviet standard of living lags behind the West, the Iron Curtain, the police state, and a powerful army will be a necessary condition for the regime's survival.

The prospects, therefore, are for the continuation of the basic structures, practices, and policies of Stalinism as they had developed by mid-century. There will, of course, be constant experimentation with new techniques of incentive and control, but the fundamental characteristics appear to be well established, with little economic or political reason for change. More than ever, sheer force would appear as the keystone of the Soviet edifice, both at home, where promises of happier days to come will carry less and less conviction as the years of strain and hardship lengthen, and abroad, where increased knowledge of Soviet realities will reduce the attraction of Stalinist ideological propaganda. This means that, in all probability, Russia will continue her restless probing in world affairs, seeking weak spots in the capitalist defenses, cautiously pressing an expansionist policy. The Stalinists will do this not only because they are convinced Marxist-Leninists firmly believing in the inevitability of their ultimate triumph, and wishing to spread their version of socialism for its own sake, but to strengthen their security at home and abroad. They will, however, probably try to stop short of acts which would bring about a general war.

It would nevertheless be a grave and perhaps suicidal error for the West to draw the implication from Soviet inefficiency, from the oppression and poverty of the masses, that Russia is militarily weak. The very concentration on power that has contributed to the miseries of the Russian people has at the same time produced great strength for war. No one can question the ability of the Soviet commanders who rose to lead the Red Army in World War II. Nor can one doubt the proved ability of the Soviet regime to mobilize its subjects for war, once they have convinced themselves the war is worth fighting. Still less is it possible, after the demonstration in Korea of the parity or even superiority of much Soviet military equipment to American materiel, to question the skill of Russian designers or that efficiency of Russian war plants to which the few who have had the chance to observe so readily testify.

But there is no real contradiction between the apparently conflicting conclusions of Soviet inefficiency in general and relatively high efficiency in matters of war. The seeming paradox merely bespeaks the regime's stress on power, the devotion of the best of their productive skills and plant to military uses. The paradox also reflects the inability of Stalinism to produce that general upward leveling of efficiency that has characterized progressive capitalist economies. With regard to the assessment of the USSR as a world power, therefore, one can only conclude that its striking force is indeed mighty, and properly to be feared. But this judgment in no way conflicts with the view that the social failures of Stalinism would influence the regime to a policy of caution in international affairs, to the avoidance if possible of a general war to which the Russian people might not freely commit themselves heart and soul.

Beginning in 1951, Soviet moves seemed to suggest that the period of dynamic aggression that had followed World War II might be coming to an end, as the efforts of the United States and its allies restored an equilibrium of power such as had existed in the 1930's. The time for overt, swift efforts to extend the Soviet power might be drawing to a temporary close, and the slower, quieter methods of Communist infiltration and organization might again be stressed, as before the war. The foreign Communist parties had been tightened by purges, as was necessary for a period of slow advance. The satellites were being more firmly bound to their Soviet master. A "peace offensive" was designed to split the West, to make the capitalist "thieves fall out," so that Stalinism might gain.

Consolidation behind the Iron Curtains and splitting the Western allies—these appeared to be the principal themes of the Nineteenth Congress of the All-Union Communist Party (Bolsheviks), which met in October, 1952. There was a good deal of tidying up: the Party name was changed to the more descriptive "Communist Party of the Soviet Union," the old emphasis on Bolshevik as distinct from Menshevik no longer being significant; the Politburo was renamed the Presidium; and the Organization Bureau became part of the Secretariat of the Central Committee. Party members were warned against continuing their sins of careerism, passivity, insensitivity to criticism, suppression of criticism, the equivalent of "com-boasts" and "com-lies," nepotism, lack of vigilance, etc.

The magnificent industrial progress of the USSR was vaunted by leading speaker Malenkov, who declared that whereas Soviet industrial output had risen from 100 in 1929 to 1266 in 1951, American industrial output had only moved from 100 to 200 over the same years and British to but 160. However, recognizing that much remained to be done before the felicity of communism would be attained, Stalin, in a commentary on economics which appeared the same week as the Party Congress met, held that real wages would have to rise by at least 100 percent, while the workday would fall to five or six hours, and the Marxian heaven would be prepared by "universal compulsory polytechnical education, so that a member of society may be able to make a free choice of occupation and not be shackled for life to any one occupation." As of this date, the state was still expected by Stalin eventually to wither away into a planning agency.

For the real world of the present, however, Malenkov and Stalin laid down a prediction upon which actual policy might more readily be based. This was that there would be relative peace between the growing and prosperous world of the Communists and the decaying world of capitalism, whereas the latter would be rent by internal struggles, in accordance with Lenin's theory of imperialism. War between the two worlds would become likely only under circumstances which invited the transformation of the Communists' struggle for peace into an effort to overthrow capitalism as such—in short, Russia would strike only at a propitious moment of capitalist disintegration.

The mixture of confidence and caution bespoke both consolidation and a reassertion of the theoretical principles which the Soviet leaders, as Marxists reading the world in Marxian terms, identified with their successes at home and abroad.[323] Genuinely peaceful co-existence between capitalism and Communism was most unlikely for two reasons. First, the restatement of the basic Lenin-Stalin line meant there was no reason to regard peaceful gestures as anything more than a tactical deviation. Second, even if the Soviet rulers were honestly deciding to relinquish plans for world Sovietization, genuinely friendly relations between the USSR and the West would hardly be possible so long as the Iron Curtain was maintained. And Russia could not drop this protective device until Soviet society could bear open and uncensored comparison with the West.

Another set of factors also dictated caution. There were signs of continued and even aggravated dissatisfaction among subject peoples and national minorities within the USSR, a dissatisfaction that naturally rose with the emphasis on Great Russia and her role of leadership (in its turn a useful improvement in the dictatorial process). Nationalism would breed even greater irritation in the satellite countries, Russia's first ramparts in case of war. And, nationalism aside, there was the great mass of dissatisfied and disaffected in Russia itself. For more than a generation they had slaved and struggled; they had rallied heroically in the German war, and saved their government along with their country. But they hoped for relaxation, for a diminution of arrests and purges, shock brigading and socialist competition, "asceticism of consumption" and propaganda pep rallies. Their hopes were dashed in the postwar policy of "restoration and further development." The greatest pains would have to be taken really to convince the Russian people that, in any future war, the Soviet state was not the aggressor.

There was more than a dispirited mass to cause worry and hesitation, however. Consider the forced laborers and their families and friends. It is surely not overburdening the imagination to suppose that prison camp inmates and those devoted to them were resentful toward the regime that inflicted these sufferings. The death rate was high in the camps, and many were released after they had served their terms, so that the number of those who had directly or

[323] For the Party Congress, new Party statutes, Malenkov's and Stalin's speeches, Stalin's commentary on economics, and a particularly vapid debate on "polytechnical education," see the *Current Digest of the Soviet Press,* September 6, September 27, October 11, October 18 (special supplement) November 1, 1952.

indirectly felt this scourge greatly exceeded the number of inmates at any given time. These people may be counted in the millions: if their families averaged three members there must have been 14 million embittered citizens of the Soviet Union at the lowest estimate, and this figure could rise as high as 40 million or more—a fifth of the total population, and a higher percentage of the adult population (without taking into account the families of former prisoners).

This argues not only for Stalinist caution, but eventually for the decay of Stalinism. Although it is quite true that the system may carry on for an indefinite period, it is by no means likely to be permanent, even if it is not destroyed in a general war. It makes too many enemies, especially among the intelligentsia who are more prone than the uneducated to be tormented by the autonomy of reason once they have begun to think. Their training and their jobs force them to think, and at the same time frustrate independent thinking. A loyal and efficient system can prevent such thinking from leading to dangerous acts only so long as there is also a secure unanimity at the very top. This was Joseph Stalin's unquestioned achievement. But would his successor be up to it? Indeed, would there be a successor as a long-reigning dictator? In the months before his death on March 5, 1953, there were increasing signs that he was paving the way for his mantle to fall on G. M. Malenkov, an unprepossessing party official. Malenkov had been given the main speaking assignment at the Party Congress, and had moved closer to Stalin in official photographs. Show trials in the satellites indicated that the process of consolidation was moving into a higher stage, and a strong note of anti-Semitism, which served a variety of political ends, also hinted at the preparation of a group of scapegoats for an internal Russian operation of the highest importance. The hearts of many Russians must have chilled, in recollection of the 1930's, when, in January, 1953, a group of Kremlin physicians, including Jews charged with being Zionist-imperialist-American agents, were accused of having arranged medically the deaths of Zhdanov and others, and of plotting further outrages. Zhdanov had been Malenkov's rival. Was this frightening remembrance of the great purge both to justify the past and to forestall, in advance of Stalin's death, opposition to the succession of Malenkov? Were

Beria, the security chief (who, it had been implied, was guilty of negligence in not preventing the doctors' "plot") and the Jewish Kaganovich (who had long been the Soviet Union's top economic administrator) marked for stellar roles in a repetition of Stalin's dramatic suppression of his opponents?

Stalin died; and Malenkov took over as Premier. But alongside him as First Deputy Premiers stood Beria and Kaganovich, their prestige enhanced, together with the veteran Molotov and the military politician Bulganin. The organizational reforms of Party and government that Stalin had instituted less than six months earlier were discarded before he had been laid to rest, the enlarged Party Presidium being cut back to the size of the old Politburo. A scant fortnight later, Malenkov, at his own request, according to the Soviet announcement, was relieved of the first Secretaryship of the Central Committee of the Communist Party, and replaced with N. S. Khrushshchev, who had earlier been Party boss in the Ukraine and had been chiefly responsible for the agro-urbanization fumble. Scarcely had the world accustomed itself to think of the Soviet Union as ruled by the triumvirate of Malenkov, Molotov, and Beria when the latter, the last of Stalin's great liquidators, was thrust from office with the usual charges of rascality. It appeared that one of his sins had been to encourage the non-Russian minorities, so that his downfall suggested a reaffirmation of Great Russian domination and centralized control.

In general, however, the post-Stalin government strove to create an atmosphere of appeasement at home by projecting a moderation of criminal laws, reducing the prices of consumers' goods, and planning a higher proportion of consumers' goods output. Stalin was almost ostentatiously forgotten, and his Party *History* replaced with one that gave Lenin unique stardom. The rule of one man was condemned, collective leadership called for. Before the fall of Beria the doctors' "plot" had been denounced as the fabrication it obviously was. After his removal the people were promised they would be protected from bureaucratic injustice on the part of the police. Abroad, there was a propaganda campaign on the theme of peace and the peaceful coexistence of Soviet socialism and western capitalism.

The successors of Stalin clearly needed time, a period free from acute problems, an interval in which domestic dissatisfaction could be induced to give way to hope for improvement, time in which to become settled and established. One could not yet perceive whether the rumblings from the Kremlin revealed a simple struggle for power within the Soviet elite, or a struggle that also involved an effort to recreate an almost mythical Leninism somehow distinct from Stalinism. Russia was yet far from facing squarely the question of how to create a prosperous society without the incentives of freedom, a contented and willing society without abolishing authoritarian rule and the privileges of a governing class.

One could only say that the death of Stalin was most likely to bring changes in the social and political structure of the Russian empire, and that the economic institutions would not be left untouched by the current of events. Perhaps, however, we had best close on a Marxist note of economic determinism, quoting, as is most fitting, Joseph Stalin:

Revolutions in the past perished because, while giving the people freedom, they were unable to bring about any serious improvement in their material and cultural conditions. Therein lay their chief weakness. Our revolution differs from all other revolutions in that it not only freed the people from tsardom and capitalism, but also brought about a radical improvement in the welfare and cultural condition of the people. Therein lies its strength and invincibility.[324]

[324] *History of the Communist Party of the Soviet Union* (Bolsheviks), p. 341. Although it is proper to attribute this quotation to Stalin, since the History was prepared by a Commission of the Central Committee of the CPSU (B), and Stalin has been credited in Russia with general and detailed supervision, it may be worth pointing out that these phrases are based upon a direct quotation from one of Stalin's speeches, which follows immediately after: "Our revolution is the only one which not only smashed the fetters of capitalism and brought the people freedom, but also succeeded in creating the material conditions of a prosperous life for the people. Therein lies the strength and invincibility of our revolution."

While this book was in press, major speeches by Malenkov and Khrushchev, in the fall of 1953, gave Soviet confirmation to the ironic interpretation of Stalin's judgment. The former, while boasting about Soviet industrial progress, conceded that the people's standard of living had not greatly benefited therefrom. The latter, while reasserting the superiority of collectivized agriculture, statistically and otherwise demonstrated its failure and announced a half-hearted NEP for the peasants. Neither speech betrayed any readiness to look at problems afresh, or to engage in anything more than a swing of the pendulum toward popular appeasement.

Once again, we may say—a last contradiction—that Stalin was both partly right, and very wrong.

NOTES ON BOOKS

The English-speaking reader who sets out to enrich his knowledge of contemporary Russia will be rather surprised by the great mass of writings available to him on what is purportedly so mysterious a subject. Much of the literature, to be sure, consists of unrestrained praise or equally unbridled criticism, but even works of this character may serve the purposes of inquiry. And there are many books and articles of excellent quality as to information and analytical insight. The reader is likely to find it curious, however, that some of the most solid productions of recent scholarship are strangely inconclusive and, if he carries on to the point of discovering what different scholarly authorities think of each other, he will learn that the most respectably accredited experts tend to look down upon writers who do take a firm position.

The cult of "objectivity" is so highly developed among some experts in Soviet studies that it is necessary to recall once again what objectivity in social analysis can really mean. It does not mean avoidance of judgments or suppression of judgments. It does not even mean the absence of "bias." After all, as British General Hilton remarked, "surely no man of ripe age can be completely unbiased unless he is an imbecile." Objectivity means a decent respect for the facts and a readiness to fit interpretations to them. And a work should be judged, not by the position or attitudes of its author, but by the accuracy of his information, his judiciousness in selection, and the consistency of his judgments with that information.

The following severely abbreviated list of books I regard as especially helpful in understanding Soviet Russia reflects the foregoing conception of objectivity, as well as, to a degree, my own "bias."

A good view of the sweep of Russian history may be obtained from Bernard Pares' *History of Russia,* or G. Vernadsky's *Political and Diplomatic History of Russia,* and, among newcomers to the field, S. Harcave's *Russia, A History.* The essential economic background can be found in G. T. Robinson's *Rural Russia Under the Old Regime* and P. I. Lyashchenko's *History of the National Economy of Russia to the 1917 Revolution.* Intrusions of the "party line" in the latter do not interfere significantly with an able and factual account. The intellectual background, which is extremely important, is more difficult to come by, but several works may be recommended: T. G. Masaryk's classic, *The Spirit of Russia* (2 vols.);

R. Hare's *Pioneers of Russian Social Thought;* the theologian N. Berdyaev's *The Russian Idea,* often brilliant but poorly organized; E. H. Carr's *Studies in Revolution.*

For the revolution itself, one may read Trotsky's monumental *History of the Russian Revolution,* in three volumes. It is, of course, not only pro-Bolshevik but intensely Trotskyite, but displays the competence and learning of one of the outstanding revolutionaries. Western requirements for good history will nevertheless be more fully met by W. H. Chamberlin's *Russian Revolution.* E. H. Carr's *The Bolshevik Revolution 1917–1923,* which has the benefit of data that have become available in recent years, is both thoughtful and sympathetic.

To a much greater extent than the American or French revolutions, the Bolshevik revolution can be seen through the life of one man, Lenin. Here David Shub's *Lenin, A Biography,* stands out as extremely well written and skillfully documented. Vernadsky's older book, *Lenin, Red Dictator,* is still very useful and provides a most lucid account of the subject's life and times. A good deal that is pertinent to both Lenin and the revolution will naturally be found in studies of his successor, of which Souvarine's *Stalin, A Critical Survey of Bolshevism* is particularly to be recommended. The more recent work of Deutscher, *Stalin, A Political Biography,* is thorough and highly competent, but is marred by a tendency toward evasion of some of the issues which Souvarine faces squarely. B. D. Wolfe's *Three Who Made a Revolution* skillfully interweaves biography, ideology, and critical source analysis. Edmund Wilson's *To the Finland Station* treats of the ideological development from Marx to Lenin and Trotsky, a briefer discussion of which may be found in R. N. Carew-Hunt, *The Theory and Practice of Communism.*

There is no one work covering the many aspects of the Stalin era. Political matters are best handled in the biographies of Stalin mentioned above. For Soviet foreign relations and policy one may consult the 1951 edition of Louis Fischer's *Soviets in World Affairs* (2 vols.), Max Beloff's two-volume *Foreign Policy of Soviet Russia,* and David J. Dallin's *Soviet Russia and the Far East* and *Russia and Postwar Europe.*

The ablest overall treatment of Soviet economic institutions, policies, and history is Harry Schwartz's *Russia's Soviet Economy,* a work rich in both fact and careful and penetrating analysis. Of earlier books, Aron Yugow's *Russia's Economic Front for War and Peace* is to be recommended. *Management in Russian Industry and Agriculture,* by Bienstock, Schwarz, and Yugow, is an able introduction to the Soviet economic system from the standpoint of organization and management. Maurice Dobb's *Soviet Economic Development Since 1917* is a most competent treatment with respect to technical economics, but either ignores the fundamental social and economic issues or gives them a Stalinist gloss. Manya Gordon's *Workers Before and After Lenin* is a powerful, factual blast at the Soviet regime, from the point of view of the welfare of the Russian people. It should be required reading for those who are prone to regard the Soviet Union as a welfare state. Isaac Deutscher's *Soviet Trade Unions* is a brief and intelligent account. In the field of agriculture and collective farming, the reader is extremely fortunate to have available Naum Jasny's remarkable achievement in research and analysis, *The Socialized Agriculture of the USSR*. The three volumes by L. E. Hubbard, *Soviet Labour and Industry, Soviet Trade and Distribution,* and *Soviet Money and Finance* remain pertinent and enlightening despite the passage of time. Harry Schwartz's *The Soviet Economy, A Selected Bibliography of Materials in English,* is an invaluable guide.

In seeking insight into Soviet society through its legal forms and philosophy, a discriminating reader will find much that is useful in Vyshinsky's *Law of the Soviet State* and J. N. Hazard, ed., *Soviet Legal Philosophy.* The uninitiated reader will do better to consult Vladimir Gsovski, *Soviet Civil Law,* which is more productive of clarification than H. J. Berman's *Justice in Russia.*

Many Soviet sources are now available to the English-speaking reader, particularly owing to the efforts of the American Council of Learned Societies, but for a severely restricted choice one would not be amiss in concentrating on Stalin's *Problems of Leninism* and the *History of the Communist Party of the Soviet Union (Bolsheviks). The Current Digest of the Soviet Press* is, of course, invaluable for Soviet news and thought since 1949.

In the broad category of works that seek to induce an understanding of the Stalinist system as a whole, G. S. Counts and N. Lodge's *The Country of the Blind* is both a valuable compilation of sources and a critical analysis. N. S. Timasheff's *The Great Retreat* is a rather original interpretation along Thermidorian lines. D. J. Dallin's *The Real Soviet Russia* is an excellent example of the frank and shrewd analysis which this author has contributed to the field. Unless he is predisposed to neo-Freudian social theory, the reader may pass lightly over G. Gorer and J. Rickman's *The People of Great Russia, A Psychological Study,* the outstanding instance to date of what Dallin has called "diaperology." The understanding it seeks to advance will be aided rather by such works as Sir John Maynard's *Russia in Flux,* or W. Weidlé's stimulating *Russia: Absent and Present,* and the concentration on a supposed Russian need for authority which results from the practice of swaddling infants has little support in concrete fact and flies in the face of both common sense and elementary logic.

There is a vast and steadily increasing literature of refugees from the USSR, naturally uneven in quality. Much of it is interesting in itself as well as being fruitful of insight to the reader who can profit from the personal narrative. What is striking about these books, from Barmine's *One Who Survived* through Kravchenko's controversial *I Chose Freedom* to such less celebrated recent volumes as Jelagin's *Taming of the Arts,* is their agreement on the basic characteristics of Stalinist society. They consequently add depth and further meaning to the conclusions drawn from more formal types of evidence.

It will not be amiss to add a word about the reliability of Soviet statistics, since every analysis of Stalinism must ultimately depend upon them. Until recent years, there were two broad classes among Western authorities on Russia: those, largely Stalinists themselves, who held that Soviet statistics were not only entirely honest, but furnished an adequate basis for favorable conclusions about the regime; and those who held that there was a great deal of concealment, but that such data as were published were entirely trustworthy. Recently a more severely critical attitude has appeared, urging that Soviet statistics are not only subject to the faults of concealment and selective revelation, but that they are, in addition, crudely doctored. Convincing evidence for this view, with respect to certain sets of Soviet figures, has been offered by Naum Jasny, in *Socialized Agriculture* and in *The Soviet Price System, Soviet Prices of Producers' Goods,* and *The Soviet Economy During the Plan Era.* Falsification aside, the greatest single distorting factor was the Soviet practice of publishing evaluations of output in terms of 1926–1927 prices, which created a severe inflationary bias in all their statistics. This system was finally abandoned in March, 1952, for one based on 1952 prices, but, to preserve the glowing statistical evidence of progress, all Soviet comparisons between years before and after 1950 (to which the new index first applied) must be calculated by a formula employing the 1926–1927 prices.

PART IV

Theories of Corporatism and an Approach to the Middle Way

13.

THE WAYS OF CORPORATISM

The Corporatist Idea

Tʜᴇ systematic ideologies of classical capitalism, democratic socialism, and Stalinism do not bear up well under examination. The first has been called the only Utopia that has never been tried—and never will be. The second may be likened to a Platonic absolute idea—its existence can only be inferred or demonstrated in the abstract, and one can never be certain that any actual society is really a concrete instance of democratic socialism, any more than one can be sure that democratic socialism is not merely a halfway house on the road to total bureaucratization. Neither classical capitalism nor democratic socialism will come into being through a fundamental and presumably inevitable historical process. We may be certain that Stalinism too will not be adopted as the result of any intrinsic social development, and while it might indeed be riding the wave of the future, this can only be a wave of successful military conquest.

One must recall the mixed and possibly even muddled concept of modern neomercantilism. There is much hope in it, partly just because it is not precise, but thus far it has been altogether too confined to the economic sphere of human interests to serve as a positive ideology. And its outstanding quality—adaptability to different historical circumstances—is shared by another concept, the doctrine of corporatism. Corporatism is truly chameleonlike in its linkage with the most diverse and contradictory political and social beliefs, and it therefore ranges in color from an anarchic democracy to nationalist totalitarianism. It was most clearly developed and formally presented by the Italian Fascists, and in this guise has little actual appeal. Its most popular expression has been that of the European Catholic democratic parties after World War II, and in this form it has less clarity. A less formal kind of corporatism is that of certain secular sociologists, historians, and economists, who form no school, and differ in many respects, but paradoxically it may turn out that they are describing the actual trend of advanced capitalist society. The defeat of fascism, in short, far from removing corporatism as an ideological issue and social option, has made it possible for one to consider its essential character and strength, unconfused by the fantasies of manic nationalism.

The basic ideas of corporatism are quite simple. Since economic interests are among the most important for most people, society should be organized along economic, that is, occupational lines, a principle that might even be extended to representative government. Although people may be equal before God, and before secular law, they are unequal in abilities and in the social importance of their work, and society must therefore recognize its separation into leaders and led, the former receiving higher rewards and prestige. In general, corporatism accepts the principle of private productive property and, far from admitting a class struggle between owners and/or managers and workers, insists on the naturalness as well as the necessity of class coöperation. Management and labor must get together, under the eyes of the state which represents all. Corporatism proclaims the organic nature of society, and claims as its justification a higher measure of social equity and security, rather than the natural laws of classical capitalism or the historical necessity of Marxism.

The foregoing would harmonize, in a general way, with all the mutually contradictory varieties of corporatism, but the details which give these generalities meaning depend upon the particular historical associations, of corporatism with Catholicism or Protestantism, of corporatism with extreme nationalism, or of corporatism with secular, bourgeois democracy. Modern corporatism developed first as a response of conservative and even reactionary thinkers to the twin challenge of individualistic, classical capitalism and political democracy following the French Revolution of 1789 and the Napoleonic Wars. It was thus a plea for the restoration of social stability by means of a tight, organic system. Later in the nineteenth century, corporatism was democratized somewhat, now appearing as a program for the improvement of the conditions of the working class, for the betterment of employer-worker relations, for countering the appeal of Marxian socialism. During and immediately after the First World War, corporatism came to the fore in Germany, in a new and secular guise which emphasized social stability and efficiency, and which was for the first time linked with the idea of the planned economy.

Despite its long history, however, corporatism struck most people as a novelty, when it reappeared, together with irresponsible nationalism, among the doctrines of the Italian Fascist state. The Nazis followed in Italy's wake, as did the Falange of Franco's Spain, Marshal Petain's Vichy regime in France, and even, in a particularly vague way, Peron in Argentina. Even before World War II, events cast doubt on the corporatist sincerity of the various fascists, and the war itself destroyed their pretensions. Corporatism itself survived, apparently entering the postwar world stronger than ever, for now it had returned to its democratic and religious affiliations of the late nineteenth century. It was indeed more democratic than ever before, since the paternalistic traits of the 1890's had yielded before the equalitarian trends of modern times. The principal exponents of corporatism following World War II, the Catholic parties of France, Italy, and Western Germany, were major mass parties, with strong popular and working-class appeal.

Secular corporatism was also restated, largely as a deduction from the bureaucratization of big business, the increased strength of labor unions, and the growth of government intervention. In this guise it served as a response to disillusionment with classical capitalism, born of the Great Depression, and disillusionment with Marxism, born of the destruction of individual liberty in Russia. Finally, corporatism gained added interest, not so much as a program of what ought to be, but as a description of the major trends operating in the Western democratic world, and as a prediction of their future development.

It is not that the word "corporatism," or the ideas it connotes, can mean anything one wishes them to mean. The story of corporatism reflects Lenin's keen but neglected observation about the relation of socialism to political democracy: the color, flavor, and real character of a social and economic system or doctrine are given by the political and ethical beliefs with which it is associated. Fascism and Catholic corporatism are not strange bedfellows; they are not bedfellows at all, for their sharply contradictory political and ethical doctrines produce equally diverse conceptions of corporatism as a way for society. Once again, therefore, the real meaning of the ideology is to be sought not so much in its abstract definitions as in its living history.

I. *Corporatism and Christianity*

The French Revolution, the horrible Reign of Terror, and the military sweeps of Napoleon shocked the collective consciousness of Europe as much as, and perhaps more than, anything that has happened since. Western civilization had of course changed in many respects since that indeterminate part of the fifteenth century by which historians generally date the end of the medieval epoch. The Reformation had shattered the ideological as well as the strictly religious overall unity of Christendom. The national states and their absolute monarchs had replaced the vague cohesiveness of a culture characterized by a large degree of local autonomy and local differences. Within each of the national societies the cultural, political, and economic autonomy of localities was steadily diminished. The ever-changing economy of capitalism, based on credit and increasingly on larger-scale industry, replaced the more or less stable relationships of towns and countrysides that had endured for centuries. The disunited Christian world expanded dramatically, bringing the other continents within its purview. Europe was remade not once but several times in the three centuries that followed the generation of Columbus and Martin Luther, but the continuity of its traditions and its essential likeness was still something one could readily grasp. The events of 1789–1815 posed a question that troubles sensitive minds of our own era. Is our civilization tending toward utter disintegration? And, much as the prophets and seers contemporary with Lenin and Hitler have evoked the collapse of the liberal ethos and value system of the nineteenth century to explain the apparent chaos of our time, the men of 1815 who sought the meaning of history pointed to the undermining of traditional philosophical attitudes, customary political and economic principles, and long-established religious beliefs to explain the lost grip of the institutions within which one could live in a comprehensible fashion. Our contemporary prophets within Western civilization call for the creation of a new value structure, or perhaps the fusion of a small portion of the old with something new, to counter the disintegrating challenge of materialism. But we have learned, over a century in which the pace of social transformation has been quickened by a permanent technological revolution, that the old order can never be restored. And we have come to doubt that it can even be readapted. To many of the prophets of 1815 it still seemed reasonable to believe that since the perils of eighteenth-century rationalism and its attendant social movements had been amply demonstrated, the obvious cure was to return to the older values and institutions which had proved their stability, only purging them of the faults and impurities born of time and change. Going back meant restoring the power of the crown and the church. Ideologically it meant rejecting rationalistic and mechanistic theories of society and taking an historical and organic view. Socially this implied a return to the conceptions of hierarchy and status or order, stability, and justice that underlay medieval town society and gild systems, and the participation in government according to social class (estates) that characterized medieval parliaments.

The idea of reincarnating the Middle Ages was naturally most congenial to conservative Roman Catholic romantics, to whom, in a sense, the Reformation could be classed with the French Revolution as an audacious human attempt to destroy divinely inspired order. The neomedievalism in the guise of which corporatism made its bow to the modern world was therefore in part a Catholic intellectual movement. And, reflecting the intensity with which Germany felt the stresses of the times, it was predominantly German.[1] The right wing of French romantic political thought made its contribution through Joseph de Maistre and the Vicomte de Bonald. But the

---

[1] The outstanding Protestant corporatists were German legal historians, such as F. C. von Savigny.

leading spokesmen for corporatism in the era of Napoleon were such German romantics as Fichte and his followers Adam Müller and Friedrich Schlegel.

The basic point to men like Müller and Schlegel was that man could not realize his potential for godliness, could not achieve a way of life favorable to Christian morality and salvation, save within a group. It was the state, and the other arms of social organization, all inspired by the Church, that raised the individual of the human species to the level of Christian man. Rationalistic individualism, spawning avaricious ambition rather than humility and the desire to do good, was thus subversive of all the fundamental aims of man. Rejecting this error, society should promote the sense of belonging and cohesiveness from which alone both order and charity could grow. Society should therefore be organized along professional or occupational lines, the lowly to seek Christian good in their stations, the higher placed devoting themselves to the just care of their fellow men. In short, these early corporatists sought the adaptation of medieval society to the nineteenth century, strengthening the binding ties by replacing the loose political structure of feudalism with the efficient central power of the modern state.

The corporatists failed utterly to advance their cause. Their political outlook was too intimately linked with the romantic reaction to the French Revolution and Napoleon to survive the onslaughts of secular liberalism and secular nationalism. Their social outlook drew little popular support from an era in which the aspirations of the middle class still fell short of full satisfaction, and in which the desires of an industrial working class still lacked clear formulation. In France, the revolutionary law that had swept away the gilds survived as a barrier to the formation of trade unions. The persistence of the gilds in the German lands was a measure of the slow development of industrialization, but it was the protective tariffs and railway building of neomercantilism rather than the further development of the gild system that attracted support and achieved success in the middle third of the nineteenth century. Post-Napoleonic corporatism, on the other hand, was little more than an ideological parallel, barely related in practical politics, to the uninspired policies of central European governments.

Whatever else the nineteenth century may have brought, it did produce an increasing democratization of society, despite the persistence of monarchy and aristocracy, and in part because of the growth of a very wealthy upper bourgeoisie. Christian corporatism shared this democratizing trend: it was, in the early years of its second phase, no longer concerned primarily with the restoration of a hierarchic social order, but rather with the improvement of the condition of the industrial working class. It was thus a very much attenuated form of corporatism, appearing under the names of Liberal Catholicism and, in England, of Protestant Christian Socialism.[2] Both emphasized the social immorality and unchristian character of unregulated industrial capitalism, both preached self-help for labor through unionization and workers' coöperatives. Both added to the climate of opinion which produced the beginnings of social legislation, especially in England, where Christian conservatives like Shaftesbury, Oastler, and Sadleir, and later Disraeli, translated into laws that desire to better the lot of the worker that had moved the Christian Socialists such as Maurice and Kingsley. From the standpoint of the development of corporatist doctrine, the beginnings of this second phase did little more than reëmphasize the need for Christians to develop some positive response to the ills of industrial capitalism.

There was less reason for the development of an active and self-consciously Christian social movement, and of a positive and self-consciously Christian social doctrine, in England than on the Continent. The garden that might have been cultivated by the established Church of England was in large part tended by Tory reformers and Tory Democrats. The independent Protestant churches strongly influenced the labor unions, the coöperatives, and, finally, the Labour Party itself. Protestant social criticism, in short, permeated many sectors of British society without constituting the basis for any unified action or cohesive movement—to which, by its very nature, Protestantism is not especially given.

On the Continent, however, particularly in France and the German Rhineland, conditions were extremely favorable to the develop-

[2] Lammenais, Lacordaire, and Ozanam were leading figures in French Liberal Catholicism which, as an intellectual tendency, ran into trouble with the Vatican. Lammenais was excommunicated in 1834. British Christian Socialism, inspired by Ludlow, Kingsley, and Maurice, blossomed in 1848 and the years immediately following.

ment of what has become known as Social Catholicism. Before the 1880's, capitalism was less subject to regulating laws than in England, labor unions were weaker, the European aristocracy showed less zeal for social reform than did British conservatives. Furthermore, Marxism had begun its permeation of European society by the time European labor began to organize effectively, posing a far more basic challenge to Catholicism even than the Reformation itself. The Church simply had to fight back against the Marxian threat to capture the steadily growing urban working class. Lastly, after 1870, the Catholic Church was directly challenged, in Germany by Bismarck's nationalist desire for uniformity, and in France by ardently anticlerical bourgeois republicanism. Unlike the Protestant churches, Catholicism was so organized as to be able to respond in a fairly systematic way[3] to the social situation of the latter part of the nineteenth century, and the soundest and longest enduring aspect of this response was Social Catholicism, a frankly corporatist doctrine and movement.

Social Catholicism blended the concern for the poor and the laborer of earlier Liberal Catholics with a program for the adaptation of the gild system to industrial needs and conditions. Compared with post-Napoleonic corporatism, this was corporatism democratized, for Social Catholics stressed not so much a functional hierarchy as the mutual interdependence and coöperation of classes. And, unlike the post-Napoleonic thinkers, Social Catholics insisted on the independence of the gild structure from the state, a position practically forced upon them by the strength of Lutheranism in Prussianized Germany and by the triumph of anticlericalism in the Third French Republic. They asked, in short, for corporatism *within* the state, but *not* for a corporate state.

The essentials of Social Catholicism, rooted in ancient Christian

[3] The unity of the Catholic Church, then or now, should not be exaggerated. There are striking differences, from country to country and even bishopric to bishopric, in the attitudes of the Catholic hierarchy toward matters of political and social policy or custom. The variation is even greater in lay acceptance, or active following, of the views expressed by the hierarchy. Catholic uniformity is maintained strictly only in respect of the essentials of the faith. The lack of unity in matters of social doctrine prevented Social Catholicism, expounded in two major papal encyclicals, from receiving greater support from Catholics, and from making far greater progress than it actually did.

doctrine, may be stated as follows. Labor is not a commodity, but partakes of the essential God-given dignity of man. Hence it is contrary to moral law to treat labor as a commodity, and it is sinful to be guided in economic life by the simple precept of maximizing one's individual gain. The laborer must work in conditions of dignity and respect, and be so rewarded as to be able to support his family and bring up his children in a Christian manner. There is no conflict inherent between employer and worker, for they are both engaged in the common task of providing the necessities or amenities of a good life. Private property is divinely sanctioned, but it is given to men as stewards to manage for the common good, rather than to be used at their whim. Hence the owner-employer has a greater measure of responsibility, commensurate with his greater wealth and higher social position, than the worker. The latter is obliged to be honest, coöperative, industrious, and loyal. The former is under these obligations too, but must in addition ensure to the best of his ability that his workers live as well and as morally as possible, on the job and off. The competition beloved of the classical economists is a law of the jungle, not of God, or man. There can be no true competition but only oppression as between the strong and the weak, between the wealthy employer and the single worker. Hence the workers must unionize. But the purpose of unions is not class struggle, but class coöperation and mutual betterment. Employers and workers should therefore belong to the same organization, built around the factory. These unions should associate in confederations of unions, sponsoring social insurance, welfare, and educational activities, all religiously inspired.

It is these confederations of unions which comprise the corporate system within the state. The social and economic role of the state itself is to be limited to such measures as the corporate entities cannot handle, and in this respect the state is to be interventionist along neomercantilist lines, never the passive policeman. But, with regard to the corporate system, the function of the state is merely to help financially or otherwise, never to dominate. Eventually the corporate entities would provide the basis for representation in the upper house of the national legislature, replacing a body based on less meaningful territorial divisions. But this functional, as distinct from geographical, representation fell far short of the corporate state, for a state that united all efforts within itself might soon challenge religion and the worship of God.

Social Catholicism thus confronted Marxian socialism with the motto of class coöperation and harmony rather than struggle, and, by its insistence on guidance by religious and ethical rather than monetary values, also condemned classical capitalism. As it happened, Social Catholics found themselves associated with Marxian socialists in fighting for social legislation and the apparatus of the welfare society. So long as the Second International ruled the Marxian world, Social Catholics and socialists would disagree violently on matters of basic doctrine, but would agree more often than not in respect of practical reform.

Since the Social Catholics believed in the voluntary formation of unions and confederations, they stressed the welfare activities, the propaganda, and the legislative campaigns that would attract adherents to their many organizations, rather than the ultimate goal of a corporate society. This objective was never lost to sight, but it was envisioned as the end product of the process of Social Catholic action and organization, rather than as the Utopia which would exert a magic pull upon potential followers. In this respect the Social Catholics differed from most orthodox Marxists, and sharply from the Leninists, who actually scorned immediate reforms, and valued organizations and party actions only insofar as they contributed to the revolution which would usher in their final goal. The Leninists were utterly unscrupulous in choosing means to achieve their end, and paid the price of perverting that end itself. The Social Catholics, like moderate and revisionist Marxians, selected means that were morally and sociologically appropriate to their long-run goal, but paid a price for their moral view of the relationship of means to ends. A flaming slogan and a hazy vision can stimulate more short-run zeal and partisan devotion than the sure-footed drudgery of education and organization. It was Catholic religious faith, and devotion to the Church, rather than Social Catholic corporatism, that inspired the leaders of Social Catholicism and gave them a hearing among Catholic peasants and workers. Practical action together with propaganda enabled them to build a movement but, as was the case with Second International Marxism, successes in the political and social arena tended even further to divert emphasis from the ideologically defined objective of a corporate society. And the very ecclesiastical origin and affiliation of Social Catholicism which guaranteed it a certain amount of support tended to limit its appeal to coreligionists.

Although the doctrine of Social Catholicism received Papal expression in the celebrated encyclical *Rerum Novarum* of Leo XIII in 1891 (reasserted on its fortieth anniversary in the *Quadrigesimo Anno* of Pius XI), Social Catholicism was born as a movement through the efforts of Wilhelm Emmanuel von Ketteler, Bishop of Mainz (1850–1877). It spread from his diocese to become an integrating force for the Catholics of southern Germany, and became part of the underlying philosophy of the Center Party, which organized the defense of Catholicism against Bismarck's assaults in the 1870's and went on to become one of the mainstays of the political and social structure of the German Empire and the Weimar Republic. A spark borrowed from this German fire rekindled the embers of Catholic social thought and action in France. Two young French officers of noble family, Albert de Mun and René de la Tour du Pin, were taken prisoner during the Franco-Prussian War of 1870 and, while interned in Germany, were inspired by one of von Ketteler's coworkers to initiate a Social Catholic movement on their return to France. From this developed a labor organization, farmers' associations, and a political party which eventually became the MRP (Mouvement Républicaine Populaire) of the Fourth French Republic. Social Catholicism became quite influential in Hapsburg Austria where, however, it tended toward a reactionary political position, with anti-Semitism playing a rather prominent role. The social doctrine was less significant in the Belgian Catholic party, and did not achieve any real importance in Italy until Don Luigi Sturzo founded the Populist Party in 1919.

Because its Catholicism limited its appeal to professing Catholics, because of its emphasis on immediate reforms and willingness to compromise with other groups, the practical successes of Social Catholicism were never more than moderate. Catholic trade unions never compared in strength with the socialist or syndicalist labor organizations; among Catholic parties, only the German Center ranked with the leaders.

The Second World War, and the years immediately following,

greatly improved the fortunes of Social Catholicism and of the Catholic political parties. No good Catholic could accept the racist theories of fascism, or the idea of an omnipotent secular state. Catholics therefore were prominent among those who resisted Hitler. In France, Social Catholics contributed more to the leadership of the underground wartime Resistance than did the better-advertised Communists. The return of peace saw the extreme right-wing movements discredited, as the old middle-class liberal groups had previously been by prewar and wartime failures. The Social Catholic outlook, middle-of-the-road between unimpeded capitalism and socialism, untainted by collaboration with the dictators, proved attractive to the electorate in France, Western Germany, and Italy, with predominantly Catholic populations who shared the general revival of religious interest and devotion born of war and chaos. In these countries Social Catholics headed or ranked high in the moderate, democratic coalitions that strove to defend the essentials of Western civilization against the extreme of the left and the threat of a resurgent right. After 1945, Adenauer's Christian Democrats in Germany, de Gasperi's Christian Democrats in Italy, and Bidault's MRP in France were at or near the top of the political ladder. "Third Force" governments everywhere, however, were forced to work in a continual state of emergency, to devote their best efforts and the greater part of their energy to economic recovery and reconstruction and to military defense. As a consequence, not only fundamental social reorganization, but the propagation of basic ideology itself, was rather slighted. What Social Catholics were actually able to begin or accomplish, therefore, did not differ essentially from the general pattern of welfare-state and neomercantilist policy that nearly all Western nations pursued after World War II. In terms of practical enactments, Social Catholic policy differed from that of British Labour particularly in rejecting a doctrinaire espousal of nationalization and equality. The institution of worker representation committees in factories, and of consultative economic assemblies associated with the national legislature, was sponsored by democratic socialists as well as Social Catholics.

To recognize the limitations of Social Catholicism is not to belittle it. The movement contributed notably to three trends that were of growing importance in the democratic West as its struggle with

Communism sharpened in the middle years of the twentieth century: a reassertion of traditional values, and of the value of the Western Christian tradition itself; a renewed awareness of the intimate relations between social and economic policy on the one hand and ethics and religion on the other; the development of corporatist practices and institutions, of the corporatist outlook, and of the view that Western civilization was evolving in a corporatist direction.

Protestant social thought and action had much the same impact, although, of course, it was less directly associated with political parties and governments. The revolt of the Christian conscience against the failings of industrial capitalism led Protestant clergy and laymen to undertake social work, to support unions and coöperatives, and to press for government intervention. Many went beyond this essentially conservative outlook to condemn capitalism as fundamentally unjust, and to associate themselves with the moderate fringes of Marxian socialism and with British Labour. More than one clergyman wrote and worked for the Fabians and the Labour Party, and more than one exponent of the "Social Gospel" that flourished in American Protestantism in the beginning of the twentieth century participated in the ephemeral rise to prominence of the American Socialist Party. The very great majority of Protestants, and their leadership, stopped far short of socialism, however.

In three Protestant conferences, held in Stockholm in 1922, Oxford in 1937, and Amsterdam in 1948, clergy and laity strove to work out guiding principles in social and economic affairs that would stand between Marxism and capitalism. The error of Marxism was held to be its belief that property is the root of human evil, thus allowing free rein to the evil inherent in the unchecked use of power. The error of doctrinal capitalism was held to be an exaggeration of individualism, the failure to understand that the inherent dignity of individual man can be realized only in community, thus allowing excessive scope for the play of individual economic power and greed. Private profit was rejected as a morally valid *basis* for an economic system, although recognized as a legitimate aspect of an economy erected on other moral foundations. Social Protestantism therefore reasserted the propositions that no man should be used as a means to any other's ends, that work must carry the quality of vocation, not merely job, that no class should presume to identify its interests with those of the community as a whole, that private property implied social responsibility, that it was the duty of the state to intervene in the interests of justice and welfare, but that there should be a great variety of social organizations, all imbued with the Christian spirit. In all these essentials, obviously, Social Protestantism and Social Catholicism were in close agreement. Indeed, observed Reinhold Niebuhr, the great American Protestant theologian,

[The] consensus of Protestant thought is the more remarkable in that it closely approaches the main emphases in the social teachings of the Catholic encyclicals since *Rerum Novarum* (1891). Whatever may be the differences in Catholic and Protestant social policy, and however much the theories may vary because of the stricter interpretation of natural law in Catholic thought, the similarities are more striking than the differences.[4]

The Protestants were more clear-cut than the Catholics in insisting on political and social democracy, and there was a stronger overtone of equalitarianism and hence less of paternalism in their outlook. They were less clear-cut in formulating the ideas of corporatism, but these basic ideas were nonetheless present: in repeated stress on the desirability of voluntary economic associations, imbued with a sense of social responsibility and subject to the arbitrament of a state representing the community as a whole; in assertions of the workers' need for a sense of status and vocation, closely resembling the views of Catholic corporatism; in the recognition of the necessity for government intervention, coupled with the fear of overcentralization of decision in the state and preference for the decentralized initiative of individuals and groups; in vigorous rejection of the idea of class struggle and the affirmation of the basic harmony among employer and worker, farmer and city dweller.[5]

[4] *Christianity and Crisis*, April 3, 1950.

[5] The social and economic views of the most representative Protestant bodies are not to be found as conveniently as those of the Vatican. Cameron P. Hall's *The Churches Deal with Economic Issues*, New York, 1949, is an extremely helpful guide to Protestant economic thinking and its literature. The reports of the Oxford and Amsterdam conferences are as authoritative as possible for world Protestantism. Among the most important statements of the Federal Council and its successor the National Council of the Churches of Christ in the U.S.A. are *The Social Ideals of the Churches*, 1932; *Report of the National*

On reflection, the corporatist tendency of Christian social thought —Protestant and Catholic—need occasion little surprise. Christianity and classical capitalism were essentially incompatible because, by subjecting all things economic to the rule of Newtonian-type laws, the classical economists effectively barred Christian ethics and Christian values from any major social influence. Christianity was incompatible with latter-day "rugged individualism" because this outlook raised a few individuals so high as to render inevitable their fall into the sin of pride, and, by the same token, condemned other, many more, individuals to the sinful suppression of individuality. Nor, in the long run, could Christians be too comfortable as socialists, for Marxism, in a sense, merely transferred the errors of rugged individualism from the economic to the political sphere, failing utterly to solve the problem of power. Christian corporatism held to a middle position with regard to the individual and the group—much as did Christian theology and morality. Taking a long historical view, the very limited approval of capitalist society which Christian social thought afforded in the middle of the twentieth century was essentially a return to the traditional Christian attitude toward business: recognition of the businessman's usefulness to society, coupled with insistence that any standards of good and bad arising from economic activity be subjected to the higher values of religion.

It would be hard indeed to think of an historical subject that has suffered more heavily at the hands of historians and sociologists than has this relationship of religion to the rise of capitalism. The generally prevailing view—an exaggerated and somewhat distorted version of the interpretations of the sociologist Max Weber and the religious historian Ernst Troeltsch—relates the rise of capitalism to the triumph of what is called the Protestant ethic.[6] Where the latter is not given as "the cause" of the triumph of capitalism in the six-

---

Study Conference on the Church and Economic Life, at Pittsburgh, 1947; *The Responsibility of Christians in an Interdependent Economic World*, statement and reports of the National Study Conference on the Church and Economic Life, Detroit, 1950. The National Council has been giving increasing attention to the task of bridging the embarrassing gap between Christian ethics and concrete economics.

[6] Max Weber, *The Protestant Ethic and the Rise of Capitalism*, London, 1930; Ernst Troeltsch, *The Social Teaching of the Christian Churches*, New York, 1931.

teenth and seventeenth centuries it is at least an indispensable, necessary factor in overcoming the anticapitalist medieval tradition. The "Protestant ethic" amounts to industriousness, thrift, sobriety, and the sense of vocation or "calling," which may be generally defined as the belief that each man is summoned by God to his particular economic activity, to which he must fully devote himself to fulfill God's will, and in which his success may be taken as evidence of God's favor. By condemning idleness and self-indulgence and praising labor and thrift, the Protestant ethic, it is said, spurred men to work and save as they otherwise would not have done, and to accumulate wealth which would be taken as a sign of God's grace. This Protestant ethic is supposed to have shattered medieval Catholic opposition to success in business and to the practices necessary thereto, particularly the taking of interest.

Now, *if* the Catholic Church had vigorously opposed the taking of interest, and *if* the triumph of capitalism had coincided geographically and temporally with the spread of Protestantism, and *if* industriousness, sobriety, thrift, and the idea of economic vocation had been first instilled in Western civilization by the Protestant Reformation, then one would be justified in seeing a close relationship between Protestantism and the rise of capitalism. The implication of such a relationship is, of course, that contemporary anti-capitalist views of the Catholic Church are reactionary, while similar views of the Protestants represent a revolution in their outlook. Further, the asserted relationship between Protestantism and early capitalism implies that the Protestant branch of Christianity was morally responsible for the evils of industrialization, and is consequently in a poor position to offer leadership in remedying these evils. Lastly, the ideological chaos of the twentieth century is diagnosed as resulting as much from disillusionment with the Protestant ethic as with economic liberalism itself.

It is obviously worth setting the historical record straight. To begin with, the medieval church's condemnations of usury applied primarily to consumers' loans, not commercial loans. The attack on usury was based on the belief that money, as such, was not productive[7] and on the doctrine that an interest-free loan in case of need was positively enjoined by Christian charity. Where the lender

[7] Classical economists could easily agree with this, by the way.

might be said to participate in the risk of a business undertaking he was, practically speaking, regarded as a silent partner and therefore entitled to a return. Where the lender sacrificed the opportunity to invest his money profitably, he was entitled to a return. The condemnation of usury was directed, then as now, by all men of good will against the extortion of high interest from the needy. In practice, it was the public small-loan lender, rather than the commercial financier who had to fear clean-up raids sponsored by ecclesiastical authorities, and whose evil practices were combated by the creation of municipal pawnshops. The church itself, from the Vatican to the monastic orders and wealthy bishoprics, did not hesitate to reap profits from the investing, lending, and transfer of funds. There were, of course, instances in which the accusation of usury furnished a secular or church leader with an excellent pretext for expropriating an enemy and adding to his own treasury, but no more than a pretext it was. In general, the attitude of the medieval church was not hostile to, and kept pace with, normal business practices.

As for the so-called Protestant ethic, it is rather older than Christianity itself, and certainly characterized medieval Catholicism. Sobriety, industriousness, thrift, and devotion to one's business for the greater glory of God are firmly recommended in, for example, such documents as *The King's Mirror* (about 1240 A.D.), in which a father advises his son, who wishes to be a merchant, to "shun like the devil himself . . . drinking, chess, harlots, quarreling and throwing dice for stakes." The *Treatise* of Pacioli (1494), the first textbook in accounting, observes:

> The end or purpose of every business man being to make lawful, and fair enough profit to keep himself substantially; but he must always commence his affairs in the name of God.

Pacioli indicates the proper relations of business and religion:

> Paul the Apostle says that no one is worthy of the crown, but he who has legitimately fought for it. . . . Give your daily attention to your affairs . . . but, above all, first always keep God before your eyes and never miss hearing Mass in the morning, bearing in mind that because of it time is never lost, as by charity riches are not wasted . . . seek you Christians first the Kingdom of Heaven and then the other temporal and

spiritual things you will easily obtain as your heavenly Father knows quite well what are your needs.[8]

These general admonitions, together with more specific recommendations on investment, partnership, and money lending, make it clear that Catholic businessmen saw no conflict between their desire for prosperity and their desire for salvation. What the Catholic Church—and the Reformers as well—opposed was the substitution of a pecuniary ethic for that of Christianity. Accumulation for its own sake was of course proscribed, but, then, it has never been defended. Protestants and Catholics alike held that the property owner had the duties of a steward, to manage his possessions according to the will of God for the common good. The same idea was stated by the rugged individualist, Andrew Carnegie, in *The Gospel of Wealth* (1900). There is no better exponent of the Protestant ethic than the modern French bourgeois, who are overwhelmingly Catholic, even when anticlerical.

Of the Reformation leaders, Luther was bitterly anticapitalist, and unfriendly to the businessman, in contradistinction, for example, to the Renaissance Popes. Calvin supported the doctrine of just price and the idea of stewardship and linked thrift with stewardship rather than with private gain as such; some of the most radical Protestants preached the good of the humble life and farming. Here was no call to rugged individualism.

It is not difficult to clarify this religious-economic muddle. Capitalism first prospered in Catholic regions: Italy, the Rhineland, France, Flanders, the London region of England. It continued to develop in France and what became Belgium, but its progress in Catholic Germany was interrupted by the Thirty Years War (1618–1648). Capitalism also flowered in Calvinist Geneva and the Netherlands, and eventually reached economically backward Calvinist Scotland. The linkage between Calvinism and capitalism results largely from the fact that in western Europe the absolute monarchs were, naturally enough, attached to the established churches, whether Catholic, Anglican, or Lutheran. Where the bourgeoisie rose against royal absolutism, as in England, Scotland, and the

---

[8] Selections from both documents are conveniently available in the Columbia source book, *Introduction to Contemporary Civilization in the West*, New York, 1946, vol. 1.

Dutch Netherlands, it also challenged the established churches. Where absolute monarchy was maintained with little challenge, as in France, Lutheran and Catholic Germany, Lutheran Scandinavia, Catholic Spain, and Catholic Flanders, the bourgeoisie gained wealth and power in accordance with the particular region's economic development, within the established church and beneath the sway of the absolute crown. But the Western world as a whole became progressively secularized from the sixteenth century on, and the doctrines of the unrepresentative sample of neo-Calvinists upon whom Weber focused his attention had already been transformed by secularization and the growth of capitalism. Christianity, Catholic or Protestant, was increasingly restricted to Sunday and holy day observance, and was thrust from the arena of public policy. In this process, a good many ecclesiastics were themselves secularized, falling into an easy acceptance of the so-called natural laws of the classical economists. Then the failings of industrial society reawakened the consciences of men, not last among them the religious leaders. Catholics, who were not tempted to flirt with equalitarianism, found it rather easy to restate their old position in new terms. What was wrong with capitalism, they held, was not private property as such, but the dehumanization of working relations owing to the growth in size of firms and factories and the disloyalty of the owners of capital to Christian social ethics. Many a Protestant did flirt with equalitarianism, but throughout the past century of the development of Christian social thought, agreement has outweighed the differences between the great branches of Christianity. Christian corporatism was therefore a modern expression of the traditional Christian view of the interrelations of individual and group, its pluralism and appeal for voluntary organization befitting the complexity and the democratization of the modern world.

The strength of Christian corporatism lies in the way it refurbishes links with honored elements of the past, in the way in which it makes the attraction of religious ideals coincide with the common sense of a middle road. Its weaknesses, as a movement, are to be found in the divisions of Christianity, in the inability of church leaders to communicate effectively at the practical levels of social debate, in secularism and anticlericalism, and, above all, in the simple fact that not enough men, and especially not enough rich and powerful men, are good enough Christians. But that, in a way, is only part of the eternal dilemma and paradox of Christianity, for if all men were good Christians there would be less need for good works of the church, and it would matter less what political, economic, or social arrangements one was living under.

II. *Corporatism and Manic Nationalism*

Ideologically, the combination of corporatism and manic nationalism equals fascism. The degree of ordinary fraud and extraordinary neurosis that infected most fascist leadership forces one to question the seriousness of any of their ideological expressions and, moreover, it is quite clear that in the practical world the essence of fascism was the organization of power to exploit weakness. But the fact remains that fascists did offer an ideology, or at least, a good many ideological pronouncements, and that these are interesting because the attraction they were able to exert provides more than one clue concerning the trends, the needs and the stresses of modern Western society.

The ideological origins of fascism may be traced back to the era of Napoleon and Metternich which saw the birth of modern corporatism, for it was out of the defeats and then the recovery of German arms and pride that there came that sentiment of nationalist inferiority-superiority that was to constitute one of the most troublesome characteristics of German culture. England, France, and even backward Russia were unified under central governments responding to their several national geniuses; only Germany among the great nations was held back as a weak and disorganized confederation and this was in large part owing to the machinations of the French, particularly Cardinal Richelieu in the seventeenth century. And yet, these early-nineteenth century nationalists felt, Germany of all nations had most to offer to the world. Distinguished and hard-working legal historians proved to their satisfaction that true democracy, the sense for equality before the law, and the sense for abiding by the law had all first really developed in the Teutonic forests. The ideals of citizenship were nowhere better understood than in the medieval German city, the aspiration of mankind for peace and unity nowhere better expressed than in the Holy Roman Empire of the Germans. Celebrated and industrious philologists, including the brothers Grimm, delved into the German past to reveal the richness of the culture created by the German race—by which word they meant, it must be understood, a linguistic and cultural, but not a biological grouping. Hegel it was who carried the concept of German excellence to its logical conclusion by making the Germans the repositories of the highest access of the world spirit. Hegel was too good a Hohenzollern monarchist and stressed the absolute character of reason and law too strongly ever to be acclaimed by the German fascists as their ancestor and, besides, he was unfortunate from their standpoint in having spawned Marx. But he certainly contributed generously to the kind of thinking that enabled later nationalists to philosophize solemnly about racist absurdities, although German fascists have generally named Adam Müller, the romantic nationalist and corporatist, as their intellectual father.

But the ideas of fascism were very long in taking hold. Not until the 1860's was the concept of race separated from its relatively harmless cultural, linguistic definition, and supplied with a new, biological meaning. A French diplomat, the Comte de Gobineau, was anxious to prove that the French nobility were inherently superior to the masses. He did this by equating the nobility with the Franks, who had taken over Gaul in the collapse of the Roman imperium, and the masses with the Gallo-Romans, the inhabitants over whom the Franks came to rule, a mixture of Celtic and Mediterranean peoples. The Franks, of course, were Germans, and Aryans, and the good Count endowed his presumed forebears with biologically inherited advantages over the lesser Gallo-Romans.[9] His discovery, published in the 1850's, did not arouse any strong reaction among the French, who are said to be easily excited, but it was hailed as a substantial contribution in Germany. Richard Wagner, much of whose music was devoted to refurbishing German legends and arousing nationalist sentiment, helped found a Gobineau Vereinigung. Wagner's son-in-law, Houston Stewart Chamberlain, whose name would probably have baffled a normal Nibelung, be-

---

[9] In its basic, linguistic meaning, the word "Aryan" refers to a group of languages, and the people speaking them, among which may be included, depending upon one's standard of definition, Iranian, Italian, Russian, French, English, German (including Yiddish, of course), and many others.

came the high propagandist of modern, extremist German nationalism, proclaiming racial superiority, the glories of war, the iniquities
of other peoples, and the German mission to rule.[10] Anti-Semitism,
an age-old prejudice which was yielding slowly to the assimilation
of the Jews and to the spread of liberal enlightenment, was revived,
reëmphasized, and reconstituted as a pseudo-philosophic and
pseudo-scientific doctrine. It was quite a success in parts of Russia,
in Austria-Hungary and France, and in Germany. After the foundation of the German Empire, historians like Heinrich von Treitschke
turned an able pen and a great deal of knowledge to the cause of
dramatizing Hegel's nationalist mission. The economist Adolf Wagner and other "socialists of the chair" modernized the German tradition of government intervention and linked ideas of the welfare state
with those of corporatism. Adolf Stoecker, a court chaplain under
Wilhelm I, preached nationalism, corporatism, and anti-Semitism
and added the hitherto missing ingredient of plain rabble rousing.
But circumstances were unpropitious, and he gained little following.

Despite its early beginnings, and almost unbroken thread of existence, German fascism had to await the social and political dislo-
cations following World War I before it could really flourish. Under
the Hohenzollerns, Christian corporatism had made little headway,
as did the secular corporatism of Adolf Wagner; anti-Semitism co-
existed with the striking assimilation of the German Jews, a good
many of whom were rather ardent German nationalists, and with the
rise of the Poles as a favorite scapegoat and internal "enemy"; the
emotions of nationalism and militarism were fully soaked up by
the Imperial Government and its splendid armed forces, and these
feelings had no cause to seek a more esoteric outlet. The established
political parties were well organized, and the German Empire was
exceedingly prosperous. For these reasons, the fascist weed matured first in the unlikely soil of Italy, where it had sprouted later
and quite independently.

Italian Fascism was created by Benito Mussolini and his coterie.
There was no Fascist movement before he founded it, no Fascist
doctrine before he decided, some time after he had risen to power,
that there ought to be one. But neither movement nor doctrine was

[10] His most famous work was *The Foundations of the Nineteenth Century*,
first published in German in 1899.

summoned into existence out of thin air, or out of elements entirely foreign to the Italian climate. Fascism appeared suddenly and freshly upon the Italian scene, and swiftly triumphed, in large part owing to the utter incompetence of Italian liberal and democratic socialist leadership. It drew nourishment above all from the weakness of its opponents, from the difficulties of reconversion to peace and from war-born social disintegration, from unsated and irresponsible postwar nationalism. It drew also upon the existence of a revolutionary syndicalist tradition in Italian labor and from the prominence of Hegelianism in Italian thought.

Syndicalism is a curious compound of a very earthy, vigorous, and even violent way of handling labor's side of industrial relations with an utterly visionary and ethereal disdain for political realities. It is the only organized heir to anarchism. Syndicalist thinking owed a great deal to the French theorist Proudhon's insistence on independent, voluntarily organized producing units, ruled by their worker-members, as the constituent entities of the free society of the future. Some syndicalists also reflected the anarchist's rejection of political government as a means of organizing society on the ground that anything other than voluntary coöperation among free producing units would mean the perpetuation of oppression. Syndicalism thus was revolutionary, organizing workers to defeat the "bosses" and to overthrow capitalist society and the state. But syndicalism rejected politics as the mere froth of social ferment, and therefore virtuously spurned the organization of workers into political parties seeking to take over the state through parliamentary, or even revolutionary, means. In the Latin countries, France, Italy, and Spain, where syndicalism throve, the practice was for workers to belong to labor unions committed to syndicalism, but to vote for socialist political parties dedicated to some form of Marxism. Syndicalism espoused violence, or at least direct action, in labor conflicts, strong-arm methods and industrial sabotage being hailed as justifiable weapons against the capitalist oppressors, preferable to negotiation or reform legislation. The weapons against the tyrannical state included the usual varieties of mass action, demonstrations and coups, capped by the supreme weapon, the general strike. By bringing all economic activity to a halt, the general strike would instantly paralyze both the bourgeoisie and the state, and enable the militant working class to overthrow them both and usher in the golden age of syndicalist society.

There was no great strain for the ordinary man in being both syndicalist and Marxian socialist, but, as the Marxian parties outside Russia lost their militancy through a growing familiarity with the real world (known as revisionism) and through the ordinary process of mellowing with age, the direct-action, violent desires bred by syndicalism were left without an organized guide in the political sphere. In Italy, after the First World War, workers took over factories through sit-in strikes, and, for a time, there appeared to be a real possibility of a leftist revolution. But this possibility had clearly ceased to exist some time before the Fascist seizure of power, and it is not correct to say that the Fascist coup was simply the direct response of Italian capitalism to the threat of a workers' revolution.

The Fascists, headed by Mussolini, himself a former Marxist editor, had formed an active force of rioters and strutters out of disillusioned socialists and syndicalists, unsettled members of the bourgeoisie, and assorted riff-raff. They staked out a profitable claim among war veterans unsuccessfully readjusted to peace and resentful at Italy's alleged mistreatment by the Allies in the share-out of the spoils of war. Indeed, it was to these heroes of a victory cheated of its fruits that the Fascists primarily directed their propaganda. Aside from some annoyingly effective violence, however, the Fascists did not accomplish very much. Just before the "March on Rome" of October, 1922, the Fascist Party membership had reached about 300,000; in the elections of May, 1921, only 22 Fascists won seats in the Italian Chamber of Deputies, compared with the Socialists' 122 and the Social Catholic Populists' 107. Fascism did not triumph through popular support, but rather through the weakness of socialist and liberal leadership. The King's refusal to sign a decree establishing martial law which, even at the very last minute, would have enabled the legal government to block Mussolini's men finally enabled Fascism to take over the government through the resignation of the Premier and Mussolini's appointment to succeed him at the head of a coalition cabinet excluding only the Marxists.

This, of course, was only a beginning for Il Duce. Having gained control of military and security forces, he began driving liberal leaders into exile, and in July, 1923, when it was apparent that he still could not win parliamentary control in an honest election, he pushed through the Acerbo Law which provided that the Party that won a plurality should receive two-thirds of the seats. Then, following a well-organized campaign to intimidate the voters, the Fascists and their allies won about sixty percent of the ballots, and the period of dictatorship could begin. After more opponents had been silenced by exile, imprisonment, murder (including that of the socialist leader Matteotti), and terror, Mussolini abandoned all but the trappings of parliamentary government, acquiring, in January, 1926, the right to issue laws by decree.

Nevertheless, the Fascist regime had not reached full flower. Its structure was not actually completed until the eve of the war that destroyed it. The basic reason was that the Fascists were consciously committed to only one element of their ideology in the early days of their movement. This was a belief in action and the will to power, derived from syndicalism and from the irrationalist philosophies of the late nineteenth and early twentieth centuries that glorified the hero and the hero-group, and their mission to transcend and to lead the common herd. The Fascists began by calling for action and the seizure of power in the name of a socialism transformed by militant nationalism, but a socialism nonetheless, so that Fascism first pretended to be a workers' movement. But, during the postwar industrial disorders, Mussolini found that greater headway could be made by demanding power to crush the socialists, in the name of the restoration of order and of a greater Italy. This sufficed through most of the 1920's, but between 1926 and 1939 the structure of the regime and of Italian society was remodeled on a thoroughly corporatist pattern.

The Fascists had, of course, invaded the field of labor organization from the beginning. It was easy for them, using the force at their disposal, to outstrip the free trade unions and secure a collective bargaining monopoly from the employers' confederation. In 1926, the state stepped into the picture overtly with a law which organized all industry, agriculture, and the professions into thirteen (later nine) confederations, each of which (with the exception of the one for professional men) had a syndicate for employers and one for employees. Strikes and lockouts were prohibited, and disputes were to be settled by negotiation or by special labor courts. In 1930 the

Council of Corporations was created to top the edifice, and to fulfill a function growing out of a reform of the parliament the year before. In 1929, the Italian Chamber of Deputies had been replaced with a body chosen by the Grand Council of the Fascist Party from nominees of the syndicates and certain other special organizations. (It should be added that the people were given the opportunity to vote for the resulting nation-wide slate.) In 1934, the existence of a corporatist society, opposed to both capitalism and socialism, was formally announced by Mussolini. The syndical structure was accordingly remodeled somewhat, twenty-two new corporations, each covering a branch of economic activity, each having Mussolini as its nominal president, being established to control and coördinate the employers' and workers' syndicates. To complete the picture, the reformed Chamber of Deputies agreed with Mussolini that it ought to be abolished, and, in 1939, it was replaced with the Chamber of Fasces and Corporations, whose six hundred members were chosen for terms lasting at Mussolini's pleasure from the membership of the Fascist Grand Council, the National Council of the Fascist Party, and the National Council of Corporations. Thus was the pattern of corporatism filled out.

The establishment of a corporatist society was quite another matter, however. So long as all important decisions were made by an avowedly totalitarian and dictatorial state, representation of the people through corporations and syndicates—functional representation—could be no more than window dressing, and the organizations themselves little more than devices for state control of their membership. They were neither the means for expressing the views of their members, nor for giving their members' lives a focus, nor yet the avenue for individual advancement in society or the device for the betterment of society as a whole. To the extent that the state provided for these functions, it did so through the single Fascist Party and its various collateral organizations, for youth, for recreation and social work. Despite the fact that the Fascist Party controlled the corporatist organizations, one might be tempted to say that the effort to make corporatism exist side by side with a one-party totalitarian state created an internal contradiction. One might be further tempted to point to this contradiction as the profound cause of the collapse of Mussolini's Italy, were it not for the many other contradictions that all reveal, as they stem from, the artificial, superficial, and stage-set character of Italian Fascism as a whole. To begin with, popular support and mass adherence, to the extent that they existed, came to Fascism as the result of its seizure of power, and not before, as a factor making the rise to power possible. Nor were the supporters of Fascism inspired by a powerful ideology in which they could fully believe. The original group were a social disarray that could find purpose in the open-ended goals of action and power for their own sakes, and could vent emotions and the desire for action in small-scale violence. Later there came the carpetbaggers, the bandwagon followers, and, very much more numerous, the conformists for safety's sake. The fabric of Fascism, in short, was terribly thin even before it had begun to wear.

Moreover, it is difficult to worship both Christ and Mammon without a good deal of cynicism. In like manner, despite the Church-state accord of 1929, it was ultimately impossible for the Italians to worship Christ as Catholics at the same time as they bent knees to a God-state whose high priest preached a kind of infallibility to which no pope ever pretended. This contradiction bred cynicism, and underscored the lack of sincerity which characterized Italian Fascism. Nor was it possible to turn a poor country, lacking essential resources, into a powerful and self-sufficient imperial nation, or to transform a peaceful populace, not bred in the tradition of disciplined, highly organized mass warfare, into a conquering nation that would restore the Imperium Romanum. And the Fascist leadership, from Mussolini down, was altogether too much given to posing and boasting for it ever to be honest or truly efficient. Perhaps one can say that corruption, fraud, and bombast are only the logical products of a regime that began by seeking power without knowing for what end.

But this trait was as proper to Fascism as were the violent nationalism, the militarism and totalitarianism. The idea of the total state gained support from the marked influence of Hegel on Italian thinkers, the idea of militarism and the glorification of power from modern nationalism and from philosophies that preached the right of the transcendant will. The exaggerated respect for action as a sufficient good came in part from these same philosophic sources and from syndicalism, but the way in which Mussolini employed it and the general character he gave his regime strongly suggest the influence of a very curious French theorist, Georges Sorel.

From the standpoint of Western, democratic capitalist civilization, Sorel, like Friedrich Nietzsche, may be described as one who did a great deal of harm, but possibly with the best of intentions. Like Nietzsche, Sorel is well worth attention, not only for his keen insights, but for the effects of his widely disseminated and disintegrating influence on European intellectuals. Like Nietzsche, Sorel was not a systematic philosopher, whose thought can be followed like a main road branching into the accepted philosophical categories. His ideas must be pulled out of polemic and tangent, and reconstructed in a manner of which he would have disapproved. Like Nietzsche, his primary concern was with what they both regarded as moral decadence, namely, the ethic of middle-class society, and with the consequent lack of moral vigor which they believed they detected. Both Nietzsche and Sorel appear to have found the source of this decline and weakness in Christianity, but for different reasons, and with different implications. While Nietzsche was a poet and philosopher, working away from the Western philosophic tradition and attempting to draw new sources of energy from it, Sorel was a civil engineer and social philosopher, in large part a Marxist, seeking to find a new source of energy in historically revealed social behavior. To Nietzsche, it was the Christian ethic as it operated in his time that undermined the potentialities of man. To Sorel, it was merely that Christianity had played out its social role, and a new force had to be found to reinvigorate the morality and the morale of Western man. The key to Sorel's judgment lies in his concept of the social myth, an idea and a goal which, true or false, attainable or unattainable, arouses sufficient ardor and loyalty among men to make them strive for it, struggling to overcome all obstacles, willing even to suffer martyrdom for its sake. The myth pulls men after it, and even if its attraction should ultimately prove to have been that of a mirage, their struggle for its attainment will not only have yielded many important accomplishments along the way, but will have brought out in them the loyalty, devotion, and honor of soldiers standing together in the field of battle. This is what Christianity accomplished in its early days, Sorel believed, but its power to uplift and energize had been dissipated through excessive ecclesiastical organization and through the association of Christianity with decadent social groups. Sorel spent his career as a social philosopher in a search for a new myth for his day.

Sorel was, in turn, orthodox Marxian socialist, revisionist, syndicalist, monarchist, and, at the close of his life, Leninist. He died in 1922, too soon to have become disillusioned with Lenin, and too early to have had the opportunity to attach his heart to Italian Fascism, although, as far back as 1912, he had favorably noticed the young socialist editor, Benito Mussolini, as one who might be seen "one day at the head of a sacred battalion, saluting with his épée the Italian banner."[11] Sorel was searching for a myth that would prove magnetic and inspiring to modern man, and dropped each affiliation as soon as he found that the ideal it held forth was powerless, or was being wrongly managed. There is no decisive reason, therefore, for him to be regarded particularly as a syndicalist, praising the myth of the general strike that would lead the working class, the least decayed sector of society, into conflict and moral greatness. He abandoned syndicalism when he decided that the French syndicalist chieftains were becoming nothing more than the leaders of another organization, concerned with organization.

Mussolini returned Sorel's compliment, writing that in the "great stream of Fascism are to be found ideas which began with Sorel" and his associates. But whereas Sorel was one who tried only to create ideas and programs on which others would act, and had little influence on any of the movements he fancied, Mussolini was a man of action who saw the utility of Sorel's concept of the myth as a means of carrying the people with him in his activity. If any one thing serves to characterize Mussolini's regime, it is his vain effort to rouse the Italian people with proclamations of the "New Italy," its "virility," the goal of a restored Roman Empire. Mussolini sought to do those things that would lend the myth some verisimilitude, the appearance of being part realized. He was therefore apt to build showily rather than well, to be cautious about truly large undertakings and heroic about small. He refurbished ruins and drained marshes, but did not tackle the problem of restoring southern Italy to fertility. He assaulted Ethiopia, certain the powers would not in-

[11] S. C. Lytle, "Georges Sorel," in E. M. Earle, ed., *Modern France*, Princeton, 1951, pp. 264 ff., p. 288.

terfere, but he was reluctant to enter Hitler's war. Indeed, one might say that Mussolini's record, like those of the other dictators, Hitler and Stalin, demonstrates both the force and the weakness of Sorel's concept of the myth. An appropriate myth is one of the demagogue's best weapons to arouse a quick enthusiasm, and it will work so long as there is created the appearance of partial realization, but it will have enduring strength only if it is independently meaningful to the individuals who are to be guided and inspired by it. In this lies democracy's strength in the West, and the reasons for the dictators' failures, for, after all, there is no reason why a myth that is consistent with the ordinary realities of life should not prove stronger in the long run than one which defies common sense and everyday observation.

The myths of Italian Fascism rang hollow, their partial realizations were seen to be fraudulent and inadequate by a people who were both Catholic and skeptical to a degree bordering on cynicism. But the lessons of seeming success were not lost on other fascists, especially the Germans, who were able to apply them in a more favorable environment. The Nazis realized the power of a social myth and, to assist in its propagation, developed the technique of the Big Lie which, they believed, if repeated often enough under a monopoly of the means of communication, could be expected to take on the aura of truth in the minds of the people.

Both Germany and the German people were a better base for the growth of truly vigorous fascism than Italy and the Italians. Germany's economy and resources and her tradition of military efficiency and militarism were a large part of the reason, and the heritage of German culture contained extremely rich veins for fascists to draw upon. Germany was, after all, the home *par excellence* of soaring philosophies which departed from the ordinary world for complex flights in the world of words, returning eventually to earth with neat conclusions that had to be imposed upon the unruly facts of life because they had been verbally demonstrated. No other nation equaled Germany's output of works glorifying war, or of systematic expositions of first the linguistic and later the biologic theory of race, and in no other major nation were racialist theories given such broad implications or taken so seriously by so many people. Moreover, Germany had traditionally had one of the strongest varieties of interventionism since the days of the Cameralists in the seventeenth century, and the tradition had been strengthened after 1870 by the growth of Marxian Socialism and by the "socialists of the chair." It was further strengthened during the First World War by the rise of secular corporatism and of the theory of the planned economy, a direct outgrowth of economic mobilization.

The impetus for an outbreak of rabid nationalism was provided by defeat in the First World War, which could be conveniently explained as the result of a sellout. The occasion for disillusionment with a parliamentary democracy whose roots were weak in any event was afforded by the Great Depression. The only missing component, party organization, was given by Hitler's Nazis, aided greatly by Stalin's German Communists.

Nazism differed from Italian Fascism in several important respects, other than the principal fact that it was far more real. For one thing, Nazi ideology clearly preceded Hitler's accession to power, and yielded to expediency thereafter, instead of itself growing as an expedient, as was the case in Italy. But the Nazis never ceased to take two ideological principles with the utmost seriousness, the German mission to conquer as a master race and anti-Semitism. Another difference, which also amounted to the preservation of an ideological principle in power, was the Nazi emphasis on a planned, state-directed economy. Italian Fascism had denied its socialistic elements even before the March on Rome; Nazism began to renege on its socialist appeals only after seizing power. But whereas the more clearly opportunistic Mussolini needed the Great Depression to inspire him to a condemnation of capitalism as well as socialism and to commit himself fully to a corporatist pattern, the Nazis were almost equally lavish in their displays of contempt for both the Western market economy and the socialism of Marx. Their own way, they insisted, was the only sound way between these two failures, but it turned out to be a statist war economy, rather than the corporatism that Nazi propaganda had previously featured.

The Nazi Party had in its infancy (1920) pledged itself to the establishment of a corporatist state, and there can be no doubt that corporatism, which rounded out the Nazi ideology, helped attract a certain amount of support, although it was certainly one of the lesser magnets in Hitler's stockroom. German corporatism had always looked back to the Middle Ages, as did the Nazis when they were not gazing even farther back to the Gods feasting and feuding in Valhalla, and it was a romantic and extremely nationalistic version of corporatism that made particular headway among Nazi intellectuals and among the more radical, leftist, or socialistic National Socialists. Its leading spokesmen were the economists Gottfried Feder and Othmar Spann, who claimed inspiration from the post-Napoleonic writer, Adam Müller. In 1933, the Nazi Party began preparations for the establishment of a corporate system, with Dr. Ley, of the Nazi Labor Front, as a leading advocate. By the end of 1934, however, corporatism had been all but officially discarded, owing to the antagonism of Nazi industrialists and bureaucrats. German society under Hitler came essentially to be a war machine. Corporatism, on the other hand, inevitably had many of the attributes of the welfare society. And, as Hermann Goering said, the Nazi choice had to be guns over butter.

In last analysis, then, Nazism was only tenuously related to corporatism, and one might again be tempted, on the basis of both German and Italian examples, to conclude that corporatism is incompatible with the totalitarian state, for corporatism creates bodies that must inevitably claim an autonomy which the dictatorship will deny. This basic conflict is deepened by another attribute of the totalitarian system: its insatiable dynamism, its stress on politics, its need to keep fighting and conquering, to rack up "unprecedented achievements." The totalitarian regime must always depend upon repression to maintain its total power at home, but if it cannot point to dramatic accomplishments, its reliance on force and fear is likely to come ever more dangerously close to being its sole foundation.

Although the historical connection between fascism and corporatism cannot be denied, it appears in the end to have been more fortuitous than essential.[12] Fascism laid claim to revolutionary nov-

[12] The existence of "clerical fascism," which refers primarily to the Austrian regime of Dollfuss and Schuschnigg prior to 1938, might appear to contradict this judgment. Clerical fascism amounted to the union of Social Catholicism and totalitarian statism, with a dash of anti-Semitism added. It lacked the dynamic quality of rabid nationalism, however, was definitely conservative in its impact, and did not rest upon a propaganda-inflamed mass movement. It was never fully totalitarian. The dictatorship of Salazar in Portugal has also been described as clerical fascism, but has been even less thoroughgoing, less severe, and less militant than the Austrian variety.

elty in all important respects. It needed a social and economic doctrine that differed both from Western capitalism and Russian Marxism, a doctrine, moreover, that had certain attractions of its own and could fulfill the need of an industrial society for organization and social discipline. In time of peace corporatism met the criteria admirably; in time of war it was superfluous, for all doctrinal requirements could be satisfied by the economy mobilized and disciplined for war in the national interest. If it does nothing else, this conclusion helps to point up the intellectual and moral bankruptcy of fascism. It was, indeed, revolutionary, but hardly new. Its actual political successes were fleeting, and resulted from the failings of its enemies more than from its own skills. Intellectually, its glorification of war was hackneyed, as was the racialist mumbo-jumbo. Totalitarianism itself did little more than fulfill ancient precepts of the political theory of pure power, whose dangers were thus more fully revealed than ever before. An element of some novelty may, perhaps, have been the systematic doctrinal evocation of the heroic leader and his elect nation, overriding all established rights and moralities and creating new values through his victories. After 1945 this must ring terribly hollow, and so point up the basic emptiness of irrationalists like Nietzsche, who carried their praise of the irrational to a logical conclusion.[13]

III. *Secular Corporatism*

Both Christian and nationalist corporatism testify to the spread of corporatist thinking in modern times, but neither promises to be Western society's ideological choice, perhaps because the first is too sublime and the second merely revolting. The prevalence of corporatist thought is brought out even more clearly by secular corporatism which, indeed, is so pervasive that one runs the risk of using it as a catch-all. No more than the religious and nationalist

[13] It will of course be objected that Nietzsche was no Nazi, or even German nationalist, and that his strictures against Christianity should not be taken at face value. This is undoubtedly so, but in no way denies that Nazism, the worst aspects of German nationalism, and anti-Christianity were all strongly supported by his writings, as they were generally, if incorrectly, construed. For this misunderstanding—if such it be—Nietzsche has only himself to blame, since he chose to be immoderate, to shock, and to be obscure.

types, however, does secular corporatism present a neat and readily acceptable ideology for the Western world. There are a number of examples of this point of view which put forward the claim that society *ought* to be organized along specified corporatist lines, for reasons of equity, security, or efficiency, rather than because of religious or nationalist presuppositions, but they share the weaknesses of all Utopian schemes. Other expositions of secular corporatism are more significant, however, for these say little of what ought to be, but a great deal of what is *going to be:* they state, in short, that Western democratic capitalism is evolving in the direction of corporatism because it is in the nature of our institutions to do so. Sociological analysis and prediction of this kind is to be taken much more seriously than the Utopian *ought,* because, if correct, it compels us to ask whether or not we should seek to reverse the corporatist trend and, if we should not, or if it is irreversible, what we should do to preserve our liberties and the energy of a free society in the coming corporatist era.

The secular pleas for corporatism are numerous and varied. One may again refer to the German tradition, beginning with Fichte and the inescapable Hegel, Adolf Wagner and the "socialists of the chair," nationalists but not prefascists, corporatists and statists but loyal to the monarchy that passed away in 1918. An interesting offshoot was the "German collective economy," in which corporatism was linked with the idea of the planned economy that had developed during the First World War, but was shorn of its monarchist attachments. Walther Rathenau and his aide Wichard von Moellendorf were the leading proponents of collective economy. Rathenau had inherited from his father sovereignty over the electrical cartel (AEG, Allgemeine Electrizitäts-Gesellschaft) and Moellendorf had been a high official of the firm. Early in the First World War, Rathenau devised and headed a supply, priorities, and allocations system which counteracted the strangling effect of the British blockade on the German war economy. Later on Rathenau and Moellendorf preached the new collective economy, combining, in essence, the old corporatist notions of vocational association and functional representation with such modern adaptations as the use of the cartels as semipublic control bodies for industries and of the state as overall economic planner. The ordinary parliament, consisting of regional representatives, would be replaced as the highest economic legislator by an economic council topping a pyramid of management-labor assemblies covering the various economic fields. Throughout the scheme ran the very modern distinctions between production for profit and production for use, between business management dedicated to the former and technician management devoted to the latter. German collective economy pulled together the predispositions of Cameralism and the neomercantilism of the nineteenth century, thoroughly refurbishing a corporatism which at heart reflected the medieval gild, accommodating it to the broad scope of the twentieth-century cartel and the efficiency gospel of the twentieth-century engineer. During the construction of the Weimar Republic, the proponents of collective economy attempted to work their scheme into the basic fabric of the new Germany, but they gained only a sop in the form of a powerless National Economic Council established alongside the Reichstag. There was a pale, and, as usual, distorted reflection of collective economy in the Nazi cartelization of industry for the purpose of economic mobilization. Totalitarianism proved incompatible with this particular kind of corporatism, for where Rathenau and Moellendorf envisaged a self-governing economy alongside the customary political state, the Nazis perforce subjected the economy completely to the state, and, in particular, to the needs of its military arm. Perhaps a truer, if embryonic, reflection of collective economy was to be seen in the labor-management industry councils established at the insistence of the unions in the German Federal Republic after World War II.

It is inevitable that corporatist schemes should be very national, if not necessarily nationalistic. The ideas and proposals of Rathenau and Moellendorf clearly mirrored certain aspects of German history, and characteristically British and American strains are to be found in the secular corporatism of the English-speaking world. English Guild socialism, linked with the names of A. J. Penty, A. R. Orage, and, above all and in its more mature years, G. D. H. Cole, had some corporatist flavor, although it was directed to and for the working class, and took over the Marxian notions of class struggle and the Marxian theory of the state as the political arm of capitalism. It reflected idealization of the medieval gild on aesthetic or moral grounds by such men as William Morris. At the same time it showed the influence of Proudhon and European syndicalism, in its emphasis on worker control of industry and in the belief of some of its more

extreme members that the political state would be entirely superfluous when the economy was organized in self-governing industrial
gilds of workers. What was characteristically British was Guild
socialism's insistence on thoroughgoing democracy, both in the tactics of persuasion relied upon to advance the movement, and in the
management of the gilds themselves. The corporatist aspects actually developed through the failure of Guild socialism as such. After
the short-lived success of some gild efforts, notably in the building
trades, the influence of Guild socialism was primarily to be seen in
the changing attitude of British Labour toward nationalization as
a mark of socialism. The problem of establishing worker control
through worker democracy in nationalized industries continued to
plague even such ardent advocates of nationalization as Aneurin
Bevan. Worker representation in the control of nationalized industries, a halfway step, was a corporatist device, save that management was public rather than private.

The underlying idea in Guild socialism was democratic pluralism,
a concept widely held in the English-speaking world and, in the
United States, closely identified with the philosopher John Dewey.
The essence of the idea was that the individual should be able to
express his interests democratically, in voluntarily joined groupings
related to each of these interests. If the various aspects of life were
thus represented by democratically operating associations and institutions—workers' groups, parents' groups, etc.—the society would
function in a truly democratic fashion. There was never, of course,
any clearly formulated pluralist movement or ideology, but, by its
very nature, pluralist thinking was more congenial to corporatism
than to either Marxian socialism or classical capitalism.

Almost peculiarly American was the corporatist thinking that developed from the writings of the original and erratic Midwestern
twentieth-century economist, Thorstein Veblen. Few American intellectuals escaped Veblen's influence, and, as the world has become
increasingly familiar with American culture, it has felt the mark of
Veblen, however indirectly. Behind Veblen's bitter shafts at what
he called the conspicuous waste of middle-class civilization, and
what he saw as the wrongheadedness of businessmen both in their
motives and their management, was a respect little short of idolatry
for the technical efficiency of the engineer. Veblen was among the
economists who most sharply defined the divorce between owner-

ship and management in business, and went on to distinguish between the business manager and the actual producer. The former
sought profits, at whatever cost in social waste; the latter sought
only the most efficient way to produce. The former was not concerned over the public welfare, and catered to the stupid whims,
prejudices, and customs of the bourgeoisie. The latter was strictly
rational, and what Veblen called the instinct of workmanship could
be fully developed and released in the technician were it not for the
bumbling overlordship of the businessman. Veblen had merely carried partial truths about social waste and irrational customs to their
logical conclusion, but he never fully elaborated the nightmare that
was incipient in his own thinking.

This was brought to pass some years after Veblen's death by the
proponents of technocracy, the rule of technicians and techniques.
Technocracy pledged a comfortable living for every American in a
halved work week, if only the economy were organized as efficiently
as the parts of an automobile engine. Inputs of work and products
were calculated in terms of units of energy, ergs, and it was clearly
proved that human beings could be much wealthier if they only
would cease being human. Technocracy flared briefly in the American press, and provided excellent opportunities for humor to liven
some of the darkest days of the depression, but it soon retired
quietly into the recesses of the newspaper morgues.

The basic idea, which the technocrats had derived from Veblen,
lived on, however, reappearing after World War II in challenging
and influential works that were better balanced and showed a
greater sense of reality than had the apostles of the slide rule. The
engineer as such was replaced with the manager, efficient both as a
producer and business organizer. The coming to power of the union
leader as one of the deciding forces in the American economy was
fully recognized. The naïve Utopian *ought* of the technocrats gave
way to the analyst's diagnosis of an inevitable development. This
trend in American postwar self-analysis amounted, in effect, to the
view that an American corporatist society was in the making (although "corporatist" and related words were not generally used), and
constituted an attempt to work out, both in analysis of current practices and in theoretical projections, the problems that corporatism
raised for a democratic society.

Three general answers to these problems, or predictions of the future, developed—two offering little hope for the preservation of political democracy, while the third was highly encouraging. The first may be called managerial corporatism, hierarchical in character (not unlike the Marxian definition of fascism without the nationalist extravagances). The second may be called laboristic corporatism, presumably equalitarian, but actually controlled by labor leaders, and likely to terminate in bureaucratic state socialism. The third, and optimistic, type may be described as democratic corporatism, essentially restricted to the economic sectors of a pluralistic society.

All three types displayed the major common characteristics of secular corporatism: emphasis on economic groups rather than individuals; acceptance of a limited sphere for government intervention; recognition of the individual's need for status and security, and for relief from the buffeting of the unregulated free market. Beyond this, however, managerial corporatism, laboristic corporatism, and democratic corporatism differed as sharply from each other as did Christian corporatism from fascism. Once again, the ultimate real character of each doctrine was governed by the system of values upon which it rested, by the limitations it envisaged for the power of leaders, by its concern for preserving the individuality of the many.[14]

During the Great Depression, when there was much talk of the "coming American fascism," and early in World War II, the tendency was to look to the business community as the creator of the forthcoming corporatist society.[15] Such was the view of James Burnham, an angry writer possessed of the certainty that often comes to learned Marxians who have left the fold without relinquishing the

[14] Terminology always creates problems. It is difficult to give words in ordinary use a special meaning, and the coinage of new terms is apt to subvert analysis into wearisome definition. Whatever choice is made is certain to be displeasing, and is unlikely to prevent confusion. The use of "corporatism" with various modifiers has at least this justification, that the various forms of corporatism do have some basic ideas and history in common. Moreover, the very diversity of corporatism has the virtue of testifying to a point that cannot be made too often, that the actual nature of a doctrine, at both practical and theoretical levels, depends upon the ethical values with which it is associated.

[15] The possibility of governmental creation of a corporatist structure attracted little interest, although NRA had been more than a hesitant step in this direction. The abrupt and definitive end of NRA may have had the salutary effect of directing attention to basic trends of social development rather than to legislative arrangements.

decisiveness of Marxian thinking. Inordinately influenced by the appearance of the moment, Burnham's *Managerial Revolution* (1941) regarded the apparent success of the German and Russian war economies as a forecast of the coming of managerial corporatism to America. Burnham modified Veblen's distinction between businessmen and engineers, recognizing it had lost most of its meaning through the steady fusion of the two groups in nonowning corporate management, and cast this new managerial class as the victor in a revised version of Marxian class struggle. The managers, in both industry and government, would take over actual sovereignty in the new society as the bourgeoisie had once displaced the feudal lords. They would institute a planned economy, drawing the laboring masses along behind them through some suitable social myths and party apparatus. The New Deal was but a primitive stage of the managerial society. November, 1940, saw the last "or, at most, the next to last," regular presidential election in which we would indulge. There would ensue an era of managerial authoritarianism from which, eventually, a new form of managerial democracy—rather limited—would emerge.

Burnham was thrown badly off course by an excess of economic determinism and love for the manipulation of abstract categories that survived his liberation from Marxism. He did not appreciate the degree to which economic forces operate within a changing social environment that can modify or even divert them, and he grossly underestimated the importance and power of the trade unions. These errors were avoided by the other leading contributors to the growing literature of corporatism. For one thing, there had been a reassessment of the nature and meaning of the large firm and of the character of competition in modern capitalism. Discarding or qualifying the unfriendly assumptions and judgments of both Marxists and classical economists, such writers as Schumpeter and Boulding had brought out the significance of the large firm as both technical innovator and factor for economic stability. Theoretical and actual case studies indicated that the objectives of monopolistic managements often were not to maximize profits and eliminate competitors, but to secure a "fair" profit (that is, one customary in the field), and to maintain the "position" of the firm among its monopolistic competitors (that is, to maintain or even moderately increase its share of the market, and to maintain its prestige). J. M. Clark, one of the most original and profound economists of modern times, had shown that the collapse of the classical theory of competition over the sale of undifferentiated products among firms too small to dominate the market, did not mean that there was no competition in an economy of very large firms. Economic doctrine needed a theory of competition that would fit contemporary practice, rather than prior assumptions concerning man and natural law and the atomistic character of producing and consuming units. And, in order to remain free and efficient, modern capitalism needed a certain amount of competition, both to prevent unhealthy concentration of power and to provide a more or less objective way of allocating resources. The decline of price competition was mitigated by the persistence of quality competition, interindustry competition, or competition of substitute commodities, among firms small or large.[16] The economists, in short, were finding ways to escape that embarrassment in the face of the large firm and the corporation in which they had been placed by the classical straitjacket.

Reconciled to the existence of the great corporation, economists as well as the rest of American society had to accustom themselves to the presence and influence of the large and powerful labor union. Not a few analysts, however, interpreted the rise of organized labor as a trend toward laboristic corporatism, which purported to be equalitarian (rather than based on an elite, as in managerial corporatism) but which was nevertheless likely to destroy the free democratic society from which it had sprung.

In less than a score of years following 1932, labor had all but reversed its long-standing position as underdog. Strengthened by government support, and by the sympathy most Americans ordinarily give the weaker competitor, organized labor boomed from a predepression strength of about 4 million to about 16 million after World War II. But this gain in numbers was not the most significant aspect of labor's rise, any more than the fact that even this swollen membership amounted to only a fourth of the total of employed persons was a sign of continuing weakness. Long before labor leaders and prolabor intellectuals and politicians had ceased declaiming

[16] J. M. Clark, "Toward a Concept of Workable Competition," *American Economic Review*, June, 1940, pp. 241 ff.

about labor's right to organize, as if that were still seriously in question, many acute observers were wondering how labor would employ powers of monopoly that greatly exceeded any ever held by a private corporation. There was greater justification for fearing the ultimate consequences of labor than of managerial monopoly. No matter how effectively cartels and lesser corporate restrictions evaded antitrust prosecution, from the standpoint of its place in society, management was no longer the confident, assertive, aggressive force it had been in the days of Theodore Roosevelt. It had become defensive and passive, and neither among the corporate stockholders nor in its own ranks was there any motivation, drive, or competition which might induce the managerial group to seek to dominate modern capitalist society in any exclusive manner. There was neither the ideological basis nor the will for the managerial elite to create a mass following to support any pretension of theirs to oligarchy. On the whole, managerial leadership found the handful of American fascist demagogues rather repulsive, and the latter, in any event, had insignificant popular backing. Management had no reason to and did not initiate inflationary pressures, nor did it firmly resist the inflationary push resulting from labor's wage demands.

Where the role of management was negative or passive, that of labor was, to the contrary, positive and active. Pessimistic observers were therefore worrying over the preservation of political democracy, of decentralization of decision, of individual liberty itself, in a society dominated by the chieftains of mighty unions and federations of unions.

It was not that either American labor or its leaders were given to communism, or socialism, or even a nonrevolutionary syndicalism. With but few exceptions of declining importance, both the rank and file and the officers of the union movement insisted on their loyalty to the society of neomercantilist, modified capitalism that had been taking shape during the second quarter of the twentieth century. They insisted that the goals of unionism were entirely consistent with this modified capitalism and with the due rights of management and ownership. The most important of these goals were the right to organize, and then to represent the workers without hindrance from management; the attainment of job security; higher earnings, both in wages and such forms as paid vacations and sick leaves; a fair share of any increase in industrial productivity. Few Americans would question the general propriety of these objectives. Another commonly stated goal, a higher share for labor of total national income, to be obtained at the expense of business profits, might arouse sharp opposition, but still would hardly seem to imply a challenge in principle to the bases of capitalism. Even "industrial democracy," the most radical and the most ideologically charged goal proposed by non-Marxist labor leaders, did not avowedly threaten the existence of private property, profits, or decentralized and nongovernmental economic decision making. "Industrial democracy" proposed that the workers, through their union representatives, share with management the responsibility and power of running the business and of planning for industry. Such a system, of course, would stretch the definition of capitalism to the breaking point and beyond, but one of the strongest arguments for it was that it offered an effective way to halt the advance of statism that otherwise seemed inevitable.[17]

"Industrial democracy" will be recognized as another name for corporatism, with a rather equalitarian and Guild socialist flavor, and may perhaps be discounted as an outburst of Utopianism on the part of some of the usually hard-headed labor leaders. But the union objectives most innocent and acceptable from the capitalist standpoint, including the right of organization itself and a share of rising productivity, tend of their own inner character to transform the practices and relations of capitalism in a corporatist direction.

If organization and representation are to be fully effective, a union can tolerate no challenge to its monopoly, from management or from nonunion labor, of the right to organize and to represent. Quite understandably, therefore, the unions are impelled to demand restrictive agreements, such as the closed shop, the union shop, or the maintenance of membership clause,[18] and even employment

---

[17] See C. E. Lindblom, *Unions and Capitalism*, New Haven, 1950, pp. 179 ff., 215 ff.

[18] Under closed-shop provisions, all employees must be members of the union at the time they are hired; under a union shop, all new employees must join the union within a period of time specified; under maintenance of membership, a worker who has joined the union cannot leave it. The last is the weakest, the first the strongest, of the common provisions protecting unions against the whittling away of their position in a shop.

through union hiring halls. Even under the less stringent arrangements, management, in effect, loses much of its power of choosing employees, and union membership, supposedly voluntary, becomes compulsory in practice for the workers. Job security, whose laudable purposes are to diminish the haunting fear of unemployment and to give the worker a sense of "belonging" and genuine participation in the firm, implies rigid seniority rules concerning layoffs and rehiring, and this often extends to promotions and job reclassifications. As a result, the employer's freedom of action is further diminished, and the worker's right to change jobs is sharply limited in practice, for he cannot do so without entering a new plant at the bottom of the seniority ladder. Paid vacations in proportion to length of employment, and the increasingly common retirement pension schemes heavily reinforce the worker's incentive to stay with one job, reducing his freedom of movement.

For the moment, we need not concern ourselves with the strictly economic effects of these and other aspects of unionization. The point to emphasize is that strong unions, effectively carrying out strictly trade-union objectives, inevitably feed the roots of corporatism, replacing the market with organized group action. As the demands for higher wages and for a share of increased productivity direct the unions to attack the traditional secrecy of company records and to question the soundness of management's policies, decisions about major aspects of the national economy are likely to be made in a corporatist fashion, through negotiations, harmonious or otherwise, between industry- and nation-wide associations of management and equally broad associations of labor.

Neither management nor government appears capable, or even desirous, of reversing this trend. In its negotiations with labor, management often represents in effect the interests of the consumer, seeking to keep costs and, ultimately, prices low, in order to maintain sales and profits. But management's zeal in defending this interest will be no stronger than the competition it has to meet, and the development of industry-wide bargaining and contract patterns affecting industry as a whole makes it ever more tempting for management to take the easy way out and secure industrial peace by passing the costs on to the consumer. Under such circumstances, only if demands were so extreme as to threaten the position of an entire industry would management be constrained to resist them with genuine determination. It is true, of course, that management is quite unwilling to consent to union infringements on its privileges of control, but here too, it has shown greater conviction in defending the form than the substance. Indeed, there are instances, the most striking being in the garment industry, in which management acts in certain respects under the supervision of the union. In any event, management will be unable to escape the further consequences of the privileges already gained by labor with the approval of the majority of the country. The employer's sovereignty is severely limited in practice; the joint management-labor consultation committee and the appearance of union representatives on corporate boards of directors are developments under way or reasonably predictable for the not too distant future.[19]

Government, which has been able at best to mitigate the effects of business monopoly, will be even less effective in limiting the monopoly power of unions. Aside from the political fact that the union members and their families are a large enough minority of the population to be able to decide any national election if they are sufficiently aroused, the nature of the union monopoly makes regulation exceedingly difficult. The monopolist attacked by the trust busters sought to gain control of the supply of a given commodity and thereby exert pressure on weaker individual buyers. He had to succeed in the hard task of barring newcomers from his chosen field. He could never escape the partial regulation of competition by substitute products. He had to be cautious in dealing with large customers. Union leadership, on the other hand, has an easier task: paradoxically, it cannot control the supply of labor, except very imperfectly, but it can control the buyer of labor, the particular employer, by means of an airtight contract. The employer, in short, is compelled to administer the union's monopoly.[20] The principal restraint upon the union is the fact that if it presses its advantage too far it may drive the employer out of business and its own members into unemployment. Under these circumstances, there is little that the government can do, in the long run, short of politically inadmissible measures such as setting wages and working conditions, or

[19] See p. 595.
[20] See Lindblom, *Unions and Capitalism*, pp. 56 ff.

enforcing labor discipline through assignment of jobs. Government can, it is true, exert pressure in the direction of moderation. It can, and undoubtedly will, develop adequate means of controlling strikes that endanger the public safety. But, ultimately, it will not be able to turn back the tide of union development that is directing the economy toward corporatism and, even if it were, there is no real pressure upon it to do so.

It would seem that only an hysterical pessimism could lead one to fear for democracy at the hands of the unions, of all great organizations those closest to the mass of the people, bodies that are avowedly democratic and led by men who are, by and large, devotedly democratic. Yet one can conceive of circumstances in which statist socialism is the only way of maintaining labor discipline, and foresee thereafter the transformation of democratic into bureaucratic socialism.[21] It is equally conceivable that labor leaders, corrupted by excessive power, might themselves be misguided into forcing the establishment of an authoritarian corporatist state and society, vaunting a sham democracy and equalitarianism which, together with a goodly share of national income would keep their rank and file contented, retaining bourgeois managers as well-paid employees, whatever their nominal status.[22] In either case, the repression of democracy would be the answer to the problem of halting inflation, inflation brought on by wage demands that, unchecked by economic forces of the capitalist market, had taken all that could be taken from the nonlabor sectors of society and threatened to outstrip the rise in productivity and productive capacity.

But what motive could bring reality to such nightmares, given the popular democracy of the unions and the sincerity of their leadership? On the one hand, it must be recognized that democratic control does not necessarily result in disinterestedness. The people can be selfish, greedy, and short-sighted. They are less likely than their leaders to understand technical and speculative arguments about the relation of profits to investment, or of wages and productivity to inflation. All people are likely to lend a ready ear to the man who promises them higher material gains. The winner of the ceaseless contest for union leadership is likely to be the one who promises.

[21] See p. 254 ff.
[22] This bears some resemblance to the Peron formula.

and secures, most. And, consciously or not, unions compete with each other for prestige within the labor movement and for larger shares of economic benefit. Hence the universal pressure for higher wages and collateral nonwage benefits. Hence the efforts, in old craft-work fields from music to typography, to fight the adoption of technological developments that eliminate jobs, or to compel make-work hiring of employees who "stand by" the new machine, earning the pay of an operator it had displaced. Hence high initiation fees for union membership or arbitrary restrictions on new members. That such measures set up a conflict between union and nonunion labor does not matter too much, for, it will be remembered, the union exercises its monopolistic control through its power over the buyer of labor, not over the supply.

On the other hand, it is generally conceded that the new genera-tion of labor leaders is better informed and more enlightened than its constituency, so that some encouragement may be drawn from the fact that the internal democracy of unions is much weaker than the friends of labor commonly presume. Insofar as the unions are a means for gaining advantages, rather than a way of life, their mem-bers' active interest in them is likely to be satisfied when such gains are achieved. Beyond this they are content to allow union activities to be the concern of the paid officers and of the organizationally minded minority of the rank and file. As in all organizations where sovereignty ultimately resides in the members, the proportion of real participants declines with size and a political machine takes over. Thereafter the power of the ordinary members of a large union lessens steadily, coming to resemble the purely nominal sovereignty of the stockholders of a great corporation.[23]

The union's leadership bureaucracy, like corporate management bureaucracy, becomes self-perpetuating and, in effect, responsible only to itself and to such external pressures as public opinion and government may apply. But while the nation benefits from the fact that the small-scale, short-term selfishness of the rank-and-file mem-ber is subordinated to the larger considerations that guide leader-ship, as the greed of the individual stockholder for immediate high dividends is subordinated to long-term policies of corporate manage-

---

[23] See, for example, J. Goldstein, *The Government of British Trade Unions,* London, 1952.

ment, the way is opened to the greater dangers of the excessive concentration of power. In the long run, moreover, there does not appear to be an adequate balance of strength between corporate and union bureaucracies. The usual ideological justification of managerial authority is based upon property rights. But the claims of property are diluted by the removal of risks, and are less persuasive than they used to be, now that they are made in behalf of apathetic and anonymous shareholders. Union leaders can summon the ideological arguments of equalitarianism and industrial democracy, and, besides, have the currents of social power running with them. One therefore cannot confidently expect that management and union will balance each other's power and thus allow the basic pattern of our institutions to survive.

This gloomy picture is essentially the one painted by Charles Lindblom's sober and searching *Unions and Capitalism* (1951), which foresaw the labor leaders driving for oligarchy not so much because of the attractions of power in itself, but because their role as chieftains of mass movements compelled them to interfere and create rigidities at every point of the capitalistic market economy, and to create inflationary pressures that ruthlessly undermined the self-adjusting free enterprise system. Since neither management nor government can halt this trend, a laboristic corporatism ruled by a union oligarchy would come into being. Although this would be no more capable than statist socialism (into which it might develop) of solving the economic and technical problems it was created to escape, it would then be too late to return to the free capitalist economy and society. The flaw in Lindblom's strong argument is that, for all practical purposes, he equates human welfare with the theoretical system of classical capitalism. Judged by this ideal standard, almost everything that has happened in the last fifty years inevitably appears as a further step into the totalitarian quicksands from which there is no escape.

This picture is altogether too dark and too certain, if one accepts the evidence of tremendous economic progress as proving that there remains a great deal of vitality to modern capitalism, a system which bears as little resemblance to the classical as to the Marxist model. It is a system which firmly resists simple definition, and allows for unorthodox conceptions of competition, for a large degree of government intervention, and for powerful unions. It is a fluid society, capable of developing in a number of directions, according to the consensus of social desire, rather than having entered upon a course whose predictable end is inevitable. The hope for a democratic corporatism is based upon this vitality and this fluidity of American society. Unlike managerial and laboristic corporatism, democratic corporatism postulates neither an elite nor drastic equalitarianism, but a pluralistic society. The concept of democratic corporatism, therefore, is restricted to the economic sectors of society, and allows for the vigorous existence of political, religious, cultural, and social institutions not subordinate to the economic groupings. Economic organization itself is not conceived narrowly in terms of labor and management alone—agriculture, the independent professions, private and public white-collar employees, these and other interests are expected to organize and make their weight and influence felt.

Accordingly, there is place in democratic corporatism for a variety of leaderships and a variety of democratic organizations. Democratic corporatism does not follow certain German thinkers and statesmen (including Bismarck), certain Social Catholics, and even some British Guild socialists, in wishing to replace the political legislature with an "economic parliament." For this would make of the legislature a body of technicians, leaving the crucial and essentially political power of decision in the hands of an increasingly unchecked executive. The concept of democratic corporatism concerns only the governance of the economy and the human relations there involved. The corporatist structure remains subject to the higher sovereignty of the nation as a whole, expressed through representative government. It remains subject to the restraining and modifying influence of voluntary groupings other than those of labor and management, in a complex society that is not destined to be simplified according to a rational blueprint. If it is to remain democratic, corporatism can neither be absorbed by the state nor itself absorb the state.

If it be agreed that the future is fluid rather than fixed, the chief problems rising from the growth of democratic corporatism are to keep government's useful and necessary role a limited one, and to adjust the relations of labor and management to prevent destructive conflicts or pressures. In working toward these ends the assumption must be made that all but a handful of the people and groups involved are free from a desire to rule or ruin, and are largely committed to customary American principles and practices of general respect for law, for negotiation and compromise.

This line of thought directs one to inquire anew into the motives that guide labor and its leaders, and to look beyond the motives to the factors that select one motive for emphasis to the neglect of another. It is no exaggeration to say that the most pessimistic estimates will be borne out unless labor develops socially responsible leadership. Labor's lateness in gaining a primary role on the American stage may have partly justified the bitterness with which its claims were asserted and pressed only a few years ago. But labor has clearly arrived, as a leading partner in our industrial economy, and bears a corresponding responsibility for the overall profitability of that economy. Undue rancor against management, wage demands that force inflation or undermine the position of nonunionized sections of society, can henceforth only bring closer the fatal choice between statist socialism and unionist oligarchy. But what grounds are there for hoping for a labor leadership and movement truly responsible to the community as a whole? Indeed, what might such responsibility mean?

If wage increases are in fact the principal objective of union activity, then a responsible attitude would appear to require labor to ask no more than is just in terms of price level, advance in productivity, and the competitive position of the industry in question. It must be conceded that what is just and reasonable under such a standard cannot be determined by any automatic formula. The celebrated agreement between General Motors and the United Automobile Workers, tying wages to a cost of living index and providing for an automatic annual increase to represent labor's share of expected improvements in productivity, may well turn out to have a built-in inflationary mechanism. Bargaining contracts will inevitably proceed by a process of trial and error, follow the leader, guesses and gambles. But there is no reason why labor leadership should not steadily gain in understanding of the basic economics involved in what amounts to national wage policy. The central federations, the CIO and AFL, are likely to gain influence over

their components at least in establishing general policy, allowing
for variation from union to union and even among locals. There is
no inherent reason why labor's wage program should be destructive,
unless labor chooses to risk statist socialism, or managerial oligarchy,
or strike out for oligarchy on its own, which is most improbable as
a deliberate choice. It is unquestionably true that even the wisest
of formulated wage policies subverts the automatically adjusting
free market. But, as J. M. Clark observes,

> On the whole, "economic law" seems to be taking on the character of
> a standard of sound policy that cannot be violated without making trouble,
> and that needs to be understood and voluntarily followed, but that is not
> self-enforcing.[24]

No one can argue that even the most public-spirited agreement on
wages between national representatives of labor and of management, with a benign federal government nodding approval, will
restore classical capitalism. Of course not. It will relegate the
theoretical model of Smith's successors even further into the shadows, but that is not the problem. The problem in respect of wages is
to develop methods and principles that, while contributing to the
formation of a democratic corporatist society, will not destroy political democracy through economic misadventures. And in this
regard, there are surely grounds for hope.

For one thing, although the prospects may favor overwhelming
union dominance over management, that day has not yet arrived.
It is as much a distortion of contemporary reality to regard management as pitifully weak in the face of labor as to continue to think of
infant labor struggling against the ruthless, rugged individualists.
Nor are management and labor left alone to fight their battles in a
sealed ring. Agriculture, professional and white-collar groups, intellectuals, have not lost their voice in American life, are creating and
perfecting their own organizations, and are far less disposed to
prejudge in labor's favor than they were a brief decade ago. Nor
does labor present a united front, and while factionalism and
internal competition are a bar to responsible statesmanship, they
are also an obstacle to premature unity behind an irresponsible
leader and a dangerous goal. And another obstacle is the probable
increase of local and sectional opposition to uniformity in labor

[24] *Alternative to Serfdom,* New York, 1948, p. 150.

organizations once the question of organization itself has been settled beyond dispute. In short, there is still time, time in which principles and practices of wage determination can be worked out that will enable a corporatist economy to operate efficiently within the framework of political democracy.[25]

The picture becomes even more favorable when it is realized that it is by no means certain that wages are indeed the crux of the problem of unionism. The tendency of labor disputes to center on wages is to some extent merely conventional, a survival from a time when the unregulated market economy was more rigorous, when economic negotiation or debate consisted largely of variations on the simple theme of supply and demand. But this convention has less and less basis in reality, and as wages move at a reasonably high level, job security becomes a prime consideration for union members, and its achievement a feather in their leader's cap. It is quite obvious that the strongest guarantee of job security is a prosperous economy and practically full employment, which enables industry more readily to bear the costs of seniority provisions, work spreading plans, and even the risks of guaranteeing a large percentage of the normal annual wage. One need not argue that the techniques derived from Keynesian economics neatly solve all problems of the business cycle, but surely there are few who would deny that society would react more intelligently and effectively to the threat of depression than it did after 1929. It is rather more likely that the least sign of a tapering off of boom-level prosperity would be generally exaggerated as a warning of collapse, so that future economic variations would be between an inflationary but prosperous condition that threatens to get out of hand and conditions of slowly advancing prices and less dazzling prosperity. One may say, in fact, that deflation (as distinct from corrective disinfla-

[25] This favorable time factor may be defined more precisely in terms of the existing social and economic checks and balances—large buyers vs. large sellers, agriculture vs. industry, as well as labor vs. management and one region vs. another. The operation of these and more strictly economic "countervailing powers" makes it possible for the economy and society to function effectively in defiance of the logic of traditional economics and political theory. New forms of competition and adjustment develop, and thereby provide time in which fundamental solutions can be worked out without catastrophe or undue discord. See J. K. Galbraith's stimulating *American Capitalism: The Concept of Countervailing Power*, Boston, 1952.

tion) is now contrary to political, if not economic, law, and the unions are one of the strongest reasons why this is so. The unions themselves, however, are responsible for a number of threats to high employment. Feather-bedding, obstruction to technological innovation, and excessive restrictions on entry into a craft or to union membership are all monopolistic devices which protect the ins and lessen the chances of employment for the outs. High wage demands and low work-load limits drive up costs and are a check to industrial expansion.

But let us place these practices in some perspective. A number of them, particularly feather-bedding, the stand-by worker, and closing the gates to craft or union entry are hardly to be defended on any ground, and the worst excesses can and should be outlawed. In the long run, however, these monopolistic tactics can delay, but can hardly prevent economically sound developments. Like the restrictive practices of monopolistic business, if not carried to excess they can serve the useful function of helping to adjust the rate of technological and social innovation to society's capacity to digest change. To the degree that large-scale enterprise benefits from certainty, union and business restrictions alike can help provide it.[26] Nor do all aspects of union monopoly work in the same direction: they may cancel each other out. Obstruction of technological innovation, for example, is in a general sense counteracted by high wage demands which compel management to hasten improvements. And the threat of revolution or dictatorship is not so close that constructive imagination does not have the time to develop workable forms of job security that are not inherently dishonest and wasteful. Retraining programs have already done much to lessen the fear of technological unemployment. A guaranteed full annual wage might, of itself, impose too great a degree of rigidity for the economy to stand, but seasonal fluctuations in business and employment can and have been reduced or eliminated in many fields, and approximations of the annual wage are by no means inconceivable. Once again, there is nothing in labor's desire for security which is inherently destructive of anything save the long-destroyed self-adjusting market of the classical economists.

The movement for job security is closely linked with the least

[26] See p. 58.

tangible and yet, to many, the most frightening of union objectives. It arises from labor's desire for a sense of belonging, for some status other than that of a commodity, for recognition of the laborer as well as his work. This feeling is of the essence of modern corporatism. Its reappearance as a social force emphasizes the decline of the wage-centered outlook that characterized labor in the past era of relatively individualistic capitalism; it constitutes a modern adaptation of the medieval gild viewpoint, which saw the job relationship as something more than a means of earning money.[27] This desire has been strongly reinforced by the widespread use of the seniority principle, in respect of layoffs and rehiring, vacations and pension rights, as a result of which employment in a given firm is apt to be an affiliation for life, rather than until another job happens to strike the worker's fancy. But the wholesome desire for status, supported by security and wage objectives and by leaders' ambitions, has led labor to undertake an assault on the hitherto sacred preserves of management. They have asked for access to confidential corporate records and have demanded a voice in the formation of all aspects of business policy, not merely those directly affecting their jobs. The general reaction of management has understandably been to double the locks on the filing cabinets and on the door of the directors' room. Having seen old established privileges whittled away, management has retired to a firm defense of its last citadel—in effect, the right to manage. In this they have had the support of most expert observers, although many have advised a policy of voluntarily informing labor of the state of the company business and of contemplated programs. It has been suggested that labor, through elected representatives, assume responsibility for administering recreation, safety, sanitation, cafeterias, vacation schedules, and the like.[28] This would be more satisfactory to labor than simple paternalism, and is likely to become quite popular, since morale and efficiency tend to rise when the workers have participated in designing, and have the responsibility for running, these collateral activities.

[27] See Frank Tannenbaum, *A Philosophy of Labor*, New York, 1951, chaps. 3–5.
[28] See, for example, P. F. Drucker, *The New Society: The Anatomy of the Industrial Order*, New York, 1949, Parts IV, VIII.

But there is no ready answer to the claim to a share of major power that is implicit in the slogan, "a right to the job." The justification for "industrial democracy" is neither especially clear nor convincing. If the function of industry is to produce, then the consumer should rule (through management). If the primary function of industry is to provide jobs, it would hardly seem to matter what is produced. Defining the objective of industry as the provision of jobs whose existence ultimately depends on satisfying the consumer does not provide an adequate case for the participation of labor in the affairs of management. On this basis the powers of management are in effect granted in recognition of proved ability to manage, and there is certainly no a priori reason why labor or its representatives should be more capable of directing production than the managers themselves.

Unwelcome, and certain to be resisted as it is, labor's demand for a voice in management is, however, a hopeful, and not essentially a revolutionary phenomenon. Viewed as a long-run phenomenon it is a sign of labor's commitment to the job and to the plant, the most profound form of good will. The very slowness with which it is likely to gain recognition is most fortunate, for, once again, time will have been afforded in which to develop principles and patterns of consultation. The social and educational gap between management and labor leadership is steadily narrowing, and another trend is slowly getting under way which could transform the whole industrial climate by placing labor's managerial aspirations on a different and firmer footing. There is every prospect that the unions will be among America's wealthy organizations. They have a certain and tax-exempt income from dues alone in excess of one billion dollars a year, and further income from three times as much invested as reserves for insurance and other benefit programs and for strike "war chests." Income has exceeded outlay, and union funds seeking investment will grow even more from the increasingly prevalent retirement pension plans. The swelling fortune of labor has been invested in real estate, in union-owned insurance companies and banks, and, in a new trend dramatically highlighted by the Automobile Workers, in the industries whose workers they represent. One can hardly exaggerate the importance and the potentialities of this development. Writes Tannenbaum:

A new source of investment from these semipublic agencies is being opened up at a time when a tendency to equalize incomes and reduce the great fortunes makes it less likely that large private savings will continue to be available. Thus one of the changes hidden in the growth of trade-unionism is the reestablishment of a proprietary interest by the workers in the industries from which they draw their living. For the worker, at least, the day of fluidity, impersonality and irresponsibility is drawing to a close. If he is going to have a pecuniary interest, he will also have to assume the moral responsibilities that a pecuniary relationship has always involved: responsibility for the property he owns, the work he does, and the quality of what he produces for the rest of the community. . . . It is not likely that these new saving institutions, for so the unions may be considered, will ever own all of modern industry. . . . But increasing ownership is a logical next step, and with it increasing responsibility.[29]

Contemporary classlike distinctions between men of management and men of labor may be expected to fade. The existence of two equally smooth roads to the top in industry, management and the union, would undermine the pressure for excessive equalization of incomes, and there would be room for adequately high rewards to the successful to provide incentives for effort and imagination. The corporatist institutions and practices that have been developing in great variety, in agriculture, the professions, and even in the arts would round out the intricate pattern of a highly organized but decentralized society. The role of government would not expand significantly, and might even contract, for security, health, and certain branches of education would be appropriate concerns of corporatist groups. Government, aside from fulfilling its traditional and unquestioned functions such as defense, administration of justice, and large-scale public works, would determine overall fiscal policy as it now does, underwrite and supervise corporatist insurance programs, and represent the total community interest when called upon to do so. The neomercantilist state would harmonize as well with a democratic corporatist society as did the royal mercantilist state of the seventeenth century with a society based upon agriculture, craft industries, commerce, and gilds. Unlike the monarchies, democratic corporatism could afford that very large degree of decentralization of decision which ensures the richness of variety and the freedom and democracy of man.

[29] *Philosophy of Labor*, p. 189.

If the reader will abide yet a further indulgence of the Utopian streak which lingers in this writer as in most, it is conceivable that contemporary American capitalism, developing into democratic corporatism, will actually bring about the Marxian nirvana of freedom from the cursed boredom of the division of labor.[30] It will do this not by wishing away the division of labor, but by carrying it to the point of efficiency where work on the job consumes less than half the waking day, and promoting leisure activity to equality with earning one's living. Thus we shall escape the gravest of the dangers that threaten freedom, the overproduction by an expanding educational system of intellectuals relative to the demand for paper workers, breeding a sense of frustration and the desire to overthrow society for the altruistic purpose of helping the working man. For it will matter less whether one works as a desk or a bench in the morning if, to paraphrase Marx, either man can as easily fish, or read, or write, or paint, or play baseball in the afternoon and evening. And, although Lord Keynes was right in saying that it is better for a man to tyrannize over his bank balance than over his fellow men, it is better yet that he tyrannize over a trout, a book, or home plate.

The sober point about this Utopian vision is that it is no more unrealistic than the dire certifications of doom to which we are so often treated. It is reasonable to say that American society appears to be changing in a corporatist direction, that this change, while rather rapid on the scale of past transformations, need not outstrip our capacity to assimilate it and adjust to it, always given the continuing vitality of the essential beliefs and institutions of the American branch of Western civilization. It is also reasonable to point to similar tendencies in other lands, western Europe, for example, and New Zealand. Corporatism may actually be strongest and farthest advanced in the United Kingdom, where the Trades Union Congress faces the Federation of British Industries, where the trade association is an active regulating force and is employed as such by the government. The trend runs strong in France and Italy, although impeded and somewhat concealed by the strength of Marxism among the working class and intellectuals. It exists in the German Federal Republic, where labor representation in heavy

[30] See p. 216.

industry management has been enacted into law. In these lands, however, statist socialism remains a strong force, and the issue between it and a decentralized democratic corporatist society is dependent upon extraneous factors, particularly the threat of Russian aggression, to a far greater extent than in the United States.

It is not Utopian, in short, to say that secular, democratic corporatism gives strong indications of being our future pattern of development. But this is not predetermined by any immutable forces of history. The future rests upon the consensus of many a group, the decisions of many an individual. At every twist and turn in that most tortuous of roads, social evolution, there are choices to be made, and they will be made in the light of some set of standards of value, some previously established judgments of what is good and what is bad. Paradoxically, the full-fashioned ideologies have failed to make way in the living society of men, while the corporatist pattern which gives a hint of fulfillment lacks an adequate theoretical expression, not only of its own content but of its relations to the noneconomic values in which we are as deeply concerned. We are therefore brought around full circle to consider the nature of an ideology of the middle way to guide contemporary America, and this paradox fittingly introduces the first question to be dealt with, whether a rigorous system is necessary.

NOTES ON BOOKS

There is no convenient, general introduction to this subject, and for this reason, possibly the best beginning will be made with a rather specialized work, R. H. Bowen's *German Theories of the Corporative State, With Special Reference to the Period 1870–1918*. F. S. Nitti's *Catholic Socialism* is seriously dated, but still useful, and a rich introduction to French Social Catholicism is to be found in P. T. Moon's *The Labor Problem and the Social Catholic Movement in France*. F. Neumann's *Behemoth* contains a good discussion of the relationship of Nazism and corporatism. From among the many good works on Italian Fascism, one may suggest W. Ebenstein's *Fascist Italy* and C. T. Schmidt's *The Corporate State in Action: Italy Under Fascism*. On postwar Social Catholicism, there is M. Einaudi and F. Goguel's *Christian Democracy in Italy and France*.

On the vexed question of "Religion and the Rise of Capitalism," one may consult R. H. Tawney's classic thus entitled, together with Max Weber's *The Protestant Ethic and the Rise of Capitalism*. A good corrective to this work is H. M. Robertson's neglected *Aspects of the Rise of Economic Individualism, A Criticism of Max Weber and His School.*

To get on the right track in studying labor in the trend toward corporatism, the reader will do best to start with Tannenbaum's *A Philosophy of Labor*, and then to take up J. M. Clark's *Alternative to Serfdom* and *Guideposts in a Time of Change*. Thereafter he will be confronted with an *embarras de richesses*, from among which one may recommend O. W. Knauth's *Managerial Enterprise*, C. E. Lindblom's *Unions and Capitalism*, J. K. Galbraith's *American Capitalism: The Concept of Countervailing Power*, and, from the library of S. H. Slichter's works, *Union Policies and Industrial Management, The Challenge of Industrial Relations,* and *The American Economy*. J. M. Clark's contribution to the symposium edited by D. M. Wright, *The Impact of the Union*, is, as usual, particularly rewarding.

14.

THE MIDDLE WAY IN THE MODERN WORLD

I. *Is a Rigorous System Necessary?*

S<small>INCE</small> the golden age of Greece, many of the ablest minds of the West have been devoted to the search for the principles upon which the best society could be built. It is one of the great ironies of this long and error-laden history that the more embracing and perfected the theory, the more skillfully fashioned its interconnections, the more rigorous the system, the less has it been worth as a guide to understanding or to action. It is ironical that idealistic philosophers of perfection like Plato, and materialistic philosophers of the ultimate freedom, like Marx, should produce systems under which living is sordid and the soul of man degraded, while some abstractions are polished to a gleaming finish which reflects the glory of a stupid or a cynical despot. It is perhaps the supreme terrestrial irony that Utopia is a prison.

It must surely give pause to the social perfectionist, to the maker of plans for the swift improvement of his fellows, to see the cause of human freedom and welfare advanced by an unprincipled ruler like Elizabeth I and set back by the incorruptible Robespierre, advanced by Stolypin, the bureaucratic minister of a worthless Tsar, and all but destroyed by Lenin, arch priest of a gospel of total liberation.

It ought certainly to shake the confidence of the cold, objective social scientist to recall that the "greatest good for the greatest number" of some of the classical economists turned into the dross of the English factory town and the wastage and tragedies of depression. For, clearly, the philosophers of society have been dogged by error, error in understanding man in their subject and man in themselves.

Social philosophies have necessarily been shorter-lived in the modern era of rapid change and easy publication, and, since the closing years of the last century, their frailty has been widely diagnosed as owing to an excess of rationalism. There consequently began a cult of the irrational, ranging the political spectrum but perhaps favoring the right wing. It included German nationalists and the syndicalist Sorel, religious and secular existentialists, and the iconoclast Nietzsche. It included Freud and the neo-Freudians, both useful healers and witch doctors to the wealthy of an industrial society. Whatever its influence on individuals in their personal lives, in the social arena this cult produced irresponsibility, or an irrational leap into the calcified rationality of Marxism, or an ecstatic embracing of one of the mountebanks of fascism, whose mystique was rationally calculated to feed upon the irrationality of man.

And yet the wisdom that steers between extremes has never been hard to discover: in the *Politics* of Aristotle, who saw the relationship between social conditions and political structure, and how each form of the latter could degenerate into an evil twin; in the *Reflections* of Edmund Burke, who loved freedom with all the ardor of a British constitutionalist, and foresaw its destruction at the hands of men who set their own conceit against the judgments of history; in the *Democracy* of de Tocqueville, who saw how endlessly complex were the intertwinings of morality, institutions, and geography, and never was so much the scientist as to forget man's capacity to choose a free, or an unfree, society. Wisdom can be discovered in the ordinary arrangements of every day, without which the intricate structure of Western civilization would tumble in ruin and starvation. It will not be taken, I hope, as undue national pride to say that as good a key as any to this wisdom of the golden mean can be found in the workings of American society, anti-intellectual, as we must admit, yet more rational and in a sense more given to theory than any other in its businesslike approach to the problems of organizing daily life.

Reason is the abundantly given source of power which moves most human works but, as every person knows, not all. One can indeed argue that intuition, insight, the emotions, habit, are subconsciously rational, and this view is implicit in the theories of many of the psychoanalysts. But this is not relevant, for the fact remains that the overt and conscious processes of reason, those which can be expressed and communicated to others rationally and which are therefore subject to the challenge of contrary reasoning, these rational processes do not apply equally well to all aspects of life, and to some very badly. Man as a social being is accordingly only partly rational, and it was the charge of having ignored this fact that was very properly leveled against the great rational system builders of the eighteenth and nineteenth centuries by the romantics, by such men as Burke, and by the later irrationalists. The rationalist system builders had mistaken the nature of man as the subject of their studies, and had elaborated theoretical structures that pertained to computing machines, not human beings.

But few indeed are the system builders, rationalist or irrationalist, who have not committed the other and equally devastating error of misunderstanding the nature of man in their own selves. Even those who judiciously recognize the limits of reason in mankind are often likely to assume that their own rational powers, as observers of mankind, are absolutely unbounded. This is regularly assumed even by the more modest theorists who concede that their conclusions can be no more than tentative because they do not yet have enough factual information or the correct theoretical concepts upon which to formulate a rigorously controlling system. Some day, they imply, the factual stockpile will be big enough, the theoretical tools at hand, and then we shall have certainty in social science.[1]

In short, they have not discarded, only renamed and redesigned

---

[1] For example, the sociologist George Lundberg (*Social Research: A Study in Methods of Gathering Data,* New York, 1942, pp. 18, 20; italicized in the original): "The complexity of human society, in other words, is largely a function of our ignorance of it." "The difficulties, therefore, which appear to preclude the possibility of a true science of society, derive from our undeveloped technique and methodology of study and our consequent unfamiliarity with the data, rather than from inherent differences in the data themselves."

the mistaken objectives, the erroneous conceptions of functions and skills, of the system builders they reject. Social scientists have, indeed, been increasingly willing to recognize that they are likely to obtain a greater measure of success when their projects are of smaller scope, when they relegate to a distant future the formulation of all-embracing systems of laws of social organization and development. In her remarkably confident *Testament for Social Science*, the English economist Barbara Wootton condemns grandiose biological analogies and Marxian constructions as "blind alleys." But once these false paths have been escaped, she seems assured, social science will be able to devise more efficient means of government compatible with freedom and, even:

If we know what mental and physical health are, and we are clear that these are the ends that we are after, then the task of devising the social and political institutions and moral codes that make these ends possible is a practical research job for the social sciences. We can get ahead with it as soon as we have freed ourselves from the obscurantism that I have described ["pre-scientific mental habits," biological analogies and the muddle derived from Marxism] . . . and we can reasonably hope that the rewards will be comparable with those of scientific inquiry in other fields.[2]

This may perhaps be an exceptionally rosy view of the eventual rich gains from grubbing research on more manageable subjects, but it reflects the same confidence in the progress of the social sciences toward command over man that underlay the frightened prediction of M. I. T.'s Dean Burchard:

We may be reasonably sure that we have not reached the end of the road, that we will not see an early moratorium on science, and that the consequences of future discoveries, wrongly used, will be even more forbidding than the consequences of the one big present threat which will not down.

Without assuming any mantle of prophecy, it is meet to suggest that the early conquest of space is probable, that large-scale biological controls are probable, and that ability to control man's thoughts with precision is by no means out of the question. Any of these is more awesome in its implications than was the mushroom cloud in 1945.[3]

[2] Barbara Wootton, *Testament for Social Science*, New York, 1950, pp. 57, 144.

[3] *New York Times*, April 1, 1949.

A similar praiseworthy fear led the distinguished American anthropologist, Margaret Mead, to warn social scientists against devising techniques for manipulating people and society toward blueprinted objectives; they must limit themselves to working out the methods of developing greater democracy. The social scientist, she writes,

. . . must lay his hands upon a process with a control none the less sure, none the less adjusted to everything he knows of the processes of culture and the peculiar nature of his own culture, for all that he cannot, nay he must not, envisage the end toward which he is setting that process in motion.[4]

Surely this is asking too much—and the wrong kind of service— of the social sciences. Having rid themselves of the "gigantomania" of biological analogies and Marxism, they are tempted, in hope or fear, with a gigantomania of a newer kind, but in its own way noxious. Those whom we may call the oversanguine social scientists will recognize that it is as absurd to expect a man to reason through his love for his wife, parents, children, or his native land as it is to use a steam shovel to transplant a bush in grandmother's rose garden. They are nevertheless prepared to use the same steam shovel to level Mount McKinley. The analogy is not unapt, for reason, when brought to do a job, is a tool of the trade, and the art of any trade is to know the limits and the capacities of its tools. The system builders fail, in short, because they try to undertake more than they can do. Why this should be so is in no way mysterious.

The poor social scientist or philosopher has one advantage over the remarkably successful physicist. The latter can never be certain that he has got to the foundation materials of his subject. The atom endured for centuries as the irreducible elemental particle, but it has since been repeatedly fractioned into more and more numerous and more and more inestimable components, until it appears to have ended, for the moment, as a series of mathematical symbols on paper or blackboard of basically mysterious composition. Not so with the student of society: his irreducible particle was and remains the human individual. And it can never be otherwise, for if one fractions this entity, the individual, one has set aside social

[4] "The Comparative Study of Culture and the Purposive Cultivation of Democratic Values," in L. Bryson and L. Finkelstein, eds., *Science, Philosophy and Religion, Second Symposium*, New York, 1942, p. 67.

analysis for individual psychology, a different field of study altogether, whose results cannot simply be totaled and presented as the
interpretation of society.

But the secureness of his "atom" is the source of the social
scientist's subsequent travails, for man acts as a whole, reasoning
mind, subconscious mind, emotions, habits, education, physique,
social and geographical environment, family, religious belief, en-
docrine system, and all. It is as if at each moment his total biography
(and, following some psychologists, some prebiography) had come
to life and were acting in him. This man has freedom of will; to
avoid an overworked controversy, let us say that, at least, he has the
freedom to choose between the feasible alternatives of which he is
aware. Will is not the same as random movement or statistical
distribution. There is always, of course, a very wide convergence of
individual wills, or society would not exist. But within the excessively broad category of "society," there are countless wills in varying degrees of controversy and coöperation. Few of these are apt to
be perfectly harmonious even in themselves. How certain would be
the results of the physicist if each of the atoms or lesser particles
within the broad category of, let us say, a lump of uranium ore, had
the power of willing its movement, of joining with other particles,
of fighting or sulking?

The successes of the natural scientist have come from his ability
to realize in fact the "other things being equal" clause so dear to the
heart of any economist. For all practical purposes, and in most
instances, the natural scientist can hold the rest of the universe, or a
selected portion of his subject matter, sufficiently "equal," or neutral
from the standpoint of his research. And, of course, he can set up
controlled experiments and count results with great accuracy. These
luxuries are denied to the student of society. His subject matter is
altogether too complex for any human mind to grasp, in sufficient
breadth and sufficient detail, in a single operation of thought. It can
never be expressed in a "field equation." The student of society
must always assume the greater part of his subject to be "equal"
while it is not so in actuality; he can never test his generalizations
save historically, which means the things he has been holding
"equal" have been changing as industriously as those whose particular change he has set out to study. When he seeks to escape

these difficulties by using the refined techniques of mathematical correlation, he confronts another peril, that of employing the neat symbols and precise methods of mathematics to represent data that are crude, and relationships that are confused. As a result, the student of society is more likely to be accurate in description than explanation of complex relationships, and in explanation of the restricted event than of the great sweep of social movement.

This argument should not in the least be taken as suggesting that the study of society is futile, or that the output of social scientists is valueless. To the contrary, the study is absolutely essential and rewarding, the results nearly always useful in some way and often a guide to wisdom in action. The argument means only that the students of society should know their own limitations and those of their subject, that they should take a resolutely agnostic view with regard to the elaboration of social laws as effective as those of physics; they should understand, in short, that it is in their own nature and in the nature of their field never to be able to understand, and never to be able to formulate in rational, communicable ways significant generalizations or laws that are universally valid. As J. M. Clark observes, there is a range of "indeterminateness" in the laws of economics (and other social sciences) within which group decisions can have decisive effect, and about which scientific prediction is feeble.[5] Once such limitations are recognized, and extravagant claims and extravagant systems abandoned, the social studies and their theories will be more useful than ever, contributing accurate if partial information and valid if partial explanation. Let us by all means be rational and use quantitative methods, and let us begin by understanding the limits of reason and of quantitative techniques.

To suggest limits to the function of the social sciences in developing an ideology and its concrete implications is neither to justify nor even condone the disdain in which the social studies are often held by the politicians and practical men who make policy. As the noted anthropologist, Ralph Linton, complains,

. . . while even the most conservative manufacturer is quick to take the advice of the chemist or engineer, the legislator rarely pays attention to

[5] D. M. Wright, ed., *The Impact of the Union, Eight Economic Theorists Evaluate the Labor Movement*, New York, 1950, p. 4.

the findings of the social scientist. Someone has said that in this age of wireless and airplanes the legislator typically keeps his ear to the ground.[6]

This is, of course, another way of saying that in some respects practical America is anti-intellectual—a fortunate trait to the extent that it makes us exceedingly skeptical of both rationalist blueprints and flights of deterministic fancy. Fortunate too in that it encourages our wisest statesmen, who do in fact make plentiful use of the social scientists as technical experts, to understand that policy making is not a technical matter, generalizing, as it were, Clemenceau's famous quip that war was too important to be left to the generals. But anti-intellectualism—the adulation of what is presumed to be practical common sense, and a contempt for theory—is often not really a rejection of theory, but rather persistence in the theory of a generation or more ago, theory that may be obsolete, but which age and familiarity have endowed with the appearance of homespun, obvious common sense. Lord Keynes observed that

Practical men who believe themselves to be quite exempt from any intellectual influence are usually the slaves of some defunct economist. Madmen in authority, who hear voices in the air, are distilling their frenzy from some academic scribbler of a few years back . . . in the field of economic and political philosophy there are not many who are influenced by new theories after they are twenty-five or thirty years of age, so that the ideas which civil servants and politicians and even demagogues apply to current events are not likely to be the newest.[7]

And yet the policy maker must always reconsider his theory, and take full advantage of whatever the technical experts can offer. He will more readily do so if the social scientists are modest in their aspirations and their claims, and if they infuse into their analyses of the present the humanizing factor of historical learning, bringing out the living nature of problems and societies the way biography breathes life into the character sketch of a man. Historical thinking can often provide a common ground for policy makers and social scientists, for many of the most successful statesmen have been given to the reading of history—not the sweeping philosophical

[6] Ralph Linton, ed., *The Science of Man in the World Crisis,* New York, 1945, p. 219.

[7] *General Theory,* pp. 383–384.

systems, from Hegel and Marx to Spengler and Toynbee, but biographies and histories of restricted scope. Some, like Theodore Roosevelt and Winston Churchill, have been historians in their own right. They have not indulged this taste purely for literary reasons, or because one can learn lessons from history, which is true only in a very roundabout sense. Consciously or unconsciously, they have grasped that the peculiar contribution of history is not to yield formulae that are readily applicable, but a depth of understanding and perspective that produces a richer insight into the present and into the likely direction of changes in the future. Historical study helps one to realize his own involvement in history, in a particular time and place, and so to escape to some extent from that self-centeredness that leads a man to think his own reason and science are the culmination and summit of wisdom, and thereby entitled to prescribe with certainty. Historical insight, like historical learning, is inordinately resistant to simple formulation and easy communication. Its achievement is more often revealed in the wisdom of the decisions it has influenced than in formal and rational argument.[8]

Is a rigorous system necessary? It is to be avoided like the plague. Can social science offer specific prescriptions as medical science can for some diseases? Rarely, if ever. When one is chanced, the complexities of life are likely to mock the conceit of man and confront him once again with the irony of undesired results and hopes betrayed. Herein is to be found the reason for the failure of some of the most ingenious conceptions in economics and politics. Take, for example, the fully planned economy (as distinct from the partially guided economy of neomercantilism). Conceived as the social and organizational counterpart to a very advanced technology, the planned economy was expected to eliminate the cultural lag between up-to-the-minute technical achievements and methods of organizing production and distribution that belonged to a less mature era. As the machine, and then the machine-tended machine, had replaced the craftsman, planning for the whole economy would replace the anarchy, chaos, and frequent irrationality of decision

[8] A psychologist might again argue that "historical insight" is merely a subconscious rational ordering of knowledge that is too complex to be ordered rationally at the conscious, communicable level of thought. Perhaps so, but the objection remains irrelevant practically.

making by thousands of independent producers ignorant of each other's intentions.

But our own experience in wartime, and that of the Soviet Union, China, Great Britain, and Scandinavia, shows that planning works best when it is confined to a relatively narrow range of more or less standardized products. All other difficulties aside, the very administrative complexity of thoroughly directing the variegated economy of the United States or western Europe, with their rich choice of styles and alternative commodities, would turn centralized planning into directed confusion and indecision, and bring the economy to a halt. Planning works best where the basic, popular standard of living is low, where decisions need to be made only with regard to essentials because luxuries are rare and unimportant. The planned economy is desirable at most for the poor country striving to create basic industries, and if imposed by political decision upon a wealthy nation would soon bring its rulers to face the choice between more planning and a lowering and simpler standard of life, and the surrender of planning to the variety, productivity and richness of decentralized choice. In short, not only will a centralized planning authority be workable only when the economy is simple, but the result of establishing such an authority must be to simplify. Russia and China have found it relatively easier to plan than Czechoslovakia, where the standard of living had to be depressed. The Western nations have found general controls more workable than precise, physical regulations, whose unwanted effects have to be corrected by further precise, physical regulations. One might almost say that if an economy is wealthy enough to justify the effort of rigorous planning, it had best not be attempted; for the poor economy to plan is essentially a waste of energy, for the unplanned progress of capitalism need offer no apologies save in terms of social costs, and these were strikingly lower than the social costs of communism.

The logic of politics may be as deceitful as that of economics. In their desire to develop the most perfect expression of the will of the people, political scientists invented proportional representation. But the will of the people can be determined only after it has been expressed, and, in practice, this means postponing, setting aside, or compromising points of disagreement and acting upon and emphasizing points of agreement. Proportional representation can effectively throttle the will of the people by rewarding political leaders for stressing differences of region, religion, class, language, or ideology. It can, and has, so well reflected the disagreements of the people as to render effective government impossible, discredit democracy, and justify dictatorship.

If we were to draw but one conclusion from the repeated failures of some of our finest minds, motivated by the very best of intentions, it might well be this: that no basis for a guiding ideology can be found either in presumed natural rights or natural laws, in deterministic theories of history, or in the psychologically, statistically, or rationally deduced principles of the social sciences. Unlike such morally neutral operations as quantitative analysis in chemistry, or solving a simultaneous equation, the elaboration of an ideology must rest upon a system of values, principles of essential good and bad which preside over the fundamental attitudes of man. The natural sciences have contributed, and can contribute, nothing to the formulation of a proper value system (although scientists as individuals in society are themselves governed by a set of values), and the efforts of naturalistic philosophies have not been conspicuously successful.[9] There remain revealed religion and history in which we may seek the source of values and the roots of an ideology.

II. *A Historical Ideology of the Middle Way*

It is most fortunate that we are not forced to choose between religion and history in the search for ideological foundations. Religion lacks force for those not already endowed with faith. And, no matter how consistent the historical reasoning, it amounts to a flat rejection of God if it pretends to be a source of ethical judgment

---

[9] I apologize for dismissing so cavalierly the many noble efforts from Aristotle to the present. But this is not a book about theories of ethics, and I can only suggest the reasons for my conclusion. If one does not believe in a God directing nature, nature must be regarded as absolutely neutral in ethical questions. Nonreligious and nonhistorical systems of ethics cannot, therefore, be derived from a law of the world of nature, but from human experience, from human reason, or from the natural order of the human organism. The first—experience—begs the question, since love, for example, is empirically better than hate only if one has established, on some prior ethical basis, a goal which love can produce and hate cannot. Nor can one derive this prior goal without

while omitting religion. An exclusive selection of either religion or history would render the ideology meaningless to many whom it must attract if it is to have any bearing in the present age. But the choice need not be made. Christianity, the dominant religion of the West, is in all its major branches thoroughly historical; Christianity is a philosophy of history. And the history of the West to any historian, whatever be his religious views, must, to a most significant degree, be a history of Christianity. This is obviously so because of the importance of the institutions of the Christian churches, but far more profoundly because the presiding values of Western civilization have been drawn from and expounded by Christianity.

Marx said, in effect, Give me the economics of a society and I will tell you how its institutions functioned, and what its history really meant. We are saying, in effect, given the values of Western civilization, we can understand the purpose of its institutions, and what its history really meant. We cannot readily equate purpose and actual conduct, for the values of the Judao-Christian tradition are linked with a Christian concept of man that denies both simple altruism and the simple logical selfishness in which Marx believed. But, for the moment, we can say that we are suggesting a way of understanding history primarily by reference to values.

No theory of history or social change, no matter how deterministic, can explain human affairs without referring to the human actors

---

having first developed some standard by which it is a good goal—and so into an infinite regression.

Reason fails to yield a stable nonreligious and nonhistorical system of ethics because the reasoner is himself involved in a religious and historical environment. In other words, he has received his ethics before starting the reasoning process, and that is why the ingenious constructions of Spinoza and other rationalists amount to an involved and clumsy assertion of the traditional Judao-Christian system, with minor variations. Moreover, reason must work from experience, so that all the difficulties of empirical ethics arise.

Naturalist ethics—in general harmony with the Judao-Christian tradition, as one might expect—have been founded upon the needs of the human organism, understood to include mental health and development. Barbara Wootton (*Testament for Social Science*, p. 181) proclaims, "Thou shalt honour the need of every human organism to persist in its own being and to reach its normal completion or actualisation." This "commandment" begs all the possible questions, for, aside from prohibiting the killing of the sane and healthy, it would in no way bar the domination of the strong, the ambitious, or the "benevolent" despot over the weak, so long as the former asserted his power and the latter were physically maintained and psychologically adjusted to slavery.

concerned. The simplest theistic interpretation, that all happenings are owing to the will of God, still means that God has elected to exert His will through certain people of His choice. Hegel's World Spirit, the Idea, functions through the individuals or nations in whom it temporarily resides. Marx's economic factors were to bring about historical change by impressing upon the rationally selfish minds of the members of a social class what their self-interest was, and what they should rationally do to advance it.[10] Obviously, a theory of social change depends on a prior theory as to how an individual or a group reaches decisions.

All such decisions deal with some aspect of the social or physical environment, but with this environment as the individual or group understands it, entirely aside from whether this understanding is accurate or not. If a village plagued by floods believes these are the work of a nine-headed demon, it will give more attention to placating the demon by suitable gifts or sacrifices than to building a dam. The village is operating on a prior theory about the powers of man, his status as subject of unseen forces, and the nature of these forces. If a tribe distributes prestige and influence in accordance with the number of shrunken heads a man accumulates, the ambitious individual will hunt heads. If a society bestows respect upon the inventor and the innovator, experiment will be encouraged; if it looks upon changes as violations of sacred prescriptions, or as threats to established order, the society is likely to remain unchanged for centuries or millennia.

The individual, in other words, seeks to express his personality, to manage his environment, according to the standards by which he has been brought up. Where, and when, a group is sufficiently close-knit to act as an entity, as in the case of a patriotic nation in time of war, the group and the individuals who compose it will choose between alternatives in accordance with the ruling values woven through its historical tradition. We are well acquainted, for example, with the Oriental soldier's readier acceptance of mass losses than that of the Western infantryman. This value-guidance theory of his-

---

[10] Theories like Spengler's, in which society follows an inherent life-cycle like that of a living being, are in a way divorced from actual contact with mankind, but such theories are no more than gigantic analogies, interesting as works of literature rather than as guides to understanding.

tory and social causation does not ignore physical environment, or individual departure from the standard social type. Directly or indirectly, all of man's decisions concern the world of nature about him, but they will be informed and guided by his prior notions about nature and the proprieties of action. No two individuals are precisely alike, but individual differences will be socially important to the extent that the values of a society reward or punish, encourage or discourage, manifestations of originality.

Nor are values necessarily fixed for all time. Even when they are first enunciated by revealed religion, their practical implications will change as the social and physical environment, modified by the historical deeds of man, presents new problems for solution. In a complex society, the practical implications of a set of values are unlikely to be perfectly harmonious with one another. And, in a society which lacks a final and universally obeyed arbiter of law, there will be disagreement as to what the ruling tradition actually implies, and even, as in modern Western civilization, as to whether or not this tradition should be seriously regarded. The nonreligious person may view the revealed religion which first expounded the value system as itself a primitive explanation of a mysterious universe, more than adequately replaced by the discoveries of science. The religious believer will insist upon the eternal truth of his faith and the eternal validity of the ethical laws derived from it.

Important though this dispute be, it need not concern us here, for, having forsworn the search for a rigorous system, trying only to suggest a workable ideology of the middle way for the present age, we need only agree that the foundations of this ideology must be sought in the value system of the Judao-Christian tradition, as the religious and ethical core of Western civilization. Given the limited objective of a workable system of guiding principles, we need not even assert the essential and absolute superiority of the Judao-Christian over other traditions; we need only argue its greater effectiveness in the secular world. We are spared the blasphemy of championing the Western over the Oriental or aboriginal concept of God.

What, then, are the cardinal values of Western civilization? The Judao-Christian tradition describes man as having been made in the image of God. Each man is therefore divinely endowed with an essential, and sacred, dignity. His individuality must be given scope to express his own worship of God and, through his works, the glory of God. All men are ultimately equal in the sight of God, and are equally capable of receiving God's grace. That they are unequal in physical and mental endowment, in worldly position and material wealth, does not diminish their essential and ultimate equality, but rather emphasizes the transient and unsubstantial character of earthly achievement and riches. The Judao-Christian tradition always gave qualified recognition to private property, and for centuries even tolerated slavery; it accepted king and Caesar. But the ascent to Heaven was held to be steeper and more uncertain for the rich and the powerful. The Old Testament records the Jewish practice of the jubilee, the year of restitution of transferred properties and of the cancellation of debts, and abounds in the repeated humiliations of kings and the mighty. The New Testament pledges the inheritance of the earth to the meek and the lowly. The medieval church, while honoring crowned heads and all but sanctifying a society of hierarchical status, praised still more the monk, and was never comfortably certain about the righteousness of mercantile wealth and customs.

Equality before God and inequality on earth, respect for the possessors of high political and material status and the penalty imposed therefor, reflect, it is true, the contrast and opposition between Heaven and earth, the otherworldly and the worldly, and the Christian distinction between the spiritual and material. But the ambivalence of the tradition in respect of mortal achievement reflects even more profoundly a concept of man that stresses his imperfections. Man is creator, yet also creature, the created. In the Fall of Man in the Garden of Eden, man committed, of the free will God had given him, the original sin of pride and pretension to being God. Thereafter the creator in him has striven, not only to master nature, as he was divinely given to do, but to order human relations in accordance with the ethical commandments of God. That he has been more successful in the former than in the latter task is owing to his creature inability fully to avoid the self-centeredness of pride. Commanded to love his neighbor as himself, he can never sufficiently escape himself for that love to be untainted by pride. His will to do good can thus never be unalloyed, and the good that he does is likely to be tainted with evil. He cannot flee the dilemma by doing nothing, for he is enjoined to work and to strive for good. To some extent achievement is consequently a measure of pride, of the pretensions of self and the opportunities for evil.

And man is limited, finite. Commanded to strive to rise toward God, he is condemned by his limitations to fail. In every human choice he makes, the fact that man cannot see with God's eye, or reason with God's mind, means that he cannot know all the consequences of his option. Hardly, therefore, can he act without some evil occurring. Moreover, even perceiving plainly what he ought morally to do, he may be unable owing to the circumstances surrounding to do as he should. He is always forced to choose one package containing good and evil over another, and cannot be certain he has chosen the better mixture. If he asserts such a certainty, he has pretended to a knowledge of consequences, of good and evil, that is beyond his powers, and is guilty of the sin of pride. In all events, he is certain of falling short of the highest goal, hence of falling into sin; and he will either enter into the guilt and awareness of guilt that comes with knowledge of sin, or into the greater sin of being unaware.

The concepts of sin and guilt have been favorite targets of those who believed in the perfectability of man through improved techniques of reasoning and education, and of the psychoanalysts who find in repression the origin of psychological disturbances. The former make claims they simply cannot fulfill, as evidenced by the failure of their rigorous systems and Utopias; the latter fail to understand that proper repression of the creature in man is but another name for civilization. These critics aside, the part played by the doctrines of man, of sin and of guilt in the shaping of Western civilization, is not adequately appreciated. In purely secular terms, these concepts lie behind the attitudes of mind that have given this civilization the dynamic quality that has made it triumph in the competition of cultures.

The Judao-Christian tradition invites man to master both nature and his individual self. Recognizing his essential dignity, it thereby recognizes his title to life, liberty, and the pusuit, if not of happiness, of salvation. The individual, in effect, is encouraged to be inquiring and inventive, to cultivate his powers of reason and to assert the dictates of his conscience. But the driving force, the moving value of the Judao-Christian tradition, rings out in the Great Commandment, "Thou shalt love the Lord thy God—and thy neighbor as thyself." This love is not sentimentality, nor, by virtue of God's entry into it, simply charity. It is a love that seeks, for the love of God, to do works that are pleasing to God, and therefore a love that strives to better and elevate one's neighbor as one would oneself. It is a positive injunction to act, a commandment to act with charity and justice, in short, to strive to see in their totality the neighbor's circumstances, failings, qualities, and problems. In its most striking decree on moral life, therefore, the Judao-Christian tradition firmly denies uninhibited individualism, and, in fact, directs man to seek salvation within a community, to which he is bound by sacred obligations of duty.[11] Because it is men who must judge, the balance between individual and community can never be perfectly just, but neither can justly trespass on the rights of the other, as men are given to see these rights. The fact that no man can achieve certainty about the most rational and the most just in effect enjoins a practice of discussion among those in the community held best qualified to judge.

But man can never fully attain his objectives, or distinguish perfectly between right and wrong. The consequent sense of falling short and the awareness of guilt are the surest motives on earth for further effort, for reassessment and reform. Here, essentially, is why Western civilization has so dynamically changed, invented, and democratized, while the great civilizations of the Orient long ago achieved an equilbrium in some ways resplendent, but moribund. Where the West, starting much later, developed its remarkable technology by conquering nature as its tradition ordained, the East, often regarding nature with mystic reverence, long ago leveled off at a stage that once surpassed the West's only to be far outstripped. Where the guilty conscience of the West prevented it from erecting suitable barriers against the claims of the lowly and oppressed, so that one after another the dikes of privilege have broken in often reluctant accordance with the commandment of love, the mighty of the Orient remained secure behind walls of caste sanctioned by religion. The concept of obligation to the community slowly inspired

[11] It was largely a secularized, latter-day version of Calvinism that praised the truly "rugged" individual, and the uninhibited piling up of wealth.

higher standards of probity among public officials in the Western world; the cheerful Oriental toleration of graft reflects, particularly in China, a concept of loyalty that is strict, but limited to a family group. Respect for the essential dignity of man and the concept of love informed one of Western civilization's greatest monuments, a legal system steadily improved by a sense of guilt at its falling short of the objective of even justice; the vaunted spirituality of the Orient, based upon a firmly dualistic distinction between soul and body, supported a degree of callousness toward human suffering far beyond the most Malthusian of nineteenth-century mill owners.

This is not to deny the long record of brutality, hate, arrogance, and mammonism that has blotted and often distorted the achievements of the West, and has made the recital of the Judao-Christian ethic appear like a mumbled hypocrisy. One had the right to expect more of Christian man, but, in terms of the Christian concept of man, one need not be surprised at his shortcomings. It is a distorted perspective, based upon an unsound theory of the perfectability of man through reason, that sees in the sins and crimes of Western man a proof of his hypocrisy in religion. The question to ask about the guiding values of the tradition is this: Are they nearer to realization now than they were two thousand years ago? It is absurd to ask, Is it possible that we fall short of them in performance? For, by the nature of man, we cannot do otherwise.

Measured against this limited but thoroughly human standard, progress toward partial realization of the traditional ethic has clearly been sufficient to encourage a continued sense of guilt over failings and continued effort toward further partial realization. Slavery vanished from the West, and its recurrence in modern times did not endure. The inadequate protection of the lowly by systems of contract has been replaced by the powerful defense of the voluntary association of free men. With all their faults, the legal structures of the Western world are a thing to marvel at, particularly the subjection of the lawmakers themselves to the law, and those branches of Anglo-American jurisprudence that reveal a preference for letting the guilty escape rather than risk ensnaring the innocent. Many crimes are still committed in the very name of the law, but fewer than in ages past.

Nor are the technical and material achievements of Western man to be sneered at, as has been made popular by the fumbling character of our efforts to achieve social control over such marvels as the automobile, the airplane, and atomic fission. They are even less to be sneered at on the ground that they are "materialistic," for this is nothing but a naïve confusion of that word of contempt. The gadgetry of the Western world, and in particular of the United States, would reflect a socially materialistic outlook only if it were developed for its own sake. Ignoring the mysteries of nuclear physics, all tangible things are material, but that has absolutely nothing to do with philosophic materialism, a system of propositions concerning ultimate reality and knowledge. Nor can any *thing* be socially or morally materialistic, or idealistic, any more than a thing can be religious or atheistic. A thing can only be put to *uses* that may be described as materialistic or not, religious or not, good or bad. To the extent that technical innovations are employed to alleviate suffering, or to reduce the burden of toil and thereby liberate human energy for more spiritual exercises, their creation and employment is not materialistic and does not reveal a materialistic attitude. Indeed, it would be difficult to conceive of a more materialistic outlook than the traditional Oriental unconcern at mass starvation, which has only recently begun to yield to Western ideas of mercy and charity.

To speak with praise of Western civilization as Western man has shaped it according to the guiding values of the Judao-Christian tradition is not to disregard its heritage from Greece and Rome, or to forget the contributions it has received from secularists and humanists, especially in modern times. But the fact remains that ancient Greece failed to endow the moderation we like to think of as one of its greatest virtues with a sufficiently dynamic quality to enable it to survive. And, despite Roman law and Roman competence, Roman Caesarism proved to be stagnant. As transformed by the Judao-Christian concepts of man and morality, much of the best in Greek and Roman civilization was perpetuated in the tradition of the West.

The view of man and history we have presented of course does not in any sense imply that Western progress was the achievement of churchgoing Christians exclusively; indeed, any such idea would flatly contradict the basic concept of man. From the limitations of his reason and of his powers of control flow good out of evil, and evil out of good. Though it be inadequate compensation for the burdens they have laid upon us, let us not forget that Hitler did more than any other modern man to destroy the respectability of racial and religious prejudice, and that Stalin's aggressiveness brought the non-Communist world a greater unity than it had ever known. Torquemada and the witch-burning Puritan divines did great evil in the belief that they were serving Christ, and Marx diverted traditional concepts of justice to the service of class hatred and strife. The intellectual, aesthetic, institutional and material creations that have entered into the main stream of Western civilization have been in a rough, human harmony with the basic value system; those that were in fundamental discord with that system, like slavery, torture, and trial by combat, have not endured.

The invention of new forms of slavery and new forms of torture, the technological perfection of trial by combat between nations, rather than individuals, points to both the strength and the weakness of an ideology grounded in history and governed by the values and the concept of man of the Judao-Christian tradition. Such an ideology can point the way forward by providing standards against which we can judge the acts and the institutions of the past and the changes whose course we must decide. Thus guided, and employing all the knowledge and techniques of our sciences, we can darkly glimpse the near future, and estimate some of the consequences of our choices. But the ultimate end of history and of society is defined as beyond the reach of our science, and many of the consequences of our acts will escape our foresight. We can rest certain of only one thing, that we shall have to decide again and again, often the same issue, in the same or in another form.

This recognition of limitations and uncertainty liberates rather than restricts, however, by guarding us against the evil consequences of precipitous actions and sharp and overreaching transformations to which we might be tempted by an unwarranted confidence in our powers of prediction and control. Our ideology will therefore be conservative, rather than radical or revolutionary. But it will not only accept, as it must, the ineluctable fact of change, it will demand change, change for the better in terms of its basic values, change for the progressive realization of those values. It must deny a return to the past as firmly as a break with the past, nor can it sanction the conceit of satisfaction and standing pat with the present. It can only be an ideology of the middle way.

Its guiding principle is to preserve or adapt those aspects of the immediate and more distant past that harmonize with the central values of Western civilization, in accordance with which innovations and novel situations must be managed. It does not pledge the future to the past, but rather takes heed of the pledge the past has given to the present and future. Its limitations enjoin a tactic of moderation, and charity in disagreement, for the concept of imperfect man labels self-righteousness as sinful, and the certainty of right as the pride that precedes a fall. At the same time it demands action and an assertion of the right as one is given to see it, and thus, as always, compels one to strive to strike the balance of the greater good and lesser evil.

This ideology sees the middle way as the only way commensurate with man, and views the panorama of Western history as a tortuous working out and selection of those institutions, principles of practice and arrangements best suited to a mankind that, by its nature, must follow the middle way or suffer painful consequences. It sees Western institutions, like individual man, as embodying a group of principles necessary to its existence but which, if followed rigorously, would prove incompatible. The dignity of man ordains freedom of action, but this must be limited by obligations to fellow men in the community, as the latter must be restricted to give scope to the former. The very existence of the community requires a certain degree of security, but this cannot be so fully organized as to stultify innovation, even at the cost of risk. Man must love peace, but not so completely as to be an accessory to wrong.

In historical terms, this ideology sees the growth of intellectual liberty and of political democracy as the most fundamental partial realizations of the basic values of Western civilization. Material advancement is their fruit, progressively liberating man from control by nature. It sees the failure of rigid economic and social arrangements in the past, and of rigorous systems in the present, as stemming from their essential incompatibility with the nature of man and with the values of our culture. It sees the disintegration of privilege and wealth derived only from the accident of birth as reflecting the tradition's emphasis on labor and distributive justice. It sees the double needs of individuality and community being met by different forms of social organization, records how fitting it is that a corporatist solution should have been chosen in the religious Middle Ages, and that a new form of corporatism should be rising in a period like the present, in which the search for the roots and inner meaning of our civilization appears to be more urgent than ever before. It sees in the record of empires, kingdoms, and republics, varying solutions to the problem of relating the needs of individual communities to those of larger sectors of Western society: the large empire loosely organizing small, but close-knit regions or cities; the modern nation, smaller than the empire, but as close-knit as the latter's subdivisions.

Viewing the Western past, and the values at the core of its tradition, such an ideology can indicate the goals we should pursue and help us select the tactics we should employ. It can neither guarantee us certainty in the short run nor describe to us our distant future; it can only help us in the inevitable human task of deciding and doing, of meeting new and old problems as they arise from our doings. It conceives of our past progress toward our goals not as an inevitable historical process, but as resulting from the fact that, however great the folly of individuals and groups, over the long years the people of the West have been wise in adhering to their fundamental value structure and casting aside that which most clearly conflicted with it. This ideology cannot even promise the certain preservation of these values, only that the decision to preserve or abandon them is ours. Subscribing to Burke's injunction not to rend the fabric of the past, it repeats de Tocqueville's warning that although our history seems to reveal a progress toward some kind of equality of condition, it is for us to choose between equality under tyranny and equality in freedom.

The goals this ideology sets forth are as familiar as a Fourth of July oration, and so they must be, for American independence is very much a part of the tradition upon which the ideology rests. The concepts of love and of the dignity of man enjoin us to seek the highest degree of individual freedom compatible with the welfare of the community as a whole and of the weak within it. We are next instructed to build the most equal opportunity for every individual to develop the best that is in him, but not to make a god of equal opportunity and thereby destroy both freedom and opportunity through rigidity. We are advised to avoid concentrations of power, to decentralize government and administration whenever possible, and to encourage nongovernmental organizations to perform whatever tasks they can, balancing such private groupings against each other, and inspecting constantly to see that they do not gather too much strength in their hands. We are not to fear, but rather to cherish, a lack of uniformity in our social arrangements, employing government ownership here, private enterprise there, administrative decision in one sphere, legislative in another. Recognizing the vitality of nationalism at the present stage of historical development, we must try to make the nation serve the ends of peace and human welfare. This means the policy of the good neighbor, not forgetting that the coöperative good neighbor is one whose house is orderly and prosperous.

With all its moderation, this ideology establishes points of no compromise. We must oppose every step that threatens freedom, and always ask ourselves whether the good that may arise from neutral behavior is overweighed by the evil of conniving, through nonintervention, in a crime. We must worry equally lest intervention in a good cause produce even greater consequences of harm. We may again have to face the terrifying decision whether it is best to plunge the world into the worst of wars, and it is only human for us to take some satisfaction in the fact that, having forsworn offensive war, the awful responsibility is in other hands. We shall have to endure insults from our enemies, and criticism, just and unjust, from our friends, replying at need, but never forgetting the price of arrogance. In seeking to reform and improve, at home and abroad, we may never forget that our conviction that we are right need not be shared by others, so that, while pursuing the right as we see it, we must count among the costs of any betterment the sense of loss and wrong, real or fancied, felt by the defeated minority.

This ideology must necessarily seem familiar to us because it seeks to bind our past with our present and future. It is worth while not because it is new, but because it enables us to see more clearly the elements of cohesion and nobility in what has been wrongly called a chaotic, unprincipled, and disintegrated civilization. It helps us to distinguish between that which is essential to our way of life and that which is incidental, needless, or even harmful. It thus helps us to know ourselves better, and more effectively to present ourselves to others, and so performs the truly useful functions of an ideology.

It is, of course, an ideology for the West and, within the fold of Western civilization, particularly for America. In a way, it consequently tends to sharpen differences between the West and the Orient, and between those who follow the Judao-Christian tradition and those who hold to its Marxist perversion. But this is inevitable, for every philosophical approach must to some extent deny every other, as the assertion that the earth is round denies the assertion that it is flat. To state that the Judao-Christian concept of man is historically correct is to declare that the Marxian and Oriental conceptions are, to the extent that they differ from it, wrong. There is no escape from this conclusion and its implications regarding the value systems of the rest of the world. If we believe in the Judao-Christian concept of man and in the related value structure, and hold that its validity is given secular proof by the history of Western civilization, the corollary is that as the world approaches unity, the sway of the Judao-Christian tradition will extend correspondingly. Indeed, it has obviously widened, particularly in recent years, and to only a very small degree owing to the military aspects of what is known as imperialism.

By enriching our perspective and diminishing the uncertainty that comes from the failure of every effort to be too certain, this historical ideology of the middle way can lend us confidence along with discrimination, and strengthen the sense of purpose which our actions show us to feel, but which we only awkwardly communicate. But it clarifies yet does not simplify, and so leaves to us the arduous yet delicate task of discovering its practical implications for the problems of the world we live in.

III. *What Is to Be Done?*[12]

It is relatively easy to explore and criticize the failings of systems of social theory, a good deal more troublesome to work out an alter-

---

[12] With apologies to the shades of Chernyshevsky and Lenin, who wrote classics of Russian literature of protest and revolution under this title. It is a good title, and might as well be put to a more constructive use.

native theoretical approach, and by far the most difficult of all to suggest what concrete decisions such an approach might require. Yet by criticizing other views one does incur the moral obligation to offer one's own, and the presentation of a different way of looking at the affairs of society requires one, in all decency, to indicate how one might go about applying this outlook to specific situations, and what the results might be.

The first step in this unenviable and unwelcome task is to clear away several obstacles in the form of popular but misleading habits of thinking. Perhaps the worst of these is what we may call the "quicksand fallacy," or the "fallacy of the logical conclusion." In recent years this has been most commonly encountered in the "creeping socialism" argument, but, since it is a favorite trick of debate, examples may be found in connection with most subjects. The form of this fallacious argument is, "If we take step A, then the next step is obviously B, and then C, and so, before anyone realizes what has happened, we will end up in the horrible situation XYZ." Now XYZ may indeed be a logical conclusion to ABC but, for the quicksand effect to take place, it must be the *only* such conclusion, and this can never be demonstrated without excessively lavish dependence on "other things being equal." In short, for this argument to have any real significance, it must be shown that, ABC having transpired, there can be no alternative sequence such as EFG leading to UVW, or HIJ to RST, or, for that matter, that ABC cannot itself be diverted by EFG and so end up in OPQ. An old instance of the fallacy is that one drink leads to another, and so to alcoholism, whereas it may as easily lead to one's becoming a teetotaler. The point is that one is rarely compelled to proceed to the logical conclusion of any process and that, in the affairs of society, men hardly ever do.

Another mental pitfall may be described as the "time-machine fallacy," or the "fallacy of simultaneity," which consists in forecasting a line of development and then treating the end result as if it were already in existence, while the surrounding environment remains unchanged. This fallacy may be exemplified by Soviet proclamations that Russia will catch up with the United States by a certain date (America presumably standing still), and in warnings that the mighty labor oligarchs *of the future* will overcome the resistance of government and business as they *presently* operate. Again, of course, "other things being equal" has sneaked in by the back door.

A third snare is the "he-too fallacy," or guilt by association, which extends much farther than the antileft campaigns in which it is especially abundant. Its weakness may be broadly exemplified by the fact that although the devil may quote Scripture, that does not make the minister of the gospel a Satanist. Persons disagreeing violently in political and social matters may favor the same thing for the same or different reasons. Among the other things held equal may be the entire purpose and character of a person or movement. A variant of this mode of confusion is the "fallacy of the burning issue," wherein people concentrate on one issue to the exclusion of others equally relevant. More than one principled pacifist, for example, has so devoutly set his eyes on peace (or, rather, the absence of war) as an absolute good that he became easy prey to aggressive Communist propaganda, or minimized the misdeeds of Hitler in an earlier decade. And more than one principled anticommunist has so girded himself against the one great foe that he has been ruthlessly used by domestic demagogues he would otherwise despise. In both instances, the burning issue has so inflamed the victim of this fallacy that, in sheer panic, he closes his mental eyes and strikes blindly at the closet target. In the first case, this will be his own government's policy of resisting aggression; in the second, it will be those branded, by whatever method, as the native votaries of the hated doctrine.

A fourth intellectual trap to be avoided is the "mirage fallacy," which may be defined as the treatment of abstract categories as if they were as solid as a granite wall. We hear of the farm vote, the city vote, the Negro vote, and other similar entities. This can mean either farmers, city folk, and Negroes in the act of voting, which has no significance, or that farmers, city dwellers, and Negroes as groups vote predominantly in a certain way. The latter is of course the significant meaning, but while it may or may not be valid for a given issue, such as the Negroes on civil rights legislation, the farmers on price supports, and city people on rent control, one cannot conclude without independent proof that the group will split in the same proportions with regard to other issues. *In other words, social categories are meaningful in respect of a specific question that is asked about society, and it is the question that determines which categories should be used.* It is a mistake, therefore, to treat these categories as if they were independent, concrete realities. To do so is to forget the obvious fact that people may constitute a group in one respect and disagree violently among themselves in others.[13]

Lastly, we may note what Arthur Koestler has called the "fallacy of the false equation," which consists in ignoring the differences in degree which form the basis for most distinctions in an imperfect world. By use of this device one can point to prison labor in Russia and the United States as if they were the same thing, or to government intervention under the New Deal and British Labour, or, for that matter, the mountains of Vermont and Colorado. This is a most effective way of obscuring issues, especially when both small and large failings can be compared to a perfect ideal, or when unequal achievements can be contrasted with an utter lack of achievement in some third place.

On the rather rash assumption that these and related intellectual fumbles have been forestalled, we may go on to the tracing out of some of the implications of an historical ideology of the middle way. The dignity of man, love, justice, the concept of man as imperfect yet striving to realize the values he holds, the acceptance of the challenge to gain dominion over nature, these we have interpreted as leading to and informing the intermediate principles by which we may be guided in making policy for our age. These intermediate principles form the link between a basic view of man and a fundamental value structure on the one hand and concrete, particular decisions on the other: political democracy; a pluralism recognizing the social role of individuals, groups, and the state, seeking to balance their activities so as to enhance both freedom and progress; decentralization of political and economic power; equality of opportunity. Now we must attempt to answer the difficult questions that arise in the process of reaching decisions: What choice will help or hinder democracy? What choice will grant too much or too little

---

[13] This line of argument is apt to disturb some social scientists, and all Marxists, by injecting doubt as to the worth of social categories, yet it can be derived from "sound social science observation" as well as in the manner above. For, as Ruth Benedict noted in *Patterns of Culture* (Pelican edition, pp. 211 ff.), concepts which imply social integration are (like economic planning, one might suggest) most applicable to simple, primitive societies and least successful in relation to the complex.

initiative and scope to the individual, group, or state? At what point may certain exercises of freedom interfere with progress, or justice? Where shall we decide for decentralization, and when might this hinder justice, progress, or the real enjoyment of freedom?

None of the answers to particular examples of these questions can pretend to certainty, nor can even tentative answers be offered to all the questions that should be asked. For no one man can assert the adequacy of his knowledge and understanding, either of the facts of the case or how the guiding values and intermediate principles should in truth be applied. An individual can only judge the facts as he knows them according to the values as he understands them. There is, in short, no room for absolutism. But neither is there an absolute relativism, only a recognition that my claim that I am right in specific judgments must rest upon a consensus of those holding to the same values and ideology, and collectively knowing the actual, existing circumstances better than any individual can know them. My conclusions about the specific implications of this ideology are to be presented, not as truths, but as judgments I believe valid, subject to the test of their fitting a broader knowledge of the facts and to the test of experience. Moreover, it is far less important whether such judgments be right or wrong than that they point to the kind of questions that should be asked by everyone making a decision in a democratic society.

It is above all essential to have a live awareness of our fundamental values, and always to test how well or how ill we are applying them in concrete decisions. A pluralistic society such as the democratic corporatism that seems in the making can survive only if there is an overriding unity in allegiance to the same values and intermediate principles, a unity strong enough to enable many autonomous bodies to exist and act freely without destroying the whole to which they belong. And our active society, one that accepts the need for group decisions rather than relying upon presumed natural laws of politics or economics, must always immerse its policy decisions in its value structure, or risk self-destruction. As Keynes once wrote:

> Dangerous acts can be done safely in a community which thinks and feels rightly, which would be the way to hell if they were executed by those who think and feel wrongly.[14]

[14] R. F. Harrod, *The Life of John Maynard Keynes,* London, 1951, p. 437.

In suggesting some of the things, dangerous and otherwise, that I believe are implied by an effort to "think and feel rightly," that is, to act in accordance with the values of the Judao-Christian tradition, caution dictates a start with predominantly political examples. For, while the various fallacies, snares, and pitfalls are rather prevalent in American discussions of economic policy, and almost as common in debates over foreign affairs, they are least troublesome in matters that are largely political. This distribution only reflects the fact that clarity goes with confidence and experience. Despite our tremendous economic achievements in production and distribution, our national aversion to theory and ideology has been a barrier to developing a sure hand in dealing with broader questions of national economy and social organization, and, until recent times, our history has exerted relatively slight pressure on us to do so. For two-thirds of our national existence we reveled in a superficially isolated position among the nations, and only during and since World War II have we begun to face up to the responsibilities of world leadership. On the other hand, we are justly proud of the political structure whose cornerstone was laid by the Founding Fathers, we are certain of its soundness, and are not easily beguiled by careless or twisted thinking.

Yet even with regard to politics it is exceedingly difficult to find the proper balance between competing objectives. On the one hand, we justly fear the ideological conflict that has embittered political life in other nations, and we fear the rigidly disciplined nation-wide party machine. On the other hand, however, we recognize the need for clear and courageous decisions about national policy, and we must confess that our major parties, as now constituted, are hardly ideal instruments for meeting this need.

Neither party stands for any systematically coördinated body of principles, or is capable of enforcing discipline either on its high command or on its subleaders. In consequence, the American parties have been aptly compared to the feudal system, in which actual power resides in the regional or district chief, whose allegiance to the higher authority may be only nominal, unless it is strengthened by the realities of power politics.

On the whole, this is extremely fortunate. If the parties were actually separated by genuine ideological disagreements, the unity and social harmony of the country would suffer irreparably. Under the present system, in which the parties are the loosest of coalitions, the sharpest issues must be compromised or glossed over within each party, so that it can get together every four years for the purpose of electing the President, chief policy maker and chief patronage dispenser. Extreme positions have been moderated within each party before they are submitted to the further compromises of a presidential campaign. The lack of party discipline guarantees the representation of regional and minority views, but not in any way that prevents unified party action, amid much self-congratulation, on matters about which there is general agreement.

The fact that our parties are not so constituted as to be a positive threat to freedom does not, however, justify smug contentment. In many areas affirmative and enduring policies are needed. The lack of them may endanger survival itself. Such national policies cannot result from the mere canceling out of intolerable extremes through the countervailing pressures of groups and sections. In a pluralistic society, the political party is the proper means whereby separate interests can not only be compromised but, through strong leadership, transcended. To urge that the national party organizations be strengthened, in opposition as well as in office, is to ignore neither the actual importance of pressure groups nor the real contribution to flexibility and democracy of our "feudal" party structure. Better organized, more cohesive, more responsible parties would still rest on their foundations in the states, and could never become overdisciplined machines. In Great Britain, strong party control tends to stifle initiative among younger members and in local areas; in the United States the looseness of party structure tends to frustrate leadership. We should strive for the middle way, safeguarded by the federal character of our government.[15]

[15] The "orthodox" view of American party politics is not only to analyze largely in terms of pressure groups and "feudalism" (A. N. Holcombe, *Our More Perfect Union*, Cambridge, 1950; D. B. Truman, *The Governmental Process: Political Interests and Public Opinion*, New York, 1951) but firmly to insist on the virtues of extreme decentralization (Herbert Agar, *The Price of Union*, Boston, 1950). The "unorthodox" approach, recognizing the fact of decentralization and its virtues up to a point, but urging a strengthening of parties under American conditions, has gained ground principally through the efforts of E. E. Schattschneider (*Party Government*, New York, 1942; *The Struggle for Party Government*, College Park, Md., 1948; and, with others, "Toward a More Responsible Two-Party System," Report of the Committee on Political Parties of the American Political Science Association, *American Political Science Review*, Supp., September, 1950, pp. 59 ff.).

We have, however, been advised to make our state and national nominating procedures more logically consistent with democracy by extending the primary. We would thereby abolish the power of "bosses in a smoke-filled room," and prevent "deals" at the quadrennial national conventions. All such suggestions are clothed in the aura of reform and righteousness, and gain support from legitimate disgust with the rule of certain party bosses and with the circus aspects of party conventions. But that does not mean that the reform might not result in greater harm than good. Conventions are as responsive to active public opinion as to the will of so-called bosses whose power, as often as not, rests in great part on their ability to diagnose the public mood. Primaries, on the other hand, open the door wide to well-organized and not necessarily benevolent minorities whenever the public at large is apathetic. Nor is there anything inherently wrong in the delegate deals that characterize political conventions. If candidate A turns over his votes to candidate B as the man closest to his own point of view who is likely to win, it is merely part of the necessary procedure of compromise.

Presidential nominating primaries would not automatically usher in an era of perfect morality. They might actually result in the selection of demagogues rather than statesmen, and in more rather than less deals. This conclusion does not derive from a distrust of the people, but from such ordinary circumstances as these: if a preeminent and generally desired candidate should, for some reason, delay his decision to run, an ambitious and presumptuous second-rater might be able to force himself on a party merely by entering the field early; or, as likely as not, the primaries might result in an oversupply of serious candidates, and deals would become a matter of dire necessity. The way to improvement is accordingly not to attempt the foolish task of debarring politicians from politics, but for the public to be actively interested in politics and reward the politicians who take a socially responsible attitude, while punishing those who do not.

More subtle and, in the long run, perhaps more serious, is the almost automatic identification of honesty in government with extension of the civil service. This is also known as ridding government of politics. Up to a point this is undoubtedly a good idea, for the nation could not support the inefficiency that a thoroughgoing spoils system, with its wholesale changes of personnel, would entail. But, beyond a point, extension of the civil service might prove harmful, and would not, of course, "take politics out of government." To the degree that a civil service is unresponsive to political pressure, moreover, it is correspondingly less flexible and more bureaucratic. For the essence of honest bureaucracy is stubborn uniformity in applying the rules. Political pressure, whether on the part of Congressmen or party leaders, may be dishonest, involving bribery, kickbacks, or connivance at lawbreaking. But it may be quite honest, smoothing the way for legitimate and even excellent appointments, contracts, or decisions. In many ways, politics and politicians perform the essential function of moderating between citizens and government, keeping the latter human, for good as well as ill.

It is often said that civil service should cover all but policy-making positions, but at the same time it is recognized that the permanent staff of an agency have a tremendous advantage over the temporary political appointee, whatever his rank. If civil service coverage is allowed to rise too high in the echelons of public office-holders, we will have unintentionally admitted bureaucratic policy-making. Nor will we be compensated with a guaranteed improvement in the quality of public servants. We shall have more specially trained experts, and fewer politicians. Since the civil service must operate within well-defined rules, this means we shall merely have a higher proportion of technicians and a lower proportion of policy makers, perhaps more decisions that are perfect in the abstract and fewer that are workable. We must not forget, moreover, that our party organizations depend for much of their vitality on jobholders and job and favor seekers. The public at large and, particularly, the "independent voter," have come increasingly to make their choice in terms of the issues as they see them, rather than according to party or under organization pressure. But without party organizations representative government would be impossible in a complex society. The public in general and especially the highminded independents find neither the time nor the interest to enter into the work of operating a political party. For those who are so interested, politics must become a profession unless they have independent incomes. We certainly do not wish to limit active participation in politics to retired magnates or men of inherited wealth.

We must therefore accept, and should cease dishonoring, the professional politician. We should merely insist that he be as competent and as honest as a man of equivalent standing in any other profession. This means more than fitting salaries for public servants. It means raising the political penalties for corruption and the political rewards for exposing it, so that the parties find it advantageous and even essential to be scrupulous about recommending for appointment men capable of the job and worthy of the trust. But the substitution of machine-corrected aptitude tests for appointment by men who can be held responsible for their choice will neither eliminate corruption nor guarantee efficiency. There is no reason to expect a higher standard of honesty in public than in private business. Indeed, rigorous honesty and strict efficiency should not be regarded as goals in themselves, but as the natural by-products of a generally high public morality, of intelligence and energy. If honesty and efficiency are deified, we shall risk copying the Soviet bureaucratic system, in which watchmen have rivaled working personnel in number, and a bureaucracy has followed the "efficiency" rules so carefully as to become ensnared in its own red tape. There is a profound lesson in the experience of a Pennsylvania firm which tried a method of keeping accounts in which all entries were evened to the dollar. This rebellion against detailed accounting "efficiency" resulted in a net saving of several thousand dollars.

Active government presents the paradox, in a democracy, of doing things the people have ordered it to do and at the same time appearing to threaten individual liberty. Much of the outcry that government is gnawing away at freedom is in fact a convenient cover for a demand to reduce the role of the state, an indirect way of reopening the question originally decided by the assignment to the state of new functions. Aside from this type of protest, however, administrative decisions do affect the lives and fortunes of citizens, and government agencies have increasingly been given quasi-judicial roles, so that the defense of the individual against arbitrary acts of government is a genuine problem. It is, moreover, one that is destined to become more serious as society and government grow more complex.

We have sought to meet this issue by laws governing administrative procedure, but, in final analysis, the citizen who feels himself wronged must have recourse either to political intervention or to the courts. The latter are overburdened, slow-moving, and not well equipped to decide cases that may be of an extremely technical, or technological, nature. We should give serious consideration to adapting to our own needs France's outstanding contribution to modern government, the Council of State. This is a judicial organization, divided into panels for utilities and similar special fields, which tries protests against administrative decisions. In our terms, it operates under law of equity. Over the years it is able to build up a body of principles and precedents which can guard the rights of the individual against arbitrary acts of administration in a more supple and effective manner than the present system relying on statutes, appeals within an administrative agency, and ultimate appeal to the regular courts. An American Court of Administrative Law would have original and appeals benches, pretrial examiners under civil service, and judges appointed by the President with the consent of the Senate. The Court would have specialized panels corresponding to the major fields of administration, all beneath an overall Appeals bench. The entire system, of course, would remain subject to the Supreme Court in all constitutional questions.[16]

A reform along such lines would do much to prevent the growth of a bureaucratic spirit among public servants, but decentralization is a more fundamental approach to keeping large-scale government compatible with a democratic society. Paradoxically, while we may have too much decentralization in party politics, we would desire more decentralization in government itself. The slogan of states' rights, as usually offered, is empty and irrelevant, an effort to block what may be necessary federal action. And decentralization should not be made a fetish, lest it undermine democracy by leading to social and economic inefficiency. Aside from such obvious areas as defense, there are instances in the conservation of natural resources where a locality cannot be trusted to serve the common good by forgoing a selfish short-run program of exploitation. Decentraliza-

---

[16] See Armin Uhler, *Review of Administrative Acts*, Michigan Legal Studies, Ann Arbor, 1942; W. Rohkam, Jr., and O. C. Pratt IV, *Studies in French Administrative Law*, Illinois Studies in the Social Sciences, vol. 28, no. 3, Urbana, 1947. The Walter-Logan Bill, embodying proposals of the American Bar Association but vetoed by Franklin D. Roosevelt, sought reform through extension and improvement of American administrative and judicial review procedures, rather than by establishing a new court system.

tion means the dispersal of control and administration, but not the abolition of unified policy. It may be objected that state governments are more easily coerced by special interests, and that it was this fact together with the inactivity of the states that compelled the federal government to step in. This is true to a very great extent, but let us not forget an earlier period prior to World War I in which states took the lead in salutary intervention and honest administration, while the record of the national government was, to say the least, tarnished. In the context of the need and demand for governmental action, states' rights can be asserted only by the states' taking it upon themselves to act. If the states do not satisfy the need for imaginative and competent government, then, of course, the federal government must try to meet it. But, in the long run, the only democratically safe answer to undue privilege and negligent government is in enlightened political leadership and an interested electorate, not in abdicating responsibility to a centralized administration, however honest and efficient.

Without suggesting a headlong retreat from federal action, or an end to coöperative federal participation in the programs of local governments, there nevertheless remain many functions in which the decentralization of initiative and administration might be worthwhile. Welfare functions, roads and waterways development, education, can generally be handled by the states, and where they exceed the capacities of an individual state, federal grants-in-aid, interstate compacts, and interstate agencies can be employed. The states themselves can delegate responsibilities to lower governments, and intercity and special authorities can be added to the range of potential agencies among which a choice can be made. Arrangements between state or local governments are difficult to negotiate, and the resulting agencies may sometimes prove to be less efficient, in a technical sense, than a centralized federal bureau. But, from the democratic standpoint, the price is worth paying because of the benefits gained in local control and responsiveness to local needs. A proliferation of diverse agencies is likely to be confusing, and to lead to a demand, every so often, for wholesale amalgamation. We must remember, however, that our smaller governmental units, from the states down, are our laboratories for experimenting with different social arrangements.

Judging the proper pace of reform is perhaps the most delicate test of the ideology of moderation we have suggested, for it directly involves the weighing of alternative bundles of mixed good and evil. Assuming that a particular reform is indisputably in harmony with the fundamental value structure, with political democracy and equality of opportunity, it is necessary first to distinguish between objectives and means. The latter must be suitable to the former, or will undermine them, but one must never so confuse ends and means that the means become the actual objective, rather than a way of attaining it. The next step is to ask whether, if the reform be carried, the injury to its opponents (either in our terms, which are presumably right, or in their terms, which are presumably wrong) may not exceed the benefit the reform brings to another sector of the community or to the community as a whole. Will pressing the reform arouse such bitterness as to exacerbate, even temporarily, the very wrong it is designed to correct? Would this bitterness result in blocking action on other matters, perhaps of equal or even greater desirability, on which there is general agreement? Does a compromise reform compromise the principle of the goal itself, merely the rate of progress toward it, or only the means of securing it? Will a proposed compromise excessively dishearten or embitter the reformers? Will it enable the opposition to coöperate part of the way? Are the reformers with whom one is making common cause more interested in a sweeping proclamation than in partial results? Are some of them trying to build a professional or political career on the issue of the particular reform, are they subverting everything else to their personal ambitions?

Questions like these are strikingly relevant to civil liberties and to such problems as the suppression of discrimination arising from racial or religious prejudice. Freedom to explore, hold, and express opinions is so very obviously the breath of democracy that all sincere democrats are not only tempted to enshrine it as an absolute right and good, but hesitate even to consider its specific meanings. To define is often to limit, and this freedom we would wish unlimited. But the hard realities of political and social conflict, of wars, soon compel us to limit the freedom of expression of those who do not themselves believe in this freedom. Soon thereafter we are likely to find that our efforts to protect freedom risk turning into a subversion of freedom. Such are the witch hunts, headline-hunting investigations, attacks on any deviation from conformity in opinion. Perhaps the worst by-product of these panics of fear is that people begin to resort to force, rather than debate, to combat opinion generally suspected of being wrong. It is force that is used, not debate, when economic boycott, picketing, and the like are invoked to throttle or punish a heretic. And in such operations an organized minority of superficially conformist antidemocrats can be even more effective than were the organized minority of Communists "boring from within."

It is no answer to such attacks on democracy to proclaim that freedom of expression is sacrosanct. It is no divinity, but a basic tradition of our society, and as such can and should be defended. First, the principles of decentralization and pluralism place the prime responsibility for countering malignant opinion in the hands of autonomous bodies, professional groups, universities. Only if this responsibility is shirked, and only as evidence of danger rises, should this task be taken over, with scrupulous regard for proper procedure, by local, and lastly, national government. Second, there is Justice Holmes's famous dictum on the "clear and present danger" as a test for the propriety of restricting freedom of expression. And in applying this dictum—which is obviously not a scientific formula but a challenge to good judgment—one may be guided by a common practice in the enforcement of the criminal law: sometimes the cost of finding and punishing a culprit may be altogether excessive in relation to the harm he has caused. In short, to enforce the law may, on net balance, be injurious to law enforcement. As a general rule, therefore, exposure and open debate should be the first weapon in any counterattack; any weapon involving force should be brought to bear only with the greatest reluctance.

As for racial or religious prejudice, no legislation or regulation can eliminate it; this can be done only by demonstrating that it is not founded on fact and that it is contrary to the accepted principles of our society. Legislation can impose the penalty of added paper work or verbal subterfuge on persons who engage in improper discrimination, but most discrimination will endure as long as the prejudice. The principal value of pressure for such legislation is that it worries the consciences of its opponents, and thus drives them to seek their own way toward partial realization of the objective. The all-or-nothing fanatic is not so much a man of principle as of arrogance; like Lenin, he is apt to be less interested in ameliorating wrongful conditions than in arousing fierce loyalty to the cause with which he has identified his own ego.

If arrogance is an obstacle to intelligent decision in domestic affairs, it is much more so in relations with other nations, where greater differences in background make it more difficult to grasp the real intent of another's policies, pronouncements, or customary practices. We may recall that the west European interprets our praise of "free enterprise" in the light of his own experience with capitalism, not ours. In the light of our past fictional isolation, we are likely to interpret alliances as regrettably necessary entanglements, whereas to the European they are as much a part of ordinary national practice as raising revenue. Some of us have been naïvely impatient over the slow progress of European federation, pointing to the speed with which the thirteen colonies got together, and forgetting they faced no obstacles of linguistic and cultural differences, diverse traditions, and strong national pride. A self-righteous attitude is not merely unintelligent, it is tantamount to sabotage of our own programs, for it can transform the ever-present barrier of national pride into a rebellion against what soon appears to be a threat to national independence itself. Yet, for all our sins in seeming to forget our oneness with many foreign countries in the essentials of outlook and institutions while vaunting our presumed superiority in respects that are relatively inconsequential, our international policy has been on the whole relatively unegoistic and far-sighted.

It is rather the European "neutralist," for example, who, arguing from both ignorance and the "fallacy of the false equation," says, in effect, that since America is materialist as proved by her mania for electric kitchen gadgets, and Russia is materialist because she is Marxian, the Europeans, who are people of culture and spirituality, should remain apart from any dispute between them. British observers and politicians, who really ought to know better, have conjured up the specter of an American military caste rushing the world into war, thereby equating American professional soldiers who, as a group, have never demonstrated much interest in or capacity for politics, with German war lords or Russian ministers belonging to ruling circles that have always operated on the principle that war is politics by other means.

And then the neutralist evokes the terror of American imperialism, summed up in the wonderful expression "Coca-colonization," revealing, through self-caricature, all the confusion and muddled thinking that has come to obscure the relations between the more and the less industrialized nations. Imperialism, as everyone knows, is a BAD THING. So universal is this judgment that one risks the censure of forward-looking, high-minded men of principle in offering even a timid defense of the labor of medical missionaries who, it seems, must have been engaged by some unfathomable cynicism in the service of heartless business bogeys. So sweeping is the condemnation of imperialism that its actual faults have been lost sight of along with its genuine benefits. No one working from an ideology based upon Judao-Christian values can rightly forget or justify monumental crimes like the Opium War, the massacres, enslavement, oppression, and exploitation that abound in the record of Westerners among peoples backward by Western standards. Nor can one defend the racial and cultural snobbery the Westerner carries not only into Asia and Africa, but into other countries that are as Western as his own.

But surely it has been no crime to introduce better techniques of managing natural resources of land, water, and subsoil, to substitute medical science for witch doctors and herbalists, to bring at least the rudiments of education to people to whom it had been denied by native rules of caste, to spread by instruction in Christianity the idea of the essential dignity of man. In the long run, it will have to be recognized that it was beneficial to mankind to acquaint the downtrodden of great Oriental nations with the concept of justifiable revolt, and even, though we pay a very heavy price for it, with the idea of nationality and with nationalism.

Are the British in India to be condemned for suppressing, through the criminal law, the Hindu custom of suttee which required a widow to burn to death on her husband's funeral pyre, or the hereditary caste or tribe of murderers, the Thugs? Or are they to be criticized for not exerting more pressure than they did against Indian customs and beliefs that stood as a bar to salutary measures? One cannot argue both ways. Assuming a common-sense toleration of most customs, no matter how strange to Western eyes, should Western imperialists, or, for that matter, native Asian or African reformers, tolerate those practices that are revolting by Western standards of justice and morality or are known to bring upon the people unnecessary afflictions? The answer depends upon whether one regards the guiding values of the Judao-Christian tradition as inherently superior to any other value system, or adopts a relativist viewpoint and holds that each set of values is a standard unto itself, and can only be judged from within, never from any external viewpoint. Under the former view, one would have to say that the Western peoples not only committed a great many wrongs, but did not do enough good, and what good they did often in the wrong manner. According to the second outlook, of cultural relativism, what we call the crimes of the Westerners were such only in so far as they violated the Western code, but all their acts, good or bad in Western eyes, must be condemned in so far as they interfered with or contradicted native customs or values. It is not easy to discover what it is that is supposed to endow any culture, or ethical code, with such sanctity; this viewpoint often culminates in the irrelevancy of a sort of anthropological stamp collecting, a mania for living museums.

And so we return to Coca-colonization. It is hard to envisage a just ground, save that of taste, for objecting to the spread of American or any other influence, provided that it is advanced by proper means. So long as hapless Frenchmen are not forced to guzzle cola beverages under the guns of the Marines, they are free, as are the Americans themselves, to drink them or not, as they choose. If American or generally Western ideas, habits, or products are freely adopted by people to whom they are new, one may indeed regret the popular taste, but one has no right to raise the cry of imperialism.

We, for our part, can undoubtedly learn a good deal from non-Western cultures, and should take every opportunity to do so. The non-Westerner, however, while welcoming Western technology, is likely to deny the Western value system, particularly since he has been given cause to suspect the sincerity of many of its adherents. He had best be warned that to accept the one without the other, unless some new ideological foundation for democracy can be discovered, risks exchanging an agrarian for a technological despotism.

Whether or not the bugaboo of imperialism will frighten much of the free world away from useful undertakings depends on how clearly each nation understands its long-run self-interest. For our part, we have made an intelligent beginning with the concept underlying the Point Four program, the export of capital and technical knowledge to regions where both can be profitably invested. It will be welcomed by any nation that has realized, as has every Chamber of Commerce, that in the long run capital investment is even more rewarding to the locality than to the investor. America, however, should not take it for granted that in any dispute between a European power and one of its colonies the latter is always right. Such an attitude is particularly unjustified when, as is so often the case, the choice is between a relatively progressive European administration which is bound eventually to disappear, and an otherwise empty native nationalism that may be little more than a cloak for corruption.

But the free world must first of all see to its defenses against the threat of Communist aggression, and our debates as to how this should be done bring out in sharp relief the social force of the guiding values of the Western tradition. It is repeatedly and correctly said that no democratic nation like the United States could even contemplate a preventive war against Russia. Since this is so, it is only tactically but not strategically important whether our forecasts of Soviet intentions and prospects are accurate or not. In either event we must be prepared to face an aggressive war. Since we will not ourselves start one, there is no real alternative to the so-called policy of containment, preventing the USSR from further advancing its empire, by maintaining force adequate for reprisal, strengthening the nations along Russia's borders, and, for long-term development, Point Four. This entire policy, as well as its corollary of treating peripheral aggressions of the Korean type in a firm but limited way, rests not only on military grounds but on the judgment that time is working for us and against Stalinism. Ideologically, we can only regard free Western society as essentially strong and capable of growth, and Soviet society as essentially stagnant, no matter how well equipped the Russian armored divisions.

When we are allied with a ruler or ruling clique whose subjects are economically depressed and socially disaffected, we face the dilemma of scrupulously respecting that nation's sovereignty and building our alliance on sand, or interfering in the nation's domestic affairs and risking the charge of imperialism. In other words, we must decide what would constitute the manifestations of love toward these foreign neighbors and what would strengthen democracy among them. Taking all their circumstances into account, to respect their national sovereignty, as we would have all nations respect ours, might only weaken democracy in their land and in the world as a whole. If this is our judgment of the actual situation, we can only choose to interfere, if we can, and as tactfully as we can. In the conditions that actually obtain, redistribution of large estates is the measure most likely to be accepted and most likely to succeed. The conservative possibilities of land reform were clearly shown by Stolypin early in this century, as its revolutionary potential was realized by Lenin and later Mao. It is, however, a good American idea, for it was Jefferson who believed a population of small, independent farmers the best foundation for a democracy. Land reform is no panacea, and may even result in a short-run reduction of agricultural output, but it is unequaled as a measure of social appeasement in backward agrarian lands, and gains time for amelioration in other respects.

But let us be warned against a dangerous illusion that often betrays the opponents of communism. The London *Economist* observed, in 1850, that "we can rely on the coming prosperity of the community to release us from all fears of socialism." A century later, the French political scientist Bertrand de Jouvenel commented in a letter to *The Economist* (May 27, 1950):

This was the opinion prevailing a hundred years ago in Liberal circles: poverty was the cause of socialism and as it receded so would socialism. Marx took it over uncritically, as he did so many other orthodox tenets, and added to it the wrong forecast that poverty would increase, and therefore socialism.

After a hundred years we find that poverty has certainly decreased; your predecessors were right in their forecast and Marx was wrong in his. But socialism has sensationally advanced; so the reasoning of both your predecessors and Marx must have been wrong. Our contemporaries who hold the same view of a simple cause-and-effect relationship must then also be presumed wrong. This is especially the case of our American friends; their public statements on the Communist menace assume as axiomatic the belief held by *The Economist* in 1850.

As man does not live by bread alone, neither will bread satisfy his social desires. The key to the attraction exercised by communism lies in the psychology of the socially and culturally uprooted, and even more in the impact of Marxism on inquiring minds not otherwise provided with a coherent outlook, a social myth or point of view. The sufferings of the poor will strengthen communism in backward countries misruled by irresponsible landlords, and there to provide bread is to serve the cause of both charity and freedom. But in the advanced nations where the crucial battles with Stalinism are joined, no degree of material comfort that can conceivably be supplied will overcome the lack of a positive ideological alternative.

We should, it goes without saying, do all in our power to strengthen the prestige of the United Nations, not so much as a means of keeping the peace, which it cannot do except in conflicts among weak states, but as a living vehicle for one of the oldest aspirations of Western civilization. From the time of Rome and of the Christian evangile, through the medieval theories of a universal imperium, the projects of eighteenth-century philosophers and the League of Woodrow Wilson, the idea of a single polity of all civilized peoples has captured much of our imagination and our hope. We can kill this hope by trying to realize it prematurely as well as by turning against it. A vision such as this is too important to trust to visionaries, and can be fulfilled only when the slow process of organic growth has, in the far distant future, brought the peoples to work together in a manner we may not now be able to envisage. There is no reason to assume that a world state, as government is now understood, is the only form within which there can be genuinely peaceful and orderly coöperation among the nations. The latter, after all, is the real goal, the form of future coöperation being irrelevant for the present and relatively unimportant in the future. But we can help or hinder progress toward this goal, help by giving the United Nations functions to perform that are within its actual capacity and by treating it with respect as the greatest international forum.

All of our potential for worthy accomplishment must depend, as the world now stands, upon our economic success and the stability of our society. In both respects, there are strong grounds for confidence and relatively less for fear. If it be correct that a so-called mature economy can continue to expand; that a neomercantilist policy can control at least the severe downward swings of the business cycle; that, given reasonably intelligent management, the kinds of competition that exist in an economy of large firms can yield a workable blend of stability and innovation; that the trend toward corporatism in both management and labor is historical and organic, rather than contrived and programmatic; that the ideological predispositions of our society can shape this trend to harmonize with economic advancement and political democracy—if these conclusions be broadly right, then it is not beyond our present competence, wisdom, or inclinations to make intelligent judgments as to what should be done in the economic and social realm.

In many cases, however, it is more significant, as well as easier, to suggest how judgments should be reached than to detail their specific content. In the field of international economics, for example, there has been a growing acceptance of the reciprocal trade program to further imports as well as exports, without permitting either foreign competition of a kind that would rapidly undermine established American industry, or a degree of protection that would effectively bar any foreign competition at all. Such a middle-of-the-road principle, with its "yes-but" overtones, can be too many things to too many men, and takes on real meaning only as it is applied to specific cases. Since it is obviously out of the question here to analyze the tariff schedule, the best we can do is to indicate some criteria by which particular rates could be decided.

If an industry is essentially incapable of meeting foreign competition, either because of scarcity or cost of materials or a necessarily high use of expensive labor, there would seem to be only two reasons which might justify its preservation by means of tariffs: first, if it is essential for national defense, and reliance on imports appears risky; second, if the industry is a large employer and represents heavy investments, so that to undermine it would injure economic stability. Protection of a new industry may be justified either on grounds of national security or because it is likely to strike roots and prosper without subsidy. There is no justification for tariffs so high as to create exceptional profits or to depress the consumption of a commodity.

The nature of these criteria implies that Congress should limit itself to establishing general principles and a fairly broad range

within ·   ι   ...al tariffs would be set by a commission, following
researc   ι nearings. If the latter's decisions were reviewable by a
qualified panel of an Administrative Court, the requirements of both
equity and economic wisdom would be more readily met than in
the past.[17]

A trend toward moderation and generally beneficial policies has
been shown by some of the largest monopolistic producers in the
domestic economy. They have been more generous in licensing
patents and processes to other firms, and have been less interested
in seeking vertical integration of an entire field, from raw material
to consumer's goods. Indeed, with the increasing importance of synthetic raw materials and standardization of manufactured components, competition even in the classical sense has actually been
stimulated by the monopolistic giants. When the latter limit their
control of the market to the basic products, relatively free competition arises among relatively small firms, as, for example, in the manufacture of consumers' goods employing synthetic fibers and in the
assembly of electrical and electronic equipment from components
produced by a few great companies.

It will, of course, be wise policy to encourage such salutary
trends: defending and developing reciprocal trade; promoting
licensing, perhaps by making it compulsory after, let us say, a ten-
year period of absolute patent monopoly; directing antimonopoly
prosecutions on a pragmatic basis. It is, of course, basic to our democracy to fight excessive concentrations of power by way of cartels
or other monopolistic devices. The Supreme Court's "rule of reason"[18] is, like Holmes' "clear and present danger," a challenge to
good judgment rather than a precise or rational formula. For this
very reason, however, it is the only *kind* of standard (as well as the
only one we have) by which conflicts between values can be analyzed and an intelligent balance reached.

It would seem, however, that the important decisions are not to
be made in such fields as antitrust policy, but rather in connection
with the control of inflation, the management of taxes and incen-

----

[17] These criteria would lead one to question the protection, for example, of
raw sugar, for whose production the United States is economically ill suited
and supplies of which are readily available in the Caribbean. The extremely
high duties on perfumes and other luxuries might also prove to be excessive.

[18] See p. 137.

tives, economic controls, and public policy toward labor organizations. These problems are intimately interrelated, and are heavily colored by social and ideological considerations. For example, the independent retailer, like the independent farmer, is part of American folklore, and government action to protect him, either by legalizing fixed resale prices or by antitrust suits against distribution chains, can ultimately be justified only on the social ground that the small retailer is a desirable element in American society, worth subsidizing at the consumer's expense. That is the decision we have apparently taken, although it is impossible to say with any certainty whether it was owing to a positive love for independent retailers or to the political weakness of the consumer's representatives—in this case the price cutters and chain stores. But it is likely that every isolated decision involving the direction of price movements will go the same way.

The most important case is in agriculture, where a policy of trying to underwrite farm income by means of the purchasing power–parity formula raised a number of embarrassing questions: Is this method one of built-in inflation? Does it produce too much bureaucracy? Does it overburden the consumer through excessively high food prices? Does it make the economy dangerously rigid? There may develop a shift away from this direct form of government intervention to corporatist methods of stabilizing agricultural income: farmers' organizations may bargain collectively with bulk-buying public agencies or with associations of processors and distributors. Such procedures are even now involved to some extent in the pricing of milk and certain specialized crops, in purchases by great food chains, and in such instances as Canadian government bulk buying of wheat at a negotiated price. As the agricultural counterpart to corporatist devices in labor and industry, these methods may be preferable to either outright government intervention or the free market, but one can scarcely doubt that their effect would be to move farm prices steadily, if unspectacularly, upward.

In short, while everyone is opposed to inflation, there appears to be no reliable way of halting any particular move to raise prices. This is substantially true even when specific wage and price controls are in effect, and such controls can be justified under the guiding principles of our society only when it is necessary to change drastically the course of the economy, in mobilization, war, or demobilization. And the general, fiscal controls over the rate of interest and volume and terms of credit, which may normally be administered by a neomercantilist state, are capable of braking, but not stopping, an upward spiral. This is not for economic but for political reasons. It is often forgotten that Keynes, like some of his eighteenth-century predecessors, was an anti-inflationist as well as antideflationist. But the general formula—expand credit, public expenditures, and public debt during depression; contract credit, cut expenditures, and reduce public debt during a boom—is not equally easy to employ in both directions. For all practical purposes, one may say that deflation is "unconstitutional"; organized labor will not tolerate wage reductions, and thus automatically places a floor, a raised floor, under prices. Credit restrictions may safely and successfully be imposed, but can of themselves only moderate the rate of advancing prices. Public expenditures are rarely subject to drastic reduction, both because a high proportion of them are fixed, for reasons of law or security, and because economy in government is something that legislators would rather talk about than bring about. High taxes imposed to meet a national emergency may survive for a time thereafter, but few politicians would suggest raising taxes in time of peace in order to check a developing boom.

The social and political pressures would all appear to work for a continually rising price level, which should occasion no surprise, for such has been the course of prices for over four centuries. There is far less danger of a runaway inflation, however, than in times past —our price level is like that of an ascending elevator but there is slight chance of its shooting through the roof. This is owing not only to our greater knowledge of economics and a better-informed public. Some of the most extreme inflationary explosions of the past resulted from deliberate political choice; others from political collapse; still others from wars fought without economic controls. Moreover, the element of speculation which operated so heavily in past inflationary movements has been replaced as a major factor by the steadier and slower social pressure of demand for higher wages. Working against this pressure is technological innovation and rising productivity, enabling the manufacturer to absorb part of the increase in wage rates.[19]

That wages should be related to productivity has been recognized by both labor and management, and certain labor contracts have tried to state this relationship in explicit terms. The assumption is made that if productivity and wages can be geared to rise at the same rate, there will be no inflationary effect. But this is a weak assumption, for a number of reasons. In the first place, productivity is by no means as easy to measure as money wages. Moreover, productivity will not rise evenly throughout industry, with the result that if, for example, the productivity and wages of steel workers both rise, then, whatever happens to the price of steel, there will be a net addition to the steel workers' demand for other products, such as clothing. If the output of clothing remains the same, its prices will rise. As a general proposition, therefore, any rise in money wages will tend to work in an inflationary direction, but less when linked to productivity than when it is entirely added to manufacturing costs."[20]

There is no reason to look forward to anything other than a generally rising price level, marked by occasional rests and even rarer slight, short-lived, declines; runaway inflation is, if anything, more unlikely than severe depression. If prices rise at a moderate rate, there need be no cause for alarm or even disturbance. But what is a moderate rate? What appears moderate to the successful commodity speculator, who is unaffected by higher prices, may seem rapid even to the rising young executive, whose promotions add more to income than do cost-of-living adjustments. It will appear to be catastrophic to one living on a fixed dollar annuity. Obviously, a moderate rate can be defined only as one that will be generally acceptable to society.

[19] Rising productivity and invention does not necessarily mean lower prices, or, more precisely, prices not so high as they would otherwise have been. Invention often yields new and necessarily more costly products to do an old job more conveniently or efficiently, as, for example, vacuum cleaners replacing the old-fashioned broom.

[20] J. M. Clark argues that given strong resistance to downward revision of wages, any unevenness in the economy—hence, any mobility and progress—will produce inflationary pressure (D. M. Wright, ed., *Impact of the Union*, pp. 20 ff.).

This is not quite the meaningless truism it appears to be. In respect of rising prices, as of the rate of interest and the level of taxes, a pattern may arise and acquire the sanction of custom, after which any marked deviation in either direction will appear untoward and even immoderate. And there are factors making for the development of such a pattern. The neomercantilist outlook which broadly characterizes contemporary America is hospitable to a steadily rising price level, as favoring high-level employment and giving confidence to business and room for the play of enterprise. Labor and management negotiators, as they gather for what is becoming a complex ritual of agreeing upon terms generally understood beforehand, gear their arguments to factors which, except under the stress of military measures, do not ordinarily fluctuate very sharply: productivity, past profits, other wage and fringe-benefit agreements, the share to taxation. We may surely expect the ritualistic aspect of collective bargaining to gain at the expense of actual debate, and with it the clearer development of a pattern of wage and other benefit increases.

There remains the problem of justice for those excluded from such patterns, pensioners and others living on fixed dollar incomes, and sufferers to a lesser degree such as unorganized workers, certain classes of civil servants, and white-collar employees. The latter groups will continue to be at a partial disadvantage until they improve their bargaining position or it becomes public and private employment policy to grant them the benefits won by union labor. Business is likely to do this more and more, if for no other reason than to forestall the organization of workers hitherto cool to unions. And civil servants have been creating more effective pressure organizations, and meeting less resistance as their place in society gains acceptance. Social security benefits which, being under the authority of Congress, can be expected to respond to a rising price level, will provide a cushion for pensioners, but recent trends in savings and in retirement plan investment are likely to accomplish even more. The increasing popularity of common stocks and investment trust shares as a form of personal savings (not, apparently, for speculative purposes as prior to 1929) and similar investment of retirement annuity funds will link such investors to the price level, and reduce an important source of dissatisfaction with its rise. But, as a matter both of equity and social stability, it must ever remain the concern of public policy that the cost of living not be allowed to break sharply with custom.

Similar concerns of policy and custom arise in connection with taxation, whose ancient function of providing revenue for the workings of government is all but lost sight of in recent discussions of the subject, which have dealt rather with the question of equity, and with the effect of taxes on incentive and on inflation. Equity, in taxation as in every other context, can be gauged only by reference to a prior ethical standard. The standard that has become dominant in the increasing democratization of Western society is ability to pay, or equality of tax burden, and this has been expressed in the steeply progressive personal income tax as well as in the political unpopularity of consumption levies such as the sales tax, which weigh proportionately more against low incomes. When taxation is proposed as a means of redistributing income, the arguments for and against can be economic, strictly speaking, only to a very limited degree. Briefly, there is the Keynesian (and traditionally mercantilist) view that excessive inequality of incomes may lead to equilibrium below full employment; on the other hand, since a greater percentage of high incomes is saved than of low, it is held that excessive equality of incomes will dry up private sources of investment capital, thereby producing either depression or socialization of investment.

Both arguments are undoubtedly correct under extreme conditions of equality or inequality, but between the extremes lies a wide range of varying possibilities that do not readily allow a neat conclusion. Much depends, for example, on the spending habits of the wealthy and the saving habits of the middle and lower income groups. Where a man is content with his fortune and is not interested in increasing it or in business activity for its own sake, he may transfer funds to exempt, low-yield securities which require less supervision by their holder. One would expect that the sense of security afforded by sustained high-level employment, high incomes, social security, and pension plans would lead to a decline of saving on the part of middle and low income groups. Recent American experience, however, while not conclusive, has been that these groups have increased their savings, placing them more and more in common stocks as a hedge against inflation. Nor may we forget that self-investment from company savings is of growing importance in corporate expansion, and that fiduciary investing agencies, from insurance companies to union pension plans, are playing an ever larger role as suppliers of the capital market.

In general, it may be said that redistribution of income, and taxation for that purpose, lose significance as the structures of a corporatist society take shape. But the relations of taxes to inflation and to incentives can never be unimportant in the management of a neo-mercantilist economic policy. This is not the place to discuss the relative merits of various taxes as anti-inflationary devices, except to record a general preference for the personal income tax if increases intended to counteract inflationary pressure are directed against the middle income groups who provide the bulk of the returns.[21]

Whatever assortment of taxes, credit restriction, and other measures is chosen to combat inflationary tendencies, it is to be assumed that tax raises and reductions will alternate as part of the general system of fiscal management. But this leaves untouched the broader questions of the effect of taxation on the incentive to work and efficiency, and of the proper place of taxation in the economy as a whole. Both these questions are linked with the problem of inflation in Colin Clark's famous thesis that taxation by all agencies (federal, state, and local, in the United States) could not exceed about 25 percent of national income without bringing on severe inflation.[22] Clark's argument, based on the experience of a number of nations,

[21] Further increases in the higher brackets would serve chiefly to support the taxpaying morale of the rest of the population, for large returns account for only a small percentage of total personal income. Adjusted gross incomes in excess of $50,000 amounted to less than 5 percent of total income before taxes and to less than 3 percent of total adjusted gross income after taxes, as of 1950.

[22] Colin Clark's thesis was stated in "Public Finance and Changes in the Value of Money," *Economic Journal,* December, 1945, pp. 371 ff., and in simplified form in "The Danger Point in Taxes," *Harper's,* December, 1950, pp. 67 ff. For critical analysis see T. Mayer and J. A. Pechman, "Mr. Colin Clark on the Limits of Taxation," *Review of Economics and Statistics,* August, 1952, pp. 232 ff.

particularly France, over the last generation, was, in effect, that taxes so reduced incentives that inflation was the only way to restore them. Aside from the fact that just about nothing was "equal" in the period Clark considered, and aside from serious objections concerning historical interpretation—indirect taxes passed on to the consumer acted precisely as price rises and induced a wage-price spiral in some of his instances—his thesis asks and answers the wrong questions. If one assumes that labor is receiving an approximately satisfactory share of national income, which holds for the United States, and that the chief vehicle for tax increases has been the personal income levy, again true of the United States, it remains to be shown how taxation could destroy incentives.

This is not easily demonstrated. Arguments to this effect hinge upon a reincarnation of the economic man, who needs increasing inducements to overcome his disinclination to work and, beyond a certain point, will find the inducement offered insufficient to outweigh his desire to go fishing. It is generally admitted that this is not particularly relevant to the top-bracket executive or engineer who, provided he has been receiving a sufficient income after taxes, will exert himself for the love of his work and because he must do so to maintain his rank, standard of living, and prestige. Above the salary range customarily attached to high corporate rank, additional pay increments are apt to be important chiefly as certificates of advancement, rather than as incentives to greater effort, and their recipient is therefore likely to work just as hard when the government takes a larger slice of additional salary as when it takes the percentage he has been accustomed to.[23] Persons below this exalted state are apt to strive harder for promotion, or take on more work, to recover the loss due to a higher tax, and wage earners in the lowest taxable brackets are likely to welcome the offer of an unemployed wife or child to seek employment. Few people calculate, save perhaps on an especially pleasant or exceedingly hot summer day, the disutility of an hour's work as compared with the hourly rate minus present and previous tax. Most people are concerned with professional or job advancement, with maintaining or advanc-

---

[23] Nor should one forget that the combination of very high incomes and very high surtaxes makes the many ingenious and legal devices for "tax reduction" exceedingly attractive.

ing their standard of living; at all events, with preventing its decline.[24]

In short, while some taxes may exert an inflationary and others an anti-inflationary influence, it is difficult to see how they can seriously affect incentives, which are shaped by the customs and values of a society and by the opportunities it affords. Moreover, one becomes even more easily accustomed to thinking in terms of "take-home pay after taxes" than one does to a higher price level; moderation in departures from the customary tax level is therefore more important to social and economic stability than the tax rate as such. And, whether taxes are inflationary depends in good part upon how their proceeds are used: it is difficult to conceive of inflation following upon a doubling of all taxes for the sole purpose of reducing the national debt.

Perhaps the most unfortunate consequence of debating the relation of taxes to incentives or of total tax revenue to inflation is that it tends to obscure the most important question, which is social and ideological rather than economic. Any tax transfers money from the public to the government for the latter, instead of the former, to spend currently, invest, or hoard. The money may be spent for the same purpose: the share of one's taxes that supports public education might conceivably equal what one would otherwise spend for private schooling. Or it may be spent for entirely different purposes, such as battleships. But the basic characteristic of taxation is that it constitutes partial socialization of consumption. A public health system like the British implies that one has, through representative government, elected to spend the money in this fashion rather than on an alternative, such as a trip abroad. As individual tastes and circumstances differ, socialized consumption inevitably involves some degree of redistribution of income and benefits which, in a democratic society, should presumably balance out in a generally fair manner. The vital question to be asked about taxation is whether the expenditures these taxes are to support should be socialized or left to individuals, to corporations, or to voluntary associations. The

---

[24] This last point is fondly known among economists as the "Duesenbury effect," because it was demonstrated in scholarly fashion by James Duesenbury. Calling something an "effect" in the style of astrophysics has an awesomely scientific effect.

health needs of an individual may be met out of his own pocket; they may be met by the state; or they may be met by his employer, or union, or a mutual insurance scheme. The first corresponds to capitalist, the second to socialist, and the last three to corporatist consumption. There is no way of calculating scientifically how the allocation to private, group, and state initiative should be made; for efficiency must be balanced against other intermediate principles, and, in general, we are directed back to our earlier considerations, and to the conclusion that a free society of open opportunity thrives on variety rather than uniformity and decentralization rather than centralization of decision.

This is neither to scorn nor excessively to limit the role of government and, in fact, as the new technology of the atom has compelled the state to undertake at least the original exploitation of that source of power, the new structures of growing corporatist society will require government to expand its role as general arbiter and inspector in the public interest. This is abundantly clear in connection with labor, for the powers of unions over their members and over the national economy require the community to intervene to protect the general welfare, as it long since has in the affairs of the great financial and manufacturing firms and of the public utilities corporations.

Labor unions are obviously organizations affected with the public interest, and yet one is necessarily more wary about supervising their conduct than that of an electric company, for they are in law voluntary associations of free men, some even practicing the secret ritual of fraternal organizations, rather than associations of property rights (like corporations). The basic values of our society therefore make intervention in the field of labor organizations a delicate matter. These values must not be contravened through excessive dictation to free citizens, and yet intervention must be undertaken, lest improper use of power similarly undermine those principles.

The nature of the dilemma is most apparent in relation to strikes that violate the law, or threaten health, security, or the functioning of the national economy. Clearly, the community should be able to defend itself against the consequences of abuse of the power to interrupt the course of business, yet we are told that any denial of the right to strike is tantamount to the institution of forced labor. A way out has been suggested through the prohibition of strikes in fields evidently affecting the public interest, in return for which the workers involved would receive something like civil service status. Aside from the fact that the very principle would tend to exaggerate social rigidities that ought not to be encouraged, it is difficult to see how its application could be reasonably limited. Steel, coal, transportation, electric power, gas, food processing and distribution—the public interest would obviously be threatened by a prolonged strike in any of these and other fields, even if it were not national in scope.

Another proposal is to face the problem squarely, distinguish between the right to strike and the right to quit, and empower the federal government to prohibit strikes held to endanger the general welfare. The right to strike carries the right to return to the job with unimpaired seniority and related privileges; there is no reason why this should be sacrosanct. The right to quit a job, on the other hand, should be limited only under total war mobilization. The practical effect of this distinction would be that anyone engaged in an illegal strike would be deemed to have quit employment, and therefore to have sacrificed seniority and other job rights. Enforcement could be assured, as S. H. Slichter suggests, by penalizing employers for rehiring illegal strikers as anything but new workers, at the initial rung of the seniority ladder.[25]

There is little doubt that such an approach would work, by dooming illegal strikes to failure, but it would seem to fall under the heading of measures that would arouse too much bitterness to be desirable. All the desired results could be obtained from the ritual of presidential "seizure" of a struck industry, provided neither side is allowed to benefit from it. The government should not employ "seizure" to impose what is in effect a new contract, but should "operate" the industry under the terms of the old contract, while collective bargaining is resumed without new benefits being retroactive. This would give labor adequate incentive to compromise, and a similar incentive could be provided for management by passing dividends and taxing away any corporate gain through the difference between old and new contracts during the period of seizure. These "penalties" could even be made flexible, at the discretion of an impartial board that has considered the merits of the case.

[25] *Trade Unions in a Free Society,* Cambridge, 1948, pp. 27–28.

It must be emphasized that the importance of such measures would lie in their mere legal existence and the possibility of their employment, rather than in actual use. Their chief function would be to add weight to the side of moderation during that indefinite period of years in which sounder motives and procedures are developed through the evolution of a democratic corporatist society.[26] The other aspects of unionism which seem to require government intervention do not, happily, raise any questions involving the risk of regimenting labor. Since the unions have not only acquired great strength in the economy, but almost the power of economic life and death over their members and other workers, the community is surely justified in insisting that this power never be used to deprive any individual of his rights as the citizen of a democratic nation. No union should have the right to deny membership to any citizen applying in good faith. Initiation fees should be limited to a moderate percentage of the individual's initial wage as a union member. Where union-shop provisions obtain, no man should be expelled from the union without due process of hearings and appeal. The conscientious objector—that nuisance precious to a democracy—should not be allowed less freedom in respect of joining a union than he is regularly granted in being released from serving in the armed forces. The unions protest that it is unfair for nonmembers to benefit from their activities as if they were dues-paying members, but the analogy with the conscientious objector to military service suggests an obvious solution: let such individuals remain outside the union, but pay the equivalent of the union dues to some appropriate charity. Excessive employment rigidity should be prevented by enabling workers to change jobs at a loss of some, but not all, their seniority. Raids on the membership of other unions by any means other than those of lawful persuasion, such as the jurisdictional strike and boycott, should be prosecuted under the antitrust laws,

[26] A minor aid to moderation worth considering would be the publication of the cost of living index, to which bargaining demands are so often linked, in two versions, one including indirect taxes in prices, as at present, and one showing the price level apart from such taxes. Labor is less likely to make private industry the target of a drive to recoup tax expenditures once the picture has been made clear for all to see. This would also tend to strengthen the public's awareness of the tax bill, and its sense of responsibility in calling for additional government expenditures.

and violence should be prosecuted under the ordinary criminal law. All union elections, as well as strike votes, should be by secret ballot, under the supervision of some public authority. Such measures as these, and others that might be suggested, are essentially of a minor character, and reflect not a distrust of unions but a recognition of their key function in a democratic, industrial society.

The practical arrangements we have suggested, whether in politics, international affairs, finance, or labor, are conceived as more or less specific implications of what we believe to be the fundamental standards of judgment and principles in our society. But we have skirted one concept which tends to color the rest of any ideology appropriate to Western civilization: the principle of equality. To define it, as we have, in terms of approximate equality of opportunity, rather than of capacity, wealth, or status, brings equality into harmony with the mixed and fluid society of neomercantilist capitalism and with the trend toward democratic corporatism. To reject this definition is to reject the entire ideological structure and its generally optimistic outlook.

Equalitarianism runs deep and strong in Western civilization: in the abstract theories of natural law propounded by Roman jurists, in the Old and New Testaments, in such sturdy assertions as that of the Leveller, Colonel Rainborough, disputing with Cromwell and the mighty of the Puritan Revolution: "For really I think that the poorest he that is in England hath a life to live, as the greatest he." Equality has been differently understood and partially realized over the centuries. The absolute monarchs largely succeeded in leveling all their subjects into an equality before the royal law. The nineteenth century saw the substantial achievement of equality at the ballot box and of equality of status, which may be described as the devaluation of advantages owing exclusively to the accident of birth. The nineteenth and twentieth centuries have also witnessed growing pressure for economic equality. But this has proved to be a misty concept, not readily defined, as the other aspects of equality have been, by such clear-cut criteria as the operation of courts of law, the presence of secret polling booths, the abolition of any genuine privileges for an hereditary nobility. Crude material equality, of income and possessions, has never been urged, even as a goal, by theorists or movements worthy of serious attention. It is not even to be found in the slogan of "higher" socialism, "From each according to his ability, to each according to his needs," since there is no reason why needs should be equal, let alone identical.

Economic equalitarianism is nevertheless widespread, in a negative as well as a positive form. The latter is reflected to some extent in pressure for higher wages, but much more significantly in the demand that the state undertake welfare functions to benefit all citizens alike, and that it underwrite individual security in employment, health, and old age. The negative sentiment of equalitarianism is expressed in the desire to reduce fortunes and incomes beyond the point necessary to prevent corruption of the state, or economic depression, from undue concentrations of wealth and power. It is most negative, and crudest, when manifested as a wish to prevent some from enjoying what is not available to all.

The building of a floor of security is quite compatible with the value structure as we have described it, so long as that which custom defines as security is not so embracing as to devour all freedom to risk and to innovate. There is little danger of any such overextension. Nor is there any need to entrust the function of providing security to the central government alone, or exclusively to government in general. Both to the extent that the desire for security arises from a simple fear of insecurity, and to the extent that it arises from equalitarianism, this desire is self-satisfying rather than self-feeding. A sense of growing security will strengthen demands for a higher standard of living and a more respected status, but not for still more security. If it be generally correct that there are good prospects for continued economic growth and for the peaceful development of democratic corporatism, equalitarianism is likely to enter into a new phase, which for want of a better term might be called "equality of personality." By this is meant (flashing back to the Utopian vision at the close of the preceding chapter) that a wealthy and democratic corporatist society would allow a sufficient variety of ways for each individual to express his personality, so that, a basic decent standard of living being secure, purely economic equalitarianism would lose its attraction.

It appears, then, that the positive forms of economic equalitarianism are consistent with an ideology of the middle way, and with the trends it suggests. This cannot be said of the negative forms, how-

ever, and whether the ideology is workable or not depends upon the
actual strength of negative equalitarianism. The latter might be defined, perhaps somewhat unkindly, as envy, or more dispassionately,
as equality for its own sake. This is clearly incompatible with the
Judao-Christian tradition, to which it does not belong. The sentiment of equality as a good in itself, though rarely stated so baldly,
derives from some of the misconceptions of eighteenth-century rationalism, particularly from Rousseau's assumption of perfect equality in a mythical presocial state of nature. The inequalities that have
come into being since that never-never time must, on this basis, be
ascribed to the errors and the selfishness of men in society. If these
are corrected, natural equality will be restored.[27]

Equalitarianism of this general character and derivation does have
support in contemporary society. It would seem to be the basis for
continued pressure for the redistribution of wealth by taxation after
the economic arguments for redistribution have all but lost their
practical significance. Economically, one would ask whether a reasonable degree of inequality seems to yield a higher national product, and the evidence appears to be that it does. If equality is taken
as a good in itself, however, such questions are irrelevant. But the
strength of negative equalitarianism should not be overestimated.
Any complex, industrial society must develop leaders, and is likely,
as in both Stalinist Russia and capitalist America, to reward them
more generously than the rank and file. If, however, leadership has
long been associated with hereditary social distinctions in a democratic country such as England, negative equalitarianism can be
expected to be vigorous while those distinctions remain important.
But it is by no means certain that it will survive the steady advance
of social equality.

In final analysis the fate of rigorous equalitarianism and, conversely, of democracy, will depend upon the outcome of the choice
as de Tocqueville saw it:

The principle of equality begets two tendencies: the one leads men
straight to independence, and may suddenly drive them into anarchy; the

---

[27] Neither this, nor any other reputable view, goes so far as to deny physical
and mental inequalities among individuals, although one sometimes may detect
a wistful note of regret over nature's imperfection. Man in the state of nature
was deemed to be equal in all other respects.

other conducts them by a longer, more secret, but more certain route, to servitude.[28]

We have, I believe, grown almost wise enough to avoid a swift and undesired descent into anarchy, although our technological skill has created the peril of chaos from atomic war. We have not irrevocably rejected that fork in the road which ends in oppression. Nor shall we ever make this most vital choice for once and all, for it is a choice that must be made afresh in each of the known and in each of the unforeseen conjunctures with which the life of society confronts us. Every such decision will be taken in the light of the values by which we are guided, and the course that is set will depend upon the nature of this prior commitment. The clarity with which we understand and apply the values of the Judao-Christian tradition that have thus far informed our history will be the measure of the wise choices we make, and the human capacity to err, of the mistaken ones. Even should society become more secular than it is, we are likely to follow that tradition because, divinely revealed to the religious, and manifested to the nonreligious in the history that carries our culture from the known past into the future whose character we must endow, it resides at the core of our ways of living and of thinking. We may even be aided by ideology, whose function it is to serve as the intermediary and the translator between essential values and the decisions to be made in the uncertain realm of social policy.

To end on a note of optimism, conditioned though it be, might seem incongruous, when one recalls that history is supposed to induce a pessimistic view of the wisdom of mankind, and that the Christian conception of man which is central to this historical ideology is itself called pessimistic. But a reasoned appraisal of history need not be pessimistic unless one measures the record by some entirely unhistorical theory of the inevitability of progress. And the Christian doctrine of man is pessimistic only when compared to the fatuous optimism of some nonhuman theory of perfectability. With regard to any residue of optimism not thereby explained, I can only plead the predispositions that come from one's own vantage point. For, it is said, America is a land of optimists.

[28] *Democracy in America*, Bradley edition, vol. 2, p. 288.

NOTES ON BOOKS

If a prophet be one who recalls a people to its highest ideals and noblest vocation, and does so not through sentimentality and mere exhortation, but by setting ideals and vocation in history and by showing the people its failings and wrongdoings; if a prophet be one who expresses in terms of the real problems of his day the values of his culture, then Reinhold Niebuhr is assuredly a prophet for twentieth-century America, and for the Western world. His writings can only be called a witness to a living faith, broadly and powerfully applied. A good introduction to Niebuhr would be to read *An Interpretation of Christian Ethics* (1935), *The Children of Light and the Children of Darkness* (1944), and *The Irony of American History* (1952).

Beyond mentioning once more writers to whom I have acknowledged a deep indebtedness (such as Burke and de Tocqueville and, among contemporaries, Keynes and Schumpeter), it would be unnecessary to suggest a list of works to go with this chapter and it might possibly prove unwelcome were I to name living authors with whom I feel intellectual and ideological kinship.

INDEX